READING POEMS

As though a tongueless nightingale should swell
Her throat in vain and die heart-
stifled, in her dell.—

A Casement tripple-arch'd and ~~diamonded~~
With many coloured glass fronted the Moon
In midst of which a shielded scutcheon shed
High blushing gules; ~~upon the herald came down~~
And only pray'd for grace and heavenly boon
The blood red gules fell on her silver cross,
~~And her white hands devout~~

There was
A Casement tripple arch'd and high
All garlanded with carven imageries
Of ~~fruits~~ trailing flowers and ~~sunny corn~~ ears of corn
A Casement high and tripple arch'd there was
All garlanded with carven imageries
Of fruits and flowers and bunches of knot grass,
And diamonded with panes of quaint device
Innumerable of stains and splendid dyes
~~As is the twisty of evening~~ ~~[illegible]~~
And in the midst whereof among thousand heraldries
And ~~twilights~~ twilight saints and dim emblazonings

Reading Poems

AN INTRODUCTION TO CRITICAL STUDY

BY

WRIGHT THOMAS, *University of Wisconsin*

AND

STUART GERRY BROWN, *Grinnell College*

OXFORD UNIVERSITY PRESS · NEW YORK · 1941

18960

PREFACE

THIS BOOK is intended, in general, for anyone who wishes to develop the skills needed in the intelligent reading of poems, and, in particular, for teachers and students in undergraduate courses in English and American poetry who may wish to emphasize the skills of reading rather than the history of poetry. It has grown out of several years of experimental work in the classroom and of study in modern criticism. The principles at which the editors have arrived will be found set forth in some detail in Part X, *On Reading Poems*. But it may be said here that the method is inductive, beginning with specific poems rather than with theories of the art of poetry. The poems themselves, which form the largest section of the book, are arranged according to generally accepted categories, but are freely grouped for purposes of study without reference to historical relations or to authorship. The names of authors are found only in the notes in Part IX; we hope that reputation will not be allowed to interfere with a reader's experience or judgment before he has actually read the poems. The book moves from relatively simple lyric poems to poems of increasing difficulty, and concludes with *The Waste Land*, mastery of which we regard as ample test of the reader's ability and maturity in the skills of reading poems. It may be necessary to add that in the earlier parts of the book a few distinctly 'bad' poems have been included, which teachers may find useful in laboratory study. The notes are intended primarily as critical guides, and often include substantial commentaries. Necessary explanatory information is given, but there are no notes of the usual historical or biographical nature. Although our collaboration has been so intimate (in discussions of the theory of teaching poems and in the classroom, long before the book was undertaken) that there could be nothing but the fullest joint responsibility, it may be said here that the notes and commentaries for Parts I, II, III, IV, and VIII were prepared by Wright Thomas, and for Parts V, VI, and VII by Stuart Brown.

The editors have made no effort to provide a critical text of the

[v]

poems, but have proceeded upon the principle of making them as 'available' as possible for the ordinary reader. For this reason spelling has been modernized and Americanized except in a few cases where old spelling or dialect forms are required for the full experience of the poem. Thus Milton, Spenser, Drayton, Burns, and the old ballads are based upon standard critical editions.

The editors of such a book as this begin to incur obligations of all sorts long before they start to prepare it. And we wish especially to acknowledge our gratitude to our students and friends whose willingness and interest in serving as 'guinea pigs' have always been a source of inspiration and encouragement. Among critics we are most deeply indebted to Mr.I.A.Richards and Mr.T.S.Eliot. In particular, from the former we have borrowed the laboratory method of studying poems as though their authorship were anonymous; and from the latter we have borrowed and attempted to extend and develop the idea of the 'objective correlative.'

We wish to express our gratitude for favors of a more personal nature to Mr.W.H.Auden and Mr.Stephen Spender, for allowing us to make transcriptions of their manuscript poems; to Mr.C.D.Abbott and Miss Mary Barnard of the Lockwood Memorial Library of the University of Buffalo, where there is a fine collection of manuscripts of modern poems; to the authorities of the Widener Library of Harvard University, for permission to print transcriptions of part of the manuscript of *The Eve of St.Agnes*; and, for other kindnesses, to Mr.Philip H.Gray, Mr.T.Sturge Moore, and Mr.F.V.Morley. Our indebtedness to Mr.T.S.Eliot is not confined to our liberal borrowing from his ideas; he has generously allowed us to make use of several of his major poems, which are central to our whole concept of the book, especially *The Waste Land* with our full notes and commentary.

Much of whatever merit this book may possess we owe to the unfailing help and encouragement of our friend Mr.Howard F. Lowry, formerly of the Oxford University Press and now Professor of English in Princeton University.

March 1, 1941.

S.G.B.
W.T.

ACKNOWLEDGMENTS

*The editors and publisher wish to offer thanks to those
who have given permission to include copyright material:*

For the poem by Conrad Aiken, to Charles Scribner's Sons.

For the poems by W.H.Auden, reprinted by permission of Random House, Inc.

For 'Nightingales' from *The Shorter Poems of Robert Bridges*, by permission of The Clarendon Press, Oxford.

For the selection from *The Collected Poems of Thomas E. Brown*, by permission of The Macmillan Company, publishers.

For the selections from *The Collected Poems of Hart Crane*, published by Liveright Publishing Corporation.

For the selections from *The Poems of Emily Dickinson*, edited by Martha Dickinson Bianchi and Alfred Leete Hampson, reprinted by permission of Little, Brown & Company.

For the selection from *The Collected Poems of H.D.*, published by Liveright Publishing Corporation.

For 'Sweeney Among the Nightingales,' 'The Love Song of J.Alfred Prufrock,' 'Portrait of a Lady,' 'The Waste Land,' 'Journey of the Magi,' and 'Marina' by T.S.Eliot, by permission of the author and of Harcourt, Brace and Company, Inc.

For 'West-Running Brook' from *West-Running Brook*, 'After Apple-Picking' and 'Mending Wall' from *North of Boston*, and 'The Tuft of Flowers' from *A Boy's Will* by Robert Frost, to Henry Holt and Company, Inc.

For 'The Darkling Thrush' and 'Dead "Wessex,"' the Dog, to the Household' from *The Collected Poems of Thomas Hardy*, by permission of The Macmillan Company, publishers.

For 'Pied Beauty,' 'The Windhover,' 'The Leaden Echo and the Golden Echo,' 'Spring and Fall,' 'I wake and feel the fell of dark,' and the Notes on Versification from the Author's Preface to *The Poems of Gerard Manely Hopkins*, by permission of Oxford University Press, London, and of the poet's family.

For 'Hell Gate,' 'Easter Hymn,' 'The Land of Biscay,' 'For My Funeral,' and 'Alta Quies' from *More Poems* by A.E.Housman, to the publishers, Alfred A. Knopf, Inc., and to the Estate of A.E.Housman. For 'The Chestnut Casts His Flambeaux,' 'The rain, it streams on stone and hillock,' and 'The night is freezing fast' from *Last Poems* and 'On moonlit heath and lonesome bank,' 'To an Athlete Dying Young,' 'With rue my heart is laden,' 'White in the moon the long road lies,' 'Is my team plowing,' and 'The Carpenter's Son' from *The Shropshire Lad* by A.E.Housman, to Henry Holt and Company, Inc.

For the poem by Robinson Jeffers, reprinted by permission of Random House, Inc.

For 'Ecce Puer' from *The Collected Poems of James Joyce*, copyright 1918, 1927, 1936, and 'Bright cap and streamers,' 'Because your voice was at my side,' 'O Sweetheart, hear you,' 'In the dark pine-wood,' and 'Now, O now, in this brown land' from *Chamber Music* by James Joyce, copyright 1918 by B.W.Huebsch, by permission of The Viking Press, Inc., New York.

[vii]

[viii]

TABLE OF CONTENTS

Part I. Lyric Poems

GROUP ONE

[x]

[xi]

Part III. Narrative and Dramatic Poems

Part IV. Satirical Poems

Part V. Pastoral Poems

PART VI. POEMS OF SERIOUS WIT AND SYMBOLISM

PART VII. POEMS OF RELIGIOUS EXPERIENCE

PART VIII. THE CREATION OF POEMS

PART IX. NOTES, 637

PART X. ON READING POEMS, 741

APPENDIX

PART I

LYRIC POEMS

GROUP ONE

1

Rest

O Earth, lie heavily upon her eyes;
Seal her sweet eyes weary of watching, Earth;
Lie close around her; leave no room for mirth
With its harsh laughter, nor for sound of sighs.
She hath no questions, she hath no replies,   5
Hushed in and curtained with a blessed dearth
Of all that irked her from the hour of birth;
With stillness that is almost Paradise.
Darkness more clear than noonday holdeth her,
Silence more musical than any song;   10
Even her very heart has ceased to stir:
Until the morning of Eternity
Her rest shall not begin nor end, but be;
And when she wakes she will not think it long.

2

Requiescat

Strew on her roses, roses,
   And never a spray of yew!
In quiet she reposes;
   Ah, would that I did too!

Her mirth the world required;   5
   She bathed it in smiles of glee.
But her heart was tired, tired,
   And now they let her be.

Her life was turning, turning,
   In mazes of heat and sound.   10
But for peace her soul was yearning,
   And now peace laps her round.

[3]

Her cabined, ample spirit,
    It fluttered and failed for breath.
Tonight it doth inherit   15
    The vasty hall of death.

3   *The Garden of Proserpine*

Here, where the world is quiet;
    Here, where all trouble seems
Dead winds' and spent waves' riot
    In doubtful dreams of dreams;
I watch the green field growing
For reaping folk and sowing,
For harvest-time and mowing,
    A sleepy world of streams.

I am tired of tears and laughter,
    And men that laugh and weep,   10
Of what may come hereafter
    For men that sow to reap;
I am weary of days and hours,
Blown buds of barren flowers,
Desires and dreams and powers
    And everything but sleep.

Here life has death for neighbor,
    And far from eye or ear
Wan waves and wet winds labor,
    Weak ships and spirits steer;   20
They drive adrift, and whither
They wot not who make thither;
But no such winds blow hither,
    And no such things grow here.

No growth of moor or coppice,
    No heather-flower or vine,
But bloomless buds of poppies,
    Green grapes of Proserpine,

[4]

Pale beds of blowing rushes
Where no leaf blooms or blushes   30
Save this whereout she crushes
    For dead men deadly wine.

Pale, without name or number,
    In fruitless fields of corn,
They bow themselves and slumber
    All night till light is born;
And like a soul belated,
In hell and heaven unmated,
By cloud and mist abated
    Comes out of darkness morn.   40

Though one were strong as seven,
    He too with death shall dwell,
Nor wake with wings in heaven,
    Nor weep for pains in hell;
Though one were fair as roses,
His beauty clouds and closes;
And well though love reposes,
    In the end it is not well.

Pale, beyond porch and portal,
    Crowned with calm leaves, she stands   50
Who gathers all things mortal
    With cold immortal hands;
Her languid lips are sweeter
Than love's who fears to greet her
To men that mix and meet her
    From many times and lands.

She waits for each and other,
    She waits for all men born;
Forgets the earth her mother,
    The life of fruits and corn;   60

[5]

And spring and seed and swallow
Take wing for her and follow
Where summer song rings hollow
　　And flowers are put to scorn.

There go the loves that wither,
　　The old loves with wearier wings;
And all dead years draw thither,
　　And all disastrous things;
Dead dreams of days forsaken,
Blind buds that snows have shaken,　　　　　　　70
Wild leaves that winds have taken,
　　Red strays of ruined springs.

We are not sure of sorrow,
　　And joy was never sure;
Today will die tomorrow;
　　Time stoops to no man's lure;
And love, grown faint and fretful,
With lips but half regretful
Sighs, and with eyes forgetful
　　Weeps that no loves endure.　　　　　　　80

From too much love of living,
　　From hope and fear set free,
We thank with brief thanksgiving
　　Whatever gods may be
That no life lives forever;
That dead men rise up never;
That even the weariest river　　　*seems contradiction*
　　Winds somewhere safe to sea.　　　　*religion*

Then star nor sun shall waken,
　　Nor any change of light;　　　　　　　90
Nor sound of waters shaken,
　　Nor any sound or sight;
Nor wintry leaves nor vernal,
Nor days nor things diurnal;
Only the sleep eternal
　　In an eternal night.

Nor skin nor hide nor fleece
   Shall cover you,
Nor curtain of crimson nor fine
Shelter of cedar-wood be over you,
   Nor the fir-tree   5
   Nor the pine.

Nor sight of whin nor gorse
   Nor river-yew,
Nor fragrance of flowering bush,
Nor wailing of reed-bird to waken you,   10
   Nor of linnet,
   Nor of thrush.

Nor word nor touch nor sight
   Of lover; you
Shall long through the night but for this: 15
The roll of the full tide to cover you
   Without question,
   Without kiss.

5   '*Fear no more*'

Fear no more the heat o' the sun,
   Nor the furious winter's rages;
Thou thy worldly task hast done,
   Home art gone, and ta'en thy wages;
Golden lads and girls all must,   5
As chimney-sweepers, come to dust.

Fear no more the frown o' the great,
   Thou art past the tyrant's stroke:
Care no more to clothe and eat;
   To thee the reed is as the oak;   10
The scepter, learning, physic, must
All follow this, and come to dust.

Fear no more the lightning-flash,
    Nor the all-dreaded thunder-stone;
Fear not slander, censure rash;   15
    Thou hast finish'd joy and moan:
All lovers young, all lovers must
Consign to thee, and come to dust.

No exorciser harm thee!
    Nor no witchcraft charm thee!   20
Ghost unlaid forbear thee!
    Nothing ill come near thee!
Quiet consummation have;
And renownèd be thy grave!

6   *'Hark, now everything is still'*

Hark, now everything is still;
The screech-owl and the whistler shrill
Call upon our dame aloud,
And bid her quickly don her shroud;
Much you had of land and rent,   5
Your length in clay's now competent.
A long war disturbed your mind;
Here your perfect peace is signed.
Of what is 't fools make such vain keeping?
Sin their conception, their birth weeping,   10
Their life a general mist of error,
Their death a hideous storm of terror.
Strew your hair with powders sweet,
Don clean linen, bathe your feet,
And, the foul fiend more to check,   15
A crucifix let bless your neck;
'Tis now full tide, 'tween night and day,
End your groan and come away.

[8]

7   *'Full fathom five thy father lies'*

Full fathom five thy father lies;
  Of his bones are coral made:
Those are pearls that were his eyes:
  Nothing of him that doth fade,
But doth suffer a sea-change
Into something rich and strange.
Sea-nymphs hourly ring his knell:
      [*Burden:* ding-dong.
Hark! now I hear them,—ding-dong, bell.

8   *'Call for the robin redbreast'*

Call for the robin redbreast and the wren,
Since o'er shady groves they hover,
And with leaves and flowers do cover
The friendless bodies of unburied men.
Call unto his funeral dole
The ant, the field-mouse, and the mole,
To rear him hillocks that shall keep him warm,
And, when gay tombs are robbed, sustain no harm;
But keep the wolf far thence, that's foe to men,
For with his nails he'll dig them up again.

9   *Dora*

She knelt upon her brother's grave,
    My little girl of six years old—
He used to be so good and brave,
    The sweetest lamb of all our fold;
He used to shout, he used to sing,   5
Of all our tribe the little king—
And so unto the turf her ear she laid,
To hark if still in that dark place he played.

    No sound! no sound!
    Death's silence was profound;   10
    And horror crept
Into her aching heart, and Dora wept.
If this is as it ought to be,
My God, I leave it unto Thee.

'A slumber did my spirit seal'

A slumber did my spirit seal;
    I had no human fears:
She seemed a thing that could not feel
    The touch of earthly years.

No motion has she now, no force;
    She neither hears nor sees;
Rolled round in earth's diurnal course,
    With rocks, and stones, and trees.

'She dwelt among the untrodden ways'

She dwelt among the untrodden ways
    Beside the springs of Dove,
A maid whom there were none to praise
    And very few to love:

A violet by a mossy stone   5
    Half hidden from the eye!
—Fair as a star, when only one
    Is shining in the sky.

She lived unknown, and few could know
    When Lucy ceased to be;   10
But she is in her grave, and, oh,
    The difference to me!

'Three years she grew'

Three years she grew in sun and shower,
Then Nature said, 'A lovelier flower
On earth was never sown;
This child I to myself will take;
She shall be mine, and I will make
A lady of my own.

'Myself will to my darling be
Both law and impulse: and with me
The girl, in rock and plain,
In earth and heaven, in glade and bower,   10
Shall feel an overseeing power
To kindle or restrain.

'She shall be sportive as the fawn
That wild with glee across the lawn
Or up the mountain springs;
And hers shall be the breathing balm,
And hers the silence and the calm
Of mute insensate things.

'The floating clouds their state shall lend
To her; for her the willow bend;   20
Nor shall she fail to see
Even in the motions of the storm
Grace that shall mold the maiden's form
By silent sympathy.

'The stars of midnight shall be dear
To her; and she shall lean her ear
In many a secret place
Where rivulets dance their wayward round,
And beauty born of murmuring sound
Shall pass into her face.   30

'And vital feelings of delight
Shall rear her form to stately height,
Her virgin bosom swell;
Such thoughts to Lucy I will give
While she and I together live
Here in this happy dell.'

Thus Nature spake—The work was done—
How soon my Lucy's race was run!
She died, and left to me
This heath, this calm, and quiet scene;   40
The memory of what has been,
And never more will be.

13   *'The night is freezing fast'*

The night is freezing fast,
   To-morrow comes December;
      And winterfalls of old
Are with me from the past;
   And chiefly I remember   5
      How Dick would hate the cold.

Fall, winter, fall; for he,
   Prompt hand and headpiece clever,
      Has woven a winter robe,
And made of earth and sea   10
   His overcoat for ever,
      And wears the turning globe.

14   *To an Athlete Dying Young*

The time you won your town the race
We chaired you through the market-place;
Man and boy stood cheering by,
And home we brought you shoulder-high.

To-day, the road all runners come,
Shoulder-high we bring you home,
And set you at your threshold down,
Townsman of a stiller town.

Smart lad, to slip betimes away
From fields where glory does not stay,   10
And early though the laurel grows
It withers quicker than the rose.

Eyes the shady night has shut
Cannot see the record cut,
And silence sounds no worse than cheers
After earth has stopped the ears.

Now you will not swell the rout
Of lads that wore their honors out,
Runners whom renown outran
And the name died before the man.   20

So set, before its echoes fade,
The fleet foot on the sill of shade,
And hold to the low lintel up
The still-defended challenge-cup.

And round that early-laurelled head
Will flock to gaze the strengthless dead,
And find unwithered on its curls
The garland briefer than a girl's.

15   *'On moonlit heath and lonesome bank'*

On moonlit heath and lonesome bank
   The sheep beside me graze;
And yon the gallows used to clank
   Fast by the four cross ways.

A careless shepherd once would keep
   The flocks by moonlight there,
And high amongst the glimmering sheep
   The dead man stood on air.

They hang us now in Shrewsbury jail;
   The whistles blow forlorn,   10
And trains all night groan on the rail
   To men that die at morn.

There sleeps in Shrewsbury jail to-night,
　　Or wakes, as may betide,
A better lad, if things went right,
　　Than most that sleep outside.

And naked to the hangman's noose
　　The morning clocks will ring
A neck God made for other use
　　Than strangling in a string.　　　　　　　　20

And sharp the link of life will snap,
　　And dead on air will stand
Heels that held up as straight a chap
　　As treads upon the land.

So here I'll watch the night and wait
　　To see the morning shine,
When he will hear the stroke of eight
　　And not the stroke of nine;

And wish my friend as sound a sleep
　　As lads' I did not know,　　　　　　　　　30
That shepherded the moonlit sheep
　　A hundred years ago.

16　　　　　*'The rain, it streams on stone and hillock'*

The rain, it streams on stone and hillock,
　　The boot clings to the clay.
Since all is done that's due and right
Let's home; and now, my lad, good-night,
　　For I must turn away.

Good-night, my lad, for nought's eternal;
　　No league of ours, for sure.
To-morrow I shall miss you less,
And ache of heart and heaviness
　　Are things that time should cure.　　　　　10

[14]

Over the hill the highway marches
   And what's beyond is wide:
Oh, soon enough will pine to nought
Remembrance and the faithful thought
   That sits the grave beside.

The skies, they are not always raining
   Nor grey the twelvemonth through;
And I shall meet good days and mirth,
And range the lovely lands of earth
   With friends no worse than you.   20

But oh, my man, the house is fallen
   That none can build again;
My man, how full of joy and woe
Your mother bore you years ago
   To-night to lie in the rain.

17   *For My Funeral*

O thou that from thy mansion
   Through time and place to roam,
Dost send abroad thy children,
   And then dost call them home,

That men and tribes and nations   5
   And all thy hand hath made
May shelter them from sunshine
   In thine eternal shade:

We now to peace and darkness
   And earth and thee restore   10
Thy creature that thou madest
   And wilt cast forth no more.

Good night. Ensured release,
Imperishable peace,
   Have these for yours.
While sky and sea and land
And earth's foundations stand   5
   And heaven endures.

When earth's foundations flee,
Nor sky nor land nor sea
   At all is found,
Content you; let them burn,   10
It is not your concern:
   Sleep on, sleep sound.

19   *Requiem*

Under the wide and starry sky,
Dig the grave and let me lie.
Glad did I live and gladly die,
And I laid me down with a will.

This be the verse you grave for me:
Here he lies where he longed to be;
Home is the sailor, home from sea,
And the hunter home from the hill.

20   *'Break, break, break'*

Break, break, break,
   On thy cold gray stones, O Sea!
And I would that my tongue could utter
   The thoughts that arise in me.

O well for the fisherman's boy,   5
   That he shouts with his sister at play!
O well for the sailor lad,
   That he sings in his boat on the bay!

And the stately ships go on
    To their haven under the hill;   10
But O for the touch of a vanished hand,
    And the sound of a voice that is still!

Break, break, break,
    At the foot of thy crags, O Sea!
But the tender grace of a day that is dead   15
    Will never come back to me.

21   *Lines for an Interment*

Now it is fifteen years you have lain in the meadow:
The boards at your face have gone through: the earth is
Packed down and the sound of the rain is fainter:
The roots of the first grass are dead:

It's a long time to lie in the earth with your honor:
The world, Soldier, the world has been moving on:

The girls wouldn't look at you twice in the cloth cap:
Six years old they were when it happened:

It bores them even in books: 'Soissons besieged!'
As for the gents they have joined the American Legion: 10

Belts and a brass band and the ladies' auxiliaries:
The Californians march in the OD silk:

We are all acting again like civilized beings:
People mention it at tea . . .

The Facts of Life we have learned are Economic:
You were deceived by the detonations of bombs:

You thought of courage and death when you thought of warfare:
Hadn't they taught you the fine words were unfortunate?

Now that we understand we judge without bias:
We feel of course for those who had to die: 20

[17]

Women have written us novels of great passion
Proving the useless death of the dead was a tragedy:

Nevertheless it is foolish to chew gall:
The foremost writers on both sides have apologized:

The Germans are back in the Midi with cropped hair:
The English are drinking the better beer in Bavaria:

You can rest now in the rain in the Belgian meadow—
Now that it's all explained away and forgotten:
Now that the earth is hard and the wood rots:

Now you are dead . . .   30

22   *Men*

(On a phrase of Apollinaire)

Our history is grave noble and tragic
We trusted the look of the sun on the green leaves
We built our towns of stone with enduring ornaments
We worked the hard flint for basins of water

We believed in the feel of the earth under us   5
We planted corn grapes apple-trees rhubarb
Nevertheless we knew others had died
Everything we have done has been faithful and dangerous

We believed in the promises made by the brows of women
We begot children at night in the warm wool   10
We comforted those who wept in fear on our shoulders
Those who comforted us had themselves vanished

We fought at the dikes in the bright sun for the pride of it
We beat drums and marched with music and laughter
We were drunk and lay with our fine dreams in the straw 15
We saw the stars through the hair of lewd women

Our history is grave noble and tragic
Many of us have died and are not remembered
Many cities are gone and their channels broken
We have lived a long time in this land and with honor   20

[18]

GROUP TWO

23 *Immortal Autumn*

I speak this poem now with grave and level voice
In praise of autumn of the far-horn-winding fall
I praise the flower-barren fields the clouds the tall
Unanswering branches where the wind makes sullen noise

I praise the fall it is the human season
                              now   5
No more the foreign sun does meddle at our earth
Enforce the green and bring the fallow land to birth
Nor winter yet weigh all with silence the pine bough

But now in autumn with the black and outcast crows
Share we the spacious world the whispering year is gone   10
There is more room to live now the once secret dawn
Comes late by daylight and the dark unguarded goes

Between the mutinous brave burning of the leaves
And winter's covering of our hearts with his deep snow
We are alone there are no evening birds we know   15
The naked moon the tame stars circle at our eaves

It is the human season on this sterile air
Do words outcarry breath the sound goes on and on
I hear a dead man's cry from autumn long since gone

I cry to you beyond upon this bitter air   20

24 *After Apple-Picking*

My long two-pointed ladder's sticking through a tree
Toward heaven still,
And there's a barrel that I didn't fill
Beside it, and there may be two or three

[19]

Apples I didn't pick upon some bough.
But I am done with apple-picking now.
Essence of winter sleep is on the night,
The scent of apples: I am drowsing off.
I cannot rub the strangeness from my sight
I got from looking through a pane of glass   10
I skimmed this morning from the drinking trough
And held against the world of hoary grass.
It melted, and I let it fall and break.
But I was well
Upon my way to sleep before it fell,
And I could tell
What form my dreaming was about to take.
Magnified apples appear and disappear,
Stem-end and blossom-end,
And every fleck of russet showing clear.   20
My instep arch not only keeps the ache,
It keeps the pressure of a ladder-round.
I feel the ladder sway as the boughs bend.
And I keep hearing from the cellar bin
The rumbling sound
Of load on load of apples coming in.
For I have had too much
Of apple-picking: I am overtired
Of the great harvest I myself desired.
There were ten thousand fruit to touch,   30
Cherish in hand, lift down, and not let fall.
For all
That struck the earth,
No matter if not bruised or spiked with stubble,
Went surely to the cider-apple heap
As of no worth.
One can see what will trouble
This sleep of mine, whatever sleep it is.
Were he not gone,
The woodchuck could say whether it's like his   40
Long sleep, as I describe its coming on,
Or just some human sleep.

To Autumn

Season of mists and mellow fruitfulness,
    Close bosom-friend of the maturing sun;
Conspiring with him how to load and bless
    With fruit the vines that round the thatch-eaves run;
To bend with apples the moss'd cottage-trees,
    And fill all fruit with ripeness to the core;
      To swell the gourd, and plump the hazel shells
With a sweet kernel; to set budding more,
    And still more, later flowers for the bees,
    Until they think warm days will never cease,   10
      For Summer has o'er-brimm'd their clammy cells.

Who hath not seen thee oft amid thy store?
    Sometimes whoever seeks abroad may find
Thee sitting careless on a granary floor,
    Thy hair soft-lifted by the winnowing wind;
Or on a half-reap'd furrow sound asleep,
    Drows'd with the fume of poppies, while thy hook
      Spares the next <u>swath</u> and all its twined flowers: *a line of grain as cut down*
And sometimes like a gleaner thou dost keep
    Steady thy laden head across a brook;   20
    Or by a cider-press, with patient look,
      Thou watchest the last oozings hours by hours.

Where are the songs of Spring? Ay, where are they?
    Think not of them, thou hast thy music too,—
While barred clouds bloom the soft-dying day,
    And touch the stubble-plains with rosy hue;
Then in a wailful choir the small gnats mourn
    Among the river sallows, borne aloft
      Or sinking as the light wind lives or dies;
And full-grown lambs loud bleat from hilly <u>bourn</u>; *stream* 30
    Hedge-crickets sing; and now with treble soft
    The redbreast whistles from a garden-croft;
      And gathering swallows twitter in the skies.

GROUP THREE

26
Fog

The fog comes
on little cat feet.
It sits looking
over harbor and city
on silent haunches
and then moves on.

27
Wind and Silver

Greatly shining,
The Autumn moon floats in the thin sky;
And the fish-ponds shake their backs and flash their dragon scales
As she passes over them.

28
Lost

Desolate and lone
All night long on the lake
Where fog trails and mist creeps,
The whistle of a boat
Calls and cries unendingly,
Like some lost child
In tears and trouble
Hunting the harbor's breast
And the harbor's eyes.

29
Grass

Pile the bodies high at Austerlitz and Waterloo.
Shovel them under and let me work—
      I am the grass; I cover all.
And pile them high at Gettysburg
And pile them high at Ypres and Verdun.
Shovel them under and let me work.
Two years, ten years, and passengers ask the conductor:

[22]

What place is this?
Where are we now?

I am the grass.
Let me work.

30
Velvet Shoes

Let us walk in the white snow
   In a soundless space;
With footsteps quiet and slow,
   At a tranquil pace,
     Under veils of white lace.   5

I shall go shod in silk,
   And you in wool,
White as a white cow's milk,
   More beautiful
     Than the breast of a gull.   10

We shall walk through the still town
   In a windless peace;
We shall step upon white down,
   Upon silver fleece,
     Upon softer than these.   15

We shall walk in velvet shoes:
   Wherever we go
Silence will fall like dews
   On white silence below.
     We shall walk in the snow.   20

31
The Solitary Reaper

Behold her, single in the field,
Yon solitary Highland lass!
Reaping and singing by herself;
Stop here, or gently pass!
Alone she cuts and binds the grain,
And sings a melancholy strain;
O listen! for the vale profound
Is overflowing with the sound.

[23]

No nightingale did ever chaunt
More welcome notes to weary bands   10
Of travelers in some shady haunt,
Among Arabian sands:
A voice so thrilling ne'er was heard
In springtime from the cuckoo-bird,
Breaking the silence of the seas
Among the farthest Hebrides.

Will no one tell me what she sings?—
Perhaps the plaintive numbers flow
For old, unhappy, far-off things,
And battles long ago;   20
Or is it some more humble lay,
Familiar matter of today?
Some natural sorrow, loss, or pain,
That has been, and may be again?

Whate'er the theme, the maiden sang
As if her song could have no ending;
I saw her singing at her work,
And o'er the sickle bending;—
I listened, motionless and still;
And, as I mounted up the hill,   30
The music in my heart I bore,
Long after it was heard no more.

32

To Night

Swiftly walk o'er the western wave,
   Spirit of Night!
Out of the misty eastern cave,
Where, all the long and lone daylight,
Thou wovest dreams of joy and fear,
Which make thee terrible and dear,—
   Swift be thy flight!

Wrap thy forms in a mantle gray,
                Star-inwrought!
Blind with thine hair the eyes of Day;   10
Kiss her until she be wearied out;
Then wander o'er city, and sea, and land,
Touching all with thine opiate wand—
                Come, long-sought!

When I arose and saw the dawn,
                I sighed for thee;
When light rode high, and the dew was gone,
And noon lay heavy on flower and tree,
And the weary Day turned to his rest,
Lingering like an unloved guest,   20
                I sighed for thee.

Thy brother Death came, and cried,
                Wouldst thou me?
Thy sweet child Sleep, the filmy-eyed,
Murmured like a noontide bee,
Shall I nestle near thy side?
Wouldst thou me?—And I replied,
                No, not thee!

Death will come when thou art dead,
                Soon, too soon;   30
Sleep will come when thou art fled;
Of neither will I ask the boon
I ask of thee, belovèd Night,—
Swift be thine approaching flight,
                Come, soon, soon!

I bring fresh showers for the thirsting flowers
    From the seas and the streams;
I bear light shade for the leaves when laid
    In their noonday dreams.
From my wings are shaken the dews that waken
    The sweet buds every one,
When rocked to rest on their mother's breast,
    As she dances about the sun.
I wield the flail of the lashing hail,
    And whiten the green plains under,   10
And then again I dissolve it in rain,
    And laugh as I pass in thunder.

I sift the snow on the mountains below,
    And their great pines groan aghast;
And all the night 'tis my pillow white,
    While I sleep in the arms of the blast.
Sublime on the towers of my skyey bowers,
    Lightning my pilot sits;
In a cavern under is fettered the thunder,
    It struggles and howls at fits;   20
Over earth and ocean, with gentle motion,
    This pilot is guiding me,
Lured by the love of the genii that move
    In the depths of the purple sea;
Over the rills, and the crags, and the hills,
    Over the lakes and the plains,
Wherever he dream, under mountain or stream,
    The Spirit he loves remains;
And I all the while bask in heaven's blue smile,
    Whilst he is dissolving in rains.   30

The sanguine sunrise, with his meteor eyes,
    And his burning plumes outspread,
Leaps on the back of my sailing rack,
    When the morning star shines dead;

As on the jag of a mountain crag,
　　Which an earthquake rocks and swings,
An eagle alit one moment may sit
　　In the light of its golden wings.
And when sunset may breathe, from the lit sea beneath,
　　Its ardors of rest and of love,　　　　　　　　　40
And the crimson pall of eve may fall
　　From the depth of heaven above,
With wings folded I rest, on mine airy nest,
　　As still as a brooding dove.

That orbèd maiden with white fire laden,
　　Whom mortals call the Moon,
Glides glimmering o'er my fleece-like floor,
　　By the midnight breezes strewn;
And wherever the beat of her unseen feet,
　　Which only the angels hear,　　　　　　　　　50
May have broken the woof of my tent's thin roof,
　　The stars peep behind her and peer;
And I laugh to see them whirl and flee,
　　Like a swarm of golden bees,
When I widen the rent in my wind-built tent,
　　Till the calm rivers, lakes, and seas,
Like strips of the sky fallen through me on high,
　　Are each paved with the moon and these.

I bind the sun's throne with a burning zone,
　　And the moon's with a girdle of pearl;　　　　60
The volcanos are dim, and the stars reel and swim,
　　When the whirlwinds my banner unfurl.
From cape to cape, with a bridge-like shape,
　　Over a torrent sea,
Sunbeam-proof, I hang like a roof,—
　　The mountains its columns be.
The triumphal arch through which I march
　　With hurricane, fire, and snow,

When the powers of the air are chained to my chair,
    Is the million-colored bow; 70
The sphere-fire above its soft colors wove,
    While the moist earth was laughing below.

I am the daughter of earth and water,
    And the nursling of the sky;
I pass through the pores of the ocean and shores;
    I change, but I cannot die.
For after the rain when with never a stain
    The pavilion of heaven is bare,
And the winds and sunbeams with their convex gleams
    Build up the blue dome of air, 80
I silently laugh at my own cenotaph,
    And out of the caverns of rain,
Like a child from the womb, like a ghost from the tomb,
    I arise and unbuild it again.

34   *A Decade*

When you came, you were like red wine and honey,
And the taste of you burnt my mouth with its sweetness.
Now you are like morning bread,
Smooth and pleasant.
I hardly taste you at all for I know your savor,
But I am completely nourished.

35   *The Bath Tub*

As a bathtub lined with white porcelain,
When the hot water gives out or goes tepid,
So is the slow cooling of our chivalrous passion,
O my much praised but-not-altogether-satisfactory lady.

36   *Pagani's, November 8*

Suddenly discovering in the eyes of the very beautiful
Normande cocotte
The eyes of the very learned British Museum assistant.

The Snare

I hear a sudden cry of pain!
There is a rabbit in a snare:
Now I hear the cry again,
But I cannot tell from where.

But I cannot tell from where   5
He is calling out for aid!
Crying on the frightened air,
Making everything afraid!

Making everything afraid!
Wrinkling up his little face!   10
As he cries again for aid;
—And I cannot find the place!

And I cannot find the place
Where his paw is in the snare!
Little One! Oh, Little One!   15
I am searching everywhere!

'Look, stranger, at this island now'

Look, stranger, at this island now
The leaping light for your delight discovers,
Stand stable here
And silent be,
That through the channels of the ear
May wander like a river
The swaying sound of the sea.

Here at the small field's ending pause
Where the chalk wall falls to the foam, and its tall ledges
Oppose the pluck   10
And knock of the tide,
And the shingle scrambles after the suck-
     ing surf, and the gull lodges
A moment on its sheer side.

[29]

Far off like floating seeds the ships
Diverge on urgent voluntary errands;
And the full view
Indeed may enter
And move in memory as now these clouds do,
That pass the harbor mirror   20
And all the summer through the water saunter.

39   *Voyages: I*

Above the fresh ruffles of the surf
Bright striped urchins flay each other with sand.
They have contrived a conquest for shell shucks,
And their fingers crumble fragments of baked weed
Gaily digging and scattering.   5

And in answer to their treble interjections
The sun beats lightning on the waves,
The waves fold thunder on the sand;
And could they hear me I would tell them:

O brilliant kids, frisk with your dog,   10
Fondle your shells and sticks, bleached
By time and the elements; but there is a line
You must not cross nor ever trust beyond it
Spry cordage of your bodies to caresses
Too lichen-faithful from too wide a breast.   15
The bottom of the sea is cruel.

40   *Voyages: II*

—And yet this great wink of eternity,
Of rimless floods, unfettered leewardings,
Samite sheeted and processioned where
Her undinal vast belly moonward bends,
Laughing the wrapt inflections of our love;

[30]

Take this Sea, whose diapason knells
On scrolls of silver snowy sentences,
The sceptered terror of whose sessions rends
As her demeanors motion well or ill,
All but the pieties of lovers' hands.   10

And onward, as bells off San Salvador
Salute the crocus lusters of the stars,
In these poinsettia meadows of her tides,—
Adagios of islands, O my Prodigal,
Complete the dark confessions her veins spell.

Mark how her turning shoulders wind the hours,
And hasten while her penniless rich palms
Pass superscription of bent foam and wave,—
Hasten, while they are true,—sleep, death, desire,
Close round one instant in one floating flower.   20

Bind us in time, O Seasons clear, and awe.
O minstrel galleons of Carib fire,
Bequeath us to no earthly shore until
Is answered in the vortex of our grave
The seal's wide spindrift gaze toward paradise.

The City in the Sea

41

Lo! Death has reared himself a throne
In a strange city lying alone
Far down within the dim West,
Where the good and the bad and the worst and the best
Have gone to their eternal rest.
There shrines and palaces and towers
(Time-eaten towers that tremble not!)
Resemble nothing that is ours.
Around, by lifting winds forgot,
Resignedly beneath the sky   10
The melancholy waters lie.

No rays from the holy heaven come down
On the long night-time of that town;
But light from out the lurid sea
Streams up the turrets silently—
Gleams up the pinnacles far and free—
Up domes—up spires—up kingly halls—
Up fanes—up Babylon-like walls—
Up shadowy long-forgotten bowers
Of sculptured ivy and stone flowers—
Up many and many a marvelous shrine
Whose wreathèd friezes intertwine
The viol, the violet, and the vine.

Resignedly beneath the sky
The melancholy waters lie.
So blend the turrets and shadows there
That all seem pendulous in air,
While from a proud tower in the town
Death looks gigantically down.

There open fanes and gaping graves
Yawn level with the luminous waves;
But not the riches there that lie
In each idol's diamond eye—
Not the gaily-jeweled dead
Tempt the waters from their bed;
For no ripples curl, alas!
Along that wilderness of glass—
No swellings tell that winds may be
Upon some far-off happier sea—
No heavings hint that winds have been
On seas less hideously serene.

But lo, a stir is in the air!
The wave—there is a movement there!
As if the towers had thrust aside,
In slightly sinking, the dull tide—
As if their tops had feebly given
A void within the filmy Heaven.

The waves have now a redder glow—
The hours are breathing faint and low—
And when, amid no earthly moans,   50
Down, down that town shall settle hence,
Hell, rising from a thousand thrones,
Shall do it reverence.

Kubla Khan

In Xanadu did Kubla Khan
A stately pleasure-dome decree:
Where Alph, the sacred river, ran
Through caverns measureless to man
    Down to a sunless sea.
So twice five miles of fertile ground
With walls and towers were girdled round:
And there were gardens bright with sinuous rills,
Where blossomed many an incense-bearing tree;
And here were forests ancient as the hills,   10
Enfolding sunny spots of greenery.

But oh! that deep romantic chasm which slanted
Down the green hill athwart a cedarn cover!
A savage place! as holy and enchanted
As e'er beneath a waning moon was haunted
By woman wailing for her demon-lover!
And from this chasm, with ceaseless turmoil seething,
As if this earth in fast thick pants were breathing,
A mighty fountain momently was forced:
Amid whose swift half-intermitted burst   20
Huge fragments vaulted like rebounding hail,
Or chaffy grain beneath the thresher's flail:
And 'mid these dancing rocks at once and ever
It flung up momently the sacred river.
Five miles meandering with a mazy motion
Through wood and dale the sacred river ran,
Then reached the caverns measureless to man,
And sank in tumult to a lifeless ocean:

And 'mid this tumult Kubla heard from far
Ancestral voices prophesying war!   30
The shadow of the dome of pleasure
Floated midway on the waves;
Where was heard the mingled measure
From the fountain and the caves.
It was a miracle of rare device,
A sunny pleasure-dome with caves of ice!

A damsel with a dulcimer
In a vision once I saw:
It was an Abyssinian maid,
And on her dulcimer she played,   40
Singing of Mount Abora.
Could I revive within me
Her symphony and song,
To such a deep delight 'twould win me,
That with music loud and long,
I would build that dome in air,
That sunny dome! those caves of ice!
And all who heard should see them there,
And all should cry, Beware! Beware!
His flashing eyes, his floating hair!   50
Weave a circle round him thrice,
And close your eyes with holy dread,
For he on honey-dew hath fed,
And drunk the milk of Paradise.

43

To Daffodils

Fair daffodils, we weep to see
    You haste away so soon;
As yet the early-rising sun
    Has not attained his noon.
        Stay, stay,   5
        Until the hasting day
        Has run
        But to the even-song;
And, having prayed together, we
        Will go with you along.   10

We have short time to stay, as you;
    We have as short a spring,
As quick a growth to meet decay,
    As you, or anything.
        We die   15
        As your hours do, and dry
        Away
        Like to the summer's rain,
Or as the pearls of morning's dew,
        Ne'er to be found again.   20

44

The Yellow Violet

When beechen buds begin to swell,
    And woods the bluebird's warble know,
The yellow violet's modest bell
    Peeps from the last year's leaves below.

Ere russet fields their green resume,
    Sweet flower, I love, in forest bare,
To meet thee, when thy faint perfume
    Alone is in the virgin air.

[35]

Of all her train, the hands of Spring
    First plant thee in the watery mold,
And I have seen thee blossoming
    Beside the snow-bank's edges cold.

Thy parent sun, who bade thee view
    Pale skies, and chilling moisture sip,
Has bathed thee in his own bright hue,
    And streaked with jet thy glowing lip.

Yet slight thy form, and low thy seat,
    And earthward bent thy gentle eye,
Unapt the passing view to meet,
    When loftier flowers are flaunting nigh.

Oft, in the sunless April day,
    Thy early smile has stayed my walk;
But midst the gorgeous blooms of May,
    I passed thee on thy humble stalk.

So they who climb to wealth forget
    The friends in darker fortunes tried.
I copied them—but I regret
    That I should ape the ways of pride.

And when again the genial hour
    Awakes the painted tribes of light,
I'll not o'erlook the modest flower
    That made the woods of April bright.

45   *'Ah, Sunflower, weary of time'*

Ah, Sunflower, weary of time,
    Who countest the steps of the sun;
Seeking after that sweet golden clime
    Where the traveler's journey is done;

Where the youth pined away with desire,
   And the pale virgin shrouded in snow,
Arise from their graves, and aspire
   Where my Sunflower wishes to go!

To a Skylark

Hail to thee, blithe Spirit!
   Bird thou never wert,
That from heaven, or near it,
   Pourest thy full heart
In profuse strains of unpremeditated art.

Higher still and higher
   From the earth thou springest
Like a cloud of fire;
   The blue deep thou wingest,
And singing still dost soar, and soaring ever singest.   10

In the golden lightning
   Of the sunken sun,
O'er which clouds are bright'ning,
   Thou dost float and run;
Like an unbodied joy whose race is just begun.

The pale purple even
   Melts around thy flight;
Like a star of heaven,
   In the broad daylight
Thou art unseen, but yet I hear thy shrill delight,   20

Keen as are the arrows
   Of that silver sphere,
Whose intense lamp narrows
   In the white dawn clear
Until we hardly see—we feel that it is there.

All the earth and air
　　With thy voice is loud,
As, when night is bare,
　　From one lonely cloud
The moon rains out her beams, and heaven is overflowed.　　30

What thou art we know not;
　　What is most like thee?
From rainbow clouds there flow not
　　Drops so bright to see
As from thy presence showers a rain of melody.

Like a poet hidden
　　In the light of thought,
Singing hymns unbidden,
　　Till the world is wrought
To sympathy with hopes and fears it heeded not:　　40

Like a high-born maiden
　　In a palace tower,
Soothing her love-laden
　　Soul in secret hour
With music sweet as love, which overflows her bower:

Like a glow-worm golden
　　In a dell of dew,
Scattering unbeholden
　　Its aërial hue
Among the flowers and grass, which screen it from the view!　　50

Like a rose embowered
　　In its own green leaves,
By warm winds deflowered,
　　Till the scent it gives
Makes faint with too much sweet those heavy-wingèd thieves:

Sound of vernal showers
　　On the twinkling grass,
Rain-awakened flowers,
　　All that ever was
Joyous, and clear, and fresh, thy music doth surpass:　　60

[38]

Teach us, sprite or bird,
    What sweet thoughts are thine:
I have never heard
    Praise of love or wine
That panted forth a flood of rapture so divine.

Chorus hymeneal,
    Or triumphal chant,
Matched with thine would be all
    But an empty vaunt,
A thing wherein we feel there is some hidden want.   70

What objects are the fountains
    Of thy happy strain?
What fields, or waves, or mountains?
    What shapes of sky or plain?
What love of thine own kind? what ignorance of pain?

With thy clear keen joyance
    Languor cannot be:
Shadow of annoyance
    Never came near thee:
Thou lovest—but ne'er knew love's sad satiety.   80

Waking or asleep,
    Thou of death must deem
Things more true and deep
    Than we mortals dream,
Or how could thy notes flow in such a crystal stream?

We look before and after,
    And pine for what is not:
Our sincerest laughter
    With some pain is fraught;
Our sweetest songs are those that tell of saddest thought.   90

Yet if we could scorn
    Hate, and pride, and fear;
If we were things born
    Not to shed a tear,
I know not how thy joy we ever should come near.

Better than all measures
  Of delightful sound,
Better than all treasures
  That in books are found,
Thy skill to poet were, thou scorner of the ground!   100

Teach me half the gladness
  That thy brain must know,
Such harmonious madness
  From my lips would flow
The world should listen then—as I am listening now.

47   *The Darkling Thrush*

I leant upon a coppice gate
    When Frost was specter-gray,
And Winter's dregs made desolate
    The weakening eye of day.
The tangled bine-stems scored the sky
    Like strings of broken lyres,
And all mankind that haunted nigh
    Had sought their household fires.

The land's sharp features seemed to be
    The Century's corpse outleant,   10
His crypt the cloudy canopy,
    The wind his death-lament.
The ancient pulse of germ and birth
    Was shrunken hard and dry,
And every spirit upon earth
    Seemed fervorless as I.

At once a voice arose among
   The bleak twigs overhead
In a full-hearted evensong
   Of joy illimited;   20
An aged thrush, frail, gaunt, and small,
   In blast-beruffled plume,
Had chosen thus to fling his soul
   Upon the growing gloom.

So little cause for carolings
   Of such ecstatic sound
Was written on terrestrial things
   Afar or nigh around,
That I could think there trembled through
   His happy good-night air   30
Some blessed Hope, whereof he knew
   And I was unaware.

48   *'Western wind, when will thou blow'*

> Western wind, when will thou blow,
>   The small rain down can rain?
> Christ, if my love were in my arms
>   And I in my bed again!

49   *'Cupid and my Campaspe played'*

> Cupid and my Campaspe played
> At cards for kisses; Cupid paid.
> He stakes his quiver, bow, and arrows,
> His mother's doves and team of sparrows,
> Loses them too; then down he throws   5
> The coral of his lip, the rose
> Growing on's cheek (but none knows how),
> With these the crystal of his brow,
> And then the dimple of his chin:
> All these did my Campaspe win.   10
> At last he set her both his eyes;
> She won, and Cupid blind did rise.
>   O Love! has she done this to thee?
>   What shall, alas, become of me?

50   *'Rose-cheeked Laura'*

> Rose-cheeked Laura, come,
> Sing thou smoothly with thy beauty's
> Silent music, either other
>   Sweetly gracing.
>
> Lovely forms do flow   5
> From concent divinely framèd;
> Heav'n is music, and thy beauty's
>   Birth is heavenly.

[42]

These dull notes we sing
Discords need for helps to grace them;   10
Only beauty purely loving
    Knows no discord,

But still moves delight,
Like clear springs renewed by flowing,
Ever perfect, ever in them-   15
    Selves eternal.

51   *'Follow your saint'*

Follow your saint, follow with accents sweet;
Haste you, sad notes, fall at her flying feet.
There, wrapped in cloud of sorrow, pity move,
And tell the ravisher of my soul I perish for her love.
But if she scorns my never-ceasing pain,   5
Then burst with sighing in her sight and ne'er return again.

All that I sung still to her praise did tend,
Still she was first, still she my songs did end.
Yet she my love and music both doth fly,
The music that her echo is and beauty's sympathy.   10
Then let my notes pursue her scornful flight:
It shall suffice that they were breathed and died for her delight.

52   *'There is a garden in her face'*

    There is a garden in her face,
Where roses and white lilies grow;
    A heav'nly paradise is that place,
Wherein all pleasant fruits do flow.
      There cherries grow which none may buy   5
      Till cherry-ripe themselves do cry.

Those cherries fairly do enclose
Of orient pearl a double row,
   Which when her lovely laughter shows,
They look like rosebuds filled with snow.   10
   Yet them nor peer nor prince can buy,
   Till cherry-ripe themselves do cry.

Her eyes like angels watch them still;
Her brows like bended bows do stand,
   Threat'ning with piercing frowns to kill   15
All that attempt with eye or hand
   Those sacred cherries to come nigh,
   Till cherry-ripe themselves do cry.

53   *'Fair and fair and twice so fair'*

Œnone

Fair and fair and twice so fair,
   As fair as any may be;
The fairest shepherd on our green,
   A love for any lady.

Paris

Fair and fair and twice so fair,
   As fair as any may be;
Thy love is fair for thee alone,
   And for no other lady.

Œnone

My love is fair, my love is gay,
As fresh as been the flowers in May,   10
And of my love my roundelay,
My merry, merry, merry roundelay
Concludes with Cupid's curse:
They that do change old love for new,
Pray gods they change for worse.

Both together

They that do change old love for new,
Pray gods they change for worse.

Œnone

Fair and fair and twice so fair,
    As fair as any may be;
The fairest shepherd on our green,   20
    A love for any lady.

Paris

Fair and fair and twice so fair,
    As fair as any may be,
Thy love is fair for thee alone,
    And for no other lady.

Œnone

My love can pipe, my love can sing,
My love can many a pretty thing,
And of his lovely praises ring
My merry, merry roundelays.
        Amen to Cupid's curse: 30
They that do change old love for new,
Pray gods they change for worse.

Paris

They that do change old love for new,
Pray gods they change for worse.

Both together

Fair and fair and twice so fair,
    As fair as any may be;
Thy love is fair for thee alone,
    And for no other lady.

[45]

Prothalamion

Calme was the day, and through the trembling ayre
Sweete breathing Zephyrus did softly play,
A gentle spirit, that lightly did delay
Hot Titans beames, which then did glyster fayre:
When I, whom sullein care,
Through discontent of my long fruitlesse stay
In princes court, and expectation vayne
Of idle hopes, which still doe fly away,
Like empty shaddowes, did aflict my brayne,
Walkt forth to ease my payne   10
Along the shoare of silver streaming Themmes;
Whose rutty bancke, the which his river hemmes,
Was paynted all with variable flowers,
And all the meades adornd with daintie gemmes,
Fit to decke maydens bowres,
And crowne their paramours,
Against the brydale day, which is not long:
    Sweete Themmes, runne softly, till I end my song.

There, in a meadow, by the rivers side,
A flocke of nymphes I chaunced to espy,   20
All lovely daughters of the flood thereby,
With goodly greenish locks all loose untyde,
As each had bene a bryde:
And each one had a little wicker basket,
Made of fine twigs entrayled curiously,
In which they gathered flowers to fill their flasket;
And with fine fingers cropt full feateously
The tender stalkes on hye.
Of every sort, which in that meadow grew,
They gathered some; the violet pallid blew,   30
The little dazie, that at evening closes,
The virgin lillie, and the primrose trew,
With store of vermeil roses,
To decke their bridegromes posies
Against the brydale day, which was not long:
    Sweete Themmes, runne softly, till I end my song.

With that I saw two swannes of goodly hewe
Come softly swimming downe along the lee;
Two fairer birds I yet did never see:
The snow which doth the top of Pindus strew   40
Did never whiter shew;
Nor Jove himselfe, when he a swan would be
For love of Leda, whiter did appeare:
Yet Leda was, they say, as white as he,
Yet not so white as these, nor nothing neare;
So purely white they were,
That even the gentle streame, the which them bare,
Seem'd foule to them, and bad his billowes spare
To wet their silken feathers, least they might
Soyle their fayre plumes with water not so fayre,   50
And marre their beauties bright,
That shone as heavens light,
Against their brydale day, which was not long:
    Sweete Themmes, runne softly, till I end my song.

Eftsoones the nymphes, which now had flowers their fill,
Ran all in haste to see that silver brood,
As they came floating on the christal flood;
Whom when they sawe, they stood amazed still,
Their wondring eyes to fill,
Them seem'd they never saw a sight so fayre,   60
Of fowles so lovely, that they sure did deeme
Them heavenly borne, or to be that same payre
Which through the skie draw Venus silver teeme;
For sure they did not seeme
To be begot of any earthly seede,
But rather angels or of angels breede:
Yet were they bred of Somers-heat, they say,
In sweetest season, when each flower and weede
The earth did fresh aray;
So fresh they seem'd as day,   70
Even as their brydale day, which was not long:
    Sweete Themmes, runne softly, till I end my song.

Then forth they all out of their baskets drew
Great store of flowers, the honour of the field,
That to the sense did fragrant odours yeild,
All which upon those goodly birds they threw,
And all the waves did strew,
That like old Peneus waters they did seeme,
When downe along by pleasant Tempes shore,
Scattred with flowres, through Thessaly they streeme,   80
That they appeare, through lillies plenteous store,
Like a brydes chamber flore.
Two of those nymphes, meane while, two garlands bound
Of freshest flowres which in that mead they found,
The which presenting all in trim array,
Their snowie foreheads therewithall they crownd,
Whil'st one did sing this lay,
Prepar'd against that day,
Against their brydale day, which was not long:
    Sweete Themmes, runne softly, till I end my song.   90

'Ye gentle birdes, the worlds faire ornament,
And heavens glorie, whom this happie hower
Doth leade unto your lovers blisfull bower,
Joy may you have and gentle hearts content
Of your loves couplement:
And let faire Venus, that is Queene of Love,
With her heart-quelling sonne upon you smile,
Whose smile, they say, hath vertue to remove
All loves dislike, and friendships faultie guile
For ever to assoile.   100
Let endlesse peace your steadfast hearts accord,
And blessèd plentie wait upon your bord;
And let your bed with pleasures chast abound,
That fruitfull issue may to you afford,
Which may your foes confound,
And make your joyes redound,
Upon your brydale day, which is not long:
    Sweete Themmes, run softlie, till I end my song.'

[48]

So ended she; and all the rest around
To her redoubled that her undersong, 110
Which said, their bridale daye should not be long.
And gentle Eccho from the neighbour ground
Their accents did resound.
So forth those joyous birdes did passe along,
Adowne the lee, that to them murmurde low,
As he would speake, but that he lackt a tong,
Yeat did by signes his glad affection show,
Making his streame run slow.
And all the foule which in his flood did dwell
Gan flock about these twaine, that did excell 120
The rest so far as Cynthia doth shend
The lesser starres. So they, enranged well,
Did on those two attend,
And their best service lend,
Against their wedding day, which was not long:
　　Sweete Themmes! run softly, till I end my song.

At length they all to mery London came,
To mery London, my most kyndly nurse,
That to me gave this lifes first native sourse;
Though from another place I take my name, 130
An house of auncient fame.
There when they came, whereas those bricky towres
The which on Themmes brode agèd backe doe ryde,
Where now the studious lawyers have their bowers,
There whylome wont the Templer Knights to byde,
Till they decayd through pride:
Next whereunto there standes a stately place,
Where oft I gayned giftes and goodly grace
Of that great lord which therein wont to dwell,
Whose want too well now feeles my freendles case: 14c
But ah! here fits not well
Olde woes, but joyes to tell
Against the bridale daye, which is not long:
　　Sweete Themmes, runne softly, till I end my song.

[49]

Yet therein now doth lodge a noble peer,
Great Englands glory and the worlds wide wonder,
Whose dreadfull name late through all Spaine did thunder,
And Hercules two pillors standing neere
Did make to quake and feare.
Faire branch of honor, flower of chevalrie,   150
That fillest England with thy triumphes fame,
Joy have thou of thy noble victorie,
And endlesse happinesse of thine owne name
That promiseth the same:
That through thy prowesse and victorious armes,
Thy country may be freed from forraine harmes;
And great Elisaes glorious name may ring
Through al the world, fil'd with thy wide alarmes,
Which some brave Muse may sing
To ages following,   160
Upon the brydale day, which is not long:
  Sweete Themmes, runne softly, till I end my song.

From those high towers this noble lord issuing,
Like radiant Hesper when his golden hayre
In th' ocean billowes he hath bathed fayre,
Descended to the rivers open vewing,
With a great traine ensuing.
Above the rest were goodly to bee seene
Two gentle knights of lovely face and feature,
Beseeming well the bower of anie queene,   170
With gifts of wit and ornaments of nature,
Fit for so goodly stature:
That like the twins of Jove they seem'd in sight,
Which decke the bauldricke of the heavens bright.
They two, forth pacing to the rivers side,
Received those two faire brides, their loves delight,
Which, at th' appointed tyde,
Each one did make his bryde,
Against their brydale day, which is not long:
  Sweete Themmes! runne softly, till I end my song.   180

55   *'Drink to me only with thine eyes'*

Drink to me only with thine eyes,
     And I will pledge with mine;
Or leave a kiss but in the cup,
     And I'll not look for wine.
The thirst that from the soul doth arise   5
     Doth ask a drink divine;
But might I of Jove's nectar sup,
     I would not change for thine.
I sent thee late a rosy wreath,
     Not so much honoring thee   10
As giving it a hope that there
     It could not withered be.
But thou thereon didst only breathe,
     And sent'st it back to me;
Since when it grows and smells, I swear,   15
     Not of itself, but thee.

56   *'Still to be neat, still to be dressed'*

Still to be neat, still be to dressed
As you were going to a feast;
Still to be powdered, still perfumed:
Lady, it is to be presumed,
Though art's hid causes are not found,   5
All is not sweet, all is not sound.

Give me a look, give me a face
That makes simplicity a grace;
Robes loosely flowing, hair as free:
Such sweet neglect more taketh me   10
Than all th' adulteries of art;
They strike mine eyes, but not my heart.

57   *Delight in Disorder*

A sweet disorder in the dress
     Kindles in clothes a wantonness;
A lawn about the shoulders thrown
     Into a fine distraction,

18960

An erring lace, which here and there   5
Enthralls the crimson stomacher,
A cuff neglectful, and thereby
Ribands to flow confusedly,
A winning wave, deserving note,
In the tempestuous petticoat,   10
A careless shoe-string, in whose tie
I see a wild civility,
Do more bewitch me than when art
Is too precise in every part.

58   *Upon Julia's Clothes*

Whenas in silks my Julia goes,
Then, then, methinks, how sweetly flows
That liquefaction of her clothes.

Next, when I cast mine eyes and see
That brave vibration each way free,
Oh, how that glittering taketh me!

59   *'Come, my Celia, let us prove'*

Come, my Celia, let us prove
While we may the sports of love;
Time will not be ours forever,
He at length our good will sever.
Spend not then his gifts in vain;   5
Suns that set may rise again,
But if once we lose this light,
'Tis with us perpetual night.
Why should we defer our joys?
Fame and rumor are but toys.   10
Cannot we delude the eyes
Of a few poor household spies?
Or his easier ears beguile,
So removèd by our wile?
'Tis no sin love's fruit to steal;   15
But the sweet theft to reveal,
To be taken, to be seen,
These have crimes accounted been.

[52]

To the virgins, to make much of time

Gather ye rosebuds while ye may,
   Old time is still a-flying,
And this same flower that smiles to-day,
   To-morrow will be dying.

The glorious lamp of heaven, the sun,   5
   The higher he's a-getting,
The sooner will his race be run,
   And nearer he's to setting.

That age is best which is the first,
   When youth and blood are warmer;   10
But being spent, the worse, and worst
   Times still succeed the former.

Then be not coy, but use your time,
   And while you may, go marry;
For having lost but once your prime,   15
   You may for ever tarry.

              Cherry-ripe

Cherry-ripe, ripe, ripe, I cry,
Full and fair ones; come and buy.
If so be you ask me where
They do grow, I answer: There,
Where my Julia's lips do smile;
There's the land, or cherry-isle,
Whose plantations fully show
All the year where cherries grow.

        '*Go and catch a falling star*'

Go and catch a falling star,
   Get with child a mandrake root, *(thought to ressemble the human shape)*
Tell me where all past years are,
   Or who cleft the devil's foot,

divided spirited [53]

Teach me to hear mermaids singing,
   Or to keep off envy's stinging,
      And find
      What wind
Serves to advance an honest mind.

If thou beest born to strange sights,   10
   Things invisible to see,
Ride ten thousand days and nights,
   Till age snow white hairs on thee,
Thou, when thou return'st, wilt tell me
All strange wonders that befell thee,
      And swear
      No where
Lives a woman true, and fair.

If thou find'st one, let me know,
   Such a pilgrimage were sweet;   20
Yet do not, I would not go,
   Though at next door we might meet;
Though she were true when you met her,
And till last you write your letter,
      Yet she
      Will be
False, ere I come, to two or three.

63   *'Why so pale and wan, fond lover?'*

Why so pale and wan, fond lover?
   Prithee, why so pale?
Will, when looking well can't move her,
   Looking ill prevail?
   Prithee, why so pale?   5

Why so dull and mute, young sinner?
   Prithee, why so mute?
Will, when speaking well can't win her,
   Saying nothing do 't?
   Prithee, why so mute?   10

Quit, quit, for shame, this will not move,
  This cannot take her.
If of herself she will not love,
  Nothing can make her.
  The devil take her!   15

64   *'Out upon it! I have loved'*

Out upon it! I have loved
  Three whole days together;
And am like to love three more,
  If it prove fair weather.

Time shall moult away his wings,   5
  Ere he shall discover
In the whole wide world again
  Such a constant lover.

But the spite on 't is, no praise
  Is due at all to me;   10
Love with me had made no stays,
  Had it any been but she.

Had it any been but she,
  And that very face,
There had been at least ere this   15
  A dozen dozen in her place.

65   *Song, by a Person of Quality*

Flutt'ring spread thy purple Pinions,
  Gentle *Cupid*, o'er my Heart;
I a Slave in thy Dominions;
  Nature must give way to Art.

Mild *Arcadians*, ever blooming,
   Nightly nodding o'er your Flocks,
See my weary Days consuming,
   All beneath yon flow'ry Rocks.

Thus the *Cyprian* Goddess weeping,
   Mourn'd *Adonis*, darling Youth: 10
Him the Boar in Silence creeping,
   Gor'd with unrelenting Tooth.

Cynthia, tune harmonious Numbers;
   Fair *Discretion*, string the Lyre;
Sooth my ever-waking Slumbers:
   Bright *Apollo*, lend thy Choir.

Gloomy *Pluto*, King of Terrors,
   Arm'd in adamantine Chains,
Lead me to the Crystal Mirrors,
   Wat'ring soft Elysian Plains.   20

Mournful Cypress, verdant Willow,
   Gilding my *Aurelia's* Brows,
Morpheus hov'ring o'er my Pillow,
   Hear me pay my dying Vows.

Melancholy smooth *Maeander*,
   Swiftly purling in a Round,
On thy Margin Lovers wander,
   With thy flow'ry Chaplets crown'd.

Thus when *Philomela* drooping,
   Softly seeks her silent Mate,   30
See the Bird of *Juno* stooping;
   Melody resigns to Fate.

'The time I've lost in wooing'

The time I've lost in wooing,
In watching and pursuing
    The light that lies
    In woman's eyes,
Has been my heart's undoing.
Though Wisdom oft has sought me,
I scorn'd the lore she brought me,
    My only books
    Were woman's looks,
And folly's all they've taught me.   10

Her smile when Beauty granted,
I hung with gaze enchanted,
    Like him, the Sprite,
    Whom maids by night
Oft meet in glen that's haunted.
Like him, too, Beauty won me,
But while her eyes were on me;
    If once their ray
    Was turn'd away,
Oh, winds could not outrun me.   20

And are those follies going?
And is my proud heart growing
    Too cold or too wise
    For brilliant eyes
Again to set it glowing?
No, vain, alas! th' endeavor
From bonds so sweet to sever;
    Poor Wisdom's chance
    Against a glance
Is now as weak as ever.   30

'Is my team plowing'

'Is my team plowing,
    That I was used to drive
And hear the harness jingle
    When I was man alive?'

Ay, the horses trample,
  The harness jingles now;
No change though you lie under
  The land you used to plow.

'Is football playing
  Along the river shore,
With lads to chase the leather,
  Now I stand up no more?'

Ay, the ball is flying,
  The lads play heart and soul;
The goal stands up, the keeper
  Stands up to keep the goal.

'Is my girl happy,
  That I thought hard to leave,
And has she tired of weeping
  As she lies down at eve?'

Ay, she lies down lightly,
  She lies not down to weep:
Your girl is well contented.
  Be still, my lad, and sleep.

'Is my friend hearty,
  Now I am thin and pine,
And has he found to sleep in
  A better bed than mine?'

Yes, lad, I lie easy,
  I lie as lads would choose;
I cheer a dead man's sweetheart—
  Never ask me whose.

To Perilla

Ah my Perilla! dost thou grieve to see
Me, day by day, to steal away from thee?
Age calls me hence, and my gray hairs bid come
And haste away to mine eternal home;
'Twill not be long, Perilla, after this,   5
That I must give thee the supremest kiss;
Dead when I am, first cast in salt, and bring
Part of the cream from that religious spring,
With which, Perilla, wash my hands and feet;
That done, then wind me in that very sheet   10
Which wrapped thy smooth limbs when thou didst implore
The gods' protection but the night before.
Follow me weeping to my turf, and there
Let fall a primrose, and with it a tear;
Then lastly, let some weekly strewings be   15
Devoted to the memory of me;
Then shall my ghost not walk about, but keep
Still in the cool and silent shades of sleep.

69   *When You are Old*

When you are old and gray and full of sleep,
And nodding by the fire, take down this book,
And slowly read, and dream of the soft look
Your eyes had once, and of their shadows deep;

How many loved your moments of glad grace,   5
And loved your beauty with love false or true;
But one man loved the pilgrim soul in you,
And loved the sorrows of your changing face.

And bending down beside the glowing bars
Murmur, a little sadly, how love fled   10
And paced upon the mountains overhead
And hid his face amid a crowd of stars.

After the fierce midsummer all ablaze
Has burned itself to ashes and expires
In the intensity of its own fires,
Then come the mellow, mild, St. Martin days
Crowned with the calm of peace, but sad with haze. 5
So after Love has led us, till he tires
Of his own throes and torments, and desires,
Comes large-eyed Friendship: with a restful gaze
He beckons us to follow, and across
Cool, verdant vales we wander free from care. 10
Is it a touch of frost lies in the air?
Why are we haunted with a sense of loss?
We do not wish the pain back, or the heat;
And yet, and yet, these days are incomplete.

71   *John Anderson, my Jo*

John Anderson, my jo, John,
 When we were first acquent,
Your locks were like the raven,
 Your bonie brow was brent:
But now your brow is beld, John, 5
 Your locks are like the snaw;
But blessings on your frosty pow,
 John Anderson, my jo!

John Anderson, my jo, John,
 We clamb the hill thegither; 10
And monie a cantie day, John,
 We've had wi' ane anither:
Now we maun totter down, John,
 And hand in hand we'll go,
And sleep thegither at the foot, 15
 John Anderson, my jo!

'O, wert thou in the cauld blast'

O, wert thou in the cauld blast,
 On yonder lea, on yonder lea,
My plaidie to the angry airt,
 I'd shelter thee, I'd shelter thee;
Or did misfortune's bitter storms   5
 Around thee blaw, around thee blaw,
Thy bield should be my bosom,
 To share it a', to share it a'.

Or were I in the wildest waste,
 Sae black and bare, sae black and bare,   10
The desert were a paradise
 If thou wert there, if thou wert there;
Or were I monarch of the globe,
 Wi' thee to reign, wi' thee to reign,
The brightest jewel in my crown   15
 Wad be my queen, wad be my queen.

Ae Fond Kiss

Ae fond kiss, and then we sever!
Ae farewell, and then forever!
Deep in heart-wrung tears I'll pledge thee;
Warring sighs and groans I'll wage thee.
Who shall say that Fortune grieves him
While the star of hope she leaves him?
Me, nae cheerfu' twinkle lights me,
Dark despair around benights me.

I'll ne'er blame my partial fancy;
Naething could resist my Nancy: 10
But to see her was to love her,
Love but her and love forever.
Had we never loved sae kindly,
Had we never loved sae blindly,
Never met, or never parted,
We had ne'er been broken-hearted.

Fare-thee-weel, thou first and fairest!
Fare-thee-weel, thou best and dearest!
Thine be ilka joy and treasure,
Peace, enjoyment, love, and pleasure!   20
Ae fond kiss, and then we sever;
Ae farewell, alas, forever!
Deep in heart-wrung tears I'll pledge thee;
Warring sighs and groans I'll wage thee.

74   *Ye Flowery Banks*

Ye flowery banks o' bonie Doon,
　　How can ye blume sae fair?
How can ye chant, ye little birds,
　　And I sae fu' o' care?

Thou'll break my heart, thou bonie bird,   5
　　That sings upon the bough;
Thou minds me o' the happy days
　　When my fause luve was true.

Thou'll break my heart, thou bonie bird,
　　That sings beside thy mate;   10
For sae I sat, and sae I sang,
　　And wist na o' my fate.

Aft hae I rov'd by bonie Doon,
　　To see the woodbine twine,
And ilka bird sang o' its luve,   15
　　And sae did I o' mine.

Wi' lightsome heart I pu'd a rose,
　　Frae aff its thorny tree;
And my fause luver staw my rose,
　　But left the thorn wi' me.   20

'O, my luv is like a red, red rose'

O, my luv is like a red, red rose,
    That's newly sprung in June:
O, my luv is like the melodie
    That's sweetly played in tune.

As fair art thou, my bonie lass,   5
    So deep in luve am I;
And I will luve thee still, my dear,
    Till a' the seas gang dry:

Till a' the seas gang dry, my dear,
    And the rocks melt wi' the sun;   10
And I will luve thee still, my dear,
    While the sands o' life shall run.

And fare thee weel, my only luve!
    And fare thee weel awhile!
And I will come again, my luve,   15
    Tho' it were ten thousand mile!

'There be none of Beauty's daughters'

There be none of Beauty's daughters
    With a magic like thee;
And like music on the waters
    Is thy sweet voice to me:
When, as if its sound were causing   5
The charmed ocean's pausing,
The waves lie still and gleaming,
And the lull'd winds seem dreaming:

And the midnight moon is weaving
    Her bright chain o'er the deep;   10
Whose breast is gently heaving,
    As an infant's asleep:
So the spirit bows before thee,
To listen and adore thee;
With a full but soft emotion,   15
Like the swell of Summer's ocean.

She walks in beauty, like the night
    Of cloudless climes and starry skies;
And all that's best of dark and bright
    Meet in her aspect and her eyes:
Thus mellow'd to that tender light   5
    Which heaven to gaudy day denies.

One shade the more, one ray the less,
    Had half impaired the nameless grace
Which waves in every raven tress,
    Or softly lightens o'er her face;   10
Where thoughts serenely sweet express
    How pure, how dear their dwelling-place.

And on that cheek, and o'er that brow,
    So soft, so calm, yet eloquent,
The smiles that win, the tints that glow,   15
    But tell of days in goodness spent,
A mind at peace with all below,
    A heart whose love is innocent!

78   *'So, we'll go no more a-roving'*

So, we'll go no more a-roving
    So late into the night,
Though the heart be still as loving,
    And the moon be still as bright.

For the sword outwears its sheath,   5
    And the soul wears out the breast,
And the heart must pause to breathe,
    And love itself have rest.

Though the night was made for loving,
    And the day returns too soon,   10
Yet we'll go no more a-roving
    By the light of the moon.

'When the lamp is shattered'

When the lamp is shattered,
The light in the dust lies dead;
When the cloud is scattered,
The rainbow's glory is shed;
When the lute is broken,
Sweet tones are remembered not;
When the lips have spoken,
Loved accents are soon forgot.

As music and splendor
Survive not the lamp and the lute,   10
The heart's echoes render
No song when the spirit is mute:—
No song but sad dirges,
Like the wind through a ruined cell,
Or the mournful surges
That ring the dead seaman's knell.

When hearts have once mingled,
Love first leaves the well-built nest;
The weak one is singled
To endure what it once possessed.   20
O Love! who bewailest
The frailty of all things here,
Why choose you the frailest
For your cradle, your home, and your bier?

Its passions will rock thee,
As the storms rock the ravens on high;
Bright reason will mock thee,
Like the sun from a wintry sky.
From thy nest every rafter
Will rot, and thine eagle home   30
Leave thee naked to laughter,
When leaves fall and cold winds come.

[65]

'Music, when soft voices die'

Music, when soft voices die,
Vibrates in the memory;
Odors, when sweet violets sicken,
Live within the sense they quicken.

Rose leaves, when the rose is dead,
Are heaped for the belovèd's bed;
And so thy thoughts, when thou art gone,
Love itself shall slumber on.

'Now sleeps the crimson petal'

Now sleeps the crimson petal, now the white;
Nor waves the cypress in the palace walk;
Nor winks the gold fin in the porphyry font.
The firefly wakens; waken thou with me.

Now droops the milk-white peacock like a ghost,   5
And like a ghost she glimmers on to me.

Now lies the Earth all Danaë to the stars,
And all thy heart lies open unto me.

Now slides the silent meteor on, and leaves
A shining furrow, as thy thoughts in me.   10

Now folds the lily all her sweetness up,
And slips into the bosom of the lake.
So fold thyself, my dearest, thou, and slip
Into my bosom and be lost in me.

To Helen

Helen, thy beauty is to me
  Like those Nicèan barks of yore,
That gently, o'er a perfumed sea,
  The weary, way-worn wanderer bore
  To his own native shore.   5

On desperate seas long wont to roam,
  Thy hyacinth hair, thy classic face,
Thy Naiad airs have brought me home
  To the glory that was Greece,
And the grandeur that was Rome.   10

Lo! in yon brilliant window-niche
  How statue-like I see thee stand,
  The agate lamp within thy hand!
Ah! Psyche, from the regions which
  Are Holy-Land!   15

83
The Sleeper

At midnight, in the month of June,
I stand beneath the mystic moon.
An opiate vapor, dewy, dim,
Exhales from out her golden rim,
And, softly dripping, drop by drop,
Upon the quiet mountain top,
Steals drowsily and musically
Into the universal valley.
The rosemary nods upon the grave;
The lily lolls upon the wave;   10
Wrapping the fog about its breast,
The ruin molders into rest;
Looking like Lethe, see! the lake
A conscious slumber seems to take,
And would not, for the world, awake.
All Beauty sleeps!—and lo! where lies
(Her casement open to the skies)
Irene, with her Destinies!

Oh, lady bright! can it be right—
This window open to the night?   20
The wanton airs, from the tree-top,
Laughingly through the lattice drop—
The bodiless airs, a wizard rout,
Flit through thy chamber in and out,
And wave the curtain canopy

[67]

So fitfully—so fearfully—
Above the closed and fringèd lid
'Neath which thy slumb'ring soul lies hid,
That, o'er the floor and down the wall,
Like ghosts the shadows rise and fall!   30
Oh, lady dear, hast thou no fear?
Why and what art thou dreaming here?
Sure thou art come o'er far-off seas,
A wonder to these garden trees!
Strange is thy pallor! strange thy dress!
Strange, above all, thy length of tress,
And this all-solemn silentness!

The lady sleeps! Oh, may her sleep,
Which is enduring, so be deep!
Heaven have her in its sacred keep!   40
This chamber changed for one more holy,
This bed for one more melancholy,
I pray to God that she may lie
For ever with unopened eye,
While the dim sheeted ghosts go by!

My love, she sleeps! Oh, may her sleep,
As it is lasting, so be deep!
Soft may the worms about her creep!
Far in the forest, dim and old,
For her may some tall vault unfold—   50
Some vault that oft hath flung its black
And wingèd panels fluttering back,
Triumphant, o'er the crested palls
Of her grand family funerals—
Some sepulchre, remote, alone,
Against whose portal she hath thrown,
In childhood many an idle stone—
Some tomb from out whose sounding door
She ne'er shall force an echo more,
Thrilling to think, poor child of sin!   60
It was the dead who groaned within.

Chamber Music

84 a

Bright cap and streamers,
  He sings in the hollow:
  Come follow, come follow,
    All you that love.
Leave dreams to the dreamers   5
  That will not after,
  That song and laughter
    Do nothing move.

With ribbons streaming
  He sings the bolder;   10
  In troop at his shoulder
    The wild bees hum.
And the time of dreaming
  Dreams is over—
  As lover to lover,   15
    Sweetheart, I come.

84 b

      *   *   *

Because your voice was at my side
  I gave him pain,
Because within my hand I held
  Your hand again.

There is no word nor any sign
  Can make amend—
He is a stranger to me now
  Who was my friend.

84 c

      *   *   *

O Sweetheart, hear you
  Your lover's tale;
A man shall have sorrow
  When friends him fail.

For he shall know then   5
  Friends be untrue
And a little ashes
  Their words come to.

But one unto him
    Will softly move
And softly woo him
    In ways of love.

His hand is under
    Her smooth round breast;
So he who has sorrow
    Shall have rest.

*   *   *

In the dark pine-wood
    I would we lay,
In deep cool shadow
    At noon of day.

How sweet to lie there,
    Sweet to kiss,
Where the great pine-forest
    Enaisled is!

Thy kiss descending
    Sweeter were
With a soft tumult
    Of thy hair.

O, unto the pine-wood
    At noon of day
Come with me now,
    Sweet love, away.

*   *   *

Now, O now, in this brown land
    Where Love did so sweet music make
We two shall wander, hand in hand,
    Forbearing for old friendship' sake,
Nor grieve because our love was gay
Which now is ended in this way.

[70]

A rogue in red and yellow dress
    Is knocking, knocking at the tree;
And all around our loneliness
    The wind is whistling merrily.   10
The leaves—they do not sigh at all
When the year takes them in the fall.

No, O now, we hear no more
    The villanelle and roundelay!
Yet will we kiss, sweetheart, before   15
    We take sad leave at close of day.
Grieve not, sweetheart, for anything—
The year, the year is gathering.

85   *'White in the moon the long road lies'*

White in the moon the long road lies,
    The moon stands blank above;
White in the moon the long road lies
    That leads me from my love.

Still hangs the hedge without a gust,   5
    Still, still the shadows stay:
My feet upon the moonlit dust
    Pursue the ceaseless way.

The world is round, so travellers tell,
    And straight though reach the track,   10
Trudge on, trudge on, 'twill all be well,
    The way will guide one back.

But ere the circle homeward hies
    Far, far must it remove:
White in the moon the long road lies   15
    That leads me from my love.

Que be-m vols mal

Note.—Anyone who has read anything of the troubadours knows
well the tale of Bertran of Born and My Lady Maent of Montaignac,
and knows also the song he made when she would none of him, the
song wherein he, seeking to find or make her equal, begs of each pre-
eminent lady of Langue d'Oc some trait or some fair semblance: thus
of Cembelins her 'esgart amoros' to wit, her love-lit glance, of Aelis
her speech free-running, of the Vicomtess of Chalais her throat and
her two hands, at Roacoart of Anhes her hair golden as Iseult's; and
even in this fashion of Lady Audiart 'although she would that ill
come unto him' he sought and praised the lineaments of the torse.
And all this to make 'Una dompna soiseubuda' a borrowed lady or as
the Italians translated it 'Una donna ideal.'

> Though thou well dost wish me ill,
> > Audiart, Audiart,
> Where thy bodice laces start
> As ivy fingers clutching through
> Its crevices,
> > Audiart, Audiart,
> Stately, tall and lovely tender
> Who shall render
> > Audiart, Audiart,
> Praises meet unto thy fashion?   10
> Here a word kiss!
> > Pass I on
> Unto Lady 'Miels-de-Ben,'
> Having praised thy girdle's scope
> How the stays ply back from it;
> I breathe no hope
> That thou shouldst . . .
> > Nay no whit
> Bespeak thyself for anything.
> Just a word in thy praise, girl,   20
> Just for the swirl
> Thy satins make upon the stair,
> 'Cause never a flaw was there

Where thy torse and limbs are met
Though thou hate me, read it set
In rose and gold.
Or when the minstrel, tale half told,
Shall burst to lilting at the praise
                    'Audiart, Audiart' . . .
Bertrans, master of his lays,   30
Bertrans of Aultaforte thy praise
Sets forth, and though thou hate me well,
Yea though thou wish me ill,
                    Audiart, Audiart.
Thy loveliness is here writ till,
                    Audiart,
Oh, till thou come again.
And being bent and wrinkled, in a form
That hath no perfect limning, when the warm
Youth dew is cold   40
Upon thy hands, and thy old soul
Scorning a new, wry'd casement,
Churlish at seemed misplacement,
Finds the earth as bitter
As now seems it sweet,
Being so young and fair
As then only in dreams,
Being then young and wry'd,
Broken of ancient pride,
Thou shalt then soften,   50
Knowing, I know not how,
Thou wert once she
                    Audiart, Audiart
For whose fairness one forgave
                    Audiart,
Audiart
            Que be-m vols mal.

87   *Spring*

When daisies pied and violets blue
    And lady-smocks all silver-white
And cuckoo-buds of yellow hue
    Do paint the meadows with delight,
The cuckoo then, on every tree,   5
Mocks married men; for thus sings he,
                    Cuckoo;
Cuckoo, cuckoo: O, word of fear,
Unpleasing to a married ear!

When shepherds pipe on oaten straws,   10
    And merry larks are plowmen's clocks,
When turtles tread, and rooks, and daws,
    And maidens bleach their summer smocks,
The cuckoo then, on every tree,
Mocks married men; for thus sings he,   15
                    Cuckoo;
Cuckoo, cuckoo: O, word of fear,
Unpleasing to a married ear!

88   *Winter*

When icicles hang by the wall,
    And Dick the shepherd blows his nail,
And Tom bears logs into the hall,
    And milk comes frozen home in pail,
When blood is nipp'd, and ways be foul,   5
Then nightly sings the staring owl,
                    Tu-who;
Tu-whit, tu-who—a merry note,
While greasy Joan doth keel the pot.

When all aloud the wind doth blow,   10
    And coughing drowns the parson's saw,
And birds sit brooding in the snow,
    And Marian's nose looks red and raw,
When roasted crabs hiss in the bowl,
Then nightly sings the staring owl,   15
            Tu-who;
Tu-whit, tu-who—a merry note,
While greasy Joan doth keel the pot.

89   *'Hark, hark! the lark'*

Hark, hark! the lark at heaven's gate sings,
    And Phœbus 'gins arise,
His steeds to water at those springs
    On chaliced flowers that lies;
And winking Mary-buds begin
    To ope their golden eyes:
With everything that pretty is,
    My lady sweet, arise:
        Arise, arise.

90   *'Where the bee sucks'*

Where the bee sucks, there suck I:
In a cowslip's bell I lie;
There I couch when owls do cry.
On the bat's back I do fly
After summer merrily:
Merrily, merrily shall I live now
Under the blossom that hangs on the bough.

91   *'Tell me where is fancy bred'*

Tell me where is fancy bred,
Or in the heart or in the head?
How begot, how nourishèd?
        Reply, reply.

[75]

It is engender'd in the eyes,
With gazing fed; and fancy dies
In the cradle where it lies.
Let us all ring fancy's knell:
I'll begin it,—Ding, dong, bell.

92   '*It was a lover and his lass*'

It was a lover and his lass,
  With a hey, and a ho, and a hey nonino,
That o'er the green corn-field did pass
  In the spring-time, the only pretty ring-time,
When birds do sing, hey ding a ding, ding!
  Sweet lovers love the spring.

Between the acres of the rye,
  With a hey, and a ho, and a hey nonino,
These pretty country folks would lie,
  In spring-time, the only pretty ring-time,   10
When birds do sing, hey ding a ding, ding!
  Sweet lovers love the spring.

This carol they began that hour,
  With a hey, and a ho, and a hey nonino,
How that a life was but a flower
  In spring-time, the only pretty ring-time,
When birds do sing, hey ding a ding, ding!
  Sweet lovers love the spring.

And therefore take the present time,
  With a hey, and a ho, and a hey nonino,   20
For love is crowned with the prime
  In spring-time, the only pretty ring-time,
When birds do sing, hey ding a ding, ding!
  Sweet lovers love the spring.

93

'Who is Silvia?'

Who is Silvia? what is she?
    That all our swains commend her?
Holy, fair, and wise is she;
    The heaven such grace did lend her,
That she might admired be.   5

Is she kind as she is fair?
    For beauty lives with kindness:
Love doth to her eyes repair,
    To help him of his blindness;
And, being help'd, inhabits there.   10

Then to Silvia let us sing,
    That Silvia is excelling;
She excels each mortal thing
    Upon the dull earth dwelling;
To her let us garlands bring.   15

94   'Take, O take those lips away'

Take, O take those lips away,
    That so sweetly were forsworn;
And those eyes, the break of day,
    Lights that do mislead the morn:
But my kisses bring again,
                        bring again,
Seals of love, but seal'd in vain,
                        seal'd in vain.

95   'When that I was and a little tiny boy'

When that I was and a little tiny boy,
    With hey, ho, the wind and the rain;
A foolish thing was but a toy,
    For the rain it raineth every day.

But when I came to man's estate,   5
    With hey, ho, the wind and the rain;
'Gainst knaves and thieves men shut their gates,
    For the rain it raineth every day.

[77]

But when I came, alas! to wive,
　With hey, ho, the wind and the rain;　　　　　　10
By swaggering could I never thrive,
　For the rain it raineth every day.

But when I came unto my beds,
　With hey, ho, the wind and the rain;
With toss-pots still had drunken heads,　　　　　15
　For the rain it raineth every day;

A great while ago the world begun,
　With hey, ho, the wind and the rain;
But that's all one, our play is done,
　And we'll strive to please you every day.　　　20

96　　　　　*'Blow, blow, thou winter wind'*

Blow, blow, thou winter wind,
Thou art not so unkind
　As man's ingratitude;
Thy tooth is not so keen,
Because thou art not seen,　　　　　　　　　　5
　Although thy breath be rude.
Heigh-ho! sing, heigh-ho! unto the green holly:
Most friendship is feigning, most loving mere folly.
　Then heigh-ho! the holly!
　　This life is most jolly.　　　　　　　　　10

Freeze, freeze, thou bitter sky,
That dost not bite so nigh
　As benefits forgot:
Though thou the waters warp,
Thy sting is not so sharp　　　　　　　　　　15
　As friend remember'd not.
Heigh-ho! sing, heigh-ho! unto the green holly:
Most friendship is feigning, most loving mere folly.
　Then heigh-ho! the holly!
　　This life is most jolly!　　　　　　　　20

[78]

97

Philomela

Hark! ah, the nightingale—
The tawny-throated!
Hark, from that moonlit cedar what a burst!
What triumph! hark!—what pain!

O wanderer from a Grecian shore,
Still, after many years, in distant lands,
Still nourishing in thy bewildered brain
That wild, unquenched, deep-sunken, old-world pain—
Say, will it never heal?   *colloquial*
And can this fragrant lawn   10
With its cool trees, and night,
And the sweet, tranquil Thames,
And moonshine, and the dew,
To thy racked heart and brain
Afford no balm?

Dost thou tonight behold,
Here, through the moonlight on this English grass,
The unfriendly palace in the Thracian wild?
Dost thou again peruse
With hot cheeks and seared eyes   20
The too clear web, and thy dumb sister's shame?
Dost thou once more assay
Thy flight, and feel come over thee,
Poor fugitive, the feathery change
Once more, and once more seem to make resound
With love and hate, triumph and agony,
Lone Daulis, and the high Cephissian vale?
Listen, Eugenia—
How thick the bursts come crowding through the leaves!
Again—thou hearest?
Eternal passion!   30
Eternal pain!

Swallow, my sister, O sister swallow,
   How can thine heart be full of the spring?
     A thousand summers are over and dead.
What hast thou found in the spring to follow?
   What hast thou found in thine heart to sing?
     What wilt thou do when the summer is shed?

O swallow, sister, O fair swift swallow,
   Why wilt thou fly after spring to the south,
     The soft south whither thine heart is set?
Shall not the grief of the old time follow?   10
   Shall not the song thereof cleave to thy mouth?
     Hast thou forgotten ere I forget?

Sister, my sister, O fleet sweet swallow,
   Thy way is long to the sun and the south;
     But I, fulfilled of my heart's desire,
Shedding my song upon height, upon hollow,
   From tawny body and sweet small mouth
     Feed the heart of the night with fire.

I the nightingale all spring through,
   O swallow, sister, O changing swallow,   20
     All spring through till the spring be done,
Clothed with the light of the night on the dew,
   Sing, while the hours and the wild birds follow,
     Take flight and follow and find the sun.

Sister, my sister, O soft light swallow,
   Though all things feast in the spring's guest-chamber,
     How hast thou heart to be glad thereof yet?
For where thou fliest I shall not follow,
   Till life forget and death remember,
     Till thou remember and I forget.   30

Swallow, my sister, O singing swallow,
   I know not how thou hast heart to sing.
      Hast thou the heart? is it all past over?
Thy lord the summer is good to follow,
   And fair the feet of thy lover the spring;
      But what wilt thou say to the spring, thy lover?

O swallow, sister, O fleeting swallow,
   My heart in me is a molten ember,
      And over my head the waves have met.
But thou wouldst tarry or I would follow,   40
   Could I forget or thou remember,
      Couldst thou remember and I forget.

O sweet stray sister, O shifting swallow,
   The heart's division divideth us.
      Thy heart is light as a leaf of a tree;
But mine goes forth among sea-gulfs hollow
   To the place of the slaying of Itylus,
      The feast of Daulis, the Thracian sea.

O swallow, sister, O rapid swallow,
   I pray thee sing not a little space.   50
      Are not the roofs and the lintels wet?
The woven web that was plain to follow,
   The small slain body, the flowerlike face,
      Can I remember if thou forget?

O sister, sister, thy first-begotten!
   The hands that cling and the feet that follow,
      The voice of the child's blood crying yet
Who hath remembered me? who hath forgotten?
   Thou hast forgotten, O summer swallow,
      But the world shall end when I forget.   60

Nightingales

Beautiful must be the mountains whence ye come,
And bright in the fruitful valleys the streams wherefrom
      Ye learn your song:
Where are those starry woods? O might I wander there,
   Among the flowers, which in that heavenly air   5
      Bloom the year long!

Nay, barren are those mountains and spent the streams:
Our song is the voice of desire, that haunts our dreams,
      A throe of the heart,
Whose pining visions dim, forbidden hopes profound,   10
   No dying cadence nor long sigh can sound,
      For all our art.

Alone, aloud in the raptured ear of men
We pour our dark nocturnal secret; and then,
      As night is withdrawn   15
From these sweet-springing meads and bursting boughs of May,
   Dream, while the innumerable choir of day
      Welcome the dawn.

100   *Ode on Melancholy*

No, no! go not to Lethe, neither twist
    Wolf's-bane, tight-rooted, for its poisonous wine;
Nor suffer thy pale forehead to be kiss'd
    By nightshade, ruby grape of Proserpine;
Make not your rosary of yew-berries,
    Nor let the beetle, nor the death-moth be
        Your mournful Psyche, nor the downy owl
A partner in your sorrow's mysteries;
    For shade to shade will come too drowsily,
        And drown the wakeful anguish of the soul.   10

But when the melancholy fit shall fall
    Sudden from heaven like a weeping cloud,
That fosters the droop-headed flowers all,
    And hides the green hill in an April shroud;
Then glut thy sorrow on a morning rose,
    Or on the rainbow of the salt sand-wave,
        Or on the wealth of globed peonies;
Or if thy mistress some rich anger shows,
    Emprison her soft hand, and let her rave,
        And feed deep, deep upon her peerless eyes.   20

She dwells with Beauty—Beauty that must die;
    And Joy, whose hand is ever at his lips
Bidding adieu; and aching Pleasure nigh,
    Turning to poison while the bee-mouth sips:
Ay, in the very temple of Delight
    Veil'd Melancholy has her sovran shrine,
        Though seen of none save him whose strenuous tongue
    Can burst Joy's grape against his palate fine;
His soul shall taste the sadness of her might,
        And be among her cloudy trophies hung.   30

My heart aches, and a drowsy numbness pains
    My sense, as though of hemlock I had drunk,
Or emptied some dull opiate to the drains
    One minute past, and Lethe-wards had sunk:
'Tis not through envy of thy happy lot,
    But being too happy in thine happiness,—
        That thou, light-wingèd Dryad of the trees,
          In some melodious plot
    Of beechen green, and shadows numberless,
      Singest of summer in full-throated ease.   10

O for a draught of vintage! that hath been
    Cool'd a long age in the deep-delvèd earth,
Tasting of Flora and the country-green,
    Dance, and Provençal song, and sunburnt mirth!
O for a beaker full of the warm South!
    Full of the true, the blushful Hippocrene,
        With beaded bubbles winking at the brim,
          And purple-stainèd mouth;
    That I might drink, and leave the world unseen,
      And with thee fade away into the forest dim: 20

Fade far away, dissolve, and quite forget
    What thou among the leaves hast never known,
The weariness, the fever, and the fret
    Here, where men sit and hear each other groan;
Where palsy shakes a few, sad, last gray hairs,
    Where youth grows pale, and specter-thin, and dies;
        Where but to think is to be full of sorrow
          And leaden-eyed despairs;
    Where Beauty cannot keep her lustrous eyes,
      Or new Love pine at them beyond to-morrow.   30

Away! away! for I will fly to thee,
    Not charioted by Bacchus and his pards,
But on the viewless wings of Poesy,
    Though the dull brain perplexes and retards:
Already with thee! tender is the night,
    And haply the Queen-Moon is on her throne,
        Cluster'd around by all her starry fays;
            But here there is no light,
    Save what from heaven is with the breezes blown
        Through verdurous glooms and winding mossy ways.   40

vegetation

I cannot see what flowers are at my feet,
    Nor what soft incense hangs upon the boughs,
But, in embalmèd darkness, guess each sweet
    Wherewith the seasonable month endows
The grass, the thicket, and the fruit-tree wild;
    White hawthorn, and the pastoral eglantine;   *sweet briar*
        Fast fading violets cover'd up in leaves;
            And mid-May's eldest child,
    The coming musk-rose, full of dewy wine,
        The murmurous haunt of flies on summer eves.   50

Darkling I listen; and, for many a time
    I have been half in love with easeful Death,
Call'd him soft names in many a musèd rhyme,
    To take into the air my quiet breath;
Now more than ever seems it rich to die,
    To cease upon the midnight with no pain,
        While thou art pouring forth thy soul abroad
            In such an ecstasy!
    Still wouldst thou sing, and I have ears in vain—
        To thy high requiem become a sod.   60

Thou wast not born for death, immortal bird!
  No hungry generations tread thee down;
The voice I hear this passing night was heard
  In ancient days by emperor and clown:
Perhaps the self-same song that found a path
    Through the sad heart of Ruth, when, sick for home,
      She stood in tears amid the alien corn;
        The same that oft-times hath
    Charm'd magic casements, opening on the foam
    Of perilous seas, in faery lands forlorn.   70

Forlorn! the very word is like a bell
  To toll me back from thee to my sole self!
Adieu! the fancy cannot cheat so well
  As she is famed to do, deceiving elf.
Adieu! adieu! thy plaintive anthem fades
    Past the near meadows, over the still stream,
      Up the hill-side; and now 'tis buried deep
        In the next valley-glades:
    Was it a vision, or a waking dream?
    Fled is that music:—do I wake or sleep?   80

102   *Ode on a Grecian Urn*

Thou still unravish'd bride of quietness,
  Thou foster-child of silence and slow time,
Sylvan historian, who canst thus express
  A flowery tale more sweetly than our rhyme:
What leaf-fring'd legend haunts about thy shape
  Of deities or mortals, or of both,
    In Tempe or the dales of Arcady?
  What men or gods are these? What maidens loth?
What mad pursuit? What struggle to escape?
    What pipes and timbrels? What wild ecstasy?   10

Heard melodies are sweet, but those unheard
  Are sweeter; therefore, ye soft pipes, play on;
Not to the sensual ear, but, more endear'd,
  Pipe to the spirit ditties of no tone:
Fair youth, beneath the trees, thou canst not leave
  Thy song, nor ever can those trees be bare;
    Bold lover, never, never canst thou kiss,
Though winning near the goal—yet, do not grieve;
    She cannot fade, though thou hast not thy bliss,
  Forever wilt thou love, and she be fair!   20

Ah, happy, happy boughs! that cannot shed
  Your leaves, nor ever bid the spring adieu;
And, happy melodist, unwearied,
  Forever piping songs forever new;
More happy love! more happy, happy love!
  Forever warm and still to be enjoy'd,
    Forever panting, and forever young;
All breathing human passion far above,
    That leaves a heart high-sorrowful and cloy'd,
  A burning forehead, and a parching tongue.   30

Who are these coming to the sacrifice?
  To what green altar, O mysterious priest,
Lead'st thou that heifer lowing at the skies,
  And all her silken flanks with garlands drest?
What little town by river or sea-shore,
  Or mountain-built with peaceful citadel,
    Is emptied of this folk, this pious morn?
And, little town, thy streets forevermore
  Will silent be; and not a soul to tell
    Why thou art desolate, can e'er return.   40

O Attic shape! fair attitude! with brede
   Of marble men and maidens overwrought,
With forest branches and the trodden weed;
   Thou, silent form! dost tease us out of thought
As doth eternity. Cold Pastoral!
   When old age shall this generation waste,
     Thou shalt remain, in midst of other woe
Than ours, a friend to man, to whom thou say'st,
'Beauty is truth, truth beauty,' that is all
   Ye know on earth, and all ye need to know.   50

103   *Ode*

Intimations of Immortality from Recollections of Early Childhood

> The Child is father of the Man;
> And I could wish my days to be
> Bound each to each by natural piety.

I

There was a time when meadow, grove, and stream,
The earth, and every common sight,
     To me did seem
     Apparelled in celestial light,
The glory and the freshness of a dream.
It is not now as it hath been of yore;—
     Turn wheresoe'er I may,
     By night or day,
The things which I have seen I now can see no more.

II

     The Rainbow comes and goes,   10
     And lovely is the Rose,
     The Moon doth with delight
Look round her when the heavens are bare,
     Waters on a starry night
     Are beautiful and fair;
   The sunshine is a glorious birth;
   But yet I know, where'er I go,
That there hath past away a glory from the earth.

III

Now, while the birds thus sing a joyous song,
   And while the young lambs bound   20
       As to the tabor's sound,
To me alone there came a thought of grief:
A timely utterance gave that thought relief,
     And I again am strong:
The cataracts blow their trumpets from the steep;
No more shall grief of mine the season wrong;
I hear the Echoes through the mountains throng,
The Winds come to me from the fields of sleep,
    And all the earth is gay;
      Land and sea   30
   Give themselves up to jollity,
    And with the heart of May
Doth every beast keep holiday;—
    Thou Child of Joy,
Shout round me, let me hear thy shouts, thou happy Shepherd-boy!

Ye blessèd Creatures, I have heard the call
    Ye to each other make; I see
The heavens laugh with you in your jubilee;
    My heart is at your festival,
    My head hath its coronal,   40
The fullness of your bliss, I feel—I feel it all.
    Oh evil day! if I were sullen
    While Earth herself is adorning,
      This sweet May-morning,
   And the children are culling
      On every side,
   In a thousand valleys far and wide,
    Fresh flowers; while the sun shines warm,
And the Babe leaps up on his mother's arm:—
    I hear, I hear, with joy I hear!   50
    —But there's a Tree, of many, one,
A single Field which I have looked upon,
Both of them speak of something that is gone:
    The Pansy at my feet
    Doth the same tale repeat:
Whither is fled the visionary gleam?
Where is it now, the glory and the dream?

Our birth is but a sleep and a forgetting:
The Soul that rises with us, our life's Star,
  Hath had elsewhere its setting,   60
   And cometh from afar:
  Not in entire forgetfulness,
  And not in utter nakedness,
But trailing clouds of glory do we come
  From God, who is our home:
Heaven lies about us in our infancy!
Shades of the prison-house begin to close
  Upon the growing Boy,
But he beholds the light, and whence it flows,
  He sees it in his joy;   70
The Youth, who daily farther from the east
  Must travel, still is Nature's priest,
  And by the vision splendid
  Is on his way attended;
At length the Man perceives it die away,
And fade into the light of common day.

VI

Earth fills her lap with pleasures of her own;
Yearnings she hath in her own natural kind,
And, even with something of a mother's mind,
   And no unworthy aim,   80
   The homely nurse doth all she can
  To make her Foster-child, her inmate Man,
   Forget the glories he hath known,
  And that imperial palace whence he came.

VII

Behold the Child among his new-born blisses,
A six years' darling of a pigmy size!
See, where 'mid work of his own hand he lies,
Fretted by sallies of his mother's kisses,
With light upon him from his father's eyes!
See, at his feet, some little plan or chart,   90
Some fragment from his dream of human life,

Shaped by himself with newly-learned art;
     A wedding or a festival,
     A mourning or a funeral;
       And this hath now his heart,
     And unto this he frames his song:
       Then will he fit his tongue
To dialogues of business, love, or strife;
     But it will not be long
     Ere this be thrown aside,   100
     And with new joy and pride
The little Actor cons another part;
Filling from time to time his 'humorous stage'
With all the Persons, down to palsied Age,
That Life brings with her in her equipage;
     As if his whole vocation
     Were endless imitation.

VIII

Thou, whose exterior semblance doth belie
     Thy soul's immensity;
Thou best philosopher, who yet dost keep   110
Thy heritage, thou eye among the blind,
That, deaf and silent, read'st the Eternal Deep,
Haunted forever by the Eternal Mind,—
     Mighty prophet! seer blest!
     On whom those truths do rest,
Which we are toiling all our lives to find,
In darkness lost, the darkness of the grave;
Thou, over whom thy Immortality
Broods like the Day, a master o'er a slave,
A Presence which is not to be put by;   120
Thou little Child, yet glorious in the might
Of heaven-born freedom on thy being's height,
Why with such earnest pains dost thou provoke
The years to bring the inevitable yoke,
Thus blindly with thy blessedness at strife?
Full soon thy Soul shall have her earthly freight,
And custom lie upon thee with a weight,
Heavy as frost, and deep almost as life!

O joy! that in our embers
Is something that doth live,   130
That nature yet remembers
What was so fugitive!
The thought of our past years in me doth breed
Perpetual benediction: not indeed
For that which is most worthy to be blest;
Delight and liberty, the simple creed
Of childhood, whether busy or at rest,
With new-fledged hope still fluttering in his breast:—
          Not for these I raise
          The song of thanks and praise;   140
        But for those obstinate questionings
        Of sense and outward things,
        Fallings from us, vanishings;
        Blank misgivings of a Creature
Moving about in worlds not realized,
High instincts before which our mortal nature
Did tremble like a guilty thing surprised:
          But for those first affections,
          Those shadowy recollections,
          Which, be they what they may,   150
Are yet the fountain-light of all our day,
Are yet a master-light of all our seeing;
        Uphold us, cherish, and have power to make
Our noisy years seem moments in the being
Of the Eternal Silence: truths that wake,
          To perish never:
Which neither listlessness, nor mad endeavor,
          Nor man nor boy,
Nor all that is at enmity with joy,
Can utterly abolish or destroy!   160
        Hence in a season of calm weather
        Though inland far we be,
Our souls have sight of that immortal sea
        Which brought us hither,

Can in a moment travel thither,
And see the children sport upon the shore,
And hear the mighty waters rolling evermore.

x

Then sing, ye Birds, sing, sing a joyous song!
     And let the young Lambs bound
     As to the tabor's sound!   170
We in thought will join your throng,
     Ye that pipe and ye that play,
     Ye that through your hearts to-day
     Feel the gladness of the May!
What though the radiance which was once so bright
Be now forever taken from my sight,
     Though nothing can bring back the hour
Of splendor in the grass, of glory in the flower;
     We will grieve not, rather find
     Strength in what remains behind;   180
     In the primal sympathy
     Which having been must ever be;
     In the soothing thoughts that spring
     Out of human suffering;
     In the faith that looks through death,
In years that bring the philosophic mind.

xi

And O, ye Fountains, Meadows, Hills, and Groves,
Forebode not any severing of our loves!
Yet in my heart of hearts I feel your might;
I only have relinquished one delight   190
To live beneath your more habitual sway.
I love the Brooks which down their channels fret,
Even more than when I tripped lightly as they;
The innocent brightness of a new-born Day
     Is lovely yet;
The Clouds that gather round the setting sun
Do take a sober coloring from an eye
That hath kept watch o'er man's mortality;
Another race hath been, and other palms are won.

[93]

Thanks to the human heart by which we live,
Thanks to its tenderness, its joys, and fears,
To me the meanest flower that blows can give
Thoughts that do often lie too deep for tears.

104   *Dejection: An Ode*

> Late, late yestreen I saw the new Moon,
> With the old Moon in her arms:
> And I fear, I fear, my Master dear!
> We shall have a deadly storm.
> > *Ballad of Sir Patrick Spence.*

I

Well! If the bard was weather-wise, who made
  The grand old ballad of *Sir Patrick Spence*,
  This night, so tranquil now, will not go hence
Unroused by winds, that ply a busier trade
Than those which mold yon cloud in lazy flakes,
Or the dull sobbing draft, that moans and rakes
Upon the strings of this Æolian lute,
    Which better far were mute.
  For lo! the New-moon winter-bright!
  And overspread with phantom light,   10
  (With swimming phantom light o'erspread
  But rimmed and circled by a silver thread)
I see the old Moon in her lap, foretelling
  The coming-on of rain and squally blast.
And oh! that even now the gust were swelling,
  And the slant night-shower driving loud and fast!
Those sounds which oft have raised me, whilst they awed,
    And sent my soul abroad,
Might now perhaps their wonted impluse give,
Might startle this dull pain, and make it move and live!   20

II

A grief without a pang, void, dark, and drear,
  A stifled, drowsy, unimpassioned grief,
  Which finds no natural outlet, no relief,
    In word, or sigh, or tear—

O Lady! in this wan and heartless mood,
To other thoughts by yonder throstle woo'd,
  All this long eve, so balmy and serene,
Have I been gazing on the western sky,
  And its peculiar tint of yellow green:
And still I gaze—and with how blank an eye! 30
And those thin clouds above, in flakes and bars,
That give away their motion to the stars;
Those stars, that glide behind them or between,
Now sparkling, now bedimmed, but always seen:
Yon crescent Moon, as fixed as if it grew
In its own cloudless, starless lake of blue;
I see them all so excellently fair,
I see, not feel, how beautiful they are!

III

  My genial spirits fail;
  And what can these avail 40
To lift the smothering weight from off my breast?
  It were a vain endeavor,
  Though I should gaze forever
On that green light that lingers in the west:
I may not hope from outward forms to win
The passion and the life, whose fountains are within.

IV

O Lady! we receive but what we give,
And in our life alone does Nature live:
Ours is her wedding garment, ours her shroud!
  And would we aught behold, of higher worth, 50
Than that inanimate cold world allowed
To the poor loveless ever-anxious crowd,
  Ah! from the soul itself must issue forth
A light, a glory, a fair luminous cloud
  Enveloping the earth—
And from the soul itself must there be sent
  A sweet and potent voice, of its own birth,
Of all sweet sounds the life and element!

V

O pure of heart! thou need'st not ask of me
What this strong music in the soul may be! 60
What, and wherein it doth exist,
This light, this glory, this fair luminous mist,
This beautiful and beauty-making power.
    Joy, virtuous Lady! Joy that ne'er was given,
Save to the pure, and in their purest hour,
Life, and life's effluence, cloud at once and shower,
Joy, Lady! is the spirit and the power,
Which wedding Nature to us gives in dower
    A new earth and new heaven,
Undreamt of by the sensual and the proud— 70
Joy is the sweet voice, Joy the luminous cloud—
    We in ourselves rejoice!
And thence flows all that charms or ear or sight,
    All melodies the echoes of that voice,
All colors a suffusion from that light.

VI

There was a time when, though my path was rough,
    This joy within me dallied with distress,
And all misfortunes were but as the stuff
    Whence Fancy made me dreams of happiness:
For hope grew round me, like the twining vine, 80
And fruits, and foliage, not my own, seemed mine.
But now afflictions bow me down to earth:
Nor care I that they rob me of my mirth;
    But oh! each visitation
Suspends what nature gave me at my birth,
    My shaping spirit of Imagination.
For not to think of what I needs must feel,
    But to be still and patient, all I can;
And haply by abstruse research to steal
    From my own nature all the natural man— 90
    This was my sole resource, my only plan:
Till that which suits a part infects the whole,
And now is almost grown the habit of my soul.

Hence, viper thoughts, that coil around my mind,
 Reality's dark dream!
I turn from you, and listen to the wind,
 Which long has raved unnoticed. What a scream
Of agony by torture lengthened out
That lute sent forth! Thou Wind, that rav'st without,
Bare crag, or mountain-tairn, or blasted tree,   100
Or pine-grove whither woodman never clomb,
Or lonely house, long held the witches' home,
 Methinks were fitter instruments for thee,
Mad lutanist! who in this month of showers,
Of dark-brown gardens, and of peeping flowers,
Mak'st Devils' yule, with worse than wintry song,
The blossoms, buds, and timorous leaves among.
 Thou actor, perfect in all tragic sounds!
Thou mighty poet, e'en to frenzy bold!
  What tell'st thou now about?   110
  'Tis of the rushing of an host in rout,
 With groans, of trampled men, with smarting wounds—
At once they groan with pain, and shudder with the cold!
But hush! there is a pause of deepest silence!
And all that noise, as of a rushing crowd,
With groans, and tremulous shudderings—all is over—
 It tells another tale, with sounds less deep and loud!
  A tale of less affright,
  And tempered with delight,
As Otway's self had framed the tender lay,— 120
  'Tis of a little child
  Upon a lonesome wild,
Not far from home, but she hath lost her way:
And now moans low in bitter grief and fear,
And now screams loud, and hopes to make her mother hear.

'Tis midnight, but small thoughts have I of sleep:
Full seldom may my friend such vigils keep!
Visit her, gentle Sleep! with wings of healing,
 And may this storm be but a mountain-birth,

May all the stars hang bright above her dwelling,
    Silent as though they watched the sleeping earth!
      With light heart may she rise,
        Gay fancy, cheerful eyes,
    Joy lift her spirit, joy attune her voice;
To her may all things live, from pole to pole,
Their life the eddying of her living soul!
    O simple spirit, guided from above,
Dear Lady! friend devoutest of my choice,
Thus mayest thou ever, evermore rejoice.

Ode to the West Wind

I

O wild West Wind, thou breath of Autumn's being,
Thou, from whose unseen presence the leaves dead
Are driven, like ghosts from an enchanter fleeing,

Yellow, and black, and pale, and hectic red,
Pestilence-stricken multitudes: O thou,
Who chariotest to their dark wintry bed

The wingèd seeds, where they lie cold and low,
Each like a corpse within its grave, until
Thine azure sister of the Spring shall blow

Her clarion o'er the dreaming earth, and fill   10
(Driving sweet buds like flocks to feed in air)
With living hues and odors plain and hill:

Wild Spirit, which art moving everywhere;
Destroyer and preserver; hear! oh, hear!

II

Thou on whose stream, mid the steep sky's commotion,
Loose clouds like earth's decaying leaves are shed,
Shook from the tangled boughs of Heaven and Ocean,

Angels of rain and lightning: there are spread
On the blue surface of thine airy surge,
Like the bright hair uplifted from the head   20

Of some fierce Mænad, even from the dim verge
Of the horizon to the zenith's height,
The locks of the approaching storm. Thou dirge

Of the dying year, to which this closing night
Will be the dome of a vast sepulcher,
Vaulted with all thy congregated might

Of vapors, from whose solid atmosphere
Black rain, and fire, and hail will burst: oh, hear!

III

Thou who didst waken from his summer dreams
The blue Mediterranean, where he lay,   30
Lulled by the coil of his crystàlline streams,

Beside a pumice isle in Baiæ's bay,
And saw in sleep old palaces and towers
Quivering within the wave's intenser day,

All overgrown with azure moss and flowers
So sweet, the sense faints picturing them! thou
For whose path the Atlantic's level powers

Cleave themselves into chasms, while far below
The sea-blooms and the oozy woods which wear
The sapless foliage of the ocean, know   40

Thy voice, and suddenly grow gray with fear,
And tremble and despoil themselves: oh, hear!

IV

If I were a dead leaf thou mightest bear;
If I were a swift cloud to fly with thee;
A wave to pant beneath thy power, and share

The impluse of thy strength, only less free
Than thou, O uncontrollable! If even
I were as in my boyhood, and could be

The comrade of thy wanderings over heaven,
As then, when to outstrip thy skyey speed   50
Scarce seemed a vision; I would ne'er have striven

As thus with thee in prayer in my sore need.
Oh, lift me as a wave, a leaf, a cloud!
I fall upon the thorns of life! I bleed!

A heavy weight of hours has chained and bowed
One too like thee: tameless, and swift, and proud.

v

Make me thy lyre, even as the forest is:
What if my leaves are falling like its own!
The tumult of thy mighty harmonies

Will take from both a deep, autumnal tone,   60
Sweet though in sadness. Be thou, Spirit fierce,
My spirit! Be thou me, impetuous one!

Drive my dead thoughts over the universe
Like withered leaves to quicken a new birth!
And, by the incantation of this verse,

Scatter, as from an unextinguished hearth
Ashes and sparks, my words among mankind!
Be through my lips to unawakened earth

The trumpet of a prophecy! O Wind,
If Winter comes, can Spring be far behind?   70

Dover Beach

The sea is calm tonight,
The tide is full, the moon lies fair
Upon the straits;—on the French coast the light
Gleams and is gone; the cliffs of England stand,
Glimmering and vast, out in the tranquil bay.
Come to the window, sweet is the night-air!
Only, from the long line of spray
Where the sea meets the moon-blanched land,
Listen! you hear the grating roar
Of pebbles which the waves draw back, and fling,   10
At their return, up the high strand,
Begin, and cease, and then again begin,
With tremulous cadence slow, and bring
The eternal note of sadness in.

Sophocles long ago
Heard it on the Ægæan, and it brought
Into his mind the turbid ebb and flow
Of human misery; we
Find also in the sound a thought,
Hearing it by this distant northern sea.   20

The Sea of Faith
Was once, too, at the full, and round earth's shore
Lay like the folds of a bright girdle furled.
But now I only hear
Its melancholy, long, withdrawing roar,
Retreating, to the breath
Of the night-wind, down the vast edges drear
And naked shingles of the world.

Ah, love, let us be true
To one another! for the world, which seems   30
To lie before us like a land of dreams,
So various, so beautiful, so new,
Hath really neither joy, nor love, nor light,
Nor certitude, nor peace, nor help for pain;
And we are here as on a darkling plain
Swept with confused alarms of struggle and flight,
Where ignorant armies clash by night.

107   *'Dover Beach'—A Note to that Poem*

The wave withdrawing
Withers with seaward rustle of flimsy water
Sucking the sand down: dragging at empty shells:
The roil after it settling: too smooth: smothered . . .

After forty a man's a fool to wait in the
Sea's face for the full force and the roaring of
Surf to come over him: droves of careening water.
After forty the tug's out and the salt and the
Sea follow it: less sound and violence:
Nevertheless the ebb has its own beauty—   10
Shells sand and all the whispering rustle.
There's earth in it then and the bubbles of foam gone.

Moreover—and this too has its lovely uses—
It's the outward wave that spills the inward forward
Tripping the proud piled mute virginal
Mountain of water in wallowing welter of light and
Sound enough—thunder for miles back: it's a fine and a
Wild smother to vanish in: pulling down—
Tripping with outward ebb the urgent inward.

Speaking alone for myself it's the steep hill and the   20
Toppling lift of the young men I am toward now—
Waiting for that as the wave for the next wave.
Let them go over us all I say with the thunder of
What's to be next in the world. It's we will be under it!

Onward led the road again
Through the sad uncolored plain
Under twilight brooding dim,
And along the utmost rim
Wall and rampart risen to sight
Cast a shadow not of night,
And beyond them seemed to glow
Bonfires lighted long ago.
And my dark conductor broke
Silence at my side and spoke,   10
Saying, 'You conjecture well:
Yonder is the gate of hell.'

Ill as yet the eyes could see
The eternal masonry,
But beneath it on the dark
To and fro there stirred a spark
And again the somber guide
Knew my question, and replied:
'At hell gate the damned in turn
Pace for sentinel and burn.'   20

Dully at the leaden sky
Staring, and with idle eye
Measuring the listless plain,
I began to think again.
Many things I thought of then,
Battle, and the loves of men,
Cities entered, oceans crossed,
Knowledge gained and virtue lost,
Cureless folly done and said,
And the lovely way that led   30
To the slimepit and the mire
And the everlasting fire.
And against a smolder dun
And a dawn without a sun

[103]

Did the nearing bastion loom,
And across the gate of gloom
Still one saw the sentry go,
Trim and burning, to and fro,
One for women to admire
In his finery of fire.   40
Something, as I watched him pace,
Minded me of time and place,
Soldiers of another corps
And a sentry known before.

   Ever darker hell on high
Reared its strength upon the sky,
And our footfall on the track
Fetched the daunting echo back.
But the soldier pacing still
The insuperable sill,   50
Nursing his tormented pride,
Turned his head to neither side,
Sunk into himself apart
And the hell-fire of his heart.
But against our entering in
From the drawbridge Death and Sin
Rose to render key and sword
To their father and their lord.
And the portress foul to see
Lifted up her eyes on me   60
Smiling, and I made reply:
'Met again, my lass,' said I.
Then the sentry turned his head,
Looked, and knew me, and was Ned.

   Once he looked, and halted straight,
Set his back against the gate,
Caught his musket to his chin,
While the hive of hell within
Sent abroad a seething hum

As of towns whose king is come   70
Leading conquest home from far
And the captives of his war,
And the car of triumph waits,
And they open wide the gates.
But across the entry barred
Straddled the revolted guard,
Weaponed and accoutered well
From the arsenals of hell;
And beside him, sick and white,
Sin to left and Death to right   80
Turned a countenance of fear
On the flaming mutineer.
Over us the darkness bowed,
And the anger in the cloud
Clenched the lightning for the stroke;
But the traitor musket spoke.

And the hollowness of hell
Sounded as its master fell,
And the mourning echo rolled
Ruin through his kingdom old,   90
Tyranny and terror flown
Left a pair of friends alone,
And beneath the nether sky
All that stirred was he and I.

Silent, nothing found to say,
We began the backward way;
And the ebbing luster died
From the soldier at my side,
As in all his spruce attire
Failed the everlasting fire.   100
Midmost of the homeward track
Once we listened and looked back;
But the city, dusk and mute,
Slept, and there was no pursuit.

[105]

'Say not the Struggle Naught Availeth'

Say not the struggle naught availeth,
   The labor and the wounds are vain,
The enemy faints not, nor faileth,
   And as things have been they remain.

If hopes were dupes, fears may be liars;   5
   It may be, in yon smoke concealed,
Your comrades chase e'en now the fliers,
   And, but for you, possess the field.

For while the tired waves, vainly breaking,
   Seem here no painful inch to gain,   10
Far back, through creeks and inlets making,
   Comes silent, flooding in, the main.

And not by eastern windows only,
   When daylight comes, comes in the light,
In front, the sun climbs slow, how slowly,   15
   But westward, look, the land is bright!

'Yes! in the sea of life enisled'

Yes! in the sea of life enisled,
With echoing straits between us thrown,
Dotting the shoreless watery wild,
We mortal millions live *alone*.
The islands feel the enclasping flow,
And then their endless bounds they know.

But when the moon their hollows lights,
And they are swept by balms of spring,
And in their glens, on starry nights,
The nightingales divinely sing;   10
And lovely notes, from shore to shore,
Across the sounds and channels pour—

Oh! then a longing like despair
Is to their farthest caverns sent;
For surely once, they feel, we were
Parts of a single continent!
Now round us spreads the watery plain—
Oh, might our marges meet again!

Who ordered, that their longing's fire
Should be, as soon as kindled, cooled?   20
Who renders vain their deep desire?—
A god, a god their severance ruled!
And bade betwixt their shores to be
The unplumbed, salt, estranging sea.

III   *The Land of Biscay*

Sons of landsmen, sons of seamen, hear the tale of grief and me,
Looking from the land of Biscay on the waters of the sea.

Looking from the land of Biscay over Ocean to the sky
On the far-beholding foreland paced at even grief and I.
There, as warm the west was burning and the east uncolored cold,
Down the waterway of sunset drove to shore a ship of gold.
Gold of mast and gold of cordage, gold of sail to sight was she,
And she glassed her ensign golden in the waters of the sea.

Oh, said I, my friend and lover, take we now that ship and sail
Outward in the ebb of hues and steer upon the sunset trail;   10
Leave the night to fall behind us and the clouding countries leave:
Help for you and me is yonder, in the havens west of eve.

Under hill she neared the harbor, till the gazer could behold
On the golden deck the steersman standing at the helm of gold,
Man and ship and sky and water burning in a single flame;
And the mariner of Ocean he was calling as he came:
From the highway of the sunset he was shouting on the sea,
'Landsman of the land of Biscay, have you help for grief and me?'

[107]

When I heard I did not answer, I stood mute and shook my head:
Son of earth and son of Ocean, much we thought and nothing said. 20
Grief and I abode the nightfall; to the sunset grief and he
Turned them from the land of Biscay on the waters of the sea.

Leaving Barra

The dazzle on the sea, my darling,
Leads from the western channel
A carpet of brilliance taking
My leave for ever of the island.

I never shall visit that island
Again with its easy tempo—
The seal sunbathing, the circuit
Of gulls on the wing for garbage.

I go to a different garbage
And scuffle for scraps of notice,   10
Pretend to ignore the stigma
That stains my life and my leisure.

For fretful even in leisure
I fidget for different values,
Restless as a gull and haunted
By a hankering after Atlantis.

I do not know that Atlantis
Unseen and uncomprehended,
Dimly divined but keenly
Felt with a phantom hunger.   20

If only I could crush the hunger
If only I could lay the phantom
Then I should no doubt be happy
Like a fool or a dog or a buddha.

O the self-abnegation of Buddha
The belief that is disbelieving
The denial of chiaroscuro   *the treatment of light and shade in art.*
Not giving a damn for existence!

But I would cherish existence
Loving the beast and the bubble   30
Loving the rain and the rainbow,
Considering philosophy alien.

For all the religions are alien
That allege that life is a fiction,
And when we agree in denial
The cock crows in the morning.

If only I could wake in the morning
And find I had learned the solution,
Wake with the knack of knowledge
Who as yet have only an inkling.   40

Though some facts foster the inkling—
The beauty of the moon and music,
The routine courage of the worker,
The gay endurance of women,

And you who to me among women
Stand for so much that I wish for,
I thank you, my dear, for the example
Of living in tune and moving.

For few are able to keep moving,
They drag and flag in the traffic;   50
While you are alive beyond question
Like the dazzle on the sea, my darling.

113   *Speech to Those who Say Comrade*

The brotherhood is not by the blood certainly:
But neither are men brothers by speech—by saying so:
Men are brothers by life lived and are hurt for it:

[109]

Hunger and hurt are the great begetters of brotherhood:
Humiliation has gotten much love:
Danger I say is the nobler father and mother:

Those are as brothers whose bodies have shared fear
Or shared harm or shared hurt or indignity.
Why are the old soldiers brothers and nearest?

For this: with their minds they go over the sea a little   10
And find themselves in their youth again as they were in
Soissons and Meaux and at Ypres and those cities:

A French loaf and the girls with their eyelids painted
Bring back to aging and lonely men
Their twentieth year and the metal odor of danger:

It is this in life which of all things is tenderest—
To remember together with unknown men the days
Common also to them and perils ended:

It is this which makes of many a generation—
A wave of men who having the same years   20
Have in common the same dead and the changes.

The solitary and unshared experience
Dies of itself like the violations of love
Or lives on as the dead live eerily:

The unshared and single man must cover his
Loneliness as a girl her shame for the way of
Life is neither by one man nor by suffering.

Who are the born brothers in truth? The puddlers
Scorched by the same flame in the same foundries:
Those who have spit on the same boards with the blood in it: 30

Ridden the same rivers with green logs:
Fought the police in the parks of the same cities:
Grinned for the same blows: the same flogging:

Veterans out of the same ships—factories—
Expeditions for fame: the founders of continents:
Those that hid in Geneva a time back:

Those that have hidden and hunted and all such—
Fought together: labored together: they carry the
Common look like a card and they pass touching.

Brotherhood! No word said can make you brothers!   40
Brotherhood only the brave earn and by danger or
Harm or by bearing hurt and by no other.

Brotherhood here in the strange world is the rich and
Rarest giving of life and the most valued:
Not to be had for a word or a week's wishing.

114   '*oh young men oh young comrades*'

oh young men oh young comrades
it is too late now to stay in those houses
your fathers built where they built you to build to breed
money on money   it is too late
to make or even to count what has been made   5
Count rather those fabulous possessions
which begin with your body and your fiery soul:—
the hairs on your head the muscles extending
in ranges with their lakes across your limbs
Count your eyes as jewels and your valued sex   10
then count the sun and the innumerable coined light
sparkling on waves and spangled under trees
It is too late to stay in great houses where the ghosts are prisoned
—those ladies like flies perfect in amber
those financiers like fossils of bones in coal.   15
Oh comrades, step beautifully from the solid wall
advance to rebuild and sleep with friend on hill
advance to rebel and remember what you have
no ghost ever had, immured in his hall.

'*Hearing of harvests rotting*'

Hearing of harvests rotting in the valleys,
Seeing at end of street the barren mountains,
Round corners coming suddenly on water,
Knowing them shipwrecked who were launched for islands,
We honor founders of these starving cities,
Whose honor is the image of our sorrow.

Which cannot see its likeness in their sorrow
That brought them desperate to the brink of valleys;
Dreaming of evening walks through learned cities,
They reined their violent horses on the mountains,   10
Those fields like ships to castaways on islands,
Visions of green to them that craved for water.

They built by rivers and at night the water
Running past windows comforted their sorrow;
Each in his little bed conceived of islands
Where every day was dancing in the valleys,
And all the year trees blossomed on the mountains,
Where love was innocent, being far from cities.

But dawn came back and they were still in cities;
No marvelous creature rose up from the water,   20
There was still gold and silver in the mountains,
And hunger was a more immediate sorrow;
Although to moping villagers in valleys
Some waving pilgrims were describing islands.

'The gods,' they promised, 'visit us from islands,
Are stalking head-up, lovely through the cities;
Now is the time to leave your wretched valleys
And sail with them across the lime-green water;
Sitting at their white sides, forget their sorrow,
The shadow cast across your lives by mountains.'   30

So many, doubtful, perished in the mountains
Climbing up crags to get a view of islands;
So many, fearful, took with them their sorrow
Which stayed them when they reached unhappy cities;
So many, careless, dived and drowned in water;
So many, wretched, would not leave their valleys.

It is the sorrow; shall it melt? Ah, water
Would gush, flush, green these mountains and these valleys,
And we rebuild our cities, not dream of islands.

116 *Sestina: Altaforte*

Loquitur: *En* Bertrans de Born.
    Dante Alighieri put this man in hell for that he was a stirrer up of strife.
    Eccovi!
    Judge ye!
    Have I dug him up again?
The scene is at his castle, Altaforte. 'Papiols' is his jongleur.
'The Leopard,' the *device* of Richard Coeur de Lion.

I

Damn it all! all this our South stinks peace.
You whoreson dog, Papiols, come! Let's to music!
I have no life save when the swords clash.
But ah! when I see the standards gold, vair, purple, opposing
And the broad fields beneath them turn crimson,
Then howl I my heart nigh mad with rejoicing.

II

In hot summer have I great rejoicing
When the tempests kill the earth's foul peace,
And the lightnings from black heav'n flash crimson,
And the fierce thunders roar me their music   10
And the winds shriek through the clouds mad, opposing,
And through all the riven skies God's swords clash.

[113]

III

Hell grant soon we hear again the swords clash!
And the shrill neighs of destriers in battle rejoicing,
Spiked breast to spiked breast opposing!
Better one hour's stour than a year's peace!
With fat boards, bawds, wine and frail music!
Bah! there's no wine like the blood's crimson!

IV

And I love to see the sun rise blood-crimson.
And I watch his spears through the dark clash   20
And it fills all my heart with rejoicing
And pries wide my mouth with fast music
When I see him so scorn and defy peace,
His lone might 'gainst all darkness opposing.

V

The man who fears war and squats opposing
My words for stour, hath no blood of crimson,
But is fit only to rot in womanish peace
Far from where worth's won and the swords clash
For the death of such sluts I go rejoicing;
Yea, I fill all the air with my music.   30

VI

Papiols, Papiols, to the music!
There's no sound like to swords swords opposing,
No cry like the battle's rejoicing
When our elbows and swords drip the crimson
And our charges 'gainst 'The Leopard's' rush clash.
May God damn for ever all who cry 'Peace!'

VII

And let the music of the swords make them crimson!
Hell grant soon we hear again the swords clash!
Hell blot black for alway the thought 'Peace'!

L'Allegro

Hence loathed Melancholy
   Of *Cerberus*, and blackest midnight born,
In *Stygian* Cave forlorn
   'Mongst horrid shapes, and shreiks, and sights unholy,
Find out som uncouth cell,
   Where brooding darknes spreads his jealous wings,
And the night-Raven sings;
   There under *Ebon* shades, and low-brow'd Rocks,
As ragged as thy Locks,
   In dark *Cimmerian* desert ever dwell.   10
But com thou Goddes fair and free,
In Heav'n ycleap'd *Euphrosyne*,
And by men, heart-easing Mirth,
Whom lovely *Venus* at a birth
With two sister Graces more
To Ivy-crowned *Bacchus* bore;
Or whether (as som Sager sing)
The frolick Wind that breathes the Spring,
Zephir with *Aurora* playing,
As he met her once a Maying,   20
There on Beds of Violets blew,
And fresh-blown Roses washt in dew,
Fill'd her with thee a daughter fair,
So bucksom, blith, and debonair.
Haste thee nymph, and bring with thee
Jest and youthful Jollity,
Quips and Cranks, and wanton Wiles,
Nods, and Becks, and Wreathèd Smiles,
Such as hang on *Hebe's* cheek,
And love to live in dimple sleek;   30
Sport that wrincled Care derides,
And Laughter holding both his sides.
Com, and trip it as ye go

[115]

On the light fantastick toe,
And in thy right hand lead with thee,
The Mountain Nymph, sweet Liberty;
And if I give thee honour due,
Mirth, admit me of thy crue
To live with her, and live with thee,
In unreprovèd pleasures free;   40
To hear the Lark begin his flight,
And singing startle the dull night,
From his watch-towre in the skies,
Till the dappled dawn doth rise;
Then to com in spight of sorrow,
And at my window bid good morrow,
Through the Sweet-Briar, or the Vine,
Or the twisted Eglantine.
While the Cock with lively din,
Scatters the rear of darknes thin,   50
And to the stack, or the Barn dore,
Stoutly struts his Dames before,
Oft list'ning how the Hounds and horn
Chearly rouse the slumbring morn,
From the side of som Hoar Hill,
Through the high wood echoing shrill.
Som time walking not unseen
By Hedge-row Elms, on Hillocks green,
Right against the Eastern gate,
Wher the great Sun begins his state,   60
Rob'd in flames, and Amber light,
The clouds in thousand Liveries dight.
While the Plowman neer at hand,
Whistles ore the Furrow'd Land,
And the Milkmaid singeth blithe,
And the Mower whets his sithe,
And every Shepherd tells his tale
Under the Hawthorn in the dale.
Streit mine eye hath caught new pleasures
Whilst the Lantskip round it measures,   70
Russet Lawns, and Fallows Gray,

Where the nibling flocks do stray,
Mountains on whose barren brest
The labouring clouds do often rest:
Meadows trim with Daisies pide,
Shallow Brooks, and Rivers wide.
Towers, and Battlements it sees
Boosom'd high in tufted Trees,
Wher perhaps som beauty lies,
The Cynosure of neighbouring eyes.   80
Hard by, a Cottage chimney smokes,
From betwixt two agèd Okes,
Where *Corydon* and *Thyrsis* met,
Are at their savory dinner set
Of Hearbs, and other Country Messes,
Which the neat-handed *Phillis* dresses;
And then in haste her Bowre she leaves,
With *Thestylis* to bind the Sheaves;
Or if the earlier season lead
To the tann'd Haycock in the Mead,   90
Som times with secure delight
The up-land Hamlets will invite,
When the merry Bells ring round,
And the jocond rebecks sound
To many a youth, and many a maid,
Dancing in the Chequer'd shade;
And young and old com forth to play
On a Sunshine Holyday,
Till the live-long day-light fail,
Then to the Spicy Nut-brown Ale,   100
With stories told of many a feat,
How *Faery Mab* the junkets eat,
She was pincht, and pull'd she sed,
And he by Friars Lanthorn led
Tells how the drudging *Goblin* swet,
To ern his Cream-bowle duly set,
When in one night, ere glimps of morn,
His shadowy Flale hath thresh'd the Corn
That ten day-labourers could not end,

Then lies him down the Lubbar Fend.   110
And stretch'd out all the Chimney's length,
Basks at the fire his hairy strength;
And Crop-full out of dores he flings,
Ere the first Cock his Mattin rings.
Thus don the Tales, to bed they creep,
By whispering Windes soon lull'd asleep.
Towred Cities please us then,
And the busie humm of men,
Where throngs of Knights and Barons bold,
In weeds of Peace high triumphs hold,   120
With store of Ladies, whose bright eies
Rain influence, and judge the prise
Of Wit, or Arms, while both contend
To win her Grace, whom all commend.
There let *Hymen* oft appear
In Saffron robe, with Taper clear,
And pomp, and feast, and revelry,
With mask, and antique Pageantry,
Such sights as youthfull Poets dream
On Summer eeves by haunted stream.   130
Then to the well-trod stage anon,
If *Jonsons* learned Sock be on,
Or sweetest *Shakespear* fancies childe,
Warble his native Wood-notes wilde,
And ever against eating Cares,
Lap me in soft *Lydian* Aires,
Married to immortal verse
Such as the meeting soul may pierce
In notes, with many a winding bout
Of lincked sweetnes long drawn out,   140
With wanton heed, and giddy cunning,
The melting voice through mazes running;
Untwisting all the chains that ty
The hidden soul of harmony.
That *Orpheus* self may heave his head
From golden slumber on a bed
Of heapt *Elysian* flowres, and hear

[118]

Such streins as would have won the ear
Of *Pluto*, to have quite set free
His half regain'd *Eurydice*.   150
These delights, if thou canst give,
Mirth with thee, I mean to live.

HENCE vain deluding joyes,
   The brood of folly without father bred,
How little you bested,
   Or fill the fixed mind with all your toyes;
Dwell in som idle brain,
   And fancies fond with gaudy shapes possess,
As thick and numberless
   As the gay motes that people the Sun Beams,
Or likest hovering dreams
   The fickle Pensioners of *Morpheus* train.   10
But hail thou Goddes, sage and holy,
Hail divinest Melancholy,
Whose Saintly visage is too bright
To hit the Sense of human sight;
And therfore to our weaker view,
Ore laid with black staid Wisdoms hue.
Black, but such as in esteem,
Prince *Memnons* sister might beseem,
Or that Starr'd *Ethiope* Queen that strove
To set her beauties praise above   20
The Sea Nymphs, and their powers offended.
Yet thou art higher far descended,
Thee bright-hair'd *Vesta* long of yore,
To solitary *Saturn* bore;
His daughter she (in *Saturns* raign,
Such mixture was not held a stain)
Oft in glimmering Bowres, and glades
He met her, and in secret shades
Of woody *Ida's* inmost grove,
While yet there was no fear of *Jove*.   30
Com pensive Nun, devout and pure,

[119]

Sober, stedfast, and demure,
All in a robe of darkest grain,
Flowing with majestick train,
And sable stole of *Cipres* Lawn,
Over thy decent shoulders drawn.
Com, but keep thy wonted state,
With eev'n step, and musing gate,
And looks commercing with the skies,
Thy rapt soul sitting in thine eyes: 40
There held in holy passion still,
Forget thy self to Marble, till
With a sad Leaden downward cast,
Thou fix them on the earth as fast.
And joyn with thee calm Peace, and Quiet,
Spare Fast, that oft with gods doth diet,
And hears the Muses in a ring,
Ay round about *Joves* Altar sing.
And adde to these retired Leasure,
That in trim Gardens takes his pleasure;   50
But first, and chiefest, with thee bring,
Him that yon soars on golden wing,
Guiding the fiery-wheeled throne,
The Cherub Contemplation,
And the mute Silence hist along,
'Less *Philomel* will daign a Song,
In her sweetest, saddest plight,
Smoothing the rugged brow of night,
While *Cynthia* checks her Dragon yoke,
Gently o're th'accustom'd Oke;   60
Sweet Bird that shunn'st the noise of folly,
Most musicall, most melancholy!
Thee Chauntress oft the Woods among,
I woo to hear thy eeven-Song;
And missing thee, I walk unseen
On the dry smooth-shaven Green,
To behold the wandring Moon,
Riding neer her highest noon,
Like one that had bin led astray

Through the Heav'ns wide pathles way;   70
And oft, as if her head she bow'd,
Stooping through a fleecy cloud.
Oft on a Plat of rising ground,
I hear the far-off *Curfeu* sound,
Over som wide-water'd shoar,
Swinging slow with sullen roar;
Or if the Ayr will not permit,
Som still removed place will fit,
Where glowing Embers through the room
Teach light to counterfeit a gloom,   80
Far from all resort of mirth,
Save the Cricket on the hearth,
Or the Belmans drousie charm,
To bless the dores from nightly harm:
Or let my Lamp at midnight hour,
Be seen in som high lonely Towr,
Where I may oft out-watch the *Bear*,
With thrice great *Hermes*, or unsphear
The spirit of *Plato* to unfold
What Worlds, or what vast Regions hold   90
The immortal mind that hath forsook
Her mansion in this fleshly nook:
And of those *Dæmons* that are found
In fire, air, flood, or under ground,
Whose power hath a true consent
With Planet, or with Element.
Som time let Gorgeous Tragedy
In Scepter'd Pall com sweeping by,
Presenting *Thebs*, or *Pelops* line,
Or the tale of *Troy* divine.   100
Or what (though rare) of later age,
Ennoblèd hath the Buskind stage.
But, O sad Virgin, that thy power
Might raise *Musæus* from his bower,
Or bid the soul of *Orpheus* sing
Such notes as warbled to the string,
Drew Iron tears down *Pluto's* cheek,

And made Hell grant what Love did seek.
Or call up him that left half told
The story of *Cambuscan* bold,   110
Of *Camball*, and of *Algarsife*,
And who had *Canace* to wife,
That own'd the vertuous Ring and Glass,
And of the wondrous Hors of Brass,
On which the *Tartar* King did ride;
And if ought els, great *Bards* beside,
In sage and solemn tunes have sung,
Of Turneys and of Trophies hung;
Of Forests, and inchantments drear,
Where more is meant then meets the ear.   120
Thus night oft see me in thy pale career,
Till civil-suited Morn appeer,
Not trickt and frounc't as she was wont,
With the Attick Boy to hunt,
But Cherchef't in a comly Cloud,
While rocking Winds are Piping loud,
Or usher'd with a shower still,
When the gust hath blown his fill,
Ending on the russling Leaves,
With minute drops from off the Eaves.   130
And when the Sun begins to fling
His flaring beams, me Goddes bring
To archèd walks of twilight groves,
And shadows brown that *Sylvan* loves
Of Pine, or monumental Oake,
Where the rude Ax with heaved stroke,
Was never heard the Nymphs to daunt,
Or fright them from their hallow'd haunt.
There in close covert by som Brook,
Where no profaner eye may look,   140
Hide me from Day's garish eie,
While the Bee with Honied thie,
That at her flowry work doth sing,
And the Waters murmuring
With such consort as they keep,

Entice the dewy-feather'd Sleep;
And let som strange mysterious dream,
Wave at his Wings in Airy stream,
Of lively portrature display'd,
Softly on my eye-lids laid.   150
And as I wake, sweet musick breath
Above, about, or underneath,
Sent by som spirit to mortals good,
Or th'unseen Genius of the Wood.
But let my due feet never fail,
To walk the studious Cloysters pale,
And love the high embowed Roof,
With antick Pillars massy proof,
And storied Windows richly dight,
Casting a dimm religious light.   160
There let the pealing Organ blow,
To the full voic'd Quire below,
In Service high, and Anthems cleer,
As may with sweetnes, through mine ear
Dissolve me into extasies,
And bring all Heav'n before mine eyes.
And may at last my weary age
Find out the peacefull hermitage,
The Hairy Gown and Mossy Cell,
Where I may sit and rightly spell   170
Of every Star that Heav'n doth shew,
And every Herb that sips the dew;
Till old experience do attain
To somthing like Prophetic strain.
These pleasures *Melancholy* give,
And I with thee will choose to live.

119   *Elegy*

WRITTEN IN A COUNTRY CHURCHYARD

The curfew tolls the knell of parting day,
    The lowing herd wind slowly o'er the lea,
The plowman homeward plods his weary way,
    And leaves the world to darkness and to me.

Now fades the glimmering landscape on the sight,
   And all the air a solemn stillness holds,
Save where the beetle wheels his droning flight,
   And drowsy tinklings lull the distant folds;

Save that from yonder ivy-mantled tower
   The moping owl does to the moon complain   10
Of such, as wandering near her secret bower,
   Molest her ancient solitary reign.

Beneath those rugged elms, that yew-tree's shade,
   Where heaves the turf in many a moldering heap,
Each in his narrow cell forever laid,
   The rude forefathers of the hamlet sleep.

The breezy call of incense-breathing morn,
   The swallow twittering from the straw-built shed,
The cock's shrill clarion, or the echoing horn,
   No more shall rouse them from their lowly bed.   20

For them no more the blazing hearth shall burn,
   Or busy housewife ply her evening care:
No children run to lisp their sire's return,
   Or climb his knees the envied kiss to share.

Oft did the harvest to their sickle yield,
   Their furrow oft the stubborn glebe has broke;
How jocund did they drive their team afield!
   How bowed the woods beneath their sturdy stroke!

Let not Ambition mock their useful toil,
   Their homely joys, and destiny obscure;   30
Nor Grandeur hear with a disdainful smile,
   The short and simple annals of the poor.

The boast of heraldry, the pomp of power,
   And all that beauty, all that wealth e'er gave,
Await alike th' inevitable hour.
   The paths of glory lead but to the grave.

Nor you, ye proud, impute to these the fault,
 If Memory o'er their tomb no trophies raise,
Where through the long-drawn aisle and fretted vault
 The pealing anthem swells the note of praise.   40

Can storied urn or animated bust
 Back to its mansion call the fleeting breath?
Can Honor's voice provoke the silent dust,
 Or Flattery soothe the dull cold ear of Death?

Perhaps in this neglected spot is laid
 Some heart once pregnant with celestial fire;
Hands that the rod of empire might have swayed,
 Or waked to ecstasy the living lyre.

But Knowledge to their eyes her ample page
 Rich with the spoils of time did ne'er unroll;   50
Chill Penury repressed their noble rage,
 And froze the genial current of the soul.

Full many a gem of purest ray serene,
 The dark unfathomed caves of ocean bear:
Full many a flower is born to blush unseen,
 And waste its sweetness on the desert air.

Some village Hampden, that, with dauntless breast
 The little tyrant of his fields withstood;
Some mute inglorious Milton here may rest,
 Some Cromwell guiltless of his country's blood.   60

Th' applause of listening senates to command,
 The threats of pain and ruin to despise,
To scatter plenty o'er a smiling land,
 And read their history in a nation's eyes,

Their lot forbade: nor circumscribed alone
 Their growing virtues, but their crimes confined;
Forbade to wade through slaughter to a throne,
 And shut the gates of mercy on mankind.

The struggling pangs of conscious truth to hide,
    To quench the blushes of ingenuous shame,   70
Or heap the shrine of Luxury and Pride
    With incense kindled at the Muse's flame.

Far from the madding crowd's ignoble strife,
    Their sober wishes never learned to stray;
Along the cool sequestered vale of life
    They kept the noiseless tenor of their way.

Yet even these bones from insult to protect,
    Some frail memorial still erected nigh,
With uncouth rhymes and shapeless sculpture decked,
    Implores the passing tribute of a sigh.   80

Their names, their years, spelt by th' unlettered Muse,
    The place of fame and elegy supply:
And many a holy text around she strews,
    That teach the rustic moralist to die.

For who, to dumb forgetfulness a prey,
    This pleasing anxious being e'er resigned,
Left the warm precincts of the cheerful day,
    Nor cast one longing lingering look behind?

On some fond breast the parting soul relies,
    Some pious drops the closing eye requires;   90
Even from the tomb the voice of Nature cries,
    Even in our ashes live their wonted fires.

For thee, who mindful of th' unhonored dead
    Dost in these lines their artless tale relate,
If chance, by lonely contemplation led,
    Some kindred spirit shall inquire thy fate,

Haply some hoary-headed swain may say,
    'Oft have we seen him at the peep of dawn
Brushing with hasty steps the dews away
    To meet the sun upon the upland lawn.   100

'There at the foot of yonder nodding beech
   That wreathes its old fantastic roots so high,
His listless length at noontide would he stretch,
   And pore upon the brook that babbles by.

'Hard by yon wood, now smiling as in scorn,
   Muttering his wayward fancies he would rove;
Now drooping, woeful-wan, like one forlorn,
   Or crazed with care, or crossed in hopeless love.

'One morn I missed him on the customed hill,
   Along the heath, and near his favorite tree;   110
Another came; nor yet beside the rill,
   Nor up the lawn, nor at the wood was he;

'The next with dirges due in sad array
   Slow through the church-way path we saw him borne,—
Approach and read (for thou canst read) the lay
   Graved on the stone beneath yon agèd thorn.'

THE EPITAPH

Here rests his head upon the lap of earth
   A youth to fortune and to fame unknown;
Fair Science frowned not on his humble birth,
   And Melancholy marked him for her own.   120

Large was his bounty, and his soul sincere;
   Heaven did a recompense as largely send:
He gave to Misery (all he had) a tear,
   He gained from Heaven ('twas all he wished) a friend.

No farther seek his merits to disclose,
   Or draw his frailties from their dread abode,
(There they alike in trembling hope repose,)—
   The bosom of his Father and his God.

[127]

120 a

In Memoriam

Old yew, which graspest at the stones
   That name the underlying dead,
   Thy fibers net the dreamless head,
Thy roots are wrapped about the bones.

The seasons bring the flower again,   5
   And bring the firstling to the flock;
   And in the dusk of thee the clock
Beats out the little lives of men.

O not for thee the glow, the bloom,
   Who changest not in any gale,   10
   Nor branding summer suns avail
To touch thy thousand years of gloom;

And gazing on thee, sullen tree,
   Sick for thy stubborn hardihood,
   I seem to fail from out my blood   15
And grow incorporate into thee.

120 b   *   *   *

Dark house, by which once more I stand
   Here in the long unlovely street,
   Doors, where my heart was used to beat
So quickly, waiting for a hand,

A hand that can be clasped no more—   5
   Behold me, for I cannot sleep,
   And like a guilty thing I creep
At earliest morning to the door.

He is not here; but far away
   The noise of life begins again,
   And ghastly through the drizzling rain   10
On the bald street breaks the blank day.

120c   *   *   *

Fair ship, that from the Italian shore
    Sailest the placid ocean-plains
    With my lost Arthur's loved remains,
Spread thy full wings, and waft him o'er.

So draw him home to those that mourn   5
    In vain; a favorable speed
    Ruffle thy mirrored mast, and lead
Through prosperous floods his holy urn.

All night no ruder air perplex
    Thy sliding keel, till Phosphor, bright   10
    As our pure love, through early light
Shall glimmer on the dewy decks.

Sphere all your lights around, above;
    Sleep, gentle heavens, before the prow;
    Sleep, gentle winds, as he sleeps now,   15
My friend, the brother of my love;

My Arthur, whom I shall not see
    Till all my widowed race be run;
    Dear as the mother to the son,
More than my brothers are to me.   20

120d   *   *   *

I hear the noise about thy keel;
    I hear the bell struck in the night;
    I see the cabin-window bright;
I see the sailor at the wheel.

Thou bring'st the sailor to his wife,   5
    And traveled men from foreign lands;
    And letters unto trembling hands;
And, thy dark freight, a vanished life.

[129]

So bring him; we have idle dreams;
 This look of quiet flatters thus   10
 Our home-bred fancies. O to us,
The fools of habit, sweeter seems

To rest beneath the clover sod,
 That takes the sunshine and the rains,
 Or where the kneeling hamlet drains   15
The chalice of the grapes of God,

Than if with thee the roaring wells
 Should gulf him fathom-deep in brine;
 And hands so often clasped in mine,
Should toss with tangle and with shells.   20

I 20 e   * * *

Calm is the morn without a sound,
 Calm as to suit a calmer grief,
 And only through the faded leaf
The chestnut pattering to the ground;

Calm and deep peace on this high wold,   5
 And on these dews that drench the furze,
 And all the silvery gossamers
That twinkle into green and gold;

Calm and still light on yon great plain
 That sweeps with all its autumn bowers, 10
 And crowded farms and lessening towers,
To mingle with the bounding main;

Calm and deep peace in this wide air,
 These leaves that redden to the fall—
 And in my heart, if calm at all,   15
If any calm, a calm despair;

Calm on the seas, and silver sleep,
 And waves that sway themselves in rest,
 And dead calm in that noble breast
Which heaves but with the heaving deep. 20

[130]

Tonight the winds begin to rise
    And roar from yonder dropping day;
    The last red leaf is whirled away,
The rooks are blown about the skies;

The forest cracked, the waters curled,   5
    The cattle huddled on the lea;
    And wildly dashed on tower and tree
The sunbeam strikes along the world.

And but for fancies, which aver
    That all thy motions gently pass   10
    Athwart a plane of molten glass,
I scarce could brook the strain and stir

That makes the barren branches loud;
    And but for fear it is not so,
    The wild unrest that lives in woe   15
Would dote and pore on yonder cloud

That rises upward always higher,
    And onward drags a laboring breast,
    And topples round the dreary west,
A looming bastion fringed with fire.   20

Be near me when my light is low,
    When the blood creeps, and the nerves prick
    And tingle; and the heart is sick,
And all the wheels of being slow.

Be near me when the sensuous frame   5
    Is racked with pangs that conquer trust;
    And Time, a maniac scattering dust,
And Life, a Fury slinging flame.

Be near me when my faith is dry,
    And men the flies of latter spring,   10
    That lay their eggs, and sting and sing
And weave their petty cells and die.

Be near me when I fade away,
    To point the term of human strife,
    And on the low dark verge of life   15
The twilight of eternal day.

120 h
            *   *   *

O yet we trust that somehow good
    Will be the final goal of ill,
    To pangs of nature, sins of will,
Defects of doubt, and taints of blood;

That nothing walks with aimless feet;   5
    That not one life shall be destroyed,
    Or cast as rubbish to the void,
When God hath made the pile complete;

That not a worm is cloven in vain;
    That not a moth with vain desire   10
    Is shriveled in a fruitless fire,
Or but subserves another's gain.

Behold, we know not anything;
    I can but trust that good shall fall
    At last—far off—at last, to all,   15
And every winter change to spring.

So runs my dream; but what am I?
    An infant crying in the night;
    An infant crying for the light,
And with no language but a cry.   20

120 i
            *   *   *

The wish, that of the living whole
    No life may fail beyond the grave,
    Derives it not from what we have
The likest God within the soul?

Are God and Nature then at strife,
    That Nature lends such evil dreams?
    So careful of the type she seems,
So careless of the single life,

That I, considering everywhere
    Her secret meaning in her deeds,
    And finding that of fifty seeds
She often brings but one to bear,

I falter where I firmly trod,
    And falling with my weight of cares
    Upon the great world's altar-stairs
That slope through darkness up to God,

I stretch lame hands of faith, and grope,
    And gather dust and chaff, and call
    To what I feel is Lord of all,
And faintly trust the larger hope.

120j

*   *   *

'So careful of the type?' but no.
    From scarpèd cliff and quarried stone
    She cries, 'A thousand types are gone;
I care for nothing, all shall go.

'Thou makest thine appeal to me.
    I bring to life, I bring to death;
    The spirit does but mean the breath.
I know no more.' And he, shall he,

Man, her last work, who seemed so fair,
    Such splendid purpose in his eyes,
    Who rolled the psalm to wintry skies,
Who built him fanes of fruitless prayer,

[133]

Who trusted God was love indeed
   And love Creation's final law—
   Though Nature, red in tooth and claw
With ravine, shrieked against his creed—

Who loved, who suffered countless ills,
   Who battled for the True, the Just,
   Be blown about the desert dust,
Or sealed within the iron hills?   20

No more? A monster then, a dream,
   A discord. Dragons of the prime,
   That tare each other in their slime,
Were mellow music matched with him.

O life as futile, then, as frail!
   O for thy voice to soothe and bless!
   What hope of answer, or redress?
Behind the veil, behind the veil.

120 k   *   *   *

When on my bed the moonlight falls,
   I know that in thy place of rest
   By that broad water of the west
There comes a glory on the walls;

Thy marble bright in dark appears,   5
   As slowly steals a silver flame
   Along the letters of thy name,
And o'er the number of thy years.

The mystic glory swims away,
   From off my bed the moonlight dies;   10
   And closing eaves of wearied eyes
I sleep till dusk is dipped in gray;

And then I know the mist is drawn,
   A lucid veil from coast to coast,
   And in the dark church like a ghost   15
Thy tablet glimmers in the dawn.

          *   *   *

As sometimes in a dead man's face,
    To those that watch it more and more,
    A likeness, hardly seen before,
Comes out—to someone of his race;

So, dearest, now thy brows are cold,   5
    I see thee what thou art, and know
    Thy likeness to the wise below,
Thy kindred with the great of old.

But there is more than I can see,
    And what I see I leave unsaid,   10
    Nor speak it, knowing Death has made
His darkness beautiful with thee.

          *   *   *

I wage not any feud with Death
    For changes wrought on form and face;
    No lower life that earth's embrace
May breed with him can fright my faith.

Eternal process moving on,   5
    From state to state the spirit walks;
    And these are but the shattered stalks,
Or ruined chrysalis of one.

Nor blame I Death, because he bare
    The use of virtue out of earth;   10
    I know transplanted human worth
Will bloom to profit, otherwhere.

For this alone on Death I wreak
    The wrath that garners in my heart:
    He put our lives so far apart   15
We cannot hear each other speak.

By night we lingered on the lawn,
　For underfoot the herb was dry;
　And genial warmth; and o'er the sky
The silvery haze of summer drawn;

And calm that let the tapers burn
　Unwavering. Not a cricket chirred;
　The brook alone far-off was heard,
And on the board the fluttering urn.

And bats went round in fragrant skies,
　And wheeled or lit the filmy shapes   10
　That haunt the dusk, with ermine capes
And woolly breasts and beaded eyes;

While now we sang old songs that pealed
　From knoll to knoll, where, couched at ease,
　The white kine glimmered, and the trees
Laid their dark arms about the field.

But when those others, one by one,
　Withdrew themselves from me and night,
　And in the house light after light
Went out, and I was all alone,   20

A hunger siezed my heart; I read
　Of that glad year which once had been,
　In those fallen leaves which kept their green,
The noble letters of the dead.

And strangely on the silence broke
　The silent-speaking words, and strange
　Was love's dumb cry defying change
To test his worth; and strangely spoke

The faith, the vigor, bold to dwell
   On doubts that drive the coward back,   30
   And keen through wordy snares to track
Suggestion to her inmost cell.

So word by word, and line by line,
   The dead man touched me from the past,
   And all at once it seemed at last
The living soul was flashed on mine,

And mine in his was wound, and whirled
   About empyreal heights of thought,
   And came on that which is, and caught
The deep pulsations of the world,   40

Æonian music measuring out
   The steps of Time—the shocks of Chance—
   The blows of Death. At length my trance
Was canceled, stricken through with doubt.

Vague words! but ah, how hard to frame
   In matter-molded forms of speech,
   Or even for intellect to reach
Through memory that which I became;

Till now the doubtful dusk revealed
   The knolls once more where, couched at ease,   50
   The white kine glimmered, and the trees
Laid their dark arms about the field;

And sucked from out the distant gloom
   A breeze began to tremble o'er
   The large leaves of the sycamore,
And fluctuate all the still perfume,

And gathering freshlier overhead,
   Rocked the full-foliaged elms, and swung
   The heavy-folded rose, and flung
The lilies to and fro, and said,   60

'The dawn, the dawn,' and died away;
    And East and West, without a breath,
    Mixed their dim lights, like life and death,
To broaden into boundless day.

120 o   *   *   *

Love is and was my lord and king,
    And in his presence I attend
    To hear the tidings of my friend,
Which every hour his couriers bring.

Love is and was my king and lord,   5
    And will be, though as yet I keep
    Within the court on earth, and sleep
Encompassed by his faithful guard,

And hear at times a sentinel
    Who moves about from place to place,   10
    And whispers to the worlds of space,
In the deep night, that all is well.

120 p   *   *   *

Thy voice is on the rolling air;
    I hear thee where the waters run;
    Thou standest in the rising sun,
And in the setting thou art fair.

What art thou then? I cannot guess;   5
    But though I seem in star and flower
    To feel thee some diffusive power,
I do not therefore love thee less.

My love involves the love before;
    My love is vaster passion now;   10
    Though mixed with God and Nature thou,
I seem to love thee more and more.

Far off thou art, but ever nigh;
    I have thee still, and I rejoice;
    I prosper, circled with thy voice;   15
I shall not lose thee though I die.

Wake! For the Sun, who scattered into flight
The Stars before him from the Field of Night,
    Drives Night along with them from Heav'n and strikes
The Sultán's Turret with a Shaft of Light.

Before the phantom of False morning died,
Methought a Voice within the Tavern cried,
    'When all the Temple is prepared within,
Why nods the drowsy Worshiper outside?'

And, as the Cock crew, those who stood before
The Tavern shouted—'Open, then, the Door!   10
    You know how little while we have to stay,
And, once departed, may return no more.'

Now the New Year reviving old Desires,
The thoughtful Soul to Solitude retires,
    Where the WHITE HAND OF MOSES on the Bough
Puts out, and Jesus from the Ground suspires.

Iram indeed is gone with all his Rose,
And Jamshyd's Sev'n-ringed Cup where no one knows;
    But still a Ruby kindles in the Vine,
And many a Garden by the Water blows.   20

And David's lips are locked; but in divine
High-piping Pehleví, with 'Wine! Wine! Wine!
    Red Wine!'—the Nightingale cries to the Rose
That sallow cheek of hers to incarnadine.

Come, fill the Cup, and in the fire of Spring
Your Winter-garment of Repentance fling;
    The Bird of Time has but a little way
To flutter—and the Bird is on the Wing.

Whether at Naishápúr or Babylon,
Whether the Cup with sweet or bitter run,   30
    The Wine of Life keeps oozing drop by drop,
The Leaves of Life keep falling one by one.

Each Morn a thousand Roses brings, you say;
Yes, but where leaves the Rose of Yesterday?
    And this first Summer month that brings the Rose
Shall take Jamshyd and Kaikobád away.

Well, let it take them! What have we to do
With Kaikobád the Great, or Kaikhosrú?
    Let Zál and Rustum bluster as they will,
Or Hátim call to Supper,—heed not you.   40

With me along the strip of Herbage strown
That just divides the desert from the sown,
    Where name of Slave and Sultán is forgot—
And Peace to Mahmúd on his golden Throne!

A Book of Verses underneath the Bough,
A Jug of Wine, a Loaf of Bread—and Thou
    Beside me singing in the Wilderness—
Oh, Wilderness were Paradise enow!

Some for the Glories of This World; and some
Sigh for the Prophet's Paradise to come;   50
    Ah, take the Cash, and let the Credit go,
Nor heed the rumble of a distant Drum!

Look to the blowing Rose about us—'Lo,
Laughing,' she says, 'into the world I blow,
    At once the silken tassel of my Purse
Tear, and its Treasure on the Garden throw.'

And those who husbanded the Golden Grain,
And those who flung it to the winds like Rain,
    Alike to no such aureate Earth are turned
As, buried once, Men want dug up again.   60

[140]

The Worldly Hope men set their Hearts upon
Turns Ashes—or it prospers; and anon,
   Like Snow upon the Desert's dusty Face,
Lighting a little hour or two—is gone.

Think, in this battered Caravanserai
Whose Portals are alternate Night and Day,
   How Sultán after Sultán with his Pomp
Abode his destined Hour, and went his way.

They say the Lion and the Lizard keep
The Courts where Jamshyd gloried and drank deep;   70
   And Bahrám, that great Hunter—the Wild Ass
Stamps o'er his Head, but cannot break his Sleep.

I sometimes think that never blows so red
The Rose as where some buried Cæsar bled;
   That every Hyacinth the Garden wears
Dropped in her Lap from some once lovely Head.

And this reviving Herb whose tender Green
Fledges the River-Lip on which we lean—
   Ah, lean upon it lightly! for who knows
From what once lovely Lip it springs unseen!   80

Ah, my Belovèd, fill the Cup that clears
TODAY of past Regrets and future Fears:
   Tomorrow!—Why, Tomorrow I may be
Myself with Yesterday's Sev'n thousand Years.

For some we loved, the loveliest and the best
That from his Vintage rolling Time hath prest,
   Have drunk their Cup a Round or two before,
And one by one crept silently to rest.

And we, that now make merry in the Room
They left, and Summer dresses in new bloom,   90
   Ourselves must we beneath the Couch of Earth
Descend—ourselves to make a Couch—for whom?

Ah, make the most of what we yet may spend,
Before we too into the Dust descend;
    Dust into Dust, and under Dust, to lie,
Sans Wine, sans Song, sans Singer, and—sans End!

Alike for those who for TODAY prepare,
And those that after some TOMORROW stare,
    A Muezzín from the Tower of Darkness cries,
'Fools, your Reward is neither Here nor There.'   100

Why, all the Saints and Sages who discussed
Of the Two Worlds so wisely—they are thrust
    Like foolish Prophets forth; their Words to Scorn
Are scattered, and their Mouths are stopped with Dust.

Myself when young did eagerly frequent
Doctor and Saint, and heard great argument
    About it and about; but evermore
Came out by the same door where in I went.

With them the seed of Wisdom did I sow,
And with mine own hand wrought to make it grow;   110
    And this was all the Harvest that I reaped—
'I came like Water, and like Wind I go.'

Into this Universe, and *Why* not knowing
Nor *Whence*, like Water willy-nilly flowing;
    And out of it, as Wind along the Waste,
I know not *Whither*, willy-nilly blowing.

What, without asking, hither hurried *Whence*?
And, without asking, *Whither* hurried hence!
    Oh, many a Cup of this forbidden Wine
Must drown the memory of that insolence!   120

Up from the Earth's Center through the Seventh Gate
I rose, and on the Throne of Saturn sate,
    And many a Knot unraveled by the Road;
But not the Master-knot of Human Fate.

[142]

There was the Door to which I found no Key;
There was the Veil through which I might not see;
　　Some little talk awhile of ME and THEE
There was—and then no more of THEE and ME.

Earth could not answer; nor the Seas that mourn
In flowing Purple, of their Lord forlorn;
　　Nor rolling Heaven, with all his Signs reveal'd
And hidden by the sleeve of Night and Morn.

Then of the THEE IN ME who works behind
The Veil, I lifted up my hands to find
　　A Lamp amid the Darkness; and I heard,
As from Without—'THE ME WITHIN THEE BLIND!'

Then to the Lip of this poor earthen Urn
I leaned, the Secret of my Life to learn;
　　And Lip to Lip it murmured—'While you live,
Drink!—for, once dead, you never shall return.'

I think the Vessel, that with fugitive
Articulation answered, once did live,
　　And drink; and Ah! the passive Lip I kissed,
How many Kisses might it take—and give!

For I remember stopping by the way
To watch a Potter thumping his wet Clay;
　　And with its all-obliterated Tongue
It murmured—'Gently, Brother, gently, pray!'

And has not such a Story from of Old
Down Man's successive generations rolled
　　Of such a clod of saturated Earth
Cast by the Maker into Human mold?

And not a drop that from our Cups we throw
For Earth to drink of, but may steal below
　　To quench the fire of Anguish in some Eye
There hidden—far beneath, and long ago.

As then the Tulip, for her morning sup
Of Heav'nly Vintage, from the soil looks up,
   Do you devoutly do the like, till Heav'n
To Earth invert you—like an empty Cup.   160

Perplexed no more with Human or Divine,
Tomorrow's tangle to the winds resign,
   And lose your fingers in the tresses of
The Cypress-slender Minister of Wine.

And if the Wine you drink, the Lip you press,
End in what All begins and ends in—Yes;
   Think that you are TODAY what YESTERDAY
You were—TOMORROW you shall not be less.

So when that Angel of the darker Drink
At last shall find you by the river-brink,   170
   And offering his Cup, invite your Soul
Forth to your Lips to quaff—you shall not shrink.

Why, if the Soul can fling the Dust aside,
And naked on the Air of Heaven ride,
   Were 't not a Shame—were 't not a Shame for him
In this clay carcass crippled to abide?

'Tis but a Tent where takes his one day's rest
A Sultán to the realm of Death addrest;
   The Sultán rises, and the dark Ferrásh
Strikes, and prepares it for another Guest.   180

And fear not lest Existence closing your
Account, and mine, should know the like no more;
   The Eternal Sákí from that Bowl has poured
Millions of Bubbles like us, and will pour.

When You and I behind the Veil are past,
Oh, but the long, long while the World shall last,
   Which of our Coming and Departure heeds
As the Sea's self should heed a pebble-cast.

A Moment's Halt—a momentary taste
Of BEING from the Well amid the Waste—   190
    And Lo!—the phantom Caravan has reached
The NOTHING it set out from—Oh, make haste!

Would you that spangle of Existence spend
About THE SECRET—quick about it, Friend!
    A Hair perhaps divides the False and True—
And upon what, prithee, does life depend?

A Hair perhaps divides the False and True—
Yes; and a single Alif were the clue—
    Could you but find it—to the Treasure-house,
And peradventure to THE MASTER too;   200

Whose secret Presence, through Creation's veins
Running Quicksilver-like, eludes your pains;
    Taking all shapes from Máh to Máhi; and
They change and perish all—but He remains;

A moment guessed—then back behind the Fold
Immersed of Darkness round the Drama rolled
    Which, for the Pastime of Eternity,
He doth Himself contrive, enact, behold.

But if in vain, down on the stubborn floor
Of Earth, and up to Heav'n's unopening Door,   210
    You gaze TODAY, while You are You—how then
TOMORROW, when You shall be You no more?

Waste not your Hour, nor in the vain pursuit
Of This and That endeavor and dispute;
    Better be jocund with the fruitful Grape
Than sadden after none, or bitter, Fruit.

You know, my Friends, with what a brave Carouse
I made a Second Marriage in my house;
    Divorced old barren Reason from my Bed,
And took the Daughter of the Vine to Spouse.   220

For 'Is' and 'Is-NOT' though with Rule and Line,
And 'UP-AND-DOWN' by Logic, I define,
    Of all that one should care to fathom, I
Was never deep in anything but—Wine.

Ah, but my Computations, People say,
Reduced the Year to better reckoning?—Nay,
    'Twas only striking from the Calendar
Unborn Tomorrow, and dead Yesterday.

And lately, by the Tavern Door agape,
Came shining through the Dusk an Angel Shape   230
    Bearing a Vessel on his Shoulder; and
He bid me taste of it; and 'twas—the Grape!

The Grape that can with Logic absolute
The Two-and-Seventy jarring Sects confute;
    The sovereign Alchemist that in a trice
Life's leaden metal into Gold transmute;

The mighty Mahmúd, Allah-breathing Lord,
That all the misbelieving and black Horde
    Of fears and Sorrows that infest the Soul
Scatters before him with his whirlwind Sword.   240

Why, be this Juice the growth of God, who dare
Blaspheme the twisted tendril as a Snare?
    A Blessing, we should use it, should we not?
And if a Curse—why, then, Who set it there?

I must abjure the Balm of Life, I must,
Scared by some After-reckoning ta'en on trust
    Or lured with Hope of some Diviner Drink,
To fill the Cup—when crumbled into Dust!

Oh threats of Hell and Hopes of Paradise!
One thing at least is certain—*This* Life flies;   250
    One thing is certain and the rest is Lies—
The Flower that once has blown forever dies.

Strange, is it not? that of the myriads who
Before us passed the door of Darkness through,
    Not one returns to tell us of the Road,
Which to discover we must travel too.

The Revelations of Devout and Learned
Who rose before us, and as Prophets burned,
    Are all but Stories, which, awoke from Sleep,
They told their comrades, and to Sleep returned.   260

I sent my Soul through the Invisible,
Some letter of that After-life to spell;
    And by and by my Soul returned to me,
And answered, 'I Myself am Heav'n and Hell'—

Heav'n but the Vision of fulfilled Desire,
And Hell the Shadow from a Soul on fire
    Cast on the Darkness into which Ourselves,
So late emerged from, shall so soon expire.

We are no other than a moving row
Of Magic Shadow-shapes that come and go   270
    Round with the Sun-illumined Lantern held
In Midnight by the Master of the Show;

But helpless Pieces of the Game He plays
Upon this Checker-board of Nights and Days;
    Hither and thither moves, and checks, and slays,
And one by one back in the Closet lays.

The Ball no question makes of Ayes and Noes,
But Here or There as strikes the Player goes;
    And He that tossed you down into the Field,
He knows about it all—HE knows—HE knows!   280

The Moving Finger writes, and, having writ,
Moves on; nor all your Piety nor Wit
    Shall lure it back to cancel half a Line,
Nor all your Tears wash out a Word of it.

And that inverted Bowl they call the Sky,
Whereunder crawling cooped we live and die,
    Lift not your hands to *It* for help—for It
As impotently moves as you or I.

With Earth's first Clay They did the Last Man knead,
And there of the Last Harvest sowed the Seed;   290
    And the first Morning of Creation wrote
What the Last Dawn of Reckoning shall read.

Yesterday *This* Day's Madness did prepare;
Tomorrow's Silence, Triumph, or Despair.
    Drink! for you know not whence you came, nor why;
Drink, for you know not why you go, nor where.

I tell you this—When, started from the Goal,
Over the flaming shoulders of the Foal
    Of Heav'n Parwín and Mushtarí they flung,
In my predestined Plot of Dust and Soul   300

The Vine had struck a fiber; which about
If clings my Being—let the Dervish flout;
    Of my Base metal may be filed a Key,
That shall unlock the Door he howls without.

And this I know: whether the one True Light
Kindle to Love, or Wrath—consume me quite,
    One Flash of It within the Tavern caught
Better than in the Temple lost outright.

What! out of senseless Nothing to provoke
A conscious Something to resent the yoke   310
    Of unpermitted Pleasure, under pain
Of Everlasting Penalties, if broke!

What! from his helpless Creature be repaid
Pure Gold for what he lent him dross-allayed—
    Sue for a Debt he never did contract,
And cannot answer—Oh, the sorry trade!

O Thou, who didst with pitfall and with gin
Beset the Road I was to wander in,
　　Thou wilt not with Predestined Evil round
Enmesh, and then impute my Fall to Sin!　　　　　320

O Thou, who Man of Baser Earth didst make,
And ev'n with Paradise devise the Snake,
　　For all the Sin wherewith the Face of Man
Is blackened—Man's forgiveness give—and take!

*　　*　　*

As under cover of departing Day
Slunk hunger-stricken Ramazán away,
　　Once more within the Potter's house alone
I stood, surrounded by the Shapes of Clay—

Shapes of all Sorts and Sizes, great and small,
That stood along the floor and by the wall;　　　　330
　　And some loquacious Vessels were; and some
Listened perhaps, but never talked at all.

Said one among them—'Surely not in vain
My substance of the common Earth was ta'en
　　And to this Figure molded, to be broke,
Or trampled back to shapeless Earth again.'

Then said a Second—'Ne'er a peevish Boy
Would break the Bowl from which he drank in joy;
　　And He that with his hand the Vessel made
Will surely not in after Wrath destroy.'　　　　340

After a momentary silence spake
Some Vessel of a more ungainly Make:
　　'They sneer at me for leaning all awry;
What! did the Hand, then, of the Potter shake?'

Whereat someone of the loquacious Lot—
I think a Súfi pipkin—waxing hot—
　　'All this of Pot and Potter—Tell me then,
Who is the Potter, pray, and who the Pot?'

'Why,' said another, 'Some there are who tell
Of one who threatens he will toss to Hell   350
   The luckless Pots he marred in making—Pish!
He's a Good Fellow, and 'twill all be well.'

'Well,' murmured one, 'Let whoso make or buy,
My Clay with long Oblivion is gone dry;
   But fill me with the old familiar Juice,
Methinks I might recover by and by.'

So while the Vessels one by one were speaking
The little Moon looked in that all were seeking;
   And then they jogged each other, 'Brother! Brother!
Now for the Porter's shoulder-knot a-creaking!'   360

*   *   *

Ah, with the Grape my fading Life provide,
And wash the Body whence the Life has died,
   And lay me, shrouded in the living Leaf,
By some not unfrequented Garden-side—

That ev'n my buried Ashes such a snare
Of Vintage shall fling up into the Air
   As not a True-believer passing by
But shall be overtaken unaware.

Indeed the Idols I have loved so long
Have done my credit in this World much wrong,   370
   Have drowned my Glory in a shallow Cup,
And sold my Reputation for a Song.

Indeed, indeed, Repentance oft before
I swore—but was I sober when I swore?
   And then and then came Spring, and Rose-in-hand
My thread-bare Penitence apieces tore.

And much as Wine has played the Infidel,
And robbed me of my Robe of Honor—Well,
   I wonder often what the Vintners buy
One-half so precious as the stuff they sell.   380

[150]

Yet Ah, that Spring should vanish with the Rose!
That Youth's sweet-scented manuscript should close!
    The Nightingale that in the branches sang,
Ah whence, and whither flown again, who knows!

Would but the Desert of the Fountain yield
One glimpse—if dimly, yet indeed, revealed,
    To which the fainting Traveler might spring,
As springs the trampled herbage of the field.

Would but some wingèd Angel ere too late
Arrest the yet unfolded Roll of Fate,   390
    And make the stern Recorder otherwise
Enregister, or quite obliterate!

Ah, Love! could you and I with Him conspire
To grasp this sorry Scheme of Things entire,
    Would not we shatter it to bits—and then
Remold it nearer to the Heart's Desire!

       *   *   *

Yon rising Moon that looks for us again—
How oft hereafter will she wax and wane;
    How oft hereafter rising look for us
Through this same Garden—and for *one* in vain!   400

And when like her, O Sákí, you shall pass
Among the Guests Star-scattered on the Grass,
    And in your joyous errand reach the spot
Where I made One—turn down an empty Glass!

122   '*Sumer is icumen in*'

Sumer is icumen in,
    Lhudé sing cuccu;
Groweth sed and bloweth med
    And springth the wudé nu.
        Sing cuccu!   5
Awé bleteth after lomb,
    Lhouth after calvé cu;
Bulluc sterteth, bucké verteth;
    Murie sing cuccu.
        Cuccu, cuccu,   10
    Wel singés thu, cuccu,
    Ne swik thu naver nu.
Sing cuccu nu! Sing cuccu!
Sing cuccu! Sing cuccu nu!

123   *Ancient Music*

Winter is icummen in,
Lhude sing Goddamm,
Raineth drop and staineth slop,
And how the wind doth ramm!
        Sing: Goddamm.   5
Skiddeth bus and sloppeth us,
An ague hath my ham.
Freezeth river, turneth liver,
        Damn you, sing: Goddamm.
Goddamm, Goddamm, 'tis why I am, Goddamm,   10
        So 'gainst the winter's balm.
Sing goddamm, damm, sing Goddamm,
Sing goddamm, sing goddamm, DAMM.

PART II

SONNETS

Loving in truth, and fain in verse my love to show,
That she, dear she, might take some pleasure of my pain,
Pleasure might cause her read, reading might make her know,
Knowledge might pity win, and pity grace obtain,—
I sought fit words to paint the blackest face of woe;
Studying inventions fine, her wits to entertain,
Oft turning others' leaves to see if thence would flow
Some fresh and fruitful showers upon my sun-burned brain.
But words came halting forth, wanting invention's stay;
Invention, nature's child, fled step-dame Study's blows,
And others' feet still seemed but strangers in my way.
Thus, great with child to speak, and helpless in my throes,
Biting my truant pen, beating myself for spite,
Fool, said my muse to me, look in thy heart and write.

124b   *   *   *

With how sad steps, O moon, thou climb'st the skies!
How silently, and with how wan a face!
What! may it be that even in heav'nly place
That busy archer his sharp arrows tries?
Sure, if that long-with-love-acquainted eyes
Can judge of love, thou feel'st a lover's case;
I read it in thy looks,—thy languished grace
To me, that feel the like, thy state descries.
Then, ev'n of fellowship, O moon, tell me,
Is constant love deemed there but want of wit?
Are beauties there as proud as here they be?
Do they above love to be loved, and yet
Those lovers scorn whom that love doth possess?
Do they call virtue there ungratefulness?

*   *   *

Come sleep! O sleep, the certain knot of peace,
The baiting place of wit, the balm of woe,
The poor man's wealth, the prisoner's release,
Th' indifferent judge between the high and low;
With shield of proof shield me from out the prease
Of those fierce darts despair at me doth throw;
O make in me those civil wars to cease;
I will good tribute pay, if thou do so.
Take thou of me smooth pillows, sweetest bed,
A chamber deaf to noise and blind to light,
A rosy garland and a weary head;
And if these things, as being thine by right,
Move not thy heavy grace, thou shalt in me,
Livelier than elsewhere, Stella's image see.

124d   *   *   *

Leave me, O love which reachest but to dust;
And thou, my mind, aspire to higher things;
Grow rich in that which never taketh rust,
Whatever fades but fading pleasure brings.
Draw in thy beams, and humble all thy might
To that sweet yoke where lasting freedoms be;
Which breaks the clouds and opens forth the light,
That doth both shine and give us sight to see.
O take fast hold; let that light be thy guide
In this small course which birth draws out to death,
And think how evil becometh him to slide,
Who seeketh heav'n, and comes of heav'nly breath.
Then farewell, world; thy uttermost I see;
Eternal Love, maintain thy life in me.

'Care-charmer sleep'

Care-charmer sleep, son of the sable night,
Brother to death, in silent darkness born,
Relieve my languish and restore the light;
With dark forgetting of my care, return.
And let the day be time enough to mourn
The shipwreck of my ill-adventured youth;
Let waking eyes suffice to wail their scorn
Without the torment of the night's untruth.
Cease, dreams, th' images of day-desires,
To model forth the passions of the morrow;
Never let rising sun approve you liars,
To add more grief to aggravate my sorrow.
Still let me sleep, embracing clouds in vain,
And never wake to feel the day's disdain.

FROM

Amoretti

Was it the worke of Nature or of Art,
Which tempred so the feature of her face,
That pride and meeknesse, mixt by equall part,
Doe both appeare t' adorne her beauties grace?
For with mild pleasance, which doth pride displace,
She to her love doth lookers eyes allure;
And with sterne countenance back again doth chace
Their looser lookes that stir up lustes impure.
With such strange termes her eyes she doth inure,
That with one looke she doth my life dismay,
And with another doth it streight recure:
Her smile me drawes, her frowne me drives away.
Thus doth she traine and teach me with her lookes:
Such art of eyes I never read in bookes.

Penelope, for her Ulisses sake,
Deviz'd a web her wooers to deceave,
In which the worke that she all day did make,
The same at night she did againe unreave.
Such subtile craft my damzell doth conceave,
Th' importune suit of my desire to shonne:
For all that I in many dayes doo weave
In one short houre I find by her undonne.
So when I thinke to end that I begonne,
I must begin and never bring to end:
For with one looke she spils that long I sponne,
And with one word my whole years work doth rend.
Such labour like the spyders web I fynd,
Whose fruitless worke is broken with least wynd.

Lyke as a ship, that through the ocean wyde
By conduct of some star doth make her way,
Whenas a storme hath dimd her trusty guyde,
Out of her course doth wander far astray;
So I, whose star, that wont with her bright ray
Me to direct, with cloudes is overcast,
Doe wander now in darknesse and dismay,
Through hidden perils round about me plast.
Yet hope I well, that when this storme is past,
My Helice, the lodestar of my lyfe,
Will shine again, and looke on me at last,
With lovely light to cleare my cloudy grief.
Till then I wander carefull comfortlesse,
In secret sorrow and sad pensivenesse.

126d   *   *   *

The weary yeare his race now having run,
The new begins his compast course anew:
With shew of morning mylde he hath begun,
Betokening peace and plenty to ensew
So let us, which this chaunge of weather vew,
Chaunge eeke our mynds, and former lives amend;
The old yeares sinnes forepast let us eschew,
And fly the faults with which we did offend.
Then shall the new yeares joy forth freshly send
Into the glooming world his gladsome ray;
And all these stormes, which now his beauty blend,
Shall turne to caulmes, and tymely cleare away.
So likewise, love, cheare you your heavy spright,
And chaunge old yeares annoy to new delight.

126e   *   *   *

One day I wrote her name upon the strand,
But came the waves and washed it away:
Agayne I wrote it with a second hand,
But came the tyde, and made my paynes his pray.
Vayne man, sayd she, that doest in vaine assay
A mortall thing so to immortalize!
For I my selve shall lyke to this decay,
And eek my name bee wyped out lykewize.
Not so (quod I) let baser things devize
To dy in dust, but you shall live by fame:
My verse your vertues rare shall eternize,
And in the hevens wryte your glorious name;
Where, whenas death shall all the world subdew,
Our love shall live, and later life renew.

127 a   *Shakespeare's Sonnets*

Shall I compare thee to a summer's day?
Thou art more lovely and more temperate:
Rough winds do shake the darling buds of May,
And summer's lease hath all too short a date;
Sometime too hot the eye of heaven shines,
And often is his gold complexion dimm'd;
And every fair from fair sometime declines,
By chance, or nature's changing course untrimm'd:
But thy eternal summer shall not fade,
Nor lose possession of that fair thou ow'st,
Nor shall Death brag thou wander'st in his shade,
When in eternal lines to time thou grow'st;
  So long as men can breathe, or eyes can see,
  So long lives this, and this gives life to thee.

127 b   *   *   *

When in disgrace with fortune and men's eyes
I all alone beweep my outcast state,
And trouble deaf heaven with my bootless cries,
And look upon myself, and curse my fate,
Wishing me like to one more rich in hope,
Featur'd like him, like him with friends possess'd,
Desiring this man's art, and that man's scope,
With what I most enjoy contented least:
Yet in these thoughts myself almost despising,
Haply I think on thee,—and then my state,
Like to the lark at break of day arising
From sullen earth, sings hymns at heaven's gate;
  For thy sweet love remember'd such wealth brings
  That then I scorn to change my state with kings.

127c   *   *   *

When to the sessions of sweet silent thought
I summon up remembrance of things past,
I sigh the lack of many a thing I sought,
And with old woes new wail my dear time's waste:
Then can I drown an eye, unus'd to flow,
For precious friends hid in death's dateless night,
And weep afresh love's long since cancell'd woe,
And moan th' expense of many a vanish'd sight:
Then can I grieve at grievances foregone,
And heavily from woe to woe tell o'er
The sad account of fore-bemoaned moan,
Which I new pay as if not paid before.
    But if the while I think on thee, dear friend,
    All losses are restor'd and sorrows end.

127d   *   *   *

Full many a glorious morning have I seen
Flatter the mountain-tops with sovereign eye,
Kissing with golden face the meadows green,
Gilding pale streams with heavenly alchemy;   *profound art of*
Anon permit the basest clouds to ride   *transmuting baser*
With ugly rack on his celestial face,   *metals into gold.*
And from the forlorn world his visage hide,
Stealing unseen to west with this disgrace.
Even so my sun one early morn did shine
With all-triumphant splendor on my brow;
But, out! alack! he was but one hour mine,
The region-cloud hath mask'd him from me now.
    Yet him for this my love no whit disdaineth;
    Suns of the world may stain when heaven's sun staineth.

*   *   *

Like as the waves make towards the pebbled shore,
So do our minutes hasten to their end;
Each changing place with that which goes before,
In sequent toil all forwards do contend.
Nativity, once in the main of light,
Crawls to maturity, wherewith being crown'd,
Crooked eclipses 'gainst his glory fight,
And Time that gave doth now his gift confound.
Time doth transfix the flourish set on youth
And delves the parallels in beauty's brow,
Feeds on the rarities of nature's truth,
And nothing stands but for his scythe to mow:
    And yet to times in hope my verse shall stand,
    Praising thy worth, despite his cruel hand.

*   *   *

When I have seen by Time's fell hand defaced
The rich proud cost of outworn buried age;
When sometime lofty towers I see down-razed,
And brass eternal slave to mortal rage;
When I have seen the hungry ocean gain
Advantage on the kingdom of the shore,
And the firm soil win of the watery main,
Increasing store with loss, and loss with store;
When I have seen such interchange of state,
Or state itself confounded to decay;
Ruin hath taught me thus to ruminate—
That Time will come and take my love away.
    This thought is as a death, which cannot choose
    But weep to have that which it fears to lose.

127 g   *   *   *

Since brass, nor stone, nor earth, nor boundless sea,
But sad mortality o'er-sways their power,
How with this rage shall beauty hold a plea,
Whose action is no stronger than a flower?
O! how shall summer's honey breath hold out
Against the wreckful siege of batt'ring days,
When rocks impregnable are not so stout,
Nor gates of steel so strong, but Time decays?
O fearful meditation! where, alack,
Shall Time's best jewel from Time's chest lie hid?
Or what strong hand can hold his swift foot back?
Or who his spoil of beauty can forbid?
    O! none, unless this miracle have might,
    That in black ink my love may still shine bright.

127 h   *   *   *

No longer mourn for me when I am dead,
Than you shall hear the surly sullen bell
Give warning to the world that I am fled
From this vile world, with vilest worms to dwell:
Nay, if you read this line, remember not
The hand that writ it; for I love you so,
That I in your sweet thoughts would be forgot,
If thinking on me then should make you woe.
O! if, I say, you look upon this verse,
When I perhaps compounded am with clay,
Do not so much as my poor name rehearse,
But let your love even with my life decay,
    Lest the wise world should look into your moan,
    And mock you with me after I am gone.

127i   *   *   *

That time of year thou mayst in me behold
When yellow leaves, or none, or few, do hang
Upon those boughs which shake against the cold,
Bare ruin'd choirs, where late the sweet birds sang.
In me thou see'st the twilight of such day
As after sunset fadeth in the west,
Which by and by black night doth take away,
Death's second self, that seals up all in rest.
In me thou see'st the glowing of such fire,
That on the ashes of his youth doth lie,
As the death-bed whereon it must expire,
Consum'd with that which it was nourish'd by.
   This thou perceiv'st, which makes thy love more strong,
   To love that well which thou must leave ere long.

127j   *   *   *

How like a winter hath my absence been
From thee, the pleasure of the fleeting year!
What freezings have I felt, what dark days seen!
What old December's bareness everywhere!
And yet this time remov'd was summer's time,
The teeming autumn, big with rich increase,
Bearing the wanton burden of the prime,
Like widow'd wombs after their lords' decease:
Yet this abundant issue seem'd to me
But hope of orphans and unfather'd fruit;
For summer and his pleasures wait on thee,
And, thou away, the very birds are mute:
   Or, if they sing, 'tis with so dull a cheer,
   That leaves look pale, dreading the winter's near.

127 k   *   *   *

When in the chronicle of wasted time
I see descriptions of the fairest wights,   *human beings*
And beauty making beautiful old rime,
In praise of ladies dead and lovely knights;
Then, in the blazon of sweet beauty's best,
Of hand, of foot, of lip, of eye, of brow,
I see their antique pen would have express'd
Even such a beauty as you master now.
So all their praises are but prophecies
Of this our time, all you prefiguring;
And, for they look'd but with divining eyes,
They had not skill enough your worth to sing:
　　For we, which now behold these present days,
　　Have eyes to wonder, but lack tongues to praise.

127 l   *   *   *

Not mine own fears, nor the prophetic soul
Of the wide world dreaming on things to come,
Can yet the lease of my true love control,
Suppos'd as forfeit to a confin'd doom.
The mortal moon hath her eclipse endur'd,
And the sad augurs mock their own presage;
Incertainties now crown themselves assur'd,
And peace proclaims olives of endless age.
Now with the drops of this most balmy time
My love looks fresh, and Death to me subscribes,
Since, spite of him, I'll live in this poor rime,
While he insults o'er dull and speechless tribes:
　　And thou in this shalt find thy monument,
　　When tyrants' crests and tombs of brass are spent.

[165]

127 m   *   *   *

O! never say that I was false of heart,
Though absence seem'd my flame to qualify.
As easy might I from myself depart
As from my soul, which in thy breast doth lie:
That is my home of love: if I have rang'd,
Like him that travels I return again,
Just to the time, not with the time exchang'd,
So that myself bring water for my stain.
Never believe, though in my nature reign'd
All frailties that besiege all kinds of blood,
That it could so preposterously be stain'd,
To leave for nothing all thy sum of good;
    For nothing this wide universe I call,
    Save thou, my rose; in it thou art my all.

127 n   *   *   *

Let me not to the marriage of true minds
Admit impediments. Love is not love
Which alters when it alteration finds,
Or bends with the remover to remove.
O, no! it is an ever-fixed mark
That looks on tempests and is never shaken;
It is the star to every wand'ring bark,
Whose worth's unknown, although his height be taken.
Love's not Time's fool, though rosy lips and cheeks
Within his bending sickle's compass come;
Love alters not with his brief hours and weeks,
But bears it out even to the edge of doom.
    If this be error, and upon me proved,
    I never writ, nor no man ever loved.

1270   *   *   *

Th' expense of spirit in a waste of shame
Is lust in action; and till action, lust
Is perjur'd, murd'rous, bloody, full of blame,
Savage, extreme, rude, cruel, not to trust:
Enjoy'd no sooner but despised straight;
Past reason hunted, and no sooner had,
Past reason hated, as a swallowed bait
On purpose laid to make the taker mad:
Mad in pursuit and in possession so;
Had, having, and in quest to have, extreme;
A bliss in proof, and prov'd, a very woe;
Before, a joy propos'd; behind, a dream.
    All this the world well knows; yet none knows well
    To shun the heaven that leads men to this hell.

127p   *   *   *

Poor soul, the center of my sinful earth,
Rebuke these rebel powers that thee array!
Why dost thou pine within and suffer dearth,
Painting thy outward walls so costly gay?
Why so large cost, having so short a lease,
Dost thou upon thy fading mansion spend?
Shall worms, inheritors of this excess,
Eat up thy charge? Is this thy body's end?
Then, soul, live thou upon thy servant's loss,
And let that pine to aggravate thy store;
Buy terms divine in selling hours of dross: *sediment; skum*
Within be fed, without be rich no more.
    So shalt thou feed on Death, that feeds on men,
    And Death once dead, there's no more dying then.

Poor   'When shrill winds shriek'

When shrill winds shriek their scream upon thine ear,
And batter the bright stars from heavenly view,
Thy heart doth shut, and clap its doors in fear,
The while mine own doth open unto you.
When April songs are flung on gentle winds,
And green of field melts into blue of sky,
Thy soul in ecstasy doth soar, and finds
Mine own in steadfast love still standing by.
And when thy flight to realms so far from here
I envy, longing for thy light-winged ease,
I comfort me that even rocks are dear,
Amid the beating of the steely seas.
In love and me thou hast the ancient core,
The changeless rock that stands forever more.

      'Death, be not proud'

Death, be not proud, though some have callèd thee
Mighty and dreadful, for thou art not so;
For those whom thou think'st thou dost overthrow
Die not, poor Death, nor yet canst thou kill me.
From rest and sleep, which but thy pictures be,
Much pleasure; then from thee much more must flow,
And soonest our best men with thee do go,
Rest of their bones, and soul's delivery.
Thou art slave to fate, chance, kings, and desperate men,
And dost with poison, war, and sickness dwell;
And poppy or charms can make us sleep as well
And better than thy stroke; why swell'st thou then?
One short sleep past, we wake eternally,
And death shall be no more; Death, thou shalt die.

How soon hath Time the suttle theef of youth,
Stoln on his wing my three and twentieth yeer!
My hasting dayes flie on with full career,
But my late spring no bud or blossom shew'th.
Perhaps my semblance might deceive the truth,
That I to manhood am arriv'd so near,
And inward ripenes doth much less appear,
That som more timely-happy spirits indu'th.
Yet be it less or more, or soon or slow,
It shall be still in strictest measure eev'n,
To that same lot, however mean, or high,
Toward which Time leads me, and the will of Heav'n;
All is, if I have grace to use it so,
As ever in my great task Masters eye.

Methought I saw my late espoused Saint
Brought to me like *Alcestis* from the grave,
Whom *Joves* great Son to her glad Husband gave,
Rescu'd from death by force though pale and faint.
Mine as whom washt from spot of child-bed taint,
Purification in the old Law did save,
And such, as yet once more I trust to have
Full sight of her in Heaven without restraint,
Came vested all in white, pure as her mind:
Her face was vail'd, yet to my fancied sight,
Love, sweetness, goodness, in her person shin'd
So clear, as in no face with more delight.
But O as to embrace me she enclin'd
I wak'd, she fled, and day brought back my night.

'When I consider how my light is spent'

When I consider how my light is spent,
E're half my days, in this dark world and wide,
And that one Talent which is death to hide,
Lodg'd with me useless, though my Soul more bent
To serve therewith my Maker, and present
My true account, least he returning chide,
Doth God exact day-labour, light deny'd,
I fondly ask; But patience to prevent
That murmur, soon replies, God doth not need
Either man's work or his own gifts, who best
Bear his milde yoak, they serve him best, his State
Is Kingly. Thousands at his bidding speed
And post o're Land and Ocean without rest:
They also serve who only stand and waite.

On the late Massacre in Piedmont

Avenge O Lord thy slaughter'd Saints, whose bones
Lie scatter'd on the Alpine mountains cold,
Ev'n them who kept thy truth so pure of old
When all our Fathers worship't Stocks and Stones,
Forget not: in thy book record their groanes
Who were thy Sheep and in their antient Fold
Slayn by the bloody *Piemontese* that roll'd
Mother with Infant down the Rocks. Their moans
The Vales redoubl'd to the Hills, and they
To Heav'n. Their martyr'd blood and ashes sow
O're all th'*Italian* fields where still doth sway
The triple Tyrant: that from these may grow
A hunder'd-fold, who having learnt thy way
Early may fly the *Babylonian* wo.

London, 1802

Milton! thou shouldst be living at this hour:
England hath need of thee: she is a fen
Of stagnant waters: altar, sword, and pen,
Fireside, the heroic wealth of hall and bower,
Have forfeited their ancient English dower
Of inward happiness. We are selfish men;
Oh! raise us up, return to us again;
And give us manners, virtue, freedom, power.
Thy soul was like a Star, and dwelt apart;
Thou hadst a voice whose sound was like the sea:
Pure as the naked heavens, majestic, free,
So didst thou travel on life's common way,
In cheerful godliness; and yet thy heart
The lowliest duties on herself did lay.

'*O friend! I know not which way I must look*'

O friend! I know not which way I must look
For comfort, being, as I am, opprest,
To think that now our life is only drest
For show; mean handiwork of craftsman, cook,
Or groom!—We must run glittering like a brook
In the open sunshine, or we are unblest:
The wealthiest man among us is the best:
No grandeur now in nature or in book
Delights us. Rapine, avarice, expense,
This is idolatry; and these we adore:
Plain living and high thinking are no more:
The homely beauty of the good old cause
Is gone; our peace, our fearful innocence,
And pure religion breathing household laws.

'The world is too much with us'

The world is too much with us; late and soon,
Getting and spending, we lay waste our powers:
Little we see in Nature that is ours;
We have given our hearts away, a sordid boon!
This sea that bares her bosom to the moon;
The winds that will be howling at all hours,
And are up-gathered now like sleeping flowers;
For this, for everything, we are out of tune;
It moves us not.—Great God! I'd rather be
A Pagan suckled in a creed outworn;
So might I, standing on this pleasant lea,
Have glimpses that would make me less forlorn;
Have sight of Proteus rising from the sea;
Or hear old Triton blow his wreathèd horn.

'It is a beauteous evening'

It is a beauteous evening, calm and free,
The holy time is quiet as a Nun
Breathless with adoration; the broad sun
Is sinking down in its tranquillity;
The gentleness of heaven broods o'er the Sea:
Listen! the mighty Being is awake,
And doth with his eternal motion make
A sound like thunder—everlastingly.
Dear Child! dear Girl; that walkest with me here,
If thou appear untouched by solemn thought,
Thy nature is not therefore less divine:
Thou liest in Abraham's bosom all the year;
And worshipp'st at the temple's inner shrine,
God being with thee when we know it not.

138   *Composed upon Westminster Bridge, September 3, 1802* – Wordsworth

Earth has not anything to show more fair:
Dull would he be of soul who could pass by
A sight so touching in its majesty:
This City now doth, like a garment, wear
The beauty of the morning; silent, bare,
Ships, towers, domes, theatres, and temples lie
Open unto the fields, and to the sky;
All bright and glittering in the smokeless air.
Never did sun more beautifully steep
In his first splendor, valley, rock, or hill;
Ne'er saw I, never felt, a calm so deep!
The river glideth at his own sweet will:
Dear God! the very houses seem asleep;
And all that mighty heart is lying still!

139   *On the Extinction of the Venetian Republic*

Once did She hold the gorgeous East in fee;
And was the safeguard of the West: the worth
Of Venice did not fall below her birth,
Venice, the eldest child of Liberty.
She was a maiden City, bright and free;
No guile seduced, no force could violate;
And, when she took unto herself a Mate,
She must espouse the everlasting Sea.
And what if she had seen those glories fade,
Those titles vanish, and that strength decay;
Yet shall some tribute of regret be paid
When her long life hath reached its final day:
Men are we, and must grieve when even the Shade
Of that which once was great is passed away.

140   *Thought of a Briton on the Subjugation of Switzerland*

Two Voices are there; one is of the sea,
One of the mountains; each a mighty Voice:
In both from age to age thou didst rejoice,
They were thy chosen music, Liberty!
There came a tyrant, and with holy glee
Thou fought'st against him; but hast vainly striven:
Thou from thy Alpine holds at length art driven,
Where not a torrent murmurs heard by thee.
Of one deep bliss thine ear hath been bereft:
Then cleave, O cleave to that which still is left;
For, high-souled Maid, what sorrow would it be
That mountain Floods should thunder as before,
And Ocean bellow from his rocky shore,
And neither awful Voice be heard by thee!

141   *On First Looking into Chapman's Homer* — Keats

Much have I travell'd in the realms of gold,
And many goodly states and kingdoms seen;
Round many western islands have I been
Which bards in fealty to Apollo hold.
Oft of one wide expanse had I been told
That deep-brow'd Homer ruled as his demesne;
Yet did I never breathe its pure serene
Till I heard Chapman speak out loud and bold:
Then felt I like some watcher of the skies
When a new planet swims into his ken;
Or like stout Cortez when with eagle eyes
He star'd at the Pacific—and all his men
Look'd at each other with a wild surmise—
Silent, upon a peak in Darien.

To Sleep

O soft embalmer of the still midnight,
Shutting, with careful fingers and benign,
Our gloom-pleas'd eyes, embower'd from the light,
Enshaded in forgetfulness divine:
O soothest Sleep! if so it please thee, close
In midst of this thine hymn my willing eyes,
Or wait the amen, ere thy poppy throws
Around my bed its lulling charities.
Then save me, or the passed day will shine
Upon my pillow, breeding many woes,—
Save me from curious conscience, that still lords
Its strength for darkness, burrowing like a mole;
Turn the key deftly in the oiled wards,
And seal the hushed casket of my soul.

'When I have fears that I may cease to be'

When I have fears that I may cease to be
Before my pen has glean'd my teeming brain,
Before high-piled books, in charact'ry,
Hold like rich garners the full ripen'd grain;
When I behold, upon the night's starr'd face,
Huge cloudy symbols of a high romance,
And think that I may never live to trace
Their shadows, with the magic hand of chance;
And when I feel, fair creature of an hour,
That I shall never look upon thee more,
Never have relish in the faery power
Of unreflecting love;—then on the shore
Of the wide world I stand alone, and think
Till love and fame to nothingness do sink.

'Bright star, would I were steadfast as thou art'

Bright star, would I were steadfast as thou art!
Not in lone splendor hung aloft the night,
And watching, with eternal lids apart,
Like Nature's patient, sleepless eremite,
The moving waters at their priestlike task
Of pure ablution round earth's human shores,
Or gazing on the new soft-fallen mask
Of snow upon the mountains and the moors:
No—yet still steadfast, still unchangeable,
Pillow'd upon my fair love's ripening breast,
To feel forever its soft fall and swell,
Awake forever in a sweet unrest.
Still, still to hear her tender-taken breath,
And so live ever—or else swoon to death.

'When our two souls stand up'

When our two souls stand up erect and strong,
Face to face, silent, drawing nigh and nigher,
Until the lengthening wings break into fire
At either curvèd point—what bitter wrong
Can the earth do to us, that we should not long
Be here contented? Think. In mounting higher,
The angels would press on us and aspire
To drop some golden orb of perfect song
Into our deep, dear silence. Let us stay
Rather on earth, Belovèd—where the unfit
Contrarious moods of men recoil away
And isolate pure spirits, and permit
A place to stand and love in for a day,
With darkness and the death-hour rounding it.

'How do I love thee?'

How do I love thee? Let me count the ways.
I love thee to the depth and breadth and height
My soul can reach, when feeling out of sight
For the ends of Being and ideal Grace.
I love thee to the level of everyday's
Most quiet need, by sun and candle-light.
I love thee freely, as men strive for Right;
I love thee purely, as they turn from Praise.
I love thee with the passion put to use
In my old griefs, and with my childhood's faith.
I love thee with a love I seemed to lose
With my lost saints—I love thee with the breath,
Smiles, tears, of all my life!—and, if God choose,
I shall but love thee better after death.

Remember

Remember me when I am gone away,
Gone far away into the silent land;
When you can no more hold me by the hand,
Nor I half turn to go yet turning stay.
Remember me when no more day by day
You tell me of our future that you planned.
Only remember me; you understand
It will be late to counsel then or pray.
Yet if you should forget me for a while
And afterwards remember, do not grieve;
For if the darkness and corruption leave
A vestige of the thoughts that once I had,
Better by far you should forget and smile
Than that you should remember and be sad.

148 a   *The House of Life*

LOVESIGHT

When do I see thee most, beloved one?
When in the light the spirits of mine eyes
Before thy face, their altar, solemnize
The worship of that Love through thee made known?
Of when in the dusk hours (we two alone)
Close-kissed and eloquent of still replies
Thy twilight-hidden glimmering visage lies,
And my soul only sees thy soul its own?
O love, my love! if I no more should see
Thyself, nor on the earth the shadow of thee,
Nor image of thine eyes in any spring—
How then should sound upon Life's darkening slope
The ground-whirl of the perished leaves of Hope,
The wind of Death's imperishable wing?

WILLOWWOOD

148 b   I

I sat with Love upon a woodside well,
Leaning across the water, I and he;
Nor ever did he speak nor looked at me,
But touched his lute wherein was audible
The certain secret thing he had to tell.
Only our mirrored eyes met silently
In the low wave; and that sound came to be
The passionate voice I knew; and my tears fell.
And at their fall, his eyes beneath grew hers;
And with his foot and with his wing-feathers
He swept the spring that watered my heart's drouth.
Then the dark ripples spread to waving hair,
And as I stooped, her own lips rising there
Bubbled with brimming kisses at my mouth.

II

And now Love sang; but his was such a song,
So meshed with half-remembrance hard to free,
As souls disused in death's sterility
May sing when the new birthday tarries long.
And I was made aware of a dumb throng
That stood aloof, one form by every tree,
All mournful forms, for each was I or she,
The shades of those our days that had no tongue.
They looked on us, and knew us and were known;
While fast together, alive from the abyss,
Clung the soul-wrung implacable close kiss;
And pity of self through all made broken moan
Which said, 'For once, for once, for once alone!'
And still Love sang, and what he sang was this:

III

'O ye, all ye that walk in Willowwood,
That walk with hollow faces burning white:
What fathom-depth of soul-struck widowhood,
What long, what longer hours, one lifelong night,
Ere ye again, who so in vain have wooed
Your last hope lost, who so in vain invite
Your lips to that their unforgotten food,
Ere ye, ere ye again shall see the light!
Alas! the bitter banks in Willowwood,
With tear-spurge wan, with blood-wort burning red.
Alas! if ever such a pillow could
Steep deep the soul in sleep till she were dead—
Better all life forget her than this thing,
That Willowwood should hold her wandering!'

So sang he; and as meeting rose and rose
Together cling through the wind's well-away
Nor change at once, yet near the end of day
The leaves drop loosened where the heart-stain glows—
So when the song died did the kiss unclose;
And her face fell back drowned, and was as gray
As its gray eyes; and if it ever may
Meet mine again I know not if Love knows.
Only I know that I leaned low and drank
A long draft from the water where she sank,
Her breath and all her tears and all her soul;
And as I leaned, I know I felt Love's face
Pressed on my neck with moan of pity and grace,
Till both our heads were in his aureole.

148f   WITHOUT HER

What of her glass without her? The blank gray
There where the pool is blind of the moon's face.
Her dress without her? The tossed empty space
Of cloud-rack whence the moon has passed away.
Her paths without her? Day's appointed sway
Usurped by desolate night. Her pillowed place
Without her? Tears, ah me! for love's good grace,
And cold forgetfulness of night or day.
What of the heart without her? Nay, poor heart,
Of thee what word remains ere speech be still?
A wayfarer by barren ways and chill,
Steep ways and weary, without her thou art,
Where the long cloud, the long wood's counterpart,
Sheds doubled darkness up the laboring hill.

What place so strange—though unrevealèd snow
With unimaginable fires arise
At the earth's end—what passion of surprise
Like frost-bound fire-girt scenes of long ago?
Lo! this is none but I this hour; and lo!
This is the very place which to mine eyes
Those mortal hours in vain immortalize,
'Mid hurrying crowds, with what alone I know.
City, of thine a single simple door,
By some new Power reduplicate, must be
Even yet my life-porch in eternity,
Even with one presence filled, as once of yore;
Or mocking winds whirl round a chaff-strown floor
Thee and thy years and these my words and me.

149   *Lucifer in Starlight*

On a starred night Prince Lucifer uprose.
Tired of his dark dominion, swung the fiend
Above the rolling ball, in cloud part screened,
Where sinners hugged their specter of repose.
Poor prey to his hot fit of pride were those.
And now upon his western wing he leaned,
Now his huge bulk o'er Afric's sands careened,
Now the black planet shadowed Arctic snows.
Soaring through wider zones that pricked his scars
With memory of the old revolt from Awe,
He reached a middle height, and at the stars,
Which are the brain of heaven, he looked, and sank.
Around the ancient track marched, rank on rank,
The army of unalterable law.

Tuscan, that wanderest through the realms of gloom,
With thoughtful pace, and sad, majestic eyes,
Stern thoughts and awful from thy soul arise,
Like Farinata from his fiery tomb.
Thy sacred song is like the trump of doom;
Yet in thy heart what human sympathies,
What soft compassion glows, as in the skies
The tender stars their clouded lamps relume!
Methinks I see thee stand, with pallid cheeks,
By Fra Hilario in his diocese,
As up the convent-walls, in golden streaks,
The ascending sunbeams mark the day's decrease;
And, as he asks what there the stranger seeks,
Thy voice along the cloister whispers, 'Peace!'

151a ### Divina Commedia

Oft have I seen at some cathedral door
A laborer, pausing in the dust and heat,
Lay down his burden, and with reverent feet
Enter, and cross himself, and on the floor
Kneel to repeat his paternoster o'er;
Far off the noises of the world retreat;
The loud vociferations of the street
Become an undistinguishable roar.
So, as I enter here from day to day,
And leave my burden at this minster gate,
Kneeling in prayer, and not ashamed to pray,
The tumult of the time disconsolate
To inarticulate murmurs dies away,
While the eternal ages watch and wait.

151b   *   *   *

How strange the sculptures that adorn these towers!
This crowd of statues, in whose folded sleeves
Birds build their nests: while canopied with leaves
Parvis and portal bloom like trellised bowers,
And the vast minster seems a cross of flowers!
But fiends and dragons on the gargoyled eaves
Watch the dead Christ between the living thieves,
And, underneath, the traitor Judas lowers!
Ah! from what agonies of heart and brain,
What exultations trampling on despair,
What tenderness, what tears, what hate of wrong,
What passionate outcry of a soul in pain,
Uprose this poem of the earth and air,
This medieval miracle of song!

151c   *   *   *

I enter, and I see thee in the gloom
Of the long aisles, O poet saturnine!
And strive to make my steps keep pace with thine.
The air is filled with some unknown perfume;
The congregation of the dead make room
For thee to pass; the votive tapers shine;
Like rooks that haunt Ravenna's groves of pine
The hovering echoes fly from tomb to tomb.
From the confessionals I hear arise
Rehearsals of forgotten tragedies,
And lamentations from the crypts below;
And then a voice celestial, that begins
With the pathetic words, 'Although your sins
As scarlet be,' and ends with 'as the snow.'

151d * * *

With snow-white veil and garments as of flame,
She stands before thee, who so long ago
Filled thy young heart with passion and the woe
From which thy song and all its splendors came;
And while with stern rebuke she speaks thy name,
The ice about thy heart melts as the snow
On mountain heights, and in swift overflow
Comes gushing from thy lips in sobs of shame.
Thou makest full confession; and a gleam,
As of the dawn on some dark forest cast,
Seems on thy lifted forehead to increase;
Lethe and Eunoe—the remembered dream
And the forgotten sorrow—bring at last
That perfect pardon which is perfect peace.

151e * * *

I lift mine eyes, and all the windows blaze
With forms of saints and holy men who died,
Here martyred and hereafter glorifed;
And the great Rose upon its leaves displays
Christ's triumph, and the angelic roundelays,
With splendor upon splendor multiplied;
And Beatrice again at Dante's side
No more rebukes, but smiles her words of praise.
And then the organ sounds, and unseen choirs
Sing the old Latin hymns of peace and love,
And benedictions of the Holy Ghost;
And the melodious bells among the spires
O'er all the house-tops and through heaven above
Proclaim the elevation of the Host!

151 f

O Star of morning and of liberty!
O bringer of the light, whose splendor shines
Above the darkness of the Apennines,
Forerunner of the day that is to be!
The voices of the city and the sea,
The voices of the mountains and the pines,
Repeat thy song, till the familiar lines
Are footpaths for the thought of Italy!
Thy fame is blown abroad from all the heights.
Through all the nations, and a sound is heard,
As of a mighty wind, and men devout,
Strangers of Rome, and the new proselytes,
In their own language hear thy wondrous word,
And many are amazed and many doubt.

152   *'As in the Midst of Battle'*

As in the midst of battle there is room
For thoughts of love, and in foul sin for mirth;
As gossips whisper of a trinket's worth
Spied by the death-bed's flickering candle-gloom;
As in the crevices of Caesar's tomb
The sweet herbs flourish on a little earth:
So in this great disaster of our birth
We can be happy, and forget our doom.
For morning, with a ray of tenderest joy
Gilding the iron heaven, hides the truth,
And evening gently woos us to employ
Our grief in idle catches. Such is youth;
Till from that summer's trance we wake, to find
Despair before us, vanity behind.

The Rustic at the Play

Our youth is like a rustic at the play
That cries aloud in simple-hearted fear,
Curses the villain, shudders at the fray,
And weeps before the maiden's wreathèd bier.
Yet once familiar with the changeful show,
He starts no longer at a brandished knife,
But, his heart chastened at the sight of woe,
Ponders the mirrored sorrows of his life.
So tutored too, I watch the moving art
Of all this magic and impassioned pain
That tells the story of the human heart
In a false instance, such as poets feign;
I smile, and keep within the parchment furled
That prompts the passions of this strutting world.

'I hereby swear that to uphold your house'

I hereby swear that to uphold your house
I would lay my bones in quick destroying lime
Or turn my flesh to timber for all time;
Cut down my womanhood; lop off the boughs
Of that perpetual ecstasy that grows
From the heart's core; condemn it as a crime
If it be broader than a beam, or climb
Above the stature that your roof allows.
I am not the hearthstone nor the cornerstone
Within this noble fabric you have builded;
Not by my beauty was its cornice gilded;
Not on my courage were its arches thrown:
My lord, adjudge my strength, and set me where
I bear a little more than I can bear.

'What lips my lips have kissed'

What lips my lips have kissed, and where, and why,
I have forgotten, and what arms have lain
Under my head till morning; but the rain
Is full of ghosts tonight, that tap and sigh
Upon the glass and listen for reply;
And in my heart there stirs a quiet pain
For unremembered lads that not again
Will turn to me at midnight with a cry.
Thus in the winter stands the lonely tree,
Nor knows what birds have vanished one by one,
Yet knows its boughs more silent than before:
I cannot say what loves have come and gone;
I only know that summer sang in me
A little while, that in me sings no more.

'You who will soon be unrecapturable'

You who will soon be unrecapturable,
You with your flair for spotted scarves and checks,
The creed I built upon your charm and sex
And *laissez-faire* I find no longer tenable;
But as the loitering senses are incapable
To hold the blend of smells or light in flecks
So knowing you whom no one could annex
Was no more durable than those are durable:
Which is why your trek to not-believed-in lands
Has dislocated the day and quenched the sun
That licked the cornice of my lonely room
Settling now to a gray and reasoned gloom
Where I shall neither recant the minutes gone
Nor fumble for the past with backward hands.

PART III

NARRATIVE AND DRAMATIC POEMS

Sir Patrick Spens

The king sits in Dumferling toune,
   Drinking the blude-reid wine:
'O whar will I get guid sailor,
   To sail this schip of mine?'

Up and spak an eldern knicht,
   Sat at the kings richt kne:
'Sir Patrick Spence is the best sailor
   That sails upon the se.'

The king has written a braid letter,
   And signd it wi his hand,   10
And sent it to Sir Patrick Spence,
   Was walking on the sand.

The first line that Sir Patrick red,
   A loud lauch lauched he;
The next line that Sir Patrick red,
   The teir blinded his ee.

'O wha is this has don this deid,
   This ill deid don to me,
To send me out this time o' the yeir,
   To sail upon the se!   20

'Mak hast, mak haste, my mirry men all,
   Our guid schip sails the morne:'
'O say na sae, my master deir,
   For I feir a deadlie storme.

'Late late yestreen I saw the new moone,
   Wi the auld moone in hir arme,
And I feir, I feir, my deir master,
   That we will cum to harme.'

O our Scots nobles wer richt laith
  To weet their cork-heild schoone;
Bot lang owre a' the play wer playd,
  Thair hats they swam aboone.   30

O lang, lang may their ladies sit,
  Wi thair fans into their hand,
Or eir they se Sir Patrick Spence
  Cum sailing to the land.

O lang, lang may the ladies stand,
  Wi thair gold kems in their hair,
Waiting for thair ain deir lords,
  For they'll se thame na mair.   40

Haf owre, haf owre to Aberdour,
  It's fiftie fadom deip,
And thair lies guid Sir Patrick Spence,
  Wi the Scots lords at his feit.

158 *Lord Randall*

Where have you been to, Randall my son?
Where have you been to, my pretty one?
I've been to my Sweetheart's, Mother,
I've been to my Sweetheart's, Mother.
Make my bed soon, for I'm sick to the heart,
And I fain would lie down.

What have you been eating, Randall my son?
What have you been eating, my pretty one?
Eels and eel broth, Mother,
Eels and eel broth, Mother.   10
Make my bed soon, for I'm sick to the heart,
And I fain would lie down.

What will you leave your Mother, Randall my son?
What will you leave your Mother, my pretty one?
My lands and houses, Mother,
My lands and houses, Mother.
Make my bed soon, for I'm sick to the heart,
And I fain would lie down.

What will you leave your brother, Randall my son?
What will you leave your brother, my pretty one?   20
My horses and cattle, Mother,
My horses and cattle, Mother.
Make my bed soon, for I'm sick to the heart,
And I fain would lie down.

What will you leave your sister, Randall my son?
What will you leave your sister, my pretty one?
My gold and silver, Mother,
My gold and silver, Mother.
Make my bed soon, for I'm sick to the heart,
And I fain would lie down.   30

What will you leave your Sweetheart, Randall my son?
What will you leave your Sweetheart, my pretty one?
A rope to hang her, Mother,
A rope to hang her, Mother.
Make my bed soon, for I'm sick to the heart,
And I fain would lie down.

159   *Mary Hamilton*

Word's gane to the kitchen,
    And word's gane to the ha,
That Marie Hamilton gangs wi bairn
    To the hichest Stewart of a'.

He's courted her in the kitchen,
    He's courted her in the ha,
He's courted her in the laigh cellar,
    And that was warst of a'.

She's tyed it in her apron
 And she's thrown it in the sea; 10
Says, Sink ye, swim ye, bonny wee babe!
 You'l neer get mair o me.

Down then cam the auld queen,
 Goud tassels tying her hair:
'O Marie, where's the bonny wee babe
 That I heard greet sae sair?'

'There was never a babe intill my room,
 As little designs to be;
It was but a touch o my sair side,
 Come oer my fair bodie.' 20

'O Marie, put on your robes o black,
 Or else your robes o brown,
For ye maun gang wi me the night,
 To see fair Edinbro town.'

'I winna put on my robes o black,
 Nor yet my robes o brown;
But I'll put on my robes o white,
 To shine through Edinbro town.'

When she gaed up the Cannogate,
 She laughd loud laughters three; 30
But whan she cam down the Cannogate
 The tear blinded her ee.

When she gaed up the Parliament stair,
 The heel cam aff her shee;
And lang or she cam down again
 She was condemnd to dee.

When she cam down the Cannogate,
 The Cannogate sae free,
Many a ladie lookd oer her window,
 Weeping for this ladie. 40

'Ye need nae weep for me,' she says,
　'Ye need nae weep for me;
For had I not slain mine own sweet babe,
　This death I wadna dee.

'Bring me a bottle of wine,' she says,
　'The best that eer ye hae,
That I may drink to my weil-wishers,
　And they may drink to me.

'Here's a health to the jolly sailors,
　That sail upon the main;
Let them never let on to my father and mother
　But what I'm coming hame.

'Here's a health to the jolly sailors,
　That sail upon the sea;
Let them never let on to my father and mother
　That I cam here to dee.

'Oh little did my mother think,
　The day she cradled me,
What lands I was to travel through,
　What death I was to dee.

'Oh little did my father think,
　The day he held up me,
What lands I was to travel through,
　What death I was to dee.

'Last night I washd the queens feet,
　And gently laid her down;
And a' the thanks I've gotten the nicht
　To be hangd in Edinbro town!

'Last nicht there was four Maries,
　The nicht there'l be but three;
There was Marie Seton, and Marie Beton,
　And Marie Carmichael, and me.'

[195]

There lived a wife at Usher's Well,
    And a wealthy wife was she;
She had three stout and stalwart sons,
    And sent them oer the sea.

They hadna been a week from her,
    A week but barely ane,
Whan word came to the carline wife
    That her three sons were gane.

They hadna been a week from her,
    A week but barely three,   10
Whan word came to the carlin wife
    That her sons she'd never see.

'I wish the wind may never cease,
    Nor fashes in the flood,
Till my three sons come hame to me,
    In earthly flesh and blood.'

It fell about the Martinmass,
    When nights are lang and mirk,
The carlin wife's three sons came hame,
    And their hats were o the birk.   20

It neither grew in syke nor ditch,
    Nor yet in ony sheugh;
But at the gates o Paradise,
    That birk grew fair eneugh.

*   *   *

'Blow up the fire, my maidens,
    Bring water from the well;
For a' my house shall feast this night,
    Since my three sons are well.'

And she has made to them a bed,
  She's made it large and wide,
And she's taen her mantle her about,
  Sat down at the bed-side.

          *   *   *

Up then crew the red, red cock,
  And up and crew the gray;
The eldest to the youngest said,
  'Tis time we were away.

The cock he hadna crawd but once,
  And clappd his wings at a',
When the youngest to the eldest said,
  Brother, we must awa.

'The cock doth craw, the day doth daw,
  The channerin worm doth chide;
Gin we be mist out o our place,
  A sair pain we maun bide.

'Fare ye weel, my mother dear!
  Fareweel to barn and byre!
And fare ye weel, the bonny lass
  That kindles my mother's fire!'

161   *The Bailiff's Daughter of Islington*

There was a youth, and a well belovd youth,
  And he was a esquire's son,
He loved the bayliff's daughter dear,
  That lived in Islington.

She was coy, and she would not believe
  That he did love her so,
No, nor at any time she would
  Any countenance to him show.

[197]

But when his friends did understand
   His fond and foolish mind,
They sent him up to fair London,
   An apprentice for to bind.

And when he had been seven long years,
   And his love he had not seen,
'Many a tear have I shed for her sake
   When she little thought of me.'

All the maids of Islington
   Went forth to sport and play;
All but the bayliff's daughter dear;
   She secretly stole away.

She put off her gown of gray,
   And put on her puggish attire;
She's up to fair London gone,
   Her true-love to require.

As she went along the road,
   The weather being hot and dry,
There was she aware of her true-love,
   At length came riding by.

She stept to him, as red as any rose,
   And took him by the bridle-ring:
'I pray you, kind sir, give me one penny,
   To ease my weary limb.'

'I prithee, sweetheart, canst thou tell me
   Where that thou wast born?'
'At Islington, kind sir,' said she,
   'Where I have had many a scorn.'

'I prithee, sweetheart, canst thou tell me
   Whether thou dost know
The bailiff's daughter of Islington?'
   'She's dead, sir, long ago.'

'Then will I sell my goodly steed,
    My saddle and my bow;
I will into some far countrey,
    Where no man doth me know.'

'O stay, O stay, thou goodly youth!
    She's alive, she is not dead;
Here she standeth by thy side,
    And is ready to be thy bride.'

'O farewel grief, and welcome joy,
    Ten thousand times and more!   50
For now I have seen my own true-love,
    That I thought I should have seen no more.'

162   *Young Waters*

    About Yule, when the wind blew cule,
        And the round tables began,
    A there is cum to our king's court
        Mony a well-favord man.

    The queen luikt owre the castle-wa,
        Beheld baith dale and down,
    And there she saw Young Waters
        Cum riding to the town.

    His footmen they did rin before,
        His horsemen rade behind;   10
    And mantel of the burning gowd
        Did keip him frae the wind.

    Gowden-graithd his horse before,
        And siller-shod behind;
    The horse Young Waters rade upon
        Was fleeter than the wind.

Out then spack a wylie lord,
  Unto the queen said he,
'O tell me wha 's the fairest face
  Rides in the company?'   20

'I've sene lord, and I've sene laird,
  And knights of high degree,
Bot a fairer face than Young Waters
  Mine eyne did never see.'

Out then spack the jealous king,
  And an angry man was he:
'O if he had bin twice as fair,
  You micht have excepted me.'

'You're neither laird nor lord,' she says,
  'Bot the king that wears the crown;   30
There is not a knight in fair Scotland
  But to thee maun bow down.'

For a' that she coud do or say,
  Appeasd he wad nae bee,
Bot for the words which she had said,
  Young Waters he maun die.

They hae taen Young Waters,
  And put fetters to his feet;
They hae taen Young Waters,
  And thrown him in dungeon deep.   40

'Aft I have ridden thro Stirling town
  In the wind bot and the weit;
Bot I neir rade thro Stirling town
  Wi fetters at my feet.

'Aft I have ridden thro Stirling town
  In the wind bot and the rain;
Bot I neir rade thro Stirling town
  Neir to return again.'

They hae taen to the heiding-hill
  His young son in his craddle,
And they hae taen to the heiding-hill   50
  His horse bot and his saddle.

They hae taen to the heiding-hill
  His lady fair to see,
And for the words the queen had spoke
  Young Waters he did die.

163   *Bonny Barbara Allan*

It was in and about the Martinmas time,
  When the green leaves were a falling,
That Sir John Graeme, in the West Country,
  Fell in love with Barbara Allan.

He sent his man down through the town,
  To the place where she was dwelling:
'O haste and come to my master dear,
  Gin ye be Barbara Allan.'

O hooly, hooly rose she up,
  To the place where he was lying,   10
And when she drew the curtain by,
  'Young man, I think you're dying.'

'O it's I'm sick, and very, very sick,
  And 'tis a' for Barbara Allan;'
'O the better for me ye 's never be,
  Tho your heart's blood were a spilling.'

'O dinna ye mind, young man,' said she,
  'When ye was in the tavern a drinking,
That ye made the healths gae round and round,
  And slighted Barbara Allan?'   20

He turned his face unto the wall,
    And death was with him dealing:
'Adieu, adieu, my dear friends all,
    And be kind to Barbara Allan.'

And slowly, slowly raise she up,
    And slowly, slowly left him,
And sighing said, she could not stay,
    Since death of life had reft him.

She had not gane a mile but twa,
    When she heard the dead-bell ringing,   30
And every jow that the dead-bell geid,
    It cry'd, Woe to Barbara Allan!

'O Mother, mother, make my bed!
    O make it saft and narrow!
Since my love died for me to-day,
    I'll die for him to-morrow.'

164   *Johnie Armstrong*

There dwelt a man in faire Westmerland,
    Ionnë Armestrong men did him call,
He had nither lands nor rents coming in,
    Yet he kept eight score men in his hall.

He had horse and harness for them all,
    Goodly steeds were all milke-white;
O the golden bands an about their necks,
    And their weapons, they were all alike.

Newes then was brought unto the king
    That there was sicke a won as hee,   10
That livëd lyke a bold out-law,
    And robbëd all the north country.

The king he writt an a letter then,
    A letter which was large and long;
He signëd it with his owne hand,
    And he promised to doe him no wrong.

When this letter came Ionnë untill,
    His heart it was as blythe as birds on the tree:
'Never was I sent for before any king,
    My father, my grandfather, nor none but mee.   20

'And if wee goe the king before,
    I would we went most orderly;
Every man of you shall have his scarlet cloak,
    Laced with silver laces three.

'Every won of you shall have his velvett coat,
    Laced with sillver lace so white;
O the golden bands an about your necks,
    Black hatts, white feathers, all alyke.'

By the morrow morninge at ten of the clock,
    Towards Edenburough gon was hee,   30
And with him all his eight score men;
    Good lord, it was a goodly sight for to see!

When Ionnë came befower the king,
    He fell downe on his knee;
'O pardon, my soveraine leige,' he said,
    'O pardon my eight score men and mee!'

Thou shalt have no pardon, thou traytor strong,
    For thy eight score men nor thee;
For tomorrow morning by ten of the clock,
    Both thou and them shall hang on the gallow-tree.   40

But Ionnë looke'd over his left shoulder,
    Good Lord, what a grevious look looked hee!
Saying, Asking grace of a graceless face—
    Why there is none for you nor me.

But Ionnë had a bright sword by his side,
   And it was made of the mettle so free,
That had not the king stept his foot aside,
   He had smitten his head from his faire boddë.

Saying, Fight on, my merry men all,
   And see that none of you be taine;
For rather then men shall say we were hange'd,
   Let them report how we were slaine.

Then, God wott, faire Eddenburrough rose,
   And so besett poore Ionnë rounde,
That fowerscore and tenn of Ionnë's best men
   Lay gasping all upon the ground.

Then like a mad man Ionnë's laide about,
   And like a mad man then fought hee,
Untill a falce Scot came Ionnë behinde,
   And runn him through the faire boddee.

Saying, Fight on, my merry men all,
   And see that none of you be taine;
For I will stand by and bleed but awhile,
   And then will I come and fight againe.

Newes then was brought to young Ionnë Armestrong,
   As he stood by his nurses knee,
Who vowed if ere he live'd for to be a man,
   O the treacherous Scots revengd hee'd be.

165   *A Lyke-Wake Dirge*

This ae nighte, this ae nighte,
   —*Every nighte and alle,*
Fire and fleet and candle-lighte,
   And Christe receive thy saule.

When thou from hence away art past,
   —*Every nighte and alle,*
To Whinny-muir thou com'st at last:
   And Christe receive thy saule.

If ever thou gavest hosen and shoon,
   —*Every nighte and alle,*   10
Sit thee down and put them on:
   And Christe receive thy saule.

If hosen and shoon thou ne'er gav'st nane
   —*Every nighte and alle,*
The whinnes sall prick thee to the bare bane;
   And Christe receive thy saule.

From Brig o' Dread when thou may'st pass,
   —*Every nighte and alle,*
To Purgatory fire thou com'st at last;
   And Christe receive thy saule.   20

If ever thou gavest meat or drink,
   —*Every nighte and alle,*
The fire sall never make thee shrink;
   And Christe receive thy saule.

If meat or drink thou ne'er gav'st nane,
   —*Every nighte and alle,*
The fire will burn thee to the bare bane;
   And Christe receive thy saule.

This ae nighte, this ae nighte,
   —*Every nighte and alle,*   30
Fire and fleet and candle-lighte,
   And Christe receive thy saule.

Faire stood the Wind for *France*,
When we our Sayles advance,
Nor now to prove our chance,
    Longer will tarry;
But putting to the Mayne,
At *Kaux*, the Mouth of *Sene*,
With all his Martiall Trayne,
    Landed King Harry.

And taking many a Fort,
Furnish'd in Warlike sort,   10
Marcheth tow'rds Agincourt,
    In happy howre;
Skirmishing day by day,
With those that stop'd his way,
Where the *French* Gen'rall lay,
    With all his Power.

Which in his Hight of Pride,
King Henry to deride,
His Ransome to provide
    To the King sending;   20
Which he neglects the while,
As from a Nation vile,
Yet with an angry smile,
    Their fall portending.

And turning to his Men,
Quoth our brave Henry then,
Though they to one be ten,
    Be not amazed.
Yet have we well begunne,
Battels so bravely wonne,   30
Have ever to the Sonne,
    By Fame beene raysed.

And for my Selfe, quoth he,
This my full rest shall be,
England ne'r mourne for Me,
   Nor more esteeme me.
Victor I will remaine,
Or on this Earth lie slaine,
Never shall Shee sustaine,
   Losse to redeeme me.   40

Poiters and *Cressy* tell,
When most their Pride did swell,
Under our Swords they fell,
   No lesse our skill is,
Then when our Grandsire Great,
Clayming the Regall Seate,
By many a Warlike feate,
   Lop'd the *French* Lillies.

The Duke of *Yorke* so dread,
The eager Vaward led;   50
With the maine, Henry sped,
   Among'st his Hench-men.
Excester had the Rere,
A Braver man not there,
O Lord, how hot they were,
   On the false *French-men*!

They now to fight are gone,
Armour on Armour shone,
Drumme now to Drumme did grone,
   To heare, was wonder;   60
That with Cryes they make,
The very Earth did shake,
Trumpet to Trumpet spake,
   Thunder to Thunder.

Well it thine Age became,
O Noble Erpingham,
Which didst the Signall ayme,
   To our hid Forces;
When from a Medow by,
Like a Storme suddenly,   70
The *English* Archery
   Stuck the *French* Horses,

With *Spanish* Ewgh so strong,
Arrowes a Cloth-yard long,
That like to Serpents stung,
   Piercing the Weather;
None from his fellow starts,
But playing Manly parts,
And like true *English* hearts,
   Stuck close together.   80

When downe their Bowes they threw,
And forth their Bilbowes drew,
And on the *French* they flew,
   Not one was tardie;
Armes were from shoulders sent,
Scalpes to the Teeth were rent,
Downe the *French* Pesants went,
   Our Men were hardie.

This while our Noble King,
His broad Sword brandishing,   90
Downe the *French* Hoast did ding,
   As to o'r-whelme it;
And many a deepe Wound lent,
His Armes with Bloud besprent,
And many a cruell Dent
   Bruised his Helmet.

Gloster, that Duke so good,
Next of the Royall Blood,
For famous England stood,
 With his brave Brother;   100
Clarence, in Steele so bright,
Though but a Maiden Knight,
Yet in that furious Fight,
 Scarce such another.

Warwick in Bloud did wade,
Oxford the Foe invade,
And cruell slaughter made,
 Still as they ran up;
Suffolke his Axe did ply,
Beaumont and Willoughby   110
Bare them right doughtily,
 Ferrers and Fanhope.

Upon Saint Crispin's day
Fought was this Noble Fray,
Which Fame did not delay,
 To *England* to carry;
O, when shall *English* Men
With such Acts fill a Pen,
Or England breed againe,
 Such a King Harry?   120

167   *Ballad of the Goodly Fere*

Simon Zelotes speaketh it somewhile after the Crucifixion.

Ha' we lost the goodliest fere o' all
For the priests and the gallows tree?
Aye lover he was of brawny men,
O' ships and the open sea.

[209]

When they came wi' a host to take Our Man
His smile was good to see;
'First let these go!' quo' our Goodly Fere,
'Or I'll see ye damned,' says he.

Aye, he sent us out through the crossed high spears,
And the scorn of his laugh rang free;   10
'Why took ye not me when I walked about
Alone in the town?' says he.

Oh, we drunk his 'Hale' in the good red wine
When we last made company;
No capon priest was the Goodly Fere
But a man o' men was he.

I ha' seen him drive a hundred men
Wi' a bundle o' cords swung free,
That they took the high and holy house
For their pawn and treasury.   20

They'll no' get him a' in a book I think,
Though they write it cunningly;
No mouse of the scrolls was the Goodly Fere
But aye loved the open sea.

If they think they ha' snared our Goodly Fere
They are fools to the last degree.
'I'll go the feast,' quo' our Goodly Fere,
'Though I go to the gallows tree.'

'Ye ha' seen me heal the lame and blind,
And wake the dead,' says he;   30
'Ye shall see one thing to master all:
'Tis how a brave man dies on the tree.'

A son of God was the Goodly Fere
That bade us his brothers be.
I ha' seen him cow a thousand men.
I have seen him upon the tree.

He cried no cry when they drave the nails
And the blood gushed hot and free;
The hounds of the crimson sky gave tongue
But never a cry cried he.   40

I ha' seen him cow a thousand men
On the hills o' Galilee;
They whined as he walked out calm between,
Wi' his eyes like the grey o' the sea,

Like the sea that brooks no voyaging
With the winds unleashed and free,
Like the sea that he cowed at Genseret
Wi' twey words spoke' suddenly.

A master of men was the Goodly Fere,
A mate of the wind and sea;   50
If they think they ha' slain our Goodly Fere
They are fools eternally.

I ha' seen him eat o' the honey-comb
Sin' they nailed him to the tree.

168   *La Belle Dame Sans Merci*

O what can ail thee, Knight-at-arms,
    Alone and palely loitering?
The sedge has withered from the Lake
    And no birds sing!

O what can ail thee, Knight-at-arms,
    So haggard, and so woe begone?
The Squirrel's granary is full
    And the harvest's done.

I see a lily on thy brow
    With anguish moist and fever dew,   10
And on thy cheeks a fading rose
    Fast withereth too.

I met a Lady in the Meads
  Full beautiful, a faery's child;
Her hair was long, her foot was light,
  And her eyes were wild.

I made a garland for her head,
  And bracelets too, and fragrant zone;
She look'd at me as she did love
  And made sweet moan.   20

I set her on my pacing steed
  And nothing else saw all day long;
For sidelong would she bend and sing
  A faery's song.

She found me roots of relish sweet
  And honey wild and manna dew;
And sure in language strange, she said
  I love thee true.

She took me to her elfin grot
  And there she wept and sigh'd full sore,   30
And there I shut her wild wild eyes
  With kisses four.

And there she lulled me asleep,
  And there I dream'd, ah woe betide!
The latest dream I ever dreamt
  On the cold hill side.

I saw pale Kings, and Princes too,
  Pale warriors, death-pale were they all;
They cried—'La belle dame sans merci
  Thee hath in thrall!'   40

I saw their starv'd lips in the gloam
  With horrid warning gaped wide,
And I awoke, and found me here
  On the cold hill's side.

And this is why I sojourn here
   Alone and palely loitering;
Though the sedge is withered from the Lake
   And no birds sing— . . .

169   *The Blessed Damozel*

   The blessed damozel leaned out
     From the gold bar of heaven;
   Her eyes were deeper than the depth
     Of waters stilled at even;
   She had three lilies in her hand,
     And the stars in her hair were seven

   Her robe, ungirt from clasp to hem,
     No wrought flowers did adorn,
   But a white rose of Mary's gift,
     For service meetly worn;   10
   Her hair that lay along her back
     Was yellow like ripe corn.

   Herseemed she scarce had been a day
     One of God's choristers;
   The wonder was not yet quite gone
     From that still look of hers;
   Albeit, to them she left, her day
     Had counted as ten years.

   (To *one* it is ten years of years.
     . . . Yet now, and in this place,   20
   Surely she leaned o'er me—her hair
     Fell all about my face . . .
   Nothing: the autumn fall of leaves.
     The whole year sets apace.)

It was the rampart of God's house
    That she was standing on;
By God built over the sheer depth
    The which is Space begun;
So high, that looking downward thence
    She scarce could see the sun.   30

It lies in heaven, across the flood
    Of ether, as a bridge.
Beneath the tides of day and night
    With flame and darkness ridge
The void, as low as where this earth
    Spins like a fretful midge.

Around her, lovers, newly met
    'Mid deathless love's acclaims,
Spoke evermore among themselves
    Their heart-remembered names;   40
And the souls mounting up to God
    Went by her like thin flames.

And still she bowed herself and stooped
    Out of the circling charm;
Until her bosom must have made
    The bar she leaned on warm,
And the lilies lay as if asleep
    Along her bended arm.

From the fixed place of heaven she saw
    Time like a pulse shake fierce   50
Through all the worlds. Her gaze still strove
    Within the gulf to pierce
Its path; and now she spoke as when
    The stars sang in their spheres.

The sun was gone now; the curled moon
    Was like a little feather
Fluttering far down the gulf; and now
    She spoke through the still weather.
Her voice was like the voice the stars
    Had when they sang together.   60

(Ah, sweet! Even now, in that bird's song,
    Strove not her accents there,
Fain to be harkened? When those bells
    Possessed the mid-day air,
Strove not her steps to reach my side
    Down all the echoing stair?)

'I wish that he were come to me,
    For he will come,' she said.
'Have I not prayed in heaven?—on earth,
    Lord, Lord, has he not prayed?   70
Are not two prayers a perfect strength?
    And shall I feel afraid?

'When round his head the aureole clings,
    And he is clothed in white,
I'll take his hand and go with him
    To the deep wells of light;
As unto a stream we will step down,
    And bathe there in God's sight.

'We two will stand beside that shrine,
    Occult, withheld, untrod,   80
Whose lamps are stirred continually
    With prayers sent up to God;
And see our old prayers, granted, melt
    Each like a little cloud.

'We two will lie i' the shadow of
    That living mystic tree
Within whose secret growth the Dove
    Is sometimes felt to be,
While every leaf that His plumes touch
    Saith His Name audibly.   90

'And I myself will teach to him,
    I myself, lying so,
The songs I sing here; which his voice
    Shall pause in, hushed and slow,
And find some knowledge at each pause,
    Or some new thing to know.'

(Alas! We two, we two, thou say'st!
    Yea, one wast thou with me
That once of old. But shall God lift
    To endless unity   100
The soul whose likeness with thy soul
    Was but its love for thee?)

'We two,' she said, 'will seek the groves
    Where the lady Mary is,
With her five handmaidens, whose names
    Are five sweet symphonies,
Cecily, Gertrude, Magdalen,
    Margaret, and Rosalys.

'Circlewise sit they, with bound locks
    And foreheads garlanded;   110
Into the fine cloth white like flame
    Weaving the golden thread,
To fashion the birth-robes for them
    Who are just born, being dead.

'He shall fear, haply, and be dumb;
    Then will I lay my cheek
To his, and tell about our love,
    Not once abashed or weak;
And the dear Mother will approve
    My pride, and let me speak.   120

'Herself shall bring us, hand in hand;
    To Him round whom all souls
Kneel, the clear-ranged unnumbered heads
    Bowed with their aureoles;
And angels meeting us shall sing
    To their citherns and citoles.

'There will I ask of Christ the Lord
    Thus much for him and me—
Only to live as once on earth
    With Love, only to be,   130
As then awhile, forever now,
    Together, I and he.'

She gazed and listened and then said,
    Less sad of speech than mild—
'All this is when he comes.' She ceased.
    The light thrilled toward her, filled
With angels in strong, level flight.
    Her eyes prayed, and she smiled.

(I saw her smile.) But soon their path
    Was vague in distant spheres;   140
And then she cast her arms along
    The golden barriers,
And laid her face between her hands,
    And wept. (I heard her tears.)

Had she come all the way for this,
To part at last without a kiss?
Yea, had she borne the dirt and rain
That her own eyes might see him slain
Beside the haystack in the floods?

Along the dripping, leafless woods,
The stirrup touching either shoe,
She rode astride as troopers do;
With kirtle kilted to her knee,
To which the mud splashed wretchedly;   10
And the wet dripped from every tree
Upon her head and heavy hair,
And on her eyelids broad and fair;
The tears and rain ran down her face.

By fits and starts they rode apace,
And very often was his place
Far off from her; he had to ride
Ahead, to see what might betide
When the roads crossed; and sometimes, when
There rose a murmuring from his men,   20
Had to turn back with promises.
Ah me! she had but little ease;
And often for pure doubt and dread
She sobbed, made giddy in the head
By the swift riding; while, for cold,
Her slender fingers scarce could hold
The wet reins; yea, and scarcely, too,
She felt the foot within her shoe
Against the stirrup; all for this,
To part at last without a kiss   30
Beside the haystack in the floods.

For when they neared that old soaked hay,
They saw across the only way
That Judas, Godmar, and the three
Red running lions dismally

Grinned from his pennon, under which
In one straight line along the ditch,
They counted thirty heads.
                            So then
While Robert turned round to his men,
She saw at once the wretched end,   40
And, stooping down, tried hard to rend
Her coif the wrong way from her head,
And hid her eyes; while Robert said,
'Nay, love, 'tis scarcely two to one;
At Poictiers where we made them run
So fast—why, sweet my love, good cheer,
The Gascon frontier is so near,
Naught after us.'
                  But 'O!' she said,
'My God! my God! I have to tread
The long way back without you; then   50
The court at Paris; those six men;
The gratings of the Chatelet;
The swift Seine on some rainy day
Like this, and people standing by,
And laughing, while my weak hands try
To recollect how strong men swim.
All this, or else a life with him,
For which I should be damned at last;
Would God that this next hour were past!'

He answered not, but cried his cry,   60
'St. George for Marny!' cheerily;
And laid his hand upon her rein.
Alas! no man of all his train
Gave back that cheery cry again;
And, while for rage his thumb beat fast
Upon his sword-hilt, someone cast
About his neck a kerchief long,
And bound him.

Then they went along
To Godmar; who said: 'Now, Jehane,
Your lover's life is on the wane   70
So fast, that, if this very hour
You yield not as my paramour,
He will not see the rain leave off;
Nay, keep your tongue from gibe and scoff,
Sir Robert, or I slay you now.'

She laid her hand upon her brow,
Then gazed upon the palm, as though
She thought her forehead bled, and 'No!'
She said, and turned her head away,
As there was nothing else to say,   80
And everything was settled; red
Grew Godmar's face from chin to head—
'Jehane, on yonder hill there stands
My castle, guarding well my lands;
What hinders me from taking you,
And doing that I list to do
To your fair willful body, while
Your knight lies dead?'

                              A wicked smile
Wrinkled her face, her lips grew thin,
A long way out she thrust her chin: 90
'You know that I should strangle you
While you were sleeping; or bite through
Your throat, by God's help; ah!' she said,
'Lord Jesus, pity your poor maid!
For in such wise they hem me in,
I cannot choose but sin and sin,
Whatever happens; yet I think
They could not make me eat or drink,
And so should I just reach my rest.'

'Nay, if you do not my behest,   100
O Jehane! though I love you well,'
Said Godmar, 'would I fail to tell
All that I know?' 'Foul lies,' she said.
'Eh? lies, my Jehane? by God's head,
At Paris folks would deem them true!
Do you know, Jehane, they cry for you:
"Jehane the brown! Jehane the brown!
Give us Jehane to burn or drown!"
Eh!—gag me Robert!—sweet my friend,
This were indeed a piteous end   110
For those long fingers, and long feet,
And long neck, and smooth shoulders sweet;
An end that few men would forget
That saw it. So, an hour yet—
Consider, Jehane, which to take
Of life or death!'

                    So, scarce awake,
Dismounting, did she leave that place,
And totter some yards; with her face
Turned upward to the sky she lay,
Her head on a wet heap of hay,   120
And fell asleep; and while she slept,
And did not dream, the minutes crept
Round to the twelve again; but she,
Being waked at last, sighed quietly,
And strangely childlike came, and said:
'I will not.' Straightway Godmar's head,
As though it hung on strong wires, turned
Most sharply round, and his face burned.

For Robert, both his eyes were dry—
He could not weep—but gloomily   130
He seemed to watch the rain; yea, too,
His lips were firm; he tried once more

To touch her lips; she reached out, sore
And vain desire so tortured them,
The poor gray lips, and now the hem
Of his sleeve brushed them.

                With a start
Up Godmar rose, thrust them apart;
From Robert's throat he loosed the bands
Of silk and mail; with empty hands
Held out, she stood and gazed, and saw,   140
The long bright blade without a flaw
Glide out from Godmar's sheath, his hand
In Robert's hair; she saw him bend
Back Robert's head; she saw him send
The thin steel down; the blow told well—
Right backward the knight Robert fell,
And moaned as dogs do, being half dead,
Unwitting, as I deem; so then
Godmar turned grinning to his men,
Who ran, some five or six, and beat   150
His head to pieces at their feet.

Then Godmar turned again and said:
'So, Jehane, the first fitte is read!
Take note, my lady, that your way
Lies backward to the Chatelet!'
She shook her head and gazed awhile
At her cold hands with a rueful smile,
As though this thing had made her mad.

This was the parting that they had
Beside the haystack in the floods.   160

171   *The Gillyflower of Gold*

A golden gillyflower today
I wore upon my helm alway,
And won the prize of this tourney.
   Hah! hah! la belle jaune giroflée.

However well Sir Giles might sit,
His sun was weak to wither it;
Lord Miles's blood was dew on it.
    Hah! hah! la belle jaune giroflée.

Although my spear in splinters flew,
From John's steel-coat, my eye was true;   10
I wheeled about, and cried for you,
    Hah! hah! la belle jaune giroflée.

Yea, do not doubt my heart was good,
Though my sword flew like rotten wood,
To shout, although I scarcely stood,
    Hah! hah! la belle jaune giroflée.

My hand was steady too, to take
My ax from round my neck, and break
John's steel-coat up for my love's sake.
    Hah! hah! la belle jaune giroflée—   20

When I stood in my tent again,
Arming afresh, I felt a pain
Take hold of me, I was so fain—
    Hah! hah! la belle jaune giroflée—

To hear *Honneur aux fils des preux!*
Right in my ears again, and shew
The gillyflower blossomed new.
    Hah! hah! la belle jaune giroflée.

The Sieur Guillaume against me came,
His tabard bore three points of flame   30
From a red heart; with little blame—
    Hah! hah! la belle jaune giroflée—

Our tough spears crackled up like straw;
He was the first to turn and draw
His sword, that had nor speck nor flaw;
    Hah! hah! la belle jaune giroflée.

But I felt weaker than a maid,
And my brain, dizzied and afraid,
Within my helm a fierce tune played,
 Hah! hah! la belle jaune giroflée,   40

Until I thought of your dear head,
Bowed to the gillyflower bed,
The yellow flowers stained with red;
 Hah! hah! la belle jaune giroflée.

Crash! how the swords met—*giroflée!*
The fierce tune in my helm would play,
La belle! la belle! jaune giroflée!
 Hah! hah! la belle jaune giroflée.

Once more the great swords met again;
'*La belle! la belle!*' but who fell then?   50
Le Sieur Guillaume, who struck down ten;
 Hah! hah! la belle jaune giroflée.

And as with mazed and unarmed face
Toward my own crown and the Queen's place,
They led me at a gentle pace—
 Hah! hah! la belle jaune giroflée—

I almost saw your quiet head
Bowed o'er the gillyflower bed,
The yellow flowers stained with red.
 Hah! hah! la belle jaune giroflée.   60

172   *The Rime of the Ancient Mariner*

PART I

It is an ancient Mariner,
And he stoppeth one of three.
'By thy long gray beard and glittering eye,
Now wherefore stopp'st thou me?

The Bridegroom's doors are opened wide,
And I am next of kin;
The guests are met, the feast is set:
May'st hear the merry din.'

He holds him with his skinny hand,
'There was a ship,' quoth he.   10
'Hold off! unhand me, gray-beard loon!'
Eftsoons his hand dropt he.

He holds him with his glittering eye—
The Wedding-Guest stood still,
And listens like a three years' child:
The Mariner hath his will.

The Wedding-Guest sat on a stone:
He cannot choose but hear;
And thus spake on that ancient man,
The bright-eyed Mariner.   20

'The ship was cheered, the harbor cleared,
Merrily did we drop
Below the kirk, below the hill,
Below the lighthouse top.

The Sun came up upon the left,
Out of the sea came he!
And he shone bright, and on the right
Went down into the sea.

Higher and higher every day,
Till over the mast at noon—'   30
The Wedding-Guest here beat his breast,
For he heard the loud bassoon.

The bride hath paced into the hall,
Red as a rose is she;
Nodding their heads before her goes
The merry minstrelsy.

The Wedding-Guest he beat his breast,
Yet he cannot choose but hear;
And thus spake on that ancient man,
The bright-eyed Mariner.   40

'And now the Storm-blast came, and he
Was tyrannous and strong:
He struck with his o'ertaking wings,
And chased us south along.

With sloping masts and dipping prow,
As who pursued with yell and blow
Still treads the shadow of his foe,
And forward bends his head,
The ship drove fast, loud roared the blast,
And southward aye we fled.   50

And now there came both mist and snow,
And it grew wondrous cold:
And ice, mast-high, came floating by,
As green as emerald.

And through the drifts the snowy clifts
Did send a dismal sheen:
Nor shapes of men nor beasts we ken—
The ice was all between.

The ice was here, the ice was there,
The ice was all around: 60
It cracked and growled, and roared and howled,
Like noises in a swound!

At length did cross an Albatross,
Thorough the fog it came;
As if it had been a Christian soul,
We hailed it in God's name.

It ate the food it ne'er had eat,
And round and round it flew.
The ice did split with a thunder-fit;
The helmsman steered us through!   70

And a good south wind sprung up behind;
The Albatross did follow,
And every day, for food or play,
Came to the mariners' hollo!

In mist or cloud, on mast or shroud,
It perched for vespers nine;
Whiles all the night, through fog-smoke white,
Glimmered the white moon-shine.'

'God save thee, ancient Mariner!
From the fiends, that plague thee thus!—   80
Why look'st thou so?'—'With my cross-bow
I shot the Albatross!'

PART II

'The Sun now rose upon the right:
Out of the sea came he,
Still hid in mist, and on the left
Went down into the sea.

And the good south wind still blew behind,
But no sweet bird did follow,
Nor any day for food or play
Came to the mariners' hollo!   90

And I had done a hellish thing,
And it would work 'em woe:
For all averred, I had killed the bird
That made the breeze to blow.
"Ah wretch!" said they, "the bird to slay,
That made the breeze to blow!"

Nor dim nor red, like God's own head,
The glorious Sun uprist:
Then all averred, I had killed the bird
That brought the fog and mist.   100
" 'Twas right," said they, "such birds to slay,
That bring the fog and mist."

The fair breeze blew, the white foam flew,
The furrow followed free;
We were the first that ever burst
Into that silent sea.

Down dropt the breeze, the sails dropt down,
'Twas sad as sad could be;
And we did speak only to break
The silence of the sea!   110

All in a hot and copper sky,
The bloody Sun, at noon,
Right up above the mast did stand,
No bigger than the Moon.

Day after day, day after day,
We stuck, nor breath nor motion;
As idle as a painted ship
Upon a painted ocean.

Water, water, everywhere,
And all the boards did shrink;   120
Water, water, everywhere,
Nor any drop to drink.

The very deep did rot: O Christ!
That ever this should be!
Yea, slimy things did crawl with legs
Upon the slimy sea.

About, about, in reel and rout
The death-fires danced at night;
The water, like a witch's oils,
Burnt green, and blue, and white. 130

And some in dreams assurèd were
Of the Spirit that plagued us so;
Nine fathom deep he had followed us
From the land of mist and snow.

And every tongue, through utter drought,
Was withered at the root;
We could not speak, no more than if
We had been choked with soot.

Ah! well-a-day! what evil looks
Had I from old and young! 140
Instead of the cross, the Albatross
About my neck was hung.

PART III

'There passed a weary time. Each throat
Was parched, and glazed each eye.
A weary time! a weary time!
How glazed each weary eye,
When looking westward, I beheld
A something in the sky.

At first it seemed a little speck,
And then it seemed a mist; 150
It moved and moved, and took at last
A certain shape, I wist.

A speck, a mist, a shape, I wist!
And still it neared and neared:
As if it dodged a water-sprite,
It plunged and tacked and veered.

With throats unslaked, with black lips baked,
We could nor laugh nor wail;
Through utter drought all dumb we stood!
I bit my arm, I sucked the blood,   160
And cried, A sail! a sail!

With throats unslaked, with black lips baked,
Agape they heard me call:
Gramercy! they for joy did grin,
And all at once their breath drew in,
As they were drinking all.

See! see! (I cried) she tacks no more!
Hither to work us weal;
Without a breeze, without a tide,
She steadies with upright keel!   170

The western wave was all a-flame.
The day was well nigh done!
Almost upon the western wave
Rested the broad bright Sun;
When that strange shape drove suddenly
Betwixt us and the Sun.

And straight the Sun was flecked with bars,
(Heaven's Mother send us grace!)
As if through a dungeon-grate he peered
With broad and burning face.   180

Alas! (thought I, and my heart beat loud)
How fast she nears and nears!
Are those her sails that glance in the Sun,
Like restless gossameres?

Are those her ribs through which the Sun
Did peer, as through a grate?
And is that Woman all her crew?
Is that a Death? and are there two?
Is Death that woman's mate?

Her lips were red, her looks were free,   190
Her locks were yellow as gold:
Her skin was as white as leprosy,
The Nightmare Life-in-Death, was she,
Who thicks man's blood with cold.

The naked hulk alongside came,
And the twain were casting dice;
"The game is done! I've won! I've won!"
Quoth she, and whistles thrice.

The Sun's rim dips; the stars rush out:
At one stride comes the dark;   200
With far-heard whisper, o'er the sea,
Off shot the spectre-bark.

We listened and looked sideways up!
Fear at my heart, as at a cup,
My life-blood seemed to sip!
The stars were dim, and thick the night,
The steersman's face by his lamp gleamed white;
From the sails the dew did drip—
Till clomb above the eastern bar
The hornèd Moon, with one bright star   210
Within the nether tip.

One after one, by the star-dogged Moon,
Too quick for groan or sigh,
Each turned his face with a ghastly pang,
And cursed me with his eye.

Four times fifty living men,
(And I heard nor sigh nor groan)
With heavy thump, a lifeless lump,
They dropped down one by one.

The souls did from their bodies fly,—
They fled to bliss or woe!
And every soul, it passed me by,
Like the whizz of my cross-bow!'

PART IV

'I fear thee, ancient Mariner!
I fear thy skinny hand!
And thou art long, and lank, and brown,
As is the ribbed sea-sand.

I fear thee and thy glittering eye,
And thy skinny hand, so brown.'—
'Fear not, fear not, thou Wedding-Guest!
This body dropt not down.

Alone, alone, all, all alone,
Alone on a wide, wide sea!
And never a saint took pity on
My soul in agony.

The many men, so beautiful!
And they all dead did lie:
And a thousand thousand slimy things
Lived on; and so did I.

I looked upon the rotting sea,
And drew my eyes away;
I looked upon the rotting deck,
And there the dead men lay.

I looked to heaven, and tried to pray;
But or ever a prayer had gusht,
A wicked whisper came, and made
My heart as dry as dust.

I closed my lids, and kept them close,
And the balls like pulses beat;
For the sky and the sea, and the sea and the sky   250
Lay like a load on my weary eye,
And the dead were at my feet.

The cold sweat melted from their limbs,
Nor rot nor reek did they:
The look with which they looked on me
Had never passed away.

An orphan's curse would drag to hell
A spirit from on high;
But oh! more horrible than that
Is the curse in a dead man's eye!   260
Seven days, seven nights, I saw that curse,
And yet I could not die.

The moving moon went up the sky,
And nowhere did abide:
Softly she was going up,
And a star or two beside—

Her beams bemocked the sultry main,
Like April hoar-frost spread;
But where the ship's huge shadow lay,
The charmèd water burnt alway   270
A still and awful red.

Beyond the shadow of the ship,
I watched the water-snakes:
They moved in tracks of shining white,
And when they reared, the elfish light
Fell off in hoary flakes.

[233]

Within the shadow of the ship
I watched their rich attire:
Blue, glossy green, and velvet black
They coiled and swam; and every track   280
Was a flash of golden fire.

O happy living things! no tongue
Their beauty might declare:
A spring of love gushed from my heart,
And I blessed them unaware:
Sure my kind saint took pity on me,
And I blessed them unaware.

The self-same moment I could pray;
And from my neck so free
The Albatross fell off, and sank   290
Like lead into the sea.

PART V

'Oh sleep! it is a gentle thing,
Beloved from pole to pole!
To Mary Queen the praise be given!
She sent the gentle sleep from Heaven,
That slid into my soul.

The silly buckets on the deck,
That had so long remained,
I dreamt that they were filled with dew;
And when I awoke, it rained.   300

My lips were wet, my throat was cold,
My garments all were dank;
Sure I had drunken in my dreams,
And still my body drank.

I moved, and could not feel my limbs:
I was so light—almost
I thought that I had died in sleep,
And was a blessèd ghost.

[234]

And soon I heard a roaring wind:
It did not come anear;
But with its sound it shook the sails,
That were so thin and sere.

The upper air burst into life!
And a hundred fire-flags sheen,
To and fro they were hurried about!
And to and fro, and in and out,
The wan stars danced between.

And the coming wind did roar more loud,
And the sails did sigh like sedge;
And the rain poured down from one black cloud;
The Moon was at its edge.

The thick black cloud was cleft, and still
The Moon was at its side:
Like water shot from some high crag,
The lightning fell with never a jag,
A river steep and wide.

The loud wind never reached the ship,
Yet now the ship moved on!
Beneath the lightning and the Moon
The dead men gave a groan.

They groaned, they stirred, they all uprose,
Nor spake, nor moved their eyes;
It had been strange, even in a dream,
To have seen those dead men rise.

The helmsman steered, the ship moved on;
Yet never a breeze up-blew;
The mariners all 'gan work the ropes,
Where they were wont to do;
They raised their limbs like lifeless tools—
We were a ghastly crew.

The body of my brother's son
Stood by me, knee to knee:
The body and I pulled at one rope,
But he said nought to me.'—

'I fear thee, ancient Mariner!'
'Be calm, thou Wedding-Guest!
'Twas not those souls that fled in pain,
Which to their corses came again,
But a troop of spirits blest:

For when it dawned—they dropped their arms,   350
And clustered round the mast;
Sweet sounds rose slowly through their mouths,
And from their bodies passed.

Around, around, flew each sweet sound,
Then darted to the Sun;
Slowly the sounds came back again,
Now mixed, now one by one.

Sometimes a-dropping from the sky
I heard the skylark sing;
Sometimes all little birds that are,   360
How they seemed to fill the sea and air
With their sweet jargoning!

And now 'twas like all instruments,
Now like a lonely flute;
And now it is an angel's song,
That makes the heavens be mute.

It ceased; yet still the sails made on
A pleasant noise till noon,
A noise like of a hidden brook
In the leafy month of June,   370
That to the sleeping woods all night
Singeth a quiet tune.

Till noon we quietly sailed on,
Yet never a breeze did breathe:
Slowly and smoothly went the ship,
Moved onward from beneath.

Under the keel nine fathom deep,
From the land of mist and snow,
The spirit slid: and it was he
That made the ship to go.   380
The sails at noon left off their tune,
And the ship stood still also.

The Sun, right up above the mast,
Had fixed her to the ocean:
But in a minute she 'gan stir,
With a short uneasy motion—
Backwards and forwards half her length
With a short uneasy motion.

Then like a pawing horse let go,
She made a sudden bound: 390
It flung the blood into my head,
And I fell down in a swound.

How long in that same fit I lay,
I have not to declare;
But ere my living life returned,
I heard and in my soul discerned
Two voices in the air.

"Is it he?" quoth one, "Is this the man?
By him who died on cross,
With his cruel bow he laid full low   400
The harmless Albatross.

The spirit who bideth by himself
In the land of mist and snow,
He loved the bird that loved the man
Who shot him with his bow."

The other was a softer voice,
As soft as honey-dew:
Quoth he, "The man hath penance done,
And penance more will do."

PART VI

First Voice

' "But tell me, tell me! speak again,   410
Thy soft response renewing—
What makes that ship drive on so fast?
What is the ocean doing?"

Second Voice

"Still as a slave before his lord,
The ocean hath no blast;
His great bright eye most silently
Up to the Moon is cast—

If he may know which way to go;
For she guides him smooth or grim.
See, brother, see! how graciously   420
She looketh down on him."

First Voice

"But why drives on that ship so fast,
Without or wave or wind?"

Second Voice

"The air is cut away before,
And closes from behind.

Fly, brother, fly! more high, more high!
Or we shall be belated:
For slow and slow that ship will go,
When the Mariner's trance is abated."

I woke, and we were sailing on   430
As in a gentle weather:
'Twas night, calm night, the moon was high;
The dead men stood together.

All stood together on the deck,
For a charnel-dungeon fitter:
All fixed on me their stony eyes,
That in the Moon did glitter.

The pang, the curse, with which they died,
Had never passed away:
I could not draw my eyes from theirs,   440
Nor turn them up to pray.

And now this spell was snapt: once more
I viewed the ocean green,
And looked far forth, yet little saw
Of what had else been seen—

Like one, that on a lonesome road
Doth walk in fear and dread,
And having once turned round walks on,
And turns no more his head;
Because he knows, a frightful fiend   450
Doth close behind him tread.

But soon there breathed a wind on me,
Nor sound nor motion made:
Its path was not upon the sea,
In ripple or in shade.

It raised my hair, it fanned my cheek
Like a meadow-gale of spring—
It mingled strangely with my fears,
Yet it felt like a welcoming.

Swiftly, swiftly flew the ship,   460
Yet she sailed softly too:
Sweetly, sweetly blew the breeze—
On me alone it blew.

Oh! dream of joy! is this indeed
The light-house top I see?
Is this the hill? is this the kirk?
Is this mine own countree?

We drifted o'er the harbor-bar,
And I with sobs did pray—
O let me be awake, my God!   470
Or let me sleep alway.

The harbor-bay was clear as glass,
So smoothly it was strewn!
And on the bay the moonlight lay,
And the shadow of the Moon.

The rock shone bright, the kirk no less,
That stands above the rock:
The moonlight steeped in silentness
The steady weathercock.

And the bay was white with silent light,   480
Till rising from the same,
Full many shapes, that shadows were,
In crimson colors came.

A little distance from the prow
Those crimson shadows were:
I turned my eyes upon the deck—
Oh, Christ! what saw I there!

Each corse lay flat, lifeless and flat,
And, by the holy rood!
A man all light, a seraph-man,   490
On every corse there stood.

This seraph-band, each waved his hand:
It was a heavenly sight!
They stood as signals to the land,
Each one a lovely light;

This seraph-band, each waved his hand,
No voice did they impart—
No voice; but oh! the silence sank
Like music on my heart.

But soon I heard the dash of oars,   500
I heard the Pilot's cheer;
My head was turned perforce away
And I saw a boat appear.

The Pilot and the Pilot's boy,
I heard them coming fast:
Dear Lord in Heaven! it was a joy
The dead men could not blast.

I saw a third—I heard his voice:
It is the Hermit good!
He singeth loud his godly hymns   510
That he makes in the wood.
He'll shrieve my soul, he'll wash away
The Albatross's blood.

PART VII

'This Hermit good lives in that wood
Which slopes down to the sea.
How loudly his sweet voice he rears!
He loves to talk with marineres
That come from a far countree.

He kneels at morn, and noon, and eve—
He hath a cushion plump: 520
It is the moss that wholly hides
The rotted old oak-stump.

The skiff-boat neared: I heard them talk,
"Why this is strange, I trow!
Where are those lights so many and fair,
That signal made but now?"

"Strange, by my faith!" the Hermit said—
"And they answered not our cheer!
The planks look warped! and see those sails,
How thin they are and sere!   530
I never saw aught like to them,
Unless perchance it were

Brown skeletons of leaves that lag
My forest-brook along;
When the ivy-tod is heavy with snow,
And the owlet whoops to the wolf below,
That eats the she-wolf's young."

"Dear Lord! it hath a fiendish look"—
(The Pilot made reply)
"I am a-feared"—"Push on, push on!"   540
Said the Hermit cheerily.

The boat came closer to the ship,
But I nor spake nor stirred;
The boat came close beneath the ship,
And straight a sound was heard.

Under the water it rumbled on,
Still louder and more dread:
It reached the ship, it split the bay;
The ship went down like lead.

Stunned by that loud and dreadful sound,   550
Which sky and ocean smote,
Like one that hath been seven days drowned
My body lay afloat;
But swift as dreams, myself I found
Within the Pilot's boat.

Upon the whirl, where sank the ship,
The boat spun round and round;
And all was still, save that the hill
Was telling of the sound.

I moved my lips—the Pilot shrieked   560
And fell down in a fit;
The holy Hermit raised his eyes,
And prayed where he did sit.

I took the oars: the Pilot's boy,
Who now doth crazy go,
Laughed loud and long, and all the while
His eyes went to and fro.
"Ha! ha!" quoth he, "full plain I see,
The Devil knows how to row."

And now, all in my own countree,   570
I stood on the firm land!
The Hermit stepped forth from the boat,
And scarcely he could stand.

"Oh shrieve me, shrieve me, holy man!"
The Hermit crossed his brow.
"Say quick," quoth he, "I bid thee say—
What manner of man art thou?"

Forthwith this frame of mine was wrenched
With a woful agony,
Which forced me to begin my tale;   580
And then it left me free.

Since then, at an uncertain hour,
That agony returns:
And till my ghastly tale is told,
This heart within me burns.

I pass, like night, from land to land;
I have strange power of speech;
That moment that his face I see,
I know the man that must hear me:
To him my tale I teach. 590

What loud uproar bursts fromt hat door!
The wedding-guests are there :
But in the garden-bower the bride
And bride-maids singing are:
And hark the little vesper bell,
Which biddeth me to prayer!

O Wedding-Guest! this soul hath been
Alone on a wide, wide sea:
So lonely 'twas, that God himself
Scarce seemèd there to be. 600

O sweeter than the marriage-feast,
'Tis sweeter far to me,
To walk together to the kirk
With a goodly company!—

To walk together to the kirk,
And all together pray,
While each to his great Father bends,
Old men, and babes, and loving friends
And youths and maidens gay!

Farewell, farewell! but this I tell 610
To thee, thou Wedding-Guest!
He prayeth well, who loveth well
Both man and bird and beast.

He prayeth best, who loveth best
All things both great and small;
For the dear God who loveth us,
He made and loveth all.'

The Mariner, whose eye is bright,
Whose beard with age is hoar,
Is gone: and now the Wedding-Guest   620
Turned from the bridegroom's door.

He went like one that hath been stunned,
And is of sense forlorn:
A sadder and a wiser man,
He rose the morrow morn.

Ulysses and the Siren

SIREN

Come, worthy Greek, Ulysses, come,
  Possess these shores with me;
The winds and seas are troublesome,
  And here we may be free.
Here may we sit and view their toil
  That travail on the deep,
And joy the day in mirth the while,
  And spend the night in sleep.

ULYSSES

Fair nymph, if fame or honor were
  To be attained with ease,   10
Then would I come and rest with thee,
  And leave such toils as these.
But here it dwells, and here must I
  With danger seek it forth;
To spend the time luxuriously
  Becomes not men of worth.

SIREN

Ulysses, O be not deceived
  With that unreal name;
This honor is a thing conceived,
  And rests on others' fame;   20

Begotten only to molest
   Our peace, and to beguile
The best thing of our life, our rest,
   And give us up to toil.

ULYSSES

Delicious nymph, suppose there were
   Nor honor nor report,
Yet manliness would scorn to wear
   The time in idle sport.
For toil doth give a better touch,
   To make us feel our joy;   30
And ease finds tediousness, as much
   As labor, yields annoy.

SIREN

Then pleasure likewise seems the shore
   Whereto tends all your toil,
Which you forgo to make it more,
   And perish oft the while.
Who may disport them diversly,
   Find never tedious day,
And ease may have variety
   As well as action may.   40

ULYSSES

But natures of the noblest frame
   These toils and dangers please,
And they take comfort in the same
   As much as you in ease,
And with the thoughts of actions past
   Are recreated still;
When pleasure leaves a touch at last
   To show that it was ill.

SIREN

That doth opinion only cause
   That's out of custom bred,   50
Which makes us many other laws
   Than ever nature did.

[246]

No widows wail for our delights,
    Our sports are without blood;
The world, we see, by warlike wights
    Receives more hurt than good.

ULYSSES

But yet the state of things require
    These motions of unrest,
And these great spirits of high desire
    Seem born to turn them best,   60
To purge the mischiefs that increase
    And all good order mar;
For oft we see a wicked peace
    To be well changed for war.

SIREN

Well, well, Ulysses, then I see
    I shall not have thee here,
And therefore I will come to thee,
    And take my fortunes there.
I must be won that cannot win,
    Yet lost were I not won;   70
For beauty hath created been
    T' undo, or be undone.

174   *Ulysses*

It little profits that an idle king,
By this still hearth, among these barren crags,
Matched with an aged wife, I mete and dole
Unequal laws unto a savage race,
That hoard, and sleep, and feed, and know not me.
I cannot rest from travel; I will drink
Life to the lees. All times I have enjoyed
Greatly, have suffered greatly, both with those
That loved me, and alone; on shore, and when
Through scudding drifts the rainy Hyades   10
Vexed the dim sea. I am become a name;

For always roaming with a hungry heart
Much have I seen and known—cities of men
And manners, climates, councils, governments,
Myself not least, but honored of them all—
And drunk delight of battle with my peers,
Far on the ringing plains of windy Troy.
I am a part of all that I have met;
Yet all experience is an arch wherethrough
Gleams that untraveled world whose margin fades   20
Forever and forever when I move.
How dull it is to pause, to make an end,
To rust unburnished, not to shine in use!
As though to breathe were life! Life piled on life
Were all too little, and of one to me
Little remains; but every hour is saved
From that eternal silence, something more,
A bringer of new things; and vile it were
For some three suns to store and hoard myself,
And this gray spirit yearning in desire   30
To follow knowledge like a sinking star,
Beyond the utmost bound of human thought.

    This is my son, mine own Telemachus,
To whom I leave the scepter and the isle—
Well-loved of me, discerning to fulfill
This labor, by slow prudence to make mild
A rugged people, and through soft degrees
Subdue them to the useful and the good.
Most blameless is he, centered in the sphere
Of common duties, decent not to fail   40
In offices of tenderness, and pay
Meet adoration to my household gods,
When I am gone. He works his work, I mine.

    There lies the port; the vessel puffs her sail;
There gloom the dark, broad seas. My mariners,
Souls that have toiled, and wrought, and thought with me—
That ever with a frolic welcome took
The thunder and the sunshine, and opposed
Free hearts, free foreheads—you and I are old;

Old age hath yet his honor and his toil. 50
Death closes all; but something ere the end,
Some work of noble note, may yet be done,
Not unbecoming men that strove with gods.
The lights begin to twinkle from the rocks;
The long day wanes; the slow moon climbs; the deep
Moans round with many voices. Come, my friends.
'Tis not too late to seek a newer world.
Push off, and sitting well in order smite
The sounding furrows; for my purpose holds
To sail beyond the sunset, and the baths 60
Of all the western stars, until I die.
It may be that the gulfs will wash us down;
It may be we shall touch the Happy Isles,
And see the great Achilles, whom we knew.
Though much is taken, much abides; and though
We are not now that strength which in old days
Moved earth and heaven, that which we are, we are—
One equal temper of heroic hearts,
Made weak by time and fate, but strong in will
To strive, to seek, to find, and not to yield. 70

175 *The Lotos-Eaters*

'Courage!' he said, and pointed toward the land,
'This mounting wave will roll us shoreward soon.'
In the afternoon they came unto a land
In which it seemed always afternoon.
All round the coast the languid air did swoon,
Breathing like one that hath a weary dream.
Full-faced above the valley stood the moon;
And, like a downward smoke, the slender stream
Along the cliff to fall and pause and fall did seem.

A land of streams! some, like a downward smoke, 10
Slow-dropping veils of thinnest lawn, did go;
And some through wavering lights and shadows broke,
Rolling a slumbrous sheet of foam below.

They saw the gleaming river seaward flow
From the inner land; far off, three mountain-tops,
Three silent pinnacles of aged snow,
Stood sunset-flushed; and, dewed with showery drops,
Up-clomb the shadowy pine above the woven copse.

The charmèd sunset lingered low adown
In the red West; through mountain clefts the dale   20
Was seen far inland, and the yellow down
Bordered with palm, and many a winding vale
And meadow, set with slender galingale;
A land where all things always seemed the same!
And round about the keel with faces pale,
Dark faces pale against that rosy flame,
The mild-eyed melancholy Lotos-eaters came.

Branches they bore of that enchanted stem,
Laden with flower and fruit, whereof they gave
To each, but whoso did receive of them   30
And taste, to him the gushing of the wave
Far far away did seem to mourn and rave
On alien shores; and if his fellow spake,
His voice was thin, as voices from the grave;
And deep-asleep he seemed, yet all awake,
And music in his ears his beating heart did make.

They sat them down upon the yellow sand
Between the sun and moon upon the shore;
And sweet it was to dream of Fatherland,
Of child, and wife, and slave; but evermore   40
Most weary seemed the sea, weary the oar,
Weary the wandering fields of barren foam.
Then someone said, 'We will return no more';
And all at once they sang, 'Our island home
Is far beyond the wave; we will no longer roam.'

I

There is sweet music here that softer falls
Than petals from blown roses on the grass,
Or night-dews on still waters between walls
Of shadowy granite, in a gleaming pass;
Music that gentlier on the spirit lies,   50
Than tired eyelids upon tired eyes;
Music that brings sweet sleep down from the blissful skies.
Here are cool mosses deep,
And through the moss the ivies creep,
And in the stream the long-leaved flowers weep,
And from the craggy ledge the poppy hangs in sleep.

2

Why are we weighed upon with heaviness,
And utterly consumed with sharp distress,
While all things else have rest from weariness?
All things have rest; why should we toil alone,   60
We only toil, who are the first of things,
And make perpetual moan,
Still from one sorrow to another thrown;
Nor ever fold our wings,
And cease from wanderings,
Nor steep our brows in slumber's holy balm;
Nor harken what the inner spirit sings,
'There is no joy but calm!'—
Why should we only toil, the roof and crown of things?

3

Lo! in the middle of the wood,   70
The folded leaf is wooed from out the bud
With winds upon the branch, and there
Grows green and broad, and takes no care,
Sun-steeped at noon, and in the moon
Nightly dew-fed; and turning yellow

Falls, and floats adown the air.
Lo! sweetened with the summer light,
The full-juiced apple, waxing over-mellow,
Drops in a silent autumn night.
All its allotted length of days   80
The flower ripens in its place,
Ripens and fades, and falls, and hath no toil,
Fast-rooted in the fruitful soil.

4

Hateful is the dark-blue sky,
Vaulted o'er the dark-blue sea.
Death is the end of life; ah, why
Should life all labor be?
Let us alone. Time driveth onward fast,
And in a little while our lips are dumb.
Let us alone. What is it that will last?   90
All things are taken from us, and become
Portions and parcels of the dreadful past.
Let us alone. What pleasure can we have
To war with evil? Is there any peace
In ever climbing up the climbing wave?
All things have rest, and ripen toward the grave
In silence—ripen, fall, and cease;
Give us long rest or death, dark death, or dreamful ease.

5

How sweet it were, hearing the downward stream
With half-shut eyes ever to seem   100
Falling asleep in a half-dream!
To dream and dream, like yonder amber light,
Which will not leave the myrrh-bush on the height;
To hear each other's whispered speech;
Eating the Lotos day by day,
To watch the crisping ripples on the beach,
And tender curving lines of creamy spray;
To lend our hearts and spirits wholly

To the influence of mild-minded melancholy;
To muse and brood and live again in memory,   110
With those old faces of our infancy
Heaped over with a mound of grass,
Two handfuls of white dust, shut in an urn of brass!

6

Dear is the memory of our wedded lives,
And dear the last embraces of our wives
And their warm tears; but all hath suffered change;
For surely now our household hearths are cold,
Our sons inherit us, our looks are strange,
And we should come like ghosts to trouble joy.
Or else the island princes over-bold   120
Have eat our substance, and the minstrel sings
Before them of the ten years' war in Troy,
And our great deeds, as half-forgotten things.
Is there confusion in the little isle?
Let what is broken so remain.
The gods are hard to reconcile;
'Tis hard to settle order once again.
There *is* confusion worse than death,
Trouble on trouble, pain on pain,
Long labor unto aged breath,   130
Sore task to hearts worn out by many wars
And eyes grown dim with gazing on the pilot-stars.

7

But, propped on beds of amaranth and moly,
How sweet—while warm airs lull us, blowing lowly—
With half-dropped eyelid still,
Beneath a heaven dark and holy,
To watch the long bright river drawing slowly
His waters from the purple hill—
To hear the dewy echoes calling
From cave to cave through the thick-twined vine—   140
To watch the emerald-colored water falling

Through many a woven acanthus-wreath divine!
Only to hear and see the far-off sparkling brine,
Only to hear were sweet, stretched out beneath the pine.

8

The Lotos blooms below the barren peak,
The Lotos blows by every winding creek;
All day the wind breathes low with mellower tone;
Through every hollow cave and alley lone
Round and round the spicy downs the yellow Lotos-dust is blown.
We have had enough of action, and of motion we,   150
Rolled to starboard, rolled to larboard, when the surge was seething
    free,
Where the wallowing monster spouted his foam-fountains in the sea.
Let us swear an oath, and keep it with an equal mind,
In the hollow Lotos-land to live and lie reclined
On the hills like gods together, careless of mankind.
For they lie beside their nectar, and the bolts are hurled
Far below them in the valleys, and the clouds are lightly curled
Round their golden houses, girdled with the gleaming world;
Where they smile in secret, looking over wasted lands,
Blight and famine, plague and earthquake, roaring deeps and fiery
    sands,   160
Clanging fights, and flaming towns, and sinking ships, and praying
    hands.
But they smile, they find a music centered in a doleful song
Steaming up, a lamentation and an ancient tale of wrong,
Like a tale of little meaning though the words are strong;
Chanted from an ill-used race of men that cleave the soil,
Sow the seed, and reap the harvest with enduring toil,
Storing yearly little dues of wheat, and wine and oil;
Till they perish and they suffer—some, 'tis whispered—down in hell
Suffer endless anguish, others in Elysian valleys dwell,
Resting weary limbs at last on beds of asphodel.   *fadeless plant* 170
Surely, surely, slumber is more sweet than toil, the shore   *of Hades*
Than labor in the deep mid-ocean, wind and wave and oar;
O rest ye, brother mariners, we will not wander more.

[254]

The woods decay, the woods decay and fall,
The vapors weep their burthen to the ground;
Man comes and tills the field and lies beneath,
And after many a summer dies the swan.
Me only cruel immortality
Consumes; I wither slowly in thine arms,
Here at the quiet limit of the world,
A white-haired shadow roaming like a dream
The ever-silent spaces of the East,
Far-folded mists, and gleaming halls of morn.   10

   Alas! for this gray shadow, once a man—
So glorious in his beauty and thy choice,
Who madest him thy chosen, that he seemed
To his great heart none other than a god!
I asked thee, 'Give me immortality.'
Then didst thou grant mine asking with a smile,
Like wealthy men who care not how they give.
But thy strong Hours indignant worked their wills,
And beat me down and marred and wasted me,
And though they could not end me, left me maimed   20
To dwell in presence of immortal youth,
Immortal age beside immortal youth,
And all I was in ashes. Can thy love,
Thy beauty, make amends, though even now,
Close over us, the silver star, thy guide,
Shines in those tremulous eyes that fill with tears
To hear me? Let me go; take back thy gift.
Why should a man desire in any way
To vary from the kindly race of men,
Or pass beyond the goal of ordinance   30
Where all should pause, as is most meet for all?

   A soft air fans the cloud apart; there comes
A glimpse of that dark world where I was born.
Once more the old mysterious glimmer steals
From thy pure brows, and from thy shoulders pure,
And bosom beating with a heart renewed.

Thy cheek begins to redden through the gloom,
Thy sweet eyes brighten slowly close to mine,
Ere yet they blind the stars, and the wild team
Which love thee, yearning for thy yoke, arise,   40
And shake the darkness from their loosened manes,
And beat the twilight into flakes of fire.

    Lo! ever thus thou growest beautiful
In silence; then, before thine answer given,
Departest, and thy tears are on my cheek.

    Why wilt thou ever scare me with thy tears,
And make me tremble lest a saying learnt,
In days far-off, on that dark earth, be true?
'The gods themselves cannot recall their gifts.'

    Ay me! ay me! with what another heart   50
In days far-off, and with what other eyes
I used to watch—if I be he that watched—
The lucid outline forming round thee; saw
The dim curls kindle into sunny rings;
Changed with thy mystic change, and felt my blood
Glow with the glow that slowly crimsoned all
Thy presence and thy portals, while I lay,
Mouth, forehead, eyelids, growing dewy-warm
With kisses balmier than half-opening buds
Of April, and could hear the lips that kissed   60
Whispering I knew not what of wild and sweet,
Like that strange song I heard Apollo sing,
While Ilion like a mist rose into towers.

    Yet hold me not forever in thine East;
How can my nature longer mix with thine?
Coldly thy rosy shadows bathe me, cold
Are all thy lights, and cold my wrinkled feet
Upon thy glimmering thresholds, when the steam
Floats up from those dim fields about the homes
Of happy men that have the power to die,   70
And grassy barrows of the happier dead.
Release me, and restore me to the ground.
Thou seest all things, thou wilt see my grave;

Thou wilt renew thy beauty morn by morn,
I earth in earth forget these empty courts,
And thee returning on thy silver wheels.

My Last Duchess

FERRARA

That's my last Duchess painted on the wall,
Looking as if she were alive. I call
That piece a wonder, now; Frà Pandolf's hands
Worked busily a day, and there she stands.
Will 't please you sit and look at her? I said
'Frà Pandolf' by design, for never read
Strangers like you that pictured countenance,
The depth and passion of its earnest glance,
But to myself they turned (since none puts by
The curtain I have drawn for you, but I)   10
And seemed as they would ask me, if they durst,
How such a glance came there; so, not the first
Are you to turn and ask thus. Sir, 'twas not
Her husband's presence only, called that spot
Of joy into the Duchess' cheek; perhaps
Frà Pandolf chanced to say, 'Her mantle laps
Over my lady's wrist too much,' or 'Paint
Must never hope to reproduce the faint
Half-flush that dies along her throat.' Such stuff
Was courtesy, she thought, and cause enough   20
For calling up that spot of joy. She had
A heart—how shall I say?—too soon made glad,
Too easily impressed; she liked whate'er
She looked on, and her looks went everywhere.
Sir, 'twas all one! My favor at her breast,
The dropping of the daylight in the West,
The bough of cherries some officious fool
Broke in the orchard for her, the white mule
She rode with round the terrace—all and each
Would draw from her alike the approving speech,   30
Or blush, at least. She thanked men,—good! but thanked

Somehow—I know not how—as if she ranked
My gift of a nine-hundred-years-old name
With anybody's gift. Who'd stoop to blame
This sort of trifling? Even had you skill
In speech—which I have not—to make your will
Quite clear to such an one, and say, 'Just this
Or that in you disgusts me; here you miss,
Or there exceed the mark'—and if she let
Herself be lessoned so, nor plainly set   40
Her wits to yours, forsooth, and made excuse—
E'en then would be some stooping; and I choose
Never to stoop. Oh, sir, she smiled, no doubt,
Whene'er I passed her; but who passed without
Much the same smile? This grew; I gave commands;
Then all smiles stopped together. There she stands
As if alive. Will 't please you rise? We'll meet
The company below, then. I repeat,
The Count your master's known munificence
Is ample warrant that no just pretense   50
Of mine for dowry will be disallowed;
Though his fair daughter's self, as I avowed
At starting, is my object. Nay, we'll go
Together down, sir. Notice Neptune, though,
Taming a sea-horse, thought a rarity,
Which Claus of Innsbruck cast in bronze for me!

178   *Andrea del Sarto*

CALLED 'THE FAULTLESS PAINTER'

But do not let us quarrel any more,
No, my Lucrezia; bear with me for once.
Sit down and all shall happen as you wish.
You turn your face, but does it bring your heart?
I'll work then for your friend's friend, never fear,
Treat his own subject after his own way,
Fix his own time, accept too his own price,
And shut the money into this small hand
When next it takes mine. Will it? tenderly?

[258]

Oh, I'll content him—but tomorrow, Love! 10
I often am much wearier than you think,
This evening more than usual, and it seems
As if—forgive now—should you let me sit
Here by the window with your hand in mine
And look a half-hour forth on Fiesole,
Both of one mind, as married people use,
Quietly, quietly the evening through,
I might get up tomorrow to my work
Cheerful and fresh as ever. Let us try.
Tomorrow, how you shall be glad for this! 20
Your soft hand is a woman of itself,
And mine the man's bared breast she curls inside.
Don't count the time lost, neither; you must serve
For each of the five pictures we require—
It saves a model. So! keep looking so—
My serpentining beauty, rounds on rounds!
—How could you ever prick those perfect ears,
Even to put the pearl there! oh, so sweet—
My face, my moon, my everybody's moon,
Which everybody looks on and calls his, 30
And, I suppose, is looked on by in turn,
While she looks—no one's: very dear, no less.
You smile? why, there's my picture ready made,
There's what we painters call our harmony!
A common grayness silvers everything—
All in a twilight, you and I alike—
You, at the point of your first pride in me
(That's gone, you know), but I, at every point;
My youth, my hope, my art, being all toned down
To yonder sober pleasant Fiesole. 40
There's the bell clinking from the chapel-top;
That length of convent-wall across the way
Holds the trees safer, huddled more inside;
The last monk leaves the garden; days decrease,
And autumn grows, autumn in everything.
Eh? the whole seems to fall into a shape
As if I saw alike my work and self

And all that I was born to be and do,
A twilight-piece. Love, we are in God's hand.
How strange now looks the life he makes us lead; 50
So free we seem, so fettered fast we are!
I feel he laid the fetter; let it lie!
This chamber, for example—turn your head—
All that's behind us! You don't understand,
Nor care to understand, about my art,
But you can hear at least when people speak;
And that cartoon, the second from the door—
It is the thing, Love! so such thing should be—
Behold Madonna!—I am bold to say.
I can do with my pencil what I know, 60
What I see, what at bottom of my heart
I wish for, if I ever wish so deep—
Do easily, too—when I say perfectly,
I do not boast, perhaps; yourself are judge,
Who listened to the Legate's talk last week,
And just as much they used to say in France.
At any rate, 'tis easy, all of it!
No sketches first, no studies—that's long past;
I do what many dream of all their lives—
Dream? strive to do, and agonize to do, 70
And fail in doing. I could count twenty such
On twice your fingers, and not leave this town,
Who strive—you don't know how the others strive
To paint a little thing like that you smeared
Carelessly passing with your robes afloat—
Yet do much less, so much less, Someone says
(I know his name, no matter)—so much less!
Well, less is more, Lucrezia; I am judged.
There burns a truer light of God in them,
In their vexed, beating, stuffed, and stopped-up brain, 80
Heart, or whate'er else, than goes on to prompt
This low-pulsed forthright craftsman's hand of mine.
Their works drop groundward, but themselves, I know,
Reach many a time a heaven that's shut to me,
Enter and take their place there sure enough,

Though they come back and cannot tell the world.
My works are nearer heaven, but I sit here.
The sudden blood of these men! at a word—
Praise them, it boils; or blame them, it boils too.
I, painting from myself and to myself,   90
Know what I do, am unmoved by men's blame
Or their praise either. Somebody remarks
Morello's outline there is wrongly traced,
His hue mistaken; what of that? or else,
Rightly traced and well ordered; what of that?
Speak as they please, what does the mountain care?
Ah, but a man's reach should exceed his grasp,
Or what's a heaven for? All is silver-gray
Placid and perfect with my art: the worse!
I know both what I want and what might gain,   100
And yet how profitless to know, to sigh,
'Had I been two, another and myself,
Our head would have o'erlooked the world!' No doubt.
Yonder's a work now, of that famous youth,
The Urbinate, who died five years ago.
('Tis copied; George Vasari sent it me.)
Well, I can fancy how he did it all,
Pouring his soul, with kings and popes to see,
Reaching, that heaven might so replenish him,
Above and through his art—for it gives way: 110
That arm is wrongly put—and there again—
A fault to pardon in the drawing's lines,
Its body, so to speak: its soul is right,
He means right—that, a child may understand.
Still, what an arm! and I could alter it;
But all the play, the insight, and the stretch—
Out of me, out of me! And wherefore out?
Had you enjoined them on me, given me soul,
We might have risen to Rafael, I and you!
Nay, Love, you did give all I asked, I think—   120
More than I merit, yes, by many times.
But had you—oh, with the same perfect brow,
And perfect eyes, and more than perfect mouth,

[261]

And the low voice my soul hears, as a bird
The fowler's pipe, and follows to the snare—
Had you, with these the same, but brought a mind!
Some women do so. Had the mouth there urged,
'God and the glory! never care for gain.
The present by the future, what is that?
Live for fame, side by side with Agnolo!   130
Rafael is waiting; up to God, all three!'
I might have done it for you. So it seems;
Perhaps not. All is as God overrules.
Beside, incentives come from the soul's self;
The rest avail not. Why do I need you?
What wife had Rafael, or has Agnolo?
In this world, who can do a thing, will not;
And who would do it, cannot, I perceive;
Yet the will's somewhat—somewhat, too, the power—
And thus we half-men struggle. At the end,   140
God, I conclude, compensates, punishes.
'Tis safer for me, if the award be strict,
That I am something underrated here,
Poor this long while, despised, to speak the truth.
I dared not, do you know, leave home all day,
For fear of chancing on the Paris lords.
The best is when they pass and look aside;
But they speak sometimes; I must bear it all.
Well may they speak! That Francis, that first time,
And that long festal year at Fontainebleau!   150
I surely then could sometimes leave the ground,
Put on the glory, Rafael's daily wear,
In that humane great monarch's golden look—
One finger in his beard or twisted curl
Over his mouth's good mark that made the smile;
One arm about my shoulder, round my neck;
The jingle of his gold chain in my ear—
I painting proudly with his breath on me,
All his Court round him, seeing with his eyes,
Such frank French eyes, and such a fire of souls   160
Profuse, my hand kept plying by those hearts;

And, best of all, this, this, this face beyond,
This in the background, waiting on my work,
To crown the issue with a last reward!
A good time, was it not, my kingly days?
And had you not grown restless . . . but I know—
'Tis done and past; 'twas right, my instinct said;
Too live the life grew, golden and not gray,
And I'm the weak-eyed bat no sun should tempt
Out of the grange whose four walls make his world.   170
How could it end in any other way?
You called me, and I came home to your heart.
The triumph was—to reach and stay there; since
I reached it ere the triumph, what is lost?
Let my hands frame your face in your hair's gold,
You beautiful Lucrezia that are mine!
'Rafael did this, Andrea painted that;
The Roman's is the better when you pray,
But still the other's Virgin was his wife'—
Men will excuse me. I am glad to judge   180
Both pictures in your presence; clearer grows
My better fortune, I resolve to think.
For, do you know, Lucrezia, as God lives,
Said one day Agnolo, his very self,
To Rafael . . . I have known it all these years . . .
(When the young man was flaming out his thoughts
Upon a palace-wall for Rome to see,
Too lifted up in heart because of it),
'Friend, there's a certain sorry little scrub
Goes up and down our Florence, none cares how,   190
Who, were he set to plan and execute
As you are, pricked on by your popes and kings,
Would bring the sweat into that brow of yours!'
To Rafael's!—And indeed the arm is wrong.
I hardly dare . . . yet, only you to see,
Give the chalk here—quick, thus the line should go!
Ay, but the soul! he's Rafael! rub it out!
Still, all I care for, if he spoke the truth
(What he? why, who but Michel Agnolo?

Do you forget already words like those?),   200
If really there was such a chance, so lost—
Is, whether you're—not grateful—but more pleased.
Well, let me think so. And you smile indeed!
This hour has been an hour! Another smile?
If you would sit thus by me every night,
I should work better, do you comprehend?
I mean that I should earn more, give you more
See, it is settled dusk now; there's a star;
Morello's gone, the watch-lights show the wall,
The cue-owls speak the name we call them by.   210
Come from the window, love—come in, at last,
Inside the melancholy little house
We built to be so gay with. God is just.
King Francis may forgive me; oft at nights
When I look up from painting, eyes tired out,
The walls become illumined, brick from brick
Distinct, instead of mortar, fierce bright gold,
That gold of his I did cement them with!
Let us but love each other. Must you go?
That Cousin here again? he waits outside?   220
Must see you—you, and not with me? Those loans?
More gaming debts to pay? you smiled for that?
Well, let smiles buy me! have you more to spend?
While hand and eye and something of a heart
Are left me, work's my ware, and what's it worth?
I'll pay my fancy. Only let me sit
The gray remainder of the evening out,
Idle, you call it, and muse perfectly
How I could paint, were I but back in France,
One picture, just one more—the Virgin's face,   230
Not yours this time! I want you at my side
To hear them—that is, Michel Agnolo—
Judge all I do and tell you of its worth.
Will you? Tomorrow, satisfy your friend.
I take the subjects for his corridor,
Finish the portrait out of hand—there, there,
And throw him in another thing or two

If he demurs; the whole should prove enough
To pay for this same Cousin's freak. Beside—
What's better and what's all I care about—   240
Get you the thirteen scudi for the ruff!
Love, does that please you? Ah, but what does he,
The Cousin! what does he to please you more?

    I am grown peaceful as old age tonight.
I regret little, I would change still less.
Since there my past life lies, why alter it?
The very wrong to Francis!—it is true
I took his coin, was tempted and complied,
And built this house and sinned, and all is said.
My father and my mother died of want.   250
Well, had I riches of my own? you see
How one gets rich! Let each one bear his lot.
They were born poor, lived poor, and poor they died;
And I have labored somewhat in my time
And not been paid profusely. Some good son
Paint my two hundred pictures—let him try!
No doubt, there's something strikes a balance. Yes,
You loved me quite enough, it seems tonight.
This must suffice me here. What would one have?
In heaven, perhaps, new chances, one more chance—   260
Four great walls in the New Jerusalem,
Meted on each side by the angel's reed,
For Leonard, Rafael, Agnolo, and me
To cover—the three first without a wife,
While I have mine! So—still they overcome
Because there's still Lucrezia—as I choose.

    Again the Cousin's whistle! Go, my Love.

Fra Lippo Lippi

I am poor brother Lippo, by your leave!
You need not clap your torches to my face.
Zooks, what's to blame? you think you see a monk!
What, 'tis past midnight, and you go the rounds,

And here you catch me at an alley's end
Where sportive ladies leave their doors ajar?
The Carmine's my cloister; hunt it up,
Do—harry out, if you must show your zeal,
Whatever rat, there, haps, on his wrong hole,
And nip each softling of a wee white mouse,   10
Weke, weke, that's crept to keep him company!
Aha, you know your betters! Then, you'll take
Your hand away that's fiddling on my throat,
And please to know me likewise. Who am I?
Why, one, sir, who is lodging with a friend
Three streets off—he's a certain . . . how d' ye call?
Master—a . . . Cosimo of the Medici,
I' the house that caps the corner. Boh! you were best!
Remember and tell me, the day you're hanged,
How you affected such a gullet's-gripe!   20
But you, sir, it concerns you that your knaves
Pick up a manner nor discredit you;
Zooks, are we pilchards, that they sweep the streets
And count fair prize what comes into their net?
He's Judas to a tittle, that man is!
Just such a face! Why, sir, you make amends.
Lord, I'm not angry! Bid your hangdogs go
Drink out this quarter-florin to the health
Of the munificent House that harbors me
(And many more beside, lads! more beside!)   30
And all's come square again. I'd like his face—
His, elbowing on his comrade in the door
With the pike and lantern—for the slave that holds
John Baptist's head a-dangle by the hair
With one hand ('Look you, now,' as who should say)
And his weapon in the other, yet unwiped!
It's not your chance to have a bit of chalk,
A wood-coal or the like? or you should see!
Yes, I'm the painter, since you style me so.
What, brother Lippo's doings, up and down,   40
You know them and they take you? like enough!
I saw the proper twinkle in your eye—

'Tell you, I liked your looks at very first.
Let's sit and set things straight now, hip to haunch.
Here's spring come, and the nights one makes up bands
To roam the town and sing out carnival,
And I've been three weeks shut within my mew,
A-painting for the great man, saints and saints
And saints again. I could not paint all night—
Ouf! I leaned out of window for fresh air.   50
There came a hurry of feet and little feet,
A sweep of lute-strings, laughs, and whifts of song—
Flower o' the broom,
Take away love, and our earth is a tomb!
Flower o' the quince,
I let Lisa go, and what good in life since?
Flower o' the thyme—and so on. Round they went.
Scarce had they turned the corner when a titter
Like the skipping of rabbits by moonlight—three slim shapes,
And a face that looked up . . . zooks, sir, flesh and blood,   60
That's all I'm made of! Into shreds it went,
Curtain and counterpane and coverlet,
All the bed-furniture—a dozen knots,
There was a ladder! Down I let myself,
Hands and feet, scrambling somehow, and so dropped,
And after them. I came up with the fun
Hard by Saint Laurence, hail fellow, well met—
Flower o' the rose,
If I've been merry, what matter who knows?
And so as I was stealing back again   70
To get to bed and have a bit of sleep
Ere I rise up tomorrow and go work
On Jerome knocking at his poor old breast
With his great round stone to subdue the flesh,
You snap me of the sudden. Ah, I see!
Though your eye twinkles still, you shake your head—
Mine's shaved—a monk, you say—the sting's in that!
If Master Cosimo announced himself,
Mum's the word naturally; but a monk!
Come, what am I a beast for? tell us, now!   80

[267]

I was a baby when my mother died
And father died and left me in the street.
I starved there, God knows how, a year or two
On fig-skins, melon-parings, rinds and shucks,
Refuse and rubbish. One fine frosty day,
My stomach being empty as your hat,
The wind doubled me up and down I went.
Old Aunt Lapaccia trussed me with one hand
(Its fellow was a stinger as I knew),
And so along the wall, over the bridge,   90
By the straight cut to the convent. Six words there,
While I stood munching my first bread that month:
'So, boy, you're minded,' quoth the good fat father,
Wiping his own mouth—'twas refection-time—
'To quit this very miserable world?
Will you renounce' . . . 'the mouthful of bread?' thought I;
By no means! Brief, they made a monk of me;
I did renounce the world, its pride and greed,
Palace, farm, villa, shop, and banking-house,
Trash, such as these poor devils of Medici   100
Have given their hearts to—all at eight years old.
Well, sir, I found in time, you may be sure,
'Twas not for nothing—the good bellyful,
The warm serge and the rope that goes all round,
And day-long blessed idleness beside!
'Let's see what the urchin's fit for'—that came next.
Not overmuch their way, I must confess.
Such a to-do! They tried me with their books;
Lord, they'd have taught me Latin in pure waste!
Flower o' the clove,   110
All the Latin I construe is 'amo,' I love!
But, mind you, when a boy starves in the streets
Eight years together, as my fortune was,
Watching folk's faces to know who will fling
The bit of half-stripped grape-bunch he desires,
And who will curse or kick him for his pains—
Which gentleman processional and fine,
Holding a candle to the Sacrament,

[268]

Will wink and let him lift a plate and catch
The droppings of the wax to sell again,   120
Or holla for the Eight and have him whipped—
How say I?—nay, which dog bites, which lets drop
His bone from the heap of offal in the street—
Why, soul and sense of him grow sharp alike;
He learns the look of things, and none the less
For admonition from the hunger-pinch.
I had a store of such remarks, be sure,
Which, after I found leisure, turned to use.
I drew men's faces on my copy-books,
Scrawled them within the antiphonary's marge, /chant   130
Joined legs and arms to the long music-notes,   (book)
Found eyes and nose and chin for A's and B's,
And made a string of pictures of the world
Betwixt the ins and outs of verb and noun,
On the wall, the bench, the door. The monks looked black.
'Nay,' quoth the Prior, 'turn him out, d' ye say?
In no wise. Lose a crow and catch a lark.
What if at last we get our man of parts,
We Carmelites, like those Camaldolese
And Preaching Friars, to do our church up fine   140
And put the front on it that ought to be!'
And hereupon he bade me daub away.
Thank you! my head being crammed, the walls a blank,
Never was such prompt disemburdening.
First, every sort of monk, the black and white,
I drew them, fat and lean; then, folk at church,
From good old gossips waiting to confess
Their cribs of barrel-droppings, candle-ends—
To the breathless fellow at the altar-foot,
Fresh from his murder, safe and sitting there   150
With the little children round him in a row
Of admiration, half for his beard and half
For that white anger of his victim's son
Shaking a fist at him with one fierce arm,
Signing himself with the other because of Christ
(Whose sad face on the cross sees only this

[269]

After the passion of a thousand years),
Till some poor girl, her apron o'er her head
(Which the intense eyes looked through), came at eve
On tiptoe, said a word, dropped in a loaf, 160
Her pair of earrings and a bunch of flowers
(The brute took growling), prayed, and so was gone.
I painted all, then cried, ' 'Tis ask and have;
Choose, for more's ready!'—laid the ladder flat,
And showed my covered bit of cloister-wall.
The monks closed in a circle and praised loud
Till checked, taught what to see and not to see,
Being simple bodies—'That's the very man!
Look at the boy who stoops to pat the dog!
That woman's like the Prior's niece who comes 170
To care about his asthma; it's the life!'
But there my triumph's straw-fire flared and funked;
Their betters took their turn to see and say;
The Prior and the learned pulled a face
And stopped all that in no time. 'How? what's here?
Quite from the mark of painting, bless us all!
Faces, arms, legs, and bodies like the true
As much as pea and pea! It's devil's-game!
Your business is not to catch men with show,
With homage to the perishable clay, 180
But lift them over it, ignore it all,
Make them forget there's such a thing as flesh.
Your business is to paint the souls of men—
Man's soul, and it's a fire, smoke . . . no, it's not . . .
It's vapor done up like a new-born babe
(In that shape when you die it leaves your mouth)—
It's . . . well, what matters talking, it's the soul!
Give us no more of body than shows soul!
Here's Giotto, with his Saint a-praising God,
That sets us praising—why not stop with him? 190
Why put all thoughts of praise out of our head
With wonder at lines, colors, and what not?
Paint the soul, never mind the legs and arms!
Rub all out, try at it a second time.

Oh, that white smallish female with the breasts,
She's just my niece . . . Herodias, I would say—
Who went and danced and got men's heads cut off!
Have it all out!' Now, is this sense, I ask?
A fine way to paint soul, by painting body
So ill the eye can't stop there, must go further   200
And can't fare worse! Thus, yellow does for white
When what you put for yellow's simply black,
And any sort of meaning looks intense
When all beside itself means and looks naught.
Why can't a painter lift each foot in turn,
Left foot and right foot, go a double step,
Make his flesh liker and his soul more like,
Both in their order? Take the prettiest face,
The Prior's niece . . . patron-saint—is it so pretty
You can't discover if it means hope, fear,   210
Sorrow or joy? won't beauty go with these?
Suppose I've made her eyes all right and blue,
Can't I take breath and try to add life's flash,
And then add soul and heighten them three-fold?
Or say there's beauty with no soul at all
(I never saw it—put the case the same);
If you get simple beauty and naught else,
You get about the best thing God invents—
That's somewhat; and you'll find the soul you have missed,
Within yourself, when you return him thanks.   220
'Rub all out!' Well, well, there's my life, in short,
And so the thing has gone on ever since.
I'm grown a man no doubt, I've broken bounds;
You should not take a fellow eight years old
And make him swear to never kiss the girls.
I'm my own master, paint now as I please—
Having a friend, you see, in the Corner-house!
Lord, it's fast holding by the rings in front—
Those great rings serve more purposes than just
To plant a flag in, or tie up a horse!   230
And yet the old schooling sticks, the old grave eyes
Are peeping o'er my shoulder as I work,

[271]

The heads shake still—'It's art's decline, my son!
You're not of the true painters, great and old;
Brother Angelico's the man, you'll find;
Brother Lorenzo stands his single peer—
Fag on at flesh, you'll never make the third!'
Flower o' the pine,
You keep your mistr . . . manners, and I'll stick to mine!
I'm not the third, then; bless us, they must know!   240
Don't you think they're the likeliest to know,
They with their Latin? So, I swallow my rage,
Clench my teeth, suck my lips in tight, and paint
To please them—sometimes do and sometimes don't;
For, doing most, there's pretty sure to come
A turn, some warm eve finds me at my saints—
A laugh, a cry, the business of the world
(*Flower o' the peach,*
Death for us all, and his own life for each!)—
And my whole soul revolves, the cup runs over,   250
The world and life's too big to pass for a dream,
And I do these wild things in sheer despite,
And play the fooleries you catch me at,
In pure rage! The old mill-horse, out at grass
After hard years, throws up his stiff heels so,
Although the miller does not preach to him
The only good of grass is to make chaff.
What would men have? Do they like grass or no—
May they or mayn't they? All I want's the thing
Settled forever one way. As it is,   260
You tell too many lies and hurt yourself;
You don't like what you only like too much,
You do like what, if given you at your word,
You find abundantly detestable.
For me, I think I speak as I was taught;
I always see the garden and God there
A-making man's wife; and, my lesson learned—
The value and significance of flesh—
I can't unlearn ten minutes afterwards.

You understand me; I'm a beast, I know. 270
But see, now—why, I see as certainly
As that the morning-star's about to shine,
What will hap some day. We've a youngster here
Comes to our convent, studies what I do,
Slouches and stares and lets no atom drop.
His name is Guidi—he'll not mind the monks—
They call him Hulking Tom, he lets them talk;
He picks my practice up—he'll paint apace,
I hope so—though I never live so long,
I know what's sure to follow. You be judge! 280
You speak no Latin more than I, belike;
However, you're my man, you've seen the world—
The beauty and the wonder and the power,
The shapes of things, their colors, lights and shades,
Changes, surprises—and God made it all!
—For what? Do you feel thankful, aye or no,
For this fair town's face, yonder river's line,
The mountain round it and the sky above,
Much more the figures of man, woman, child,
These are the frame to? What's it all about? 290
To be passed over, despised? or dwelt upon,
Wondered at? Oh, this last of course!—you say.
But why not do as well as say—paint these
Just as they are, careless what comes of it?
God's works—paint any one, and count it crime
To let a truth slip. Don't object, 'His works
Are here already; nature is complete:
Suppose you reproduce her—which you can't—
There's no advantage! you must beat her, then.'
For, don't you mark? we're made so that we love 300
First when we see them painted, things we have passed
Perhaps a hundred times nor cared to see;
And so they are better, painted—better to us,
Which is the same thing. Art was given for that;
God uses us to help each other so,
Lending our minds out. Have you noticed, now,
Your cullion's hanging face? A bit of chalk,

[273]

And trust me but you should, though! How much more,
If I drew higher things with the same truth!
That were to take the Prior's pulpit-place,   310
Interpret God to all of you! Oh, oh,
It makes me mad to see what men shall do
And we in our graves! This world's no blot for us,
Nor blank; it means intensely, and means good—
To find its meaning is my meat and drink.
'Aye, but you don't so instigate to prayer!'
Strikes in the Prior; 'when your meaning's plain
It does not say to folk—remember matins,
Or, mind you fast next Friday!' Why, for this
What need of art at all? A skull and bones,   320
Two bits of stick nailed crosswise, or, what's best,
A bell to chime the hour with, does as well.
I painted a Saint Laurence six months since
At Prato, splashed the fresco in fine style;
'How looks my painting, now the scaffold's down?'
I ask a brother. 'Hugely,' he returns—
'Already not one phiz of your three slaves
Who turn the Deacon off his toasted side,
But's scratched and prodded to our heart's content,
The pious people have so eased their own   330
With coming to say prayers there in a rage;
We get on fast to see the bricks beneath.
Expect another job this time next year,
For pity and religion grow i' the crowd—
Your painting serves its purpose!' Hang the fools!

   —That is—you'll not mistake an idle word
Spoke in a huff by a poor monk, God wot,
Tasting the air this spicy night, which turns
The unaccustomed head like Chianti wine!
Oh, the church knows! don't misreport me, now!   340
It's natural a poor monk out of bounds
Should have his apt word to excuse himself,
And hearken how I plot to make amends.
I have bethought me: I shall paint a piece

. . . There's for you! Give me six months, then go, see
Something in Sant' Ambrogio's! Bless the nuns!
They want a cast o' my office. I shall paint
God in the midst, Madonna and her babe,
Ringed by a bowery, flowery angel-brood,
Lilies and vestments and white faces, sweet   350
As puff on puff of grated orris-root
When ladies crowd to Church at midsummer.
And then i' the front, of course a saint or two—
Saint John, because he saves the Florentines,
Saint Ambrose, who puts down in black and white
The convent's friends and gives them a long day,
And Job, I must have him there past mistake,
The man of Uz (and Us without the z,
Painters who need his patience). Well, all these
Secured at their devotion, up shall come   360
Out of a corner when you least expect,
As one by a dark stair into a great light,
Music and talking, who but Lippo! I!—
Mazed, motionless, and moonstruck—I'm the man!
Back I shrink—what is this I see and hear?
I, caught up with my monk's-things by mistake,
My old serge gown and rope that goes all round,
I, in this presence, this pure company!
Where's a hole, where's a corner for escape?
Then steps a sweet angelic slip of a thing   370
Forward, puts out a soft palm: 'Not so fast!'
—Addresses the celestial presence, 'Nay,
He made you and devised you, after all,
Though he's none of you! Could Saint John there draw—
His camel-hair make up a painting-brush?
We come to brother Lippo for all that,
Iste perfecit opus!' So, all smile—
I shuffle sideways with my blushing face
Under the cover of a hundred wings
Thrown like a spread of kirtles when you're gay   380
And play hot cockles, all the doors being shut,
Till, wholly unexpected, in there pops

The hothead husband! Thus I scuttle off
To some safe bench behind, not letting go
The palm of her, the little lily thing
That spoke the good word for me in the nick,
Like the Prior's niece . . . Saint Lucy, I would say.
And so all's saved for me, and for the church
A pretty picture gained. Go, six months hence!
Your hand, sir, and good-by; no lights, no lights!   390
The street's hushed, and I know my own way back,
Don't fear me! There's the gray beginning. Zooks!

180

Cino

ITALIAN CAMPAGNA 1309, THE OPEN ROAD

Bah! I have sung women in three cities,
But it is all the same;
And I will sing of the sun.

Lips, words, and you snare them,
Dreams, words, and they are as jewels,
Strange spells of old deity,
Ravens, nights, allurement:
And they are not;
Having become the souls of song.

Eyes, dreams, lips, and the night goes.   10
Being upon the road once more,
They are not.
Forgetful in their towers of our tuneing
Once for Wind-runeing
They dream us-toward and
Sighing, say, 'Would Cino,
Passionate Cino, of the wrinkling eyes,
Gay Cino, of quick laughter,
Cino, of the dare, the jibe,
Frail Cino, strongest of his tribe   20
That tramp old ways beneath the sun-light,
Would Cino of the Luth were here!'

[276]

Once, twice, a year—
Vaguely thus word they:
  'Cino?' 'Oh, eh, Cino Polnesi
  The singer is't you mean?'
  'Ah yes, passed once our way,
  A saucy fellow, but . . .
  (Oh, they are all one these vagabonds),
  Peste! 'tis his own songs?   30
  Or some other's that he sings?
  But *you*, My Lord, how with your city?'

But you 'My Lord,' God's pity!
And all I knew were out, My Lord, you
Were Lack-land Cino, e'en as I am,
O Sinistro.

I have sung women in three cities.
But it is all one.
I will sing of the sun.
  . . . eh? . . . they mostly had grey eyes,   40
But it is all one, I will sing of the sun.

  'Pollo Phoibee, old tin pan, you
  Glory to Zeus' aegis-day,
  Shield o' steel-blue, th' heaven o'er us
  Hath for boss thy luster gay!

  'Pollo Phoibee, to our way-fare
  Make thy laugh our wander-lied;
  Bid thy 'fulgence bear away care.
  Cloud and rain-tears pass they fleet!

  Seeking e'er the new-laid rast-way   50
  To the gardens of the sun . . .

         *   *   *

I have sung women in three cities.
But it is all one.

I will sing of the white birds
In the blue waters of heaven,
The clouds that are spray to its sea.

Patterns

I walk down the garden-paths,
And all the daffodils
Are blowing, and the bright blue squills.
I walk down the patterned garden-paths
In my stiff, brocaded gown.
With my powdered hair and jeweled fan,
I too am a rare
Pattern. As I wander down
The garden-paths.

My dress is richly figured,   10
And the train
Makes a pink and silver stain
On the gravel, and the thrift
Of the borders.
Just a plate of current fashion,
Tripping by in high-heeled, ribboned shoes.
Not a softness anywhere about me,
Only whalebone and brocade.
And I sink on a seat in the shade
Of a lime tree. For my passion   20
Wars against the stiff brocade.
The daffodils and squills
Flutter in the breeze
As they please.
And I weep;
For the lime tree is in blossom
And one small flower has dropped upon my bosom.

And the plashing of waterdrops
In the marble fountain
Comes down the garden-paths.   30
The dripping never stops.

[278]

Underneath my stiffened gown
Is the softness of a woman bathing in a marble basin,
A basin in the midst of hedges grown
So thick, she cannot see her lover hiding,
But she guesses he is near,
And the sliding of the water
Seems the stroking of a dear
Hand upon her.
What is Summer in a fine brocaded gown!   40
I should like to see it lying in a heap upon the ground.
All the pink and silver crumpled up on the ground.

I would be the pink and silver as I ran along the paths,
And he would stumble after,
Bewildered by my laughter.
I should see the sun flashing from his sword-hilt and the buckles on
    his shoes.
I would choose
To lead him in a maze along the patterned paths,
A bright and laughing maze for my heavy-booted lover.
Till he caught me in the shade,   50
And the buttons of his waistcoat bruised my body as he clasped me,
Aching, melting, unafraid.
With the shadows of the leaves and the sundrops,
And the plopping of the waterdrops,
All about us in the open afternoon—
I am very like to swoon
With the weight of this brocade,
For the sun sifts through the shade.

Underneath the fallen blossom
In my bosom   60
Is a letter I have hid.
It was brought to me this morning by a rider from the Duke.
'Madam, we regret to inform you that Lord Hartwell
Died in action Thursday se'nnight.'
As I read it in the white, morning sunlight,

The letters squirmed like snakes.
'Any answer, Madam,' said my footman.
'No,' I told him.
'See that the messenger takes some refreshment.
No, no answer.'   70
And I walked into the garden,
Up and down the patterned paths,
In my stiff, correct brocade.
The blue and yellow flowers stood up proudly in the sun,
Each one.
I stood upright too,
Held rigid to the pattern
By the stiffness of my gown;
Up and down I walked,
Up and down.   80

In a month he would have been my husband.
In a month, here, underneath this lime,
We would have broke the pattern;
He for me, and I for him,
He as Colonel, I as Lady,
On this shady seat.
He had a whim
That sunlight carried blessing.
And I answered, 'It shall be as you have said.'
Now he is dead.   90

In Summer and in Winter I shall walk
Up and down
The patterned garden-paths
In my stiff, brocaded gown.
The squills and daffodils
Will give place to pillared roses, and to asters, and to snow.
I shall go
Up and down
In my gown.
Gorgeously arrayed,   100
Boned and stayed.

And the softness of my body will be guarded from embrace
By each button, hook, and lace.
For the man who should loose me is dead,
Fighting with the Duke in Flanders,
In a pattern called a war.
Christ! What are patterns for?

Slow quiet Low

182 *Richard Cory*

Whenever Richard Cory went down town,
    We people on the pavement looked at him:
He was a gentleman from sole to crown,
    Clean favored, and imperially slim.

And he was always quietly arrayed,   5
    And he was always human when he talked;
But still he fluttered pulses when he said,
    'Good-morning,' and he glittered when he walked.

And he was rich—yes, richer than a king—
    And admirably schooled in every grace: 10
In fine, we thought that he was everything
    To make us wish that we were in his place.

So on we worked, and waited for the light,
    And went without the meat, and cursed the bread;
And Richard Cory, one calm summer night,   15
    Went home and put a bullet through his head.

183 *Miniver Cheevy*

Miniver Cheevy, child of scorn,
    Grew lean while he assailed the seasons;
He wept that he was ever born,
    And he had reasons.

Miniver loved the days of old
    When swords were bright and steeds were prancing;
The vision of a warrior bold
    Would set him dancing.

[281]

Miniver sighed for what was not,
    And dreamed, and rested from his labors;
He dreamed of Thebes and Camelot,
    And Priam's neighbors.

Miniver mourned the ripe renown
    That made so many a name so fragrant;
He mourned Romance, now on the town,
    And Art, a vagrant.

Miniver loved the Medici,
    Albeit he had never seen one;
He would have sinned incessantly
    Could he have been one.

Miniver cursed the commonplace
    And eyed a khaki suit with loathing;
He missed the medieval grace
    Of iron clothing.

Miniver scorned the gold he sought,
    But sore annoyed was he without it;
Miniver thought, and thought, and thought,
    And thought about it.

Miniver Cheevy, born too late,
    Scratched his head and kept on thinking;
Miniver coughed, and called it fate,
    And kept on drinking.

Mr. Flood's Party

Old Eben Flood, climbing alone one night
Over the hill between the town below
And the forsaken upland hermitage
That held as much as he should ever know
On earth again of home, paused warily.
The road was his with not a native near;
And Eben, having leisure, said aloud,
For no man else in Tilbury Town to hear:

'Well, Mr. Flood, we have the harvest moon
Again, and we may not have many more;   10
The bird is on the wing, the poet says,
And you and I have said it here before.
Drink to the bird.' He raised up to the light
The jug that he had gone so far to fill,
And answered huskily: 'Well, Mr. Flood,
Since you propose it, I believe I will.'

Alone, as if enduring to the end
A valiant armor of scarred hopes outworn,
He stood there in the middle of the road
Like Roland's ghost winding a silent horn.   20
Below him, in the town among the trees,
Where friends of other days had honored him,
A phantom salutation of the dead
Rang thinly till old Eben's eyes were dim.

Then, as a mother lays her sleeping child
Down tenderly, fearing it may awake,
He set the jug down slowly at his feet
With trembling care, knowing that most things break;
And only when assured that on firm earth
It stood, as the uncertain lives of men   30
Assuredly did not, he paced away,
And with his hand extended paused again:

'Well, Mr. Flood, we have not met like this
In a long time; and many a change has come
To both of us, I fear, since last it was
We had a drop together. Welcome home!'
Convivially returning with himself,
Again he raised the jug up to the light;
And with an acquiescent quaver said:
'Well, Mr. Flood, if you insist, I might.   40

'Only a very little, Mr. Flood—
For auld lang syne. No more, sir; that will do.'
So, for the time, apparently it did,
And Eben evidently thought so too;
For soon amid the silver loneliness
Of night he lifted up his voice and sang,
Secure, with only two moons listening,
Until the whole harmonious landscape rang—

'For auld lang syne.' The weary throat gave out,
The last word wavered; and the song being done,   50
He raised again the jug regretfully
And shook his head, and was again alone.
There was not much that was ahead of him,
And there was nothing in the town below—
Where strangers would have shut the many doors
That many friends had opened long ago.

185   *The Tuft of Flowers*

I went to turn the grass once after one
Who mowed it in the dew before the sun.

The dew was gone that made his blade so keen
Before I came to view the leveled scene.

I looked for him behind an isle of trees;
I listened for his whetstone on the breeze.

But he had gone his way, the grass all mown,
And I must be, as he had been,—alone,

'As all must be,' I said within my heart,
'Whether they work together or apart.'   10

But as I said it, swift there passed me by
On noiseless wing a bewildered butterfly,

Seeking with memories grown dim over night
Some resting flower of yesterday's delight.

[284]

And once I marked his flight go round and round,
As where some flower lay withering on the ground.

And then he flew as far as eye could see,
And then on tremulous wing came back to me.

I thought of questions that have no reply,
And would have turned to toss the grass to dry;　　20

But he turned first, and led my eye to look
At a tall tuft of flowers beside a brook,

A leaping tongue of bloom the scythe had spared
Beside a reedy brook the scythe had bared.

I left my place to know them by their name,
Finding them butterfly-weed when I came.

The mower in the dew had loved them thus,
By leaving them to flourish, not for us,

Nor yet to draw one thought of ours to him,
But from sheer morning gladness at the brim.　　30

The butterfly and I had lit upon,
Nevertheless, a message from the dawn,

That made me hear the wakening birds around,
And hear his long scythe whispering to the ground,

And feel a spirit kindred to my own;
So that henceforth I worked no more alone;

But glad with him, I worked as with his aid,
And weary, sought at noon with him the shade;

And dreaming, as it were, held brotherly speech
With one whose thought I had not hoped to reach.　　40

'Men work together,' I told him from the heart,
'Whether they work together or apart.'

Something there is that doesn't love a wall,
That sends the frozen-ground-swell under it,
And spills the upper boulders in the sun;
And makes gaps even two can pass abreast.
The work of hunters is another thing:
I have come after them and made repair
Where they have left not one stone on a stone,
But they would have the rabbit out of hiding,
To please the yelping dogs. The gaps I mean,
No one has seen them made or heard them made,   10
But at spring mending-time we find them there.
I let my neighbor know beyond the hill;
And on a day we meet to walk the line
And set the wall between us once again.
We keep the wall between us as we go.
To each the boulders that have fallen to each.
And some are loaves and some so nearly balls
We have to use a spell to make them balance:
'Stay where you are until our backs are turned!'
We wear our fingers rough with handling them.   20
Oh, just another kind of out-door game,
One on a side. It comes to little more:
There where it is we do not need the wall:
He is all pine and I am apple orchard.
My apple trees will never get across
And eat the cones under his pines, I tell him.
He only says, 'Good fences make good neighbors.'
Spring is the mischief in me, and I wonder
If I could put a notion in his head:
'*Why* do they make good neighbors? Isn't it   30
Where there are cows? But here there are no cows.
Before I built a wall I'd ask to know
What I was walling in or walling out,
And to whom I was like to give offense.
Something there is that doesn't love a wall,
That wants it down.' I could say 'Elves' to him,

But it's not elves exactly, and I'd rather
He said it for himself. I see him there
Bringing a stone grasped firmly by the top
In each hand, like an old-stone savage armed.   40
He moves in darkness as it seems to me,
Not of woods only and the shade of trees.
He will not go behind his father's saying,
And he likes having thought of it so well
He says again, 'Good fences make good neighbors.'

'Fred, where is north?'

              'North? North is there, my love.
The brook runs west.'

               'West-running Brook then call it.'
(West-running Brook men call it to this day.)
'What does it think it's doing running west
When all the other country brooks flow east
To reach the ocean? It must be the brook
Can trust itself to go by contraries
The way I can with you—and you with me—
Because we're—we're—I don't know what we are.
What are we?'

        'Young or new?'

                'We must be something.   10
We've said we two. Let's change that to we three.
As you and I are married to each other,
We'll both be married to the brook. We'll build
Our bridge across it, and the bridge shall be
Our arm thrown over it asleep beside it.
Look, look, it's waving to us with a wave
To let us know it hears me.'

              'Why, my dear,
That wave's been standing off this jut of shore—'
(The black stream, catching on a sunken rock,
Flung backward on itself in one white wave,   20
And the white water rode the black forever,

Not gaining but not losing, like a bird
While feathers from the struggle of whose breast
Flecked the dark stream and flecked the darker pool
Below the point, and were at last driven wrinkled
In a white scarf against the far shore alders.)
'That wave's been standing off this jut of shore
Ever since rivers, I was going to say,
Were made in heaven. It wasn't waved to us.'

'It wasn't, yet it was. If not to you   30
It was to me—in an annunciation.'

'Oh, if you take it off to lady-land,
As 'twere the country of the Amazons
We men must see you to the confines of
And leave you there, ourselves forbid to enter,—
It is your brook! I have no more to say.'

'Yes, you have, too. Go on. You thought of something.'

'Speaking of contraries, see how the brook
In that white wave runs counter to itself.
It is from that in water we were from   40
Long, long before we were from any creature.
Here we, in our impatience of the steps,
Get back to the beginning of beginnings,
The stream of everything that runs away.
Some say existence like a Pirouot
And Pirouette, forever in one place,
Stands still and dances, but it runs away,
It seriously, sadly, runs away
To fill the abyss' void with emptiness.
It flows beside us in this water brook,   50
But it flows over us. It flows between us
To separate us for a panic moment.
It flows between us, over us, and *with* us.
And it is time, strength, tone, light, life and love
And even substance lapsing unsubstantial;

The universal cataract of death
That spends to nothingness—and unresisted,
Save by some strange resistance in itself,
Not just a swerving, but a throwing back,
As if regret were in it and were sacred.   60
It has this throwing backward on itself
So that the fall of most of it is always
Raising a little, sending up a little.
Our life runs down in sending up the clock.
The brook runs down in sending up our life.
The sun runs down in sending up the brook.
And there is something sending up the sun.
It is this backward motion toward the source,
Against the stream, that most we see ourselves in,
The tribute of the current to the source.   70
It is from this in nature we are from.
It is most us.'
        'Today will be the day
You said so.'
         'No, today will be the day
You said the brook was called West-running Brook.'

'Today will be the day of what we both said.'

188   Frescoes for Mr. Rockefeller's City . . .

I

LANDSCAPE AS A NUDE

She lies on her left side her flank golden:
Her hair is burned black with the strong sun:
The scent of her hair is of rain in the dust on her shoulders:
She has brown breasts and the mouth of no other country:

Ah she is beautiful here in the sun where she lies:
She is not like the soft girls naked in vineyards
Nor the soft naked girls of the English islands
Where the rain comes in with the surf on an east wind:

Hers is the west wind and the sunlight: the west
Wind is the long clean wind of the continents—
The wind turning with earth: the wind descending
Steadily out of the evening and following on:

The wind here where she lies is west: the trees
Oak ironwood cottonwood hickory: standing in
Great groves they roll on the wind as the sea would:
The grasses of Iowa Illinois Indiana

Run with the plunge of the wind as a wave tumbling:

Under her knees there is no green lawn of the Florentines:
Under her dusty knees is the corn stubble:
Her belly is flecked with the flickering light of the corn:

She lies on her left side her flank golden:
Her hair is burned black with the strong sun:
The scent of her hair is of dust and of smoke on her shoulders:
She has brown breasts and the mouth of no other country:

2

WILDWEST

There were none of my blood in this battle:
There were Minneconjous: Sans Arcs: Brules:
Many nations of Sioux: they were few men galloping:

This would have been in the long days in June:
They were galloping well deployed under the plum-trees:
They were driving riderless horses: themselves they were few: 30

Crazy Horse had done it with a few numbers:
Crazy Horse was small for a Lakota:
He was riding always alone thinking of something:

He was standing alone by the picket lines by the ropes:
He was young then: he was thirty when he died:
Unless there were children to talk to he took no notice:

When the soldiers came for him there on the other side
On the Greasy Grass in the villages we were shouting
'Hoka Hey! Crazy Horse will be riding!'

They fought in the water: horses and men were drowning: 40
They rode on the butte: dust settled in sunlight:
Hoka Hey! they lay on the bloody ground:

No one could tell of the dead which man was Custer . . .
That was the end of his luck: by that river:
The soldiers beat him at Slim Buttes once:

They beat him at Willow Creek when the snow lifted:
The last time they beat him was the Tongue:
He had only the meat he had made and of that little:

Do you ask why he should fight? It was his country:
My God should he not fight? It was his: 50
But after the Tongue there were no herds to be hunting:

He cut the knots of the tails and he led them in:
He cried out 'I am Crazy Horse! Do not touch me!'
There were many soldiers between and the gun glinting . . .

And a Mister Josiah Perham of Maine had much of the
land Mister Perham was building the Northern Pacific
railroad that is Mister Perham was saying at lunch that

forty say fifty millions of acres in gift and
government grant outright ought to be worth a
wide price on the Board at two-fifty and   60

later a Mister Cooke had relieved Mister Perham and
later a Mister Morgan relieved Mister Cooke:
Mister Morgan converted at prices current:

It was all prices to them: they never looked at it:
why should they look at the land: they were Empire Builders:
it was all in the bid and the asked and the ink on their books . . .

[291]

When Crazy Horse was there by the Black Hills
His heart would be big with the love he had for that country
And all the game he had seen and the mares he had ridden

And how it went out from you wide and clean in the sunlight   70

3
Burying Ground by the Ties

Ayee! Ai! This is heavy earth on our shoulders:
There were none of us born to be buried in this earth:
Niggers we were Portuguese Magyars Polacks:

We were born to another look of the sky certainly:
Now we lie here in the river pastures:
We lie in the mowings under the thick turf:

We hear the earth and the all-day rasp of the grasshoppers:
It was we laid the steel on this land from ocean to ocean:
It was we (if you know) put the U. P. through the passes

Bringing her down into Laramie full load   80
Eighteen mile on the granite anticlinal
Forty-three foot to the mile and the grade holding:

It was we did it: hunkies of our kind:
It was we dug the caved-in holes for the cold water:
It was we built the gully spurs and the freight sidings:

Who would do it but we and the Irishmen bossing us?
It was all foreign-born men there were in this country:
It was Scotsmen Englishmen Chinese Squareheads Austrians . . .

Ayee! but there's weight to the earth under it:
Nor for this did we come out—to be lying here   90
Nameless under the ties in the clay cuts:

There's nothing good in the world but the rich will buy it:
Everything sticks to the grease of a gold note—
Even a continent—even a new sky!

Do not pity us much for the strange grass over us:
We laid the steel to the stone stock of these mountains:
The place of our graves is marked by the telegraph poles!

It was not to lie in the bottoms we came out
And the trains going over us here in the dry hollows . . .

4

OIL PAINTING OF THE ARTIST AS THE ARTIST

The plump Mr. Pl'f is washing his hands of America: 100
The plump Mr. Pl'f is in ochre with such hair:

America is in blue-black-grey-green-sandcolor:
America is a continent—many lands:

The plump Mr. Pl'f is washing his hands of America:
He is pictured at Pau on the *place* and his eyes glaring:

He thinks of himself as an exile from all this:
As an émigré from his own time into history—

(History being an empty house without owners
A practical man may get in by the privy stones—

The dead are excellent hosts: they have no objections—   110
And once in he can nail the knob on the next one

Living the life of a classic in bad air with
Himself for the Past and his face in the glass for Posterity)

The Cinquecento is nothing at all like Nome
Or Natchez or Wounded Knee or the Shenandoah:

Your vulgarity Tennessee: your violence Texas:
The rocks under your fields Ohio Connecticut:

Your clay Missouri your clay: you have driven him out:
You have shadowed his life Appalachians purple mountains:

[293]

There is much too much of your flowing Mississippi: 120
He prefers a tidier stream with a terrace for trippers and

Cypresses mentioned in Horace or Henry James:
He prefers a country where everything carries the name of a

Countess or real king or an actual palace or
Something in Prose and the stock prices all in Italian:

There is more shade for an artist under a fig
Than under the whole damn range (he finds) of the Big Horns

5

EMPIRE BUILDERS

The Museum Attendant:

This is *The Making of America in Five Panels:*

This is Mister Harriman making America:
Mister-Harriman-is-buying-the-Union-Pacific-at-Seventy: 130
The Santa Fe is shining on his hair:

This is Commodore Vanderbilt making America:
Mister-Vanderbilt-is-eliminating-the-short-interest-in-Hudson:
Observe the carving on the rocking chair:

This is J. P. Morgan making America:
(The Tennessee Coal is behind to the left of the Steel Company:)
Those in mauve are braces he is wearing:

This is Mister Mellon making America:
Mister-Mellon-is-represented-as-a-symbolical-figure-in-aluminum-
Strewing-bank-stocks-on-a-burnished-stair: 140

This is the Bruce is the Barton making America:
Mister-Barton-is-selling-us-Doctor's-Deliciousest-Dentifrice:
This is he in beige with the canary:

You have just beheld the Makers making America:
This is *The Making of America in Five Panels:*
America lies to the west-southwest of the Switch-Tower:
There is nothing to see of America but land:

The Original Document
under the Panel Paint:

'To Thos. Jefferson Esq. his obd't serv't   150
M. Lewis: captain: detached:
                                    Sir:

Having in mind your repeated commands in this matter:
And the worst half of it done and the streams mapped:

And we here on the back of this beach beholding the
Other ocean—two years gone and the cold

Breaking with rain for the third spring since St. Louis:
The crows at the fishbones on the frozen dunes:

The first cranes going over from south north:
And the river down by a mark of the pole since the morning: 160

And time near to return, and a ship (Spanish)
Lying in for the salmon: and fearing chance or the

Drought or the Sioux should deprive you of these discoveries—
Therefore we sent by sea in this writing:

                                                        Above the
Platte there were long plains and a clay country:
Rim of the sky far off: grass under it:

Dung for the cook fires by the sulphur licks:
After that there were low hills and the sycamores:

And we poled up by the Great Bend in the skiffs: 170
The honey bees left us after the Osage River:

The wind was west in the evenings and no dew and the
Morning Star larger and whiter than usual—

The winter rattling in the brittle haws:
The second year there was sage and the quail calling:

All that valley is good land by the river:
Three thousand miles and the clay cliffs and

Rue and beargrass by the water banks
And many birds and the brant going over and tracks of

Bear elk wolves marten: the buffalo   180
Numberless so that the cloud of their dust covers them:

The antelope fording the fall creeks: and the mountains and
Grazing lands and the meadow lands and the ground

Sweet and open and well-drained:
                                        We advise you to
Settle troops at the forks and to issue licenses:

Many men will have living on these lands:
There is wealth in the earth for them all and the wood standing

And wild birds on the water where they sleep:
There is stone in the hills for the towns of a great people . . .'   190

You have just beheld the Makers making America:

They screwed her scrawny and gaunt with their seven-year panics:
They bought her back on their mortgages old-whore-cheap:
They fattened their bonds at her breasts till the thin blood ran
    from them:

Men have forgotten how full clear and deep
The Yellowstone moved on the gravel and grass grew
When the land lay waiting for her westward people!

6

BACKGROUND WITH REVOLUTIONARIES

And the corn singing Millennium!
Lenin! Millennium! Lennium!

When they're shunting the cars on the Katy a mile off   200
When they're shunting the cars when they're shunting the cars on the Katy
You can hear the clank of the couplings riding away

Also Comrade Devine who writes of America
Most instructively having in 'Seventy-four
Crossed to the Hoboken side on the Barclay Street Ferry

She sits on a settle in the State of North Dakota
O she sits on a settle in the State of North Dakota
She can hear the engines whistle over Iowa and Idaho

Also Comrade Edward Remington Ridge
Who has prayed God since the April of 'Seventeen   210
To replace in his life his lost (M. E.) religion

And The New York Daily Worker *goes a 'blowing over Arkansas*
The New York Daily Worker *goes a 'blowing over Arkansas*
The grasses let it go along the Ozarks over Arkansas

Even Comrade Grenadine Grilt who has tried since
August tenth for something to feel about strongly in
Verses—his personal passions having tired

I can tell my land by the jays in the apple-trees
Tell my land by the jays in the apple-trees
I can tell my people by the blue-jays in the apple-trees   220

Aindt you read in d'books you are all brudders?
D' glassic historic objective broves you are brudders!
You and d' Wops and d' Chinks you are all brudders!
Havend't you got it d' same ideology? Havend't you?

[297]

When it's yesterday in Oregon it's one A M in Maine
And she slides: and the day slides: and it runs: runs over us:
And the bells strike twelve strike twelve strike twelve
In Marblehead in Buffalo in Cheyenne in Cherokee
Yesterday runs on the states like a crow's shadow

For Marx has said to us Workers what do you need?   230
And Stalin has said to us Starvers what do you need?
You need the Dialectical Materialism!

She's a tough land under the corn mister:
She has changed the bone in the cheeks of many races:
She has winced the eyes of the soft Slavs with her sun on them:
She has tried the fat from the round rumps of Italians:
Even the voice of the English has gone dry
And hard on the tongue and alive in the throat speaking:

She's a tough land under the oak-trees mister:
It may be she can change the word in the book   240
As she changes the bone of a man's head in his children:
It may be that the earth and the men remain . . .

There is too much sun on the lids of my eyes to be listening

189   ## Hero and Leander

FIRST SESTIAD

On Hellespont, guilty of true love's blood,
In view, and opposite, two cities stood,
Sea-borderers, disjoined by Neptune's might;
The one Abydos, the other Sestos hight.
At Sestos, Hero dwelt; Hero the fair,
Whom young Apollo courted for her hair,
And offered as a dower his burning throne,
Where she should sit for men to gaze upon.
The outside of her garments were of lawn,
The lining purple silk, with gilt stars drawn;   10
Her wide sleeves green, and bordered with a grove

[298]

Where Venus in her naked glory strove
To please the careless and disdainful eyes
Of proud Adonis, that before her lies;
Her kirtle blue, whereon was many a stain,
Made with the blood of wretched lovers slain.
Upon her head she ware a myrtle wreath,
From whence her veil reached to the ground beneath.
Her veil was artificial flowers and leaves,
Whose workmanship both man and beast deceives;   20
Many would praise the sweet smell as she passed,
When 'twas the odor which her breath forth cast;
And there for honey bees have sought in vain,
And, beat from thence, have lighted there again.
About her neck hung chains of pebble-stone,
Which, lightened by her neck, like diamonds shone.
She ware no gloves, for neither sun nor wind
Would burn or parch her hands, but to her mind,
Or warm or cool them, for they took delight
To play upon those hands, they were so white.   30
Buskins of shells all silvered, usèd she,
And branched with blushing coral to the knee,
Where sparrows perched, of hollow pearl and gold,
Such as the world would wonder to behold;
Those with sweet water oft her handmaid fills,
Which, as she went, would chirrup through the bills.
Some say, for her the fairest Cupid pined,
And, looking in her face, was strooken blind.
But this is true: so like was one the other,
As he imagined Hero was his mother;   40
And oftentimes into her bosom flew,
About her naked neck his bare arms threw,
And laid his childish head upon her breast,
And with still panting rocked, there took his rest.
So lovely fair was Hero, Venus' nun,
As nature wept, thinking she was undone,
Because she took more from her than she left
And of such wondrous beauty her bereft;
Therefore, in sign her treasure suffered wrack,

Since Hero's time hath half the world been black.   50
Amorous Leander, beautiful and young,
(Whose tragedy divine Musæus sung)
Dwelt at Abydos; since him dwelt there none
For whom succeeding times make greater moan.
His dangling tresses that were never shorn,
Had they been cut and unto Colchis borne,
Would have allured the vent'rous youth of Greece
To hazard more than for the Golden Fleece.
Fair Cynthia wished his arms might be her sphere;
Grief makes her pale, because she moves not there.   60
His body was as straight as Circe's wand;
Jove might have sipped out nectar from his hand.
Even as delicious meat is to the taste,
So was his neck in touching, and surpassed
The white of Pelops' shoulder. I could tell ye
How smooth his breast was, and how white his belly,
And whose immortal fingers did imprint
That heavenly path, with many a curious dint,
That runs along his back; but my rude pen
Can hardly blazon forth the loves of men,   70
Much less of powerful gods; let it suffice
That my slack muse sings of Leander's eyes,
Those orient cheeks and lips, exceeding his
That leapt into the water for a kiss
Of his own shadow, and despising many,
Died ere he could enjoy the love of any.
Had wild Hippolytus Leander seen,
Enamored of his beauty had he been;
His presence made the rudest peasant melt,
That in the vast uplandish country dwelt;   80
The barbarous Thracian soldier, moved with nought,
Was moved with him, and for his favor sought.
Some swore he was a maid in man's attire,
For in his looks were all that men desire:
A pleasant smiling cheek, a speaking eye,
A brow for love to banquet royally;
And such as knew he was a man, would say,

[300]

Leander, thou art made for amorous play;
Why art thou not in love, and loved of all?
Though thou be fair, yet be not thine own thrall. 90
   The men of wealthy Sestos every year,
For his sake whom their goddess held so dear,
Rose-cheeked Adonis, kept a solemn feast.
Thither resorted many a wand'ring guest
To meet their loves; such as had none at all,
Came lovers home from this great festival.
For every street, like to a firmament,
Glistered with breathing stars, who, where they went,
Frighted the melancholy earth, which deemed
Eternal heaven to burn, for so it seemed 100
As if another Phaeton had got
The guidance of the sun's rich chariot.
But, far above the loveliest, Hero shined,
And stole away th' enchanted gazer's mind;
For like sea-nymphs' inveigling harmony,
So was her beauty to the standers by.
Nor that night-wand'ring pale and wat'ry star
(When yawning dragons draw her thirling car
From Latmos' mount up to the gloomy sky,
Where, crowned with blazing light and majesty, 110
She proudly sits) more over-rules the flood,
Than she the hearts of those that near her stood.
Even as when gaudy nymphs pursue the chase,
Wretched Ixion's shaggy-footed race,
Incensed with savage heat, gallop amain
From steep pine-bearing mountains to the plain,
So ran the people forth to gaze upon her,
And all that viewed her were enamored on her.
And as in fury of a dreadful fight,
Their fellows being slain or put to flight, 120
Poor soldiers stand with fear of death dead-strooken,
So at her presence all, surprised and tooken,
Await the sentence of her scornful eyes;
He whom she favors lives, the other dies.
There might you see one sigh, another rage,

[301]

And some, their violent passions to assuage,
Compile sharp satires; but alas, too late,
For faithful love will never turn to hate.
And many, seeing great princes were denied,
Pined as they went, and thinking on her, died. 130
On this feast day, oh, cursed day and hour!
Went Hero thorough Sestos, from her tower
To Venus' temple, where unhappily,
As after chanced, they did each other spy.
So fair a church as this had Venus none;
The walls were of discolored jasper stone,
Wherein was Proteus carvèd, and o'erhead
A lively vine of green sea-agate spread,
Where by one hand light-headed Bacchus hung,
And with the other wine from grapes out-wrung. 140
Of crystal shining fair the pavement was;
The town of Sestos called it Venus' glass;
There might you see the gods in sundry shapes,
Committing heady riots, incest, rapes;
For know that underneath this radiant floor
Was Danaë's statue in a brazen tower;
Jove slyly stealing from his sister's bed
To dally with Idalian Ganymed,
And for his love Europa bellowing loud,
And tumbling with the rainbow in a cloud; 150
Blood-quaffing Mars heaving the iron net
Which limping Vulcan and his Cyclops set;
Love kindling fire to burn such towns as Troy;
Silvanus weeping for the lovely boy
That now is turned into a cypress tree,
Under whose shade the wood-gods love to be.
And in the midst a silver altar stood;
There Hero sacrificing turtles' blood,
Veiled to the ground, veiling her eyelids close,
And modestly they opened as she rose; 160
Thence flew love's arrow with the golden head,
And thus Leander was enamorèd.
Stone still he stood, and evermore he gazed,

Till with the fire that from his count'nance blazed,
Relenting Hero's gentle heart was strook;
Such force and virtue hath an amorous look.
　　It lies not in our power to love or hate,
For will in us is over-ruled by fate.
When two are stripped, long ere the course begin
We wish that one should lose, the other win;　　170
And one especially do we affect
Of two gold ingots, like in each respect.
The reason no man knows, let it suffice,
What we behold is censured by our eyes.
Where both deliberate, the love is slight;
Who ever loved, that loved not at first sight?
　　He kneeled, but unto her devoutly prayed;
Chaste Hero to herself thus softly said:
Were I the saint he worships, I would hear him;
And as she spake these words, came somewhat near him.　180
He started up; she blushed as one ashamed;
Wherewith Leander much more was inflamed.
He touched her hand; in touching it she trembled;
Love deeply grounded hardly is dissembled.
These lovers parlèd by the touch of hands;
True love is mute, and oft amazèd stands.
Thus while dumb signs their yielding hearts entangled,
The air with sparks of living fire was spangled,
And night, deep drenched in misty Acheron,
Heaved up her head, and half the world upon　　190
Breathed darkness forth (dark night is Cupid's day).
And now begins Leander to display
Love's holy fire with words, with sighs, and tears,
Which like sweet music entered Hero's ears;
And yet at every word she turned aside,
And always cut him off as he replied.
At last, like to a bold sharp sophister,
With cheerful hope thus he accosted her:
　　Fair creature, let me speak without offense;
I would my rude words had the influence　　200
To lead thy thoughts as thy fair looks do mine!

Then shouldst thou be his prisoner who is thine.
Be not unkind and fair; misshapen stuff
Are of behavior boisterous and rough.
Oh, shun me not, but hear me ere you go,
God knows I cannot force love, as you do.
My words shall be as spotless as my youth,
Full of simplicity and naked truth.
This sacrifice, whose sweet perfume descending
From Venus' altar to your footsteps bending, 210
Doth testify that you exceed her far,
To whom you offer, and whose nun you are.
Why should you worship her? her you surpass
As much as sparkling diamonds flaring glass.
A diamond set in lead his worth retains;
A heavenly nymph, beloved of human swains,
Receives no blemish, but ofttimes more grace;
Which makes me hope, although I am but base,
Base in respect of thee, divine and pure,
Dutiful service may thy love procure, 220
And I in duty will excel all other,
As thou in beauty dost exceed Love's mother.
Nor heaven, nor thou, were made to gaze upon;
As heaven preserves all things, so save thou one.
A stately builded ship, well rigged and tall,
The ocean maketh more majestical;
Why vowest thou then to live in Sestos here,
Who on love's seas more glorious would appear?
Like untuned golden strings all women are,
Which long time lie untouched, will harshly jar. 230
Vessels of brass, oft handled, brightly shine;
What difference betwixt the richest mine
And basest mold, but use? for both, not used,
Are of like worth. Then treasure is abused,
When misers keep it; being put to loan,
In time it will return us two for one.
Rich robes themselves and others do adorn;
Neither themselves nor others, if not worn.
Who builds a palace, and rams up the gate,

Shall see it ruinous and desolate.   240
Ah, simple Hero, learn thyself to cherish!
Lone women, like to empty houses, perish.
Less sins the poor rich man that starves himself
In heaping up a mass of drossy pelf,
Than such as you; his golden earth remains,
Which after his decease some other gains;
But this fair gem, sweet in the loss alone,
When you fleet hence, can be bequeathed to none.
Or if it could, down from th' enameled sky
All heaven would come to claim this legacy,   250
And with intestine broils the world destroy,
And quite confound nature's sweet harmony.
Well therefore by the gods decreed it is
We human creatures should enjoy that bliss.
One is no number; maids are nothing, then,
Without the sweet society of men.
Wilt thou live single still? one shalt thou be
Though never-singling Hymen couple thee.
Wild savages, that drink of running springs,
Think water far excels all earthly things,   260
But they that daily taste neat wine, despise it;
Virginity, albeit some highly prize it,
Compared with marriage, had you tried them both,
Differs as much as wine and water doth.
Base bullion for the stamp's sake we allow;
Even so for men's impression do we you,
By which alone, our reverend fathers say,
Women receive perfection every way.
This idol which you term virginity
Is neither essence subject to the eye,   270
No, nor to any one exterior sense,
Nor hath it any place of residence,
Nor is 't of earth or mold celestial,
Or capable of any form at all.
Of that which hath no being, do not boast;
Things that are not at all, are never lost.
Men foolishly do call it virtuous;

What virtue is it, that is born with us?
Much less can honor be ascribed thereto;
Honor is purchased by the deeds we do.   280
Believe me, Hero, honor is not won
Until some honorable deed be done.
Seek you, for chastity, immortal fame,
And know that some have wronged Diana's name?
Whose name is it, if she be false or not,
So she be fair, but some vile tongues will blot?
But you are fair, ay me, so wondrous fair,
So young, so gentle, and so debonair,
As Greece will think, if thus you live alone,
Some one or other keeps you as his own.   290
Then, Hero, hate me not, nor from me fly
To follow swiftly blasting infamy.
Perhaps thy sacred priesthood makes thee loath;
Tell me, to whom mad'st thou that heedless oath?
     To Venus, answered she, and as she spake,
Forth from those two tralucent cisterns brake
A stream of liquid pearl, which down her face
Made milk-white paths, whereon the gods might trace
To Jove's high court. He thus replied: The rites
In which love's beauteous empress most delights   300
Are banquets, Doric music, midnight revel,
Plays, masks, and all that stern age counteth evil.
Thee as a holy idiot doth she scorn,
For thou, in vowing chastity, hast sworn
To rob her name and honor, and thereby
Commit'st a sin far worse than perjury,
Even sacrilege against her deity,
Through regular and formal purity.
To expiate which sin, kiss and shake hands;
Such sacrifice as this Venus demands.   310
     Thereat she smiled, and did deny him so
As, put thereby, yet might he hope for mo.
Which makes him quickly reinforce his speech,
And her in humble manner thus beseech:
     Though neither gods nor men may thee deserve,

[306]

Yet for her sake whom you have vowed to serve,
Abandon fruitless cold virginity,
The gentle queen of love's sole enemy.
Then shall you most resemble Venus' nun,
When Venus' sweet rites are performed and done.   320
Flint-breasted Pallas joys in single life,
But Pallas and your mistress are at strife.
Love, Hero, then, and be not tyrannous,
But heal the heart that thou hast wounded thus;
Nor stain thy youthful years with avarice;
Fair fools delight to be accounted nice.
The richest corn dies if it be not reaped;
Beauty alone is lost, too warily kept.
These arguments he used, and many more,
Wherewith she yielded, that was won before.   330
Hero's looks yielded, but her words made war;
Women are won when they begin to jar.
Thus having swallowed Cupid's golden hook,
The more she strived, the deeper was she strook;
Yet, evilly feigning anger, strove she still,
And would be thought to grant against her will.
So having paused a while, at last she said:
Who taught thee rhetoric to deceive a maid?
Ay me! such words as these should I abhor,
And yet I like them for the orator.   340
    With that Leander stooped to have embraced her,
But from his spreading arms away she cast her,
And thus bespake him: Gentle youth, forbear
To touch the sacred garments which I wear.
    Upon a rock, and underneath a hill,
Far from the town, where all is whist and still
Save that the sea playing on yellow sand
Sends forth a rattling murmur to the land,
Whose sound allures the golden Morpheus
In silence of the night to visit us,   350
My turret stands; and there, God knows, I play
With Venus' swans and sparrows all the day.
A dwarfish beldame bears me company,

That hops about the chamber where I lie,
And spends the night, that might be better spent,
In vain discourse and apish merriment.
Come thither. As she spake this, her tongue tripped,
For unawares, Come thither, from her slipped;
And suddenly her former color changed,
And here and there her eyes through anger ranged.   360
And like a planet moving several ways
At one self instant, she, poor soul, assays,
Loving, not to love at all, and every part
Strove to resist the motions of her heart;
And hands so pure, so innocent, nay such
As might have made heaven stoop to have a touch,
Did she uphold to Venus, and again
Vowed spotless chastity, but all in vain.
Cupid beats down her prayers with his wings;
Her vows above the empty air he flings;   370
All deep enraged, his sinewy bow he bent,
And shot a shaft that burning from him went;
Wherewith she, strooken, looked so dolefully,
As made Love sigh to see his tyranny.
And as she wept, her tears to pearl he turned,
And wound them on his arm, and for her mourned.
Then towards the palace of the Destinies,
Laden with languishment and grief, he flies,
And to those stern nymphs humbly made request,
Both might enjoy each other, and be blest.   380
But with a ghastly dreadful countenance,
Threat'ning a thousand deaths at every glance,
They answered Love, nor would vouchsafe so much
As one poor word, their hate to him was such.
Hearken awhile, and I will tell you why:
Heaven's wingèd herald, Jove-born Mercury,
The self-same day that he asleep had laid
Enchanted Argus, spied a country maid,
Whose careless hair, instead of pearl t' adorn it,
Glistered with dew, as one that seemed to scorn it;   390
Her breath as fragrant as the morning rose,

Her mind pure, and her tongue untaught to gloze;
Yet proud she was, for lofty pride that dwells
In towered courts is oft in shepherds' cells,
And too too well the fair vermilion knew,
And silver tincture of her cheeks, that drew
The love of every swain. On her this god
Enamored was, and with his snaky rod
Did charm her nimble feet, and made her stay,
The while upon a hillock down he lay, 400
And sweetly on his pipe began to play,
And with smooth speech her fancy to assay;
Till in his twining arms he locked her fast,
And then he wooed with kisses, and at last,
As shepherds do, her on the ground he laid,
And tumbling in the grass, he often strayed
Beyond the bounds of shame, in being bold
To eye those parts which no eye should behold.
And like an insolent commanding lover,
Boasting his parentage, would needs discover 410
The way to new Elysium; but she,
Whose only dower was her chastity,
Having striv'n in vain, was now about to cry,
And crave the help of shepherds that were nigh.
Herewith he stayed his fury, and began
To give her leave to rise; away she ran;
After went Mercury, who used such cunning,
As she, to hear his tale, left off her running;
Maids are not won by brutish force and might,
But speeches full of pleasure and delight; 420
And knowing Hermes courted her, was glad
That she such loveliness and beauty had
As could provoke his liking, yet was mute,
And neither would deny nor grant his suit.
Still vowed he love, she wanting no excuse
To feed him with delays, as women use,
Or thirsting after immortality—
All women are ambitious naturally—
Imposed upon her lover such a task

As he ought not perform, nor yet she ask.
A draught of flowing nectar she requested,
Wherewith the king of gods and men is feasted.
He, ready to accomplish what she willed,
Stole some from Hebe (Hebe Jove's cup filled)
And gave it to his simple rustic love;
Which being known (as what is hid from Jove?)
He inly stormed, and waxed more furious
Than for the fire filched by Prometheus,
And thrusts him down from heaven; he wand'ring here
In mournful terms, with sad and heavy cheer,
Complained to Cupid. Cupid, for his sake,
To be revenged on Jove did undertake;
And those on whom heaven, earth, and hell relies,
I mean the adamantine Destinies,
He wounds with love, and forced them equally
To dote upon deceitful Mercury.
They offered him the deadly fatal knife
That shears the slender threads of human life;
At his fair-feathered feet the engines laid
Which th' earth from ugly Chaos' den upweighed;
These he regarded not, but did entreat
That Jove, usurper of his father's seat,
Might presently be banished into hell,
And aged Saturn in Olympus dwell.
They granted what he craved, and once again
Saturn and Ops began their golden reign.
Murder, rape, war, lust, and treachery
Were with Jove closed in Stygian empery.
But long this blessed time continued not;
As soon as he his wishèd purpose got,
He, reckless of his promise, did despise
The love of th' everlasting Destinies.
They seeing it, both Love and him abhorred,
And Jupiter unto his place restored.
And but that Learning, in despite of Fate,
Will mount aloft, and enter heaven gate,
And to the seat of Jove itself advance,

Hermes had slept in hell with Ignorance;
Yet as a punishment they added this,
That he and Poverty should always kiss.   470
And to this day is every scholar poor;
Gross gold from them runs headlong to the boor.
Likewise, the angry sisters thus deluded,
To venge themselves on Hermes, have concluded
That Midas' brood shall sit in Honor's chair,
To which the Muses' sons are only heir;
And fruitful wits that inaspiring are,
Shall, discontent, run into regions far;
And few great lords in virtuous deeds shall joy,
But be surprised with every garish toy;   480
And still enrich the lofty servile clown,
Who with encroaching guile keeps learning down.
Then muse not Cupid's suit no better sped,
Seeing in their loves the Fates were injurèd.

SECOND SESTIAD

By this, sad Hero, with love unacquainted,
Viewing Leander's face, fell down and fainted.
He kissed her and breathed life into her lips,
Wherewith, as one displeased, away she trips.
Yet as she went, full often looked behind,
And many poor excuses did she find
To linger by the way, and once she stayed
And would have turned again, but was afraid,
In off'ring parley, to be counted light.
So on she goes, and in her idle flight,   10
Her painted fan of curlèd plumes let fall,
Thinking to train Leander therewithal.
He, being a novice, knew not what she meant,
But stayed, and after her a letter sent,
Which joyful Hero answered in such sort
As he had hope to scale the beauteous fort
Wherein the liberal graces locked their wealth,
And therefore to her tower he got by stealth.
Wide open stood the door, he need not climb;

And she herself, before the 'pointed time,   20
Had spread the board, with roses strewed the room,
And oft looked out, and mused he did not come.
At last he came; oh, who can tell the greeting
These greedy lovers had at their first meeting.
He asked, she gave, and nothing was denied;
Both to each other quickly were affied.
Look how their hands, so were their hearts united,
And what he did she willingly requited.
Sweet are the kisses, the embracements sweet,
When like desires and affections meet;   30
For from the earth to heaven is Cupid raised,
Where fancy is in equal balance peised.
Yet she this rashness suddenly repented,
And turned aside, and to herself lamented,
As if her name and honor had been wronged
By being possessed of him for whom she longed;
Ay, and she wished, albeit not from her heart,
That he would leave her turret and depart.
The mirthful god of amorous pleasure smiled
To see how he this captive nymph beguiled;   40
For hitherto he did but fan the fire,
And kept it down that it might mount the higher.
Now waxed she jealous lest his love abated,
Fearing her own thoughts made her to be hated.
Therefore unto him hastily she goes,
And like light Salmacis, her body throws
Upon his bosom, where with yielding eyes
She offers up herself, a sacrifice
To slake his anger if he were displeased.
Oh, what god would not therewith be appeased?   50
Like Æsop's cock, this jewel he enjoyed,
And as a brother with his sister toyed,
Supposing nothing else was to be done,
Now he her favor and goodwill had won.
But know you not that creatures wanting sense
By nature have a mutual appetence,
And wanting organs to advance a step,

[312]

Moved by love's force, unto each other lep?
Much more in subjects having intellect,
Some hidden influence breeds like effect.   60
Albeit Leander, rude in love and raw,
Long dallying with Hero, nothing saw
That might delight him more, yet he suspected
Some amorous rites or other were neglected.
Therefore unto his body hers he clung;
She, fearing on the rushes to be flung,
Strived with redoubled strength; the more she strived,
The more a gentle pleasing heat revived,
Which taught him all that elder lovers know;
And now the same gan so to scorch and glow,   70
As in plain terms, yet cunningly, he craved it;
Love always makes those eloquent that have it.
She, with a kind of granting, put him by it,
And ever as he thought himself most nigh it,
Like to the tree of Tantalus she fled,
And, seeming lavish, saved her maidenhead.
Ne'er king more sought to keep his diadem,
Than Hero this inestimable gem.
Above our life we love a steadfast friend,
Yet when a token of great worth we send,   80
We often kiss it, often look thereon,
And stay the messenger that would be gone;
No marvel then though Hero would not yield
So soon to part from that she dearly held;
Jewels being lost are found again, this never;
'Tis lost but once, and once lost, lost forever.

    Now had the morn espied her lover's steeds,
Whereat she starts, puts on her purple weeds,
And, red for anger that he stayed so long,
All headlong throws herself the clouds among.   90
And now Leander, fearing to be missed,
Embraced her suddenly, took leave, and kissed.
Long was he taking leave, and loath to go,
And kissed again, as lovers use to do.
Sad Hero wrung him by the hand and wept,

Saying, Let your vows and promises be kept.
Then, standing at the door, she turned about,
As loath to see Leander going out.
And now the sun that through th' horizon peeps,
As pitying these lovers, downward creeps,   100
So that in silence of the cloudy night,
Though it was morning, did he take his flight.
But what the secret trusty night concealed,
Leander's amorous habit soon revealed;
With Cupid's myrtle was his bonnet crowned,
About his arms the purple riband wound
Wherewith she wreathed her largely-spreading hair;
Nor could the youth abstain, but he must wear
The sacred ring wherewith she was endowed,
When first religious chastity she vowed;   110
Which made his love through Sestos to be known,
And thence unto Abydos sooner blown
Than he could sail, for incorporeal Fame,
Whose weight consists in nothing but her name,
Is swifter than the wind, whose tardy plumes
Are reeking water and dull earthly fumes.
Home, when he came, he seemed not to be there,
But like exilèd air thrust from his sphere,
Set in a foreign place; and straight from thence,
Alcides like, by mighty violence   120
He would have chased away the swelling main
That him from her unjustly did detain.
Like as the sun in a diameter
Fires and inflames objects removèd far,
And heateth kindly, shining lat'rally,
So beauty sweetly quickens when 'tis nigh,
But being separated and removed,
Burns where it cherished, murders where it loved.
Therefore even as an index to a book,
So to his mind was young Leander's look.   130
Oh, none but gods have power their love to hide;
Affection by the count'nance is descried.
The light of hidden fire itself discovers,

And love that is concealed betrays poor lovers.
His secret flame apparently was seen;
Leander's father knew where he had been,
And for the same mildly rebuked his son,
Thinking to quench the sparkles new begun.
But love, resisted once, grows passionate,
And nothing more than counsel lovers hate;   140
For as a hot proud horse highly disdains
To have his head controlled, but breaks the reins,
Spits forth the ringled bit, and with his hooves
Checks the submissive ground, so he that loves,
The more he is restrained, the worse he fares.
What is it now but mad Leander dares?
O Hero, Hero! thus he cried full oft,
And then he got him to a rock aloft,
Where having spied her tower, long stared he on 't,
And prayed the narrow toiling Hellespont   150
To part in twain, that he might come and go;
But still the rising billows answered no.
With that he stripped him to the iv'ry skin,
And crying, Love, I come, leaped lively in.
Whereat the sapphire-visaged god grew proud,
And made his cap'ring Triton sound aloud,
Imagining that Ganymede, displeased,
Had left the heavens; therefore on him he seized.
Leander strived; the waves about him wound,
And pulled him to the bottom, where the ground   160
Was strewed with pearl, and in low coral groves
Sweet singing mermaids sported with their loves
On heaps of heavy gold, and took great pleasure
To spurn in careless sort the shipwreck treasure.
For here the stately azure palace stood,
Where kingly Neptune and his train abode.
The lusty god embraced him, called him love,
And swore he never should return to Jove.
But when he knew it was not Ganymede,
For under water he was almost dead,   170
He heaved him up, and looking on his face,

Beat down the bold waves with his triple mace,
Which mounted up, intending to have kissed him,
And fell in drops like tears, because they missed him.
Leander, being up, began to swim,
And looking back, saw Neptune follow him;
Whereat aghast, the poor soul gan to cry:
Oh, let me visit Hero ere I die!
The god put Helle's bracelet on his arm,
And swore the sea should never do him harm.   180
He clapped his plump cheeks, with his tresses played,
And smiling wantonly, his love bewrayed.
He watched his arms, and as they opened wide,
At every stroke betwixt them would he slide,
And steal a kiss, and then run out and dance,
And as he turned, cast many a lustful glance,
And threw him gaudy toys to please his eye,
And dive into the water, and there pry
Upon his breast, his thighs, and every limb,
And up again, and close beside him swim,   190
And talk of love. Leander made reply:
You are deceived, I am no woman, I.
Thereat smiled Neptune, and then told a tale
How that a shepherd, sitting in a vale,
Played with a boy so fair and kind,
As for his love both earth and heaven pined;
That of the cooling river durst not drink
Lest water-nymphs should pull him from the brink;
And when he sported in the fragrant lawns,
Goat-footed satyrs and up-staring fauns   200
Would steal him thence. Ere half this tale was done,
Ay me, Leander cried, th' enamored sun,
That now should shine on Thetis' glassy bower,
Descends upon my radiant Hero's tower.
Oh, that these tardy arms of mine were wings!
And as he spake, upon the waves he springs.
Neptune was angry that he gave no ear,
And in his heart revenging malice bear;
He flung at him his mace, but as it went

He called it in, for love made him repent. 210
The mace returning back, his own hand hit,
As meaning to be venged for darting it.
When this fresh bleeding wound Leander viewed,
His color went and came, as if he rued
The grief which Neptune felt. In gentle breasts
Relenting thoughts, remorse, and pity rests;
And who have hard hearts and obdurate minds
But vicious, hare-brained, and illit'rate hinds?
The god, seeing him with pity to be moved,
Thereon concluded that he was beloved. 220
(Love is too full of faith, too credulous,
With folly and false hope deluding us.)
Wherefore, Leander's fancy to surprise,
To the rich oceàn for gifts he flies.
'Tis wisdom to give much; a gift prevails
When deep persuading oratory fails.
By this, Leander being near the land,
Cast down his weary feet, and felt the sand.
Breathless albeit he were, he rested not
Till to the solitary tower he got, 230
And knocked and called, at which celestial noise
The longing heart of Hero much more joys
Than nymphs or shepherds when the timbrel rings,
Or crooked dolphin when the sailor sings;
She stayed not for her robes, but straight arose,
And drunk with gladness, to the door she goes;
Where seeing a naked man, she screeched for fear,
(Such sights as this to tender maids are rare)
And ran into the dark herself to hide.
Rich jewels in the dark are soonest spied; 240
Unto her was he led, or rather drawn,
By those white limbs which sparkled through the lawn.
The nearer that he came, the more she fled,
And seeking refuge, slipped into her bed.
Whereon Leander sitting, thus began,
Through numbing cold all feeble, faint, and wan:
    If not for love, yet, love, for pity sake,

Me in thy bed and maiden bosom take;
At least vouchsafe these arms some little room,
Who, hoping to embrace thee, cheerly swoom;   250
This head was beat with many a churlish billow,
And therefore let it rest upon thy pillow.
Herewith affrighted Hero shrunk away,
And in her lukewarm place Leander lay,
Whose lively heat like fire from heaven fet,
Would animate gross clay, and higher set
The drooping thoughts of base declining souls,
Than dreary Mars carousing nectar bowls.
His hands he cast upon her like a snare;
She, overcome with shame and sallow fear,   260
Like chaste Diana, when Actæon spied her,
Being suddenly betrayed, dived down to hide her;
And as her silver body downward went,
With both her hands she made the bed a tent,
And in her own mind thought herself secure,
O'ercast with dim and darksome coverture.
And now she lets him whisper in her ear,
Flatter, entreat, promise, protest, and swear;
Yet ever as he greedily assayed
To touch those dainties, she the harpy played,   270
And every limb did, as a soldier stout,
Defend the fort and keep the foeman out;
For though the rising iv'ry mount he scaled,
Which is with azure circling lines empaled,
Much like a globe (a globe may I term this,
By which love sails to regions full of bliss)
Yet there with Sisyphus he toiled in vain,
Till gentle parley did the truce obtain.
Wherein Leander on her quivering breast,
Breathless spoke something, and sighed out the rest;   280
Which so prevailed, as he with small ado
Enclosed her in his arms and kissed her too.
And every kiss to her was as a charm,
And to Leander as a fresh alarm,
So that the truce was broke, and she, alas,

Poor silly maiden, at his mercy was.
Love is not full of pity, as men say,
But deaf and cruel where he means to prey.
Even as a bird, which in our hands we wring,
Forth plunges and oft flutters with her wing,   290
She trembling strove; this strife of hers, like that
Which made the world, another world begat
Of unknown joy. Treason was in her thought,
And cunningly to yield herself she sought.
Seeming not won, yet won she was at length;
In such wars women use but half their strength.
Leander now, like Theban Hercules,
Entered the orchard of th' Hesperides,
Whose fruit none rightly can describe but he
That pulls or shakes it from the golden tree.   300
And now she wished this night were never done,
And sighed to think upon th' approaching sun;
For much it grieved her that the bright daylight
Should know the pleasure of this blessed night,
And them like Mars and Erycine displayed,
Both in each other's arms chained as they laid.
Again she knew not how to frame her look,
Or speak to him who in a moment took
That which so long so charily she kept;
And fain by stealth away she would have crept,   310
And to some corner secretly have gone,
Leaving Leander in the bed alone.
But as her naked feet were whipping out,
He on the sudden clinged her so about,
That mermaid-like unto the floor she slid,
One half appeared, the other half was hid.
Thus near the bed she blushing stood upright,
And from her countenance behold ye might
A kind of twilight break, which through the hair,
As from an orient cloud, glimpse here and there;   320
And round about the chamber this false morn
Brought forth the day before the day was born.
So Hero's ruddy cheek Hero betrayed,

And her all naked to his sight displayed;
Whence his admiring eyes more pleasure took
Than Dis on heaps of gold fixing his look.
By this, Apollo's golden harp began
To sound forth music to the oceàn;
Which watchful Hesperus no sooner heard,
But he the day-bright-bearing car prepared,   330
And ran before, as harbinger of light,
And with his flaring beams mocked ugly night
Till she, o'ercome with anguish, shame, and rage,
Danged down to hell her loathsome carriage.
Desunt nonnulla.

190

The Eve of St. Agnes

St. Agnes' Eve—Ah, bitter chill it was!
The owl, for all his feathers, was a-cold;
The hare limp'd trembling through the frozen grass,
And silent was the flock in woolly fold:
Numb were the beadsman's fingers, while he told
His rosary, and while his frosted breath,
Like pious incense from a censer old,
Seem'd taking flight for heaven, without a death,
Past the sweet Virgin's picture, while his prayer he saith.

His prayer he saith, this patient, holy man;   10
Then takes his lamp, and riseth from his knees,
And back returneth, meager, barefoot, wan,
Along the chapel aisle by slow degrees:
The sculptur'd dead, on each side, seem to freeze,
Emprison'd in black, purgatorial rails:
Knights, ladies, praying in dumb orat'ries,
He passeth by; and his weak spirit fails
To think how they may ache in icy hoods and mails.

[320]

Northward he turneth through a little door,
And scarce three steps, ere Music's golden tongue 20
Flatter'd to tears this aged man and poor;
But no—already had his deathbell rung:
The joys of all his life were said and sung:
His was harsh penance on St. Agnes' Eve:
Another way he went, and soon among
Rough ashes sat he for his soul's reprieve,
And all night kept awake, for sinners' sake to grieve.

That ancient beadsman heard the prelude soft;
And so it chanc'd, for many a door was wide,
From hurry to and fro. Soon, up aloft, 30
The silver, snarling trumpets 'gan to chide:
The level chambers, ready with their pride,
Were glowing to receive a thousand guests:
The carved angels, ever eager-eyed,
Star'd, where upon their heads the cornice rests,
With hair blown back, and wings put cross-wise on their breasts.

At length burst in the argent revelry,
With plume, tiara, and all rich array,
Numerous as shadows haunting fairily
The brain, new stuff'd, in youth, with triumphs gay 40
Of old romance. These let us wish away,
And turn, sole-thoughted, to one lady there,
Whose heart had brooded, all that wintry day,
On love, and wing'd St. Agnes' saintly care,
As she had heard old dames full many times declare.

They told her how, upon St. Agnes' Eve,
Young virgins might have visions of delight,
And soft adorings from their loves receive
Upon the honey'd middle of the night,
If ceremonies due they did aright; 50
As, supperless to bed they must retire,
And couch supine their beauties, lily white;
Nor look behind, nor sideways, but require
Of Heaven with upward eyes for all that they desire.

Full of this whim was thoughtful Madeline:
The music, yearning like a god in pain,
She scarcely heard: her maiden eyes divine,
Fix'd on the floor, saw many a sweeping train
Pass by—she heeded not at all: in vain
Came many a tiptoe, amorous cavalier,   60
And back retir'd; not cool'd by high disdain,
But she saw not: her heart was otherwhere:
She sigh'd for Agnes' dreams, the sweetest of the year.

She danc'd along with vague, regardless eyes,
Anxious her lips, her breathing quick and short:
The hallow'd hour was near at hand: she sighs
Amid the timbrels, and the throng'd resort
Of whisperers in anger, or in sport;
'Mid looks of love, defiance, hate, and scorn,
Hoodwink'd with faery fancy; all amort,   70
Save to St. Agnes and her lambs unshorn,
And all the bliss to be before tomorrow morn.

So, purposing each moment to retire,
She linger'd still. Meantime, across the moors,
Had come young Porphyro, with heart on fire
For Madeline. Beside the portal doors,
Buttress'd from moonlight, stands he, and implores
All saints to give him sight of Madeline,
But for one moment in the tedious hours,
That he might gaze and worship all unseen;   80
Perchance speak, kneel, touch, kiss—in sooth such things have been.

He ventures in: let no buzz'd whisper tell:
All eyes be muffled, or a hundred swords
Will storm his heart, Love's fev'rous citadel:
For him, those chambers held barbarian hordes,
Hyena foemen, and hot-blooded lords,
Whose very dogs would execrations howl
Against his lineage: not one breast affords
Him any mercy, in that mansion foul,
Save one old beldame, weak in body and in soul.   90

Ah, happy chance! the aged creature came,
Shuffling along with ivory-headed wand,
To where he stood, hid from the torch's flame,
Behind a broad hall-pillar, far beyond
The sound of merriment and chorus bland:
He startled her; but soon she knew his face,
And grasp'd his fingers in her palsied hand,
Saying, 'Mercy, Porphyro! hie thee from this place:
They are all here tonight, the whole blood-thirsty race!

'Get hence! get hence! there's dwarfish Hildebrand;   100
He had a fever late, and in the fit
He cursed thee and thine, both house and land:
Then there's that old Lord Maurice, not a whit
More tame for his gray hairs—Alas me! flit!
Flit like a ghost away.'—'Ah, gossip dear,
We're safe enough; here in this armchair sit,
And tell me how'—'Good Saints! not here, not here;
Follow me, child, or else these stones will be thy bier.'

He follow'd through a lowly arched way,
Brushing the cobwebs with his lofty plume,   110
And as she mutter'd 'Well-a—well-a-day!'
He found him in a little moonlight room,
Pale, lattic'd, chill, and silent as a tomb.
'Now tell me where is Madeline,' said he,
'O tell me, Angela, by the holy loom
Which none but secret sisterhood may see,
When they St. Agnes' wool are weaving piously.'

'St. Agnes! Ah! it is St. Agnes' Eve—
Yet men will murder upon holy days:
Thou must hold water in a witch's sieve,   120
And be liege-lord of all the elves and fays,
To venture so: it fills me with amaze
To see thee, Porphyro!—St. Agnes' Eve!
God's help! my lady fair the conjuror plays
This very night: good angels her deceive!
But let me laugh awhile, I've mickle time to grieve.'

[323]

Feebly she laugheth in the languid moon,
While Porphyro upon her face doth look,
Like puzzled urchin on an aged crone
Who keepeth clos'd a wond'rous riddle-book,   130
As spectacled she sits in chimney nook.
But soon his eyes grew brilliant, when she told
His lady's purpose; and he scarce could brook
Tears, at the thought of those enchantments cold,
And Madeline asleep in lap of legends old.

Sudden a thought came like a full-blown rose,
Flushing his brow, and in his pained heart
Made purple riot: then doth he propose
A stratagem, that makes the beldame start:
'A cruel man and impious thou art: 140
Sweet lady, let her pray, and sleep, and dream
Alone with her good angels, far apart
From wicked men like thee. Go, go!—I deem
Thou canst not surely be the same that thou didst seem.'

'I will not harm her, by all saints I swear,'
Quoth Porphyro: 'O may I ne'er find grace
When my weak voice shall whisper its last prayer,
If one of her soft ringlets I displace,
Or look with ruffian passion in her face:
Good Angela, believe me by these tears;   150
Or I will, even in a moment's space,
Awake, with horrid shout, my foemen's ears,
And beard them, though they be more fang'd than wolves and bears.'

'Ah! why wilt thou affright a feeble soul?
A poor, weak, palsy-stricken, churchyard thing,
Whose passing-bell may ere the midnight toll;
Whose prayers for thee, each morn and evening,
Were never miss'd.'—Thus plaining, doth she bring
A gentler speech from burning Porphyro;
So woful, and of such deep sorrowing,   160
That Angela gives promise she will do
Whatever he shall wish, betide her weal or woe.

Which was, to lead him, in close secrecy,
Even to Madeline's chamber, and there hide
Him in a closet, of such privacy
That he might see her beauty unespied,
And win perhaps that night a peerless bride,
While legion'd fairies pac'd the coverlet,
And pale enchantment held her sleepy-eyed.
Never on such a night have lovers met,   170
Since Merlin paid his demon all the monstrous debt.

'It shall be as thou wishest,' said the dame:
'All cates and dainties shall be stored there
Quickly on this feast-night: by the tambour frame
Her own lute thou wilt see: no time to spare,
For I am slow and feeble, and scarce dare
On such a catering trust my dizzy head.
Wait here, my child, with patience; kneel in prayer
The while. Ah! thou must needs the lady wed,
Or may I never leave my grave among the dead.'   180

So saying, she hobbled off with busy fear.
The lover's endless minutes slowly pass'd;
The dame return'd, and whisper'd in his ear
To follow her; with aged eyes aghast
From fright of dim espial. Safe at last,
Through many a dusky gallery, they gain
The maiden's chamber, silken, hush'd, and chaste;
Where Porphyro took covert, pleas'd amain.
His poor guide hurried back with agues in her brain.

Her falt'ring hand upon the balustrade,   190
Old Angela was feeling for the stair,
When Madeline, St. Agnes' charmed maid,
Rose, like a mission'd spirit, unaware:
With silver taper's light, and pious care,
She turn'd, and down the aged gossip led
To a safe level matting. Now prepare,
Young Porphyro, for gazing on that bed;
She comes, she comes again, like ringdove fray'd and fled.

[325]

Out went the taper as she hurried in;
Its little smoke, in pallid moonshine, died: 200
She clos'd the door, she panted, all akin
To spirits of the air, and visions wide:
No uttered syllable, or, woe betide!
But to her heart, her heart was voluble,
Paining with eloquence her balmy side;
As though a tongueless nightingale should swell
Her throat in vain, and die, heart-stifled, in her dell.

A casement high and triple-arch'd there was,
All garlanded with carven imag'ries
Of fruits, and flowers, and bunches of knot-grass,   210
And diamonded with panes of quaint device,
Innumerable of stains and splendid dyes,
As are the tiger-moth's deep-damask'd wings;
And in the midst, 'mid thousand heraldries,
And twilight saints, and dim emblazonings,
A shielded scutcheon blush'd with blood of queens and kings.

Full on this casement shone the wintry moon,
And threw warm gules on Madeline's fair breast,
As down she knelt for heaven's grace and boon;
Rose-bloom fell on her hands, together prest,   220
And on her silver cross soft amethyst,
And on her hair a glory, like a saint:
She seem'd a splendid angel, newly drest,
Save wings, for heaven:—Porphyro grew faint:
She knelt, so pure a thing, so free from mortal taint.

Anon his heart revives: her vespers done,
Of all its wreathed pearls her hair she frees;
Unclasps her warmed jewels one by one;
Loosens her fragrant bodice; by degrees
Her rich attire creeps rustling to her knees: 230
Half-hidden, like a mermaid in sea-weed,
Pensive awhile she dreams awake, and sees
In fancy, fair St. Agnes in her bed,
But dares not look behind, or all the charm is fled.

Soon, trembling in her soft and chilly nest,
In sort of wakeful swoon, perplex'd she lay,
Until the poppied warmth of sleep oppress'd
Her soothed limbs, and soul fatigued away;
Flown, like a thought, until the morrow-day;
Blissfully haven'd both from joy and pain;　　　　　240
Clasp'd like a missal where swart Paynims pray;
Blinded alike from sunshine and from rain,
As though a rose should shut, and be a bud again.

Stol'n to this paradise, and so entranced,
Porphyro gazed upon her empty dress,
And listen'd to her breathing, if it chanced
To wake into a slumberous tenderness;
Which when he heard, that minute did he bless,
And breath'd himself: then from the closet crept,
Noiseless as fear in a wide wilderness,　　　　　250
And over the hush'd carpet, silent, stept,
And 'tween the curtain peep'd, where, lo!—how fast she slept.

Then by the bed-side, where the faded moon
Made a dim, silver twilight, soft he set
A table, and, half anguish'd, threw thereon
A cloth of woven crimson, gold, and jet:—
O for some drowsy Morphean amulet!
The boisterous, midnight, festive clarion,
The kettle-drum, and far-heard clarinet,
Affray his ears, though but in dying tone:—　　　　　260
The hall door shuts again, and all the noise is gone.

And still she slept an azure-lidded sleep,
In blanched linen, smooth, and lavender'd,
While he from forth the closet brought a heap
Of candied apple, quince, and plum, and gourd;
With jellies soother than the creamy curd,
And lucent syrups, tinct with cinnamon;
Manna and dates, in argosy transferr'd
From Fez; and spiced dainties, every one,
From silken Samarcand to cedar'd Lebanon.　　　　　270

These delicates he heap'd with glowing hand
On golden dishes and in baskets bright
Of wreathed silver: sumptuous they stand
In the retired quiet of the night,
Filling the chilly room with perfume light.—
'And now, my love, my seraph fair, awake!
Thou art my heaven, and I thine eremite:
Open thine eyes, for meek St. Agnes' sake,
Or I shall drowse beside thee, so my soul doth ache.'

Thus whispering, his warm, unnerved arm   280
Sank in her pillow. Shaded was her dream
By the dusk curtains:—'twas a midnight charm
Impossible to melt as iced stream:
The lustrous salvers in the moonlight gleam;
Broad golden fringe upon the carpet lies:
It seem'd he never, never could redeem
From such a steadfast spell his lady's eyes;
So mus'd awhile, entoil'd in woofed phantasies.

Awakening up, he took her hollow lute,—
Tumultuous,—and, in chords that tenderest be,   290
He play'd an ancient ditty, long since mute,
In Provence call'd, 'La belle dame sans mercy:'
Close to her ear touching the melody;—
Wherewith disturb'd, she utter'd a soft moan:
He ceased—she panted quick—and suddenly
Her blue affrayed eyes wide open shone:
Upon his knees he sank, pale as smooth-sculptured stone.

Her eyes were open, but she still beheld,
Now wide awake, the vision of her sleep:
There was a painful change, that nigh expell'd   300
The blisses of her dream so pure and deep
At which fair Madeline began to weep,
And moan forth witless words with many a sigh;
While still her gaze on Porphyro would keep;
Who knelt, with joined hands and piteous eye,
Fearing to move or speak, she look'd so dreamingly.

[328]

'Ah, Porphyro!' said she, 'but even now
Thy voice was at sweet tremble in mine ear,
Made tuneable with every sweetest vow;
And those sad eyes were spiritual and clear: 310
How chang'd thou art! how pallid, chill, and drear!
Give me that voice again, my Porphyro,
Those looks immortal, those complainings dear!
Oh leave me not in this eternal woe,
For if thou diest, my love, I know not where to go.'

Beyond a mortal man impass'd far
At these voluptuous accents, he arose,
Ethereal, flush'd, and like a throbbing star
Seen mid the sapphire heaven's deep repose;
Into her dream he melted, as the rose   320
Blendeth its odor with the violet,—
Solution sweet: meantime the frostwind blows
Like Love's alarum pattering the sharp sleet
Against the window-panes; St. Agnes' moon hath set.

'Tis dark: quick pattereth the flaw-blown sleet:
'This is no dream, my bride, my Madeline!'
'Tis dark: the iced gusts still rave and beat:
'No dream, alas! alas! and woe is mine!
Porphyro will leave me here to fade and pine.—
Cruel! what traitor could thee hither bring?   330
I curse not, for my heart is lost in thine,
Though thou forsakest a deceived thing;—
A dove forlorn and lost with sick unpruned wing.'

'My Madeline! sweet dreamer! lovely bride!
Say, may I be for aye thy vassal blest?
Thy beauty's shield, heart-shap'd and vermeil-dyed?
Ah, silver shrine, here will I take my rest
After so many hours of toil and quest,
A famish'd pilgrim,—sav'd by miracle.
Though I have found, I will not rob thy nest   340
Saving of thy sweet self; if thou think'st well
To trust, fair Madeline, to no rude infidel.

[329]

'Hark! 'tis an elfin-storm from faery land,
Of haggard seeming, but a boon indeed:
Arise—arise! the morning is at hand;—
The bloated wassaillers will never heed:—
Let us away, my love, with happy speed;
There are no ears to hear, or eyes to see,—
Drown'd all in Rhenish and the sleepy mead:
Awake! arise! my love, and fearless be,   350
For o'er the southern moors I have a home for thee.'

She hurried at his words, beset with fears,
For there were sleeping dragons all around,
At glaring watch, perhaps, with ready spears—
Down the wide stairs a darkling way they found.—
In all the house was heard no human sound.
A chain-droop'd lamp was flickering by each door;
The arras, rich with horseman, hawk, and hound,
Flutter'd in the besieging wind's uproar;
And the long carpets rose along the gusty floor.   360

They glide, like phantoms, into the wide hall;
Like phantoms, to the iron porch, they glide;
Where lay the porter in uneasy sprawl,
With a huge empty flagon by his side:
The wakeful bloodhound rose, and shook his hide,
But his sagacious eye an inmate owns:
By one and one, the bolts full easy slide:—
The chains lie silent on the footworn stones;—
The key turns, and the door upon its hinges groans.

And they are gone: aye, ages long ago   370
These lovers fled away into the storm.
That night the Baron dreamt of many a woe,
And all his warrior-guests, with shade and form
Of witch, and demon, and large coffin-worm,
Were long be-nightmar'd. Angela the old
Died palsy-twitch'd, with meager face deform;
The beadsman after thousand aves told,
For aye unsought-for slept among his ashes cold.

BOOK I

Deep in the shady sadness of a vale
Far sunken from the healthy breath of morn,
Far from the fiery noon, and eve's one star,
Sat gray-hair'd Saturn, quiet as a stone,
Still as the silence round about his lair;
Forest on forest hung about his head
Like cloud on cloud. No stir of air was there,
Not so much life as on a summer's day
Robs not one light seed from the feather'd grass,
But where the dead leaf fell, there did it rest.   10
A stream went voiceless by, still deadened more
By reason of his fallen divinity
Spreading a shade; the Naiad 'mid her reeds
Press'd her cold finger closer to her lips.

Along the margin-sand large footmarks went,
No further than to where his feet had stray'd,
And slept there since. Upon the sodden ground
His old right hand lay nerveless, listless, dead,
Unsceptered; and his realmless eyes were closed;
While his bow'd head seem'd list'ning to the Earth,   20
His ancient mother, for some comfort yet.

It seem'd no force could wake him from his place;
But there came one, who with a kindred hand
Touch'd his wide shoulders, after bending low
With reverence, though to one who knew it not.
She was a Goddess of the infant world;
By her in stature the tall Amazon
Had stood a pigmy's height: she would have ta'en
Achilles by the hair and bent his neck;
Or with a finger stay'd Ixion's wheel.   30
Her face was large as that of Memphian sphinx,
Pedestal'd haply in a palace court,
When sages look'd to Egypt for their lore.

But oh! how unlike marble was that face:
How beautiful, if sorrow had not made
Sorrow more beautiful than Beauty's self.
There was a listening fear in her regard,
As if calamity had but begun;
As if the vanward clouds of evil days
Had spent their malice, and the sullen rear   40
Was with its stored thunder laboring up.
One hand she press'd upon that aching spot
Where beats the human heart, as if just there,
Though an immortal, she felt cruel pain:
The other upon Saturn's bended neck
She laid, and to the level of his ear
Leaning with parted lips, some words she spake
In solemn tenor and deep organ tone:
Some mourning words, which in our feeble tongue
Would come in these like accents; O how frail   50
To that large utterance of the early Gods!
'Saturn, look up!—though wherefore, poor old King?
I have no comfort for thee, no not one:
I cannot say, "O wherefore sleepest thou?"
For heaven is parted from thee, and the earth
Knows thee not, thus afflicted, for a God;
And ocean too, with all its solemn noise,
Has from thy scepter pass'd; and all the air
Is emptied of thine hoary majesty.
Thy thunder, conscious of the new command,   60
Rumbles reluctant o'er our fallen house;
And thy sharp lightning in unpractic'd hands
Scorches and burns our once serene domain.
O aching time! O moments big as years!
All as ye pass swell out the monstrous truth,
And press it so upon our weary griefs
That unbelief has not a space to breathe.
Saturn, sleep on:—O thoughtless, why did I
Thus violate thy slumbrous solitude?
Why should I ope thy melancholy eyes?   70
Saturn, sleep on! while at thy feet I weep.'

As when, upon a tranced summer-night,
Those green-rob'd senators of mighty woods,
Tall oaks, branch-charmed by the earnest stars,
Dream, and so dream all night without a stir,
Save from one gradual solitary gust
Which comes upon the silence, and dies off,
As if the ebbing air had but one wave;
So came these words and went; the while in tears
She touch'd her fair large forehead to the ground, 80
Just where her falling hair might be outspread
A soft and silken mat for Saturn's feet.
One moon, with alteration slow, had shed
Her silver seasons four upon the night,
And still these two were postured motionless,
Like natural sculpture in cathedral cavern;
The frozen God still couchant on the earth,
And the sad Goddess weeping at his feet:
Until at length old Saturn lifted up
His faded eyes, and saw his kingdom gone, 90
And all the gloom and sorrow of the place,
And that fair kneeling Goddess; and then spake,
As with a palsied tongue, and while his beard
Shook horrid with such aspen-malady:
'O tender spouse of gold Hyperion,
Thea, I feel thee ere I see thy face;
Look up, and let me see our doom in it;
Look up, and tell me if this feeble shape
Is Saturn's; tell me, if thou hear'st the voice
Of Saturn; tell me, if this wrinkling brow, 100
Naked and bare of its great diadem,
Peers like the front of Saturn. Who had power
To make me desolate? whence came the strength?
How was it nurtur'd to such bursting forth,
While Fate seem'd strangled in my nervous grasp?
But it is so; and I am smother'd up,
And buried from all godlike exercise
Of influence benign on planets pale,
Of admonitions to the winds and seas,

Of peaceful sway above man's harvesting,   110
And all those acts which Deity supreme
Doth ease its heart of love in.—I am gone
Away from my own bosom: I have left
My strong identity, my real self,
Somewhere between the throne, and where I sit
Here on this spot of earth. Search, Thea, search!
Open thine eyes eterne, and sphere them round
Upon all space: space starr'd, and lorn of light;
Space region'd with life-air; and barren void;
Spaces of fire, and all the yawn of hell.—   120
Search, Thea, search! and tell me, if thou seest
A certain shape or shadow, making way
With wings or chariot fierce to repossess
A heaven he lost erewhile: it must—it must
Be of ripe progress—Saturn must be King.
Yes, there must be a golden victory;
There must be Gods thrown down, and trumpets blown
Of triumph calm, and hymns of festival
Upon the gold clouds metropolitan,
Voices of soft proclaim, and silver stir   130
Of strings in hollow shells; and there shall be
Beautiful things made new, for the surprise
Of the sky-children; I will give command:
Thea! Thea! Thea! where is Saturn?'

    This passion lifted him upon his feet,
And made his hands to struggle in the air,
His Druid locks to shake and ooze with sweat,
His eyes to fever out, his voice to cease.
He stood, and heard not Thea's sobbing deep;
A little time, and then again he snatch'd   140
Utterance thus.—'But cannot I create?
Cannot I form? Cannot I fashion forth
Another world, another universe,
To overbear and crumble this to naught?
Where is another chaos? Where?'—That word
Found way unto Olympus, and made quake

The rebel three.—Thea was startled up,
And in her bearing was a sort of hope,
As thus she quick-voic'd spake, yet full of awe.

'This cheers our fallen house: come to our friends,   150
O Saturn! come away, and give them heart;
I know the covert, for thence came I hither.'
Thus brief; then with beseeching eyes she went
With backward footing through the shade a space:
He follow'd, and she turn'd to lead the way
Through aged boughs, that yielded like the mist
Which eagles cleave upmounting from their nest.

   Meanwhile in other realms big tears were shed,
More sorrow like to this, and such like woe,
Too huge for mortal tongue or pen of scribe: 160
The Titans fierce, self-hid, or prison-bound,
Groan'd for the old allegiance once more,
And listen'd in sharp pain for Saturn's voice.
But one of the whole mammoth-brood still kept
His sov'reignty, and rule, and majesty;—
Blazing Hyperion on his orbed fire
Still sat, still snuff'd the incense, teeming up
From man to the sun's God; yet insecure:
For as among us mortals omens drear
Fright and perplex, so also shuddered he—   170
Not at dog's howl, or gloom-bird's hated screech,
Or the familiar visiting of one
Upon the first toll of his passing-bell,
Or prophesyings of the midnight lamp;
But horrors, portion'd to a giant nerve,
Oft made Hyperion ache. His palace bright
Bastion'd with pyramids of glowing gold,
And touch'd with shade of bronzed obelisks,
Glar'd a blood-red through all its thousand courts,
Arches, and domes, and fiery galleries;   180
And all its curtains of Aurorian clouds
Flush'd angerly: while sometimes eagle's wings,

Unseen before by Gods or wondering men,
Darken'd the place; and neighing steeds were heard,
Not heard before by Gods or wondering men.
Also, when he would taste the spicy wreaths
Of incense, breath'd aloft from sacred hills,
Instead of sweets, his ample palate took
Savor of poisonous brass and metal sick:
And so, when harbor'd in the sleepy west,   190
After the full completion of fair day,—
For rest divine upon exalted couch
And slumber in the arms of melody,
He pac'd away the pleasant hours of ease
With stride colossal, on from hall to hall;
While far within each aisle and deep recess,
His winged minions in close clusters stood,
Amaz'd and full of fear; like anxious men
Who on wide plains gather in panting troops,
When earthquakes jar their battlements and towers.   200
Even now, while Saturn, rous'd from icy trance,
Went step for step with Thea through the woods,
Hyperion, leaving twilight in the rear,
Came slope upon the threshold of the west;
Then, as was wont, his palace-door flew ope
In smoothest silence, save what solemn tubes,
Blown by the serious Zephyrs, gave of sweet
And wandering sounds, slow-breathed melodies;
And like a rose in vermeil tint and shape,
In fragrance soft, and coolness to the eye,   210
That inlet to severe magnificence
Stood full blown, for the God to enter in.

    He enter'd, but he enter'd full of wrath;
His flaming robes stream'd out beyond his heels,
And gave a roar, as if of earthly fire,
That scar'd away the meek ethereal Hours
And made their dove-wings tremble. On he flared,
From stately nave to nave, from vault to vault,
Through bowers of fragrant and enwreathed light,

And diamond-paved lustrous long arcades,   220
Until he reach'd the great main cupola;
There standing fierce beneath, he stamp'd his foot,
And from the basements deep to the high towers
Jarr'd his own golden region; and before
The quavering thunder thereupon had ceas'd,
His voice leapt out, despite of godlike curb,
To this result: 'O dreams of day and night!
O monstrous forms! O effigies of pain!
O specters busy in a cold, cold gloom!
O lank-ear'd Phantoms of black-weeded pools!   230
Why do I know ye? why have I seen ye? why
Is my eternal essence thus distraught
To see and to behold these horrors new?
Saturn is fallen, am I too to fall?
Am I to leave this haven of my rest,
This cradle of my glory, this soft clime,
This calm luxuriance of blissful light,
These crystalline pavilions, and pure fanes,
Of all my lucent empire? It is left
Deserted, void, nor any haunt of mine.   240
The blaze, the splendor, and the symmetry,
I cannot see—but darkness, death and darkness.
Even here, into my center of repose,
The shady visions come to domineer,
Insult, and blind, and stifle up my pomp.—
Fall!—No, by Tellus and her briny robes!
Over the fiery frontier of my realms
I will advance a terrible right arm
Shall scare that infant thunderer, rebel Jove,
And bid old Saturn take his throne again.'—
He spake, and ceas'd, the while a heavier threat   250
Held struggle with his throat but came not forth;
For as in theatres of crowded men
Hubbub increases more they call out 'Hush!'
So at Hyperion's words the Phantoms pale
Bestirr'd themselves, thrice horrible and cold;
And from the mirror'd level where he stood

A mist arose, as from a scummy marsh.
At this, through all his bulk an agony
Crept gradual, from the feet unto the crown,   260
Like a lithe serpent vast and muscular
Making slow way, with head and neck convuls'd
From over-strained might. Releas'd, he fled
To the eastern gates, and full six dewy hours
Before the dawn in season due should blush,
He breath'd fierce breath against the sleepy portals,
Clear'd them of heavy vapors, burst them wide
Suddenly on the ocean's chilly streams.
The planet orb of fire, whereon he rode
Each day from east to west the heavens through,   270
Spun round in sable curtaining of clouds;
Not therefore veiled quite, blindfold, and hid,
But ever and anon the glancing spheres,
Circles, and arcs, and broad-belting colure,
Glow'd through, and wrought upon the muffling dark
Sweet-shaped lightnings from the nadir deep
Up to the zenith,—hieroglyphics old
Which sages and keen-eyed astrologers
Then living on the earth, with laboring thought
Won from the gaze of many centuries: 280
Now lost, save what we find on remnants huge
Of stone, or marble swart; their import gone,
Their wisdom long since fled.—Two wings this orb
Possess'd for glory, two fair argent wings,
Ever exalted at the God's approach:
And now, from forth the gloom their plumes immense
Rose, one by one, till all outspreaded were;
While still the dazzling globe maintain'd eclipse,
Awaiting for Hyperion's command.
Fain would he have commanded, fain took throne   290
And bid the day begin, if but for change.
He might not:—No, though a primeval God:
The sacred seasons might not be disturb'd.
Therefore the operations of the dawn
Stay'd in their birth, even as here 'tis told.

Those silver wings expanded sisterly,
Eager to sail their orb; the porches wide
Open'd upon the dusk demesnes of night;
And the bright Titan, frenzied with new woes,
Unus'd to bend, by hard compulsion bent   300
His spirit to the sorrow of the time;
And all along a dismal rack of clouds,
Upon the boundaries of day and night,
He stretch'd himself in grief and radiance faint.
There as he lay, the Heaven with its stars
Look'd down on him with pity, and the voice
Of Cœlus, from the universal space,
Thus whisper'd low and solemn in his ear.
'O brightest of my children dear, earthborn
And sky-engendered, Son of Mysteries   310
All unrevealed even to the powers
Which met at thy creating; at whose joys
And palpitations sweet, and pleasures soft,
I, Cœlus, wonder, how they came and whence;
And at the fruits thereof what shapes they be,
Distinct, and visible; symbols divine,
Manifestations of that beauteous life
Diffus'd unseen throughout eternal space:
Of these new-form'd art thou, oh brightest child!
Of these, thy brethren and the Goddesses!   320
There is sad feud among ye, and rebellion
Of son against his sire. I saw him fall,
I saw my first-born tumbled from his throne!
To me his arms were spread, to me his voice
Found way from forth the thunders round his head!
Pale wox I, and in vapors hid my face.
Art thou, too, near such doom? vague fear there is:
For I have seen my sons most unlike Gods.
Divine ye were created, and divine
In sad demeanor, solemn, undisturb'd,   330
Unruffled, like high Gods, ye liv'd and ruled:
Now I behold in you fear, hope, and wrath;
Actions of rage and passion; even as

[339]

I see them, on the mortal world beneath,
In men who die.—This is the grief, O Son!
Sad sign of ruin, sudden dismay, and fall!
Yet do thou strive; as thou art capable,
As thou canst move about, an evident God;
And canst oppose to each malignant hour
Ethereal presence:—I am but a voice;   340
My life is but the life of winds and tides,
No more than winds and tides can I avail:—
But thou canst.—Be thou therefore in the van
Of circumstance; yea, seize the arrow's barb
Before the tense string murmur.—To the earth!
For there thou wilt find Saturn, and his woes.
Meantime I will keep watch on thy bright sun,
And of thy seasons be a careful nurse.'—
Ere half this region-whisper had come down,
Hyperion arose, and on the stars   350
Lifted his curved lids, and kept them wide
Until it ceas'd; and still he kept them wide:
And still they were the same bright, patient stars.
Then with a slow incline of his broad breast,
Like to a diver in the pearly seas,
Forward he stoop'd over the airy shore,
And plung'd all noiseless into the deep night.

BOOK II

Just at the self-same beat of Time's wide wings
Hyperion slid into the rustled air,
And Saturn gain'd with Thea that sad place
Where Cybele and the bruis'd Titans mourn'd.
It was a den where no insulting light
Could glimmer on their tears; where their own groans
They felt, but heard not, for the solid roar
Of thunderous waterfalls and torrents hoarse,
Pouring a constant bulk, uncertain where.
Crag jutting forth to crag, and rocks that seem'd   10
Ever as if just rising from a sleep,
Forehead to forehead with their monstrous horns;

And thus in thousand hugest phantasies
Made a fit roofing to this nest of woe.
Instead of thrones, hard flint they sat upon,
Couches of rugged stone, and slaty ridge
Stubborn'd with iron. All were not assembled:
Some chain'd in torture, and some wandering.
Cœus, and Gyges, and Briareüs,
Typhon, and Dolor, and Porphyrion,   20
With many more, the brawniest in assault,
Were pent in regions of laborious breath;
Dungeon'd in opaque element, to keep
Their clenched teeth still clench'd, and all their limbs
Lock'd up like veins of metal, crampt and screw'd;
Without a motion, save of their big hearts
Heaving in pain, and horribly convuls'd
With sanguine, feverous, boiling gurge of pulse.
Mnemosyne was straying in the world;
Far from her moon had Phœbe wandered;   30
And many else were free to roam abroad,
But for the main, here found they covert drear.
Scarce images of life, one here, one there,
Lay vast and edgeways; like a dismal cirque
Of Druid stones, upon a forlorn moor,
When the chill rain begins at shut of eve,
In dull November, and their chancel vault,
The Heaven itself, is blinded throughout night.
Each one kept shroud, nor to his neighbor gave
Or word, or look, or action of despair.   40
Creüs was one; his ponderous iron mace
Lay by him, and a shatter'd rib of rock
Told of his rage, ere he thus sank and pined.
Iäpetus another; in his grasp,
A serpent's plashy neck; its barbed tongue
Squeez'd from the gorge, and all its uncurl'd length
Dead; and because the creature could not spit
Its poison in the eyes of conquering Jove.
Next Cottus: prone he lay, chin uppermost,
As though in pain; for still upon the flint   50

He ground severe his skull, with open mouth
And eyes at horrid working. Nearest him
Asia, born of most enormous Caf,
Who cost her mother Tellus keener pangs,
Though feminine, than any of her sons:
More thought than woe was in her dusky face,
For she was prophesying of her glory;
And in her wide imagination stood
Palm-shaded temples, and high rival fanes,
By Oxus or in Ganges' sacred isles.   60
Even as Hope upon her anchor leans,
So leant she, not so fair, upon a tusk
Shed from the broadest of her elephants.
Above her, on a crag's uneasy shelve,
Upon his elbow rais'd, all prostrate else,
Shadow'd Enceladus; once tame and mild
As grazing ox unworried in the meads;
Now tiger-passion'd, lion-thoughted, wroth,
He meditated, plotted, and even now
Was hurling mountains in that second war,   70
Not long delay'd, that scar'd the younger Gods
To hide themselves in forms of beast and bird.
Not far hence Atlas; and beside him prone
Phorcus, the sire of Gorgons. Neighbor'd close
Oceanus, and Tethys, in whose lap
Sobb'd Clymene among her tangled hair.
In midst of all lay Themis, at the feet
Of Ops the queen all clouded round from sight;
No shape distinguishable, more than when
Thick night confounds the pine-tops with the clouds: 80
And many else whose names may not be told.
For when the Muse's wings are air-ward spread,
Who shall delay her flight? And she must chant
Of Saturn, and his guide, who now had climb'd
With damp and slippery footing from a depth
More horrid still. Above a somber cliff
Their heads appear'd, and up their stature grew
Till on the level height their steps found ease:

Then Thea spread abroad her trembling arms
Upon the precincts of this nest of pain,   90
And sidelong fix'd her eye on Saturn's face:
There saw she direst strife; the supreme God
At war with all the frailty of grief,
Of rage, or fear, anxiety, revenge,
Remorse, spleen, hope, but most of all despair.
Against these plagues he strove in vain; for Fate
Had pour'd a mortal oil upon his head,
A disanointing poison: so that Thea,
Affrighted, kept her still, and let him pass
First onwards in, among the fallen tribe.   100

      As with us mortal men, the laden heart
Is persecuted more, and fever'd more,
When it is nighing to the mournful house
Where other hearts are sick of the same bruise;
So Saturn, as he walk'd into the midst,
Felt faint, and would have sunk among the rest,
But that he met Enceladus's eye,
Whose mightiness, and awe of him, at once
Came like an inspiration; and he shouted,
'Titans, behold your God!' at which some groan'd;   110
Some started on their feet; some also shouted;
Some wept, some wail'd,—all bow'd with reverence;
And Ops, uplifting her black folded veil,
Show'd her pale cheeks, and all her forehead wan,
Her eyebrows thin and jet, and hollow eyes.
There is a roaring in the bleak-grown pines
When Winter lifts his voice; there is a noise
Among immortals when a God gives sign,
With hushing finger, how he means to load
His tongue with the full weight of utterless thought,   120
With thunder, and with music, and with pomp:
Such noise is like the roar of bleak-grown pines:
Which, when it ceases in this mountain'd world,
No other sound succeeds; but ceasing here,
Among these fallen, Saturn's voice therefrom

Grew up like organ, that begins anew
Its strain, when other harmonies, stopt short,
Leave the dinn'd air vibrating silverly.
Thus grew it up—'Not in my own sad breast,
Which is its own great judge and searcher out,   130
Can I find reason why ye should be thus:
Not in the legends of the first of days,
Studied from that old spirit-leaved book
Which starry Uranus with finger bright
Sav'd from the shores of darkness, when the waves
Low-ebb'd still hid it up in shallow gloom;—
And the which book ye know I ever kept
For my firm-based footstool.—Ah, infirm!
Not there, nor in sign, symbol, or portent
Of element, earth, water, air, and fire,—   140
At war, at peace, or inter-quarreling
One against one, or two, or three, or all
Each several one against the other three,
As fire with air loud warring when rainfloods
Drown both, and press them both against earth's face,
Where, finding sulphur, a quadruple wrath
Unhinges the poor world;—not in that strife,
Wherefrom I take strange lore, and read it deep,
Can I find reason why ye should be thus:
No, nowhere can unriddle, though I search,   150
And pore on Nature's universal scroll
Even to swooning, why ye, Divinities,
The first-born of all shap'd and palpable Gods,
Should cower beneath what, in comparison,
Is untremendous might. Yet ye are here,
O'erwhelm'd, and spurn'd, and batter'd, ye are here!
O Titans, shall I say, "Arise!"—Ye groan:
Shall I say "Crouch!"—Ye groan. What can I then?
O Heaven wide! O unseen parent dear!
What can I? Tell me, all ye brethren Gods,   160
How we can war, how engine our great wrath!
O speak your counsel now, for Saturn's ear
Is all a-hunger'd. Thou, Oceanus,

Ponderest high and deep; and in thy face
I see, astonied, that severe content
Which comes of thought and musing: give us help!'

    So ended Saturn; and the God of the Sea,
Sophist and sage, from no Athenian grove,
But cogitation in his watery shades,
Arose, with locks not oozy, and began,   170
In murmurs, which his first-endeavoring tongue
Caught infant-like from the far-foamed sands.
'O ye, whom wrath consumes! who, passion-stung,
Writhe at defeat, and nurse your agonies!
Shut up your senses, stifle up your ears,
My voice is not a bellows unto ire.
Yet listen, ye who will, whilst I bring proof
How ye, perforce, must be content to stoop:
And in the proof much comfort will I give,
If ye will take that comfort in its truth.   180
We fall by course of Nature's law, not force
Of thunder, or of Jove. Great Saturn, thou
Hast sifted well the atom-universe;
But for this reason, that thou art the King,
And only blind from sheer supremacy,
One avenue was shaded from thine eyes,
Through which I wandered to eternal truth.
And first, as thou wast not the first of powers,
So art thou not the last; it cannot be:
Thou are not the beginning nor the end.   190
From chaos and parental darkness came
Light, the first fruits of that intestine broil,
That sullen ferment, which for wondrous ends
Was ripening in itself. The ripe hour came,
And with it light, and light, engendering
Upon its own producer, forthwith touch'd
The whole enormous matter into life.
Upon that very hour, our parentage,
The Heavens and the Earth, were manifest:
Then thou first-born, and we the giant-race,   200

Found ourselves ruling new and beauteous realms
Now comes the pain of truth, to whom 'tis pain;
O folly! for to bear all naked truths,
And to envisage circumstance, all calm,
That is the top of sovereignty. Mark well!
As Heaven and Earth are fairer, fairer far
Than Chaos and blank Darkness, though once chiefs;
And as we show beyond that Heaven and Earth
In form and shape compact and beautiful,
In will, in action free, companionship,   210
And thousand other signs of purer life;
So on our heels a fresh perfection treads,
A power more strong in beauty, born of us
And fated to excel us, as we pass
In glory that old Darkness: nor are we
Thereby more conquer'd, than by us the rule
Of shapeless Chaos. Say, doth the dull soil
Quarrel with the proud forests it hath fed,
And feedeth still, more comely than itself?
Can it deny the chiefdom of green groves?   220
Or shall the tree be envious of the dove
Because it cooeth, and hath snowy wings
To wander wherewithal and find its joys?
We are such forest-trees, and our fair boughs
Have bred forth, not pale solitary doves,
But eagles golden-feather'd, who do tower
Above us in their beauty, and must reign
In right thereof; for 'tis the eternal law
That first in beauty should be first in might:
Yea, by that law, another race may drive   230
Our conquerors to mourn as we do now.
Have ye beheld the young God of the Seas,
My dispossessor? Have ye seen his face?
Have ye beheld his chariot, foam'd along
By noble winged creatures he hath made?
I saw him on the calmed waters scud,
With such a glow of beauty in his eyes,
That it enforc'd me to bid sad farewell

To all my empire: farewell sad I took,
And hither came, to see how dolorous fate   240
Had wrought upon ye; and how I might best
Give consolation in this woe extreme.
Receive the truth, and let it be your balm.'

   Whether through pos'd conviction, or disdain,
They guarded silence, when Oceanus
Left murmuring, what deepest thought can tell?
But so it was, none answer'd for a space,
Save one whom none regarded, Clymene;
And yet she answer'd not, only complain'd,
With hectic lips, and eyes up-looking mild,   250
Thus wording timidly among the fierce:
'O Father, I am here the simplest voice,
And all my knowledge is that joy is gone,
And this thing woe crept in among our hearts,
There to remain forever, as I fear:
I would not bode of evil, if I thought
So weak a creature could turn off the help
Which by just right should come of mighty Gods;
Yet let me tell my sorrow, let me tell
Of what I heard, and how it made me weep,   260
And know that we had parted from all hope.
I stood upon a shore, a pleasant shore,
Where a sweet clime was breathed from a land
Of fragrance, quietness, and trees, and flowers.
Full of calm joy it was, as I of grief;
Too full of joy, and soft delicious warmth;
So that I felt a movement in my heart
To chide, and to reproach that solitude
With songs of misery, music of our woes;
And sat me down, and took a mouthed shell   270
And murmur'd into it, and made melody—
O melody no more! for while I sang,
And with poor skill let pass into the breeze
The dull shell's echo, from a bowery strand
Just opposite, an island of the sea,

[347]

There came enchantment with the shifting wind,
That did both drown and keep alive my ears.
I threw my shell away upon the sand,
And a wave fill'd it, as my sense was fill'd
With that new blissful golden melody.   280
A living death was in each gush of sounds,
Each family of rapturous hurried notes,
That fell, one after one, yet all at once,
Like pearl beads dropping sudden from their string:
And then another, then another strain,
Each like a dove leaving its olive perch,
With music wing'd instead of silent plumes,
To hover round my head, and make me sick
Of joy and grief at once. Grief overcame,
And I was stopping up my frantic ears,   290
When, past all hindrance of my trembling hands,
A voice came sweeter, sweeter than all tune,
And still it cried, "Apollo! young Apollo!
The morning-bright Apollo! young Apollo!"
I fled, it follow'd me, and cried "Apollo!"
O Father, and O Brethren, had ye felt
Those pains of mine; O Saturn, hadst thou felt,
Ye would not call this too-indulged tongue
Presumptuous, in thus venturing to be heard.'

   So far her voice flow'd on, like timorous brook   300
That, lingering along a pebbled coast,
Doth fear to meet the sea: but sea it met,
And shudder'd; for the overwhelming voice
Of huge Enceladus swallow'd it in wrath:
The ponderous syllables, like sullen waves
In the half-glutted hollows of reef-rocks,
Came booming thus, while still upon his arm
He lean'd; not rising, from supreme contempt.
'Or shall we listen to the over-wise,
Or to the over-foolish, giant Gods?   310
Not thunderbolt on thunderbolt, till all
That rebel Jove's whole armory were spent,

Not world on world upon these shoulders piled,
Could agonize me more than baby-words
In midst of this dethronement horrible.
Speak! roar! shout! yell! ye sleepy Titans all.
Do ye forget the blows, the buffets vile?
Are ye not smitten by a youngling arm?
Dost thou forget, sham Monarch of the Waves,
Thy scalding in the seas? What! have I rous'd   320
Your spleens with so few simple words as these?
O joy! for now I see ye are not lost:
O joy! for now I see a thousand eyes
Wide-glaring for revenge!'—As this he said,
He lifted up his stature vast, and stood,
Still without intermission speaking thus:
'Now ye are flames, I'll tell you how to burn,
And purge the ether of our enemies;
How to feed fierce the crooked stings of fire,
And singe away the swollen clouds of Jove,   330
Stifling that puny essence in its tent.
O let him feel the evil he hath done;
For though I scorn Oceanus's lore,
Much pain have I for more than loss of realms:
The days of peace and slumberous calm are fled;
Those days, all innocent of scathing war,
When all the fair Existences of heaven
Came open-eyed to guess what we would speak:—
That was before our brows were taught to frown,
Before our lips knew else but solemn sounds;   340
That was before we knew the winged thing,
Victory, might be lost, or might be won.
And be ye mindful that Hyperion,
Our brightest brother, still is undisgraced—
Hyperion, lo! his radiance is here!'

    All eyes were on Enceladus's face,
And they beheld, while still Hyperion's name
Flew from his lips up to the vaulted rocks,
A pallid gleam across his features stern:

Not savage, for he saw full many a God 350
Wroth as himself. He look'd upon them all,
And in each face he saw a gleam of light,
But splendider in Saturn's, whose hoar locks
Shone like the bubbling foam about a keel
When the prow sweeps into a midnight cove.
In pale and silver silence they remain'd,
Till suddenly a splendor, like the morn,
Pervaded all the beetling gloomy steeps,
All the sad spaces of oblivion,
And every gulf, and every chasm old, 360
And every height, and every sullen depth,
Voiceless, or hoarse with loud tormented streams:
And all the everlasting cataracts,
And all the headlong torrents far and near,
Mantled before in darkness and huge shade,
Now saw the light and made it terrible.
It was Hyperion:—a granite peak
His bright feet touch'd, and there he stay'd to view
The misery his brilliance had betray'd
To the most hateful seeing of itself. 370
Golden his hair of short Numidian curl,
Regal his shape majestic, a vast shade
In midst of his own brightness, like the bulk
Of Memnon's image at the set of sun
To one who travels from the dusking East:
Sighs, too, as mournful as that Memnon's harp,
He utter'd, while his hands contemplative
He press'd together, and in silence stood.
Despondence seiz'd again the fallen Gods
At sight of the dejected King of Day, 380
And many hid their faces from the light:
But fierce Enceladus sent forth his eyes
Among the brotherhood; and, at their glare,
Uprose Iäpetus, and Creüs too,
And Phorcus, sea-born, and together strode
To where he towered on his eminence.
There those four shouted forth old Saturn's name;

Hyperion from the peak loud answered, 'Saturn!'
Saturn sat near the Mother of the Gods,
In whose face was no joy, though all the Gods   390
Gave from their hollow throats the name of 'Saturn!'

BOOK III

Thus in alternate uproar and sad peace,
Amazed were those Titans utterly.
O leave them, Muse! O leave them to their woes;
For thou art weak to sing such tumults dire:
A solitary sorrow best befits
Thy lips, and antheming a lonely grief.
Leave them, O Muse! for thou anon wilt find
Many a fallen old Divinity
Wandering in vain about bewildered shores.
Meantime touch piously the Delphic harp,   10
And not a wind of heaven but will breathe
In aid soft warble from the Dorian flute;
For lo! 'tis for the Father of all verse.
Flush every thing that hath a vermeil hue,
Let the rose glow intense and warm the air,
And let the clouds of even and of morn
Float in voluptuous fleeces o'er the hills;
Let the red wine within the goblet boil,
Cold as a bubbling well; let faint-lipp'd shells,
On sands, or in great deeps, vermilion turn   20
Through all their labyrinths; and let the maid
Blush keenly, as with some warm kiss surpris'd.
Chief isle of the embowered Cyclades,
Rejoice, O Delos, with thine olives green,
And poplars, and lawn-shading palms, and beech,
In which the Zephyr breathes the loudest song,
And hazels thick, dark-stemm'd beneath the shade:
Apollo is once more the golden theme!
Where was he, when the Giant of the Sun
Stood bright, amid the sorrow of his peers?   30
Together had he left his mother fair
And his twin-sister sleeping in their bower,

[351]

And in the morning twilight wandered forth
Beside the osiers of a rivulet,
Full ankle-deep in lilies of the vale.
The nightingale had ceas'd, and a few stars
Were lingering in the heavens, while the thrush
Began calm-throated. Throughout all the isle
There was no covert, no retired cave
Unhaunted by the murmurous noise of waves,   40
Though scarcely heard in many a green recess.
He listen'd, and he wept, and his bright tears
Went trickling down the golden bow he held.
Thus with half-shut suffused eyes he stood,
While from beneath some cumbrous boughs hard by
With solemn step an awful Goddess came,
And there was purport in her looks for him,
Which he with eager guess began to read
Perplex'd, the while melodiously he said:
'How cam'st thou over the unfooted sea?   50
Or hath that antique mien and robed form
Mov'd in these vales invisible till now?
Sure I have heard those vestments sweeping o'er
The fallen leaves, when I have sat alone
In cool mid-forest. Surely I have traced
The rustle of those ample skirts about
These grassy solitudes, and seen the flowers
Lift up their heads, as still the whisper pass'd.
Goddess! I have beheld those eyes before,
And their eternal calm, and all that face,   60
Or I have dream'd.'—'Yes,' said the supreme shape,
'Thou hast dream'd of me; and awaking up
Didst find a lyre all golden by thy side,
Whose strings touch'd by thy fingers, all the vast
Unwearied ear of the whole universe
Listen'd in pain and pleasure at the birth
Of such new tuneful wonder. Is't not strange
That thou shouldst weep, so gifted? Tell me, youth,
What sorrow thou canst feel; for I am sad
When thou dost shed a tear: explain thy griefs   70

To one who in this lonely isle hath been
The watcher of thy sleep and hours of life,
From the young day when first thy infant hand
Pluck'd witless the weak flowers, till thine arm
Could bend that bow heroic to all times.
Show thy heart's secret to an ancient Power
Who hath forsaken old and sacred thrones
For prophecies of thee, and for the sake
Of loveliness new born.'—Apollo then,
With sudden scrutiny and gloomless eyes,   80
Thus answer'd, while his white melodious throat
Throbb'd with the syllables.—'Mnemosyne!
Thy name is on my tongue, I know not how;
Why should I tell thee what thou so well seest?
Why should I strive to show what from thy lips
Would come no mystery? For me, dark, dark,
And painful vile oblivion seals my eyes:
I strive to search wherefore I am so sad,
Until a melancholy numbs my limbs;
And then upon the grass I sit, and moan,   90
Like one who once had wings.—O why should I
Feel curs'd and thwarted, when the liegeless air
Yields to my step aspirant? why should I
Spurn the green turf as hateful to my feet?
Goddess benign, point forth some unknown thing:
Are there not other regions than this isle?
What are the stars? There is the sun, the sun!
And the most patient brilliance of the moon!
And stars by thousands! Point me out the way
To any one particular beauteous star,   100
And I will fit into it with my lyre,
And make its silvery splendor pant with bliss.
I have heard the cloudy thunder: Where is power?
Whose hand, whose essence, what divinity
Makes this alarum in the elements,
While I here idle listen on the shores
In fearless yet in aching ignorance?
O tell me, lonely Goddess, by thy harp,

That waileth every morn and eventide,
Tell me why thus I rave, about these groves! 110
Mute thou remainest—mute! yet I can read
A wondrous lesson in thy silent face:
Knowledge enormous makes a God of me.
Names, deeds, gray legends, dire events, rebellions,
Majesties, sovran voices, agonies,
Creations and destroyings, all at once
Pour into the wide hollows of my brain,
And deify me, as if some blithe wine
Or bright elixir peerless I had drunk,
And so become immortal.'—Thus the God, 120
While his enkindling eyes, with level glance
Beneath his white soft temples, steadfast kept
Trembling with light upon Mnemosyne.
Soon wild commotions shook him, and made flush
All the immortal fairness of his limbs;
Most like the struggle at the gate of death;
Or liker still to one who should take leave
Of pale immortal death, and with a pang
As hot as death's is chill, with fierce convulse
Die into life: so young Apollo anguish'd: 130
His very hair, his golden tresses famed
Kept undulation round his eager neck.
During the pain Mnemosyne upheld
Her arms as one who prophesied.—At length
Apollo shriek'd;—and lo! from all his limbs
Celestial——

*   *   *

PART IV

SATIRICAL POEMS

All human things are subject to decay
And, when Fate summons, monarchs must obey.
This Flecknoe found, who, like Augustus, young
Was called to empire and had governed long,
In prose and verse was owned without dispute
Through all the realms of *Nonsense* absolute.
This aged prince, now flourishing in peace
And blessed with issue of a large increase,
Worn out with business, did at length debate
To settle the succession of the State;   10
And pondering which of all his sons was fit
To reign and wage immortal war with wit,
Cried, ''Tis resolved, for Nature pleads that he
'Should only rule who most resembles me.
'Shadwell alone my perfect image bears,
'Mature in dullness from his tender years;
'Shadwell alone of all my sons is he
'Who stands confirmed in full stupidity.
'The rest to some faint meaning make pretence,
'But Shadwell never deviates into sense.   20
'Some beams of wit on other souls may fall,
'Strike through and make a lucid interval;
'But Shadwell's genuine night admits no ray,
'His rising fogs prevail upon the day.
'Besides, his goodly fabric fills the eye
'And seems designed for thoughtless majesty.
'Thoughtless as monarch oaks that shade the plain
'And, spread in solemn state, supinely reign.
'Heywood and Shirley were but types of thee,
'Thou last great prophet of tautology.   30
'Even I, a dunce of more renown than they,
'Was sent before but to prepare thy way,
'And coarsely clad in Norwich drugget came
'To teach the nations in thy greater name.

'My warbling lute, the lute I whilom strung,
'When to King John of Portugal I sung,
'Was but the prelude to that glorious day,
'When thou on silver Thames didst cut thy way,
'With well-timed oars before the royal barge,
'Swelled with the pride of thy celestial charge,   40
'And, big with hymn, commander of an host;
'The like was ne'er in Epsom blankets tost.
'Methinks I see the new Arion sail,
'The lute still trembling underneath thy nail.
'At thy well-sharpened thumb from shore to shore
'The treble squeaks for fear, the basses roar;
'Echoes from Pissing-alley Shadwell call,
'And Shadwell they resound from Aston-hall.
'About thy boat the little fishes throng,
'As at the morning toast that floats along.   50
'Sometimes, as prince of thy harmonious band,
'Thou wieldst thy papers in thy threshing hand;
'St. André's feet ne'er kept more equal time,
'Not even the feet of thy own *Psyche's* rhyme:
'Though they in number as in sense excel,
'So just, so like tautology, they fell
'That, pale with envy, Singleton forswore
'The lute and sword which he in triumph bore,
'And vowed he ne'er would act Villerius more.'
Here stopped the good old sire and wept for joy,   60
In silent raptures of the hopeful boy.
All arguments, but most his plays, persuade,
That for anointed dullness he was made.

   Close to the walls which fair Augusta bind,
(The fair Augusta much to fears inclined,)
An ancient fabric raised to inform the sight
There stood of yore, and Barbican it hight;
A watch-tower once, but now, so fate ordains,
Of all the pile an empty name remains;
From its old ruins brothel-houses rise,   70
Scenes of lewd loves and of polluted joys,
Where their vast courts the mother-strumpets keep,

And, undisturbed by watch, in silence sleep.
Near these a Nursery erects its head,
Where queens are formed and future heroes bred,
Where unfledged actors learn to laugh and cry,
Where infant punks their tender voices try,
And little Maximins the gods defy.
Great Fletcher never treads in buskins here,
Nor greater Jonson dares in socks appear; 80
But gentle Simkin just reception finds
Amidst this monument of vanished minds;
Pure clinches the suburbian Muse affords
And Panton waging harmless war with words.
Here Flecknoe, as a place to fame well known,
Ambitiously designed his Shadwell's throne.
For ancient Decker prophesied long since
That in this pile should reign a mighty prince,
Born for a scourge of wit and flail of sense,
To whom true dullness should some *Psyches* owe, 90
But worlds of *Misers* from his pen should flow;
Humorists and hypocrites it should produce,
Whole Raymond families and tribes of Bruce.
　　Now Empress Fame had published the renown
Of Shadwell's coronation through the town.
Roused by report of Fame, the nations meet
From near Bunhill and distant Watling-street.
No Persian carpets spread the imperial way,
But scattered limbs of mangled poets lay;
From dusty shops neglected authors come, 100
Martyrs of pies and relics of the bum.
Much Heywood, Shirley, Ogleby there lay,
But loads of Shadwell almost choked the way.
Bilked stationers for yeomen stood prepared
And Herringman was captain of the guard.
The hoary prince in majesty appeared,
High on a throne of his own labors reared.
At his right hand our young Ascanius sat,
Rome's other hope and pillar of the State.
His brows thick fogs instead of glories grace, 110

And lambent dullness played around his face.
As Hannibal did to the altars come,
Sworn by his sire a mortal foe to Rome;
So Shadwell swore, nor should his vow be vain,
That he till death true dullness would maintain;
And, in his father's right and realm's defense,
Ne'er to have peace with wit nor truce with sense.
The king himself the sacred unction made,
As king by office and as priest by trade.
In his sinister hand, instead of ball,   120
He placed a mighty mug of potent ale.
Love's Kingdom to his right he did convey,
At once his scepter and his rule of sway;
Whose righteous lore the prince had practiced young
And from whose loins recorded *Psyche* sprung.
His temples, last, with poppies were o'erspread,
That nodding seemed to consecrate his head.
Just at that point of time, if fame not lie,
On his left hand twelve reverend owls did fly.
So Romulus, 'tis sung, by Tiber's brook,   130
Presage of sway from twice six vultures took.
The admiring throng loud acclamations make
And omens of his future empire take.
The sire then shook the honors of his head,
And from his brows damps of oblivion shed
Full on the filial dullness: long he stood,
Repelling from his breast the raging God;
At length burst out in this prophetic mood:
      'Heavens bless my son! from Ireland let him reign
'To far Barbadoes on the western main;   140
'Of his dominion may no end be known
'And greater than his father's be his throne;
'Beyond *Love's Kingdom* let him stretch his pen!'
He paused, and all the people cried 'Amen.'
Then thus continued he: 'My son, advance
'Still in new impudence, new ignorance.
'Success let others teach, learn thou from me
'Pangs without birth and fruitless industry.

[360]

'Let "Virtuosos" in five years be writ,
'Yet not one thought accuse thy toil of wit.   150
'Let gentle George in triumph tread the stage,
'Make Dorimant betray, and Loveit rage;
'Let Cully, Cockwood, Fopling, charm the pit,
'And in their folly show the writer's wit.
'Yet still thy fools shall stand in thy defense
'And justify their author's want of sense.
'Let them be all by thy own model made
'Of dullness and desire no foreign aid,
'That they to future ages may be known,
'Not copies drawn, but issue of thy own.   160
'Nay, let thy men of wit too be the same,
'All full of thee and differing but in name.
'But let no alien Sedley interpose
'To lard with wit thy hungry *Epsom* prose.
'And when false flowers of rhetoric thou wouldst cull,
'Trust nature, do not labor to be dull;
'But write thy best and top; and in each line
'Sir Formal's oratory will be thine.
'Sir Formal, though unsought, attends thy quill
'And does thy northern dedications fill.   170
'Nor let false friends seduce thy mind with praise
'And uncle Ogleby thy envy raise.
'Thou art my blood, where Jonson has no part:
'What share have we in nature or in art?
'Where did his wit on learning fix a brand
'And rail at arts he did not understand?
'Where made he love in Prince Nicander's vein
'Or swept the dust in *Psyche's* humble strain?
'Where sold he bargains, "whip-stitch, kiss my arse,"
'Promised a play and dwindled to a farce?   180
'When did his Muse from Fletcher scenes purloin,
'As thou whole Eth'rege dost transfuse to thine?
'But so transfused as oil on waters flow,
'His always floats above, thine sinks below.
'This is thy province, this thy wondrous way,
'New humors to invent for each new play:

[361]

'This is that boasted bias of thy mind,
'By which one way to dullness 'tis inclined,
'Which makes thy writings lean on one side still,
'And, in all changes, that way bends thy will.   190
'Nor, let thy mountain belly make pretense
'Of likeness; thine's a tympany of sense.
'A tun of man in thy large bulk is writ,
'But sure thou art but a kilderkin of wit.
'Like mine, thy gentle numbers feebly creep;
'Thy tragic Muse gives smiles, thy comic sleep.
'With whate'er gall thou setst thyself to write,
'Thy inoffensive satires never bite;
'In thy felonious heart though venom lies,
'It does but touch thy Irish pen, and dies.   200
'Thy genius calls thee not to purchase fame
'In keen Iambics, but mild Anagram.
'Leave writing plays, and choose for thy command
'Some peaceful province in Acrostic land.
'There thou mayest wings display and altars raise,
'And torture one poor word ten thousand ways;
'Or, if thou wouldst thy different talents suit,
'Set thy own songs, and sing them to thy lute.'
He said, but his last words were scarcely heard,
For Bruce and Longville had a trap prepared,   210
And down they sent the yet declaiming bard.
Sinking he left his drugget robe behind,
Borne upwards by a subterranean wind.
The mantle fell to the young prophet's part
With double portion of his father's art.

193   *Mr. Pope*

When Alexander Pope strolled in the city
Strict was the glint of pearl and gold sedans.
Ladies leaned out, more out of fear than pity;
For Pope's tight back was rather a goat's than man's.

One often thinks the urn should have more bones   5
Than skeletons provide for speedy dust;
The urn gets hollow, cobwebs brittle as stones
Weave to the funeral shell a frivolous rust.

And he who dribbled couplets like the snake
Coiled to a lithe precision in the sun,   10
Is missing. The jar is empty; you may break
It only to find that Mr. Pope is gone.

What requisitions of a verity
Prompted the wit and rage between his teeth
One cannot say: around a crooked tree   15
A mortal climbs whose name should be a wreath.

Epistle to Dr. Arbuthnot

P.   SHUT, shut the door, good John! fatigued, I said,
Tie up the knocker, say I'm sick, I'm dead.
The Dog-star rages! nay 'tis past a doubt,
All Bedlam, or Parnassus, is let out:
Fire in each eye, and papers in each hand,
They rave, recite, and madden round the land.
      What walls can guard me, or what shades can hide?
They pierce my thickets, through my Grot they glide;
By land, by water, they renew the charge;
They stop the chariot, and they board the barge.   10
No place is sacred, not the Church is free;
Even Sunday shines no Sabbath-day to me;
Then from the Mint walks forth the Man of rhyme,
Happy to catch me just at Dinner-time.
      Is there a Parson, much bemused in beer,
A maudlin Poetess, a rhyming Peer,
A Clerk, foredoomed his father's soul to cross,
Who pens a Stanza, when he should *engross* ?
Is there, who, locked from ink and paper, scrawls
With desp'rate charcoal round his darkened walls?   20
All fly to TWIT'NAM, and in humble strain

Apply to me, to keep them mad or vain.
Arthur, whose giddy son neglects the Laws,
Imputes to me and my damned works the cause:
Poor Cornus sees his frantic wife elope,
And curses Wit, and Poetry, and Pope.

  Friend to my Life! (which did not you prolong,
The world had wanted many an idle song)
What *Drop* or *Nostrum* can this plague remove?
Or which must end me, a Fool's wrath or love?   30
A dire dilemma! either way I'm sped,
If foes, they write, if friends, they read me dead.
Seized and tied down to judge, how wretched I!
Who can't be silent, and who will not lie.
To laugh, were want of goodness and of grace,
And to be grave, exceeds all Power of face.
I sit with sad civility, I read
With honest anguish, and an aching head;
And drop at last, but in unwilling ears,
This saving counsel, 'Keep your piece nine years.'   40

  'Nine years!' cries he, who high in Drury-lane,
Lulled by soft Zephyrs through the broken pane,
Rhymes ere he wakes, and prints before *Term* ends,
Obliged by hunger, and request of friends:
'The piece, you think, is incorrect? why, take it,
I'm all submission, what you'd have it, make it.'

  Three things another's modest wishes bound,
My Friendship, and a Prologue, and ten pound.

  Pitholeon sends to me: 'You know his Grace,
I want a Patron; ask him for a Place.'   50
' "Pitholeon libeled me," '—'but here's a letter
Informs you, Sir, 'twas when he knew no better.
Dare you refuse him? Curll invites to dine,
He'll write a *Journal*, or he'll turn Divine.'

  Bless me! a packet.—' 'Tis a stranger sues,
A Virgin Tragedy, an Orphan Muse.'
If I dislike it, 'Furies, death and rage!'
If I approve, 'Commend it to the Stage.'
There (thank my stars) my whole Commission ends,

The Players and I are, luckily, no friends.   60
Fired that the house reject him, ' 'Sdeath I'll print it,
And shame the fools——Your Int'rest, Sir, with Lintot!'
"Lintot, dull rogue! will think your price too much:"
'Not, Sir, if you revise it, and retouch.'
All my demurs but double his Attacks;
At last he whispers, 'Do; and we go snacks.'
Glad of a quarrel, straight I clap the door,
'Sir, let me see your works and you no more.'
    'Tis sung, when Midas' Ears began to spring,
(Midas, a sacred person and a king)   70
His very Minister who spied them first,
(Some say his Queen) was forced to speak, or burst.
And is not mine, my friend, a sorer case,
When every coxcomb perks them in my face?
A.   Good friend, forbear! you deal in dang'rous things.
I'd never name Queens, Ministers, or Kings;
Keep close to Ears, and those let asses prick;
'Tis nothing— P.   Nothing? if they bite and kick?
Out with it, DUNCIAD! let the secret pass,
That secret to each fool, that he's an Ass: 80
The truth once told (and wherefore should we lie?)
The Queen of Midas slept, and so may I.
    You think this cruel? take it for a rule,
No creature smarts so little as a fool.
Let peals of laughter, Codrus! round thee break,
Thou unconcerned canst hear the mighty crack:
Pit, Box, and gall'ry in convulsions hurled,
Thou stand'st unshook amidst a bursting world.
Who shames a Scribbler? break one cobweb through,
He spins the slight, self-pleasing thread anew: 90
Destroy his fib or sophistry, in vain,
The creature's at his dirty work again,
Throned in the centre of his thin designs,
Proud of a vast extent of flimsy lines!
Whom have I hurt? has Poet yet, or Peer,
Lost the arched eye-brow, or Parnassian sneer?
And has not Colley still his Lord, and whore?

His Butchers Henley, his free-masons Moore?
Does not one table Bavius still admit?
Still to one Bishop Philips seem a wit?   100
Still Sappho— A.   Hold! for God's sake—you'll offend,
No Names!—be calm!—learn prudence of a friend!
I too could write, and I am twice as tall;
But foes like these— P.   One Flatt'rer's worse than all.
Of all mad creatures, if the learned are right,
It is the slaver kills, and not the bite.
A fool quite angry is quite innocent:
Alas! 'tis ten times worse when they *repent*.

     One dedicates in high heroic prose,
And ridicules beyond a hundred foes: 110
One from all Grubstreet will my fame defend,
And, more abusive, calls himself my friend.
This prints my *Letters*, that expects a bribe,
And others roar aloud, 'Subscribe, subscribe.'

     There are, who to my person pay their court:
I cough like *Horace*, and, though lean, am short,
Ammon's great son one shoulder had too high,
Such *Ovid's* nose, and 'Sir! you have an Eye'—
Go on, obliging creatures, make me see
All that disgraced my Betters, met in me.   120
Say for my comfort, languishing in bed,
'Just so immortal *Maro* held his head:'
And when I die, be sure you let me know
Great *Homer* died three thousand years ago.

     Why did I write? what sin to me unknown
Dipt me in ink, my parents', or my own?
As yet a child, nor yet a fool to fame,
I lisped in numbers, for the numbers came.
I left no calling for this idle trade,
No duty broke, no father disobeyed.   130
The Muse but served to ease some friend, not Wife,
To help me through this long disease, my Life,
To second, ARBUTHNOT! thy Art and Care,
And teach the Being you preserved, to bear.

     But why then publish? *Granville* the polite,

And knowing *Walsh*, would tell me I could write;
Well-natured *Garth* inflamed with early praise;
And *Congreve* loved, and *Swift* endured my lays;
The courtly *Talbot, Somers, Sheffield* read;
Even mitred *Rochester* would nod the head,   140
And *St. John's* self (great *Dryden's* friends before)
With open arms received one Poet more.
Happy my studies, when by these approved!
Happier their author, when by these beloved!
From these the world will judge of men and books,
Not from the *Burnets, Oldmixons,* and *Cookes.*

   Soft were my numbers; who could take offense,
While pure Description held the place of Sense?
Like gentle *Fanny's* was my flowery theme,
A painted mistress, or a purling stream.   150
Yet then did *Gildon* draw his venal quill;—
I wished the man a dinner, and sat still.
Yet then did *Dennis* rave in furious fret;
I never answered,—I was not in debt.
If want provoked, or madness made them print,
I waged no war with *Bedlam* or the *Mint.*

   Did some more sober Critic come abroad;
If wrong, I smiled; if right, I kissed the rod.
Pains, reading, study, are their just pretense,
And all they want is spirit, taste, and sense.   160
Commas and points they set exactly right,
And 'twere a sin to rob them of their mite.
Yet ne'er one sprig of laurel graced these ribalds,
From slashing *Bentley* down to pidling *Tibalds*:
Each wight, who reads not, and but scans and spells,
Each Word-catcher, that lives on syllables,
Even such small Critics some regard may claim,
Preserved in *Milton's* or in *Shakespeare's* name.
Pretty! in amber to observe the forms
Of hairs, or straws, or dirt, or grubs, or worms!   170
The things, we know, are neither rich nor rare,
But wonder how the devil they got there.

   Were others angry: I excused them too;

Well might they rage, I gave them but their due.
A man's true merit 'tis not hard to find;
But each man's secret standard in his mind,
That Casting-weight pride adds to emptiness,
This, who can gratify? for who can *guess*?
The Bard whom pilfered Pastorals renown,
Who turns a Persian tale for half a Crown,   180
Just writes to make his barrenness appear,
And strains, from hard-bound brains, eight lines a year;
He, who still wanting, though he lives on theft,
Steals much, spends little, yet has nothing left:
And He, who now to sense, now nonsense leaning,
Means not, but blunders round about a meaning:
And He, whose fustian's so sublimely bad,
It is not Poetry, but prose run mad:
All these, my modest Satire bade *translate*,
And owned that nine such Poets made a *Tate*.   190
How did they fume, and stamp, and roar, and chafe!
And swear, not ADDISON himself was safe.

   Peace to all such! but were there One whose fires
True Genius kindles, and fair Fame inspires;
Blest with each talent and each art to please,
And born to write, converse, and live with ease:
Should such a man, too fond to rule alone,
Bear, like the Turk, no brother near the throne.
View him with scornful, yet with jealous eyes,
And hate for arts that caused himself to rise;   200
Damn with faint praise, assent with civil leer,
And without sneering, teach the rest to sneer;
Willing to wound, and yet afraid to strike,
Just hint a fault, and hesitate dislike;
Alike reserved to blame, or to commend,
A tim'rous foe, and a suspicious friend;
Dreading even fools, by Flatt'rers besieged,
And so obliging, that he ne'er obliged;
Like *Cato*, give his little Senate laws,
And sit attentive to his own applause;   210
While Wits and Templars every sentence raise,

And wonder with a foolish face of praise:—
Who but must laugh, if such a man there be?
Who would not weep, if ATTICUS were he?
    What though my Name stood rubric on the walls,
Or plaistered posts, with claps, in capitals?
Or smoking forth, a hundred hawkers' load,
On wings of winds came flying all abroad?
I sought no homage from the Race that write;
I kept, like *Asian* Monarchs, from their sight: 220
Poems I heeded (now be-rhymed so long)
No more than thou, great GEORGE! a birth-day song.
I ne'er with wits or witlings passed my days,
To spread about the itch of verse and praise;
Nor like a puppy, daggled through the town,
To fetch and carry sing-song up and down;
Nor at Rehearsals sweat, and mouthed, and cried,
With handkerchief and orange at my side.
But sick of fops, and poetry, and prate,
To *Bufo* left the whole *Castalian* state.   230
    Proud as *Apollo* on his forkèd hill,
Sat full-blown *Bufo*, puffed by every quill;
Fed with soft Dedication all day long,
Horace and he went hand in hand in song.
His Library (where busts of Poets dead
And a true *Pindar* stood without a head,)
Received of wits an undistinguished race,
Who first his judgment asked, and then a place:
Much they extolled his pictures, much his seat,
And flattered every day, and some days eat: 240
Till grown more frugal in his riper days,
He paid some bards with port, and some with praise;
To some a dry rehearsal was assigned,
And others (harder still) he paid in kind.
Dryden alone (what wonder?) came not nigh,
Dryden alone escaped this judging eye:
But still the *Great* have kindness in reserve,
He helped to bury whom he helped to starve.
    May some choice patron bless each grey goose quill!

May every *Bavius* have his *Bufo* still! 250
So, when a Statesman wants a day's defense,
Or Envy holds a whole week's war with Sense,
Or simple pride for flatt'ry makes demands,
May dunce by dunce be whistled off my hands!
Blest be the *Great*! for those they take away,
And those they left me; for they left me GAY;
Left me to see neglected Genius bloom,
Neglected die, and tell it on his tomb:
Of all thy blameless life the sole return
My Verse, and QUEENSB'RY weeping o'er thy urn! 260
    Oh let me live my own, and die so too!
(To live and die is all I have to do:)
Maintain a Poet's dignity and ease,
And see what friends, and read what books I please;
Above a Patron, though I condescend
Sometimes to call a minister my friend.
I was not born for Courts or great affairs;
I pay my debts, believe, and say my prayers;
Can sleep without a Poem in my head;
Nor know, if *Dennis* be alive or dead. 270
    Why am I asked what next shall see the light?
Heavens! was I born for nothing but to write?
Has Life no joys for me? or, (to be grave)
Have I no friend to serve, no soul to save?
'I found him close with *Swift*'—"Indeed? no doubt,"
(Cries prating *Balbus*) "something will come out."
'Tis all in vain, deny it as I will.
"No, such a Genius never can lie still;"
And then for mine obligingly mistakes
The first Lampoon Sir *Will*. or *Bubo* makes. 280
Poor guiltless I! and can I choose but smile,
When every Coxcomb knows me by my *Style*?
    Curst be the verse, how well soe'er it flow,
That tends to make one worthy man my foe,
Give Virtue scandal, Innocence a fear,
Or from the soft-eyed Virgin steal a tear!
But he who hurts a harmless neighbor's peace,

Insults fallen worth, or Beauty in distress,
Who loves a Lie, lame slander helps about,
Who writes a Libel, or who copies out: 290
That Fop, whose pride affects a patron's name,
Yet absent, wounds an author's honest fame:
Who can *your* merit *selfishly* approve,
And show the *sense* of it without the *love*;
Who has the vanity to call you friend,
Yet wants the honor, injured, to defend;
Who tells whate'er you think, whate'er you say,
And, if he lie not, must at least betray:
Who to the *Dean*, and *silver bell* can swear,
And sees at *Canons* what was never there;   300
Who reads, but with a lust to misapply,
Make Satire a Lampoon, and Fiction, Lie.
A lash like mine no honest man shall dread,
But all such babbling blockheads in his stead.
    Let *Sporus* tremble— A.   What? that thing of silk,
Sporus, that mere white curd of Ass's milk?
Satire or sense, alas! can *Sporus* feel?
Who breaks a butterfly upon a wheel?
P.   Yet let me flap this bug with gilded wings,
This painted child of dirt, that stinks and stings;   310
Whose buzz the witty and the fair annoys,
Yet wit ne'er tastes, and beauty ne'er enjoys:
So well-bred spaniels civilly delight
In mumbling of the game they dare not bite.
Eternal smiles his emptiness betray,
As shallow streams run dimpling all the way.
Whether in florid impotence he speaks,
And, as the prompter breathes, the puppet squeaks;
Or at the ear of *Eve*, familiar Toad,
Half froth, half venom, spits himself abroad,   320
In puns, or politics, or tales, or lies,
Or spite, or smut, or rhymes, or blasphemies.
His wit all see-saw, between *that* and *this*,
Now high, now low, now master up, now miss,
And he himself one vile Antithesis.

[371]

Amphibious thing! that acting either part,
The trifling head or the corrupted heart,
Fop at the toilet, flatt'rer at the board,
Now trips a Lady, and now struts a Lord.
Eve's tempter thus the Rabbins have exprest,   330
A Cherub's face, a reptile all the rest;
Beauty that shocks you, parts that none will trust;
Wit that can creep, and pride that licks the dust.

    Not Fortune's worshipper, nor fashion's fool,
Not Lucre's madman, nor Ambition's tool,
Not proud, nor servile;—be one Poet's praise,
That, if he pleased, he pleased by manly ways:
That Flatt'ry, even to Kings, he held a shame,
And thought a Lie in verse or prose the same.
That not in Fancy's maze he wandered long,   340
But stooped to Truth, and moralized his song:
That not for Fame, but Virtue's better end,
He stood the furious foe, the timid friend,
The damning critic, half approving wit,
The coxcomb hit, or fearing to be hit;
Laughed at the loss of friends he never had,
The dull, the proud, the wicked, and the mad;
The distant threats of vengeance on his head
The blow unfelt, the tear he never shed;
The tale revived, the lie so oft o'erthrown,   350
Th' imputed trash, and dulness not his own;
The morals blackened when the writings scape,
The libeled person, and the pictured shape;
Abuse, on all he loved, or loved him, spread,
A friend in exile, or a father, dead;
The whisper, that to greatness still too near,
Perhaps, yet vibrates on his Sov'REIGN's ear:—
Welcome for thee, fair *Virtue*! all the past;
For thee, fair Virtue! welcome even the *last*!

    A.   But why insult the poor, affront the great?   360
P.   A knave's a knave, to me, in every state:
Alike my scorn, if he succeed or fail,
Sporus at court, or *Japhet* in a jail,

A hireling scribbler, or a hireling peer,
Knight of the post corrupt, or of the shire;
If on a Pillory, or near a Throne,
He gain his Prince's ear, or lose his own.

Yet soft by nature, more a dupe than wit,
Sappho can tell you how this man was bit;
This dreaded Sat'rist *Dennis* will confess   370
Foe to his pride, but friend to his distress:
So humble, he has knocked at *Tibbald's* door,
Has drunk with *Cibber*, nay, has rhymed for *Moore*.
Full ten years slandered, did he once reply?
Three thousand suns went down on *Welsted's* lie.
To please a Mistress one aspersed his life;
He lashed him not, but let her be his wife.
Let *Budgel* charge low *Grubstreet* on his quill,
And write whate'er he pleased, except his Will;
Let the two *Curlls* of Town and Court, abuse   ⸰380
His father, mother, body, soul, and muse.
Yet why? that Father held it for a rule,
It was a sin to call our neighbor fool:
That harmless Mother thought no wife a whore:
Hear this, and spare his family, *James Moore*!
Unspotted names, and memorable long!
If there be force in Virtue, or in Song.

Of gentle blood (part shed in Honor's cause,
While yet in *Britain* Honor had applause)   389
Each parent sprung— A.   What fortune, pray?— P.   Their own,
And better got, than *Bestia's* from the throne.
Born to no Pride, inheriting no Strife,
Nor marrying Discord in a noble wife,
Stranger to civil and religious rage,
The good man walked innoxious through his age.
Nor Courts he saw, no suits would ever try,
Nor dared an Oath, nor hazarded a Lie.
Un-learned, he knew no schoolman's subtle art,
No language, but the language of the heart.
By Nature honest, by Experience wise,   400
Healthy by temp'rance, and by exercise;

His life, though long, to sickness past unknown,
His death was instant, and without a groan.
O grant me, thus to live, and thus to die!
Who sprung from Kings shall know less joy than I.
　　O Friend! may each domestic bliss be thine!
Be no unpleasing Melancholy mine:
Me, let the tender office long engage,
To rock the cradle of reposing Age,
With lenient arts extend a Mother's breath,　　　410
Make Languor smile, and smooth the bed of Death,
Explore the thought, explain the asking eye,
And keep a while one parent from the sky!
On cares like these if length of days attend,
May Heaven, to bless those days, preserve my friend
Preserve him social, cheerful, and serene,
And just as rich as when he served a QUEEN.
A.　　Whether that blessing be denied or given,
Thus far was right, the rest belongs to Heaven.

195　　　　　　*The Rape of the Lock*

CANTO I

WHAT dire offense from am'rous causes springs,
What mighty contests rise from trivial things,
I sing—This verse to CARYL, Muse! is due:
This, even Belinda may vouchsafe to view:
Slight is the subject, but not so the praise,
If She inspire, and He approve my lays.
　　Say what strange motive, Goddess! could compel
A well-bred Lord t' assault a gentle Belle?
O say what stranger cause, yet unexplored,
Could make a gentle Belle reject a Lord?　　　10
In tasks so bold, can little men engage,
And in soft bosoms dwells such mighty Rage?
　　Sol through white curtains shot a tim'rous ray,
And oped those eyes that must eclipse the day:
Now lap-dogs give themselves the rousing shake,
And sleepless lovers, just at twelve, awake:

Thrice rung the bell, the slipper knocked the ground,
And the pressed watch returned a silver sound.
Belinda still her downy pillow prest,
Her guardian SYLPH prolonged the balmy rest: 20
'Twas He had summoned to her silent bed
The morning-dream that hovered o'er her head;
A Youth more glitt'ring than a Birth-night Beau,
(That even in slumber caused her cheek to glow)
Seemed to her ear his winning lips to lay,
And thus in whispers said, or seemed to say.
   Fairest of mortals, thou distinguished care
Of thousand bright Inhabitants of Air!
If e'er one vision touched thy infant thought,
Of all the Nurse and all the Priest have taught;   30
Of airy Elves by moonlight shadows seen,
The silver token, and the circled green,
Or virgins visited by Angel-powers,
With golden crowns and wreaths of heav'nly flowers;
Hear and believe! thy own importance know,
Nor bound thy narrow views to things below.
Some secret truths, from learnèd pride concealed,
To Maids alone and Children are revealed:
What though no credit doubting Wits may give?
The Fair and Innocent shall still believe.   40
Know, then, unnumbered Spirits round thee fly,
The light Militia of the lower sky:
These, though unseen, are ever on the wing,
Hang o'er the Box, and hover round the Ring.
Think what an equipage thou hast in Air,
And view with scorn two Pages and a Chair.
As now your own, our beings were of old,
And once inclosed in Woman's beauteous mould;
Thence, by a soft transition, we repair
From earthly Vehicles to these of air.   50
Think not, when Woman's transient breath is fled,
That all her vanities at once are dead;
Succeeding vanities she still regards,
And though she plays no more, o'erlooks the cards.

Her joy in gilded Chariots, when alive,
And love of Ombre, after death survive.
For when the Fair in all their pride expire,
To their first Elements their Souls retire:
The Sprites of fiery Termagants in Flame
Mount up, and take a Salamander's name.   60
Soft yielding minds to Water glide away,
And sip, with Nymphs, their elemental Tea.
The graver Prude sinks downward to a Gnome,
In search of mischief still on Earth to roam.
The light Coquettes in Sylphs aloft repair,
And sport and flutter in the fields of Air.

 Know further yet; whoever fair and chaste
Rejects mankind, is by some Sylph embraced:
For Spirits, freed from mortal laws, with ease
Assume what sexes and what shapes they please.   70
What guards the purity of melting Maids,
In courtly balls, and midnight masquerades,
Safe from the treach'rous friend, the daring spark,
The glance by day, the whisper in the dark,
When kind occasion prompts their warm desires,
When music softens, and when dancing fires?
'Tis but their Sylph, the wise Celestials know,
Though Honor is the word with Men below.

 Some nymphs there are, too conscious of their face,
For life predestined to the Gnomes' embrace.   80
These swell their prospects and exalt their pride,
When offers are disdained, and love denied:
Then gay Ideas crowd the vacant brain,
While Peers, and Dukes, and all their sweeping train,
And Garters, Stars, and Coronets appear,
And in soft sounds, Your Grace salutes their ear.
'Tis these that early taint the female soul,
Instruct the eyes of young Coquettes to roll,
Teach Infant-cheeks a bidden blush to know,
And little hearts to flutter at a Beau.   90

 Oft, when the world imagine women stray,
The Sylphs through mystic mazes guide their way,

Through all the giddy circle they pursue,
And old impertinence expel by new.
What tender maid but must a victim fall
To one man's treat, but for another's ball?
When Florio speaks what virgin could withstand,
If gentle Damon did not squeeze her hand?
With varying vanities, from every part,
They shift the moving Toyshop of their heart;   100
Where wigs with wigs, with sword-knots sword-knots strive,
Beaux banish beaux, and coaches coaches drive.
This erring mortals Levity may call;
Oh blind to truth! the Sylphs contrive it all.
    Of these am I, who they protection claim,
A watchful sprite, and Ariel is my name.
Late, as I ranged the crystal wilds of air,
In the clear Mirror of thy ruling Star
I saw, alas! some dread event impend,
Ere to the main this morning sun descend,   110
But heaven reveals not what, or how, or where:
Warned by the Sylph, oh pious maid, beware!
This to disclose is all thy guardian can:
Beware of all, but most beware of Man!
    He said; when Shock, who thought she slept too long,
Leaped up, and waked his mistress with his tongue.
'Twas then, Belinda, if report say true,
Thy eyes first opened on a Billet-doux;
Wounds, Charms, and Ardors were no sooner read,
But all the Vision vanished from thy head.   120
    And now, unveiled, the Toilet stands displayed,
Each silver Vase in mystic order laid.
First, robed in white, the Nymph intent adores,
With head uncovered, the Cosmetic powers.
A heav'nly image in the glass appears,
To that she bends, to that her eyes she rears;
Th' inferior Priestess, at her altar's side,
Trembling begins the sacred rites of Pride.
Unnumbered treasures ope at once, and here
The various off'rings of the world appear;   130

From each she nicely culls with curious toil,
And decks the Goddess with the glitt'ring spoil.
This casket India's glowing gems unlocks,
And all Arabia breathes from yonder box.
The Tortoise here and Elephant unite,
Transformed to combs, the speckled, and the white.
Here files of pins extend their shining rows,
Puffs, Powders, Patches, Bibles, Billet-doux.
Now awful Beauty puts on all its arms;
The fair each moment rises in her charms,   140
Repairs her smiles, awakens every grace,
And calls forth all the wonders of her face;
Sees by degrees a purer blush arise,
And keener lightnings quicken in her eyes.
The busy Sylphs surround their darling care,
These set the head, and those divide the hair,
Some fold the sleeve, whilst others plait the gown;
And Betty's praised for labors not her own.

CANTO II

Not with more glories, in th' etherial plain,
The Sun first rises o'er the purpled main,
Than, issuing forth, the rival of his beams
Launched on the bosom of the silver Thames.
Fair Nymphs, and well-drest Youths around her shone,
But every eye was fixed on her alone.
On her white breast a sparkling Cross she wore,
Which Jews might kiss, and Infidels adore.
Her lively looks a sprightly mind disclose,
Quick as her eyes, and as unfixed as those: 10
Favors to none, to all she smiles extends;
Oft she rejects, but never once offends.
Bright as the sun, her eyes the gazers strike,
And, like the sun, they shine on all alike.
Yet graceful ease, and sweetness void of pride,
Might hide her faults, if Belles had faults to hide:
If to her share some female errors fall,
Look on her face, and you'll forget 'em all.

This Nymph, to the destruction of mankind,
Nourished two Locks, which graceful hung behind   20
In equal curls, and well conspired to deck
With shining ringlets the smooth iv'ry neck.
Love in these labyrinths his slaves detains,
And mighty hearts are held in slender chains.
With hairy springes we the birds betray,
Slight lines of hair surprise the finny prey,
Fair tresses man's imperial race ensnare,
And beauty draws us with a single hair.

Th' advent'rous Baron the bright locks admired;
He saw, he wished, and to the prize aspired.   30
Resolved to win, he meditates the way,
By force to ravish, or by fraud betray;
For when success a Lover's toil attends,
Few ask, if fraud or force attained his ends.

For this, ere Phœbus rose, he had implored
Propitious heaven, and every power adored,
But chiefly Love—to Love an Altar built,
Of twelve vast French Romances, neatly gilt.
There lay three garters, half a pair of gloves;
And all the trophies of his former loves;   40
With tender Billet-doux he lights the pyre,
And breathes three am'rous sighs to raise the fire.
Then prostrate falls, and begs with ardent eyes
Soon to obtain, and long possess the prize:
The powers gave ear, and granted half his prayer,
The rest, the winds dispersed in empty air.

But now secure the painted vessel glides,
The sun-beams trembling on the floating tides:
While melting music steals upon the sky,
And softened sounds along the waters die;   50
Smooth flow the waves, the Zephyrs gently play,
Belinda smiled, and all the world was gay.
All but the Sylph—with careful thoughts opprest,
Th' impending woe sat heavy on his breast.
He summons strait his Denizens of air;
The lucid squadrons round the sails repair:

Soft o'er the shrouds aërial whispers breathe,
That seemed but Zephyrs to the train beneath.
Some to the sun their insect-wings unfold,
Waft on the breeze, or sink in clouds of gold;   60
Transparent forms, too fine for mortal sight,
Their fluid bodies half dissolved in light,
Loose to the wind their airy garments flew,
Thin glitt'ring textures of the filmy dew,
Dipt in the richest tincture of the skies,
Where light disports in ever-mingling dyes,
While every beam new transient colors flings,
Colors that change whene'er they wave their wings.
Amid the circle, on the gilded mast,
Superior by the head, was Ariel placed;   70
His purple pinions opening to the sun,
He raised his azure wand, and thus begun.
    Ye Sylphs and Sylphids, to your chief give ear!
Fays, Fairies, Genii, Elves, and Dæmons, hear!
Ye know the spheres and various tasks assigned
By laws eternal to th' aërial kind.
Some in the fields of purest Æther play,
And bask and whiten in the blaze of day.
Some guide the course of wand'ring orbs on high,
Or roll the planets through the boundless sky.   80
Some less refined, beneath the moon's pale light
Pursue the stars that shoot athwart the night,
Or suck the mists in grosser air below,
Or dip their pinions in the painted bow,
Or brew fierce tempests on the wintry main,
Or o'er the glebe distil the kindly rain.
Others on earth o'er human race preside,
Watch all their ways, and all their actions guide:
Of these the chief the care of Nations own,
And guard with Arms divine the British Throne.   90
    Our humbler province is to tend the Fair,
Not a less pleasing, though less glorious care;
To save the powder from too rude a gale,
Nor let th' imprisoned essences exhale;

To draw fresh colors from the vernal flowers;
To steal from rainbows e'er they drop in showers
A brighter wash; to curl their waving hairs,
Assist their blushes, and inspire their airs;
Nay oft, in dreams, invention we bestow,
To change a Flounce, or add a Furbelow.   100
    This day, black Omens threat the brightest Fair,
That e'er deserved a watchful spirit's care;
Some dire disaster, or by force, or slight;
But what, or where, the fates have wrapt in night.
Whether the nymph shall break Diana's law,
Or some frail China jar receive a flaw;
Or stain her honor or her new brocade;
Forget her prayers, or miss a masquerade;
Or lose her heart, or necklace, at a ball;
Or whether Heaven has doomed that Shock must fall.   110
Haste, then, ye spirits! to your charge repair:
The flutt'ring fan be Zephyretta's care;
The drops to thee, Brillante, we consign;
And, Momentilla, let the watch be thine;
Do thou, Crispissa, tend her fav'rite Lock;
Ariel himself shall be the guard of Shock.
    To fifty chosen Sylphs, of special note,
We trust th' important charge, the Petticoat:
Oft have we known that seven-fold fence to fail,
Though stiff with hoops, and armed with ribs of whale;   120
Form a strong line about the silver bound,
And guard the wide circumference around.
    Whatever spirit, careless of his charge,
His post neglects, or leaves the fair at large,
Shall feel sharp vengeance soon o'ertake his sins,
Be stopped in vials, or transfixed with pins;
Or plunged in lakes of bitter washes lie,
Or wedged whole ages in a bodkin's eye:
Gums and Pomatums shall his flight restrain,
While clogged he beats his silken wings in vain;   130
Or Alum styptics with contracting power
Shrink his thin essence like a riveled flower:

Or, as Ixion fixed, the wretch shall feel
The giddy motion of the whirling Mill,
In fumes of burning Chocolate shall glow,
And tremble at the sea that froths below!
    He spoke; the spirits from the sails descend;
Some, orb in orb, around the nymph extend;
Some thrid the mazy ringlets of her hair;
Some hang upon the pendants of her ear: 140
With beating hearts the dire event they wait,
Anxious, and trembling for the birth of Fate.

CANTO III

Close by those meads, forever crowned with flowers,
Where Thames with pride surveys his rising towers,
There stands a structure of majestic frame,
Which from the neighb'ring Hampton takes its name.
Here Britain's statesmen oft the fall foredoom
Of foreign Tyrants and of Nymphs at home;
Here thou, great Anna! whom three realms obey,
Dost sometimes counsel take—and sometimes Tea.
    Hither the heroes and the nymphs resort,
To taste awhile the pleasures of a Court;   10
In various talk th' instructive hours they past,
Who gave the ball, or paid the visit last;
One speaks the glory of the British Queen,
And one describes a charming Indian screen;
A third interprets motions, looks, and eyes;
At every word a reputation dies.
Snuff, or the fan, supply each pause of chat,
With singing, laughing, ogling, *and all that.*
    Meanwhile, declining from the noon of day,
The sun obliquely shoots his burning ray;   20
The hungry Judges soon the sentence sign,
And wretches hang that jury-men may dine;
The merchant from th' Exchange returns in peace,
And the long labors of the Toilet cease.
Belinda now, whom thirst of fame invites,
Burns to encounter two advent'rous Knights,

At Ombre singly to decide their doom;
And swells her breast with conquests yet to come.
Straight the three bands prepare in arms to join,
Each band the number of the sacred nine.   30
Soon as she spreads her hand, th' aërial guard
Descend, and sit on each important card:
First Ariel perched upon a Matadore,
Then each, according to the rank they bore;
For Sylphs, yet mindful of their ancient race,
Are, as when women, wondrous fond of place.

    Behold, four Kings in majesty revered,
With hoary whiskers and a forky beard;
And four fair Queens whose hands sustain a flower,
Th' expressive emblem of their softer power;   40
Four Knaves in garbs succinct, a trusty band,
Caps on their heads, and halberts in their hand;
And particolored troops, a shining train,
Draw forth to combat on the velvet plain.

    The skilful Nymph reviews her force with care:
Let Spades be trumps! she said, and trumps they were.

    Now move to war her sable Matadores,
In show like leaders of the swarthy Moors.
Spadillio first, unconquerable Lord!
Led off two captive trumps, and swept the board.   50
As many more Manillio forced to yield,
And marched a victor from the verdant field.
Him Basto followed, but his fate more hard
Gained but one trump and one Plebeian card.
With his broad sabre next, a chief in years,
The hoary Majesty of Spades appears,
Puts forth one manly leg, to sight revealed,
The rest, his many-colored robe concealed.
The rebel Knave, who dares his prince engage,
Proves the just victim of his royal rage.   60
Even mighty Pam, that Kings and Queens o'erthrew
And mowed down armies in the fights of Lu,
Sad chance of war! now destitute of aid,
Falls undistinguished by the victor spade!

Thus far both armies to Belinda yield;
Now to the Baron fate inclines the field.
His warlike Amazon her host invades,
Th' imperial consort of the crown of Spades.
The Club's black Tyrant first her victim dyed,
Spite of his haughty mien, and barb'rous pride: 70
What boots the regal circle on his head,
His giant limbs, in state unwieldy spread;
That long behind he trails his pompous robe,
And, of all monarchs, only grasps the globe?
    The Baron now his Diamonds pours apace;
Th' embroidered King who shows but half his face,
And his refulgent Queen, with powers combined
Of broken troops an easy conquest find.
Clubs, Diamonds, Hearts, in wild disorder seen,
With throngs promiscuous strow the level green.   80
Thus when dispersed a routed army runs,
Of Asia's troops, and Afric's sable sons,
With like confusion different nations fly,
Of various habit, and of various dye,
The pierced battalions dis-united fall,
In heaps on heaps; one fate o'erwhelms them all.
    The Knave of Diamonds tries his wily arts,
And wins (oh shameful chance!) the Queen of Hearts.
At this, the blood the virgin's cheek forsook,
A livid paleness spreads o'er all her look;   90
She sees, and trembles at th' approaching ill,
Just in the jaws of ruin, and Codille.
And now (as oft in some distempered State)
On one nice Trick depends the general fate.
An Ace of Hearts steps forth: The King unseen
Lurked in her hand, and mourned his captive Queen:
He springs to Vengeance with an eager pace,
And falls like thunder on the prostrate Ace.
The nymph exulting fills with shouts the sky;
The walls, the woods, and long canals reply.   100
    Oh thoughtless mortals! ever blind to fate,
Too soon dejected, and too soon elate.

Sudden, these honors shall be snatched away,
And cursed for ever this victorious day.
 For lo! the board with cups and spoons is crowned,
The berries crackle, and the mill turns round;
On shining Altars of Japan they raise
The silver lamp; the fiery spirits blaze:
From silver spouts the grateful liquors glide,
While China's earth receives the smoking tide: 110
At once they gratify their scent and taste,
And frequent cups prolong the rich repast.
Straight hover round the Fair her airy band;
Some, as she sipped, the fuming liquor fanned,
Some o'er her lap their careful plumes displayed,
Trembling, and conscious of the rich brocade.
Coffee, (which makes the politician wise,
And see through all things with his half-shut eyes)
Sent up in vapors to the Baron's brain
New Stratagems, the radiant Lock to gain.   120
Ah cease, rash youth! desist ere 'tis too late,
Fear the just Gods, and think of Scylla's Fate!
Changed to a bird, and sent to flit in air,
She dearly pays for Nisus' injured hair!
 But when to mischief mortals bend their will,
How soon they find fit instruments of ill!
Just then, Clarissa drew with tempting grace
A two-edged weapon from her shining case:
So Ladies in Romance assist their Knight,
Present the spear, and arm him for the fight.   130
He takes the gift with rev'rence, and extends
The little engine on his fingers' ends;
This just behind Belinda's neck he spread,
As o'er the fragrant steams she bends her head.
Swift to the Lock a thousand Sprites repair,
A thousand wings, by turns, blow back the hair;
And thrice they twitched the diamond in her ear;
Thrice she looked back, and thrice the foe drew near.
Just in that instant, anxious Ariel sought
The close recesses of the Virgin's thought;   140

[385]

As on the nosegay in her breast reclined,
He watched th' Ideas rising in her mind,
Sudden he viewed, in spite of all her art,
An earthly Lover lurking at her heart.
Amazed, confused, he found his power expired,
Resigned to fate, and with a sigh retired.

The Peer now spreads the glitt'ring Forfex wide,
T' inclose the Lock; now joins it, to divide.
Even then, before the fatal engine closed,
A wretched Sylph too fondly interposed;   150
Fate urged the shears, and cut the Sylph in twain,
(But airy substance soon unites again)
The meeting points the sacred hair dissever
From the fair head, forever, and forever!

Then flashed the living lightning from her eyes,
And screams of horror rend th' affrighted skies.
Not louder shrieks to pitying heaven are cast,
When husbands, or when lap-dogs breathe their last;
Or when rich China vessels fall'n from high,
In glitt'ring dust and painted fragments lie!   160

Let wreaths of triumph now my temples twine,
(The victor cried) the glorious Prize is mine!
While fish in streams, or birds delight in air,
Or in a coach and six the British Fair,
As long as Atalantis shall be read,
Or the small pillow grace a Lady's bed,
While visits shall be paid on solemn days,
When num'rous wax-lights in bright order blaze,
While nymphs take treats, or assignations give,
So long my honor, name, and praise shall live!   170
What Time would spare, from Steel receives its date,
And monuments, like men, submit to fate!
Steel could the labor of the Gods destroy,
And strike to dust th' imperial towers of Troy;
Steel could the works of mortal pride confound,
And hew triumphal arches to the ground.
What wonder then, fair nymph! thy hairs should feel,
The conq'ring force of unresisted steel?

[386]

But anxious cares the pensive nymph oppressed,
And secret passions labored in her breast.
Not youthful kings in battle seized alive,
Not scornful virgins who their charms survive,
Not ardent lovers robbed of all their bliss,
Not ancient ladies when refused a kiss,
Not tyrants fierce that unrepenting die,
Not Cynthia when her manteau's pinned awry,
E'er felt such rage, resentment, and despair,
As thou, sad Virgin! for thy ravished Hair.   10
    For, that sad moment, when the Sylphs withdrew
And Ariel weeping from Belinda flew,
Umbriel, a dusky, melancholy sprite,
As ever sullied the fair face of light,
Down to the central earth, his proper scene,
Repaired to search the gloomy Cave of Spleen.
    Swift on his sooty pinions flits the Gnome,
And in a vapour reached the dismal dome.
No cheerful breeze this sullen region knows,
The dreaded East is all the wind that blows.   20
Here in a grotto, sheltered close from air,
And screened in shades from day's detested glare,
She sighs forever on her pensive bed,
Pain at her side, and Megrim at her head.
    Two handmaids wait the throne: alike in place,
But diff'ring far in figure and in face.
Here stood Ill-nature like an ancient maid,
Her wrinkled form in black and white arrayed;
With store of prayers, for mornings, nights, and noons,
Her hand is filled; her bosom with lampoons.   30
    There Affectation, with a sickly mien,
Shows in her cheek the roses of eighteen,
Practised to lisp, and hang the head aside,
Faints into airs, and languishes with pride,
On the rich quilt sinks with becoming woe,
Wrapt in a gown, for sickness, and for show.
The fair ones feel such maladies as these,

When each new night-dress gives a new disease.
   A constant Vapor o'er the palace flies;
Strange phantoms rising as the mists arise;   40
Dreadful, as hermit's dreams in haunted shades,
Or bright, as visions of expiring maids.
Now glaring fiends, and snakes on rolling spires,
Pale specters, gaping tombs, and purple fires:
Now lakes of liquid gold, Elysian scenes,
And crystal domes, and angels in machines.
   Unnumbered throngs on every side are seen,
Of bodies changed to various forms by Spleen.
Here living Tea-pots stand, one arm held out,
One bent; the handle this, and that the spout: 50
A Pipkin there, like Homer's Tripod walks;
Here sighs a Jar, and there a Goose-pie talks;
Men prove with child, as powerful fancy works,
And maids turned bottles, call aloud for corks.
   Safe past the Gnome through this fantastic band,
A branch of healing Spleenwort in his hand.
Then thus addressed the power: 'Hail, wayward Queen!
Who rule the sex to fifty from fifteen:
Parent of vapors and of female wit,
Who give th' hysteric or poetic fit,   60
On various tempers act by various ways,
Make some take physic, others scribble plays;
Who cause the proud their visits to delay,
And send the godly in a pet to pray.
A nymph there is, that all thy power disdains,
And thousands more in equal mirth maintains.
But oh! if e'er thy Gnome could spoil a grace,
Or raise a pimple on a beauteous face,
Like Citron-waters matrons' cheeks inflame,
Or change complexions at a losing game;   70
If e'er with airy horns I planted heads,
Or rumpled petticoats, or tumbled beds,
Or caus'd suspicion when no soul was rude,
Or discomposed the head-dress of a Prude,
Or e'er to costive lap-dog gave disease,

Which not the tears of brightest eyes could ease:
Hear me, and touch Belinda with chagrin,
That single act gives half the world the spleen.'
    The Goddess with a discontented air
Seems to reject him, though she grants his prayer.   80
A wondrous Bag with both her hands she binds,
Like that where once Ulysses held the winds;
There she collects the force of female lungs,
Sighs, sobs, and passions, and the war of tongues.
A Vial next she fills with fainting fears,
Soft sorrows, melting griefs, and flowing tears.
The Gnome rejoicing bears her gifts away,
Spreads his black wings, and slowly mounts to day.
    Sunk in Thalestris' arms the nymph he found,
Her eyes dejected and her hair unbound.   90
Full o'er their heads the swelling bag he rent,
And all the Furies issued at the vent.
Belinda burns with more than mortal ire,
And fierce Thalestris fans the rising fire.
'Oh wretched maid!' she spread her hands, and cried,
(While Hampton's echoes, 'Wretched maid!' replied)
'Was it for this you took such constant care
The bodkin, comb, and essence to prepare?
For this your locks in paper durance bound,
For this with torturing irons wreathed around?   100
For this with fillets strained your tender head,
And bravely bore the double loads of lead?
Gods! shall the ravisher display your hair,
While the Fops envy, and the Ladies stare!
Honor forbid! at whose unrivaled shrine
Ease, pleasure, virtue, all our sex resign.
Methinks already I your tears survey,
Already hear the horrid things they say,
Already see you a degraded toast,
And all your honor in a whisper lost!   110
How shall I, then, your helpless fame defend?
'Twill then be infamy to seem your friend!
And shall this prize, th' inestimable prize,

Exposed through crystal to the gazing eyes,
And heightened by the diamond's circling rays,
On that rapacious hand forever blaze?
Sooner shall grass in Hyde-park Circus grow,
And wits take lodgings in the sound of Bow;
Sooner let earth, air, sea, to Chaos fall,
Men, monkeys, lap-dogs, parrots, perish all!'   120
    She said; then raging to Sir Plume repairs,
And bids her Beau demand the precious hairs:
(Sir Plume of amber snuff-box justly vain,
And the nice conduct of a clouded cane)
With earnest eyes, and round unthinking face,
He first the snuff-box opened, then the case,
And thus broke out—'My Lord, why, what the devil?
Z—ds! damn the lock! 'fore Gad, you must be civil!
Plague on't! 'tis past a jest—nay prithee, pox!
Give her the hair'—he spoke, and rapped his box.   130
    'It grieves me much' (replied the Peer again)
'Who speaks so well should ever speak in vain.
But by this Lock, this sacred Lock I swear,
(Which never more shall join its parted hair;
Which never more its honors shall renew,
Clipped from the lovely head where late it grew)
That while my nostrils draw the vital air,
This hand, which won it, shall for ever wear.'
He spoke, and speaking, in proud triumph spread
The long-contended honours of her head.   140
    But Umbriel, hateful Gnome! forbears not so;
He breaks the Vial whence the sorrows flow.
Then see! the nymph in beauteous grief appears,
Her eyes half-languishing, half-drowned in tears;
On her heaved bosom hung her drooping head,
Which, with a sigh, she raised; and thus she said.
    'Forever cursed be this detested day,
Which snatched my best, my fav'rite curl away!
Happy! ah ten times happy had I been,
If Hampton-Court these eyes had never seen!   150
Yet am not I the first mistaken maid,

By love of Courts to numerous ills betrayed.
Oh had I rather un-admired remained
In some lone isle, or distant Northern land;
Where the gilt Chariot never marks the way,
Where none learn Ombre, none e'er taste Bohea!
There kept my charms concealed from mortal eye,
Like roses, that in deserts bloom and die.
What moved my mind with youthful Lords to roam?
Oh had I stayed, and said my prayers at home! 160
'Twas this, the morning omens seemed to tell,
Thrice from my trembling hand the patch-box fell;
The tott'ring China shook without a wind,
Nay, Poll sat mute, and Shock was most unkind!
A Sylph too warned me of the threats of fate,
In mystic visions, now believed too late!
See the poor remnants of these slighted hairs!
My hands shall rend what even thy rapine spares:
These in two sable ringlets taught to break,
Once gave new beauties to the snowy neck; 170
The sister-lock now sits uncouth, alone,
And in its fellow's fate foresees its own;
Uncurled it hangs, the fatal shears demands,
And tempts once more, thy sacrilegious hands.
Oh hadst thou, cruel! been content to seize
Hairs less in sight, or any hairs but these!'

CANTO V

SHE said: the pitying audience melt in tears.
But Fate and Jove had stopped the Baron's ears.
In vain Thalestris with reproach assails,
For who can move when fair Belinda fails?
Not half so fixed the Trojan could remain,
While Anna begged and Dido raged in vain.
Then grave Clarissa graceful waved her fan;
Silence ensued, and thus the nymph began.
    'Say why are Beauties praised and honored most,
The wise man's passion, and the vain man's toast? 10
Why decked with all that land and sea afford,

[391]

Why Angels called, and Angel-like adored?
Why round our coaches crowd the white-gloved Beaux,
Why bows the side-box from its inmost rows;
How vain are all these glories, all our pains,
Unless good sense preserve what beauty gains:
That men may say, when we the front-box grace:
"Behold the first in virtue as in face!"
Oh! if to dance all night, and dress all day,
Charmed the small-pox, or chased old-age away;   20
Who would not scorn what housewife's cares produce,
Or who would learn one earthly thing of use?
To patch, nay ogle, might become a Saint,
Nor could it sure be such a sin to paint.
But since, alas! frail beauty must decay,
Curled or uncurled, since Locks will turn to grey;
Since painted, or not painted, all shall fade,
And she who scorns a man, must die a maid;
What then remains but well our power to use,
And keep good-humor still whate'er we lose?   30
And trust me, dear! good-humor can prevail,
When airs, and flights, and screams, and scolding fail.
Beauties in vain their pretty eyes may roll;
Charms strike the sight, but merit wins the soul.'
    So spoke the Dame, but no applause ensued;
Belinda frowned, Thalestris called her Prude.
'To arms, to arms!' the fierce Virago cries,
And swift as lightning to the combat flies.
All side in parties, and begin th' attack;
Fans clap, silks rustle, and tough whalebones crack;   40
Heroes' and Heroines' shouts confus'dly rise,
And bass and treble voices strike the skies.
No common weapons in their hands are found,
Like Gods they fight, nor dread a mortal wound.
    So when bold Homer makes the Gods engage,
And heavenly breasts with human passions rage;
'Gainst Pallas, Mars; Latona, Hermes arms;
And all Olympus rings with loud alarms:
Jove's thunder roars, heaven trembles all around,

Blue Neptune storms, the bellowing deeps resound: 50
Earth shakes her nodding towers, the ground gives way,
And the pale ghosts start at the flash of day!
    Triumphant Umbriel on a sconce's height
Clapped his glad wings, and sat to view the fight:
Propped on their bodkin spears, the Sprites survey
The growing combat, or assist the fray.
    While through the press enraged Thalestris flies,
And scatters death around from both her eyes,
A Beau and Witling perished in the throng,
One died in metaphor, and one in song.   60
'O cruel nymph! a living death I bear,'
Cried Dapperwit, and sunk beside his chair.
A mournful glance Sir Fopling upwards cast,
'Those eyes are made so killing'—was his last.
Thus on Mæander's flowery margin lies
Th' expiring Swan, and as he sings he dies.
    When bold Sir Plume had drawn Clarissa down,
Chloe stepped in, and killed him with a frown;
She smiled to see the doughty hero slain,
But, at her smile, the Beau revived again.   70
    Now Jove suspends his golden scales in air,
Weighs the Men's wits against the Lady's hair;
The doubtful beam long nods from side to side;
At length the wits mount up, the hairs subside.
    See, fierce Belinda on the Baron flies,
With more than usual lightning in her eyes:
Nor feared the Chief th' unequal fight to try,
Who sought no more than on his foe to die.
But this bold Lord with manly strength endued,
She with one finger and a thumb subdued: 80
Just where the breath of life his nostrils drew,
A charge of Snuff the wily virgin threw;
The Gnomes direct, to every atom just,
The pungent grains of titillating dust.
Sudden, with starting tears each eye o'erflows,
And the high dome re-echoes to his nose.
    Now meet thy fate, incensed Belinda cried,

And drew a deadly bodkin from her side.
(The same, his ancient personage to deck,
Her great great grandsire wore about his neck, 90
In three seal-rings; which after, melted down,
Formed a vast buckle for his widow's gown:
Her infant grandame's whistle next it grew,
The bells she jingled, and the whistle blew;
Then in a bodkin graced her mother's hairs,
Which long she wore, and now Belinda wears.)
 'Boast not my fall' (he cried) 'insulting foe!
Thou by some other shalt be laid as low,
Nor think, to die dejects my lofty mind:
All that I dread is leaving you behind! 100
Rather than so, ah let me still survive,
And burn in Cupid's flames—but burn alive.'
 'Restore the Lock!' she cries; and all around
'Restore the Lock!' the vaulted roofs rebound.
Not fierce Othello in so loud a strain
Roared for the handkerchief that caused his pain.
But see how oft ambitious aims are crossed,
And chiefs contend till all the prize is lost!
The Lock, obtained with guilt, and kept with pain,
In every place is sought, but sought in vain: 110
With such a prize no mortal must be blest,
So heaven decrees! with heaven who can contest?
 Some thought it mounted to the Lunar sphere,
Since all things lost on earth are treasured there.
There Hero's wits are kept in pond'rous vases,
And beau's in snuff-boxes and tweezer-cases.
There broken vows and death-bed alms are found,
And lovers' hearts with ends of riband bound,
The courtier's promises, and sick man's prayers,
The smiles of harlots, and the tears of heirs, 120
Cages for gnats, and chains to yoke a flea,
Dried butterflies, and tomes of casuistry.
 But trust the Muse—she saw it upward rise,
Though marked by none but quick, poetic eyes:
(So Rome's great founder to the heavens withdrew,

To Proculus alone confessed in view)
A sudden Star, it shot through liquid air,
And drew behind a radiant trail of hair.
Not Berenice's Locks first rose so bright,
The heavens bespangling with disheveled light.   130
The Sylphs behold it kindling as it flies,
And pleased pursue its progress through the skies.
   This the Beau monde shall from the Mall survey,
And hail with music its propitious ray.
This the blest Lover shall for Venus take,
And send up vows from Rosamonda's lake.
This Partridge soon shall view in cloudless skies,
When next he looks through Galileo's eyes;
And hence th' egregious wizard shall foredoom
The fate of Louis, and the fall of Rome.   140
   Then cease, bright Nymph! to mourn thy ravished hair,
Which adds new glory to the shining sphere!
Not all the tresses that fair head can boast,
Shall draw such envy as the Lock you lost.
For, after all the murders of your eye,
When, after millions slain, yourself shall die:
When those fair suns shall set, as set they must,
And all those tresses shall be laid in dust,
This Lock, the Muse shall consecrate to fame,
And 'midst the stars inscribe Belinda's name.   150

196   *The Vision of Judgment*

Saint Peter sat by the celestial gate:
   His keys were rusty, and the lock was dull,
So little trouble had been given of late;
   Not that the place by any means was full,
But since the Gallic era 'eighty-eight'
   The devils had ta'en a longer, stronger pull,
And 'a pull all together,' as they say
At sea—which drew most souls another way.

The angels all were singing out of tune,
    And hoarse with having little else to do,   10
Excepting to wind up the sun and moon,
    Or curb a runaway young star or two,
Or wild colt of a comet, which too soon
    Broke out of bounds o'er the ethereal blue,
Splitting some planet with its playful tail,
As boats are sometimes by a wanton whale.

The guardian seraphs had retired on high,
    Finding their charges past all care below;
Terrestrial business fill'd nought in the sky
    Save the recording angel's black bureau;   20
Who found, indeed, the facts to multiply
    With such rapidity of vice and woe,
That he had stripp'd off both his wings in quills,
And yet was in arrear of human ills.

His business so augmented of late years,
    That he was forced, against his will no doubt
(Just like those cherubs, earthly ministers),
    For some resource to turn himself about,
And claim the help of his celestial peers,
    To aid him ere he should be quite worn out   30
By the increased demand for his remarks:
Six angels and twelve saints were named his clerks.

This was a handsome board—at least for heaven;
  . And yet they had even then enough to do,
So many conquerors' cars were daily driven,
    So many kingdoms fitted up anew;
Each day too slew its thousands six or seven,
    Till at the crowning carnage, Waterloo,
They threw their pens down in divine disgust—
The page was so besmear'd with blood and dust.   40

[396]

This by the way; 'tis not mine to record
    What angels shrink from: even the very devil
On this occasion his own work abhorr'd,
    So surfeited with the infernal revel:
Though he himself had sharpen'd every sword,
    It almost quench'd his innate thirst of evil.
(Here Satan's sole good work deserves insertion—
'Tis, that he has both generals in reversion.)

Let's skip a few short years of hollow peace,
    Which peopled earth no better, hell as wont,   50
And heaven none—they form the tyrant's lease,
    With nothing but new names subscribed upon 't;
'Twill one day finish: meantime they increase,
    'With seven heads and ten horns,' and all in front,
Like Saint John's foretold beast; but ours are born
Less formidable in the head than horn.

In the first year of freedom's second dawn
    Died George the Third; although no tyrant, one
Who shielded tyrants, till each sense withdrawn
    Left him nor mental nor external sun: 60
A better farmer ne'er brush'd dew from lawn,
    A worse king never left a realm undone!
He died—but left his subjects still behind,
One half as mad—and t'other no less blind.

He died!—his death made no great stir on earth:
    His burial made some pomp; there was profusion
Of velvet, gilding, brass, and no great dearth
    Of aught but tears—save those shed by collusion.
For these things may be bought at their true worth;
    Of elegy there was the due infusion—   70
Bought also; and the torches, cloaks, and banners,
Heralds, and relics of old Gothic manners,

[397]

Form'd a sepulchral melodrame. Of all
    The fools who flock'd to swell or see the show,
Who cared about the corpse? The funeral
    Made the attraction, and the black the woe.
There throbb'd not there a thought which pierced the pall;
    And when the gorgeous coffin was laid low,
It seem'd the mockery of hell to fold
The rottenness of eighty years in gold.   80

So mix his body with the dust! It might
    Return to what it *must* far sooner, were
The natural compound left alone to fight
    Its way back into earth, and fire, and air;
But the unnatural balsams merely blight
    What nature made him at his birth, as bare
As the mere million's base unmummied clay—
Yet all his spices but prolong decay.

He's dead—and upper earth with him has done;
    He's buried; save the undertaker's bill,   90
Or lapidary scrawl, the world is gone
    For him, unless he left a German will:
But where's the proctor who will ask his son?
    In whom his qualities are reigning still,
Except that household virtue, most uncommon,
Of constancy to a bad, ugly woman.

'God save the king!' It is a large economy
    In God to save the like; but if he will
Be saving, all the better; for not one am I
    Of those who think damnation better still: 100
I hardly know too if not quite alone am I
    In this small hope of bettering future ill
By circumscribing, with some slight restriction,
The eternity of hell's hot jurisdiction.

I know this is unpopular; I know
　　'Tis blasphemous; I know one may be damn'd
For hoping no one else may e'er be so;
　　I know my catechism; I know we're cramm'd
With the best doctrine till we quite o'erflow;
　　I know that all save England's church have shamm'd,　110
And that the other twice two hundred churches
And synagogues have made a *damn'd* bad purchase.

God help us all! God help me too! I am,
　　God knows, as helpless as the devil can wish,
And not a whit more difficult to damn,
　　Than is to bring to land a late-hook'd fish,
Or to the butcher to purvey the lamb;
　　Not that I'm fit for such a noble dish,
As one day will be that immortal fry
Of almost everybody born to die.　　　　　　120

Saint Peter sat by the celestial gate,
　　And nodded o'er his keys; when, lo! there came
A wondrous noise he had not heard of late—
　　A rushing sound of wind, and stream, and flame;
In short, a roar of things extremely great,
　　Which would have made aught save a saint exclaim;
But he, with first a start and then a wink,
Said, 'There's another star gone out, I think!'

But ere he could return to his repose,
　　A cherub flapp'd his right wing o'er his eyes—　　130
At which St. Peter yawn'd, and rubb'd his nose:
　　'Saint porter,' said the angel, 'prithee rise!'
Waving a goodly wing, which glow'd, as glows
　　An earthly peacock's tail, with heavenly dyes:
To which the saint replied, 'Well, what's the matter?
'Is Lucifer come back with all this clatter?'

'No,' quoth the cherub; 'George the Third is dead.'
   'And who *is* George the Third?' replied the apostle:
'*What George? what Third?*'—'The king of England,' said
   The angel. 'Well! he won't find kings to jostle   140
Him on his way; but does he wear his head?
   Because the last we saw here had a tussle,
And ne'er would have got into heaven's good graces,
Had he not flung his head in all our faces.

'He was, if I remember, king of France;
   That head of his, which could not keep a crown
On earth, yet ventured in my face to advance
   A claim to those of martyrs—like my own:
If I had had my sword, as I had once
   When I cut ears off, I had cut him down;   150
But having but my *keys*, and not my brand,
I only knock'd his head from out his hand.

'And then he set up such a headless howl,
   That all the saints came out and took him in;
And there he sits by St. Paul, cheek by jowl;
   That fellow Paul—the parvenù! The skin
Of St. Bartholomew, which makes his cowl
   In heaven, and upon earth redeem'd his sin,
So as to make a martyr, never sped
Better than did this weak and wooden head.   160

'But had it come up here upon its shoulders,
   There would have been a different tale to tell:
The fellow-feeling in the saint's beholders
   Seems to have acted on them like a spell,
And so this very foolish head heaven solders
   Back on its trunk: it may be very well,
And seems the custom here to overthrow
Whatever has been wisely done below.'

The angel answer'd, 'Peter! do not pout:
    The king who comes has head and all entire,   170
And never knew much what it was about;
    He did as doth the puppet—by its wire,
And will be judged like all the rest, no doubt:
    My business and your own is not to inquire
Into such matters, but to mind our cue—
Which is to act as we are bid to do.'

While thus they spake, the angelic caravan,
    Arriving like a rush of mighty wind,
Cleaving the fields of space, as doth the swan
    Some silver stream (say Ganges, Nile, or Inde,   180
Or Thames, or Tweed), and 'midst them an old man
    With an old soul, and both extremely blind,
Halted before the gate, and in his shroud
Seated their fellow traveler on a cloud.

But bringing up the rear of this bright host
    A Spirit of a different aspect waved
His wings, like thunder-clouds above some coast
    Whose barren beach with frequent wrecks is paved;
His brow was like the deep when tempest-toss'd;
    Fierce and unfathomable thoughts engraved   190
Eternal wrath on his immortal face,
And *where* he gazed a gloom pervaded space.

As he drew near, he gazed upon the gate
    Ne'er to be enter'd more by him or sin,
With such a glance of supernatural hate,
    As made Saint Peter wish himself within;
He patter'd with his keys at a great rate,
    And sweated through his apostolic skin:
Of course his perspiration was but ichor,
Or some such other spiritual liquor.   200

The very cherubs huddled all together,
    Like birds when soars the falcon; and they felt
A tingling to the tip of every feather,
    And form'd a circle like Orion's belt
Around their poor old charge; who scarce knew whither
    His guards had led him, though they gently dealt
With royal manes (for by many stories,
And true, we learn the angels are all Tories).

As things were in this posture, the gate flew
    Asunder, and the flashing of its hinges   210
Flung over space an universal hue
    Of many-color'd flame, until its tinges
Reach'd even our speck of earth, and made a new
    Aurora borealis spread its fringes
O'er the North Pole; the same seen, when ice-bound,
By Captain Parry's crew, in 'Melville's Sound.'

And from the gate thrown open issued beaming
    A beautiful and mighty Thing of Light,
Radiant with glory, like a banner streaming
    Victorious from some world-o'erthrowing fight: 220
My poor comparisons must needs be teeming
    With earthly likenesses, for here the night
Of clay obscures our best conceptions, saving
Johanna Southcote, or Bob Southey raving.

'Twas the archangel Michael; all men know
    The make of angels and archangels, since
There's scarce a scribbler has not one to show,
    From the fiends' leader to the angels' prince;
There also are some altar-pieces, though
    I really can't say that they much evince   230
One's inner notions of immortal spirits;
But let the connoisseurs explain *their* merits.

Michael flew forth in glory and in good;
    A goodly work of him from whom all glory
And good arise; the portal past—he stood;
    Before him the young cherubs and saints hoary—
(I say *young*, begging to be understood
    By looks, not years; and should be very sorry
To state, they were not older than St. Peter,
But merely that they seem'd a little sweeter).   240

The cherubs and the saints bow'd down before
    That arch-angelic hierarch, the first
Of essences angelical, who wore
    The aspect of a god; but this ne'er nursed
Pride in his heavenly bosom, in whose core
    No thought, save for his Maker's service, durst
Intrude, however glorified and high;
He knew him but the viceroy of the sky.

He and the somber, silent Spirit met—
    They knew each other both for good and ill;   250
Such was their power, that neither could forget
    His former friend and future foe; but still
There was a high, immortal, proud regret
    In either's eye, as if 'twere less their will
Than destiny to make the eternal years
Their date of war, and their 'champ clos' the spheres.

But here they were in neutral space: we know
    From Job, that Satan hath the power to pay
A heavenly visit thrice a year or so;
    And that the 'sons of God,' like those of clay,   260
Must keep him company; and we might show
    From the same book, in how polite a way
The dialogue is held between the Powers
Of Good and Evil—but 'twould take up hours.

And this is not a theologic tract,
    To prove with Hebrew and with Arabic,
If Job be allegory or a fact,
    But a true narrative; and thus I pick
From out the whole but such and such an act
    As sets aside the slightest thought of trick.   270
'Tis every tittle true, beyond suspicion,
And accurate as any other vision.

The spirits were in neutral space, before
    The gate of heaven; like eastern thresholds is
The place where Death's grand cause is argued o'er,
    And souls despatch'd to that world or to this;
And therefore Michael and the other wore
    A civil aspect; though they did not kiss,
Yet still between his Darkness and his Brightness
There pass'd a mutual glance of great politeness.   280

The Archangel bow'd, not like a modern beau,
    But with a graceful Oriental bend,
Pressing one radiant arm just where below
    The heart in good men is supposed to tend;
He turn'd as to an equal, not too low,
    But kindly; Satan met his ancient friend
With more hauteur, as might an old Castilian
Poor noble meet a mushroom rich civilian.

He merely bent his diabolic brow
    An instant; and then raising it, he stood   290
In act to assert his right or wrong, and show
    Cause why King George by no means could or should
Make out a case to be exempt from woe
    Eternal, more than other kings, endued
With better sense and hearts, whom history mentions,
Who long have 'paved hell with their good intentions.'

Michael began: 'What wouldst thou with this man,
  Now dead, and brought before the Lord? What ill
Hath he wrought since his mortal race began,
  That thou canst claim him? Speak! and do thy will,   300
If it be just: if in this earthly span
  He hath been greatly failing to fulfil
His duties as a king and mortal, say,
And he is thine; if not, let him have way.'

'Michael!' replied the Prince of Air, even here
  Before the gate of him thou servest, must
I claim my subject: and will make appear
  That as he was my worshiper in dust,
So shall he be in spirit, although dear
  To thee and thine, because nor wine nor lust   310
Were of his weaknesses; yet on the throne
He reign'd o'er millions to serve me alone.

'Look to *our* earth, or rather *mine*; it was,
  Once, more thy master's: but I triumph not
In this poor planet's conquest; nor, alas!
  Need he thou servest envy me my lot:
With all the myriads of bright worlds which pass
  In worship round him, he may have forgot
Yon weak creation of such paltry things:
I think few worth damnation save their kings,—   320

'And these but as a kind of quit-rent, to
  Assert my right as lord; and even had
I such an inclination, 'twere (as you
  Well know) superfluous; they are grown so bad,
That hell has nothing better left to do
  Than leave them to themselves: so much more mad
And evil by their own internal curse,
Heaven cannot make them better, nor I worse.

[405]

'Look to the earth, I said, and say again:
    When this old, blind, mad, helpless, weak, poor worm   330
Began in youth's first bloom and flush to reign,
    The world and he both wore a different form,
And much of earth and all the watery plain
    Of ocean call'd him king: through many a storm
His isles had floated on the abyss of time;
For the rough virtues chose them for their clime.

'He came to his scepter young; he leaves it old:
    Look to the state in which he found his realm,
And left it; and his annals too behold,
    How to a minion first he gave the helm;   340
How grew upon his heart a thirst for gold,
    The beggar's vice, which can but overwhelm
The meanest hearts; and for the rest, but glance
Thine eye along America and France.

' 'Tis true, he was a tool from first to last
    (I have the workmen safe); but as a tool
So let him be consumed. From out the past
    Of ages, since mankind have known the rule
Of monarchs—from the bloody rolls amass'd
    Of sin and slaughter—from the Cæsar's school,   350
Take the worst pupil; and produce a reign
More drench'd with gore, more cumber'd with the slain.

'He ever warr'd with freedom and the free:
    Nations as men, home subjects, foreign foes,
So that they utter'd the word "Liberty!"
    Found George the Third their first opponent. Whose
History was ever stain'd as his will be
    With national and individual woes?
I grant his household abstinence; I grant
His neutral virtues, which most monarchs want;   360

'I know he was a constant consort; own
    He was a decent sire, and middling lord.
All this is much, and most upon a throne;
    As temperance, if at Apicius' board,
Is more than at an anchorite's supper shown.
    I grant him all the kindest can accord;
And this was well for him, but not for those
Millions who found him what oppression chose.

'The New World shook him off; the Old yet groans
    Beneath what he and his prepared, if not   370
Completed; he leaves heirs on many thrones
    To all his vices, without what begot
Compassion for him—his tame virtues; drones
    Who sleep, or despots who have now forgot
A lesson which shall be re-taught them, wake
Upon the thrones of earth; but let them quake!

'Five millions of the primitive, who hold
    The faith which makes ye great on earth, implored
A *part* of that vast *all* they held of old,—
    Freedom to worship—not alone your Lord,   380
Michael, but you, and you, Saint Peter! Cold
    Must be your souls, if you have not abhorr'd
The foe to Catholic participation
In all the license of a Christian nation.

'True! he allow'd them to pray God; but as
    A consequence of prayer, refused the law
Which would have placed them upon the same base
    With those who did not hold the saints in awe.'
But here Saint Peter started from his place,
    And cried, 'You may the prisoner withdraw: 390
Ere heaven shall ope her portals to this Guelph,
While I am guard, may I be damn'd myself!

'Sooner will I with Cerberus exchange
    My office (and *his* is no sinecure)
Than see this royal Bedlam bigot range
    The azure fields of heaven, of that be sure!'
'Saint!' replied Satan, 'you do well to avenge
    The wrongs he made your satellites endure;
And if to this exchange you should be given,
I'll try to coax *our* Cerberus up to heaven!'   400

Here Michael interposed: 'Good saint! and devil!
    Pray, not so fast; you both outrun discretion.
Saint Peter! you were wont to be more civil!
    Satan! excuse this warmth of his expression,
And condescension to the vulgar's level:
    Even saints sometimes forget themselves in session.
Have you got more to say?'—'No.'—'If you please,
I'll trouble you to call your witnesses.'

Then Satan turn'd and waved his swarthy hand,
    Which stirr'd with its electric qualities   410
Clouds farther off than we can understand,
    Although we find him sometimes in our skies.
Infernal thunder shook both sea and land
    In all the planets, and hell's batteries
Let off the artillery, which Milton mentions
As one of Satan's most sublime inventions.

This was a signal unto such damn'd souls
    As have the privilege of their damnation
Extended far beyond the mere controls
    Of worlds past, present, or to come; no station   420
Is theirs particularly in the rolls
    Of hell assign'd; but where their inclination
Or business carries them in search of game,
They may range freely—being damn'd the same.

[408]

They're proud of this—as very well they may,
   It being a sort of knighthood, or gilt key
Stuck in their loins; or like to an 'entré'
   Up the back stairs, or such free-masonry.
I borrow my comparisons from clay,
   Being clay myself. Let not those spirits be   430
Offended with such base low likenesses;
We know their posts are nobler far than these.

When the great signal ran from heaven to hell—
   About ten million times the distance reckon'd
From our sun to its earth, as we can tell
   How much time it takes up, even to a second,
For every ray that travels to dispel
   The fogs of London, through which, dimly beacon'd,
The weathercocks are gilt some thrice a year,
If that the *summer* is not too severe: 440

I say that I can tell—'twas half a minute;
   I know the solar beams take up more time
Ere, pack'd up for their journey, they begin it;
   But then their telegraph is less sublime,
And if they ran a race, they would not win it
   'Gainst Satan's couriers bound for their own clime.
The sun takes up some years for every ray
To reach its goal—the devil not half a day.

Upon the verge of space, about the size
   Of half-a-crown, a little speck appear'd   450
(I've seen a something like it in the skies
   In the Ægean, ere a squall); it near'd,
And, growing bigger, took another guise;
   Like an aërial ship it tack'd, and steer'd,
Or *was* steer'd (I am doubtful of the grammar
Of the last phrase, which makes the stanza stammer;—

But take your choice); and then it grew a cloud;
  And so it was—a cloud of witnesses.
But such a cloud! No land e'er saw a crowd
  Of locusts numerous as the heavens saw these;   460
They shadow'd with their myriads space; their loud
  And varied cries were like those of wild geese
(If nations may be liken'd to a goose),
And realized the phrase of 'hell broke loose.'

Here crash'd a sturdy oath of stout John Bull,
  Who damn'd away his eyes as heretofore:
There Paddy brogued 'By Jasus!'—'What's your wull?'
  The temperate Scot exclaim'd: the French ghost swore
In certain terms I shan't translate in full,
  As the first coachman will; and 'midst the war,   470
The voice of Jonathan was heard to express,
'*Our* president is going to war, I guess.'

Besides there were the Spaniard, Dutch, and Dane;
  In short, an universal shoal of shades,
From Otaheite's isle to Salisbury Plain,
  Of all climes and professions, years and trades,
Ready to swear against the good king's reign,
  Bitter as clubs in cards are against spades:
All summon'd by this grand 'subpœna,' to
Try if kings mayn't be damn'd like me or you.   480

When Michael saw this host, he first grew pale,
  As angels can; next, like Italian twilight,
He turn'd all colors—as a peacock's tail,
  Or sunset streaming through a Gothic skylight
In some old abbey, or a trout not stale,
  Or distant lightning on the horizon *by* night,
Or a fresh rainbow, or a grand review
Of thirty regiments in red, green, and blue.

Then he address'd himself to Satan: 'Why—
   My good old friend, for such I deem you, though   490
Our different parties make us fight so shy,
   I ne'er mistake you for a *personal* foe;
Our difference is *political*, and I
   Trust that, whatever may occur below,
You know my great respect for you: and this
Makes me regret whate'er you do amiss—

'Why, my dear Lucifer, would you abuse
   My call for witnesses? I did not mean
That you should half of earth and hell produce;
   'Tis even superfluous, since two honest, clean,   500
True testimonies are enough: we lose
   Our time, nay, our eternity, between
The accusation and defence: if we
Hear both, 'twill stretch our immortality.'

Satan replied, 'To me the matter is
   Indifferent, in a personal point of view:
I can have fifty better souls than this
   With far less trouble than we have gone through
Already; and I merely argued his
   Late majesty of Britain's case with you   510
Upon a point of form: you may dispose
Of him; I've kings enough below, God knows!'

Thus spoke the Demon (late call'd 'multi-faced'
   By multo-scribbling Southey). 'Then we'll call
One or two persons of the myriads placed
   Around our congress, and dispense with all
The rest,' quoth Michael: 'Who may be so graced
   As to speak first? there's choice enough—who shall
It be?' Then Satan answer'd, 'There are many;
But you may choose Jack Wilkes as well as any.'   520

A merry, cock-eyed, curious-looking sprite
　　Upon the instant started from the throng,
Dress'd in a fashion now forgotten quite;
　　For all the fashions of the flesh stick long
By people in the next world; where unite
　　All the costumes since Adam's, right or wrong,
From Eve's fig-leaf down to the petticoat,
Almost as scanty, of days less remote.

The spirit look'd around upon the crowds
　　Assembled, and exclaim'd, 'My friends of all　　530
The spheres, we shall catch cold amongst these clouds;
　　So let's to business: why this general call?
If those are freeholders I see in shrouds,
　　And 'tis for an election that they bawl,
Behold a candidate with unturn'd coat!
Saint Peter, may I count upon your vote?'

'Sir,' replied Michael, 'you mistake; these things
　　Are of a former life, and what we do
Above is more august; to judge of kings
　　Is the tribunal met: so now you know.'　　540
'Then I presume those gentlemen with wings,'
　　Said Wilkes, 'are cherubs; and that soul below
Looks much like George the Third, but to my mind
A good deal older—Bless me! is he blind?'

'He is what you behold him, and his doom
　　Depends upon his deeds,' the Angel said;
'If you have aught to arraign in him, the tomb
　　Gives license to the humblest beggar's head
To lift itself against the loftiest.'—'Some,'
　　Said Wilkes, 'don't wait to see them laid in lead,　　550
For such a liberty—and I, for one,
Have told them what I thought beneath the sun.'

[412]

'*Above* the sun repeat, then, what thou hast
    To urge against him,' said the Archangel. 'Why,'
Replied the spirit, 'since old scores are past,
    Must I turn evidence? In faith, not I.
Besides, I beat him hollow at the last,
    With all his Lords and Commons: in the sky
I don't like ripping up old stories, since
His conduct was but natural in a prince.   560

'Foolish, no doubt, and wicked, to oppress
    A poor unlucky devil without a shilling;
But then I blame the man himself much less
    Than Bute and Grafton, and shall be unwilling
To see him punish'd here for their excess,
    Since they were both damn'd long ago, and still in
Their place below: for me, I have forgiven,
And vote his "habeas corpus" into heaven.'

'Wilkes,' said the Devil, 'I understand all this;
    You turn'd to half a courtier ere you died,   570
And seem to think it would not be amiss
    To grow a whole one on the other side
Of Charon's ferry; you forget that *his*
    Reign is concluded; whatsoe'er betide,
He won't be sovereign more: you've lost your labor,
For at the best he will be but your neighbor.

'However, I knew what to think of it,
    When I beheld you in your jesting way,
Flitting and whispering round about the spit
    Where Belial, upon duty for the day,   580
With Fox's lard was basting William Pitt,
    His pupil; I knew what to think, I say:
That fellow even in hell breeds farther ills;
I'll have him *gagg'd*—'twas one of his own bills.

[413]

'Call Junius!' From the crowd a shadow stalk'd,
  And at the name there was a general squeeze,
So that the very ghosts no longer walk'd
  In comfort, at their own aërial ease,
But were all ramm'd, and jamm'd (but to be balk'd,
  As we shall see), and jostled hands and knees,   590
Like wind compress'd and pent within a bladder,
Or like a human colic, which is sadder.

The shadow came—a tall, thin, gray-hair'd figure,
  That look'd as it had been a shade on earth;
Quick in its motions, with an air of vigor,
  But nought to mark its breeding or its birth;
Now it wax'd little, then again grew bigger,
  With now an air of gloom, or savage mirth;
But as you gazed upon its features, they
Changed every instant—to *what*, none could say.   600

The more intently the ghosts gazed, the less
  Could they distinguish whose the features were;
The Devil himself seem'd puzzled even to guess;
  They varied like a dream—now here, now there;
And several people swore from out the press,
  They knew him perfectly; and one could swear
He was his father; upon which another
Was sure he was his mother's cousin's brother:

Another, that he was a duke, or knight,
  An orator, a lawyer, or a priest,   610
A nabob, a man-midwife; but the wight
  Mysterious changed his countenance at least
As oft as they their minds; though in full sight
  He stood, the puzzle only was increased;
The man was a phantasmagoria in
Himself—he was so volatile and thin.

The moment that you had pronounced him *one*,
    Presto! his face changed, and he was another;
And when that change was hardly well put on,
    It varied, till I don't think his own mother   620
(If he had a mother) would her son
    Have known, he shifted so from one to t'other;
Till guessing from a pleasure grew a task,
At this epistolary 'Iron Mask.'

For sometimes he like Cerberus would seem—
    'Three gentlemen at once' (as sagely says
Good Mrs. Malaprop); then you might deem
    That he was not even *one*; now many rays
Were flashing round him; and now a thick steam
    Hid him from sight—like fogs on London days: 630
Now Burke, now Tooke, he grew to people's fancies,
And certes often like Sir Philip Francis.

I've an hypothesis—'tis quite my own;
    I never let it out till now, for fear
Of doing people harm about the throne,
    And injuring some minister or peer,
On whom the stigma might perhaps be blown;
    It is—my gentle public, lend thine ear!
'Tis, that what Junius we are wont to call
Was *really*, *truly*, nobody at all.   640

I don't see wherefore letters should not be
    Written without hands, since we daily view
Them written without heads; and books, we see,
    Are fill'd as well without the latter too:
And really till we fix on somebody
    For certain sure to claim them as his due,
Their author, like the Niger's mouth, will bother
The world to say if *there* be mouth or author.

'And who and what art thou?' the Archangel said.
    'For *that* you may consult my title-page,'   650
Replied this mighty shadow of a shade:
    'If I have kept my secret half an age,
I scarce shall tell it now.'—'Canst thou upbraid,'
    Continued Michael, 'George Rex, or allege
Aught further?' Junius answer'd, 'You had better
First ask him for *his* answer to my letter:

'My charges upon record will outlast
    The brass of both his epitaph and tomb.'
'Repent'st thou not,' said Michael, 'of some past
    Exaggeration? something which may doom   660
Thyself if false, as him if true? Thou wast
    Too bitter—is it not so?—in thy gloom
Of passion?'—'Passion!' cried the phantom dim,
'I loved my country, and I hated him.

'What I have written, I have written: let
    The rest be on his head or mine!' So spoke
Old 'Nominis Umbra'; and while speaking yet,
    Away he melted in celestial smoke.
Then Satan said to Michael, 'Don't forget
    To call George Washington, and John Horne Tooke,   670
And Franklin';—but at this time there was heard
A cry for room, though not a phantom stirr'd.

At length with jostling, elbowing, and the aid
    Of cherubim appointed to that post,
The devil Asmodeus to the circle made
    His way, and look'd as if his journey cost
Some trouble. When his burden down he laid,
    'What's this?' cried Michael; 'why, 'tis not a ghost?'
'I know it,' quoth the incubus; 'but he
Shall be one, if you leave the affair to me.   680

[416]

'Confound the renegado! I have sprain'd
    My left wing, he's so heavy; one would think
Some of his works about his neck were chain'd.
    But to the point; while hovering o'er the brink
Of Skiddaw (where as usual it still rain'd),
    I saw a taper, far below me, wink,
And stooping, caught this fellow at a libel—
No less on history than the Holy Bible.

'The former is the devil's scripture, and
    The latter yours, good Michael: so the affair   690
Belongs to all of us, you understand.
    I snatch'd him up just as you see him there,
And brought him off for sentence out of hand:
    I've scarcely been ten minutes in the air—
At least a quarter it can hardly be:
I dare say that his wife is still at tea.'

Here Satan said, 'I know this man of old,
    And have expected him for some time here;
A sillier fellow you will scarce behold,
    Or more conceited in his petty sphere: 700
But surely it was not worth while to fold
    Such trash below your wing, Asmodeus dear:
We had the poor wretch safe (without being bored
With carriage) coming of his own accord.

'But since he's here, let's see what he has done.'
    'Done!' cried Asmodeus, 'he anticipates
The very business you are now upon,
    And scribbles as if head clerk to the Fates.
Who knows to what his ribaldry may run,
    When such an ass as this, like Balaam's, prates?'   710
'Let's hear,' quoth Michael, 'what he has to say:
You know we're bound to that in every way.'

Now the bard, glad to get an audience, which
    By no means often was his case below,
Began to cough, and hawk, and hem, and pitch
    His voice into that awful note of woe
To all unhappy hearers within reach
    Of poets when the tide of rhyme 's in flow;
But stuck fast with his first hexameter,
Not one of all whose gouty feet would stir.   720

But ere the spavin'd dactyls could be spurr'd
    Into recitative, in great dismay
Both cherubim and seraphim were heard
    To murmur loudly through their long array;
And Michael rose ere he could get a word
    Of all his founder'd verses under way,
And cried, 'For God's sake, stop, my friend! 'twere best—
Non Di, non homines—you know the rest.'

A general bustle spread throughout the throng,
    Which seem'd to hold all verse in detestation;   730
The angels had of course enough of song
    When upon service; and the generation
Of ghosts had heard too much in life, not long
    Before, to profit by a new occasion:
The monarch, mute till then, exclaim'd, 'What! what!
Pye come again? No more—no more of that!'

The tumult grew; an universal cough
    Convulsed the skies, as during a debate,
When Castlereagh has been up long enough
    (Before he was first minister of state,   740
I mean—*the slaves hear now*); some cried 'Off! off!'
    As at a farce; till, grown quite desperate,
The bard Saint Peter pray'd to interpose
(Himself an author) only for his prose.

The varlet was not an ill-favor'd knave;
 A good deal like a vulture in the face,
With a hook nose and a hawk's eye, which gave
 A smart and sharper-looking sort of grace
To his whole aspect, which, though rather grave,
 Was by no means so ugly as his case;   750
But that, indeed, was hopeless as can be,
Quite a poetic felony '*de se.*'

Then Michael blew his trump, and still'd the noise
 With one still greater, as is yet the mode
On earth besides; except some grumbling voice,
 Which now and then will make a slight inroad
Upon decorous silence, few will twice
 Lift up their lungs when fairly overcrow'd;
And now the bard could plead his own bad cause,
With all the attitudes of self-applause.   760

He said (I only give the heads)—he said,
 He meant no harm in scribbling; 'twas his way
Upon all topics; 'twas, besides, his bread,
 Of which he butter'd both sides; 'twould delay
Too long the assembly (he was pleased to dread),
 And take up rather more time than a day,
To name his works—he would but cite a few—
Wat Tyler—Rhymes on Blenheim—Waterloo.

He had written praises of a regicide;
 He had written praises of all kings whatever;   770
He had written for republics far and wide,
 And then against them bitterer than ever;
For pantisocracy he once had cried
 Aloud, a scheme less moral than 'twas clever;
Then grew a hearty anti-jacobin—
Had turn'd his coat—and would have turn'd his skin.

He had sung against all battles, and again
    In their high praise and glory; he had call'd
Reviewing 'the ungentle craft,' and then
    Become as base a critic as e'er crawl'd—   780
Fed, paid, and pamper'd by the very men
    By whom his muse and morals had been maul'd:
He had written much blank verse, and blanker prose,
And more of both than anybody knows.

He had written Wesley's life:—here turning round
    To Satan, 'Sir, I'm ready to write yours,
In two octavo volumes, nicely bound,
    With notes and preface, all that most allures
The pious purchaser; and there's no ground
    For fear, for I can choose my own reviewers: 790
So let me have the proper documents,
That I may add you to my other saints.'

Satan bow'd, and was silent. 'Well, if you,
    With amiable modesty, decline
My offer, what says Michael? There are few
    Whose memoirs could be render'd more divine.
Mine is a pen of all work; not so new
    As it was once, but I would make you shine
Like your own trumpet. By the way, my own
Has more of brass in it, and is as well blown.   800

'But talking about trumpets, here's my *Vision*!
    Now you shall judge, all people; yes, you shall
Judge with my judgment, and by my decision
    Be guided who shall enter heaven or fall.
I settle all these things by intuition,
    Times present, past, to come, heaven, hell, and all,
Like King Alphonso. When I thus see double,
I save the Deity some worlds of trouble.'

He ceased, and drew forth an MS.; and no
    Persuasion on the part of devils, saints,   810
Or angels, now could stop the torrent; so
    He read the first three lines of the contents;
But at the fourth, the whole spiritual show
    Had vanish'd, with variety of scents,
Ambrosial and sulphureous, as they sprang,
Like lightning, off from his 'melodious twang.'

Those grand heroics acted as a spell:
    The angels stopp'd their ears and plied their pinions;
The devils ran howling, deafen'd, down to hell;
    The ghosts fled, gibbering, for their own dominions   820
(For 'tis not yet decided where they dwell,
    And I leave every man to his opinions);
Michael took refuge in his trump—but, lo!
His teeth were set on edge, he could not blow!

Saint Peter, who has hitherto been known
    For an impetuous saint, upraised his keys,
And at the fifth line knock'd the poet down;
    Who fell like Phaeton, but more at ease,
Into his lake, for there he did not drown;
    A different web being by the Destinies   830
Woven for the Laureate's final wreath, whene'er
Reform shall happen either here or there.

He first sank to the bottom—like his works,
    But soon rose to the surface—like himself;
For all corrupted things are buoy'd like corks,
    By their own rottenness, light as an elf,
Or wisp that flits o'er a morass: he lurks,
    It may be, still, like dull books on a shelf,
In his own den, to scrawl some 'Life' or 'Vision,'
As Welborn says—'the devil turn'd precisian.'   840

As for the rest, to come to the conclusion
    Of this true dream, the telescope is gone
Which kept my optics free from all delusion,
    And show'd me what I in my turn have shown;
All I saw farther, in the last confusion,
    Was, that King George slipp'd into heaven for one;
And when the tumult dwindled to a calm,
I left him practicing the hundredth psalm.

PART V

PASTORAL POEMS

197

The Passionate Shepherd to His Love

Come live with me and be my love,
And we will all the pleasures prove
That valleys, groves, hills, and fields,
Woods, or steepy mountain yields.

And we will sit upon the rocks,
Seeing the shepherds feed their flocks,
By shallow rivers to whose falls
Melodious birds sing madrigals.

And I will make thee beds of roses
And a thousand fragrant posies,   10
A cap of flowers, and a kirtle
Embroidered all with leaves of myrtle;

A gown made of the finest wool
Which from our pretty lambs we pull;
Fair linèd slippers for the cold,
With buckles of the purest gold;

A belt of straw and ivy buds,
With coral clasps and amber studs:
And if these pleasures may thee move,
Come live with me, and be my love.   20

The shepherds' swains shall dance and sing
For thy delight each May morning:
If these delights thy mind may move,
Then live with me and be my love.

198

The Nymph's Reply to the Shepherd

If all the world and love were young,
And truth in every shepherd's tongue,
These pretty pleasures might me move
To live with thee and be thy love.

[425]

Time drives the flocks from field to fold
When rivers rage and rocks grow cold,
And Philomel becometh dumb;
The rest complains of cares to come.

The flowers do fade, and wanton fields
To wayward winter reckoning yields;   10
A honey tongue, a heart of gall,
Is fancy's spring, but sorrow's fall.

Thy gowns, thy shoes, thy beds of roses,
Thy cap, thy kirtle, and thy posies
Soon break, soon wither, soon forgotten,—
In folly ripe, in reason rotten.

Thy belt of straw and ivy buds,
Thy coral clasps and amber studs,
All these in me no means can move
To come to thee and be thy love.   20

But could youth last and love still breed,
Had joys no date nor age no need,
Then these delights my mind might move
To live with thee and be thy love.

199   *Corinna's Going a-Maying*

Get up, get up for shame, the blooming morn
Upon her wings presents the god unshorn.
  See how Aurora throws her fair
  Fresh-quilted colors through the air;
  Get up, sweet slug-a-bed, and see
  The dew bespangling herb and tree.
Each flower has wept and bowed toward the east
Above an hour since, yet you not dressed;
  Nay, not so much as out of bed.
  When all the birds have matins said,   10
  And sung their thankful hymns, 'tis sin,

Nay, profanation to keep in,
Whenas a thousand virgins on this day
Spring, sooner than the lark, to fetch in May.

Rise and put on your foliage, and be seen
To come forth like the springtime, fresh and green,
    And sweet as Flora. Take no care
    For jewels for your gown or hair;
    Fear not, the leaves will strew
    Gems in abundance upon you;   20
Besides, the childhood of the day has kept,
Against you come, some orient pearls unwept;
    Come and receive them while the light
    Hangs on the dew-locks of the night,
    And Titan on the eastern hill
    Retires himself, or else stands still
Till you come forth. Wash, dress, be brief in praying:
Few beads are best when once we go a-maying.

Come, my Corinna, come; and coming, mark
How each field turns a street, each street a park   30
    Made green and trimmed with trees; see how
    Devotion gives each house a bough
    Or branch; each porch, each door, ere this,
    An ark, a tabernacle is,
Made up of white-thorn neatly interwove,
As if here were those cooler shades of love.
    Can such delights be in the street
    And open fields, and we not see't?
    Come, we'll abroad, and let's obey
    The proclamation made for May,   40
And sin no more, as we have done, by staying;
But, my Corinna, come, let's go a-maying.

There's not a budding boy or girl this day
But is got up, and gone to bring in May.
    A deal of youth, ere this, is come
    Back, and with white-thorn laden, home.

[427]

Some have despatched their cakes and cream
  Before that we have left to dream;
And some have wept, and wooed, and plighted troth,
And chose their priest, ere we can cast off sloth;   50
    Many a green-gown has been given,
    Many a kiss, both odd and even,
    Many a glance too has been sent
    From out the eye, love's firmament,
Many a jest told of the keys betraying
This night, and locks picked, yet we're not a-maying.

Come, let us go while we are in our prime,
And take the harmless folly of the time.
    We shall grow old apace, and die
    Before we know our liberty.   60
    Our life is short, and our days run
    As fast away as does the sun;
And as a vapor, or a drop of rain
Once lost, can ne'er be found again,
    So when or you or I are made
    A fable, song, or fleeting shade,
    All love, all liking, all delight
    Lies drowned with us in endless night.
Then while time serves, and we are but decaying,
Come, my Corinna, come, let's go a-maying.   70

200   *To Phyllis, to Love and Live with Him*

    Live, live with me, and thou shalt see
    The pleasures I'll prepare for thee:
    What sweets the country can afford
    Shall bless thy bed and bless thy board.
    The soft sweet moss shall be thy bed,
    With crawling woodbine overspread,
    By which the silver-shedding streams
    Shall gently melt thee into dreams.
    Thy clothing, next, shall be a gown
    Made of the fleece's purest down.   10

The tongues of kids shall be thy meat,
Their milk thy drink; and thou shalt eat
The paste of filberts for thy bread
With cream of cowslips butterèd.
Thy feasting-tables shall be hills
With daisies spread, and daffodils,
Where thou shalt sit, and redbreast by,
For meat, shall give thee melody.
I'll give thee chains and carcanets
Of primroses and violets.   20
A bag and bottle thou shalt have,
That richly wrought, and this as brave,
So that as either shall express
The wearer's no mean shepherdess.
At shearing-times, and yearly wakes,
When Themilis his pastime makes,
There thou shalt be, and be the wit,
Nay more, the feast, and grace of it.
On holy days when virgins meet
To dance the hays with nimble feet,   30
Thou shalt come forth, and then appear
The queen of roses for that year,
And having danced, 'bove all the best,
Carry the garland from the rest.
In wicker baskets maids shall bring
To thee, my dearest shepherdling,
The blushing apple, bashful pear,
And shame-faced plum, all simp'ring there.
Walk in the groves, and thou shalt find
The name of Phyllis in the rind   40
Of every straight and smooth-skin tree,
Where kissing that, I'll twice kiss thee.
To thee a sheep-hook I will send,
Bepranked with ribands, to this end,
This, this alluring hook might be
Less for to catch a sheep, than me.
Thou shalt have possets, wassails fine,
Not made of ale, but spicèd wine,

To make thy maids and self free mirth,
All sitting near the glitt'ring hearth.   50
Thou shalt have ribands, roses, rings,
Gloves, garters, stockings, shoes, and strings
Of winning colors, that shall move
Others to lust, but me to love.
These, nay and more, thine own shall be,
If thou wilt love and live with me.

Summer

A Shepherd's Boy (he seeks no better name)
Led forth his flocks along the silver Thame,
Where dancing sun-beams on the waters played,
And verdant alders formed a quiv'ring shade.
Soft as he mourned, the streams forgot to flow,
The flocks around a dumb compassion show,
The Naiads wept in every watery bower,
And Jove consented in a silent shower.
    Accept, O Garth, the Muse's early lays,
That adds this wreath of Ivy to thy Bays;   10
Hear what from Love unpracticed hearts endure,
From Love, the sole disease thou canst not cure.
    Ye shady beeches, and ye cooling streams,
Defense from Phœbus', not from Cupid's beams,
To you I mourn, nor to the deaf I sing,
The woods shall answer, and their echo ring.
The hills and rocks attend my doleful lay,
Why art thou prouder and more hard than they?
The bleating sheep with my complaints agree,
They parched with heat, and I inflamed by thee.   20
The sultry Sirius burns the thirsty plains,
While in thy heart eternal winter reigns.
    Where stray ye, Muses, in what lawn or grove,
While your Alexis pines in hopeless love?
In those fair fields where sacred Isis glides,
Or else where Cam his winding vales divides?
As in the crystal spring I view my face,

Fresh rising blushes paint the watery glass;
But since those graces please thy eyes no more,
I shun the fountains which I sought before.   30
Once I was skilled in every herb that grew,
And every plant that drinks the morning dew;
Ah, wretched shepherd, what avails thy art,
To cure thy lambs, but not to heal thy heart!

    Let other swains attend the rural care,
Feed fairer flocks, or richer fleeces shear:
But nigh yon' mountain let me tune my lays,
Embrace my Love, and bind my brows with bays.
That flute is mine which Colin's tuneful breath
Inspired when living, and bequeathed in death;   40
He said; Alexis, take this pipe, the same
That taught the groves my Rosalinda's name:
But now the reeds shall hang on yonder tree,
For ever silent, since despised by thee.
Oh! were I made by some transforming power
The captive bird that sings within thy bower!
Then might my voice thy listening ears employ,
And I those kisses he receives, enjoy.

    And yet my numbers please the rural throng,
Rough Satyrs dance, and Pan applauds the song: 50
The Nymphs, forsaking every cave and spring,
Their early fruit, and milk-white turtles bring;
Each am'rous nymph prefers her gifts in vain,
On you their gifts are all bestowed again.
For you the swains the fairest flowers design,
And in one garland all their beauties join;
Accept the wreath which you deserve alone,
In whom all beauties are compris'd in one.

    See what delights in sylvan scenes appear!
Descending Gods have found Elysium here.   60
In woods bright Venus with Adonis strayed,
And chaste Diana haunts the forest-shade.
Come, lovely nymph, and bless the silent hours,
When swains from shearing seek their nightly bowers
When weary reapers quit the sultry field,

And crowned with corn their thanks to Ceres yield.
This harmless grove no lurking viper hides,
But in my breast the serpent Love abides
Here bees from blossoms sip the rosy dew,
But your Alexis knows no sweets but you.   70
Oh deign to visit our forsaken seats,
The mossy fountains, and the green retreats!
Where'er you walk, cool gales shall fan the glade;
Trees, where you sit, shall crowd into a shade;
Where'er you tread, the blushing flowers shall rise,
And all things flourish where you turn your eyes.
Oh! how I long with you to pass my days,
Invoke the Muses, and resound your praise!
Your praise the birds shall chant in every grove,
And winds shall waft it to the powers above,   80
But would you sing, and rival Orpheus' strain,
The wond'ring forests soon should dance again;
The moving mountains hear the powerful call,
And headlong streams hang listening in their fall!
    But see, the shepherds shun the noonday heat,
The lowing herds to murm'ring brooks retreat,
To closer shades the panting flocks remove;
Ye Gods! and is there no relief for Love?
But soon the sun with milder rays descends
To the cool ocean, where his journey ends.   90
On me love's fiercer flames for ever prey,
By night he scorches, as he burns by day.

202   *Ode to Evening*

If aught of oaten stop or pastoral song
May hope, chaste Eve, to soothe thy modest ear,
        Like thy own solemn springs,
        Thy springs and dying gales,

O nymph reserved, while now the bright-haired sun
Sits in yon western tent, whose cloudy skirts,
        With brede ethereal wove,
        O'erhang his wavy bed:

Now air is hushed, save where the weak-eyed bat,
With short, shrill shriek, flits by on leathern wing;   10
        Or where the beetle winds
        His small but sullen horn,

As oft he rises 'midst the twilight path,
Against the pilgrim borne in heedless hum:
        Now teach me, maid composed,
        To breathe some softened strain,

Whose numbers, stealing through thy darkening vale,
May not unseemly with its stillness suit,
        As, musing slow, I hail
        Thy genial loved return!   20

For when thy folding-star, arising, shows
His paly circlet, at his warning lamp
        The fragrant Hours, and elves
        Who slept in flowers the day,

And many a nymph who wreathes her brows with sedge,
And sheds the freshening dew, and, lovelier still,
        The pensive Pleasures sweet,
        Prepare thy shadowy car.

Then lead, calm votaress, where some sheety lake
Cheers the lone heath, or some time-hallowed pile   30
        Or upland fallows grey
        Reflect its last cool gleam.

But when chill blustering winds or driving rain
Forbid my willing feet, be mine the hut
        That from the mountain's side
        Views wilds, and swelling floods,

And hamlets brown, and dim-discovered spires,
And hears their simple bell, and marks o'er all
        Thy dewy fingers draw
        The gradual dusky veil.   40

While Spring shall pour his showers, as oft he wont,
And bathe thy breathing tresses, meekest Eve;
    While Summer loves to sport
    Beneath thy lingering light;

While sallow Autumn fills thy lap with leaves;
Or Winter, yelling through the troublous air,
    Affrights thy shrinking train,
    And rudely rends thy robes;

So long, sure-found beneath the sylvan shed,
Shall Fancy, Friendship, Science, rose-lipped Health,   50
    Thy gentlest influence own,
    And hymn thy favorite name!

203   *The Scholar-Gypsy*

Go, for they call you, shepherd, from the hill;
    Go, shepherd, and untie the wattled cotes!
    No longer leave thy wistful flock unfed,
    Nor let thy bawling fellows rack their throats,
        Nor the cropped herbage shoot another head.
            But when the fields are still,
    And the tired men and dogs all gone to rest,
        And only the white sheep are sometimes seen
        Cross and recross the strips of moon-blanched green,
Come, shepherd, and again begin the quest!   10

Here, where the reaper was at work of late—
    In this high field's dark corner, where he leaves
        His coat, his basket, and his earthen cruse,
    And in the sun all morning binds the sheaves,
        Then here, at noon, comes back his stores to use—
            Here will I sit and wait,
    While to my ear from uplands far away
        The bleating of the folded flocks is borne,
        With distant cries of reapers in the corn—
All the live murmur of a summer's day.   20

Screened is this nook o'er the high, half-reaped field,
    And here till sun-down, shepherd! will I be.
        Through the thick corn the scarlet poppies peep,
    And round green roots and yellowing stalks I see
        Pale pink convolvulus in tendrils creep;
            And air-swept lindens yield
    Their scent, and rustle down their perfumed showers
        Of bloom on the bent grass where I am laid,
        And bower me from the August sun with shade;
    And the eye travels down to Oxford's towers.   30

And near me on the grass lies Glanvil's book—
    Come, let me read the oft-read tale again!
        The story of the Oxford scholar poor,
    Of pregnant parts and quick inventive brain,
        Who, tired of knocking at preferment's door,
            One summer-morn forsook
    His friends, and went to learn the gypsy-lore,
        And roamed the world with that wild brotherhood,
        And came, as most men deemed, to little good,
    But came to Oxford and his friends no more.   40

But once, years after, in the country-lanes,
    Two scholars, whom at college erst he knew,
        Met him, and of his way of life inquired;
    Whereat he answered that the gypsy-crew,
        His mates, had arts to rule as they desired
            The workings of men's brains,
    And they can bind them to what thoughts they will.
        'And I,' he said, 'the secret of their art,
        When fully learned, will to the world impart;
    But it needs heaven-sent moments for this skill.'   50

This said, he left them, and returned no more.—
    But rumors hung about the country-side,
        That the lost Scholar long was seen to stray,
    Seen by rare glimpses, pensive and tongue-tied,
        In hat of antique shape, and cloak of gray,

[435]

The same the gypsies wore.
Shepherds had met him on the Hurst in spring;
   At some lone alehouse in the Berkshire moors,
   On the warm ingle-bench, the smock-frocked boors
Had found him seated at their entering.   60

But, 'mid their drink and clatter, he would fly.
   And I myself seem half to know thy looks,
     And put the shepherds, wanderer! on thy trace;
   And boys who in lone wheatfields scare the rooks
     I ask if thou hast passed their quiet place;
       Or in my boat I lie
Moored to the cool bank in the summer-heats,
   'Mid wide grass meadows which the sunshine fills,
   And watch the warm, green-muffled Cumner hills,
And wonder if thou haunt'st their shy retreats.   70

For most, I know, thou lov'st retired ground!
   Thee at the ferry Oxford riders blithe,
     Returning home on summer-nights, have met
   Crossing the stripling Thames at Bab-lock-hithe,
     Trailing in the cool stream thy fingers wet,
       As the punt's rope chops round;
   And leaning backward in a pensive dream,
     And fostering in thy lap a heap of flowers
     Plucked in shy fields and distant Wychwood bowers,
And thine eyes resting on the moonlit stream.   80

And then they land, and thou art seen no more!—
   Maidens, who from the distant hamlets come
     To dance around the Fyfield elm in May,
   Oft through the darkening fields have seen thee roam,
     Or cross a stile into the public way.
       Oft thou hast given them store
Of flowers—the frail-leafed, white anemōne,   *wind flower*
   Dark bluebells drenched with dews of summer eves,
   And purple orchises with spotted leaves—
But none hath words she can report of thee.   90

And, above Godstow Bridge, when hay-time's here
    In June, and many a scythe in sunshine flames,
        Men who through those wide fields of breezy grass
    Where black-winged swallows haunt the glittering Thames,
        To bathe in the abandoned lasher pass,
            Have often passed thee near
    Sitting upon the river bank o'ergrown;
        Marked thine outlandish garb, thy figure spare,
        Thy dark vague eyes, and soft abstracted air—
    But, when they came from bathing, thou wast gone!   100

At some lone homestead in the Cumner hills,
    Where at her open door the housewife darns,
        Thou hast been seen, or hanging on a gate
    To watch the threshers in the mossy barns.
        Children, who early range these slopes and late
            For cresses from the rills,
    Have known thee eying, all an April-day,
        The springing pastures and the feeding kine;
        And marked thee, when the stars come out and shine,
    Through the long dewy grass move slow away.   110

In autumn, on the skirts of Bagley Wood—
    Where most the gypsies by the turf-edged way
        Pitch their smoked tents, and every bush you see
    With scarlet patches tagged and shreds of gray,
        Above the forest-ground called Thessaly—
            The blackbird, picking food,
    Sees thee, nor stops his meal, nor fears at all;
        So often has he known thee past him stray,
        Rapt, twirling in thy hand a withered spray,
    And waiting for the spark from heaven to fall.   120

And once, in winter, on the causeway chill
    Where home through flooded fields foot-travelers go,
        Have I not passed thee on the wooden bridge,
    Wrapped in thy cloak and battling with the snow,
        Thy face tow'rd Hinksey and its wintry ridge?

And thou hast climbed the hill,
And gained the white brow of the Cumner range;
   Turned once to watch, while thick the snowflakes fall,
   The line of festal light in Christ-Church hall—
Then sought thy straw in some sequestered grange.   130

But what—I dream! Two hundred years are flown
   Since first thy story ran through Oxford halls,
     And the grave Glanvil did the tale inscribe
   That thou wert wandered from the studious walls
     To learn strange arts, and join a gypsy tribe;
       And thou from earth art gone
   Long since, and in some quiet churchyard laid—
     Some country-nook, where o'er thy unknown grave
     Tall grasses and white flowering nettles wave,
Under a dark, red-fruited yew-tree's shade.   140

—No, no, thou hast not felt the lapse of hours!
   For what wears out the life of mortal men?
     'Tis that from change to change their being rolls;
   'Tis that repeated shocks, again, again,
     Exhaust the energy of strongest souls
       And numb the elastic powers,
   Till having used our nerves with bliss and teen,
     And tired upon a thousand schemes our wit,
     To the just-pausing Genius we remit
Our worn-out life, and are—what we have been.   150

Thou hast not lived, why should'st thou perish, so?
   Thou hadst *one* aim, *one* business, *one* desire;
     Else wert thou long since numbered with the dead!
   Else hadst thou spent, like other men, thy fire!
     The generations of thy peers are fled,
       And we ourselves shall go;
   But thou possessest an immortal lot,
     And we imagine thee exempt from age
     And living as thou liv'st on Glanvil's page,
Because thou hadst—what we, alas! have not.   160

For early didst thou leave the world, with powers
    Fresh, undiverted to the world without,
        Firm to their mark, not spent on other things;
    Free from the sick fatigue, the languid doubt,
        Which much to have tried, in much been baffled, brings.
           O life unlike to ours!
    Who fluctuate idly without term or scope,
        Of whom each strives, nor knows for what he strives,
        And each half lives a hundred different lives;
    Who wait like thee, but not, like thee, in hope.   170

Thou waitest for the spark from heaven! and we,
    Light half-believers of our casual creeds,
        Who never deeply felt, nor clearly willed,
    Whose insight never has borne fruit in deeds,
        Whose vague resolves never have been fulfilled;
           For whom each year we see
    Breeds new beginnings, disappointments new;
        Who hesitate and falter life away,
        And lose tomorrow the ground won today—
    Ah! do not we, wanderer! await it too?   180

Yes, we await it!—but it still delays,
    And then we suffer! and amongst us one,
        Who most hast suffered, takes dejectedly
    His seat upon the intellectual throne;
        And all his store of sad experience he
           Lays bare of wretched days;
   Tells us his misery's birth and growth and signs,
        And how the dying spark of hope was fed,
        And how the breast was soothed, and how the head,
    And all his hourly varied anodynes. *drug which relieves pain.*   190

This for our wisest! and we others pine,
    And wish the long unhappy dream would end,
        And waive all claim to bliss, and try to bear;
    With close-lipped patience for our only friend,
        Sad patience, too near neighbor to despair—

But none has hope like thine!
Thou through the fields and through the woods dost stray,
   Roaming the country-side, a truant boy,
   Nursing thy project in unclouded joy,
And every doubt long blown by time away.   200

O born in days when wits were fresh and clear,
   And life ran gayly as the sparkling Thames;
      Before this strange disease of modern life,
   With its sick hurry, its divided aims,
      Its head o'ertaxed, its palsied hearts, was rife—
        Fly hence, our contact fear!
Still fly, plunge deeper in the bowering wood!
    Averse, as Dido did with gesture stern
    From her false friend's approach in Hades turn,
Wave us away, and keep thy solitude!   210

Still nursing the unconquerable hope,
   Still clutching the inviolable shade,
     With a free, onward impulse brushing through,
   By night, the silvered branches of the glade—
     Far on the forest-skirts, where none pursue,
       On some mild pastoral slope
    Emerge, and resting on the moonlit pales
     Freshen thy flowers as in former years
     With dew, or listen with enchanted ears,
From the dark dingles, to the nightingales!   220

But fly our paths, our feverish contact fly!
   For strong the infection of our mental strife,
     Which, though it gives no bliss, yet spoils for rest;
   And we should win thee from thy own fair life,
     Like us distracted, and like us unblest.
       Soon, soon thy cheer would die,
Thy hopes grow timorous, and unfixed thy powers,
    And thy clear aims be cross and shifting made;
    And then thy glad perennial youth would fade,
Fade, and grow old at last, and die like ours.   230

Then fly our greetings, fly our speech and smiles!
—As some grave Tyrian trader, from the sea,
     Descried at sunrise an emerging prow
Lifting the cool-haired creepers stealthily,
     The fringes of a southward-facing brow
          Among the Ægæan isles;
And saw the merry Grecian coaster come,
     Freighted with amber grapes, and Chian wine,
     Green, bursting figs, and tunnies steeped in brine—
And knew the intruders on his ancient home,   240

The young light-hearted masters of the waves—
     And snatched his rudder, and shook out more sail;
          And day and night held on indignantly
O'er the blue Midland waters with the gale,
     Betwixt the Syrtes and soft Sicily,
          To where the Atlantic raves
Outside the western straits; and unbent sails
     There, where down cloudy cliffs, through sheets of foam,
     Shy traffickers, the dark Iberians come;
And on the beach undid his corded bales.   250

Eclogue by a Five-Barred Gate

                   (DEATH AND TWO SHEPHERDS)

D. There is no way here, shepherds, read the wooden sign,
     Your road is a blind road, all this land is mine.
 1. But your fields, mister, would do well for our sheep.
 2. They could shelter from the sun where the low hills dip.
D. I have sheep of my own, see them over there.
 1. There seems no nater in 'em, they look half dead.
 2. They be no South Downs, they look so thin and bare.
D. More than half, shepherds, they are more than half dead.
     But where are your own flocks you have been so talking of?
 1. Right here at our elbow—
 2.   Or they *was* so just now.   10
D. That's right, shepherd, they was so just now.
     Your sheep are gone, they can't speak for you,

I must have your credentials, sing me who you are.
1. I am a shepherd of the Theocritean breed,
   Been pasturing my songs, man and boy, this thirty year—
2. And for me too my pedigree acceptances
   Have multiplied beside the approved streams.
D. This won't do, shepherds, life is not like that,
   And when it comes to death I may say he is not like that.
   Have you never thought of Death?
1.   Only off and on,   20
   Thanatos in Greek, the accent proparoxytone—
2. That's not what he means, he means the thing behind the word
   Same as took Alice White the time she had her third—
D. Cut out for once the dialect and the pedantry,
   I thought a shepherd was a poet—
1.   On his flute—
2.   On his oat—
D. I thought he was a poet and could quote the prices
   Of significant living and decent dying, could lay the rails level on
     the sleepers
   To carry the powerful train of abstruse thought—
1. What an idea!
2.   But certainly poets are sleepers,
   The sleeping beauty behind the many-colored hedge—   30
D. All you do is burke the other and terrible beauty, all you do is
     hedge
   And shirk the inevitable issue, all you do
   Is shear your sheep to stop your ears.
   Poetry you think is only the surface vanity,
   The painted nails, the hips narrowed by fashion,
   The hooks and eyes of words; but it is not that only,
   And it is not only the curer sitting by the wayside,
   Phials on his trestle, his palms grown thin as wafers
   With blessing the anonymous heads;
   And poetry is not only the bridging of two-banked rivers.   40
2. Whoever heard of a river without a further bank?
D. You two never heard of it.
   Tell me now, I have heard the cuckoo, there is tar on your shoes,
   I surmise that spring is here—

[442]

2.   Spring be here truly,
   On Bank Holiday I wore canvas shoes,
   Could feel the earth—
D.   And that being so, tell me
   Don't you ever feel old?
2.   There's a question now.
1. It is a question we all have to answer,
   And I may say that when I smell the beans or hear the thrush
   I feel a wave intensely bitter-sweet and topped with silver—   50
D. There you go again, your self-congratulation
   Blunts all edges, insulates with wool
   No spark of reality possible.
   Can't you peel off for even a moment that conscious face?
   All time is not your tear-off jotter, you cannot afford to scribble
   So many so false answers.
   This escapism of yours is blasphemy,
   An immortal cannot blaspheme for one way or another
   His trivialities will pattern in the end;
   But for you your privilege and panic is to be mortal   60
   And with Here and Now for your anvil
   You must strike while the iron is hot—
2.   He is an old man,
   That is why he talks so.
D.   Can't you understand me?
   Look, I will set you a prize like any of your favorites,
   Like any Tityrus or tired Damon;
   Sing me, each in turn, what dream you had last night
   And if either's dream rings true, to him I will open my gate:
2. Ho, here's talking.
1.   Let me collect myself.
D. Collect yourself in time for if you win my prize—   70
2. I'm going to sing first, I had a rare dream.
1. Your dream is nothing—
D.   The more nothing the better.
1. My dream will word well—
2.   But not wear well—
D. No dreams wear at all as dreams.
   Water appears tower only while in well—

All from the same comes, the same drums sound
In the pulsation of all the bulging suns,
And no clock whatever, while winding or running down,
Makes any difference to time however the long-legged weights
Straggle down the cottage wall or the child grows leggy too—   80

1. I do not like your talking.

2.   It gives giddiness
Like the thrumming of the telephone wires in an east wind
With the bellyache and headache and nausea.

D. It is not my nature to talk, so sing your pieces
And I will try, what is repugnant too, to listen.

1. Last night as the bearded lips of sleep
Closed with the slightest sigh on me and I sank through the blue
    soft caves
Picked with light delicate as the chink of coins
Or stream on the pebbles I was caught by hands
And a face was swung in my eyes like a lantern   90
Swinging on the neck of a snake.
And that face I knew to be God and I woke,
And now I come to look at yours, stranger,
There is something in the lines of it—

D.   Your dream, shepherd,
Is good enough of its kind. Now let us hear yours.

2. Well, I dreamt it was a hot day, the territorials
Were out on melting asphalt under the howitzers,
The brass music bounced on the houses. Come
I heard a cry as it were a water-nymph, come and fulfill me
And I sped floating, my feet plashing in the tops of the wheat   100
But my eyes were blind,
I found her with my hands lying on the drying hay,
Wet heat in the deeps of the hay as my hand delved,
And I possessed her, gross and good like the hay,
And she went and my eyes regained sight and the sky was full of
    ladders
Angels ascending and descending with a shine like mackerel—
Now I come to tell it it sounds like nonsense.

D. Thank you, gentlemen, these two dreams are good,
Better than your daytime madrigals.

[444]

If you really wish I will give you both the prize,   110
But take another look at my land before you choose it.
1. It looks colder now.
2.   The sheep have not moved.
1. I have a fancy there is no loving there
Even among sheep.
D.   They do not breed or couple.
1. & 2. And what about us, shall we enjoy it there?
D. *Enjoy what there?*
2. Why, life in your land.
D. I will open this gate that you may see for yourselves.
1. You go first.
2.   Well, you come too.
1. & 2. We will go together to these pastures new . . .   120
D. So; they are gone; life in my land . . .
There is no life as there is no land.
They are gone and I am alone
With a gate the façade of a mirage.

205   *Lycidas*

YET once more, O ye Laurels, and once more
Ye Myrtles brown, with Ivy never-sear,
I com to pluck your Berries harsh and crude,
And with forc'd fingers rude,
Shatter your leaves before the mellowing year.
Bitter constraint, and sad occasion dear,
Compels me to disturb your season due:
For *Lycidas* is dead, dead ere his prime
Young *Lycidas*, and hath not left his peer:
Who would not sing for *Lycidas*? he knew   10
Himself to sing, and build the lofty rhyme.
He must not flote upon his watry bear
Unwept, and welter to the parching wind,
Without the meed of som melodious tear.
   Begin then, Sisters of the sacred well,
That from beneath the seat of *Jove* doth spring,
Begin, and somwhat loudly sweep the string.

Hence with denial vain, and coy excuse,
So may som gentle Muse
With lucky words favour my destin'd Urn,   20
And as he passes turn,
And bid fair peace be to my sable shrowd.
For we were nurst upon the self-same hill,
Fed the same flock, by fountain, shade, and rill.
    Together both, ere the high Lawns appear'd
Under the opening eye-lids of the morn,
We drove a field, and both together heard
What time the Gray-fly winds her sultry horn,
Batt'ning our flocks with the fresh dews of night,
Oft till the Star that rose, at Ev'ning, bright   30
Toward Heav'ns descent had slop'd his westering wheel.
Mean while the Rural ditties were not mute,
Temper'd to th'Oaten Flute;
Rough *Satyrs* danc'd, and *Fauns* with clov'n heel,
From the glad sound would not be absent long,
And old *Damætas* lov'd to hear our song.
    But O the heavy change, now thou art gon,
Now thou art gon, and never must return!
Thee Shepherd, thee the Woods, and desert Caves,
With wilde Thyme and the gadding Vine o'regrown,   40
And all their echoes mourn.
The Willows, and the Hazle Copses green,
Shall now no more be seen,
Fanning their joyous Leaves to thy soft layes.
As killing as the Canker to the Rose,
Or Taint-worm to the weanling Herds that graze,
Or Frost to Flowers, that their gay wardrop wear,
When first the White thorn blows;
Such, *Lycidas*, thy loss to Shepherds ear.
    Where were ye Nymphs when the remorseless deep   50
Clos'd o're the head of your lov'd *Lycidas*?
For neither were ye playing on the steep,
Where your old *Bards*, the famous *Druids* ly,
Nor on the shaggy top of *Mona* high,
Nor yet where *Deva* spreads her wisard stream:

Ay me, I fondly dream!
Had ye bin there—for what could that have don?
What could the Muse her self that *Orpheus* bore,
The Muse her self, for her inchanting son
Whom Universal nature did lament,   60
When by the rout that made the hideous roar,
His goary visage down the stream was sent,
Down the swift *Hebrus* to the *Lesbian* shore.
    Alas! What boots it with uncessant care
To tend the homely slighted Shepherds trade,
And strictly meditate the thankles Muse,
Were it not better don as others use,
To sport with *Amaryllis* in the shade,
Or with the tangles of *Neæra's* hair?
Fame is the spur that the clear spirit doth raise   70
(That last infirmity of Noble mind)
To scorn delights, and live laborious dayes;
But the fair Guerdon when we hope to find,
And think to burst out into sudden blaze,
Comes the blind *Fury* with th'abhorred shears,
And slits the thin spun life. But not the praise,
Phœbus repli'd, and touch'd my trembling ears;
Fame is no plant that grows on mortal soil,
Nor in the glistering foil
Set off to th'world, nor in broad rumour lies,   80
But lives and spreds aloft by those pure eyes,
And perfet witnes of all judging *Jove*;
As he pronounces lastly on each deed,
Of so much fame in Heav'n expect thy meed.
    O Fountain *Arethuse*, and thou honour'd floud,
Smooth-sliding *Mincius*, crown'd with vocall reeds,
That strain I heard was of a higher mood:
But now my Oate proceeds,
And listens to the Herald of the Sea
That came in *Neptune's* plea,   90
He ask'd the Waves, and ask'd the Fellon winds,
What hard mishap hath doom'd this gentle swain?
And question'd every gust of rugged wings

[447]

That blows from off each beaked Promontory,
They knew not of his story,
And sage *Hippotades* their answer brings,
That not a blast was from his dungeon stray'd,
The Ayr was calm, and on the level brine,
Sleek *Panope* with all her sisters play'd.
It was that fatall and perfidious Bark   100
Built in th'eclipse, and rigg'd with curses dark,
That sunk so low that sacred head of thine.
    Next *Camus*, reverend Sire, went footing slow,
His Mantle hairy, and his Bonnet sedge,
Inwrought with figures dim, and on the edge
Like to that sanguine flower inscrib'd with woe.
Ah; Who hath reft (quoth he) my dearest pledge?
Last came, and last did go,
The Pilot of the *Galilean* lake,
Two massy Keyes he bore of metals twain,   110
(The Golden opes, the Iron shuts amain)
He shook his Miter'd locks, and stern bespake,
How well could I have spar'd for thee, young swain,
Anow of such as for their bellies sake,
Creep and intrude, and climb into the fold?
Of other care they little reck'ning make,
Then how to scramble at the shearers feast,
And shove away the worthy bidden guest.
Blind mouthes! that scarce themselves know how to hold
A Sheep-hook, or have learn'd ought els the least   120
That to the faithfull Herdmans art belongs!
What recks it them? What need they? They are sped;
And when they list, their lean and flashy songs
Grate on their scrannel Pipes of wretched straw,
The hungry Sheep look up, and are not fed,
But swoln with wind, and the rank mist they draw,
Rot inwardly, and foul contagion spread:
Besides what the grim Woolf with privy paw
Daily devours apace, and nothing sed,
But that two-handed engine at the door,   130
Stands ready to smite once, and smite no more.

Return *Alpheus*, the dread voice is past,
That shrunk thy streams; Return *Sicilian* Muse,
And call the Vales, and bid them hither cast
Their Bels, and Flourets of a thousand hues.
Ye valleys low where the milde whispers use,
Of shades and wanton winds, and gushing brooks,
On whose fresh lap the swart Star sparely looks,
Throw hither all your quaint enameld eyes,
That on the green terf suck the honied showres,   140
And purple all the ground with vernal flowres.
Bring the rathe Primrose that forsaken dies.
The tufted Crow-toe, and pale Gessamine,
The white Pink, and the Pansie freakt with jeat,
The glowing Violet.
The Musk-rose, and the well attir'd Woodbine.
With Cowslips wan that hang the pensive hed,
And every flower that sad embroidery wears:
Bid *Amaranthus* all his beauty shed,
And Daffadillies fill their cups with tears,   150
To strew the Laureat Herse where *Lycid* lies.
For so to interpose a little ease,
Let our frail thoughts dally with false surmise.
Ay me! Whilst thee the shores, and sounding Seas
Wash far away, where ere thy bones are hurld,
Whether beyond the stormy *Hebrides*,
Where thou perhaps under the whelming tide
Visit'st the bottom of the monstrous world;
Or whether thou to our moist vows deny'd,
Sleep'st by the fable of *Bellerus* old,   160
Where the great vision of the guarded Mount
Looks toward *Namancos* and *Bayona's* hold;
Look homeward Angel now, and melt with ruth.
And, O ye *Dolphins*, waft the haples youth.
    Weep no more, woful Shepherds weep no more,
For *Lycidas* your sorrow is not dead,
Sunk though he be beneath the watry floar,
So sinks the day-star in the Ocean bed,
And yet anon repairs his drooping head,

And tricks his beams, and with new spangled Ore, 170
Flames in the forehead of the morning sky:
So *Lycidas* sunk low, but mounted high,
Through the dear might of him that walk'd the waves
Where other groves, and other streams along,
With *Nectar* pure his oozy Lock's he laves,
And hears the unexpressive nuptiall Song,
In the blest Kingdoms meek of joy and love.
There entertain him all the Saints above,
In solemn troops, and sweet Societies
That sing, and singing in their glory move, 180
And wipe the tears for ever from his eyes.
Now *Lycidas* the Shepherds weep no more;
Hence forth thou art the Genius of the shore,
In thy large recompense, and shalt be good
To all that wander in that perilous flood.
    Thus sang the uncouth Swain to th'Okes and rills,
While the still morn went out with Sandals gray,
He touch'd the tender stops of various Quills,
With eager thought warbling his *Dorick* lay:
And now the Sun had stretch'd out all the hills, 190
And now was dropt into the Western bay;
At last he rose, and twitch'd his Mantle blew:
To morrow to fresh Woods, and Pastures new.

206 *Adonais*

I weep for Adonais—he is dead!
Oh weep for Adonais! though our tears
Thaw not the frost which binds so dear a head!
And thou, sad Hour, selected from all years
To mourn our loss, rouse thy obscure compeers,
And teach them thine own sorrow! Say: 'With me
Died Adonais; till the Future dares
Forget the Past, his fate and fame shall be
An echo and a light unto Eternity!'

Where wert thou, mighty Mother, when he lay,   10
When thy son lay, pierced by the shaft which flies
In darkness? where was lorn Urania
When Adonais died? With veilèd eyes,
'Mid listening Echoes, in her paradise
She sate, while one, with soft enamored breath,
Rekindled all the fading melodies,
With which, like flowers that mock the corse beneath,
He had adorned and hid the coming bulk of death.

Oh, weep for Adonais—he is dead!
Wake, melancholy Mother, wake and weep!   20
Yet wherefore? Quench within their burning bed
Thy fiery tears, and let thy loud heart keep
Like his, a mute and uncomplaining sleep;
For he is gone, where all things wise and fair
Descend. Oh, dream not that the amorous Deep
Will yet restore him to the vital air;
Death feeds on his mute voice, and laughs at our despair.

Most musical of mourners, weep again!
Lament anew, Urania!—He died,
Who was the sire of an immortal strain,   30
Blind, old, and lonely, when his country's pride,
The priest, the slave, and the liberticide,
Trampled and mocked with many a loathèd rite
Of lust and blood; he went, unterrified,
Into the gulf of death; but his clear Sprite
Yet reigns o'er earth, the third among the sons of light.

Most musical of mourners, weep anew!
Not all to that bright station dared to climb;
And happier they their happiness who knew,
Whose tapers yet burn through that night of time   40
In which suns perished; others more sublime,
Struck by the envious wrath of man or God,
Have sunk, extinct in their refulgent prime;
And some yet live, treading the thorny road,
Which leads, through toil and hate, to Fame's serene abode.

[451]

But now, thy youngest, dearest one has perished,
The nursing of thy widowhood, who grew,
Like a pale flower by some sad maiden cherished,
And fed with true-love tears instead of dew;
Most musical of mourners, weep anew!   50
Thy extreme hope, the loveliest and the last,
The bloom, whose petals nipped before they blew,
Died on the promise of the fruit, is waste;
The broken lily lies—the storm is overpast.

To that high Capital, where kingly Death
Keeps his pale court in beauty and decay,
He came; and bought, with price of purest breath,
A grave among the eternal.—Come away!
Haste, while the vault of blue Italian day
Is yet his fitting charnel-roof! while still   60
He lies, as if in dewy sleep he lay;
Awake him not! surely he takes his fill
Of deep and liquid rest, forgetful of all ill.

He will awake no more, oh, never more!
Within the twilight chamber spreads apace
The shadow of white Death, and at the door
Invisible Corruption waits to trace
His extreme way to her dim dwelling-place;
The eternal Hunger sits, but pity and awe
Soothe her pale rage, nor dares she to deface.   70
So fair a prey, till darkness, and the law
Of change, shall o'er his sleep the mortal curtain draw.

Oh, weep for Adonais!—The quick Dreams,
The passion-wingèd ministers of thought,
Who were his flocks, whom near the living streams
Of his young spirit he fed, and whom he taught
The love which was its music, wander not,—
Wander no more, from kindling brain to brain,
But droop there, whence they sprung; and mourn their lot
Round the cold heart, where, after their sweet pain,   80
They ne'er will gather strength, or find a home again.

And one with trembling hands clasps his cold head,
And fans him with her moonlight wings, and cries;
'Our love, our hope, our sorrow, is not dead;
See, on the silken fringe of his faint eyes,
Like dew upon a sleeping flower, there lies
A tear some Dream has loosened from his brain.'
Lost Angel of a ruined paradise!
She knew not 'twas her own; as with no stain
She faded, like a cloud which had outwept its rain.   90

One from a lucid urn of starry dew
Washed his light limbs as if embalming them;
Another clipped her profuse locks, and threw
The wreath upon him, like an anadem,
Which frozen tears instead of pearls begem;
Another in her wilful grief would break
Her bow and winged reeds, as if to stem
A greater loss with one which was more weak;
And dull the barbèd fire against his frozen cheek.

Another Splendor on his mouth alit,   100
That mouth, whence it was wont to draw the breath
Which gave it strength to pierce the guarded wit,
And pass into the panting heart beneath
With lightning and with music: the damp death
Quenched its caress upon his icy lips;
And, as a dying meteor stains a wreath
Of moonlight vapor, which the cold night clips,
It flushed through his pale limbs, and passed to its eclipse.

And others came—Desires and Adorations,
Wingèd Persuasions and veiled Destinies,   110
Splendors, and Glooms, and glimmering Incarnations
Of hopes and fears, and twilight Fantasies;
And Sorrow, with her family of Sighs,
And Pleasure, blind with tears, led by the gleam
Of her own dying smile instead of eyes,
Came in slow pomp;—the moving pomp might seem
Like pageantry of mist on an autumnal stream.

All he had loved, and molded into thought,
From shape, and hue, and odor, and sweet sound,
Lamented Adonais. Morning sought   120
Her eastern watch-tower, and her hair unbound,
Wet with the tears which should adorn the ground,
Dimmed the aëreal eyes that kindle day;
Afar the melancholy thunder moaned,
Pale Ocean in unquiet slumber lay,
And the wild winds flew round, sobbing in their dismay.

Lost Echo sits amid the voiceless mountains,
And feeds her grief with his remembered lay,
And will no more reply to winds or fountains,
Or amorous birds perched on the young green spray,   130
Or herdsman's horn, or bell at closing day;
Since she can mimic not his lips, more dear
Than those for whose disdain she pined away
Into a shadow of all sounds:—a drear
Murmur, between their songs, is all the woodmen hear.

Grief made the young Spring wild, and she threw down
Her kindling buds, as if she Autumn were,
Or they dead leaves; since her delight is flown,
For whom should she have waked the sullen year?
To Phœbus was not Hyacinth so dear   140
Nor to himself Narcissus, as to both
Thou, Adonais: wan they stand and sere
Amid the faint companions of their youth,
With dew all turned to tears; odor, to sighing ruth.

Thy spirit's sister, the lorn nightingale
Mourns not her mate with such melodious pain;
Not so the eagle, who like thee could scale
Heaven, and could nourish in the sun's domain
Her mighty youth with morning, doth complain,
Soaring and screaming round her empty nest,   150
As Albion wails for thee: the curse of Cain
Light on his head who pierced thy innocent breast,
And scared the angel soul that was its earthly guest!

Ah, woe is me! Winter is come and gone,
But grief returns with the revolving year;
The airs and streams renew their joyous tone;
The ants, the bees, the swallows reappear;
Fresh leaves and flowers deck the dead Seasons' bier;
The amorous birds now pair in every brake,
And build their mossy homes in field and brere;   160
And the green lizard, and the golden snake,
Like unimprisoned flames, out of their trance awake.

Through wood and stream and field and hill and ocean
A quickening life from the Earth's heart has burst
As it has ever done, with change and motion,
From the great morning of the world when first
God dawned on Chaos; in its stream immersed,
The lamps of Heaven flash with a softer light;
All baser things pant with life's sacred thirst;
Diffuse themselves; and spend in love's delight,   170
The beauty and the joy of their renewèd might.

The leprous corpse, touched by this spirit tender,
Exhales itself in flowers of gentle breath;
Like incarnations of the stars, when splendor
Is changed to fragrance, they illumine death
And mock the merry worm that wakes beneath;
Nought we know dies. Shall that alone which knows
Be as a sword consumed before the sheath
By sightless lightning?—the intense atom glows
A moment, then is quenched in a most cold repose.   180

Alas! that all we loved of him should be,
But for our grief, as if it had not been,
And grief itself be mortal! Woe is me!
Whence are we, and why are we? of what scene
The actors or spectators? Great and mean
Meet massed in death, who lends what life must borrow.
As long as skies are blue, and fields are green,
Evening must usher night, night urge the morrow,
Month follow month with woe, and year wake year to sorrow.

He will awake no more, oh, never more!
'Wake thou,' cried Misery, 'childless Mother, rise
Out of thy sleep, and slake, in thy heart's core,
A wound more fierce than his, with tears and sighs.'
And all the Dreams that watched Urania's eyes,
And all the Echoes whom their sister's song
Had held in holy silence, cried: 'Arise!'
Swift as a Thought by the snake Memory stung,
From her ambrosial rest the fading Splendor sprung.

She rose like an autumnal Night, that springs
Out of the East, and follows wild and drear
The golden Day, which, on eternal wings,
Even as a ghost abandoning a bier,
Had left the Earth a corpse;—sorrow and fear
So struck, so roused, so rapt Urania;
So saddened round her like an atmosphere
Of stormy mist; so swept her on her way
Even to the mournful place where Adonais lay.

Out of her secret paradise she sped.
Through camps and cities rough with stone, and steel,
And human hearts, which to her airy tread
Yielding not, wounded the invisible
Palms of her tender feet where'er they fell:
And barbèd tongues, and thoughts more sharp than they,
Rent the soft Form they never could repel,
Whose sacred blood, like the young tears of May,
Paved with eternal flowers that undeserving way.

In the death-chamber for a moment Death,
Shamed by the presence of that living Might,
Blushed to annihilation, and the breath
Revisited those lips, and Life's pale light
Flashed through those limbs, so late her dear delight.
'Leave me not wild and drear and comfortless,
As silent lightning leaves the starless night!
Leave me not!' cried Urania: her distress
Roused Death: Death rose and smiled, and met her vain caress.

'Stay yet awhile! speak to me once again;
Kiss me, so long but as a kiss may live;
And in my heartless breast and burning brain
That word, that kiss, shall all thoughts else survive,
With food of saddest memory kept alive,   230
Now thou art dead, as if it were a part
Of thee, my Adonais! I would give
All that I am to be as thou now art!
But I am chained to Time, and cannot thence depart!

'O gentle child, beautiful as thou wert,
Why didst thou leave the trodden paths of men
Too soon, and with weak hands though mighty heart
Dare the unpastured dragon in his den?
Defenseless as thou wert, oh, where was then
Wisdom the mirrored shield, or scorn the spear?   240
Or hadst thou waited the full cycle when
Thy spirit should have filled its crescent sphere,
The monsters of life's waste had fled from thee like deer.

'The herded wolves, bold only to pursue;
The obscene ravens, clamorous o'er the dead;
The vultures to the conqueror's banner true
Who feed where Desolation first has fed,
And whose wings rain contagion;—how they fled,
When, like Apollo, from his golden bow
The Pythian of the age one arrow sped   250
And smiled!—The spoilers tempt no second blow,
They fawn on the proud feet that spurn them lying low.

'The sun comes forth, and many reptiles spawn;
He sets, and each ephemeral insect then
Is gathered into death without a dawn,
And the immortal stars awake again;
So is it in the world of living men:
A godlike mind soars forth, in its delight
Making earth bare and veiling heaven, and when
It sinks, the swarms that dimmed or shared its light   260
Leave to its kindred lamps the spirit's awful night.'

Thus ceased she: and the mountain shepherds came,
Their garlands sere, their magic mantles rent;
The Pilgrim of Eternity, whose fame
Over his living head like Heaven is bent,
An early but enduring monument,
Came, veiling all the lightnings of his song
In sorrow; from her wilds Ierne sent
The sweetest lyrist of her saddest wrong,
And love taught grief to fall like music from his tongue.   270

Midst others of less note, came one frail Form,
A phantom among men; companionless
As the last cloud of an expiring storm
Whose thunder is its knell; he, as I guess,
Had gazed on Nature's naked loveliness,
Actæon-like, and now he fled astray
With feeble steps o'er the world's wilderness,
And his own thoughts, along that rugged way,
Pursued, like raging hounds, their father and their prey.

A pardlike Spirit beautiful and swift—   280
A Love in desolation masked;—a Power
Girt round with weakness;—it can scarce uplift
The weight of the superincumbent hour;
It is a dying lamp, a falling shower,
A breaking billow;—even whilst we speak
Is it not broken? On the withering flower
The killing sun smiles brightly: on a cheek
The life can burn in blood, even while the heart may break.

His head was bound with pansies overblown,
And faded violets, white, and pied, and blue;   290
And a light spear topped with a cypress cone,
Round whose rude shaft dark ivy-tresses grew
Yet dripping with the forest's noonday dew,
Vibrated, as the ever-beating heart
Shook the weak hand that grasped it; of that crew
He came the last, neglected and apart;
A herd-abandoned deer struck by the hunter's dart.

[458]

All stood aloof, and at his partial moan
Smiled through their tears; well knew that gentle band
Who in another's fate now wept his own,   300
As in the accents of an unknown land
He sung new sorrow; sad Urania scanned
The stranger's mien, and murmured: 'Who art thou?'
He answered not, but with a sudden hand
Made bare his branded and ensanguined brow,
Which was like Cain's or Christ's—oh! that it should be so!

What softer voice is hushed over the dead?
Athwart what brow is that dark mantle thrown?
What form leans sadly o'er the white death-bed,
In mockery of monumental stone,   310
The heavy heart heaving without a moan?
If it be he, who, gentlest of the wise,
Taught, soothed, loved, honored the departed one,   .
Let me not vex, with inharmonious sighs,
The silence of that heart's accepted sacrifice.

Our Adonais has drunk poison—oh,
What deaf and viperous murderer could crown
Life's early cup with such a draught of woe?
The nameless worm would now itself disown:
It felt, yet could escape, the magic tone   320
Whose prelude held all envy, hate, and wrong,
But what was howling in one breast alone,
Silent with expectation of the song,
Whose master's hand is cold, whose silver lyre unstrung.

Live thou, whose infamy is not thy fame!
Live! fear no heavier chastisement from me,
Thou noteless blot on a remembered name!
But be thyself, and know thyself to be!
And ever at thy season be thou free
To spill the venom when thy fangs o'erflow: 330
Remorse and Self-Contempt shall cling to thee;
Hot Shame shall burn upon thy secret brow,
And like a beaten hound tremble thou shalt—as now.

[459]

Nor let us weep that our delight is fled
Far from these carrion kites that scream below;
He wakes or sleeps with the enduring dead;
Thou canst not soar where he is sitting now.—
Dust to the dust! but the pure spirit shall flow
Back to the burning fountain whence it came,
A portion of the Eternal, which must glow   340
Through time and change, unquenchably the same,
Whilst thy cold embers choke the sordid hearth of shame.

Peace, peace! he is not dead, he doth not sleep—
He hath awakened from the dream of life—
'Tis we, who, lost in stormy visions, keep
With phantoms an unprofitable strife,
And in mad trance, strike with our spirit's knife
Invulnerable nothings. *We* decay
Like corpses in a charnel; fear and grief
Convulse us and consume us day by day,   350
And cold hopes swarm like worms within our living clay.

He has outsoared the shadow of our night;
Envy and calumny and hate and pain,
And that unrest which men miscall delight,
Can touch him not and torture not again;
From the contagion of the world's slow stain
He is secure, and now can never mourn
A heart grown cold, a head grown gray in vain;
Nor, when the spirit's self has ceased to burn,
With sparkless ashes load an unlamented urn.   360

He lives, he wakes—'tis Death is dead, not he;
Mourn not for Adonais.—Thou young Dawn,
Turn all thy dew to splendor, for from thee
The spirit thou lamentest is not gone;
Ye caverns and ye forests, cease to moan!
Cease, ye faint flowers and fountains, and thou air,
Which like a mourning veil thy scarf hadst thrown
O'er the abandoned Earth, now leave it bare
Even to the joyous stars which smile on its despair!

He is made one with Nature: there is heard   370
His voice in all her music, from the moan
Of thunder, to the song of night's sweet bird;
He is a presence to be felt and known
In darkness and in light, from herb and stone,
Spreading itself where'er that Power may move
Which has withdrawn his being to its own;
Which wields the world with never-wearied love,
Sustains it from beneath, and kindles it above.

He is a portion of the loveliness
Which once he made more lovely: he doth bear   380
His part, while the one Spirit's plastic stress
Sweeps through the dull dense world, compelling there,
All new successions to the forms they wear,
Torturing the unwilling dross that checks its flight
To its own likeness, as each mass they bear;
And bursting in its beauty and its might
From trees and beasts and men into the Heaven's light.

The splendors of the firmament of time
May be eclipsed, but are extinguished not;
Like stars to their appointed height they climb,   390
And death is a low mist which cannot blot
The brightness it may veil. When lofty thought
Lifts a young heart above its mortal lair,
And love and life contend in it for what
Shall be its earthly doom, the dead live there
And move like winds of light on dark and stormy air.

The inheritors of unfulfilled renown
Rose from their thrones, built beyond mortal thought,
Far in the Unapparent. Chatterton
Rose pale,—his solemn agony had not   400
Yet faded from him; Sidney, as he fought
And as he fell and as he lived and loved
Sublimely mild, a Spirit without spot,
Arose; and Lucan, by his death approved:
Oblivion as they rose shrank like a thing reproved.

And many more, whose names on earth are dark,
But whose transmitted effluence cannot die
So long as fire outlives the parent spark,
Rose, robed in dazzling immortality.
'Thou art become as one of us,' they cry,   410
'It was for thee yon kingless sphere has long
Swung blind in unascended majesty,
Silent alone amid an heaven of song.
Assume thy wingèd throne, thou Vesper of our throng!'

Who mourns for Adonais? Oh, come forth,
Fond wretch! and know thyself and him aright.
Clasp with thy panting soul the pendulous earth;
As from a center, dart thy spirit's light
Beyond all world's, until its spacious might
Satiate the void circumference: then shrink   420
Even to a point within our day and night;
And keep thy heart light lest it make thee sink
When hope has kindled hope, and lured thee to the brink.

Or go to Rome, which is the sepulcher,
Oh, not of him, but of our joy: 'tis nought
That ages, empires, and religions there
Lie buried in the ravage they have wrought;
For such as he can lend,—they borrow not
Glory from those who made the world their prey;
And he is gathered to the kings of thought   430
Who waged contention with their time's decay,
And of the past are all that cannot pass away.

Go thou to Rome,—at once the Paradise,
The grave, the city, and the wilderness;
And where its wrecks like shattered mountains rise,
And flowering weeds and fragrant copses dress
The bones of Desolation's nakedness,
Pass, till the Spirit of the spot shall lead
Thy footsteps to a slope of green access
Where, like an infant's smile, over the dead   440
A light of laughing flowers along the grass is spread;

And gray walls molder round, on which dull Time
Feeds, like slow fire, upon a hoary brand;
And one keen pyramid with wedge sublime,
Pavilioning the dust of him who planned
This refuge for his memory, doth stand
Like flame transformed to marble; and beneath,
A field is spread, on which a newer band
Have pitched in Heaven's smile their camp of death,
Welcoming him we lose with scarce extinguished breath.   450

Here pause: these graves are all too young as yet
To have outgrown the sorrow which consigned
Its charge to each; and if the seal is set,
Here, on one fountain of a mourning mind,
Break it not thou! too surely shalt thou find
Thine own well full, if thou returnest home,
Of tears and gall. From the world's bitter wind
Seek shelter in the shadow of the tomb.
What Adonais is, why fear we to become?

The One remains, the many change and pass;   460
Heaven's light forever shines, Earth's shadows fly;
Life, like a dome of many-colored glass,
Stains the white radiance of Eternity,
Until Death tramples it to fragments.—Die,
If thou wouldst be with that which thou dost seek!
Follow where all is fled!—Rome's azure sky,
Flowers, ruins, statues, music, words, are weak
The glory they transfuse with fitting truth to speak.

Why linger, why turn back, why shrink, my heart?
Thy hopes are gone before: from all things here   470
They have departed; thou shouldst now depart!
A light is passed from the revolving year,
And man, and woman; and what still is dear
Attracts to crush, repels to make thee wither.
The soft sky smiles,—the low wind whispers near:
'Tis Adonais calls! oh, hasten thither,
No more let Life divide what Death can join together.

[463]

That Light whose smile kindles the Universe,
That Beauty in which all things work and move,
That Benediction which the eclipsing Curse   480
Of birth can quench not, that sustaining Love
Which through the web of being blindly wove
By man and beast and earth and air and sea,
Burns bright or dim, as each are mirrors of
The fire for which all thirst; now beams on me,
Consuming the last clouds of cold mortality.

The breath whose might I have invoked in song
Descends on me; my spirit's bark is driven,
Far from the shore, far from the trembling throng
Whose sails were never to the tempest given;   490
The massy earth and spherèd skies are riven!
I am borne darkly, fearfully, afar:
Whilst, burning through the inmost veil of Heaven,
The soul of Adonais, like a star,
Beacons from the abode where the Eternal are.

207   *Thyrsis*

How changed is here each spot man makes or fills!
  In the two Hinkseys nothing keeps the same;
    The village street its haunted mansion lacks,
  And from the sign is gone Sibylla's name,
    And from the roofs the twisted chimney-stacks—
      Are ye too changed, ye hills?
  See, 'tis no foot of unfamiliar men
    Tonight from Oxford up your pathway strays!
    Here came I often, often, in old days—
  Thyrsis and I; we still had Thyrsis then.   10

Runs it not here, the track by Childsworth Farm,
  Past the high wood, to where the elm-tree crowns
    The hill behind whose ridge the sunset flames?
  The signal-elm, that looks on Ilsley Downs,
    The Vale, the three lone weirs, the youthful Thames?—
      This winter-eve is warm,
  Humid the air! leafless, yet soft as spring,
    The tender purple spray on copse and briers!
    And that sweet city with her dreaming spires,
  She needs not June for beauty's heightening,   20

Lovely all times she lies, lovely tonight!—
  Only, methinks, some loss of habit's power
    Befalls me wandering through this upland dim.
  Once passed I blindfold here, at any hour;
    Now seldom come I, since I came with him.
      That single elm-tree bright
  Against the west—I miss it! is it gone?
    We prized it dearly; while it stood, we said,
    Our friend, the gypsy-scholar, was not dead;
  While the tree lived, he in these fields lived on.   30

Too rare, too rare, grow now my visits here,
  But once I knew each field, each flower, each stick;
    And with the country-folk acquaintance made
  By barn in threshing-time, by new-built rick.
    Here, too, our shepherd-pipes we first assayed.
      Ah me! this many a year
  My pipe is lost, my shepherd's holiday!
    Needs must I lose them, needs with heavy heart
    Into the world and wave of men depart;
  But Thyrsis of his own will went away.   40

It irked him to be here; he could not rest.
    He loved each simple joy the country yields,
        He loved his mates; but yet he could not keep,
    For that a shadow lowered on the fields,
        Here with the shepherds and the silly sheep.
           Some life of men unblest
    He knew, which made him droop, and filled his head.
        He went; his piping took a troubled sound
        Of storms that rage outside our happy ground;
    He could not wait their passing, he is dead.   50

So, some tempestuous morn in early June,
    When the year's primal burst of bloom is o'er,
        Before the roses and the longest day—
    When garden-walks and all the grassy floor
        With blossoms red and white of fallen May
           And chestnut-flowers are strewn—
    So have I heard the cuckoo's parting cry,
        From the wet field, through the vexed garden-trees,
        Come with the volleying rain and tossing breeze:
    The bloom is gone, and with the bloom go I!   60

Too quick despairer, wherefore wilt thou go?
    Soon will the high Midsummer pomps come on,
        Soon will the musk carnations break and swell,
    Soon shall we have gold-dusted snapdragon,
        Sweet-William with his homely cottage-smell,
           And stocks in fragrant blow;
    Roses that down the alleys shine afar,
        And open, jasmine-muffled lattices,
        And groups under the dreaming garden-trees,
    And the full moon, and the white evening-star.   70

He hearkens not! light comer, he is flown!
　　What matters it? next year he will return,
　　　　And we shall have him in the sweet spring-days,
　　With whitening hedges, and uncrumpling fern,
　　　　And bluebells trembling by the forest-ways,
　　　　　　And scent of hay new-mown.
　　But Thyrsis never more we swains shall see;
　　　　See him come back, and cut a smoother reed,
　　　　And blow a strain the world at last shall heed—
　　For Time, not Corydon, hath conquered thee!　　　　80

Alack, for Corydon no rival now!—
　　But when Sicilian shepherds lost a mate,
　　　　Some good survivor with his flute would go,
　　Piping a ditty sad for Bion's fate;
　　　　And cross the unpermitted ferry's flow,
　　　　　　And relax Pluto's brow,
　　And make leap up with joy the beauteous head
　　　　Of Proserpine, among whose crownèd hair
　　　　Are flowers first opened on Sicilian air,
　　And flute his friend, like Orpheus, from the dead.　　　90

O easy access to the hearer's grace
　　When Dorian shepherds sang to Proserpine!
　　　　For she herself had trod Sicilian fields,
　　She knew the Dorian water's gush divine,
　　　　She knew each lily white which Enna yields,
　　　　　　Each rose with blushing face;
　　She loved the Dorian pipe, the Dorian strain.
　　　　But, ah, of our poor Thames she never heard!
　　　　Her foot the Cumner cowslips never stirred;
　　And we should tease her with our plaint in vain!　　　100

[467]

Well! wind-dispersed and vain the words will be,
   Yet, Thyrsis, let me give my grief its hour
      In the old haunt, and find our tree-topped hill!
   Who, if not I, for questing here hath power?
      I know the wood which hides the daffodil,
         I know the Fyfield tree,
      I know what white, what purple fritillaries
         The grassy harvest of the river-fields,
         Above by Ensham, down by Sandford, yields,
   And what sedged brooks are Thames's tributaries;   110

I know these slopes; who knows them if not I?—
   But many a dingle on the loved hill-side,
      With thorns once studded, old, white-blossomed trees,
   Where thick the cowslips grew, and far descried
      High towered the spikes of purple orchises,
         Hath since our day put by
      The coronals of that forgotten time;
         Down each green bank hath gone the plowboy's team,
         And only in the hidden brookside gleam
   Primroses, orphans of the flowery prime.   120

Where is the girl, who by the boatman's door,
   Above the locks, above the boating throng,
      Unmoored our skiff when through the Wytham flats,
   Red loosestrife and blond meadow-sweet among
      And darting swallows and light water-gnats,
         We tracked the shy Thames shore?
   Where are the mowers, who, as the tiny swell
      Of our boat passing heaved the river-grass,
      Stood with suspended scythe to see us pass?—
   They all are gone, and thou art gone as well!   130

Yes, thou art gone! and round me too the night
   In ever-nearing circle weaves her shade.
      I see her veil draw soft across the day,
   I feel her slowly chilling breath invade
      The cheek grown thin, the brown hair sprent with gray;

I feel her finger light
Laid pausefully upon life's headlong train—
　The foot less prompt to meet the morning dew,
　The heart less bounding at emotion new,
And hope, once crushed, less quick to spring again.　　140

And long the way appears, which seemed so short
　To the less practiced eye of sanguine youth;
　　And high the mountain-tops, in cloudy air,
　The mountain-tops where is the throne of Truth,
　　Tops in life's morning-sun so bright and bare!
　　　Unbreachable the fort
　Of the long-battered world uplifts its wall;
　　And strange and vain the earthly turmoil grows,
　　And near and real the charm of thy repose,
And night as welcome as a friend would fall.　　150

But hush! the upland hath a sudden loss
　Of quiet!—Look, adown the dusk hill-side,
　　A troop of Oxford hunters going home,
　As in old days, jovial and talking, ride!
　　From hunting with the Berkshire hounds they come.
　　　Quick! let me fly, and cross
　Into yon farther field!—'Tis done; and see,
　　Backed by the sunset, which doth glorify
　　The orange and pale violet evening-sky,
Bare on its lonely ridge, the Tree! the Tree!　　160

I take the omen! Eve lets down her veil,
　The white fog creeps from bush to bush about,
　　The west unflushes, the high stars grow bright,
　And in the scattered farms the lights come out.
　　I cannot reach the signal-tree tonight,
　　　Yet, happy omen, hail!
　Hear it from thy broad lucent Arno-vale
　　(For there thine earth-forgetting eyelids keep
　　The morningless and unawakening sleep
Under the flowery oleanders pale),　　170

[469]

Hear it, O Thyrsis, still our tree is there!—
    Ah, vain! These English fields, this upland dim,
      These brambles pale with mist engarlanded,
    That lone, sky-pointing tree, are not for him;
      To a boon southern country he is fled,
        And now in happier air,
    Wandering with the great Mother's train divine
      (And purer or more subtle soul than thee,
      I trow, the mighty Mother doth not see)
    Within a folding of the Apennine,   180

Thou hearest the immortal chants of old!—
    Putting his sickle to the perilous grain
      In the hot cornfield of the Phrygian king,
    For thee the Lityerses-song again
      Young Daphnis with his silver voice doth sing;
        Sings his Sicilian fold,
    His sheep, his hapless love, his blinded eyes—
      And how a call celestial round him rang,
      And heavenward from the fountain-brink he sprang,
    And all the marvel of the golden skies.   190

There thou art gone, and me thou leavest here
    Sole in these fields! yet will I not despair.
      Despair I will not, while I yet descry
    'Neath the mild canopy of English air
      That lonely tree against the western sky.
        Still, still these slopes, 'tis clear,
    Our Gypsy-Scholar haunts, outliving thee!
      Fields where soft sheep from cages pull the hay,
      Woods with anemones in flower till May,
    Know him a wanderer still; then why not me?   200

A fugitive and gracious light he seeks,
    Shy to illumine; and I seek it too.
      This does not come with houses or with gold,
    With place, with honor, and a flattering crew;
      'Tis not in the world's market bought and sold—

But the smooth-slipping weeks
 Drop by, and leave its seeker still untired;
  Out of the heed of mortals he is gone,
  He wends unfollowed, he must house alone;
 Yet on he fares, by his own heart inspired.   210

Thou too, O Thyrsis, on like quest wast bound;
 Thou wanderedst with me for a little hour!
  Men gave thee nothing; but this happy quest,
 If men esteemed thee feeble, gave thee power,
  If men procured thee trouble, gave thee rest.
   And this rude Cumner ground,
 Its fir-topped Hurst, its farms, its quiet fields,
  Here cam'st thou in thy jocund youthful time,
  Here was thine height of strength, thy golden prime!
 And still the haunt beloved a virtue yields.   220

What though the music of thy rustic flute
 Kept not for long its happy, country tone;
  Lost it too soon, and learned a stormy note
 Of men contention-tossed, of men who groan,
  Which tasked thy pipe too sore, and tired thy throat—
   It failed, and thou wast mute!
 Yet hadst thou alway visions of our light,
  And long with men of care thou couldst not stay,
  And soon thy foot resumed its wandering way,
 Left human haunt, and on alone till night.   230

Too rare, too rare, grow now my visits here!
 'Mid city-noise, not, as with thee of yore,
  Thyrsis! in reach of sheep-bells is my home.
 —Then through the great town's harsh, heart-wearying roar,
  Let in thy voice a whisper often come,
   To chase fatigue and fear:
 Why faintest thou? I wandered till I died.
  Roam on! The light we sought is shining still.
  Dost thou ask proof? Our tree yet crowns the hill,
 Our Scholar travels yet the loved hill-side.   240

[471]

PART VI

POEMS OF SERIOUS WIT AND SYMBOLISM

Mark but this flea, and mark in this,
How little that which thou deny'st me is;
It sucked me first, and now sucks thee,
And in this flea our two bloods mingled be;
Thou know'st that this cannot be said
A sin, nor shame, nor loss of maidenhead;
    Yet this enjoys before it woo,
    And pampered swells with one blood made of two,
    And this, alas, is more than we would do.

Oh stay, three lives in one flea spare,   10
Where we almost, yea, more than married are.
This flea is you and I, and this
Our marriage bed, and marriage temple is;
Though parents grudge, and you, w' are met,
And cloistered in these living walls of jet.
    Though use make you apt to kill me,
    Let not to that, self-murder added be,
    And sacrilege, three sins in killing three.

Cruel and sudden, hast thou since
Purpled thy nail in blood of innocence?   20
Wherein could this flea guilty be,
Except in that drop which it sucked from thee?
Yet thou triumph'st and say'st that thou
Find'st not thyself, nor me the weaker now;
    'Tis true, then learn how false fears be:
    Just so much honor, when thou yield'st to me,
    Will waste, as this flea's death took life from thee.

The Bait

    Come live with me, and be my love,
    And we will some new pleasures prove,
    Of golden sands, and crystal brooks,
    With silken lines, and silver hooks.

There will the river whispering run,
Warmed by thy eyes more than the sun.
And there the'enamored fish will stay,
Begging themselves they may betray.

When thou wilt swim in that live bath,
Each fish, which every channel hath,   10
Will amorously to thee swim,
Gladder to catch thee, than thou him.

If thou, to be so seen, beest loath,
By sun or moon, thou dark'nest both;
And if myself have leave to see,
I need not their light, having thee.

Let others freeze with angling reeds,
And cut their legs with shells and weeds,
Or treacherously poor fish beset
With strangling snare, or windowy net.   20

Let coarse bold hands from slimy nest
The bedded fish in banks out-wrest,
Or curious traitors, sleave-silk flies,
Bewitch poor fishes' wand'ring eyes.

For thee, thou need'st no such deceit,
For thou thyself art thine own bait;
That fish that is not catched thereby,
Alas, is wiser far than I

The Ecstasy

Where, like a pillow on a bed,
   A pregnant bank swelled up to rest
The violet's reclining head,
   Sat we two, one another's best.
Our hands were firmly cèmented
   With a fast balm, which thence did spring;
Our eye-beams twisted, and did thread

Our eyes upon one double string;
So to'entergraft our hands, as yet
    Was all the means to make us one,   10
And pictures in our eyes to get
    Was all our propagation.
As 'twixt two equal armies fate
    Suspends uncertain victory,
Our souls, which to advance their state
    Were gone out, hung 'twixt her and me.
And whilst our souls negotiate there,
    We like sepulchral statues lay;
All day, the same our postures were,
    And we said nothing, all the day.   20
If any, so by love refined
    That he soul's language understood,
And by good love were grown all mind,
    Within convenient distance stood,
He, though he knew not which soul spake,
    Because both meant, both spake the same,
Might thence a new concoction take
    And part far purer than he came.
This ecstasy doth unperplex,
    We said, and tell us what we love: 30
We see by this it was not sex,
    We see we saw not what did move;
But as all several souls contain
    Mixture of things, they know not what,
Love these mixed souls doth mix again
    And makes both one, each this and that.
A single violet transplant,
    The strength, the color, and the size,
All which before was poor and scant,
    Redoubles still, and multiplies.   40
When love with one another so
    Interinanimates two souls,
That abler soul, which thence doth flow,
    Defects of loneliness controls.
We then, who are this new soul, know

Of what we are composed and made,
For th' atomies of which we grow
    Are souls, whom no change can invade.
But oh, alas, so long, so far,
    Our bodies why do we forbear?   50
They are ours, though not we; we are
    The intelligences, they the sphere.
We owe them thanks, because they thus
    Did us to us at first convey,
Yielded their forces, sense, to us,
    Nor are dross to us, but allay.
On man heaven's influence works not so,
    But that it first imprints the air;
For soul into the soul may flow,
    Though it to body first repair.   60
As our blood labors to beget
    Spirits, as like souls as it can,
Because such fingers need to knit
    That subtle knot which makes us man,
So must pure lovers' souls descend
    T' affections, and to faculties,
Which sense may reach and apprehend,
    Else a great prince in prison lies.
To' our bodies turn we then, that so
    Weak men on love revealed may look;   70
Love's mysteries in souls do grow,
    But yet the body is his book.
And if some lover, such as we,
    Have heard this dialogue of one,
Let him still mark us, he shall see
    Small change when we' are to bodies gone.

211

The Good-morrow

I wonder by my troth, what thou and I
Did, till we loved? Were we not weaned till then,
But sucked on country pleasures, childishly?
Or snorted we in the seven sleepers' den?

'Twas so; but this, all pleasures fancies be.
If ever any beauty I did see,
Which I desired, and got, 'twas but a dream of thee.

And now good morrow to our waking souls,
Which watch not one another out of fear;
For love all love of other sights controls,   10
And makes one little room an everywhere.
Let sea-discoverers to new worlds have gone,
Let maps to other, worlds on worlds have shown;
Let us possess one world, each hath one, and is one.

My face in thine eye, thine in mine appears,
And true plain hearts do in the faces rest;
Where can we find two better hemispheres
Without sharp north, without declining west?
Whatever dies was not mixed equally;
If our two loves be one, or thou and I   20
Love so alike that none do slacken, none can die.

212   *The Anniversary*

All kings, and all their favorites,
    All glory of honors, beauties, wits,
The sun itself, which makes times as they pass,
Is elder by a year now, than it was
When thou and I first one another saw;
All other things to their destruction draw,
    Only our love hath no decay;
This no to-morrow hath, nor yesterday,
Running, it never runs from us away,
But truly keeps his first, last, everlasting day.   10

    Two graves must hide thine and my corse;
    If one might, death were no divorce.
Alas, as well as other princes, we,
Who prince enough in one another be,
Must leave at last in death these eyes and ears,

Oft fed with true oaths, and with sweet salt tears;
      But souls where nothing dwells but love,
All other thoughts being inmates, then shall prove
This, or a love increasèd there above,
When bodies to their graves, souls from their graves, remove.   20

      And then we shall be throughly blest,
      But we no more than all the rest;
Here upon earth we'are kings, and none but we
Can be such kings, nor of such subjects be.
Who is so safe as we, where none can do
Treason to us, except one of us two?
      True and false fears let us refrain;
Let us love nobly, and live, and add again
Years and years unto years, till we attain
To write threescore; this is the second of our reign.   30

Song

            Sweetest love, I do not go
                  For weariness of thee,
            Nor in hope the world can show
                  A fitter love for me;
                        But since that I
            Must die at last, 'tis best,
            To use myself in jest
                  Thus by feigned deaths to die.

            Yesternight the sun went hence,
                  And yet is here to-day;   10
            He hath no desire nor sense,
                  Nor half so short a way;
                        Then fear not me,
            But believe that I shall make
            Speedier journeys, since I take
                  More wings and spurs than he.

Oh, how feeble is man's power,
　　That if good fortune fall,
Cannot add another hour,
　　Nor a lost hour recall!
　　　　But come bad chance,
And we join to'it our strength,
And we teach it art and length,
　　Itself o'er us to'advance.

When thou sigh'st, thou sigh'st not wind,
　　But sigh'st my soul away;
When thou weep'st, unkindly kind,
　　My life's blood doth decay.
　　　　It cannot be
That thou lov'st me, as thou say'st,
If in thine my life thou waste;
　　Thou art the best of me.

Let not thy divining heart
　　Forethink me any ill,
Destiny may take thy part,
　　And may thy fears fulfill;
　　　　But think that we
Are but turned aside to sleep;
They who one another keep
　　Alive, ne'er parted be.

214　　*A Valediction Forbidding Mourning*

As virtuous men pass mildly away,
　　And whisper to their souls to go,
Whilst some of their sad friends do say,
　　The breath goes now, and some say, No;

So let us melt, and make no noise,
　　No tear-floods, nor sigh-tempests move;
'Twere profanation of our joys
　　To tell the laity our love.

Moving of th' earth brings harms and fears,
    Men reckon what it did and meant;   10
But trepidation of the spheres,
    Though greater far, is innocent.

Dull sublunary lovers' love,
    Whose soul is sense, cannot admit
Absence, because it doth remove
    Those things which elemented it.

But we by a love so much refined
    That ourselves know not what it is,
Inter-assurèd of the mind,
    Careless eyes, lips, hands to miss.   20

Our two souls therefore, which are one,
    Though I must go, endure not yet
A breach, but an expansïon,
    Like gold to airy thinness beat.

If they be two, they are two so
    As stiff twin compasses are two;
Thy soul, the fixed foot, makes no show
    To move, but doth if the'other do.

And though it in the center sit,
    Yet when the other far doth roam,   30
It leans, and hearkens after it,
    And grows erect as that comes home.

Such wilt thou be to me who must,
    Like th' other foot, obliquely run;
Thy firmness makes my circle just,
    And makes me end where I begun.

215   *The Funeral*

Whoever comes to shroud me, do not harm
            Nor question much
That subtile wreath of hair which crowns my arm;
The mystery, the sign you must not touch,

For 'tis my outward soul,
Viceroy to that, which unto heaven being gone,
    Will leave this to control
And keep these limbs, her provinces, from dissolution.

For if the sinewy thread my brain lets fall
    Through every part,   10
Can tie those parts, and make me one of all,
Those hairs, which upward grew, and strength and art
    Have from a better brain,
Can better do'it; except she meant that I
    By this should know my pain,
As prisoners then are manacled, when they'are condemned to die.

Whate'er she meant by'it, bury it with me,
    For since I am
Love's martyr, it might breed idolatry
If into others' hands these relics came;   20
    As 'twas humility
To afford to it all that a soul can do,
    So 'tis some bravery,
That since you would have none of me, I bury some of you.

216   *A Nocturnal upon Saint Lucy's Day*

'Tis the year's midnight, and it is the day's,
Lucy's, who scarce seven hours herself unmasks;
    The sun is spent, and now his flasks
    Send forth light squibs, no constant rays;
      The world's whole sap is sunk;
The general balm th' hydroptic earth hath drunk,
Whither, as to the bed's feet, life is shrunk,
Dead and interred; yet all these seem to laugh,
Compared with me, who am their epitaph.

Study me then, you who shall lovers be   10
At the next world, that is, at the next spring;
    For I am every dead thing,
    In whom Love wrought new alchemy.

For his art did express
A quintessence even from nothingness,
From dull privations, and lean emptiness;
He ruined me, and I am re-begot
Of absence, darkness, death—things which are not.

All others from all things draw all that's good,
Life, soul, form, spirit, whence they being have;   20
   I, by Love's limbec, am the grave   *dose*
   Of all that's nothing. Oft a flood
      Have we two wept, and so
Drowned the whole world, us two; oft did we grow
To be two chaoses, when we did show
Care to aught else; and often absences
Withdrew our souls, and made us carcasses.

But I am by her death, which word wrongs her,
Of the first nothing the elixir grown;
   Were I a man, that I were one   30
   I needs must know; I should prefer,
      If I were any beast,
Some ends, some means; yea plants, yea stones detest
And love; all, all some properties invest;
If I an ordinary nothing were,
As shadow, a light and body must be here.

But I am none; nor will my sun renew.
You lovers, for whose sake the lesser sun
   At this time to the Goat is run
   To fetch new lust, and give it you,   40
      Enjoy your summer all;
Since she enjoys her long night's festival,
Let me prepare towards her, and let me call
This hour her vigil, and her eve, since this
Both the year's and the day's deep midnight is.

[484]

On His Mistress

By our first strange and fatal interview,
By all desires which thereof did ensue,
By our long starving hopes, by that remorse
Which my words' masculine persuasive force
Begot in thee, and by the memory
Of hurts which spies and rivals threatened me,
I calmly beg; but by thy father's wrath,
By all pains, which want and divorcement hath,
I conjure thee; and all the oaths which I
And thou have sworn to seal joint constancy,   10
Here I unswear, and overswear them thus:
Thou shalt not love by ways so dangerous.
Temper, O fair love, love's impetuous rage,
Be my true mistress still, not my feigned page;
I'll go, and by thy kind leave, leave behind
Thee, only worthy to nurse in my mind
Thirst to come back; oh, if thou die before,
My soul from other lands to thee shall soar.
Thy else almighty beauty cannot move
Rage from the seas, nor thy love teach them love,   20
Nor tame wild Boreas' harshness; thou hast read
How roughly he in pieces shiverèd
Fair Orithea, whom he swore he loved.
Fall ill or good, 'tis madness to have proved
Dangers unurged; feed on this flattery,
That absent lovers one in th' other be.
Dissemble nothing, not a boy, nor change
Thy body's habit, nor mind's; be not strange
To thyself only; all will spy in thy face
A blushing womanly discovering grace.   30
Richly clothed apes are called apes; and as soon
Eclipsed as bright, we call the moon the moon.
Men of France, changeable chameleons,
Spitals of diseases, shops of fashions,
Love's fuelers, and the rightest company
Of players which upon the world's stage be,

Will quickly know thee, and no less, also!
Th' indifferent Italian, as we pass
His warm land, well content to think thee page,
Will hunt thee with such lust and hideous rage   40
As Lot's fair guests were vexed. But none of these,
Nor spongy hydroptic Dutch shall thee displease,
If thou stay here. Oh, stay here! for, for thee,
England is only a worthy gallery
To walk in expectation, till from thence
Our greatest King call thee to his presènce.
When I am gone, dream me some happiness,
Nor let thy looks our long hid love confess,
Nor praise, nor dispraise me, nor bless nor curse
Openly love's force, nor in bed fright thy nurse   50
With midnight's startings, crying out, Oh, oh,
Nurse, oh, my love is slain, I saw him go
O'er the white Alps alone; I saw him, I,
Assailed, fight, taken, stabbed, bleed, fall, and die.
Augur me better chance, except dread Jove
Think it enough for me to'have had thy love.

Mark Antony

When as the nightingale chanted her vespers,
And the wild forester couched on the ground,
Venus invited me in the evening whispers
Unto a fragrant field with roses crowned,
    Where she before had sent
    My wishes' complement;
    Unto my heart's content
    Played with me on the green.
      Never Mark Antony
      Dallied more wantonly   10
      With the fair Egyptian Queen.

First on her cherry cheeks I mine eyes feasted,
Thence fear of surfeiting made me retire;
Next on her warmer lips, which when I tasted,
My duller spirits made active as fire.

Then we began to dart,
Each at another's heart,
Arrows that knew no smart,
Sweet lips and smiles between.
   Never Mark Antony   20
   Dallied more wantonly
   With the fair Egyptian Queen.

Wanting a glass to plait her amber tresses,
Which like a bracelet rich deckèd mine arm,
Gaudier than Juno wears when as she graces
Jove with embraces more stately than warm;
   Then did she peep in mine
   Eyes' humor crystalline;
   I in her eyes was seen,
   As if we one had been.   30
   Never Mark Antony
   Dallied more wantonly
   With the fair Egyptian Queen.

Mystical grammar of amorous glances;
Feeling of pulses, the physic of love;
Rhetorical courtings and musical dances;
Numb'ring of kisses arithmetic prove;
   Eyes like astronomy;
   Straight-limbed geometry;
   In her arts' ingeny   40
   Our wits were sharp and keen.
   Never Mark Antony
   Dallied more wantonly
   With the fair Egyptian Queen.

219   *To His Coy Mistress*

Had we but world enough, and time,
This coyness, lady, were no crime.
We would sit down and think which way
To walk, and pass our long love's day;

Thou by the Indian Ganges' side
Shouldst rubies find; I by the tide
Of Humber would complain. I would
Love you ten years before the Flood;
And you should, if you please, refuse
Till the conversion of the Jews.   10
My vegetable love should grow
Vaster than empires, and more slow.
An hundred years should go to praise
Thine eyes, and on thy forehead gaze;
Two hundred to adore each breast,
By thirty thousand to the rest;
An age at least to every part,
And the last age should show your heart.
For, lady, you deserve this state,
Nor would I love at lower rate.   20
    But at my back I always hear
Time's wingèd chariot hurrying near;
And yonder all before us lie
Deserts of vast eternity.
Thy beauty shall no more be found,
Nor in thy marble vault shall sound
My echoing song; then worms shall try
That long preserved virginity,
And your quaint honor turn to dust,
And into ashes all my lust.   30
The grave's a fine and private place,
But none, I think, do there embrace.
    Now therefore, while the youthful hue
Sits on thy skin like morning dew,
And while thy willing soul transpires
At every pore with instant fires,
Now let us sport us while we may;
And now, like am'rous birds of prey,
Rather at once our time devour,
Than languish in his slow-chapped power.   40
Let us roll all our strength, and all
Our sweetness, up into one ball;

And tear our pleasures with rough strife
Thorough the iron gates of life.
Thus, though we cannot make our sun
Stand still, yet we will make him run.

You, Andrew Marvell

And here face down beneath the sun
And here upon earth's noonward height
To feel the always coming on
The always rising of the night

To feel creep up the curving east
The earthy chill of dusk and slow
Upon those under lands the vast
And ever climbing shadow grow

And strange at Ecbatan the trees
Take leaf by leaf the evening strange   10
The flooding dark about their knees
The mountains over Persia change

And now at Kermanshah the gate
Dark empty and the withered grass
And through the twilight now the late
Few travelers in the westward pass

And Baghdad darken and the bridge
Across the silent river gone
And through Arabia the edge
Of evening widen and steal on   20

And deepen on Palmyra's street
The wheel rut in the ruined stone
And Lebanon fade out and Crete
High through the clouds and overblown

And over Sicily the air
Still flashing with the landward gulls
And loom and slowly disappear
The sails above the shadowy hulls

And Spain go under and the shore
Of Africa the gilded sand   30
And evening vanish and no more
The low pale light across that land

Nor now the long light on the sea

And here face downward in the sun
To feel how swift how secretly
The shadow of the night comes on . . .

221   *The Mower to the Glow-worms*

Ye living lamps, by whose dear light
The nightingale does sit so late,
And studying all the summer night,
Her matchless songs does meditate;

Ye county comets that portend   5
No war nor prince's funeral,
Shining unto no higher end
Than to presage the grass's fall;

Ye glow-worms, whose officious flame
To wand'ring mowers shows the way,   10
That in the night have lost their aim,
And after foolish fires do stray;

Your courteous lights in vain you waste,
Since Juliana here is come,
For she my mind hath so displaced   15
That I shall never find my home.

222

'Past ruin'd Ilion Helen lives'

Past ruin'd Ilion Helen lives,
    Alcestis rises from the shades;
Verse calls them forth; 'tis verse that gives
    Immortal youth to mortal maids.

Soon shall Oblivion's deepening veil
    Hide all the peopled hills you see,
The gay, the proud, while lovers hail
    These many summers you and me.

On Seeing a Hair of Lucretia Borgia

Borgia, thou once wert almost too august
And high for adoration; now thou'rt dust;
All that remains of thee these plaits unfold,
Calm hair, meandering in pellucid gold.

Days

Daughters of Time, the hypocritic Days,
Muffled and dumb like barefoot dervishes,
And marching single in an endless file,
Bring diadems and fagots in their hands.
To each they offer gifts after his will,
Bread, kingdoms, stars, and sky that holds them all.
I, in my pleached garden, watched the pomp,
Forgot my morning wishes, hastily
Took a few herbs and apples, and the Day
Turned and departed silent. I, too late,
Under her solemn fillet saw the scorn.

The Express

After the first powerful plain manifesto
The black statement of pistons, without more fuss
But gliding like a queen, she leaves the station.
Without bowing and with restrained unconcern

She passes the houses which humbly crowd outside,
The gasworks and at last the heavy page
Of death, printed by gravestones in the cemetery.
Beyond the town there lies the open country
Where, gathering speed, she acquires mystery,
The luminous self-possession of ships on ocean.   10
It is now she begins to sing—at first quite low
Then loud, and at last with a jazzy madness—
The song of her whistle screaming at curves,
Of deafening tunnels, brakes, innumerable bolts.
And always light, aerial, underneath
Goes the elate metre of her wheels.
Steaming through metal landscape on her lines
She plunges new eras of wild happiness
Where speed throws up strange shapes, broad curves
And parallels clean like the steel of guns.   20
At last, further than Edinburgh or Rome,
Beyond the crest of the world, she reaches night
Where only a low streamline brightness
Of phosphorus on the tossing hills is white.
Ah, like a comet through flame she moves entranced
Wrapt in her music no bird song, no, nor bough
Breaking with honey buds, shall ever equal.

226   *'I like to see it lap the miles'*

I like to see it lap the miles,
And lick the valleys up,
And stop to feed itself at tanks;
And then, prodigious, step

Around a pile of mountains,   5
And, supercilious, peer
In shanties by the sides of roads;
And then a quarry pare

To fit its sides, and crawl between,
Complaining all the while   10
In horrid, hooting stanza;
Then chase itself down hill

And neigh like Boanerges;
Then, punctual as a star,
Stop—docile and omnipotent—   15
At its own stable door.

227   *'There's a certain slant of light'*

There's a certain slant of light,
On winter afternoons,
That oppresses, like the weight
Of cathedral tunes.

Heavenly hurt it gives us;   5
We can find no scar,
But internal difference
Where the meanings are.

None may teach it anything,
'Tis the seal, despair,—   10
An imperial affliction
Sent us of the air.

When it comes, the landscape listens,
Shadows hold their breath;
When it goes, 'tis like the distance   15
On the look of death.

228   *'I died for beauty'*

I died for beauty, but was scarce
Adjusted in the tomb,
When one who died for truth was lain
In an adjoining room.

[493]

He questioned softly why I failed?
'For beauty,' I replied.
'And I for truth,—the two are one;
We brethren are,' he said.

And so, as kinsmen met a night,
We talked between the rooms,   10
Until the moss had reached our lips,
And covered up our names.

229   *'I heard a fly buzz when I died'*

I heard a fly buzz when I died;
    The stillness round my form
Was like the stillness in the air
    Between the heaves of storm.

The eyes beside had wrung them dry,   5
    And breaths were gathering sure
For that last onset, when the king
    Be witnessed in his power.

I willed my keepsakes, signed away
    What portion of me I   10
Could make assignable,—and then
    There interposed a fly,

With blue, uncertain, stumbling buzz,
    Between the light and me;
And then the windows failed, and then   15
    I could not see to see.

230   *The Leaden Echo and the Golden Echo*

THE LEADEN ECHO

How to kéep—is there ány any, is there none such, nowhere known
        some, bow or brooch or braid or brace, láce, latch or catch
        or key to keep
Back beauty, keep it, beauty, beauty, beauty, . . . from vanishing
        away?

[494]

Ó, is there no frowning of these wrinkles, rankèd wrinkles deep,
Dówn? no waving off of these most mournful messengers, still mes-
        sengers, sad and stealing messengers of gray?
No, there's none, there's none—O no there's none,   5
Nor can you long be, what you now are, called fair,
Do what you may do, what, do what you may,
And wisdom is early to despair:
Be beginning; since, no, nothing can be done
To keep at bay   10
Age and age's evils, hoar hair,
Ruck and wrinkle, drooping, dying, death's worst, winding sheets,
        tombs and worms and tumbling to decay;
So be beginning, be beginning to despair.
O, there's none; no no no there's none:
    Be beginning to despair, to despair,   15
    Despair, despair, despair, despair.

                    THE GOLDEN ECHO

    Spare!
There ís one, yes, I have one (Hush there!);
Only not within seeing of the sun,
Not within the singeing of the strong sun,
Tall sun's tingeing, or treacherous the tainting of the earth's air,
Somewhere elsewhere there is ah well where! one,
Óne. Yes I can tell such a key, I do know such a place,
Where whatever's prized and passes of us, everything that's fresh and
        fast flying of us, seems to us sweet of us and swiftly away
        with, done away with, undone,
Undone, done with, soon done with, and yet dearly and dangerously
        sweet
Of us, the wimpled-water-dimpled, not-by-morning-matchèd face, 10
The flower of beauty, fleece of beauty, too too apt to, ah! to fleet,
Never fleets móre, fastened with the tenderest truth
To its own best being and its loveliness of youth: it is an everlasting-
        ness of, O it is an all youth!
Come then, your ways and airs and looks, locks, maiden gear, gal-
        lantry and gaiety and grace,

                    [495]

Winning ways, airs innocent, maiden manners, sweet looks, loose
    locks, long locks, lovelocks, gaygear, going gallant, girl-
    grace—
Resign them, sign them, seal them, send them, motion them with
    breath,
And with sighs soaring, soaring síghs deliver
Them; beauty-in-the-ghost, deliver it, early now, long before death
Give beauty back, beauty, beauty, beauty, back to God, beauty's
    self and beauty's giver.
See; not a hair is, not an eyelash, not the least lash lost; every hair   20
Is, hair of the head, numbered.
Nay, what we had lighthanded left in surly the mere mold
Will have waked and have waxed and have walked with the wind
    what while we slept,
This side, that side hurling a heavyheaded hundredfold
What while we, while we slumbered.
O then, weary then whý should we tread? O why are we so haggard
    at the heart, so care-coiled, care-killed, so fagged, so fashed,
    so cogged, so cumbered,
When the thing we freely fórfeit is kept with fonder a care,
Fonder a care kept than we could have kept it, kept
Far with fonder a care (and we, we should have lost it) finer, fonder
A care kept.—Where kept? Do but tell us where kept, where.—   30
Yonder.—What high as that!We follow, now we follow.—Yonder,
    yes yonder, yonder,
Yonder.

231   *The Leaden Echo and the Golden Echo*

THE LEADEN ECHO

How keep beauty? is there any way?
Is there nowhere any means to have it stay?
Will no bow or brooch or braid,
Brace or lace
Latch or catch   5
Or key to lock the door lend aid
Before beauty vanishes away?

No, no, there's none,
Nor can you long be fair;
Soon your best is done, 10
Wisdom must be early to despair:
Look now for age, hoar hair,
Winding sheets and tumbling to decay;
Even now to-day
Be beginning to despair, 15
Despair, despair.

THE GOLDEN ECHO

Spare!
There's one
Though not within the seeing of the sun,
One way to hold sweet looks, girl grace,
Youth and the not-by-morning matched face—
Resign them, yea, deliver
Beauty back to Beauty's self and giver—
Back to God . . . Every lash and tress
Is hair of the head numbered
Its heavy hundredfold has . . . yes,
Waked and waxed and walked with the wind 10
Where that but breathes to bless
Has more joy but to find . . .
O why so cogged, fashed, cumbered,
So teased but to continue fair?
Freely forfeit what were kept
With fonder a care
E'en though we surly slept,
With care far fonder!
Is kept where?
So high as that? Yes, yonder! 20
Follow! There!
There! There!

'All lovely things will have an ending'

All lovely things will have an ending,
All lovely things will fade and die,
And youth, that's now so bravely spending,
Will beg a penny by and by.

Fine ladies all are soon forgotten,   5
And goldenrod is dust when dead,
The sweetest flesh and flowers are rotten
And cobwebs tent the brightest head.

Come back, true love! Sweet youth, return!—
But time goes on, and will, unheeding,   10
Though hands will reach, and eyes will yearn,
And the wild days set true hearts bleeding.

Come back, true love! Sweet youth, remain!—
But goldenrod and daisies wither,
And over them blows autumn rain,   15
They pass, they pass, and know not whither.

'With rue my heart is laden'

With rue my heart is laden
    For golden friends I had,
For many a rose-lipt maiden
    And many a lightfoot lad.

By brooks too broad for leaping
    The lightfoot boys are laid;
The rose-lipt girls are sleeping
    In fields where roses fade.

'Euclid alone has looked on Beauty bare'

Euclid alone has looked on Beauty bare.
Let all who prate of Beauty hold their peace,
And lay them prone upon the earth and cease
To ponder on themselves, the while they stare

At nothing, intricately drawn nowhere
In shapes of shifting lineage; let geese
Gabble and hiss, but heroes seek release
From dusty bondage into luminous air.
O blinding hour, O holy, terrible day,
When first the shaft into his vision shone
Of light anatomized! Euclid alone
Has looked on Beauty bare. Fortunate they
Who, though once only and then but far away,
Have heard her massive sandal set on stone.

5

10

235   *'What is beauty, saith my sufferings, then?'*

What is beauty, saith my sufferings, then?
If all the pens that ever poets held
Had fed the feeling of their masters' thoughts,
And every sweetness that inspir'd their hearts,
Their minds, and muses on admired themes;
If all the heavenly quintessence they still
From their immortal flowers of poesy,
Wherein, as in a mirror, we perceive
The highest reaches of a human wit;
If these had made one poem's period,
And all combin'd in beauty's worthiness,
Yet should there hover in their restless heads
One thought, one grace, one wonder, at the least,
Which into words no virtue can digest.

5

10

236   *On Growing Old*

Be with me, Beauty, for the fire is dying;
My dog and I are old, too old for roving;
Man, whose young passion sets the spindrift flying,
Is soon too lame to march, too cold for loving.
I take the book and gather to the fire,
Turning old yellow leaves; minute by minute,
The clock ticks to my heart; a withered wire
Moves a thin ghost of music in the spinet.

I cannot sail your seas, I cannot wander
Your cornland, nor your hill-land nor your valleys,   10
Ever again, nor share the battle yonder
Where the young knight the broken squadron rallies.
Only stay quiet while my mind remembers
The beauty of fire from the beauty of embers.

Beauty, have pity, for the strong have power,
The rich their wealth, the beautiful their grace,
Summer of man its sunlight and its flower,
Spring time of man all April in a face.
Only, as in the jostling in the Strand,
Where the mob thrusts or loiters or is loud   20
The beggar with the saucer in his hand
Asks only a penny from the passing crowd,
So, from this glittering world with all its fashion,
Its fire and play of men, its stir, its march,
Let me have wisdom, Beauty, wisdom and passion,
Bread to the soul, rain where the summers parch.
Give me but these, and though the darkness close
Even the night will blossom as the rose.

237   *Peter Quince at the Clavier*

I

Just as my fingers on these keys
Make music, so the self-same sounds
On my spirit make a music too.

Music is feeling then, not sound;
And thus it is that what I feel,
Here in this room, desiring you,

Thinking of your blue-shadowed silk,
Is music. It is like the strain
Waked in the elders by Susanna:

Of a green evening, clear and warm,　　　　　　10
She bathed in her still garden, while
The red-eyed elders, watching, felt

The basses of their being throb
In witching chords, and their thin blood
Pulse pizzicati of Hosanna.

II

In the green evening, clear and warm,
Susanna lay.
She searched
The touch of springs,
And found　　　　　　　　　　　　　　20
Concealed imaginings.
She sighed
For so much melody.

Upon the bank she stood
In the cool
Of spent emotions.
She felt, among the leaves,
The dew
Of old devotions.

She walked upon the grass,　　　　　　　　30
Still quavering.
The winds were like her maids,
On timid feet,
Fetching her woven scarves,
Yet wavering.

A breath upon her hand
Muted the night.
She turned—
A cymbal clashed,
And roaring horns.　　　　　　　　　　　40

III

Soon, with a noise like tambourines,
Came her attendant Byzantines.

They wondered why Susanna cried
Against the elders by her side:

And as they whispered, the refrain
Was like a willow swept by rain.

Anon their lamps' uplifted flame
Revealed Susanna and her shame.

And then the simpering Byzantines,
Fled, with a noise like tambourines. 50

IV

Beauty is momentary in the mind—
The fitful tracing of a portal;
But in the flesh it is immortal.

The body dies; the body's beauty lives.
So evenings die, in their green going,
A wave, interminably flowing.

So gardens die, their meek breath scenting
The cowl of Winter, done repenting.
So maidens die to the auroral
Celebration of a maiden's choral. 60

Susanna's music touched the bawdy strings
Of those white elders; but, escaping,
Left only Death's ironic scraping.
Now in its immortality, it plays
On the clear viol of her memory,
And makes a constant sacrament of praise.

O Galuppi, Baldassare, this is very sad to find!
I can hardly misconceive you; it would prove me deaf and blind;
But although I take your meaning, 'tis with such a heavy mind!

Here you come with your old music, and here's all the good it brings.
What, they lived once thus at Venice where the merchants were the
  kings,
Where St. Mark's is, where the Doges used to wed the sea with rings?

Aye, because the sea's the street there; and 'tis arched by—what you
  call—
Shylock's bridge with houses on it, where they kept the carnival.
I was never out of England—it's as if I saw it all.

Did young people take their pleasure when the sea was warm in
  May?   10
Balls and masks begun at midnight, burning ever to mid-day,
When they made up fresh adventures for the morrow, do you say?

Was a lady such a lady, cheeks so round and lips so red—
On her neck the small face buoyant, like a bell-flower on its bed,
O'er the breast's superb abundance where a man might base his
  head?

Well, and it was graceful of them—they'd break talk off and afford—
She, to bite her mask's black velvet—he, to finger on his sword,
While you sat and played Toccatas, stately at the clavichord?

What? Those lesser thirds so plaintive, sixths diminished, sigh on
  sigh,
Told them something? Those suspensions, those solutions—'Must we
  die?'   20
Those commiserating sevenths—'Life might last! we can but try!'

'Were you happy?'—'Yes.'—'And are you still as happy?'—'Yes.
   And you?'
—'Then, more kisses!'—'Did *I* stop them, when a million seemed so
   few?'
Hark, the dominant's persistence till it must be answered to!

So, an octave struck the answer. Oh, they praised you, I dare say!
'Brave Galuppi! that was music! good alike at grave and gay!
I can always leave off talking when I hear a master play!'

Then they left you for their pleasure; till in due time, one by one,
Some with lives that came to nothing, some with deeds as well un-
   done,
Death stepped tacitly and took them where they never see the sun.   30

But when I sit down to reason, think to take my stand nor swerve,
While I triumph o'er a secret wrung from nature's close reserve,
In you come with your cold music till I creep through every nerve.

Yes, you, like a ghostly cricket, creaking where a house was burned:
'Dust and ashes, dead and done with, Venice spent what Venice
   earned.
The soul, doubtless, is immortal—where a soul can be discerned.

'Yours for instance: you know physics, something of geology,
Mathematics are your pastime; souls shall rise in their degree;
Butterflies may dread extinction—you'll not die, it cannot be!

'As for Venice and her people, merely born to bloom and drop,   40
Here on earth they bore their fruitage, mirth and folly were the crop;
What of soul was left, I wonder, when the kissing had to stop?

'Dust and ashes!' So you creak it, and I want the heart to scold.
Dear dead women, with such hair, too—what's become of all the
   gold
Used to hang and brush their bosoms? I feel chilly and grown old.

[504]

239

Spring and Fall:

TO A YOUNG CHILD

Márgarét, are you griéving
Over Goldengrove unleaving?
Leáves, líke the things of man, you
With your fresh thoughts care for, can you?
Áh! ás the heart grows older   5
It will come to such sights colder
By and by, nor spare a sigh
Though worlds of wanwood leafmeal lie;
And yet you wíll weep and know why.
Now no matter, child, the name: 10
Sórrow's spríngs áre the same.
Nor mouth had, no nor mind, expressed
What heart heard of, ghost guessed:
It ís the blight man was born for,
It is Margaret you mourn for.   15

The Windhover:

TO CHRIST OUR LORD

I caught this morning morning's minion, kingdom of daylight's dau-
    phin, dapple-dawn-drawn Falcon, in his riding
  Of the rolling level underneath him steady air, and striding
High there, how he rung upon the rein of a wimpling wing
In his ecstasy! then off, off forth on swing,
    As a skate's heel sweeps smooth on a bow-bend: the hurl and
    gliding   5
  Rebuffed the big wind. My heart in hiding
Stirred for a bird,—the achieve of, the mastery of the thing!

Brute beauty and valor and act, oh, air, pride, plume, here
    Buckle! And the fire that breaks from thee then, a billion
Times told lovelier, more dangerous, O my chevalier!   10

  No wonder of it: shéer plód makes plow down sillion
Shine, and blue-bleak embers, ah my dear,
    Fall, gall themselves, and gash gold-vermilion.

Ecce Puer

Of the dark past
A child is born
With joy and grief
My heart is torn

Calm in his cradle   5
The living lies.
May love and mercy
Unclose his eyes!

Young life is breathed
On the glass;   10
The world that was not
Comes to pass.

A child is sleeping:
An old man gone.
O, father forsaken,   15
Forgive your son!

242   *O Virtuous Light*

A private madness has prevailed
Over the pure and valiant mind;
The instrument of reason failed
And the star-gazing eyes struck blind.

Sudden excess of light has wrought
Confusion in the secret place
Where the slow miracles of thought
Take shape through patience into grace.

Mysterious as steel and flint
The birth of this destructive spark   10
Whose inward growth has power to print
Strange suns upon the natural dark.

[506]

O break the walls of sense in half
And make the spirit fugitive!
This light begotten of itself
Is not a light by which to live!

The fire of farthing tallow dips
Dispels the menace of the skies
So it illuminate the lips
And enter the discerning eyes.   20

O virtuous light, if thou be man's
Or matter of the meteor stone,
Prevail against this radiance
Which is engendered of its own!

243   *Dead 'Wessex,' the Dog, to the Household*

Do you think of me at all,
        Wistful ones?
Do you think of me at all
        As if nigh?
Do you think of me at all
At the creep of evenfall,
Or when the sky-birds call
        As they fly?

Do you look for me at times,
        Wistful ones?   10
Do you look for me at times
        Strained and still?
Do you look for me at times,
When the hour for walking chimes,
On that grassy path that climbs
        Up the hill?

You may hear a jump or trot,
        Wistful ones,
You may hear a jump or trot—
        Mine, as 'twere—   20

You may hear a jump or trot
On the stair or path or plot;
But I shall cause it not,
    Be not there.

Should you call as when I knew you,
    Wistful ones,
Should you call as when I knew you,
    Shared you home;
Should you call as when I knew you,
I shall not turn to view you,
I shall not listen to you,
    Shall not come. 30

244   *Janet Waking*

Beautifully Janet slept
Till it was deeply morning. She woke then
And thought about her dainty-feathered hen,
To see how it had kept.

One kiss she gave her mother,
Only a small one gave she to her daddy
Who would have kissed each curl of his shining baby;
No kiss at all for her brother.

'Old Chucky, Old Chucky!' she cried,
Running on little pink feet upon the grass 10
To Chucky's house, and listening. But alas,
Her Chucky had died.

It was a transmogrifying bee
Came droning down on Chucky's old bald head
And sat and put the poison. It scarcely bled,
But how exceedingly

And purply did the knot
Swell with the venom and communicate
Its rigor! Now the poor comb stood up straight
But Chucky did not. 20

So there was Janet
Kneeling on the wet grass, crying her brown hen
(Translated far beyond the daughters of men)
To rise and walk upon it.

And weeping fast as she had breath
Janet implored us, 'Wake her from her sleep!'
And would not be instructed in how deep
Was the forgetful kingdom of death.

245   *Here Lies a Lady*

Here lies a lady of beauty and high degree.
Of chills and fever she died, of fever and chills,
The delight of her husband, her aunts, an infant of three,
And of medicos marveling sweetly on her ills.

For either she burned, and her confident eyes would blaze,   5
And her fingers fly in a manner to puzzle their heads—
What was she making? Why, nothing; she sat in a maze
Of old scraps of laces, snipped into curious shreds—

Or this would pass, and the light of her fire decline   9
Till she lay discouraged and cold as a thin stalk white and blown,
And would not open her eyes, to kisses, to wine;
The sixth of these states was her last; the cold settled down.

Sweet ladies, long may ye bloom, and toughly I hope ye may thole,
But was she not lucky? In flowers and lace and mourning,
In love and great honor we bade God rest her soul   15
After six little spaces of chill, and six of burning.

246   *The Too-Late Born*

We too, we too, descending once again
The hills of our own land, we too have heard
Far off—Ah, que ce cor a longue haleine—
The horn of Roland in the passages of Spain,

The first, the second blast, the failing third,   5
And with the third turned back and climbed once more
The steep road southward, and heard faint the sound
Of swords, of horses, the disastrous war,
And crossed the dark defile at last, and found
At Roncevaux upon the darkening plain   10
The dead against the dead and on the silent ground
The silent slain—

247   *Moving In*

Is it your hope, hope's hearth, heart's home, here at the lane's end?
Deeds are signed, structure is sound though century-old;
Redecorated throughout, all modern convenience, the cable extended;
Need grope no more in corners nor cower from dark and cold.

Who between town and country dreams of contact with the two worlds
Earthquake will wake, a chasm at his feet, crack of doom overhead.
What deeds can survive, what stone can shoulder the shock of a new world?
Dark and cold, dancing no spark, when the cable is dead.

Fear you not ghosts of former tenants, a fell visitation
From them whose haunts you have sealed, whose secrets you haled to light?   10
Gay as grass are you? Tough as granite? But they are patient,
Waiting for you to weaken, awaiting a sleepless night.

You have cut down the yews, say you, for a broader view? No churchyard
Emblems shall bind or blind you? But see, the imperative brow
Frowns of the hills, offers no compromise, means far harder
Visions than valley steeples call to, a stricter vow.

Though your wife is chaste, though your children lustily throng, though laughing
    Raise you a record crop, yet do you wrong your powers,
Flattered no longer by isolation nor satisfied loving.
Not box hedge where the birds nest, not embankments of flowers   20

Guard from regret. No private good will let you forget all
Those, time's accessories, whose all is a leaden arc
Between work and sleep; who might have been men, brighter metal,
Proudly reaped the light, passed peacefully into dark.

248   *'Rest from loving and be living'*

        Rest from loving and be living.
        Fallen is fallen past retrieving
        The unique flyer dawn's dove
        Arrowing down feathered with fire.

        Cease denying, begin knowing.   5
        Comes peace this way here comes renewing
        With dower of bird and bud knocks
        Loud on winter wall on death's door.

        Here's no meaning but of morning.
        Naught soon of night but stars remaining,   10
        Sink lower, fade, as dark womb
        Recedes creation will step clear.

249   *'I hear the cries of evening'*

        I hear the cries of evening, while the paw
        Of dark creeps up the turf;
        Sheep's bleating, swaying gulls' cry, the rook's caw,
        The hammering surf.

        I am inconstant yet this constancy   5
        Of natural rest twangs at my heart;
        Town-bred, I feel the roots of each earth-cry
        Tear me apart.

These are the creakings of the dusty day
When the dog night bites sharp,   10
These fingers grip my soul and tear away
And pluck me like a harp.

I feel this huge sphere turn, the great wheel sing
While beasts move to their ease:
Sheep's love, gulls' peace—I feel my chattering   15
Uncared by these.

250   *'Not palaces, an era's crown'*

Not palaces, an era's crown
Where the mind dwells, intrigues, rests;
The architectural gold-leaved flower
From people ordered like a single mind,
I build. This only what I tell:
It is too late for rare accumulation
For family pride, for beauty's filtered dusts;
I say, stamping the words with emphasis,
Drink from here energy and only energy,
As from the electric charge of a battery,   10
To will this Time's change.
Eye, gazelle, delicate wanderer,
Drinker of horizon's fluid line;
Ear that suspends on a chord
The spirit drinking timelessness;
Touch, love, all senses;
Leave your gardens, your singing feasts,
Your dreams of suns circling before our sun,
Of heaven after our world.
Instead, watch images of flashing brass   20
That strike the outward sense, the polished will
Flag of our purpose which the wind engraves.
No spirit seek here rest. But this: No man
Shall hunger: Man shall spend equally.
Our goal which we compel: Man shall be man.
—That program of the antique Satan

[512]

Bristling with guns on the indented page
With battleship towering from hilly waves:
For what? Drive of a ruined purpose
Destroying all but its age-long exploiters.   30
Our program like this, yet opposite,
Death to the killers, bringing light to life.

251   *'He will watch the hawk'*

He will watch the hawk with an indifferent eye
            Or pitifully;
Nor on those eagles that so feared him, now
            Will strain his brow;
Weapons men use, stone, sling and strong-thewed bow   5
            He will not know.

This aristocrat, superb of all instinct,
            With death close linked
Had paced the enormous cloud, almost had won
            War on the sun;   10
Till now, like Icarus mid-ocean-drowned,
            Hands, wings, are found.

252   *'Sir, no man's enemy'*

Sir, no man's enemy, forgiving all
But will his negative inversion, be prodigal:
Send to us power and light, a sovereign touch
Curing the intolerable neural itch,
The exhaustion of weaning, the liar's quinsy,   5
And the distortions of ingrown virginity.
Prohibit sharply the rehearsed response
And gradually correct the coward's stance;
Cover in time with beams those in retreat
That, spotted, they turn though the reverse were great;   10
Publish each healer that in city lives
Or country houses at the end of drives;
Harrow the house of the dead; look shining at
New styles of architecture, a change of heart.

[513]

253

'Doom is dark and deeper'

Doom is dark and deeper than any sea-dingle.
Upon what man it fall
In spring, day-wishing flowers appearing,
Avalanche sliding, white snow from rock-face,
That he should leave his house,
No cloud-soft hand can hold him, restraint by women;
But ever that man goes
Through place-keepers, through forest trees,
A stranger to strangers over undried sea,
Houses for fishes, suffocating water,   10
Or lonely on fell as chat,
By pot-holed becks
A bird stone-haunting, an unquiet bird.

There head falls forward, fatigued at evening,
And dreams of home,
Waving from window, spread of welcome,
Kissing of wife under single sheet;
But waking sees
Bird-flocks nameless to him, through doorway voices
Of new men making another love.   20

Save him from hostile capture,
From sudden tiger's spring at corner;
Protect his house,
His anxious house where days are counted
From thunderbolt protect,
From gradual ruin spreading like a stain;
Converting number from vague to certain,
Bring joy, bring day of his returning,
Lucky with day approaching, with leaning dawn.

254

'Between attention and attention'

Between attention and attention
The first and last decision
Is mortal distraction
Of earth and air,

Further and nearer,
The vague wants
Of days and nights,
And personal error;
And the fatigued face,
Taking the strain   10
Of the horizontal force
And the vertical thrust,
Makes random answer
To the crucial test;
The uncertain flesh
Scraping back chair
From the wrong train,
Falling in slush,
Before a friend's friends
Or shaking hands   20
With a snub-nosed winner.

The opening window, closing door,
Open, close, but not
To finish or restore;
These wishes get
No further than
The edges of the town,
And leaning asking from the car
Cannot tell us where we are;
While the divided face   30
Has no grace,
No discretion,
No occupation
But registering
Acreage, mileage,
The easy knowledge
Of the virtuous thing.

Control of the passes was, he saw, the key
To this new district, but who would get it?
He, the trained spy, had walked into the trap
For a bogus guide, seduced with the old tricks.

At Greenhearth was a fine site for a dam   5
And easy power, had they pushed the rail
Some stations nearer. They ignored his wires.
The bridges were unbuilt and trouble coming.

The street music seemed gracious now to one
For weeks up in the desert. Woken by water   10
Running away in the dark, he often had
Reproached the night for a companion
Dreamed of already. They would shoot, of course,
Parting easily who were never joined.

256   *'Consider this and in our time'*

Consider this and in our time
As the hawk sees it or the helmeted airman:
The clouds rift suddenly—look there
At cigarette-end smoldering on a border
At the first garden party of the year.
Pass on, admire the view of the massif
Through plate-glass windows of the Sport Hotel;
Join there the insufficient units
Dangerous, easy, in furs, in uniform
And constellated at reserved tables   10
Supplied with feelings by an efficient band
Relayed elsewhere to farmers and their dogs
Sitting in kitchens in the stormy fens.

Long ago, supreme Antagonist,
More powerful than the great northern whale
Ancient and sorry at life's limiting defect,
In Cornwall, Mendip, or the Pennine moor

Your comments on the highborn mining-captains,
Found they no answer, made them wish to die
—Lie since in barrows out of harm.   20
You talk to your admirers every day
By silted harbors, derelict works,
In strangled orchards, and the silent comb
Where dogs have worried or a bird was shot.
Order the ill that they attack at once:
Visit the ports and, interrupting
The leisurely conversation in the bar
Within a stone's throw of the sunlit water,
Beckon your chosen out. Summon
Those handsome and diseased youngsters, those women   30
Your solitary agents in the country parishes;
And mobilize the powerful forces latent
In soils that make the farmer brutal
In the infected sinus, and the eyes of stoats.
Then, ready, start your rumor, soft
But horrifying in its capacity to disgust
Which, spreading magnified, shall come to be
A polar peril, a prodigious alarm,
Scattering the people, as torn-up paper
Rags and utensils in a sudden gust,   40
Seized with immeasurable neurotic dread.

Financier, leaving your little room
Where the money is made but not spent,
You'll need your typist and your boy no more;
The game is up for you and for the others,
Who, thinking, pace in slippers on the lawns
Of College Quad or Cathedral Close,
Who are born nurses, who live in shorts
Sleeping with people and playing fives.
Seekers after happiness, all who follow   50
The convolutions of your simple wish,
It is later than you think; nearer that day
Far other than that distant afternoon
Amid rustle of frocks and stamping feet

They gave the prizes to the ruined boys.
You cannot be away, then, no
No though you pack to leave within an hour,
Escaping humming down arterial roads:
The date was yours; the prey to fugues,
Irregular breathing and alternate ascendancies   60
After some haunted migratory years
To disintegrate on an instant in the explosion of mania
Or lapse for ever into a classic fatigue.

257   *'Where do They come from?'*

I

Where do They come from? Those whom we so much dread
As on our dearest location falls the chill
      Of the crooked wing and endangers
      The melting friend, the aqueduct, the flower.

2

Terrible Presences that the ponds reflect
Back at the famous, and when the blond boy
      Bites eagerly into the shining
      Apple, emerge in their shocking fury.

3

And we realize the woods are deaf and the sky
Nurses no one, and we are awake and these   10
      Like farmers have purpose and knowledge,
      And towards us their hate is directed.

4

We are the barren pastures to which they bring
The resentment of outcasts; on us they work
      Out their despair; they wear our weeping
      As the disgraceful badge of their exile.

[518]

5

O we conjured them here like a lying map;
Desiring the extravagant joy of life
    We lured with a mirage of orchards
    Fat in the lazy climate of refuge.   20

6

Our money sang like streams on the aloof peaks
Of our thinking that beckoned them on like girls;
    Our culture like a West of wonder
    Shone a solemn promise in their faces.

7

We expected the beautiful or the wise
Ready to see a charm in our childish fib,
    Pleased to find nothing but stones and
    Able at once to create a garden.

8

But those who come are not even children with
The big indiscriminate eyes we had lost,   30
    Occupying our narrow spaces
    With their anarchist vivid abandon.

9

They arrive, already adroit, having learned
Restraint at the table of a father's rage;
    In a mother's distorting mirror
    They discovered the Meaning of Knowing.

10

These pioneers have long adapted themselves
To the night and the nightmare; they come equipped
    To reply to terror with terror,
    With lies to unmask the least deception.   40

11

For a future of marriage nevertheless
The bed is prepared; though all our whiteness shrinks
   From the hairy and clumsy bridegroom,
   We conceive in the shuddering instant.

12

For the barren must wish to bear though the Spring
Punish; and the crooked that dreads to be straight
   Cannot alter its prayer but summons
   Out of the dark a horrible rector.

13

O the striped and vigorous tiger can move
With style through the borough of murder; the ape   50
   Is really at home in the parish
   Of grimacing and licking: but we have

14

Failed as their pupils. Our tears well from a love
We have never outgrown; our cities predict
   More than we hope; even our armies
   Have to express our need of forgiveness.

258   *The Hebrides*

On those islands
The west wind drops its messages of indolence
No one hurries, the Gulf Stream warms the gnarled
Rampart of gneiss, the feet of the peasant years
Pad up and down their sentry-beat not challenging
Any comer for the password—only Death
Comes through unchallenged in his general's cape.
The houses straggle on the umber moors,
The Aladdin lamp mutters in the boarded room
Where a woman smoors the fire of fragrant peat.   10
No one repeats the password for it is known,
All is known before it comes to the lips—

[520]

Instinctive wisdom. Over the fancy vases
The photos with the wrinkles taken out,
The enlarged portraits of the successful sons
Who married wealth in Toronto or New York,
Cajole the lonely evenings of the old
Who live embanked by memories of labor
And child-bearing and scriptural commentaries.
On those islands   20
The boys go poaching their ancestral rights—
The Ossianic salmon who take the yellow
Tilt of the river with a magnet's purpose—
And listen breathless to the tales at the ceilidh
Among the peat-smoke and the smells of dung
That fill the felted room from the cave of the byre.
No window opens of the windows sunk like eyes
In a four-foot wall of stones casually picked
From the knuckly hills on which these houses crawl
Like black and legless beasts who breath in their sleep   30
Among the piles of peat and pooks of hay—
A brave oasis in the indifferent moors.
And while the stories circulate like smoke,
The sense of life spreads out from the one-eyed house
In wider circles through the lake of night
In which articulate man has dropped a stone—
In wider circles round the black-faced sheep,
Wider and fainter till they hardly crease
The ebony heritage of the herded dead.
On those islands   40
The tinkers whom no decent girl will go with,
Preserve the Gaelic tunes unspoiled by contact
With the folk-fancier or the friendly tourist,
And preserve the knowledge of horse-flesh and preserve
The uncompromising empire of the rogue.
On those islands
The tethered cow grazes among the orchises
And figures in blue calico turn by hand
The ground beyond the plow, and the bus, not stopping,
Drops a parcel for the lonely household   50

Where men remembering stories of eviction
Are glad to have their land though mainly stones—
The honored bones which still can hoist a body.
On those islands
There is echo of the leaping fish, the identical
Sound that cheered the chiefs at ease from slaughter;
There is echo of baying hounds of a lost breed
And echo of MacCrimmon's pipes lost in the cave;
And seals cry with the voices of the drowned.
When men go out to fish, no one must say 'Good luck'   60
And the confidences told in a boat at sea
Must be as if printed on the white ribbon of a wave
Withdrawn as soon as printed—so never heard.
On those islands
The black minister paints the tour of hell
While the unregenerate drink from the bottle's neck
In gulps like gauntlets thrown at the devil's head
And spread their traditional songs across the hills
Like fraying tapestries of fights and loves,
The boar-hunt and the rope let down at night—   70
Lost causes and lingering home-sickness.
On those islands
The fish come singing from the drunken sea,
The herring rush the gunwales and sort themselves
To cram the expectant barrels of their own accord—
Or such is the dream of the fisherman whose wet
Leggings hang on the door as he sleeps returned
From a night when miles of net were drawn up empty.
On those islands
A girl with candid eyes goes out to marry   80
An independent tenant of seven acres
Who goes each year to the south to work on the roads
In order to raise a rent of forty shillings,
And all the neighbors celebrate their wedding
With drink and pipes and the walls of the barn reflect
The crazy shadows of the whooping dancers.
On those islands
Where many live on the dole or on old-age pensions

And many waste with consumption and some are drowned
And some of the old stumble in the midst of sleep   90
Into the pot-hole hitherto shunned in dreams
Or falling from the cliff among the shrieks of gulls
Reach the bottom before they have time to wake—
Whoever dies on the islands and however
The whole of the village goes into three-day mourning,
The afflicted home is honored and the shops are shut
For on those islands
Where a few surnames cover a host of people
And the art of being a stranger with your neighbor
Has still to be imported, death is still   100
No lottery ticket in a public lottery—
The result to be read on the front page of a journal—
But a family matter near to the whole family.
On those islands
Where no train runs on rails and the tyrant time
Has no clock-towers to signal people to doom
With semaphore ultimatums tick by tick,
There is still peace though not for me and not
Perhaps for long—still peace on the bevel hills
For those who still can live as their fathers lived   110
On those islands.

259   *Song*

        The sunlight on the garden
        Hardens and grows cold,
        We cannot cage the minute
        Within its nets of gold;
        When all is told
        We cannot beg for pardon.

        Our freedom as free lances
        Advances towards its end;
        The earth compels, upon it
        Sonnets and birds descend;   10
        And soon, my friend,
        We shall have no time for dances.

[523]

The sky was good for flying
Defying the church bells
And every evil iron
Siren and what it tells:
The earth compels,
We are dying, Egypt, dying

And not expecting pardon,
Hardened in heart anew,   20
But glad to have sat under
Thunder and rain with you,
And grateful too
For sunlight in the garden.

260   *Bagpipe Music*

It's no go the merrygoround, it's no go the rickshaw,
All we want is a limousine and ticket for the peepshow.
Their knickers are made of crêpe-de-chine, their shoes are made of
    python,
Their halls are lined with tiger rugs and their walls with heads of
    bison.

John MacDonald found a corpse, put it under the sofa,
Waited till it came to life and hit it with a poker,
Sold its eyes for souvenirs, sold its blood for whiskey,
Kept its bones for dumb-bells to use when he was fifty.

It's no go the Yogi-Man, it's no go Blavatsky,
All we want is a bank balance and a bit of skirt in a taxi.   10

Annie MacDougall went to milk, caught her foot in the heather,
Woke to hear a dance record playing of Old Vienna.
It's no go your maidenheads, it's no go your culture,
All we want is a Dunlop tyre and the devil mend the puncture.

The Laird o'Phelps spent Hogmannay declaring he was sober;
Counted his feet to prove the fact and found he had one foot over.
Mrs. Carmichael had her fifth, looked at the job with repulsion,
Said to the midwife 'Take it away; I'm through with overproduction.'

It's no go the gossip column, it's no go the Ceilidh,
All we want is a mother's help and a sugar-stick for the baby.   20

Willie Murray cut his thumb, couldn't count the damage,
Took the hide of an Ayrshire cow and used it for a bandage.
His brother caught three hundred cran when the seas were lavish,
Threw the bleeders back in the sea and went upon the parish.

It's no go the Herring Board, it's no go the Bible,
All we want is a packet of fags when our hands are idle.

It's no go the picture palace, it's no go the stadium,
It's no go the country cot with a pot of pink geraniums.
It's no go the Government grants, it's no go the elections,
Sit on your arse for fifty years and hang your hat on a pension.   30

It's no go my honey love, it's no go my poppet;
Work your hands from day to day, the winds will blow the profit.
The glass is falling hour by hour, the glass will fall for ever,
But if you break the bloody glass you won't hold up the weather.

261   *Portrait d'une Femme*

Your mind and you are our Sargasso Sea,
London has swept about you this score years
And bright ships left you this or that in fee:
Ideas, old gossip, oddments of all things,
Strange spars of knowledge and dimmed wares of price.
Great minds have sought you—lacking someone else.
You have been second always. Tragical?
No. You preferred it to the usual thing:
One dull man, dulling and uxorious,
One average mind—with one thought less, each year.   10
Oh, you are patient. I have seen you sit
Hours, where something might have floated up.
And now you pay one. Yes, you richly pay.
You are a person of some interest, one comes to you
And takes strange gain away:

[525]

Trophies fished up; some curious suggestion;
Fact that leads nowhere; and a tale for two,
Pregnant with mandrakes, or with something else
That might prove useful and yet never proves,
That never fits a corner or shows use,   20
Or finds its hour upon the loom of days:
The tarnished, gaudy, wonderful old work;
Idols, and ambergris and rare inlays.
These are your riches, your great store; and yet
For all this sea-hoard of deciduous things,
Strange woods half sodden, and new brighter stuff:
In the slow float of differing light and deep,
No! there is nothing! In the whole and all,
Nothing that's quite your own.
                                        Yet this is you.

262   *Portrait of a Lady*

> *Thou hast committed—*
> *Fornication: but that was in another country,*
> *And besides, the wench is dead.*
>   THE JEW OF MALTA

                                 I

Among the smoke and fog of a December afternoon
You have the scene arrange itself—as it will seem to do—
With 'I have saved this afternoon for you';
And four wax candles in the darkened room,
Four rings of light upon the ceiling overhead,
And atmosphere of Juliet's tomb
Prepared for all the things to be said, or left unsaid.
We have been, let us say, to hear the latest Pole
Transmit the Preludes, through his hair and finger-tips.
'So intimate, this Chopin, that I think his soul   10
Should be resurrected only among friends
Some two or three, who will not touch the bloom
That is rubbed and questioned in the concert room.'
—And so the conversation slips
Among velleities and carefully caught regrets

Through attenuated tones of violins
Mingled with remote cornets
And begins.
'You do not know how much they mean to me, my friends,
And how, how rare and strange it is, to find   20
In a life composed so much, so much of odds and ends
(For indeed I do not love it . . . you knew? You are not blind!
How keen you are!)
To find a friend who has these qualities,
Who has, and gives
Those qualities upon which friendship lives.
How much it means that I say this to you—
Without these friendships—life, what *cauchemar*!'

Among the windings of the violins
And the ariettes   30
Of cracked cornets
Inside my brain a dull tom-tom begins
Absurdly hammering a prelude of its own,
Capricious monotone
That is at least one definite 'false note.'
—Let us take the air, in a tobacco trance,
Admire the monuments,
Discuss the late events,
Correct our watches by the public clocks,
Then sit for half an hour and drink our bocks.   40

II

Now that lilacs are in bloom
She has a bowl of lilacs in her room
And twists one in her fingers while she talks.
'Ah, my friend, you do not know, you do not know
What life is, you should hold it in your hands';
(Slowly twisting the lilac stalks)
'You let it flow from you, you let it flow,
And youth is cruel, and has no remorse
And smiles at situations which it cannot see.'
I smile, of course,   50

And go on drinking tea.
'Yet with these April sunsets, that somehow recall
My buried life, and Paris in the Spring,
I feel immeasurably at peace, and find the world
To be wonderful and youthful, after all.'

The voice returns like the insistent out-of-tune
Of a broken violin on an August afternoon:
'I am always sure that you understand
My feelings, always sure that you feel,
Sure that across the gulf you reach your hand.   60

You are invulnerable, you have no Achilles' heel.
You will go on, and when you have prevailed
You can say: at this point many a one has failed.
But what have I, but what have I, my friend,
To give you, what can you receive from me?
Only the friendship and the sympathy
Of one about to reach her journey's end.

I shall sit here, serving tea to friends. . . .'

I take my hat: how can I make a cowardly amends
For what she has said to me?   70
You will see me any morning in the park
Reading the comics and the sporting page.
Particularly I remark
An English countess goes upon the stage.
A Greek was murdered at a Polish dance,
Another bank defaulter has confessed.
I keep my countenance,
I remain self-possessed
Except when a street piano, mechanical and tired
Reiterates some worn-out common song   80
With the smell of hyacinths across the garden
Recalling things that other people have desired.
Are these ideas right or wrong?

[528]

The October night comes down; returning as before
Except for a slight sensation of being ill at ease
I mount the stairs and turn the handle of the door
And feel as if I had mounted on my hands and knees.
'And so you are going abroad; and when do you return?
But that's a useless question.
You hardly know when you are coming back,   90
You will find so much to learn.'
My smile falls heavily among the bric-à-brac.

'Perhaps you can write to me.'
My self-possession flares up for a second;
This is as I had reckoned.
'I have been wondering frequently of late
(But our beginnings never know our ends!)
Why we have not developed into friends.'
I feel like one who smiles, and turning shall remark
Suddenly, his expression in a glass.   100
My self-possession gutters; we are really in the dark.

'For everybody said so, all our friends,
They all were sure our feelings would relate
So closely! I myself can hardly understand.
We must leave it now to fate.
You will write, at any rate.
Perhaps it is not too late.
I shall sit here, serving tea to friends.'

And I must borrow every changing shape
To find expression . . . dance, dance   110
Like a dancing bear,
Cry like a parrot, chatter like an ape.
Let us take the air, in a tobacco trance—

Well! and what if she should die some afternoon,
Afternoon gray and smoky, evening yellow and rose;
Should die and leave me sitting pen in hand
With the smoke coming down above the housetops;

Doubtful, for a while
Not knowing what to feel or if I understand
Or whether wise or foolish, tardy or too soon . . .   120
Would she not have the advantage, after all?
This music is successful with a 'dying fall'
Now that we talk of dying—
And should I have the right to smile?

The Love Song of J. Alfred Prufrock

> *S'io credesse che mia risposta fosse*
> *A persona che mai tornasse al mondo,*
> *Questa fiamma staria senza piu scosse.*
> *Ma perciocche giammai di questo fondo*
> *Non torno vivo alcun, s'i' odo il vero,*
> *Senza tema d'infamia ti rispondo.*

Let us go then, you and I,
When the evening is spread out against the sky
Like a patient etherized upon a table;
Let us go, through certain half-deserted streets,
The muttering retreats
Of restless nights in one-night cheap hotels
And sawdust restaurants with oyster-shells:
Streets that follow like a tedious argument
Of insidious intent
To lead you to an overwhelming question. . . .   10
Oh, do not ask, 'What is it?'
Let us go and make our visit.

In the room the women come and go
Talking of Michelangelo.

The yellow fog that rubs its back upon the window-panes,
The yellow smoke that rubs its muzzle on the window-panes,
Licked its tongue into the corners of the evening,
Lingered upon the pools that stand in drains,
Let fall upon its back the soot that falls from chimneys,
Slipped by the terrace, made a sudden leap,   20
And seeing that it was a soft October night,
Curled once about the house, and fell asleep.

And indeed there will be time
For the yellow smoke that slides along the street,
Rubbing its back upon the window-panes;
There will be time, there will be time
To prepare a face to meet the faces that you meet;
There will be time to murder and create,
And time for all the works and days of hands
That lift and drop a question on your plate;   30
Time for you and time for me,
And time yet for a hundred indecisions,
And for a hundred visions and revisions,
Before the taking of a toast and tea.

In the room the women come and go
Talking of Michelangelo.

And indeed there will be time
To wonder, 'Do I dare?' and, 'Do I dare?'
Time to turn back and descend the stair,
With a bald spot in the middle of my hair—   40
(They will say: 'How his hair is growing thin!')
My morning coat, my collar mounting firmly to the chin,
My necktie rich and modest, but asserted by a simple pin—
(They will say: 'But how his arms and legs are thin!')
Do I dare
Disturb the universe?
In a minute there is time
For decisions and revisions which a minute will reverse.

For I have known them all already, known them all:—
Have known the evenings, mornings, afternoons,   50
I have measured out my life with coffee spoons;
I know the voices dying with a dying fall
Beneath the music from a farther room.
    So how should I presume?

And I have known the eyes already, known them all—
The eyes that fix you in a formulated phrase,
And when I am formulated, sprawling on a pin,
When I am pinned and wriggling on the wall,
Then how should I begin
To spit out all the butt-ends of my days and ways? 60
    And how should I presume?

And I have known the arms already, known them all—
Arms that are braceleted and white and bare
(But in the lamplight, downed with light brown hair!)
Is it perfume from a dress
That makes me so digress?
Arms that lie along a table, or wrap about a shawl.
    And should I then presume?
    And how should I begin?

                    .   .   .

Shall I say, I have gone at dusk through narrow streets 70
And watched the smoke that rises from the pipes
Of lonely men in shirt-sleeves, leaning out of windows? . . .

I should have been a pair of ragged claws
Scuttling across the floors of silent seas.

                    .   .   .

And the afternoon, the evening, sleeps so peacefully!
Smoothed by long fingers,
Asleep . . . tired . . . or it malingers,
Stretched on the floor, here beside you and me.
Should I, after tea and cakes and ices,
Have the strength to force the moment to its crisis? 80
But though I have wept and fasted, wept and prayed,
Though I have seen my head (grown slightly bald) brought in upon a
        platter,
I am no prophet—and here's no great matter;
I have seen the moment of my greatness flicker,
And I have seen the eternal Footman hold my coat, and snicker,
And in short, I was afraid.

And would it have been worth it, after all,
After the cups, the marmalade, the tea,
Among the porcelain, among some talk of you and me,
Would it have been worth while,   90
To have bitten off the matter with a smile,
To have squeezed the universe into a ball
To roll it toward some overwhelming question,
To say: 'I am Lazarus, come from the dead,
Come back to tell you all, I shall tell you all'—
If one, settling a pillow by her head,
      Should say: 'That is not what I meant at all.
      That is not it, at all.'

And would it have been worth it, after all,
Would it have been worth while,   100
After the sunsets and the dooryards and the sprinkled streets,
After the novels, after the teacups, after the skirts that trail along the
      floor—
And this, and so much more?—
It is impossible to say just what I mean!
But as if a magic lantern threw the nerves in patterns on a screen:
Would it have been worth while
If one, settling a pillow or throwing off a shawl,
And turning toward the window, should say:
      'That is not it at all,
      That is not what I meant, at all.'   110

                          .   .   .

No! I am not Prince Hamlet, nor was meant to be;
Am an attendant lord, one that will do
To swell a progress, start a scene or two,
Advise the prince; no doubt, an easy tool,
Deferential, glad to be of use,
Politic, cautious, and meticulous;
Full of high sentence, but a bit obtuse;
At times, indeed, almost ridiculous—
Almost, at times, the Fool.

I grow old. . . . I grow old. . . .
I shall wear the bottoms of my trousers rolled.

Shall I part my hair behind? Do I dare to eat a peach?
I shall wear white flannel trousers, and walk upon the beach.
I have heard the mermaids singing, each to each.

I do not think that they will sing to me.

I have seen them riding seaward on the waves
Combing the white hair of the waves blown back
When the wind blows the water white and black.

We have lingered in the chambers of the sea
By sea-girls wreathed with seaweed red and brown
Till human voices wake us, and we drown.

264   *Sweeney Among the Nightingales*

ὤμοι, πέπληγμαι καιρίαν πληγὴν ἔσω.

Apeneck Sweeney spreads his knees
Letting his arms hang down to laugh,
The zebra stripes along his jaw
Swelling to maculate giraffe.

The circles of the stormy moon
Slide westward toward the River Plate,
Death and the Raven drift above
And Sweeney guards the hornèd gate.

Gloomy Orion and the Dog
Are veiled; and hushed the shrunken seas;   10
The person in the Spanish cape
Tries to sit on Sweeney's knees

Slips and pulls the table cloth
Overturns a coffee-cup,
Reorganized upon the floor
She yawns and draws a stocking up;

[534]

The silent man in mocha brown
Sprawls at the window-sill and gapes;
The waiter brings in oranges
Bananas figs and hothouse grapes;   20

The silent vertebrate in brown
Contracts and concentrates, withdraws;
Rachel *née* Rabinovitch
Tears at the grapes with murderous paws;

She and the lady in the cape
Are suspect, thought to be in league;
Therefore the man with heavy eyes
Declines the gambit, shows fatigue,

Leaves the room and reappears
Outside the window, leaning in,   30
Branches of wistaria
Circumscribe a golden grin;

The host with someone indistinct
Converses at the door apart,
The nightingales are singing near
The Convent of the Sacred Heart,

And sang within the bloody wood
When Agamemnon cried aloud,
And let their liquid siftings fall
To stain the stiff dishonored shroud.   40

265   *Marina*

Quis hic locus, quae regio, quae mundi plaga?

What seas what shores what grey rocks and what islands
What water lapping the bow
And scent of pine and the woodthrush singing through the fog
What images return
O my daughter.

Those who sharpen the tooth of the dog, meaning
Death
Those who glitter with the glory of the humming-bird, meaning
Death   10
Those who sit in the sty of contentment, meaning
Death
Those who suffer the ecstasy of the animals, meaning
Death

Are become unsubstantial, reduced by a wind,
A breath of pine, and the woodsong fog
By this grace dissolved in place

What is this face, less clear and clearer
The pulse in the arm, less strong and stronger—
Given or lent? more distant than stars and nearer than the eye   20

Whispers and small laughter between leaves and hurrying feet
Under sleep, where all the waters meet.

Bowsprit cracked with ice and paint cracked with heat.
I made this, I have forgotten
And remember.
The rigging weak and the canvas rotten
Between one June and another September.
Made this unknowing, half conscious, unknown, my own.

The garboard strake leaks, the seams need calking.
This form, this face, this life   30
Living to live in a world of time beyond me; let me
Resign my life for this life, my speech for that unspoken,
The awakened, lips parted, the hope, the new ships.

What seas what shores what granite islands towards my timbers
And woodthrush calling through the fog
My daughter.

PART VII

POEMS OF RELIGIOUS EXPERIENCE

Adieu, farewell earth's bliss,
This world uncertain is;
Fond are life's lustful joys,
Death proves them all but toys,
None from his darts can fly.
I am sick, I must die.
   Lord, have mercy on us!

Rich men, trust not in wealth,
Gold cannot buy you health;
Physic himself must fade,   10
All things to end are made,
The plague full swift goes by;
I am sick, I must die.
   Lord, have mercy on us!

Beauty is but a flower
Which wrinkles will devour:
Brightness falls from the air,
Queens have died young and fair,
Dust hath closed Helen's eye.
I am sick, I must die.   20
   Lord, have mercy on us!

Strength stoops unto the grave,
Worms feed on Hector brave,
Swords may not fight with fate.
Earth still holds ope her gate;
Come! come! the bells do cry.
I am sick, I must die.
   Lord, have mercy on us!

Wit with his wantonness
Tasteth death's bitterness;   30
Hell's executioner
Hath no ears for to hear

What vain art can reply.
I am sick, I must die.
            Lord, have mercy on us!

Haste, therefore, each degree,
To welcome destiny.
Heaven is our heritage,
Earth but a player's stage;
Mount we unto the sky.   40
I am sick, I must die.
            Lord, have mercy on us!

267   *Crossing the Bar*

Sunset and evening star,
    And one clear call for me!
And may there be no moaning of the bar,
    When I put out to sea,

But such a tide as moving seems asleep,   5
    Too full for sound and foam,
When that which drew from out the boundless deep
    Turns again home.

Twilight and evening bell,
    And after that the dark!   10
And may there be no sadness of farewell,
    When I embark;

For though from out our bourn of Time and Place
    The flood may bear me far,
I hope to see my Pilot face to face   15
    When I have crossed the bar.

268   *Good Friday,* 1613. *Riding Westward*

Let man's soul be a sphere, and then in this
The intelligence that moves, devotion is;
And as the other spheres, by being grown
Subject to foreign motion, lose their own,

And being by others hurried every day
Scarce in a year their natural form obey,
Pleasure or business, so, our souls admit
For their first mover, and are whirled by it.
Hence is 't that I am carried towards the west
This day, when my soul's form bends towards the east.   10
There I should see a sun, by rising set,
And by that setting, endless day beget;
But that Christ on this cross did rise and fall,
Sin had eternally benighted all.
Yet dare I 'almost be glad I do not see
That spectacle of too much weight for me.
Who sees God's face, that is self life, must die;
What a death were it then to see God die!
It made his own lieutenant, nature, shrink;
It made his footstool crack, and the sun wink.   20
Could I behold those hands which span the poles
And tune all spheres at once, pierced with those holes?
Could I behold that endless height, which is
Zenith to us and our antipodes,
Humbled below us? or that blood which is
The seat of all our souls, if not of his,
Made dirt of dust, or that flesh which was worn
By God for his apparel, ragg'd and torn?
If on these things I durst not look, durst I
Upon his miserable mother cast mine eye,   30
Who was God's partner here, and furnished thus
Half of that sacrifice which ransomed us?
Though these things, as I ride, be from mine eye,
They 'are present yet unto my memory,
For that looks towards them; and thou look'st towards me,
O Savior, as thou hang'st upon the tree;
I turn my back to thee but to receive
Corrections, till thy mercies bid thee leave.
Oh, think me worth thine anger, punish me,
Burn off my rusts, and my deformity;   40
Restore thine image, so much, by thy grace,
That thou mayst know me, and I'll turn my face.

At the round earth's imagined corners, blow
Your trumpets, angels; and arise, arise
From death, you numberless infinities
Of souls, and to your scattered bodies go;
All whom the flood did, and fire shall o'erthrow,   5
All whom war, dearth, age, agues, tyrannies,
Despair, law, chance hath slain, and you whose eyes
Shall behold God and never taste death's woe.
But let them sleep, Lord, and me mourn a space,
For if above all these my sins abound,   10
'Tis late to ask abundance of thy grace
When we are there; here on this lowly ground
Teach me how to repent; for that's as good
As if thou'hadst sealed my pardon with thy blood.

270   *The Night*

John iii. 2

Through that pure virgin-shrine,
That sacred veil drawn o'er thy glorious noon,
That men might look and live, as glow-worms shine,
        And face the moon,
    Wise Nicodemus saw such light
    As made him know his God by night.

    Most blest believer he!
Who in that land of darkness and blind eyes
Thy long-expected healing wings could see
        When thou didst rise,   10
    And what can never more be done,
    Did at midnight speak with the Sun!

    Oh, who will tell me where
He found thee at that dead and silent hour!
What hallowed solitary ground did bear
        So rare a flower,
    Within whose sacred leaves did lie
    The fullness of the deity.

No mercy-seat of gold,
No dead and dusty cherub, nor carved stone,   20
But his own living works did my Lord hold
    And lodge alone,
    Where trees and herbs did watch and peep
    And wonder, while the Jews did sleep.

Dear night! this world's defeat;
The stop to busy fools; care's check and curb;
The day of spirits; my soul's calm retreat
    Which none disturb;
    Christ's progress, and his prayer time;
    The hours to which high heaven doth chime;   30

God's silent, searching flight;
When my Lord's head is filled with dew, and all
His locks are wet with the clear drops of night;
    His still, soft call;
    His knocking time; the soul's dumb watch,
    When spirits their fair kindred catch.

Were all my loud, evil days
Calm and unhaunted as is thy dark tent,
Whose peace but by some angel's wing or voice
    Is seldom rent,   40
    Then I in heaven all the long year
    Would keep, and never wander here.

But living where the sun
Doth all things wake, and where all mix and tire
Themselves and others, I consent and run
    To ev'ry mire,
    And by this world's ill-guiding light,
    Err more than I can do by night.

There is in God, some say,
A deep but dazzling darkness, as men here   50
Say it is late and dusky, because they
    See not all clear;
  Oh, for that night, where I in him
  Might live invisible and dim!

The Waterfall

With what deep murmurs through time's silent stealth
Doth thy transparent, cool, and wat'ry wealth
    Here flowing fall,
    And chide, and call,
As if his liquid, loose retínue stayed
Ling'ring, and were of this steep place afraid,
    The common pass
    Where, clear as glass,
    All must descend—
    Not to an end,   10
But quickened by this deep and rocky grave,
Rise to a longer course more bright and brave.

  Dear stream! dear bank, where often I
  Have sat and pleased my pensive eye,
  Why, since each drop of thy quick store
  Runs thither whence it flowed before,
  Should poor souls fear a shade or night,
  Who came, sure, from a sea of light?
  Or since those drops are all sent back
  So sure to thee, that none doth lack,   20
  Why should frail flesh doubt any more
  That what God takes he'll not restore?

  O useful element and clear!
  My sacred wash and cleanser here,
  My first consigner unto those
  Fountains of life where the Lamb goes!
  What sublime truths and wholesome themes

Lodge in thy mystical deep streams!
Such as dull man can never find
Unless that spirit lead his mind   30
Which first upon thy face did move,
And hatched all with his quick'ning love.
As this loud brook's incessant fall
In streaming rings restagnates all,
Which reach by course the bank, and then
Are no more seen, just so pass men.
O my invisible estate,
My glorious liberty, still late!
Thou art the channel my soul seeks,
Not this with cataracts and creeks.   40

Mount of Olives [1]

Sweet sacred hill! on whose fair brow
My Savior sat, shall I allow
   Language to love
And idolize some shade or grove,
Neglecting thee? Such ill-placed wit,
Conceit, or call it what you please,
    Is the brain's fit,
    And mere disease.

Cotswold and Cooper's, both have met
With learned swains, and echo yet   10
   Their pipes and wit;
But thou sleep'st in a deep neglect,
Untouched by any; and what need
The sheep bleat thee a silly lay,
    That heard'st both reed
    And sheep-ward play?

Yet if poets mind thee well,
They shall find thou art their hill,
   And fountain too,
Their Lord with thee had most to do;   20

He wept once, walked whole nights on thee,
And from thence, his suff'rings ended,
    Unto glory
    Was attended.

Being there, this spacious ball
Is but his narrow footstool all,
    And what we think
Unsearchable, now with one wink
He doth comprise; but in this air
When he did stay to bear our ill   30
    And sin, this hill
    Was then his chair.

273   *The World*

I saw eternity the other night
Like a great ring of pure and endless light,
    All calm as it was bright;
And round beneath it, time in hours, days, years,
    Driv'n by the spheres,
Like a vast shadow moved, in which the world
    And all her train were hurled:
The doting lover in his quaintest strain
    Did there complain;
Near him his lute, his fancy, and his flights,   10
    Wit's sour delights,
With gloves and knots, the silly snares of pleasure,
    Yet his dear treasure,
All scattered lay, while he his eyes did pore
    Upon a flower.

The darksome statesman, hung with weights and woe,
Like a thick midnight fog moved there so slow
    He did not stay, nor go;
Condemning thoughts, like sad eclipses, scowl
    Upon his soul,   20
And clouds of crying witnesses without

Pursued him with one shout;
Yet digged the mole, and lest his ways be found
      Worked underground,
Where he did clutch his prey, but One did see
      That policy;
Churches and altars fed him; perjuries
      Were gnats and flies;
It rained about him blood and tears, but he
      Drank them as free.   30

The fearful miser on a heap of rust
Sat pining all his life there, did scarce trust
      His own hands with the dust,
Yet would not place one piece above, but lives
      In fear of thieves.
Thousands there were as frantic as himself,
      And hugged each one his pelf:
The downright epicure placed heav'n in sense,
      And scorned pretense;
While others, slipped into a wide excess,   40
      Said little less;
The weaker sort slight trivial wares enslave,
      Who think them brave;
And poor despisèd truth sat counting by
      Their victory.

Yet some, who all this while did weep and sing,
And sing and weep, soared up into the ring;
      But most would use no wing.
O fools, said I, thus to prefer dark night
      Before true light,   50
To live in grots and caves, and hate the day
      Because it shows the way,
The way which from this dead and dark abode
      Leads up to God,
A way where you might tread the sun, and be
      More bright than he.

But as I did their madness so discuss,
One whispered thus:
This ring the bridegroom did for none provide
But for his bride.   60

274   *The Pulley*

When God at first made man,
Having a glass of blessings standing by,
Let us, said he, pour on him all we can.
Let the world's riches, which dispersèd lie,
    Contract into a span.   5

So strength first made a way,
Then beauty flowed, then wisdom, honor, pleasure.
When almost all was out, God made a stay,
Perceiving that alone of all his treasure
    Rest in the bottom lay.   10

For if I should, said he,
Bestow this jewel also on my creature,
He would adore my gifts instead of me,
And rest in nature, not the God of nature;
    So both should losers be.   15

Yet let him keep the rest,
But keep them with repining restlessness.
Let him be rich and weary, that at least,
If goodness lead him not, yet weariness
    May toss him to my breast.   20

275   *Eden*

A learned and happy ignorance
Divided me
From all the vanity,
From all the sloth, care, sorrow, that advance

[548]

The madness and the misery
Of men. No error, no distraction, I
Saw cloud the earth, or overcast the sky.

I knew not that there was a serpent's sting,
                Whose poison shed
            On men did overspread   10
The world, nor did I dream of such a thing
        As sin, in which mankind lay dead.
They all were brisk and living things to me,
Yea pure and full of immortality.

Joy, pleasure, beauty, kindness, charming love,
                Sleep, life, and light,
            Peace, melody—my sight,
Mine ears, and heart did fill and freely move;
        All that I saw did me delight;
The universe was then a world of treasure,   20
To me an universal world of pleasure.

Unwelcome penitence I then thought not on;
                Vain costly toys,
            Swearing and roaring boys,
Shops, markets, taverns, coaches, were unknown,
        So all things were that drown my joys;
No thorns choked up my path, nor hid the face
Of bliss and glory, nor eclipsed my place.

Only what Adam in his first estate,
                Did I behold;   30
            Hard silver and dry gold
As yet lay underground; my happy fate
        Was more acquainted with the old
And innocent delights which he did see
In his original simplicity.

Those things which first his Eden did adorn,
            My infancy
        Did crown; simplicity
Was my protection when I first was born.
        Mine eyes those treasures first did see   40
Which God first made; the first effects of love
My first enjoyments upon earth did prove,

And were so great, and so divine, so pure,
            So fair and sweet,
        So true, when I did meet
Them here at first they did my soul allure,
        And drew away mine infant feet
Quite from the works of men, that I might see
The glorious wonders of the Deity.

Wonder

276

        How like an angel came I down!
            How bright are all things here!
When first among his works I did appear,
        Oh, how their glory did me crown!
The world resembled his eternity,
            In which my soul did walk;
            And ev'rything that I did see
            Did with me talk.

        The skies in their magnificence,
            The lovely lively air,   10
Oh, how divine, how soft, how sweet, how fair!
        The stars did entertain my sense,
And all the works of God so bright and pure,
            So rich and great, did seem,
            As if they ever must endure
            In my esteem.

        A native health and innocence
            Within my bones did grow,
And while my God did all his glories show,
        I felt a vigor in my sense   20

That was all spirit; I within did flow
    With seas of life like wine;
  I nothing in the world did know,
    But 'twas divine.

  Harsh rugged objects were concealed;
    Oppressions, tears, and cries,
Sins, griefs, complaints, dissensions, weeping eyes,
    Were hid, and only things revealed
Which heavenly spirits and the angels prize:
    The state of innocence   30
   And bliss, not trades and poverties,
    Did fill my sense.

  The streets seemed paved with golden stones,
    The boys and girls all mine—
To me how did their lovely faces shine!
    The sons of men all holy ones,
In joy and beauty then appeared to me;
    And ev'rything I found,
  While like an angel I did see,
    Adorned the ground.   40

  Rich diamonds, and pearl, and gold
    Might ev'rywhere be seen;
Rare colors, yellow, blue, red, white, and green,
    Mine eyes on ev'ry side behold;
All that I saw a wonder did appear,
    Amazement was my bliss,
  That and my wealth met ev'rywhere;
    No joy to this!

  Cursed, ill-devised proprieties,
    With envy, avarice,   50
And fraud, those fiends that spoil ev'n paradise,
    Were not the object of mine eyes;

Nor hedges, ditches, limits, narrow bounds,
    I dreamt not aught of those,
But in surveying all men's grounds
    I found repose.

For property itself was mine,
    And hedges, ornaments,
Walls, houses, coffers, and their rich contents,
    To make me rich combine.   60
Clothes, costly jewels, laces, I esteemed
    My wealth, by others worn,
For me they all to wear them seemed,
    When I was born.

277

Tintern Abbey

Five years have past; five summers, with the length
Of five long winters! and again I hear
These waters, rolling from their mountain-springs
With a soft inland murmur.—Once again
Do I behold these steep and lofty cliffs,
That on a wild secluded scene impress
Thoughts of more deep seclusion; and connect
The landscape with the quiet of the sky.
The day is come when I again repose
Here, under this dark sycamore, and view   10
These plots of cottage-ground, these orchard-tufts,
Which at this season, with their unripe fruits,
Are clad in one green hue, and lose themselves
'Mid groves and copses. Once again I see
These hedgerows, hardly hedgerows, little lines
Of sportive wood run wild: these pastoral farms,
Green to the very door; and wreaths of smoke
Sent up, in silence, from among the trees!
With some uncertain notice, as might seem
Of vagrant dwellers in the houseless woods,   20
Or of some hermit's cave, where by his fire

The hermit sits alone.

                    These beauteous forms,
Through a long absence, have not been to me
As is a landscape to a blind man's eye:
But oft, in lonely rooms, and 'mid the din
Of towns and cities, I have owed to them,
In hours of weariness, sensations sweet,
Felt in the blood, and felt along the heart;
And passing even into my purer mind,
With tranquil restoration:—feelings too   30
Of unremembered pleasure: such, perhaps,
As have no slight or trivial influence
On that best portion of a good man's life,
His little, nameless, unremembered acts
Of kindness and of love. Nor less, I trust,
To them I may have owed another gift,
Of aspect more sublime; that blessed mood,
In which the burthen of the mystery,
In which the heavy and the weary weight
Of all this unintelligible world,   40
Is lightened:—that serene and blessed mood,
In which the affections gently lead us on,—
Until, the breath of this corporeal frame
And even the motion of our human blood
Almost suspended, we are laid asleep
In body, and become a living soul:
While with an eye made quiet by the power
Of harmony, and the deep power of joy,
We see into the life of things.

                        If this
Be but a vain belief, yet, oh! how oft—   50
In darkness and amid the many shapes
Of joyless daylight; when the fretful stir
Unprofitable, and the fever of the world,
Have hung upon the beatings of my heart—
How oft, in spirit, have I turned to thee,
O sylvan Wye! thou wanderer thro' the woods,
How often has my spirit turned to thee!

And now, with gleams of half-extinguished thought,
With many recognitions dim and faint,
And somewhat of a sad perplexity,   60
The picture of the mind revives again:
While here I stand, not only with the sense
Of present pleasure, but with pleasing thoughts
That in this moment there is life and food
For future years. And so I dare to hope,
Though changed, no doubt, from what I was when first
I came among these hills; when like a roe
I bounded o'er the mountains, by the sides
Of the deep rivers, and the lonely streams,
Wherever nature led: more like a man   70
Flying from something that he dreads than one
Who sought the thing he loved. For nature then
(The coarser pleasures of my boyish days,
And their glad animal movements all gone by)
To me was all in all.—I cannot paint
What then I was. The sounding cataract
Haunted me like a passion: the tall rock,
The mountain, and the deep and gloomy wood,
Their colors and their forms, were then to me
An appetite; a feeling and a love,   80
That had no need of a remoter charm,
By thought supplied, nor any interest
Unborrowed from the eye.—That time is past,
And all its aching joys are now no more,
And all its dizzy raptures. Not for this
Faint I, nor mourn nor murmur; other gifts
Have followed; for such loss, I would believe,
Abundant recompense. For I have learned
To look on nature, not as in the hour
Of thoughtless youth; but hearing oftentimes   90
The still, sad music of humanity,
Nor harsh nor grating, though of ample power
To chasten and subdue. And I have felt
A presence that disturbs me with the joy
Of elevated thoughts; a sense sublime

Of something far more deeply interfused,
Whose dwelling is the light of setting suns,
And the round ocean and the living air,
And the blue sky, and in the mind of man:
A motion and a spirit, that impels   100
All thinking things, all objects of all thought,
And rolls through all things. Therefore am I still
A lover of the meadows and the woods,
And mountains; and of all that we behold
From this green earth; of all the mighty world
Of eye, and ear,—both what they half create,
And what perceive; well pleased to recognize
In nature and the language of the sense
The anchor of my purest thoughts, the nurse,
The guide, the guardian of my heart, and soul   110
Of all my moral being.
                            Nor perchance,
If I were not thus taught, should I the more
Suffer my genial spirits to decay:
For thou art with me here upon the banks
Of this fair river; thou my dearest friend,
My dear, dear friend; and in thy voice I catch
The language of my former heart, and read
My former pleasures in the shooting lights
Of thy wild eyes. Oh! yet a little while
May I behold in thee what I was once,   120
My dear, dear sister! and this prayer I make,
Knowing that Nature never did betray
The heart that loved her; 'tis her privilege,
Through all the years of this our life, to lead
From joy to joy: for she can so inform
The mind that is within us, so impress
With quietness and beauty, and so feed
With lofty thoughts, that neither evil tongues,
Rash judgments, nor the sneers of selfish men,
Nor greetings where no kindness is, nor all   130
The dreary intercourse of daily life,
Shall e'er prevail against us, or disturb

Our cheerful faith, that all which we behold
Is full of blessings. Therefore let the moon
Shine on thee in thy solitary walk;
And let the misty mountain-winds be free
To blow against thee: and, in after years,
When these wild ecstasies shall be matured
Into a sober pleasure; when thy mind
Shall be a mansion for all lovely forms,   140
Thy memory be as a dwelling-place
For all sweet sounds and harmonies; oh! then,
If solitude, or fear, or pain, or grief,
Should be thy portion, with what healing thoughts
Of tender joy wilt thou remember me,
And these my exhortations! Nor, perchance—
If I should be where I no more can hear
Thy voice, nor catch from thy wild eyes these gleams
Of past existence—wilt thou then forget
That on the banks of this delightful stream   150
We stood together; and that I, so long
A worshipper of Nature, hither came
Unwearied in that service: rather say
With warmer love—oh! with far deeper zeal
Of holier love. Nor wilt thou then forget
That after many wanderings, many years
Of absence, these steep woods and lofty cliffs,
And this green pastoral landscape, were to me
More dear, both for themselves and for thy sake!

278   *On the Morning of Christs Nativity*

I

THIS is the Month, and this the happy morn
Wherein the Son of Heav'ns eternal King,
Of wedded Maid, and Virgin Mother born,
Our great redemption from above did bring;
For so the holy sages once did sing,
    That he our deadly forfeit should release,
And with his Father work us a perpetual peace.

[556]

The glorious Form, that Light unsufferable,
And that far-beaming blaze of Majesty,
Wherwith he wont at Heav'ns high Councel-Table,　　　10
To sit the midst of Trinal Unity,
He laid aside; and here with us to be,
　　Forsook the Courts of everlasting Day,
And chose with us a darksom House of mortal Clay.

III

Say Heav'nly Muse, shall not thy sacred vein
Afford a present to the Infant God?
Hast thou no vers, no hymn, or solemn strein,
To welcom him to this his new abode,
Now while the Heav'n by the Suns team untrod,
　　Hath took no print of the approching light,　　　20
And all the spangled host keep watch in squadrons bright?

IV

See how from far upon the Eastern rode
The Star-led Wisards haste with odours sweet,
O run, prevent them with thy humble ode,
And lay it lowly at his blessed feet;
Have thou the honour first, thy Lord to greet,
　　And joyn thy voice unto the Angel Quire,
From out his secret Altar toucht with hallow'd fire.

THE HYMN

I

It was the Winter wilde,
While the Heav'n-born-childe,　　　30
　　All meanly wrapt in the rude manger lies;
Nature in aw to him
Had doff't her gawdy trim,
　　With her great Master so to sympathize:
It was no season then for her
To wanton with the Sun her lusty Paramour.

Only with speeches fair
She woo's the gentle Air
   To hide her guilty front with innocent Snow,
And on her naked shame,   40
Pollute with sinfull blame,
   The Saintly Vail of Maiden white to throw,
Confounded, that her Makers eyes
Should look so neer upon her foul deformities.

III

But he her fears to cease,
Sent down the meek-eyd Peace,
   She crown'd with Olive green, came softly sliding
Down through the turning sphear
His ready Harbinger,
   With Turtle wing the amorous clouds dividing,   50
And waving wide her mirtle wand,
She strikes a universall Peace through Sea and Land.

IV

No War, or Battails sound
Was heard the World around,
   The idle spear and shield were high up hung;
The hooked Chariot stood
Unstain'd with hostile blood,
   The Trumpet spake not to the armed throng,
And Kings sate still with awfull eye,
As if they surely knew their sovran Lord was by.   60

V

But peacefull was the night
Wherin the Prince of light
   His raign of peace upon the earth began:
The Windes with wonder whist,
Smoothly the waters kist,
   Whispering new joyes to the milde Ocean,
Who now hath quite forgot to rave,
While Birds of Calm sit brooding on the charmed wave.

VI

The Stars with deep amaze
Stand fixt in stedfast gaze,   70
    Bending one way their pretious influence,
And will not take their flight,
For all the morning light,
    Or *Lucifer* that often warn'd them thence;
But in their glimmering Orbs did glow,
Untill their Lord himself bespake, and bid them go.

VII

And though the shady gloom
Had given day her room,
    The Sun himself with-held his wonted speed,
And hid his head for shame,   80
As his inferiour flame,
    The new enlightn'd world no more should need;
He saw a greater Sun appear
Then his bright Throne, or burning Axletree could bear.

VIII

The Shepherds on the Lawn,
Or ere the point of dawn,
    Sate simply chatting in a rustick row;
Full little thought they than,
That the mighty *Pan*
    Was kindly com to live with them below;   90
Perhaps their loves, or els their sheep,
Was all that did their silly thoughts so busie keep.

IX

When such musick sweet
Their hearts and ears did greet,
    As never was by mortall finger strook,
Divinely-warbled voice
Answering the stringed noise,
    As all their souls in blisfull rapture took:
The Air such pleasure loth to lose,
With thousand echo's still prolongs each heav'nly close.   100

X

Nature that heard such sound
Beneath the hollow round
   Of *Cynthia's* seat, the Airy region thrilling,
Now was almost won
To think her part was don,
   And that her raign had here its last fulfilling;
She knew such harmony alone
Could hold all Heav'n and Earth in happier union.

XI

At last surrounds their sight
A Globe of circular light,   110
   That with long beams the shame-fac't night array'd,
The helmed Cherubim
And sworded Seraphim,
   Are seen in glittering ranks with wings displaid,
Harping in loud and solemn quire,
With unexpressive notes to Heav'ns new-born Heir.

XII

Such musick (as 'tis said)
Before was never made,
   But when of old the sons of morning sung,
While the Creator Great   120
His constellations set,
   And the well-ballanc't world on hinges hung,
And cast the dark foundations deep,
And bid the weltring waves their oozy channel keep.

XIII

Ring out ye Crystall sphears,
Once bless our human ears,
   (If ye have power to touch our senses so)
And let your silver chime
Move in melodious time;
   And let the Base of Heav'ns deep Organ blow,   130
And with your ninefold harmony
Make up full consort to th'Angelike symphony.

XIV

For if such holy Song
Enwrap our fancy long,
 Time will run back, and fetch the age of gold,
And speckl'd vanity
Will sicken soon and die,
 And leprous sin will melt from earthly mould,
And Hell it self will pass away,
And leave her dolorous mansions to the peering day.   140

XV

Yea Truth, and Justice then
Will down return to men,
 Th'enameld *Arras* of the Rain-bow wearing,
And Mercy set between,
Thron'd in Celestiall sheen,
 With radiant feet the tissued clouds down stearing,
And Heav'n as at som festivall,
Will open wide the Gates of her high Palace Hall.

XVI

But wisest Fate sayes no,
This must not yet be so,   150
 The Babe lies yet in smiling Infancy,
That on the bitter cross
Must redeem our loss;
 So both himself and us to glorifie:
Yet first to those ychain'd in sleep,
The wakefull trump of doom must thunder through the deep,

XVII

With such a horrid clang
As on mount *Sinai* rang
 While the red fire, and smouldring clouds out brake:
The aged Earth agast   160
With terrour of that blast,
 Shall from the surface to the center shake,
When at the worlds last session,
The dreadfull Judge in middle Air shall spread his throne.

XVIII

And then at last our bliss
Full and perfect is,
　　But now begins; for from this happy day
Th'old Dragon under ground
In straiter limits bound,
　　Not half so far casts his usurped sway,　　　　　　170
And wrath to see his Kingdom fail,
Swindges the scaly Horrour of his foulded tail.

XIX

The Oracles are dumm,
No voice or hideous humm
　　Runs through the arched roof in words deceiving.
Apollo from his shrine
Can no more divine,
　　With hollow shreik the steep of *Delphos* leaving.
No nightly trance, or breathed spell,
Inspire's the pale-ey'd Priest from the prophetic cell.　　　180

XX

The lonely mountains o're,
And the resounding shore,
　　A voice of weeping heard, and loud lament;
From haunted spring, and dale
Edg'd with poplar pale,
　　The parting Genius is with sighing sent,
With flowre-inwov'n tresses torn
The Nimphs in twilight shade of tangled thickets mourn.

XXI

In consecrated Earth,
And on the holy Hearth,　　　　　　190
　　The *Lars*, and *Lemures* moan with midnight plaint,
In Urns, and Altars round,
A drear, and dying sound
　　Affrights the *Flamins* at their service quaint;
And the chill Marble seems to sweat,
While each peculiar power forgoes his wonted seat.

XXII

Peor, and *Baalim*,

Forsake their Temples dim,

   With that twise-batter'd god of *Palestine*,

And mooned *Ashtaroth*,   200

Heav'ns Queen and Mother both,

   Now sits not girt with Tapers holy shine,

The Libyc *Hammon* shrinks his horn,

In vain the *Tyrian* Maids their wounded *Thamuz* mourn.

And sullen *Moloch* fled,

Hath left in shadows dred,

   His burning Idol all of blackest hue,

In vain with Cymbals ring,

They call the grisly king,

   In dismall dance about the furnace blue;   210

The brutish gods of *Nile* as fast,

Isis and *Orus*, and the Dog *Anubis* hast.

Nor is *Osiris* seen

In *Memphian* Grove, or Green,

   Trampling the unshowr'd Grasse with lowings loud:

Nor can he be at rest

Within his sacred chest,

   Naught but profoundest Hell can be his shroud,

In vain with Timbrel'd Anthems dark

The sable-stoled Sorcerers bear his worshipt Ark.   220

He feels from *Juda's* Land

The dredded Infants hand,

   The rayes of *Bethlehem* blind his dusky eyn;

Nor all the gods beside,

Longer dare abide,

   Not *Typhon* huge ending in snaky twine:

Our Babe to shew his Godhead true,

Can in his swadling bands controul the damned crew.

So when the Sun in bed,
Curtain'd with cloudy red, 230
   Pillows his chin upon an Orient wave,
The flocking shadows pale,
Troop to th'infernall jail,
   Each fetter'd Ghost slips to his severall grave,
And the yellow-skirted *Fayes*,
Fly after the Night-steeds, leaving their Moon-lov'd maze.

XXVII

But see the Virgin blest,
Hath laid her Babe to rest.
   Time is our tedious Song should here have ending,
Heav'ns youngest teemed Star, 240
Hath fixt her polisht Car,
   Her sleeping Lord with Handmaid Lamp attending:
And all about the Courtly Stable,
Bright-harnest Angels sit in order serviceable.

279   *The Divine Image*

To Mercy, Pity, Peace, and Love
All pray in their distress;
And to these virtues of delight
Return their thankfulness.

For Mercy, Pity, Peace, and Love 5
Is God, our Father dear,
And Mercy, Pity, Peace, and Love
Is man, His child and care.

For Mercy has a human heart,
Pity a human face, 10
And Love, the human form divine,
And Peace, the human dress.

Then every man, of every clime,
That prays in his distress,
Prays to the human form divine, 15
Love, Mercy, Pity, Peace.

And all must love the human form,
In heathen, Turk, or Jew;
Where Mercy, Love, and Pity dwell
There God is dwelling too. 20

280   *'And did those feet in ancient time'*

(FROM *Milton*)

And did those feet in ancient time
 Walk upon England's mountains green?
And was the holy Lamb of God
 On England's pleasant pastures seen?

And did the countenance divine 5
 Shine forth upon our clouded hills?
And was Jerusalem builded here
 Among these dark Satanic mills?

Bring me my bow of burning gold!
 Bring me my arrows of desire! 10
Bring me my spear! O clouds, unfold!
 Bring me my chariot of fire!

I will not cease from mental fight,
 Nor shall my sword sleep in my hand,
Till we have built Jerusalem 15
 In England's green and pleasant land.

281   *Holy Thursday*

Is this a holy thing to see
In a rich and fruitful land,
Babes reduced to misery,
Fed with cold and usurous hand?

[565]

Is that trembling cry a song?   5
Can it be a song of joy?
And so many children poor?
It is a land of poverty!

And their sun does never shine,
And their fields are bleak and bare,   10
And their ways are filled with thorns:
It is eternal winter there.

For where'er the sun does shine,
And where'er the rain does fall,
Babe can never hunger there,   15
Nor poverty the mind appall.

The Tiger

Tiger! Tiger! burning bright
In the forests of the night,
What immortal hand or eye
Could frame thy fearful symmetry?

In what distant deeps or skies
Burnt the fire of thine eyes?
On what wings dare he aspire?
What the hand dare seize the fire?

And what shoulder, and what art,
Could twist the sinews of thy heart?   10
And when thy heart began to beat,
What dread hand? and what dread feet?

What the hammer? what the chain?
In what furnace was thy brain?
What the anvil? what dread grasp
Dare its deadly terrors clasp?

When the stars threw down their spears,
And watered heaven with their tears,
Did he smile his work to see?
Did he who made the Lamb make thee?   20

Tiger! Tiger! burning bright
In the forests of the night,
What immortal hand or eye,
Dare frame thy fearful symmetry?

283   *The Sheaves*

Where long the shadows of the wind had rolled,
Green wheat was yielding to the change assigned;
And as by some vast magic undivined
The world was turning slowly into gold.
Like nothing that was ever bought or sold   5
It waited there, the body and the mind;
And with a mighty meaning of a kind
That tells the more the more it is not told.

So in a land where all days are not fair,
Fair days went on till on another day   10
A thousand golden sheaves were lying there,
Shining and still, but not for long to stay—
As if a thousand girls with golden hair
Might rise from where they slept and go away.

284   *The Waste Places*

As a naked man I go
    Through the desert sore afraid,
Holding up my head, although
    I am as frightened as a maid.

The couching lion there I saw
    From barren rocks lift up his eye,
He parts the cactus with his paw,
    He stares at me as I go by.

He would follow on my trace
    If he knew I was afraid, 10
If he knew my hardy face
    Hides the terrors of a maid.

In the night he rises, and
    He stretches forth, he snuffs the air,
He roars and leaps along the sand,
    He creeps and watches everywhere.

His burning eyes, his eyes of bale,
    Through the darkness I can see;
He lashes fiercely with his tail,
    He would love to spring at me. 20

I am the lion in his lair,
    I am the fear that frightens me,
I am the desert of despair,
    And the nights of agony.

Night or day, whate'er befall,
    I must walk that desert land,
Until I can dare to call
    The lion out to lick my hand.

285 *Eloïsa to Abelard*

ARGUMENT

ABELARD and Eloïsa flourished in the twelfth Century; they were two of the most distinguished Persons of their age in learning and beauty, but for nothing more famous than for their unfortunate passion. After a long course of calamities, they retired each to a several Convent, and consecrated the remainder of their days to religion. It was many years after this separation, that a letter of Abelard's to a Friend, which contained the history of his misfortune, fell into the hands of Eloïsa. This awakening all her Tenderness, occasioned those celebrated letters (out of which the following is partly extracted) which gives so lively a picture of the struggles of grace and nature, virtue and passion.

    IN these deep solitudes and awful cells,
    Where heavenly-pensive contemplation dwells,
    And ever-musing melancholy reigns;
    What means this tumult in a Vestal's veins?

Why rove my thoughts beyond this last retreat?
Why feels my heart its long-forgotten heat?
Yet, yet I love!—From Abelard it came,
And Eloïsa yet must kiss the name.
    Dear fatal name! rest ever unrevealed,
Nor pass these lips in holy silence sealed: 10
Hide it, my heart, within that close disguise,
Where mixed with God's, his loved Idea lies:
O write it not my hand—the name appears
Already written—wash it out, my tears!
In vain lost Eloïsa weeps and prays,
Her heart still dictates, and her hand obeys.
    Relentless walls! whose darksome round contains
Repentant sighs, and voluntary pains:
Ye rugged rocks! which holy knees have worn;
Ye grots and caverns shagged with horrid thorn!   20
Shrines! where their vigils pale-eyed virgins keep,
And pitying saints, whose statues learn to weep!
Though cold like you, unmoved and silent grown,
I have not yet forgot myself to stone.
All is not Heaven's while Abelard has part,
Still rebel nature holds out half my heart;
Nor prayers nor fasts its stubborn pulse restrain,
Nor tears for ages taught to flow in vain.
    Soon as thy letters trembling I unclose,
That well-known name awakens all my woes.   30
Oh name for ever sad! for ever dear!
Still breathed in sighs, still ushered with a tear.
I tremble too, where'er my own I find,
Some dire misfortune follows close behind.
Line after line my gushing eyes o'erflow,
Led through a sad variety of woe:
Now warm in love, now with'ring in my bloom,
Lost in a convent's solitary gloom!
There stern Religion quenched th' unwilling flame,
There died the best of passions, Love and Fame.   40
    Yet write, oh write me all, that I may join
Griefs to thy griefs, and echo sighs to thine.

Nor foes nor fortune take this power away;
And is my Abelard less kind than they?
Tears still are mine, and those I need not spare,
Love but demands what else were shed in prayer;
No happier task these faded eyes pursue;
To read and weep is all they now can do.

    Then share thy pain, allow that sad relief;
Ah, more than share it, give me all thy grief.   50
Heaven first taught letters for some wretch's aid,
Some banished lover, or some captive maid;
They live, they speak, they breathe what love inspires,
Warm from the soul, and faithful to its fires,
The virgin's wish without her fears impart,
Excuse the blush, and pour out all the heart,
Speed the soft intercourse from soul to soul,
And waft a sigh from Indus to the Pole.

    Thou know'st how guiltless first I met thy flame,
When Love approached me under Friendship's name;   60
My fancy formed thee of angelic kind,
Some emanation of th' all-beauteous Mind.
Those smiling eyes, attemp'ring every ray,
Shone sweetly lambent with celestial day.
Guiltless I gazed; heaven listened while you sung;
And truths divine came mended from that tongue.
From lips like those what precept failed to move?
Too soon they taught me 'twas no sin to love:
Back through the paths of pleasing sense I ran,
Nor wished an Angel whom I loved a Man.   70
Dim and remote the joys of saints I see;
Nor envy them that heaven I lose for thee.

    How oft, when pressed to marriage, have I said,
Curse on all laws but those which love has made?
Love, free as air, at sight of human ties,
Spreads his light wings, and in a moment flies.
Let wealth, let honor, wait the wedded dame,
August her deed, and sacred be her fame;
Before true passion all those views remove,
Fame, wealth, and honor! what are you to Love?   80

The jealous God, when we profane his fires,
Those restless passions in revenge inspires,
And bids them make mistaken mortals groan,
Who seek in love for aught but love alone.
Should at my feet the world's great master fall,
Himself, his throne, his world, I'd scorn 'em all:
Not Cæsar's empress would I deign to prove;
No, make me mistress to the man I love;
If there be yet another name more free,
More fond than mistress, make me that to thee!   90
Oh! happy state! when souls each other draw,
When love is liberty, and nature law:
All then is full, possessing, and possessed,
No craving void left aching in the breast:
Even thought meets thought, ere from the lips it part,
And each warm wish springs mutual from the heart.
This sure is bliss (if bliss on earth there be)
And once the lot of Abelard and me.

    Alas, how changed! what sudden horrors rise!
A naked Lover bound and bleeding lies!   100
Where, where was Eloïse? her voice, her hand,
Her poniard, had opposed the dire command.
Barbarian, stay! that bloody stroke restrain;
The crime was common, common be the pain.
I can no more; by shame, by rage suppressed,
Let tears, and burning blushes speak the rest.

    Canst thou forget that sad, that solemn day,
When victims at yon altar's foot we lay?
Canst thou forget what tears that moment fell,
When, warm in youth, I bade the world farewell?   110
As with cold lips I kissed the sacred veil,
The shrines all trembled, and the lamps grew pale:
Heaven scarce believed the Conquest it surveyed,
And Saints with wonder heard the vows I made.
Yet then, to those dread altars as I drew,
Not on the Cross my eyes were fixed, but you:
Not grace, or zeal, love only was my call,
And if I lose thy love, I lose my all.

[571]

Come! with thy looks, thy words, relieve my woe;
Those still at least are left thee to bestow.   120
Still on that breast enamored let me lie,
Still drink delicious poison from thy eye,
Pant on thy lip, and to thy heart be pressed;
Give all thou canst—and let me dream the rest.
Ah no! instruct me other joys to prize,
With other beauties charm my partial eyes,
Full in my view set all the bright abode,
And make my soul quit Abelard for God.

   Ah, think at least thy flock deserves thy care,
Plants of thy hand, and children of thy prayer.   130
From the false world in early youth they fled,
By thee to mountains, wilds, and deserts led.
You raised these hallowed walls; the desert smiled,
And Paradise was opened in the Wild.
No weeping orphan saw his father's stores
Our shrines irradiate, or emblaze the floors;
No silver saints, by dying misers given,
Here bribed the rage of ill-requited heaven:
But such plain roofs as Piety could raise,
And only vocal with the Maker's praise.   140
In these lone walls (their days eternal bound)
These moss-grown domes with spiry turrets crowned,
Where awful arches make a noon-day night,
And the dim windows shed a solemn light;
Thy eyes diffused a reconciling ray,
And gleams of glory brightened all the day.
But now no face divine contentment wears,
'Tis all blank sadness, or continual tears.
See how the force of others' prayers I try,
(O pious fraud of am'rous charity!)   150
But why should I on others' prayers depend?
Come thou, my father, brother, husband, friend!
Ah let thy handmaid, sister, daughter move,
And all those tender names in one, thy love!
The darksome pines that o'er yon rocks reclined
Wave high, and murmur to the hollow wind,

The wandering streams that shine between the hills,
The grots that echo to the tinkling rills,
The dying gales that pant upon the trees,
The lakes that quiver to the curling breeze;   160
No more these scenes my meditation aid,
Or lull to rest the visionary maid.
But o'er the twilight groves and dusky caves,
Long-sounding aisles, and intermingled graves,
Black Melancholy sits, and round her throws
A death-like silence, and a dead repose:
Her gloomy presence saddens all the scene,
Shades every flower, and darkens every green,
Deepens the murmur of the falling floods,
And breathes a browner horror on the woods.   170

    Yet here for ever, ever must I stay;
Sad proof how well a lover can obey!
Death, only death, can break the lasting chain:
And here, even then, shall my cold dust remain,
Here all its frailties, all its flames resign,
And wait till 'tis no sin to mix with thine.
    Ah wretch! believe the spouse of God in vain,
Confessed within the slave of love and man.
Assist me, heaven! but whence arose that prayer?
Sprung it from piety, or from despair?   180
Even here, where frozen chastity retires,
Love finds an altar for forbidden fires.
I ought to grieve, but cannot what I ought;
I mourn the lover, not lament the fault;
I view my crime, but kindle at the view,
Repent old pleasures, and solicit new;
Now turned to heaven, I weep my past offense,
Now think of thee, and curse my innocence.
Of all affliction taught a lover yet,
'Tis sure the hardest science to forget!   190
How shall I lose the sin, yet keep the sense,
And love th' offender, yet detest th' offense?
How the dear object from the crime remove,
Or how distinguish penitence from love?

[573]

Unequal task! a passion to resign,
For hearts so touched, so pierced, so lost as mine.
Ere such a soul regains its peaceful state,
How often must it love, how often hate!
How often hope, despair, resent, regret,
Conceal, disdain,—do all things but forget.   200
But let heaven seize it, all at once 'tis fired:
Not touched, but rapt; not wakened, but inspired!
Oh come! oh teach me nature to subdue,
Renounce my love, my life, myself—and you.
Fill my fond heart with God alone, for he
Alone can rival, can succeed to thee.

   How happy is the blameless Vestal's lot!
The world forgetting, by the world forgot:
Eternal sunshine of the spotless mind!
Each prayer accepted, and each wish resigned;   210
Labor and rest, that equal periods keep;
'Obedient slumbers that can wake and weep;'
Desires composed, affections ever even;
Tears that delight, and sighs that waft to heaven.
Grace shines around her with serenest beams,
And whisp'ring Angels prompt her golden dreams.
For her th' unfading rose of Eden blooms,
And wings of Seraphs shed divine perfumes,
For her the Spouse prepares the bridal ring,
For her white virgins Hymenæals sing,   220
To sounds of heavenly harps she dies away,
And melts in visions of eternal day.

   Far other dreams my erring soul employ,
Far other raptures, of unholy joy:
When at the close of each sad, sorrowing day,
Fancy restores what vengeance snatched away,
Then conscience sleeps, and leaving nature free,
All my loose soul unbounded springs to thee.
Oh curst, dear horrors of all-conscious night;
How glowing guilt exalts the keen delight!   230
Provoking Dæmons all restraint remove,
And stir within me every source of love.

I hear thee, view thee, gaze o'er all thy charms,
And round thy phantom glue my clasping arms.
I wake:—no more I hear, no more I view,
The phantom flies me, as unkind as you.
I call aloud; it hears not what I say:
I stretch my empty arms; it glides away.
To dream once more I close my willing eyes;
Ye soft illusions, dear deceits, arise!   240
Alas, no more! methinks we wand'ring go
Through dreary wastes, and weep each other's woe,
Where round some mold'ring tower pale ivy creeps,
And low-browed rocks hang nodding o'er the deeps.
Sudden you mount, you beckon from the skies;
Clouds interpose, waves roar, and winds arise.
I shriek, start up, the same sad prospect find,
And wake to all the griefs I left behind.
    For thee the fates, severely kind, ordain
A cool suspense from pleasure and from pain;   250
Thy life a long dead calm of fixed repose;
No pulse that riots, and no blood that glows.
Still as the sea, ere winds were taught to blow,
Or moving spirit bade the waters flow;
Soft as the slumbers of a saint forgiven,
And mild as opening gleams of promised heaven.
    Come, Abelard! for what hast thou to dread?
The torch of Venus burns not for the dead.
Nature stands checked; Religion disapproves;
Even thou art cold—yet Eloïsa loves.   260
Ah hopeless, lasting flames! like those that burn
To light the dead, and warm th' unfruitful urn.
    What scenes appear where'er I turn my view?
The dear Ideas, where I fly, pursue,
Rise in the grove, before the altar rise,
Stain all my soul, and wanton in my eyes.
I waste the Matin lamp in sighs for thee,
Thy image steals between my God and me,
Thy voice I seem in every hymn to hear,
With every bead I drop too soft a tear.   270

When from the censer clouds of fragrance roll,
And swelling organs lift the rising soul,
One thought of thee puts all the pomp to flight,
Priests, tapers, temples, swim before my sight:
In seas of flame my plunging soul is drowned,
While Altars blaze, and Angels tremble round.
　　While prostrate here in humble grief I lie,
Kind, virtuous drops just gath'ring in my eye,
While praying, trembling, in the dust I roll,
And dawning grace is opening on my soul:　　　　　　　280
Come, if thou dar'st, all charming as thou art!
Oppose thyself to heaven; dispute my heart;
Come, with one glance of those deluding eyes
Blot out each bright Idea of the skies;
Take back that grace, those sorrows, and those tears;
Take back my fruitless penitence and prayers;
Snatch me, just mounting, from the blest abode;
Assist the fiends, and tear me from my God!
　　No, fly me, fly me, far as Pole from Pole;
Rise Alps between us! and whole oceans roll!　　　　　　290
Ah, come not, write not, think not once of me,
Nor share one pang of all I felt for thee.
Thy oaths I quit, thy memory resign;
Forget, renounce me, hate whate'er was mine.
Fair eyes, and tempting looks (which yet I view!)
Long loved, adored ideas, all adieu!
Oh Grace serene! oh virtue heavenly fair!
Divine oblivion of low-thoughted care!
Fresh blooming Hope, gay daughter of the sky!
And Faith, our early immortality!　　　　　　　　　　　300
Enter, each mild, each amicable guest;
Receive, and wrap me in eternal rest!
　　See in her cell sad Eloïsa spread,
Propt on some tomb, a neighbor of the dead.
In each low wind methinks a Spirit calls,
And more than Echoes talk along the walls.
Here, as I watched the dying lamps around,
From yonder shrine I heard a hollow sound.

'Come, sister, come!' (it said, or seemed to say)
'Thy place is here, sad sister, come away!   310
Once like thyself, I trembled, wept, and prayed,
Love's victim then, though now a sainted maid:
But all is calm in this eternal sleep;
Here grief forgets to groan, and love to weep,
Even superstition loses every fear:
For God, not man, absolves our frailties here.'
    I come, I come! prepare your roseate bowers,
Celestial palms, and ever-blooming flowers.
Thither, where sinners may have rest, I go,
Where flames refined in breasts seraphic glow: 320
Thou, Abelard! the last sad office pay,
And smooth my passage to the realms of day;
See my lips tremble, and my eye-balls roll,
Suck my last breath, and catch my flying soul!
Ah no—in sacred vestments may'st thou stand,
The hallowed taper trembling in thy hand,
Present the Cross before my lifted eye,
Teach me at once, and learn of me to die.
Ah then, thy once-loved Eloïsa see!
It will be then no crime to gaze on me.   330
See from my cheek the transient roses fly!
See the last sparkle languish in my eye!
'Til every motion, pulse, and breath be o'er;
And even my Abelard be loved no more.
O Death all-eloquent! you only prove
What dust we dote on, when 'tis man we love.
    Then too, when fate shall thy fair frame destroy,
(That cause of all my guilt, and all my joy)
In trance ecstatic may thy pangs be drowned,
Bright clouds descend, and Angels watch thee round,   340
From opening skies may streaming glories shine,
And saints embrace thee with a love like mine.
    May one kind grave unite each hapless name,
And graft my love immortal on thy fame!
Then, ages hence, when all my woes are o'er,
When this rebellious heart shall beat no more;

[577]

If ever chance two wand'ring lovers brings
To Paraclete's white walls and silver springs,
O'er the pale marble shall they join their heads,
And drink the falling tears each other sheds; 350
Then sadly say, with mutual pity moved,
'Oh may we never love as these have loved!'
From the full choir when loud Hosannas rise,
And swell the pomp of dreadful sacrifice,
Amid that scene if some relenting eye
Glance on the stone where our cold relics lie,
Devotion's self shall steal a thought from heaven,
One human tear shall drop and be forgiven.
And sure, if fate some future bard shall join
In sad similitude of griefs to mine, 360
Condemned whole years in absence to deplore,
And image charms he must behold no more;
Such if there be, who loves so long, so well;
Let him our sad, our tender story tell;
The well-sung woes will soothe my pensive ghost;
He best can paint 'em who shall feel 'em most.

286   *Easter Hymn*

If in that Syrian garden, ages slain,
You sleep, and know not you are dead in vain,
Nor even in dreams behold how dark and bright
Ascends in smoke and fire by day and night
The hate you died to quench and could but fan, 5
Sleep well and see no morning, son of man.

But if, the grave rent and the stone rolled by,
At the right hand of majesty on high
You sit, and sitting so remember yet
Your tears, your agony and bloody sweat, 10
Your cross and passion and the life you gave,
Bow hither out of heaven and see and save.

'A cold coming we had of it,
Just the worst time of the year
For a journey, and such a long journey:
The ways deep and the weather sharp,
The very dead of winter.'
And the camels galled, sore-footed, refractory,
Lying down in the melting snow.
There were times we regretted
The summer palaces on slopes, the terraces,
And the silken girls bringing sherbet.   10
Then the camel men cursing and grumbling
And running away, and wanting their liquor and women,
And the night-fires going out, and the lack of shelters,
And the cities hostile and the towns unfriendly
And the villages dirty and charging high prices:
A hard time we had of it.
At the end we preferred to travel all night,
Sleeping in snatches,
With the voices singing in our ears, saying
That this was all folly.   20

Then at dawn we came down to a temperate valley,
Wet, below the snow line, smelling of vegetation;
With a running stream and a water-mill beating the darkness,
And three trees on the low sky,
And an old white horse galloped away in the meadow.
Then we came to a tavern with vine-leaves over the lintel,
Six hands at an open door dicing for pieces of silver,
And feet kicking the empty wine-skins.
But there was no information, and so we continued
And arrived at evening, not a moment too soon   30
Finding the place; it was (you may say) satisfactory.

All this was a long time ago, I remember,
And I would do it again, but set down
This set down
This: were we led all that way for

Birth or Death? There was a Birth, certainly,
We had evidence and no doubt. I had seen birth and death,
But had thought they were different; this Birth was
Hard and bitter agony for us, like Death, our death.
We returned to our places, these Kingdoms,   40
But no longer at ease here, in the old dispensation,
With an alien people clutching their gods.
I should be glad of another death.

288   *To Jesus on His Birthday*

For this your mother sweated in the cold,
For this you bled upon the bitter tree:
A yard of tinsel ribbon bought and sold;
A paper wreath; a day at home for me.
The merry bells ring out, the people kneel;   5
Up goes the man of God before the crowd;
With voice of honey and with eyes of steel
He drones your humble gospel to the proud.
Nobody listens. Less than the wind that blows
Are all your words to us you died to save.   10
O Prince of Peace! O Sharon's dewy Rose!
How mute you lie within your vaulted grave.
    The stone the angel rolled away with tears
    Is back upon your mouth these thousand years.

289   *The Carpenter's Son*

'Here the hangman stops his cart:
Now the best of friends must part.
Fare you well, for ill fare I:
Live, lads, and I will die.

'Oh, at home had I but stayed
'Prenticed to my father's trade,
Had I stuck to plane and adze,
I had not been lost, my lads.

[580]

'Then I might have built perhaps
Gallows-trees for other chaps,
Never dangled on my own,
Had I but left ill alone.

'Now, you see, they hang me high,
And the people passing by
Stop to shake their fists and curse;
So 'tis come from ill to worse.

'Here hang I, and right and left
Two poor fellows hang for theft:
All the same's the luck we prove,
Though the midmost hangs for love.

'Comrades all, that stand and gaze,
Walk henceforth in other ways;
See my neck and save your own:
Comrades all, leave ill alone.

'Make some day a decent end,
Shrewder fellows than your friend.
Fare you well, for ill fare I:
Live, lads, and I will die.'

290

'The Chestnut Casts His Flambeaux'

The chestnut casts his flambeaux, and the flowers
   Stream from the hawthorn on the wind away,
The doors clap to, the pane is blind with showers.
   Pass me the can, lad; there's an end of May.

There's one spoilt spring to scant our mortal lot,
   One season ruined of our little store.
May will be fine next year as like as not:
   Oh ay, but then we shall be twenty-four.

We for a certainty are not the first
  Have sat in taverns while the tempest hurled   10
Their hopeful plans to emptiness, and cursed
  Whatever brute and blackguard made the world.

It is in truth iniquity on high
  To cheat our sentenced souls of aught they crave,
And mar the merriment as you and I
  Fare on our long fool's-errand to the grave.

Iniquity it is; but pass the can.
  My lad, no pair of kings our mothers bore;
Our only portion is the estate of man:
  We want the moon, but we shall get no more.   20

If here to-day the cloud of thunder lours
  To-morrow it will hie on far behests;
The flesh will grieve on other bones than ours
  Soon, and the soul will mourn in other breasts.

The troubles of our proud and angry dust
  Are from eternity, and shall not fail.
Bear them we can, and if we can we must.
  Shoulder the sky, my lad, and drink your ale.

291   *Shine, Perishing Republic*

While this America settles in the mold of its vulgarity,
    heavily thickening to empire,
And protest, only a bubble in the molten mass, pops and
    sighs out, and the mass hardens,

I sadly remember that the flower fades to make fruit,   5
    the fruit rots to make earth.
Out of the mother; and through the spring exultances,
    ripeness and decadence; and home to the mother.

You making haste haste on decay: not blameworthy; life is
  good, be it stubbornly long or suddenly   10
A mortal splendor: meteors are not needed less than
  mountains: shine, perishing republic.

But for my children, I would rather have them keep their distance
  from the thickening center; corruption
Never has been compulsory, when the cities lie at the   15
  monster's feet there are left the mountains.

And boys, be in nothing so moderate as in love of man, a
  clever servant, insufferable master.
There is the trap that catches noblest spirits, that caught—
  they say—God, when he walked on earth.   20

Of Course I Prayed

              Of course I prayed—
              And did God care?
              He cared as much as
              On the air
              A bird had stamped her foot   5
              And cried 'Give me!'

              My reason, life,
              I had not had, but for yourself.
              'Twere better charity
              To leave me in the atom's tomb,   10
              Merry and nought and gay and numb,
              Than this smart misery.

293   *Hymn to Earth*

              Farewell, incomparable element,
              Whence man arose, where he shall not return;
              And hail, imperfect urn
              Of his last ashes, and his firstborn fruit;
              Farewell, the long pursuit,

                            [583]

And all the adventures of his discontent;
The voyages which sent
His heart averse from home:
Metal of clay, permit him that he come
To thy slow-burning fire as to a hearth;   10
Accept him as a particle of earth.

Fire, being divided from the other three,
It lives removed, or secret at the core;
Most subtle of the four,
When air flies not, nor water flows,
It disembodied goes,
Being light, elixir of the first decree,
More volatile than he;
With strength and power to pass
Through space, where never his least atom was: 20
He has no part in it, save as his eyes
Have drawn its emanation from the skies.

A wingless creature heavier than air,
He is rejected of its quintessence;
Coming and going hence,
In the twin minutes of his birth and death,
He may inhale as breath,
As breath relinquish heaven's atmosphere,
Yet in it have no share,
Nor can survive therein   30
Where its outer edge is filtered pure and thin:
It doth but lend its crystal to his lungs
For his early crying, and his final songs.

The element of water has denied
Its child; it is no more his element;
It never will relent;
Its silver harvests are more sparsely given
Than the rewards of heaven,
And he shall drink cold comfort at its side:
The water is too wide: 40
The seamew and the gull

Feather a nest made soft and pitiful
Upon its foam; he has not any part
In the long swell of sorrow at its heart.

Hail and farewell, beloved element,
Whence he departed, and his parent once;
See where thy spirit runs
Which for so long hath had the moon to wife;
Shall this support his life
Until the arches of the waves be bent   50
And grow shallow and spent?
Wisely it cast him forth
With his dead weight of burdens nothing worth,
Leaving him, for the universal years,
A little seawater to make his tears.

Hail element of earth, receive thy own,
And cherish, at thy charitable breast,
This man, this mongrel beast:
He plows the sand, and, at his hardest need,
He sows himself for seed;   60
He plows the furrow, and in this lies down
Before the corn is grown;
Between the apple bloom
And the ripe apple is sufficient room
In time, and matter, to consume his love
And make him parcel of a cypress grove.

Receive him as thy lover for an hour
Who will not weary, by a longer stay,
The kind embrace of clay;
Even within thine arms he is dispersed   70
To nothing, as at first;
The air flings downward from its four-quartered tower
Him whom the flames devour;
At the full tide, at the flood,
The sea is mingled with his salty blood:
The traveler dust, although the dust be vile,
Sleeps as thy lover for a little while.

[585]

The Kingdom of God

'IN NO STRANGE LAND'

O world invisible, we view thee,
O world intangible, we touch thee,
O world unknowable, we know thee,
Inapprehensible, we clutch thee!

Does the fish soar to find the ocean,
The eagle plunge to find the air—
That we ask of the stars in motion
If they have rumor of thee there?

Now where the wheeling systems darken,
And our benumbed conceiving soars!—   10
The drifts of pinions, would we hearken,
Beats at our own clay-shuttered doors.

The angels keep their ancient places—
Turn but a stone, and start a wing!
'Tis ye, 'tis your estrangèd faces,
That miss the many-splendored thing.

But (when so sad thou canst not sadder)
Cry—and upon thy so sore loss
Shall shine the traffic of Jacob's ladder
Pitched betwixt Heaven and Charing Cross.   20

Yea, in the night, my Soul, my daughter,
Cry—clinging Heaven by the hems;
And lo, Christ walking on the water,
Not of Genesareth, but Thames!

The Toys

295

My little Son, who look'd from thoughtful eyes
And moved and spoke in quiet grown-up wise,
Having my law the seventh time disobey'd,
I struck him, and dismiss'd
With hard words and unkiss'd,
His Mother, who was patient, being dead.

[586]

Then, fearing lest his grief should hinder sleep,
I visited his bed,
But found him slumbering deep,
With darken'd eyelids, and their lashes yet   10
From his late sobbing wet.
And I, with moan,
Kissing away his tears, left others of my own;
For, on a table drawn beside his head,
He had put, within his reach,
A box of counters and a red-vein'd stone,
A piece of glass abraded by the beach
And six or seven shells,
A bottle with bluebells
And two French copper coins, ranged there with careful art,   20
To comfort his sad heart.
So when that night I pray'd
To God, I wept, and said:
Ah, when at last we lie with tranced breath,
Not vexing Thee in death,
And Thou rememberest of what toys
We made our joys,
How weakly understood,
Thy great commanded good,
Then, fatherly not less   30
Than I whom Thou hast molded from the clay,
Thou'lt leave Thy wrath, and say,
'I will be sorry for their childishness.'

296   '*I wake and feel the fell of dark*'

I wake and feel the fell of dark, not day.
What hours, O what black hoürs we have spent
This night! what sights you, heart, saw; ways you went!
And more must, in yet longer light's delay.
        With witness I speak this. But where I say   5
Hours I mean years, mean life. And my lament
Is cries countless, cries like dead letters sent
To dearest him that lives alas! away.

[587]

I am gall, I am heartburn. God's most deep decree
Bitter would have me taste: my taste was me;   10
Bones built in me, flesh filled, blood brimmed the curse.
    Selfyeast of spirit a dull dough sours. I see
The lost are like this, and their scourge to be
As I am mine, their sweating selves; but worse.

297   *Pied Beauty*

Glory be to God for dappled things—
    For skies of couple-color as a brinded cow;
        For rose-moles all in stipple upon trout that swim;
Fresh-firecoal chestnut-falls; finches' wings;
    Landscape plotted and pieced—fold, fallow, and plough;
        And áll trádes, their gear and tackle and trim.

All things counter, original, spare, strange;
    Whatever is fickle, freckled (who knows how?)
        With swift, slow; sweet, sour; adazzle, dim;
He fathers-forth whose beauty is past change:
                    Praise him.

298   *Sailing to Byzantium*

That is no country for old men. The young
In one another's arms, birds in the trees
—Those dying generations—at their song,
The salmon-falls, the mackerel-crowded seas,
Fish, flesh, or fowl, commend all summer long
Whatever is begotten, born, and dies.
Caught in that sensual music all neglect
Monuments of unaging intellect.

An aged man is but a paltry thing,
A tattered coat upon a stick, unless   10
Soul clap its hands and sing, and louder sing
For every tatter in its mortal dress,

Nor is there singing school but studying
Monuments of its own magnificence;
And therefore I have sailed the seas and come
To the holy city of Byzantium.

O sages standing in God's holy fire
As in the gold mosaic of a wall,
Come from the holy fire, perne in a gyre,
And be the singing-masters of my soul.   20
Consume my heart away; sick with desire
And fastened to a dying animal
It knows not what it is; and gather me
Into the artifice of eternity.

Once out of nature I shall never take
My bodily form from any natural thing,
But such a form as Grecian goldsmiths make
Of hammered gold and gold enameling
To keep a drowsy Emperor awake;
Or set upon a golden bough to sing   30
To lords and ladies of Byzantium
Of what is past, or passing, or to come.

299   *Byzantium*

The unpurged images of day recede;
The Emperor's drunken soldiery are abed;
Night resonance recedes, night-walkers' song
After great cathedral gong;
A starlit or a moonlit dome disdains
All that man is,
All mere complexities,
The fury and the mire of human veins.

Before me floats an image, man or shade,
Shade more than man, more image than a shade;   10
For Hades' bobbin bound in mummy-cloth
May unwind the winding path;

A mouth that has no moisture and no breath
Breathless mouths may summon;
I hail the superhuman;
I call it death-in-life and life-in-death.

Miracle, bird or golden handiwork,
More miracle than bird or handiwork,
Planted on the star-lit golden bough,
Can like the cocks of Hades crow,   20
Or, by the moon embittered, scorn aloud
In glory of changeless metal
Common bird or petal
And all complexities of mire or blood.

At midnight on the Emperor's pavement flit
Flames that no fagot feeds, nor steel has lit,
Nor storm disturbs, flames begotten of flame,
Where blood-begotten spirits come
And all complexities of fury leave,
Dying into a dance,   30
An agony of trance,
An agony of flame that cannot singe a sleeve.

Astraddle on the dolphin's mire and blood,
Spirit after spirit! The smithies break the flood,
The golden smithies of the Emperor!
Marbles of the dancing floor
Break bitter furies of complexity,
Those images that yet
Fresh images beget,
That dolphin-torn, that gong-tormented sea.   40

The Second Coming

Turning and turning in the widening gyre
The falcon cannot hear the falconer;
Things fall apart; the center cannot hold;
Mere anarchy is loosed upon the world,

The blood-dimmed tide is loosed, and everywhere
The ceremony of innocence is drowned;
The best lack all conviction, while the worst
Are full of passionate intensity.

Surely some revelation is at hand;
Surely the Second Coming is at hand. 10
The Second Coming! Hardly are those words out
When a vast image out of *Spiritus Mundi*
Troubles my sight: somewhere in sands of the desert
A shape with lion body and the head of a man,
A gaze blank and pitiless as the sun,
Is moving its slow thighs, while all about it
Reel shadows of the indignant desert birds.
The darkness drops again; but now I know
That twenty centuries of stony sleep
Were vexed to nightmare by a rocking cradle, 20
And what rough beast, its hour come round at last,
Slouches towards Bethlehem to be born?

301 *The Waste Land*

"Nam Sibyllam quidem Cumis ego ipse oculis meis vidi
in ampulla pendere, et cum illi pueri dicerent: Σίβυλλα
τι θέλεις; respondebat illa: άπο θανεῖν θέλω."

I. THE BURIAL OF THE DEAD

April is the cruelest month, breeding
Lilacs out of the dead land, mixing
Memory and desire, stirring
Dull roots with spring rain.
Winter kept us warm, covering
Earth in forgetful snow, feeding
A little life with dried tubers.
Summer surprised us, coming over the Starnbergersee
With a shower of rain; we stopped in the colonnade,
And went on in sunlight, into the Hofgarten, 10
And drank coffee, and talked for an hour.
Bin gar keine Russin, stamm' aus Litauen, echt deutsch.

And when we were children, staying at the archduke's,
My cousin's, he took me out on a sled,
And I was frightened. He said, Marie,
Marie, hold on tight. And down we went.
In the mountains, there you feel free.
I read, much of the night, and go south in the winter.
What are the roots that clutch, what branches grow   20
Out of this stony rubbish? Son of man,
You cannot say, or guess, for you know only
A heap of broken images, where the sun beats,
And the dead tree gives no shelter, the cricket no relief,
And the dry stone no sound of water. Only
There is shadow under this red rock,
(Come in under the shadow of this red rock),
And I will show you something different from either
Your shadow at morning striding behind you
Or your shadow at evening rising to meet you;
I will show you fear in a handful of dust.   30
            Frisch weht der Wind
            Der Heimat zu
            Mein Irisch Kind,
            Wo weilest du?
'You gave me hyacinths first a year ago;
'They called me the hyacinth girl.'
—Yet when we came back, late, from the hyacinth garden,
Your arms full, and your hair wet, I could not
Speak, and my eyes failed, I was neither
Living nor dead, and I knew nothing,   40
Looking into the heart of light, the silence.
Oed' und leer das Meer.

Madame Sosostris, famous clairvoyante,
Had a bad cold, nevertheless
Is known to be the wisest woman in Europe,
With a wicked pack of cards. Here, said she,
Is your card, the drowned Phoenician Sailor,
(Those are pearls that were his eyes. Look!)
Here is Belladonna, the Lady of the Rocks,

The lady of situations.   50
Here is the man with three staves, and here the Wheel,
And here is the one-eyed merchant, and this card,
Which is blank, is something he carries on his back,
Which I am forbidden to see. I do not find
The Hanged Man. Fear death by water.
I see crowds of people, walking round in a ring.
Thank you. If you see dear Mrs. Equitone,
Tell her I bring the horoscope myself:
One must be so careful these days.

Unreal City,   60
Under the brown fog of a winter dawn,
A crowd flowed over London Bridge, so many,
I had not thought death had undone so many.
Sighs, short and infrequent, were exhaled,
And each man fixed his eyes before his feet.
Flowed up the hill and down King William Street,
To where Saint Mary Woolnoth kept the hours
With a dead sound on the final stroke of nine.
There I saw one I knew, and stopped him, crying: 'Stetson!
'You who were with me in the ships at Mylae!   70
'That corpse you planted last year in your garden,
'Has it begun to sprout? Will it bloom this year?
'Or has the sudden frost disturbed its bed?
'Oh keep the Dog far hence, that's friend to men,
'Or with his nails he'll dig it up again!
'You! hypocrite lecteur!—mon semblable,—mon frère!'

II. A GAME OF CHESS

The Chair she sat in, like a burnished throne,
Glowed on the marble, where the glass
Held up by standards wrought with fruited vines
From which a golden Cupidon peeped out   80
(Another hid his eyes behind his wing)
Doubled the flames of seven branched candelabra
Reflecting light upon the table as
The glitter of her jewels rose to meet it,

[593]

From satin cases poured in rich profusion;
In vials of ivory and colored glass
Unstoppered, lurked her strange synthetic perfumes,
Unguent, powdered, or liquid—troubled, confused
And drowned the sense in odors; stirred by the air
That freshened from the window, these ascended   90
In fattening the prolonged candle-flames,
Flung their smoke into the laquearia,
Stirring the pattern on the coffered ceiling.
Huge sea-wood fed with copper
Burned green and orange, framed by the colored stone,
In which sad light a carvèd dolphin swam.
Above the antique mantel was displayed
As though a window gave upon the sylvan scene
The change of Philomel, by the barbarous king
So rudely forced; yet there the nightingale   100
Filled all the desert with inviolable voice
And still she cried, and still the world pursues,
'Jug Jug' to dirty ears.
And other withered stumps of time
Were told upon the walls; staring forms
Leaned out, leaning, hushing the room enclosed.
Footsteps shuffled on the stair.
Under the firelight, under the brush, her hair
Spread out in fiery points
Glowed into words, then would be savagely still.   110

'My nerves are bad tonight. Yes, bad. Stay with me.
'Speak to me. Why do you never speak. Speak.
    'What are you thinking of? What thinking? What?
'I never know what you are thinking. Think.'

I think we are in rats' alley
Where the dead men lost their bones.

'What is that noise?'
              The wind under the door.
'What is that noise now? What is the wind doing?'

                                    'Do
'You know nothing? Do you see nothing? Do you remember
'Nothing?'

            I remember
Those are pearls that were his eyes.

'Are you alive or not? Is there nothing in your head?'
                                                   But
O O O O that Shakespeherian Rag—
It's so elegant
So intelligent   130
'What shall I do now? What shall I do?'
'I shall rush out as I am, and walk the street
'With my hair down, so. What shall we do tomorrow?
'What shall we ever do?'
                        The hot water at ten.
And if it rains, a closed car at four.
And we shall play a game of chess,
Pressing lidless eyes and waiting for a knock upon the door.

When Lil's husband got demobbed, I said—
I didn't mince my words, I said to her myself,   140
HURRY UP PLEASE ITS TIME
Now Albert's coming back, make yourself a bit smart.
He'll want to know what you done with that money he gave you
To get yourself some teeth. He did, I was there.
You have them all out, Lil, and get a nice set,
He said, I swear, I can't bear to look at you.
And no more can't I, I said, and think of poor Albert,
He's been in the army four years, he wants a good time,
And if you don't give it him, there's others will, I said.
Oh is there, she said. Something o'that, I said.   150
Then I'll know who to thank, she said, and give me a straight look.
HURRY UP PLEASE ITS TIME
If you don't like it you can get on with it, I said.
Others can pick and choose if you can't.

But if Albert makes off, it won't be for lack of telling.
You ought to be ashamed, I said, to look so antique.
(And her only thirty-one.)
I can't help it, she said, pulling a long face,
It's them pills I took, to bring it off, she said.
(She's had five already, and nearly died of young George.)   160
The chemist said it would be all right, but I've never been the same.
You *are* a proper fool, I said.
Well, if Albert won't leave you alone, there it is, I said,
What you get married for if you don't want children?
HURRY UP PLEASE ITS TIME
Well, that Sunday Albert was home, they had a hot gammon,
And they asked me in to dinner, to get the beauty of it hot—
HURRY UP PLEASE ITS TIME
HURRY UP PLEASE ITS TIME
Goonight Bill. Goonight Lou. Goonight May. Goonight.   170
Ta ta. Goonight. Goonight.
Good night, ladies, good night, sweet ladies, good night, good night.

III. THE FIRE SERMON

The river's tent is broken: the last fingers of leaf
Clutch and sink into the wet bank. The wind
Crosses the brown land, unheard. The nymphs are departed.
Sweet Thames, run softly, till I end my song.
The river bears no empty bottles, sandwich papers,
Silk handkerchiefs, cardboard boxes, cigarette ends
Or other testimony of summer nights. The nymphs are departed.
And their friends, the loitering heirs of city directors;   180
Departed, have left no addresses.
By the waters of Leman I sat down and wept . . .
Sweet Thames, run softly till I end my song,
Sweet Thames, run softly, for I speak not loud or long.
But at my back in a cold blast I hear
The rattle of the bones, and chuckle spread from ear to ear.
A rat crept softly through the vegetation
Dragging its slimy belly on the bank
While I was fishing in the dull canal
On a winter evening round behind the gashouse   190

[596]

Musing upon the king my brother's wreck
And on the king my father's death before him.
White bodies naked on the low damp ground
And bones cast in a little low dry garret,
Rattled by the rat's foot only, year to year.
But at my back from time to time I hear
The sound of horns and motors, which shall bring
Sweeney to Mrs. Porter in the spring.
O the moon shone bright on Mrs. Porter
And on her daughter   200
They wash their feet in soda water
Et O ces voix d'enfants, chantant dans la coupole!

Twit twit twit
Jug jug jug jug jug jug
So rudely forc'd.
Tereu

Unreal City
Under the brown fog of a winter noon
Mr. Eugenides, the Smyrna merchant
Unshaven, with a pocket full of currants   210
C. i. f. London: documents at sight,
Asked me in demotic French
To luncheon at the Cannon Street Hotel
Followed by a weekend at the Metropole.
At the violet hour, when the eyes and back
Turn upward from the desk, when the human engine waits
Like a taxi throbbing waiting,
I Tiresias, though blind, throbbing between two lives,
Old man with wrinkled female breasts, can see
At the violet hour, the evening hour that strives   220
Homeward, and brings the sailor home from the sea,
The typist home at teatime, clears her breakfast, lights
Her stove, and lays out food in tins.
Out of the window perilously spread
Her drying combinations touched by the sun's last rays,
On the divan are piled (at night her bed)

[597]

Stockings, slippers, camisoles, and stays.
I Tiresias, old man with wrinkled dugs
Perceived the scene, and foretold the rest—
I too awaited the expected guest.   230
He, the young man carbuncular, arrives,
A small house agent's clerk, with one bold stare,
One of the low on whom assurance sits
As a silk hat on a Bradford millionaire.
The time is now propitious, as he guesses,
The meal is ended, she is bored and tired,
Endeavors to engage her in caresses
Which still are unreproved, if undesired.
Flushed and decided, he assaults at once;
Exploring hands encounter no defense;   240
His vanity requires no response,
And makes a welcome of indifference.
(And I Tiresias have foresuffered all
Enacted on this same divan or bed;
I who have sat by Thebes below the wall
And walked among the lowest of the dead.)
Bestows one final patronizing kiss,
And gropes his way, finding the stairs unlit . . .

She turns and looks a moment in the glass,
Hardly aware of her departed lover;   250
Her brain allows one half-formed thought to pass:
'Well now that's done: and I'm glad it's over.'
When lovely woman stoops to folly and
Paces about her room again, alone,
She smooths her hair with automatic hand,
And puts a record on the gramophone.

'This music crept by me upon the waters'
And along the Strand, up Queen Victoria Street.
O City city, I can sometimes hear
Beside a public bar in Lower Thames Street,   260
The pleasant whining of a mandolin
And a clatter and a chatter from within

Where fishmen lounge at noon: where the walls
Of Magnus Martyr hold
Inexplicable splendor of Ionian white and gold.

> The river sweats
> Oil and tar
> The barges drift
> With the turning tide
> Red sails   270
> Wide
> To leeward, swing on the heavy spar.
> The barges wash
> Drifting logs
> Down Greenwich reach
> Past the Isle of Dogs.
>> Weialala leia
>> Wallala leialala

> Elizabeth and Leicester
> Beating oars   280
> The stern was formed
> A gilded shell
> Red and gold
> The brisk swell
> Rippled both shores
> Southwest wind
> Carried down stream
> The peal of bells
> White towers
>> Weialala leia   290
>> Wallala leialala

'Trams and dusty trees.
Highbury bore me. Richmond and Kew
Undid me. By Richmond I raised my knees
Supine on the floor of a narrow canoe.'

'My feet are at Moorgate, and my heart
Under my feet. After the event
He wept. He promised "a new start."
I made no comment. What should I resent?'

'On Margate Sands.   300
I can connect
Nothing with nothing
The broken fingernails of dirty hands.
My people humble people who expect
Nothing.'
                    la la

To Carthage then I came
Burning burning burning burning
O Lord Thou pluckest me out
O Lord Thou pluckest   310

    burning

                    IV. DEATH BY WATER
Phlebas the Phoenician, a fortnight dead,
Forgot the cry of gulls, and the deep sea swell
And the profit and loss.
                    A current under sea
Picked his bones in whispers. As he rose and fell
He passed the stages of his age and youth
Entering the whirlpool.
                    Gentile or Jew
O you who turn the wheel and look to windward,   320
Consider Phlebas, who was once handsome and tall as you.

                    V. WHAT THE THUNDER SAID
After the torchlight red on sweaty faces
After the frosty silence in the gardens
After the agony in stony places
The shouting and the crying
Prison and palace and reverberation
Of thunder of spring over distant mountains

He who was living is now dead
We who were living are now dying
With a little patience   330

Here is no water but only rock
Rock and no water and the sandy road
The road winding above among the mountains
Which are mountains of rock without water
If there were water we should stop and drink
Amongst the rock one cannot stop or think
Sweat is dry and feet are in the sand
If there were only water amongst the rock
Dead mountain mouth of carious teeth that cannot spit
Here one can neither stand nor lie nor sit   340
There is not even silence in the mountains
But dry sterile thunder without rain
There is not even solitude in the mountains
But red sullen faces sneer and snarl
From doors of mudcracked houses
                        If there were water
    And no rock
    If there were rock
    And also water
    And water
    A spring   350
    A pool among the rock
    If there were the sound of water only
    Not the cicada
    And dry grass singing
    But sound of water over a rock
    Where the hermit-thrush sings in the pine trees
    Drip drop drip drop drop drop drop
    But there is no water

Who is the third who walks always beside you?
When I count, there are only you and I together   360
But when I look ahead up the white road
There is always another one walking beside you

Gliding wrapped in a brown mantle, hooded
I do not know whether a man or a woman
—But who is that on the other side of you?

What is that sound high in the air
Murmur of maternal lamentation
Who are those hooded hordes swarming
Over endless plains, stumbling in cracked earth
Ringed by the flat horizon only   370
What is the city over the mountains
Cracks and reforms and bursts in the violet air
Falling towers
Jerusalem Athens Alexandria
Vienna London
Unreal

A woman drew her long black hair out tight
And fiddled whisper music on those strings
And bats with baby faces in the violet light
Whistled, and beat their wings   380
And crawled head downward down a blackened wall
And upside down in air were towers
Tolling reminiscent bells, that kept the hours
And voices singing out of empty cisterns and exhausted wells.

In this decayed hole among the mountains
In the faint moonlight, the grass is singing
Over the tumbled graves, about the chapel
There is the empty chapel, only the wind's home.
It has no windows, and the door swings,
Dry bones can harm no one.   390
Only a cock stood on the rooftree
Co co rico co co rico
In a flash of lightning. Then a damp gust
Bringing rain

Ganga was sunken, and the limp leaves
Waited for rain, while the black clouds
Gathered far distant, over Himavant.
The jungle crouched, humped in silence.

Then spoke the thunder
DA   400
Datta: what have we given?
My friend, blood shaking my heart
The awful daring of a moment's surrender
Which an age of prudence can never retract
By this, and this only, we have existed
Which is not to be found in our obituaries
Or in memories draped by the beneficent spider
Or under seals broken by the lean solicitor
In our empty rooms
DA   410
Dayadhvam: I have heard the key
Turn in the door once and turn once only
We think of the key, each in his prison
Thinking of the key, each confirms a prison
Only at nightfall, ethereal rumors
Revive for a moment a broken Coriolanus
DA
Damyata: The boat responded
Gaily, to the hand expert with sail and oar
The sea was calm, your heart would have responded   420
Gaily, when invited, beating obedient
To controlling hands

                             I sat upon the shore
Fishing, with the arid plain behind me
Shall I at least set my lands in order?
London Bridge is falling down falling down falling down
Poi s'ascose nel fico che gli affina
Quando fiam uti chelidon—O swallow swallow
Le Prince d'Aquitaine à la tour abolie
These fragments I have shored against my ruins   430
Why then Ile fit you. Hieronymo's mad againe.
Datta. Dayadhvam. Damyata.
         Shantih shantih shantih

(1833)

PART THE FIRST.

I

On either side the river lie
Long fields of barley and of rye,
That clothe the wold, and meet the sky.
And thro' the field the road runs by
  To manytowered Camelot.
The yellowleavèd waterlily,
The greensheathèd daffodilly,
Tremble in the water chilly,
  Round about Shalott.

2

Willows whiten, aspens shiver,   10
The sunbeam-showers break and quiver
In the stream that runneth ever
By the island in the river,
  Flowing down to Camelot.
Four gray walls and four gray towers
Overlook a space of flowers,
And the silent isle imbowers
  The Lady of Shalott.

The Lady of Shalott
(1842)

PART I

I

On either side the river lie
Long fields of barley and of rye,
That clothe the wold and meet the sky;
And through the field the road runs by
     To many-towered Camelot;
And up and down the people go,
Gazing where the lilies blow
Round an island there below,
     The island of Shalott.

2

Willows whiten, aspens quiver,   10
Little breezes dusk and shiver
Through the wave that runs forever
By the island in the river
     Flowing down to Camelot.
Four gray walls, and four gray towers,
Overlook a space of flowers,
And the silent isle embowers
     The Lady of Shalott.

Underneath the bearded barley,
The reaper, reaping late and early,   20
Hears her ever chanting cheerly,
Like an angel, singing clearly,
  O'er the stream of Camelot.
Piling the sheaves in furrows airy,
Beneath the moon, the reaper weary
Listening whispers, ' 'tis the fairy
  Lady of Shalott.'

4

The little isle is all inrailed
With a rose-fence, and overtrailed
With roses: by the marge unhailed   30
The shallop flitteth silkensailed,
  Skimming down to Camelot.
A pearlgarland winds her head:
She leaneth on a velvet bed,
Full royally apparellèd,
  The Lady of Shalott.

PART THE SECOND.

I

No time hath she to sport and play:
A charmèd web she weaves alway.
A curse is on her, if she stay
Her weaving, either night or day,   40
  To look down to Camelot.
She knows not what the curse may be;
Therefore she weaveth steadily,
Therefore no other care hath she,
  The Lady of Shalott.

3

By the margin, willow-veiled,
Slide the heavy barges trailed   20
By slow horses; and unhailed
The shallop flitteth silken-sailed
    Skimming down to Camelot:
But who hath seen her wave her hand?
Or at the casement seen her stand?
Or is she known in all the land,
    The Lady of Shalott?

4

Only reapers, reaping early
In among the bearded barley,
Hear a song that echoes cheerly   30
From the river winding clearly,
    Down to towered Camelot;
And by the moon the reaper weary,
Piling sheaves in uplands airy,
Listening, whispers, ' 'Tis the fairy
    Lady of Shalott.'

PART 2

I

There she weaves by night and day
A magic web with colors gay.
She has heard a whisper say,
A curse is on her if she stay   40
    To look down to Camelot.
She knows not what the curse may be,
And so she weaveth steadily,
And little other care hath she,
    The Lady of Shalott.

She lives with little joy or fear.
Over the water, running near,
The sheepbell tinkles in her ear.
Before her hangs a mirror clear,
    Reflecting towered Camelot.   50
And, as the mazy web she whirls,
She sees the surly village-churls,
And the red cloaks of market-girls,
    Pass onward from Shalott.

3

Sometimes a troop of damsels glad,
An abbot on an ambling pad,
Sometimes a curly shepherd lad,
Or longhaired page, in crimson clad,
    Goes by to towered Camelot.
And sometimes thro' the mirror blue,   60
The knights come riding, two and two.
She hath no loyal knight and true,
    The Lady of Shalott.

4

But in her web she still delights
To weave the mirror's magic sights:
For often thro' the silent nights
A funeral, with plumes and lights
    And music, came from Camelot.
Or, when the moon was overhead,
Came two young lovers, lately wed: 70
'I am half-sick of shadows,' said
    The Lady of Shalott.

And moving through a mirror clear
That hangs before her all the year,
Shadows of the world appear.
There she sees the highway near
      Winding down to Camelot;   50
There the river eddy whirls,
And there the surly village-churls,
And the red cloaks of market girls,
      Pass onward from Shalott.

3

Sometimes a troop of damsels glad,
An abbot on an ambling pad,
Sometimes a curly shepherd-lad,
Or long-haired page in crimson clad,
      Goes by to towered Camelot;
And sometimes through the mirror blue   60
The knights come riding two and two;
She hath no loyal knight and true,
      The Lady of Shalott.

4

But in her web she still delights
To weave the mirror's magic sights,
For often through the silent nights
A funeral, with plumes and lights
      And music, went to Camelot;
Or when the moon was overhead,
Came two young lovers lately wed;   70
'I am half sick of shadows,' said
      The Lady of Shalott.

I

A bowshot from her bower-eaves.
He rode between the barleysheaves:
The sun came dazzling thro' the leaves,
And flamed upon the brazen greaves
  Of bold Sir Launcelot.
A redcross knight for ever kneeled
To a lady in his shield,
That sparkled on the yellow field,   80
  Beside remote Shalott.

2

The gemmy bridle glittered free,
Like to some branch of stars we see
Hung in the golden galaxy.
The bridle-bells rang merrily,
  As he rode down from Camelot.
And, from his blazoned baldric slung,
A mighty silver bugle hung,
And, as he rode, his armour rung,
  Beside remote Shalott.   90

3

All in the blue unclouded weather,
Thickjewelled shone the saddle-leather.
The helmet, and the helmet-feather
Burned like one burning flame together,
  As he rode down from Camelot.
As often thro' the purple night,
Below the starry clusters bright,
Some bearded meteor, trailing light,
  Moves over green Shalott.

I

A bow-shot from her bower-eaves,
He rode between the barley-sheaves;
The sun came dazzling through the leaves,
And flamed upon the brazen greaves
     Of bold Sir Lancelot.
A red-cross knight forever kneeled
To a lady in his shield,
That sparkled on the yellow field,   80
     Beside remote Shalott.

2

The gemmy bridle glittered free,
Like to some branch of stars we see
Hung in the golden Galaxy.
The bridle bells rang merrily
     As he rode down to Camelot;
And from his blazoned baldric slung
A mighty silver bugle hung,
And as he rode his armor rung,
     Beside remote Shalott.   90

3

All in the blue unclouded weather
Thick-jewelled shone the saddle-leather,
The helmet and the helmet-feather
Burned like one burning flame together
     As he rode down to Camelot;
As often through the purple night,
Below the starry clusters bright,
Some bearded meteor, trailing light,
     Moves over still Shalott.

His broad clear brow in sunlight glowed. 100
On burnished hooves his warhorse trode.
From underneath his helmet flowed
His coalblack curls, as on he rode,
  As he rode down from Camelot.
From the bank, and from the river,
He flashed into the crystal mirror,
'Tirra lirra, tirra lirra,'
  Sang Sir Launcelot.

5

She left the web: she left the loom:
She made three paces thro' the room: 110
She saw the waterflower bloom:
She saw the helmet and the plume:
  She looked down to Camelot.
Out flew the web, and floated wide,
The mirror cracked from side to side,
'The curse is come upon me,' cried
  The Lady of Shalott.

PART THE FOURTH.

I

In the stormy eastwind straining
The pale-yellow woods were waning,
The broad stream in his banks complaining, 120
Heavily the low sky raining
  Over towered Camelot:
Outside the isle a shallow boat
Beneath a willow lay afloat,
Below the carven stern she wrote,
  THE LADY OF SHALOTT.

His broad clear brow in sunlight glowed;   100
On burnished hooves his war-horse trode;
From underneath his helmet flowed
His coal-black curls as on he rode,
  As he rode down to Camelot.
From the bank and from the river
He flashed into the crystal mirror,
'Tirra lirra,' by the river
  Sang Sir Lancelot.

5

She left the web, she left the loom,
She made three paces through the room,   110
She saw the water-lily bloom,
She saw the helmet and the plume,
  She looked down to Camelot.
Out flew the web and floated wide;
The mirror cracked from side to side;
'The curse is come upon me,' cried
  The Lady of Shalott.

PART 4

I

In the stormy east-wind straining,
The pale yellow woods were waning,
The broad stream in his banks complaining,   120
Heavily the low sky raining
  Over towered Camelot;
Down she came and found a boat
Beneath a willow left afloat,
And round about the prow she wrote
  The Lady of Shalott.

A cloudwhite crown of pearl she dight.
All raimented in snowy white
That loosely flew, (her zone in sight,
Clasped with one blinding diamond bright,)   130
    Her wide eyes fixed on Camelot,
Though the squally eastwind keenly
Blew, with folded arms serenely
By the water stood the queenly
    Lady of Shalott.

3

With a steady, stony glance—
Like some bold seer in a trance,
Beholding all his own mischance,
Mute, with a glassy countenance—
    She looked down to Camelot.   140
It was the closing of the day,
She loosed the chain, and down she lay,
The broad stream bore her far away,
    The Lady of Shalott.

4

As when to sailors while they roam,
By creeks and outfalls far from home,
Rising and dropping with the foam,
From dying swans wild warblings come,
    Blown shoreward; so to Camelot
Still as the boathead wound along   150
The willowy hills and fields among,
They heard her chanting her deathsong,
    The Lady of Shalott.

And down the river's dim expanse
Like some bold seër in a trance,
Seeing all his own mischance—
With a glassy countenance 130
        Did she look to Camelot.
And at the closing of the day
She loosed the chain, and down she lay;
The broad stream bore her far away,
        The Lady of Shalott.

3

Lying, robed in snowy white
That loosely flew to left and right—
The leaves upon her falling light—
Through the noises of the night
        She floated down to Camelot; 140
And as the boat-head wound along
The willowy hills and fields among,
They heard her singing her last song,
        The Lady of Shalott.

A longdrawn carol, mournful, holy,
She chanted loudly, chanted lowly,
Till her eyes were darkened wholly,
And her smooth face sharpened slowly
  Turned to towered Camelot:
For ere she reached upon the tide
The first house by the waterside,   160
Singing in her song she died,
  The Lady of Shalott.

    6

Under tower and balcony,
By gardenwall and gallery,
A pale, pale corpse she floated by,
Deadcold, between the houses high,
  Dead into towered Camelot.
Knight and burgher, lord and dame,
To the plankèd wharfage came:
Below the stern they read her name,   170
  'The Lady of Shalott.'

    7

They crossed themselves, their stars they blest,
Knight, minstrel, abbot, squire and guest.
There lay a parchment on her breast,
That puzzled more than all the rest,
  The wellfed wits at Camelot.
'*The web was woven curiously*
The charm is broken utterly,
Draw near and fear not—this is I,
  The Lady of Shalott.'   180

4

Heard a carol, mournful, holy,
Chanted loudly, chanted lowly,
Till her blood was frozen slowly,
And her eyes were darkened wholly,
        Turned to towered Camelot.
For ere she reached upon the tide   150
The first house by the water-side,
Singing in her song she died,
        The Lady of Shalott.

5

Under tower and balcony,
By garden-wall and gallery,
A gleaming shape she floated by,
Dead-pale between the houses high,
        Silent into Camelot.
Out upon the wharfs they came,
Knight and burgher, lord and dame,   160
And round the prow they read her name,
        The Lady of Shalott.

6

Who is this? and what is here?
And in the lighted palace near
Died the sound of royal cheer;
And they crossed themselves for fear,
        All the knights at Camelot.
But Lancelot mused a little space;
He said, 'She has a lovely face;
God in his mercy lend her grace,   170
        The Lady of Shalott.'

BY JOHN KEATS

[stanza 24, lines 208–216]

A 1   A Casement ~~ach'd~~ tripple archd and diamonded
  2   With many coloured glass fronted the Moon
                   wereof
  3   In midst ~~of which~~ a shilded scutcheon shed
  4   High blushing gules: ~~upon she kneeled saintly~~ down
  5   And inly prayed for grace and heavenly boon
  6   The blood red gules fell on her silver cross
  7   And ~~her~~ white(est) hands devout

       There was
B 1   A Casement tipple archd and high
  2   All garlanded with carven imageries
  3   Of fruits & ~~trailing~~ flowers and sunny corn
                              ears parchd

C 1   A Casement high and tripple archd there was
  2   All gardneded with carven imageries
  3   Of fruits and flowers and bunches of knot grass;
  4   And diamonded with panes of quaint device
  5   Innumerable of stains and splendid dies
                sunset
       As is the tger moths ~~rich~~ deep ~~damasked~~ wjngs
  6   ~~As is the wing of evening tiger moths;~~
                whereft   thousand
  7   ~~And~~ in ~~the~~ midst 'momg ~~man~~ heraldries
  8   And ~~dim twilight~~ twilight saints and dim emblasonings
  9   A shielded scutcheon blushd with Blood of Queens & Kings

[stanza 25, lines 217–225]

  1   Full on this Casement shone the wintry moon
                warm rich   breast
  2   And threw ~~red~~ gules on Madelines fair ~~face~~
  3   As down she kneel'd for heavens grace and boon
                              fell
       ~~And~~ rose ~~with red~~ bloom on her hang togeth
  4   ~~Tinging her pious~~ hands ~~together~~ prest

5 And ~~on her~~ silver cross soft Amethyst

(on her inserted above)

6 And on her hair a glory like a Saint's

7 Shee seem'd ~~like an immortal agel drest~~
silvery angel newly drest,

8 Save wings, for heaven—~~Porphyro~~ grew faint
(Lionel above Porphyro)

9 She knelt too pure a thing, too free from motal taint

[stanza 26, lines 226–234]

A 1 But soon his heart revives—her prayers said

2 She ~~lays aside her veil~~
pearled
strips her hair of all its ~~wreathed pearl~~

3 ~~Unclasps her bosom jewels~~
~~And twists it in one knot upon her head~~

B 1 But soon his heart revives—her prayers(ing) ~~soon~~ done,

2 Sh(Of) all her(its) wreathed pearl she strips her hair

3 Unclasps her warmed jewels one by one

4 Loosens ~~her boddice from her~~
her bursting
~~her Boddice lace~~ string
~~her Boddice and her bosom bar~~
her

[Here Keats begins a new sheet]

Loosens her fragrant ~~boddice~~ and doth bare

5 Her

26

C 1 ~~But soon~~ his heart revives—her praying done
Anon

2 Of all its wreathéd pearl her hair she ~~strips~~
frees

3 Unclasps her warmed jewels one by one

4 Loosens her fragrant boddice: ~~and down slips~~
by degrees
to her knees

5 Her sweet attire ~~falls light creeps down by~~
creeps rustling to her knees

6 Half hidden like a ~~Syren of the Sea~~
Mermaid in sea weed

7 ~~And more melodious~~ dreaming
She stands awhile in thought, and sees

8 In fancy fair Saint Agnes in her bed

9 But dares not look behind or all the charm is ~~fled~~ dead

[621]

[stanza 27, lines 235–243]

1 ~~Then stepping forth she slips~~
   ~~The charm fled not—she did not look behid;~~ nd
   But (Soon) trembling in her soft and chilly ^nest

2 ~~She ly and had not seen her—~~
   ~~She lay; and as and till the poppied warmth of sleep~~
   /She lay, /in sort of wakeful swoon perplext)

3 Util the poppied warmth of sleep opprest

4 Her soothed Limbs, and Soul fatigued away;

5 Flown like a thought until the morrow day;

6 Blisfully havend both from jory and pain

   Clasped   shut clasped
7 ~~Shut~~ like a ^Missal where swart paynims pray—

8 ~~Dead to~~ Blinded alike from Sunshine and from rain

          ~~close~~ shut
9 As though a rose should ~~shut~~ and be a bud again

[stanza 28, lines 244–252]

1 ~~Her slumrous breathing~~
   ~~The listning Porphyro her breathing heard~~
   ~~And when~~
   ~~The entranced Porphyro stol'n to Paradise~~
   Stol'n to this Paradize and so entrance'd

          Porphyro
2 ~~Porphyro~~ gazed upon her empty dress

3 And listen to her breathing, if it chanc'd

4 To wake into a slumbrous tenderness

5 Which when he heard ~~he breath'd himself~~
                    that minute did he bless

6 And breath'd himself: then from the closet crept

   Silent
   Noiseless   ~~amid~~   in a wild (wide)
7 ~~Silent~~ as Fear, ~~and~~   ?   ~~not with~~ a wildeness

                    hush'd
8 And on (over) the ~~silent~~ carpet ~~hushing~~ silent stept

9 And 'tween the Curtains peep'd, and lo! how fast she slept

[622]

[stanza 29, lines 253–261]

1 Then ~~on~~ by the bed side where the fading Moon

2 Made an illumed twilight soft he set

       and with anguish   spread

3 A Table, ~~light, and stilly threw~~ theron

4 A Cloth of woven crimson gold and jet—

5 O for some drowy morphean amulet:

         festive   ~~Ball~~

6 The boisterous midnight ^Clarions of the ~~feast~~

7 ~~Sounded though faint and far away~~

  ~~Came Sound in his ears~~

  And kettle drums and far heard clarinet

8 ~~Reach'd his scar'd ears~~

            in

  Affray'd his ears though but ~~with~~ faintest tones:

                                is

9 The Hall door shuts again and all the noise was(is) gone;

[stanza 30, lines 262–270]

  ~~But~~

1 ~~And still she slept:~~

  And still she slept an azure-lidded sleep

2 In blanched linen smooth and lavender'd;

3 While he from frorth the closet brought a heap

       ~~fruits~~

4 Of candied ~~sweets~~ ~~sweets with~~ and plumb and gourd

      apple   Quince

                creamed

5 With jellies soother than the ~~dairy~~ curd

         'tinct

6 And lucent syrups ~~smooth~~ with crannamon

7 ~~And sugar'd dates from that o'er Euphrates fard~~

       ~~in Brigantine transferred~~

               ~~transferred~~

  Manna and daites in Bragine ~~wild transferrd~~

         ~~and Manna~~

7a ~~And Manna wild and~~| ~~Bragantine~~

                ~~sugar'd~~ dates transferrd

  argosy [in left margin]

8 ~~In Brigantine from Fez~~

  From fez—and spiced danties every one

     ~~glutted~~

9 From ~~wealthy~~ Sarmarchand to cedard lebanon

    silken

[623]

BY STEPHEN SPENDER

[Draft A]

1   After the first powerful plain manifesto,

               black
2   The ~~clear~~ statement of pistons, without more fuss

3   But gliding like a queen   ~~-?-~~   she leaves the station:

4   Without bowing and with restrained unconcern

           passes   which
5   She ~~notices~~ the houses humbly crowd~~ing~~ outside

6   And then the gasworks and at last the ~~printed~~ psalm

           printed
7   Of death ~~written~~ by gravestones in the cemetery.

8   Beyond the town lies the open country

9   Where, gathering speed, she acquires mystery   [ocean.

10   ~~Like~~ t[T]he luminous self-possession ~~possession~~ of ships on

          now
11   It is ~~then~~ she begins to sing—at first low

12   And then loud and at last with mad joy—

13   The ~~strange~~ song of her whistle screaming round corners,

14   ~~And~~ o[O]f drums in tunnels, ~~and~~ of her innumerable bolts,

15   ~~And~~ a [A] swaying melody of tearing speed:

16   And always light, ariel, under~~neath~~ this

17   Is the tapping metre of her wheels.

18   We travel further than Edinburgh or Rome

                                wild
19   ~~For we~~ r[R]each[ing] new eras of ~~insane~~ happiness

20   When night falls

                        Explore new areas of happiness   }
                             "   "   eras of wild happiness }

[*The Express*]

[Draft B]

1 After the first powerful plain manifesto
2 The black statement of pistons, without more fuss
3 But gliding like a queen she leaves the station.
4 Without bowing and with restrained unconcern
5 She passes the houses which humbly crowd outside,
6 The gasworks, and at last the heavy page
7 Of death printed by gravestones in the cemetery.
8 Beyond the town there lies the open country
9 Where, gathering speed, she acquires mystery,
10 The luminous self-possession of ships on ocean.
11 It is now she begins to sing—at first quite low
12 And then loud and at last with ~~mad joy~~ a jazzy madness
13 The song of her whistle screaming ~~round~~ at corners
14 Of tunnels, of brakes, of innumerable bolts:
15 ~~The swaying melody of tearing speed:~~
16 And always light, aeriel ~~under this~~ underneath
17 Is the tapping metre of her wheels.
18 ~~Travellers go~~ Her passengers —(further than Edinburgh or Rome,)—
19 ~~Plunging[e]~~ Explore new ~~areas~~ eras are of ~~wild~~ wild happiness
20 At night when ~~flapping screens of~~ the dark gusts knock the glass
21 ~~Knock on the glass,~~ and only the low stream-line brightness
22 Of moonlight on the waving hills ~~relieves~~ is white.

[625]

[Draft C]

1   After the first powerful plain manifestoe

2   The black statement of pistons, without more fuss

3   But gliding like a queen, she leaves the station.

4   Without bowing and with restrained unconcern

5   She passes the houses which humbly crowd outside,

6   The gas-works, and at last the heavy page
    ~~And~~

7   Of death printed by gravestones in the cemetery.

8   Beyond the town there lies the open country

9   Where, gathering speed, she acquires mystery,

10   The luminous self-possession of ships on ocean.

11   It is now she begins to sing—at first quite low,

12   ~~And~~ Then loud, and at last with a jazzy madness—

13   The song of her whistle screaming at corners

14   Of ~~blindi~~ deafening tunnels, brakes, innumerable bolts;

15   And always light, aeriel, underneath

16   Is [Goes] the ~~tapping~~ ^{raving} metre of her wheels.

17   Her passengers (further than Edinburgh or Rome)

18   Explore new eras of wild happiness

19   At night when dark flags ~~touch the glass~~ knock the glass

20   And only the low stream-line brightness

21   Of moonlight on the tossing hills is white.

22   ~~Entranced~~ ^{Rapt in what} by a symphony [ies] they dream

23   Of ~~gleaming~~ ^{tapping} metals, and ~~sharp~~ strange shapes entrance

24   Them in their rigid ~~folds.~~ ^{lines} Nor bird song, no nor bough

25   Breaking with honeyed buds, nor dreams of India

26   And ~~tracing~~ ^{hunting} through thick leaves the ~~rare p~~ ^{jeweled} jeweled tiger,

27   So rules with stamped and iron image   ~~Can build~~

28   The strange world where they turn, as this

29   Of jetting steam and rods . . .   She stops

30   Ruled round with iron lines

31   They watch the images of power that stamp their brain

32   Impressed by thunder of waters & tearing steam

33   And roar of furnace[s] that mould natures.

[*The Express*]

[Draft D]

1 After the first powerful plain manifestoe
2 The black statement of pistons, without more fuss
3 But gliding like a queen, she leaves the station.
4 Without bowing and with restrained unconcern
5 She passes the houses which humbly crowd outside,
6 The gasworks and at last the heavy page
7 Of death printed by gravestones in the cemetery.
8 Beyond the town there lies the open country
9 Where, gathering speed, she acquires mystery,
10 The luminous self-possession of ships ~~at~~ on ocean.
11 It is now she begins to sing—at first quite low
12 Then loud and at last with a jazzy madness—
13 The song of her whistle screaming at corners,
14 Of deafening tunnels, brakes, innumerable bolts:
15 And always light, aeriel, underneath
              elate
16 Goes the ~~raving~~ metre of her wheels.
17 Her passengers, (further than Edinburgh or Rome),
18 Explore new eras of wild happiness
19 At night when dark flags knock the glass
20 And only the low stream-line brightness
21 Of moonlight on the tossing hills is white
22 T[t]hey are wrapt in music no bird song nor bough
  ~~oh,~~
23 **Breaking** with honey buds, nor tale from India
24 ~~Of~~ h[H]unting through dripping boughs the precious tiger,—
     Can build   iron
25 ~~Creates.~~   ~~They are~~ r[R]uled round with   lines
                                builds
26 ~~And stamped with~~ ? imagery ~~which makes~~ new ~~worlds:~~
27 ~~This strange new world~~
28 And strange new forms of rods and jets of steam
29 Stamp on their brains an image of new worlds   ~~[by steam~~
30 ~~Their brains are stamped pressed on by with forms poured on~~
31 The images of power stamp their brain
  They watch
32 ~~And of works whose fires~~
33 ~~And of metals moulten to create new works worlds~~
34 And hear

[627]

[*The Express*]

[Draft E]

1   After the first powerful plain manifesto,

2   The black statement of pistons, without more fuss

3   But gliding like a queen she leaves the station.

4   Without bowing and with restrained unconcern

5   She passes the houses which humbly crowd outside,

6   The gasworks, and at last the heavy page

7   Of death printed by gravestones in the cemetery.

8   Beyond the town there lies the open country

9   Where, gathering speed, she acquires mystery

10   The luminous self-possession of ships on ocean.

11   It is now she begins to sing—at first quite low

12   Then loud, and at last with a jazzy madness—

13   The song of her whistle screaming at corners,

14   Of deafening tunnels, brakes, innumerable bolts.

15   And always light, aeriel underneath

16   Goes the elate metre of her wheels.

17   Steaming through ~~shining~~ [metal] landscape on her ~~shining metals~~ [line,

18   She plunges new eras of wild happiness

19   Where speed ~~evokes new~~ [throws up] shapes, ~~vast~~ [strange broad] ~~clean~~ curves

20   And parallels ~~with their air as clean as guns~~ [~~like white bursts from~~ clean like steel of guns]

21   At last, further than Edinburgh or Rome,

22   She reaches night beyond the crest of the world

23   Where only ~~the~~ a low stream-line brightness

24   ~~Like~~ Of phosphorus on the hills is white.

25   ~~Her passengers are rapt in~~

26   Like a comet with flame she moves ~~with music~~ entranced

27   Rapt with her music no bird song nor bough

28   Breaking with honey bud shall ever equal.

[*The Express*]

[Draft F]

1   After the first powerful plain manifesto
2   The black statement of pistons, without more fuss
3   But gliding like a queen she leaves the station.
4   Without bowing and with restrained unconcern
5   She passes the houses which humbly crowd outside,
6   The gasworks, and at last the heavy page
7   Of death printed by gravestones in the cemetery.
8   Beyond the town there lies the open country
9   Where, gathering speed, she acquires mystery,
10   The luminous self-possession of ships on ~~ocean~~ ocean.
11   It is now she begins to sing—at first quite low
12   Then loud, and at last with a jazzy madness—
13   The song of her whistle screaming at corners,
14   Of deafening tunnels, brakes, innumerable ~~wh~~ bolts.
15   And always light, aeriel, underneath
16   Goes the elate metre of her wheels.
17   Steaming through metal landscape on her lines
18   She plunges new eras of wild happiness
19   Her speed throws up strange shapes, broad curves
20   And parallels clean like the steel of guns.
21   At last, further than Edinburgh or Rome
22   ~~She reaches night~~
23   Beyond the crest of the world, she reaches night
24   Where only a low stream-line brightness
25   Of phosphorus on the tossing hills is white.
26   Ah, like a comet through flame, she moves entranced
27   Wrapped in her music no bird song, no, nor bough
28   Breaking with honey buds shall ever equal.

THE MANUSCRIPT OF
'Where do They come from?'

BY W. H. AUDEN

[1]

1   Where do they come from ~~the terrible~~ ^{whom we so much} ~~those terrible presences~~ we dread

2   ~~That suddenly ?(On) ?(In) ?(our) dearest familiar locations~~

3   ~~That Over our dearest locations they cast~~ *In   In   On our dearest locations falls the chill*

4   ~~That endanger our dearest locations~~

5   ~~A chilling crooked wing~~

6   Of their crooked wing and endangers

7   The ~~loving~~ melting friend, the acqueduct, the flower.

[2]

1   Terrible presences that the ponds reflect

2   ~~Back~~ At(To) the married and ~~strong,~~ ^{well-born} and when the boy ^{fair}

3   Bites eagerly ~~upon~~ into the shining ~~apple~~

4   Apple, emerge in their shocking fury

[3]

1   ~~And we realize that~~

2   And we realize the woods ~~to be~~ are deaf and the sky

3   Nurses no one and we are awake and these,

4   Like ~~captains~~ farmers have purpose and knowledge

5   ~~But on to us their hate is directed~~ ^{Of what we had failed}

6   But upon us their hate is directed

[4]

1   We are the barren ~~earth fields~~ pastures, to which they bring

2   The instincts of ~~auto~~ outcasts, ~~they attack us~~ ^{on ? ? work} ?

3   ~~In despair? ?, weary,~~

[6]

Our money sang like streams on

1   The aloof peaks ~~of our tr tho~~

      ~~high~~   on   them   ~~them~~ like young

2   Of our thinking beckoned ~~them~~ on like girls

3   Our culture like a West of wonder

4   ~~The Whereof Our culture like a sunset~~

         promise

5   Shone a solemn ~~answer~~ in their faces

6   Of our thinking that beckons them on like girls

[5]

1   ~~We called~~ O we conjured them here like a lying map

        extravagant

2   Desiring the joy of ~~j~~ life

       lured them   [chards

3   We ~~enticed them hither here~~ with a mirage of or-

      fat(Fat)

    fruit grown ~~big~~ in the lazy climate of refuge

4   Of ~~refuge, orchards~~

[7]

1   We expected the beautiful and the wise

   Ready   ~~Able~~ to   see

2   ~~Like ?~~ ~~laugh~~ ~~find~~ a charm in the childish fib

      Quite glad   and ~~able~~

3   ~~Quite pleased~~ to find nothing but rock, ~~and~~

     ?(Able)   ?   ~~day~~ to

4   ~~Able in~~ a ~~day~~ to create a garden

[8]

1   But   Those who came were not even children with

2   The ~~round-eyed in~~ large indiscriminate eyes we had lost

3   ~~And The anarchists abandon of movement~~

           spaces

4   Occupying our narrow ~~places~~

       vivid

5   With their anarchist abandon ~~of movement~~

1 ~~In boroughs of hunger they had learnt~~
       ~~restrained~~   from the lands

2 ~~They arrive, already~~ adroit, ~~from the lands~~
       adroit

                      ~~forgotten boroughs~~

3 ~~Of restraint~~ Policed by restraint, Boroughs of hunger ~~where~~
                        acquired
                  they had ~~learnt~~ restraint

4   ~~In the boroughs of failure, knowledge~~

5   ~~How to accept the~~

6 ~~They had already~~ acquired ~~restraint.~~

7 They arrive already adroit, having learnt

8 Restraint in the boroughs of a father's rage

     island
     ~~coast~~   sorrow

9 In the ~~valleys~~ of a mothers ~~sorrow~~ ~~weeping~~

10 They Discovered the meaning of ~~knowledge~~ knowing.

    ~~For years~~   long

1 ~~These pioneers~~ ~~long ago~~ these pioneers have adapted themselves
                        come

2 To the night and the nightmare. They ~~came~~ equipped

3 To meet any terror with terror

                least
         can unmask the ~~slightest~~ deception

4 ~~They~~ have (Their) lies ~~to unmask~~

1 ~~Coarse clumsy bridgegroom~~   ~~and the bed~~ and we
         ?   ?   ?   ?

2 Are ready   ?   Yet all our ~~soft~~ whiteness shrinks
                hairy and clumsy

3 Flinches From these ~~coarse and~~ clumsy bridgegrooms

4 It is our hour of marriage nevertheless.   [shrinks

5 These(The) beds are(is) ready, though all ~~wh~~ our whiteness

6 From these(the) hairy and clumsy bridgegroom

7 ~~As approaches~~ the moment of conception approaches

[12]

1. ~~For all must wish fruition, ?~~ ~~?~~ ~~?~~ ~~?~~ ~~?~~
2. ~~In a few A blessing ? a punishment~~
   barren
3. For the ~~bar sterile~~ must wish to bear, though ~~it dread~~ the spring
4. ~~The anguish of spring, and the crooked must wish~~
5. ~~To be straight~~
   a   that dreads to be straight
6. Punishes, ~~and the crooked wish to be straight though~~ it dreads
   prayer but
7. Cannot alter its ~~wish, and~~ summons
   Out of the dark
8. ~~To come a horrib ?~~ (a) horrible rector

[13]

1. ~~For we can not~~ win in trials of body with ease
2. ~~Only And the striped and vigorous tiger moves~~
3. ~~Until~~ O the striped and vigorous tiger can move
4. In the world of body as an ape in style
   parish
5. The ape is at home in the ~~parish~~
6. ~~Of lust and eating at last, but we were never~~
7. Of grimacing and licking, but ~~never we have~~ we ~~were~~ are

[14]

Our hot tears
1. ~~Never completed our lives~~ ~~Our cities~~
   ~~We await~~
2. Not their indifferent pupils. ~~We are weak~~
3. ~~In spite of our cities.~~
4. ~~More than we hope with our cities. Our And our tears~~
   ~~express~~ promise
5. Even for other nations. We ~~promise~~ more
   ~~towns~~ armies
6. Than we hope with our ~~cities~~
   ~~The~~ Failures as pupils
   ~~swift~~   Our tears well ~~up~~ from a love
7. ~~Not~~ their ~~indifferent~~ pupils. ~~Our wretched tears~~
8. ~~Even for other nations. We promise more~~ Our tears
   our
9. ~~Than we hope with our tears, and armies~~
   ~~different~~ bitter wrong
10. ~~And~~ For a ~~different other nations.~~ Our cities predict
11. More than we hope. Even our armies
    Only
12. ~~Have to~~ express our need of forgiveness
13. We are never outg

[633]

PART IX

NOTES

NOTES

The purpose of each of the explanatory and critical notes is to help the reader to come to a more complete comprehension of the poem, *after* he has read the poem *as a poem*—that is, in the plain text. A perfect reader needs no notes; others may find them useful tools with which to work. The reader should assume that, without assistance, he can comprehend most of the poems in this book; if he encounters, at first reading, some words or references that he does not know, he had best take them in his stride, without feeling disturbed by a momentary blankness, and move on into the poem. Frequently the blank space is not so blank if taken in its context. Later the reader may turn to the dictionary or to these notes for help—and then return to the poem. These notes give a minimum of information. They are more extensive in critical annotations on many poems. These critical observations are intended to be useful and not necessarily authoritative; perhaps many of them will be most useful when they stimulate readers to disagree. Sometimes help is offered the reader in the form of questions. On many poems, no help is offered; the reader should feel complimented. It is assumed that he has read the essay in Part X.

At the beginning of the note on each poem, the name of the author and the date of first book publication are given. When a number of poems in a series are printed in sequence (as *Shakespeare's Sonnets*), this information is given only at the beginning of the sequence.

I

LYRIC POEMS

The poems in Part I have been arranged in several groups, usually to bring together a number of poems on the same 'subject.' The purpose, however, is not to indicate that the poems are alike, but, on the contrary, to enable the reader to discover that the 'subject' is a very poor indication of what the *poem* is. The same 'subject' will produce in ten poets (or in the same poet) ten different responses, each expressed in a unique poem. Comparison of two similar experiences is useful if the reader comes to comprehend more clearly the qualities in each experience which make it itself.

[Poem 1]

GROUP ONE

1–22. These poems are on the 'subject' of death. The notes suggest a few comparisons of poems that may help the reader to a more complete comprehension of each poem. An alert reader will discover other useful comparisons.

1, Christina Rossetti, *Rest*, 1849. The experience of this poem is centered in an intense feeling of the blessed rest of death, the death of a woman. Her life had been harsh, so that death is a relief. But the poet is aware of the harshness of her life only as something put aside, and her death seems less a relief from pain than an entrance into a positive happiness. The dominant feeling in the experience is an intense and serious joy. We may suppose that the poet perhaps began with a feeling of relief, a negative emotion; but, if so, the feeling has changed until now it is a positive emotion of joy, with undertones of relief. The poet assumes that the dead woman feels this same joy: he is both contemplating the woman's happiness and also sharing in it. And here is the crucial point of the experience: how can one feel a positive joy in the absolute rest of the grave—absolute rest, the absence of anything, nothingness, a void, a vacuum—where no experience exists? The *logical* answer is that no positive feeling can exist in nothingness. But the poet *does* feel. How is this possible? Since feeling cannot exist in a world of nothingness, it attaches itself to things in the world of something. The act is a logical contradiction, a paradox; it is possible only because feeling can make 'things' *mean* whatever we *want* them to mean. Things in themselves have no meaning for us; we create their meaning. Here the poet's feeling forces *things* to mean what *no-thing* means. And, even further, the poet's feeling forces *no-things* to mean what *things* mean. The experience has an essential quality of paradox in it, and the statements used to express and communicate the experience involve paradoxical meanings.

The poem begins (ll. 1–4) by reversing the feeling of revulsion that we ordinarily have toward the sensation of earth pressing on the eyes and body of a buried woman; the pressure of the earth is realized fully and insisted on: *lie heavily, lie close, leave no room*. The dominant feeling then reverses the meaning of laughter in the living world and rejects it, as it rejects the *sound of sighs*, for there is room for nothing under the heavy earth. In ll. 6–7 the feeling uses the paradoxical image of a curtain of *dearth* shielding her now from pain. From this point on, the experience ignores her life and centers the feeling on the no-things of the grave, *stillness, darkness, silence*, whose meanings are given through self-contradictory statements. And in ll. 12–14 the dominant feeling forces its meaning on a whole set of contradictions. Eternity will have a morning, her rest did not begin, her rest is eternal (*shall not begin nor end, but be*) and will end when she wakes, at the beginning of Eternity. These lines communicate the meaning by pushing the method to an extreme, and are perhaps not wholly successful. The feeling here is based on a sense of happy

[638]

[Poem 2]

rest infinitely long, and all of the statements have this meaning. There seems
to be an implied image here, that of a person's sound sleep during the night
until morning; the most satisfying sleep seems, when we wake, to have been
the shortest. Since Eternity cannot begin, she will lie forever in a rest so satisfying that, *if* she woke on some impossibly distant morning, she would think
her sleep had been short.

But to some readers these last three lines may have other meanings. Consider these comments and conclusions: 'She will sleep until she wakes in
Heaven. If this is true, why does the poet think the nothingness of the grave
a greater happiness than the joys of Heaven? Besides, doesn't the soul go to
Heaven immediately after death?' Another comment: '*The morning of Eternity* is the Judgment Day; *when she wakes* means her body will be resurrected.
Since I don't believe in the resurrection of the body, I cannot follow the poet
here, and the poem breaks down.'

Consider this comment on l. 11: 'Since she is dead, of course her heart has
stopped. We don't need to be told what we already know.' Is the purpose of
this line to give us information? What is the full meaning of *very*? of *stir*?

Read ll. 1–2 aloud and listen to the rhythms and qualities of sound. Do
they support the sense and feeling? In the phrase *heavily upon her*, there is no
decided stress on any one of the last five syllables. In l. 2, listen to the
stresses in *Seal . . . sweet eyes weary*, and to the play of alliteration and of one
particular vowel-sound. Do the rhymes help hold together lines that are a
unit in their meaning?

2, Matthew Arnold, *Requiescat*, 1853. The title means 'may she rest.' The
yew tree, frequently found in English graveyards, is a traditional symbol of
grief.

The feeling here is similar to the feeling of *Rest*. But this poem, ignoring the
physical grave, includes only the experiences of her disembodied spirit in
death; the images are not sensory except in the last stanza. The images of her
life are more sensory. The structure of the experience is repetition of contrasts, the past and the present. Compare this with the structure of *Rest*,
where sustained attention is focused on the present, while the past is involved
by implication, chiefly through paradox. The verse form of each poem is a
part of its structure of repetition or of sustained continuity.

Is this a just comment: '*Rest* forces the imagination to create the desired
rest out of the most stubborn materials, to turn defeat into victory, and, by the
intensity of its feeling, horror into peace. *Requiescat* invites us too easily by its
obvious contrasts; we flop for peace, of course, in this stage-managed world—
just as the poet does in his facile and irrelevant, *Ah! would that I did too.* Only
in the last stanza does death seem to have more importance than an afternoon nap; and here the *vasty hall of death* suddenly sends over us a strange
chill of terror, lonely and alien. Where now is our facile peace? And on this
we strew roses, roses—to the easy rhythms of an unchanging lilt.'

[Poem 3]

3, A. C. Swinburne, *The Garden of Proserpine*, 1866. Proserpine is the Queen of Hades, the Kingdom of the Dead, in classical mythology. References to Hades and its people are so frequently found in poems that a reader should know something about the place. In Greek stories Hades is usually a region underground, but often it is in the far West, beyond the Pillars of Hercules (Gibraltar), by the Ocean Stream, into which the sun and stars go down. Hades is separated from the world of the living by the river Styx, over which the dead are ferried by Charon; in the region are other rivers, Acheron, river of Woe, Phlegethon, river of Fire, Cocytus, river of Wailing, Lethe, river of Forgetfulness. Most of the dead dwell on a dim plain, mere shades of themselves, strengthless phantoms of bodies, living a faint existence, without pleasure or pain. A few of the heroic dead (Menelaus, Achilles, etc.) are taken, with all the powers of body and spirit undiminished, to live immortal in another part of the region, the Elysian Fields, where they have perfect joy; this region is usually thought of as lying beyond the Western Ocean, where it is also called Islands of the Blessed, the Fortunate Isles, or the Happy Isles. A third part of Hades is Tartarus, where a few people are punished for their great sins or crimes (Tantalus, Sisyphus, etc.). In some stories the World of the Dead is an enormous house, entered by a low doorway. The King of the dead is Pluto (also called Dis), who drives a chariot with black horses. His queen is Persephone, also called Proserpina and Proserpine. She once lived in the Vale of Enna, in Sicily, a beautiful maiden goddess, the daughter of Demeter (Ceres), goddess of the Earth, of vegetation, and especially of grain (which is called 'corn' in Britain). Pluto fell in love with Persephone and secretly carried her to Hades to be his unwilling queen. Her mother, whose grief caused all vegetation to die, sought her over the whole world; Zeus finally decreed that Persephone should live six months as Queen of Hades and six months with Demeter on earth; when Persephone is on earth, vegetation grows, when she is in Hades, it dies.

In *The Garden of Proserpine* the poet is in the grove or garden sacred to her at the entrance to the World of the Dead. The grief-stricken Queen wears a crown of her sacred poppies, the flower of oblivion, from which she crushes the wine of sleep.

The sound of this poem is a very important element of the experience. It must be read aloud, not too fast, with a slight pause at the end of each line, until your ear comes to expect the patterned rhythm of each line and of each stanza, and to expect the pattern of rhyme: the alternating feminine and masculine at the start, the triple feminine insistently holding its cadence, and then the same masculine of the firm close. Your ear should hear the frequent alliteration, which is usually of consonant sounds; read the poem aloud once, very slowly, consciously exaggerating your lip movements—notice the repetitions of the muscular movement of your lips and tongue; these kinetic sensations help us 'hear' the sounds of consonants.

[Poem 4]

Consider these two comments:

The images, the sights, of this poem are so vague and unformed, so miscellan-
eous and brief, that when I sit down to write about it, I can remember only a
confused jumble of vague sensations—very irritating.

The above reader misses the 'point' of this experience; I too cannot remember
the separate images; the only way I can remember the poem is to *hear* it, just as I
can remember music only by hearing it in my mind. It is too long to 'remember'
adequately; but its length is almost necessary for its full effect when read aloud.
In fact, this poem, as an *adequate* experience, ceases to exist when its sounds (its
rhythms, rhymes, alliterations) cease their long-sustained flow into my ears.
While these sounds are moving through my consciousness, carrying with them the
brief half-seen images, I can feel the poet's feeling of weariness, his pale longing
for sleep. My feeling can exist only while I am in a kind of hypnotic state—and
this is the work of the sounds; in this hypnotic dream, the images are completely
adequate—more, they are perfectly *right*, just the sort of slow procession of dim
forms suited to a world of dreams—any sharp outline would be an intrusion, an
alien solid among shifting shadows. The only fixed shape here is the impassive
figure of Proserpine, waiting in forgetful stillness,

> *Pale, beyond porch and portal,*
> *Crowned with calm leaves, she stands,*

while around her shadows move; the *things* of life (ships, men) lose shape, and
the *spiritual* of life (love, dreams) assume form—all equally shadows in the World
of the Dead. The poet's experience may have originated in a feeling of weariness
or in trying to realize the Greek conception of the world of the dead. Whatever
the origin, in the poem itself the feeling finds its perfect 'objective correlative' in
Proserpine and the shades of Hades—and only by finding its perfect 'objective
correlative' could the experience of weariness bring the poet the complete satisfaction which is obviously here, the complete realization of emotion, the full enjoyment of death.

Consider this comment: 'This poem is just like *Rest*: both poets want rest.'
Does this statement help us to understand, or prevent us from understanding,
the two poems?

4, H.D. (Hilda Doolittle), *Lethe*, 1924. *You* may be alive or dead; *you* when
dead will retain full consciousness, memory, and all the earthly desires; but
you will be physically impotent, cut off from life, like the weak shades of
Hades. *Lethe* is the river in Hades whose waters rising over the dead can
bring forgetfulness of life. *Whin* and *gorse* are names for the same thing, a
prickly, thorny, unattractive shrub.
The structure of most of this poem is built on insistent repetition of syntax
and rhythm in corresponding lines in the first two stanzas. What is the effect?
What is the effect of using two pairs of words which mean the same thing,

skin nor hide, whin nor gorse? When this tight syntax is loosened suddenly, beginning with l. 14, what is the effect? What is the importance of the experience of ll. 14–18 in the whole experience? What is the full meaning of the last line?

5, William Shakespeare, '*Fear no more the heat o' the sun*,' 1623. From *Cymbeline*, written about 1610. A dirge to be sung. What are the two themes of each of the first three stanzas? The same themes are in *The Garden of Proserpine*. Compare the two poets' attitudes toward them. How do the images and use of sound in '*Fear no more*' help to communicate the quality of feeling? How deeply felt are the ills of this world? The last two lines of stanzas 1–3 are a sort of refrain, with variations; do the three couplets carry different tones of feeling? Would the poem be better without the last stanza?

    l. 11. *physic*. Medical science.
    l. 18. *consign to thee*. Agree with you (a legal term).

6, John Webster, '*Hark, now everything is still*,' 1623. From *The Duchess of Malfi*.

7, William Shakespeare, '*Full fathom five thy father lies*,' 1623. From *The Tempest*, written about 1611. A song. Does a clear visualization of ll. 2–3 help or hinder your feeling that the sea-change is into *something rich and strange*?

8, John Webster, '*Call for the robin redbreast*,' 1612. From *The White Devil*. A dirge to be sung. Charles Lamb compared this to '*Full fathom five*': 'As that is of the water, watery; so this is of the earth, earthy. Both have that intenseness of feeling, which seems to resolve itself into the elements which it contemplates.'

9, Thomas E. Brown, *Dora*, 1900. Is the center of this experience the feeling of the poet or the feeling of Dora? Are the two fused into a unified experience for you? What do the last two lines mean? Compare this poem with the following two poems.

10, William Wordsworth, '*A slumber did my spirit seal*,' 1800. In spite of its brevity, this poem is an experience of great intensity and depth. The meaning of death arises from a realization of sudden and shocking change: from his earlier sense of only her *vitality*, his dream-like (as it now seems) absorption in a living being exempt from mortal change—to his present full-daylight awareness that she is now only a *thing*. His imagination, shocked from its dream of illusion, has now carried him, as it were, to a point in outer space, from which his purged eyes, looking down on the revolving earth, can nevertheless see with painful clarity this still and senseless thing rolled round with rocks, and stones, and trees.

The communication of this experience is an astonishing achievement in economy of means. Every simple statement (which often seems to say and even repeat only obvious facts), almost every word, is charged with extraordinary meaning as a part of the whole experience. The center of the experience, the feeling, is never 'said'; the poet names his earlier state of consciousness, *a slumber*; but there is no name for *this* moment of feeling, this penetrating imaginative seeing of the terrible meaning lying, as it were, within the simple facts. Only the facts are given the reader; he must use these, as the poet did, to create the meaning, the poem.

11, William Wordsworth, '*She dwelt among the untrodden ways*,' 1800. In this and the following poem, the poet's love for the living woman is fully realized. What quality does this give to his grief?

12, William Wordsworth, '*Three years she grew*,' 1800.

13, A. E. Housman, '*The night is freezing fast*,' 1922. Compare the closing image with that of '*A slumber did my spirit seal*.' Can you visualize the image here? The poet's feeling is not simple, but complex. What are its elements? Can grotesque wit arouse serious feeling?

14, A. E. Housman, *To an Athlete Dying Young*, 1896. In many of Housman's poems he calls a man 'lad,' a common practice in western England. The *sill of shade* (l. 22) is the doorway of the house of Hades (see the note to poem No. 3, *The Garden of Proserpine*, on the Greek World of the Dead). The experience is unified and the feeling expressed by what set of objects and actions used as 'objective correlatives'? How does the second stanza communicate depth and power of feeling? The feeling in ll. 9–20 is one of relief, somewhat bitter. Does this change in the last two stanzas? Does this poem have a more adequate 'objective correlative' for the feeling of the pain of life than has poem No. 2, *Requiescat*, or poem No. 3, *The Garden of Proserpine*? The latter poem and the present poem both close in the Greek World of the Dead; are the poets' feelings the same?

15, A. E. Housman, '*On moonlit heath and lonesome bank*,' 1896. Men who had stolen sheep were once hanged in chains at crossroads, and their bodies left as examples; they were said to be keeping their sheep by moonlight. What sets of images express the two main feelings? How does the poet make us feel that hanging at the crossroads is to be resented less than hanging in jail? What is the effect of the sounds in l. 11? of the pun on *ring* in l. 18? of *string* in l. 20? How do you hear the rhythm of l. 8? The poem ends with the scene of the opening. Why?

16, A. E. Housman, '*The rain, it streams on stone and hillock*,' 1922. Where is the poet standing? The poem opens with rain and ends with it. Why? Why does the poet engage in the prolonged and rather repetitive series of 'realistic' and platitudinous reflections, ll. 6–20? About whom is the poet talking most of the time? What happens when he isn't?

17, A. E. Housman, *For My Funeral*, 1936. In this and the following poem, the speakers believe that the dead men have found *peace*. What is the full meaning of *peace* in each poem? What traditional images of God's love are parts of the experience of *For My Funeral*? Is there any image contrary to tradition?

In the Old Testament, when Job had been filled with bitter despair by the afflictions which God had rained upon him, he cried out to God in these words:

> *Wherefore then hast thou brought me forth out of the womb? Oh that I had given up the ghost, and no eye had seen me!*
>
> *I should have been as though I had not been; I should have been carried from the womb to the grave.*
>
> *Are not my days few? cease then, and let me alone, that I may take comfort a little,*
>
> *Before I go whence I shall not return, even to the land of darkness and the shadow of death;*
>
> *A land of darkness, as darkness itself; and of the shadow of death, without any order, and where the light is as darkness.*

What is the meaning of *darkness* in Housman's poem?

18, A. E. Housman, *Alta Quies*, 1936. The title means 'Deep Rest.'

19, R. L. Stevenson, *Requiem*, 1887. The title, meaning 'Rest,' is the first word of a Mass for the dead, 'Rest eternal give them, O Lord.'

20, Alfred Tennyson, '*Break, break, break*,' 1842. How does the poet express the thoughts that his tongue could not utter? Is the grief here more or less complex than the grief in poem No. 16, '*The rain, it streams on stone and hillock*'?

21, Archibald MacLeish, *Lines for an Interment*, 1933. The soldier was the poet's brother. What is the dominant feeling in this poem? How is it affected by other emotions of the poet? Are the people of this poem the *men* of the following poem?

22, Archibald MacLeish, *Men*, 1929. Do the images of this poem evoke the feeling that men's history is *grave noble and tragic*?

Group Two

23–5. These three poems are full of the things of autumn. In each poem what is the feeling or attitude or psychological state, of which the things are 'objective correlatives'? In which poem is an idea a significant element in the experience? What is the idea? Compare the meaning, in *Immortal Autumn* and *To Autumn*, of the same things: *the flower-barren fields* and the *stubble-plains*, the *sun* (and its work), the *birds*. What determines the differences in their meaning?

23, Archibald MacLeish, *Immortal Autumn*, 1929. What is the meaning of *immortal* in the title? of *human* (l. 5)? Does *human* here have the same meaning as *men* in poem No. 22? What does l. 18 mean? Is the quality of the whole experience in part determined by the absence of punctuation? How? Try reading this poem aloud, without pauses at the places where punctuation would normally be used, but with changes of inflections and tones of voice at these places.

24, Robert Frost, *After Apple-Picking*, 1914. Consider the woodchuck.

25, John Keats, *To Autumn*, 1820. Does the division into stanzas correspond to the organization of the things, the sensory stimuli? In particular, consider the place of the second stanza in the whole organization. What is the effect of bringing Spring into the experience? Do you notice many places where the quality of the word-sounds particularly supports the experience, as in the last line of stanza 2? How urgent is the sense of iambic rhythm? Does this support what might be called the 'tempo' of the poet's sensory and emotional experience? Has the poet been successful in controlling (i.e. reversing) your normal response to the words *clammy* and *oozings*? Can you describe adequately the feeling that arises from the last line? Is the poem a completely happy experience?

Group Three

26–42. These poems should be read with an especial awareness of images. Images are used in different poems in different ways. Some need to be clearly visualized; others are most effective when they are not sharply seen; others depend on what might be called our 'idea' of them. The important thing is what the reader *does* with them.

His response is partly his own natural, 'free,' response to the image itself, his response to the image in no particular context. For example, his response to 'cat feet' may be something like this: the pleasant sight of a sleeping cat's feet tucked up close against its stomach, relaxed, soft, motionless. Or it may be this: the sight of feet stealthily stepping toward a bird, tense and silent, until suddenly the two front feet come together, trembling as the muscles get set for the spring; and then the front feet savagely stabbing the struggling bird to earth. Such 'free' responses depend on the reader's previous experience of 'cat feet.' But in the poem, the reader's response is only partly 'free.' It is also 'controlled,' by its context, by the rest of the poem, particularly by the reader's response to what precedes the image.

For instance, 'cat feet' is in the second line of poem No. 26, *Fog*. The first line is

The fog comes

The reader understands that there is fog (white mist, drifting, soft, shapeless) in motion. Then the line:

on little cat feet.

The reader's response to *cat feet* is 'controlled' by his understanding of the first line: there is motion, so that the 'free' response (mentioned first above) of a sleeping cat cannot occur; there is soft drifting motion, so that the 'free' response (second above) of the tense, purposeful feet stalking a bird cannot occur. Neither of the 'free' responses fits the context; the response that does fit must be a sense of a soft drifting motion. In making the appropriate response, the reader selects the relaxed softness and rejects the motionlessness of the first 'free' response and selects the motion (and rejects the tense purposefulness) of the second, and thus creates the sense of soft drifting motion. This description, of course, is not psychologically accurate: the reader does not consciously select and reject, nor is he aware of either of the 'free' responses. For the response he does have is *pre*-controlled, so that (if he is a skillful reader) he has only the appropriate response and is not aware of the many other possible responses to *cat feet* that would be inappropriate here. (A poor poem, of course, may not effectively control the response, but may allow an incongruous or even a ridiculous response to occur. This is a very common fault in poor poems. If a poem deliberately permits or even encourages an incongruous response, the result is wit or humor.) But if a reader should have an inappropriate response, he may suspect two reasons: either the poem is at fault or the reader is unskillful. If the latter is true, the reader should consciously consider other possible responses and select the most appropriate. Even if he fails to find a fitting response and so fails to comprehend the image, the effort will probably increase his skill. It is an error to suppose that he cannot learn to handle images more effectively. Good reading is a skill. If we understand how a process works, we can learn to use it better.

These two lines of fog and cat feet can show us several more important characteristics of images. In l. 1 *fog* gives us a sense of shapelessness. But *cat feet* gives us a sense of definite shape, outline, form—no matter what the feet are doing. How can we 'see' *fog* moving *on little cat feet?* We cannot see it, and if we try to see it we are only confused and frustrated. What have we done that is wrong? We have acted on the assumption that the poem means that the 'sight' of fog is like the 'sight' of cat feet. We have assumed that there should be some exact visual correspondence between the image (*cat feet*) and the object (*fog*), that the image can be applied directly to the object, as a yardstick can be applied to an object to show us its length. This assumption is wrong, fatally wrong. And it constantly brings frustration and irritation to many readers. Very seldom can an image in a poem be applied directly to the object. That is not its use. Its use is this: the reader's response to *cat feet* may begin as a 'sight' but it almost instantly becomes a 'feeling' about the 'sight.' This 'feeling' corresponds to his 'feeling' about *fog*. Here an important point may be noticed. The response to the image, as we have seen, is not 'free' but is 'controlled' by the context. However, if a certain reader has a habitual, fixed, and strong response to cats, the context may be unable to control his response here. If this reader has a phobia about cats, his response to *cat feet* will be a feeling of strong revulsion—which is not at all his normal feeling about *fog*. Thus his whole response to these two lines may be just confusion; or the whole response may be dominated by his feeling about cats and hence fog will be, momentarily, a repulsive thing. Such a response would be abnormal. But it reveals clearly an important fact about normal responses: not only is our feeling about the image controlled by our feeling about the object, but our feeling about the object is also controlled by our feeling about the image. That is, the two feelings tend to control and change each other, to fuse together into a third feeling, a feeling about *cat-feet-fog*. This third feeling is a unified, coherent fusion of similar elements in two feelings—it is our final response to these two lines.

We may notice further that this discussion has been stumbling around awkwardly trying to describe our feelings about *fog* and about *cat feet*. We could fill pages with such description without adequately explaining just what our feelings are. Here lies the difference between explanatory description of feeling and poetic evocation of feeling. This poem does not explain or describe feeling; it evokes feeling—or rather, it gives the reader the words which arouse certain feelings and the reader creates from these several feelings a composite feeling. These two lines do not describe feeling about fog; by using the image of *cat feet* they evoke our feeling of the fog. This is our experience in reading the poem.

It may be well to summarize the points we have made in this discussion of images. (1) A reader's response to an image is partly 'free' and partly 'controlled' by the context, the rest of the poem. (2) An image usually cannot be applied directly to the object; the total responses, including feeling, interact and fuse together to create a unified experience. (3) The most important function of images is to evoke feeling.

The poems of this group are of particular interest for their images. In each poem consider carefully how the images are to be used by the reader.

26, Carl Sandburg, *Fog*, 1916.

27, Amy Lowell, *Wind and Silver*, 1925. How does this poem control your response to *dragon scales*?

28, Carl Sandburg, *Lost*, 1916. Often an image may be 'hidden,' so to speak: consider *mist creeps*. What happens if you directly apply to *harbor* the visual images of the last two lines?

29, Carl Sandburg, *Grass*, 1918. In this poem is the feeling of *grass* the usual feeling of grass covering graves? Is your feeling about grass the center of the experience?

30, Elinor Wylie, *Velvet Shoes*, 1921. Read this aloud for rhythm and quality of sound. Are all the images effectively controlled? Consider *white cow's milk*.

31, William Wordsworth, *The Solitary Reaper*, 1807. The poet had seen in the Scotch Highlands fields that (as he wrote) 'were quietly—might I be allowed to say pensively?—enlivened by small companies of reapers' or by a single reaper singing. He had also read in Thomas Wilkinson's *Tours of the British Mountains* this sentence:

Passed a female who was reaping alone: she sung in Erse [Gaelic], as she bended over her sickle; the sweetest human voice I ever heard: her strains were tenderly melancholy, and felt delicious, long after they were heard no more.

How does the poet create, from these materials, the experience in the poem? Particularly, how does the poem communicate the feeling which is stated in the prose in the words *pensively enlivened . . . sweetest human voice . . . tenderly melancholy . . . felt delicious*? Read aloud several times ll. 13–16.

32, P. B. Shelley, *To Night*, 1824. After reading this poem, did you want to ask 'why did the poet want night to come?' If you did, read it aloud, slowly, several times—and use the images.

33, P. B. Shelley, *The Cloud*, 1820. The scientific fact about the H_2O of the cloud is *I change but I cannot die*. How does it feel to be immortal H_2O?

34, Amy Lowell, *A Decade*, 1919.

35, Ezra Pound, *The Bath Tub*, 1916. Compare this poem with *A Decade*.

36, Ezra Pound, *Pagani's, November 8*, 1915. A *cocotte* is a stage or two beyond a coquette.

37, James Stephens, *The Snare*, 1915. Images and sounds combine to create the feeling of this poem. What is the feeling?

38, W. H. Auden, '*Look, stranger, at this island now*,' 1937.

39, Hart Crane, *Voyages: I*, 1926. Feeling for the sea is at the center of the experiences of this and the following poem. In each the image of a woman appears. What is the complex feeling in ll. 14–16 of this poem? How is it related to his feeling for the children and their feeling for the sea? Consider this comment: 'The poet is worried because there isn't any life-guard around.'

40, Hart Crane, *Voyages: II*, 1926. This poem communicates its meaning chiefly through the images. The syntax of ordinary statements is almost entirely absent. The feeling is one of almost mystical union with the sea, a love that accepts the terror as well as the beauty of the sea.

41, E. A. Poe, *The City in the Sea*, 1831. (An earlier title was *The City of Sin*.) Compare the meaning of death, given here in this great image, with that in poem No. 3, *The Garden of Proserpine*.

42, S. T. Coleridge, *Kubla Khan*, 1816. Written in 1798. This poem came to the poet in a dream: sights, sounds, words—complete as it stands, a fragment, but one of the most subtle and impressive experiences ever communicated by language. It has, as a whole, no structure of 'plain sense.' Our experience arises from its sound and its succession of images. Professor J. L. Lowes, in *The Road to Xanadu*, pp. 343–434, has brilliantly traced the creation of this poem in the sleeping poet's mind, whose subconscious powers gave unity and form to hundreds of details, from dozens of books, that had lodged in the poet's memory. It is a book that should be read by everyone interested in poems. Here is Coleridge's own note to the poem:

Of the Fragment of Kubla Khan

The following fragment is here published at the request of a poet of great and deserved celebrity [Lord Byron], and, as far as the author's own opinions are concerned, rather as a psychological curiosity, than on the ground of any supposed *poetic* merits.

In the summer of the year 1797, the author, then in ill health, had retired to a lonely farmhouse between Porlock and Linton, on the Exmoor confines of Somerset and Devonshire. In consequence of a slight indisposition, an anodyne had been prescribed, from the effects of which he fell asleep in his chair at the moment that he was reading the following sentence, or words of the same substance, in *Purchas's Pilgrimage*: 'Here the Khan Kubla commanded a palace to be built, and a stately garden thereunto. And thus ten miles of fertile ground were inclosed with a wall.' The author continued for about three hours in a profound sleep, at least of the external senses, during which time he has the most vivid confidence, that he could not have composed less than from two to three hundred lines; if that indeed can be called composition in which all the images rose up before him as *things*, with a parallel production of the correspondent expressions, without any sensation or consciousness of effort. On awaking he appeared to himself to have a distinct recollection of the whole, and taking his pen, ink, and paper, instantly and eagerly wrote down the lines that are here preserved. At this moment he was unfortunately called out by a person on business from Porlock, and detained by him above an hour, and on his return to his room, found, to his no small surprise and mortification, that though he still retained some vague and dim recollection of the general purport of the vision, yet, with the exception of some eight or ten scattered lines and images, all the rest has passed away like the images on the surface of a stream into which a stone has been cast, but, alas! without the after restoration of the latter!

GROUP FOUR

43–7. In each of these poems a flower or a bird is thought of as having some relation to human beings. In effect, the flower or bird is an image of some human fact or experience; or the reverse is true. How effective is the image? Two points of the discussion on the group of poems, Nos. 26–42, should be particularly remembered. How does the image correspond to the object? We said that the visual image is not applied directly to the object, but that their common quality is usually the feelings they arouse in the reader. We also said that these feelings interact and fuse together in a unified experience—not an experience of *fog* to which is added an experience of *cat feet*, but an experience of *cat-feet-fog*.

43, Robert Herrick, *To Daffodils*, 1648. For further discussion of this poem see the introductory note to Part VI, *Serious Wit and Symbolism*. At the center of this experience is the sweet-sad feeling of the brevity of human life. This feeling could find its 'objective correlatives' in the events of human life from birth to death; but the small number of words would hardly be enough to communicate the sensory experience of these events. In this poem a feeling is evoked by one image of a life whose time is so short that its life-span of a day can be an immediate sensory experience. The poem begins with this; but the feeling then fuses with another feeling which arises, not from a sensory experience, but from *thinking about* the human life-span of three score and ten years. The experience moves from feeling *for* the daffodils to feeling *with* them. And in the second stanza this feeling does something remarkable: it holds together as a unified experience two time-senses based on two vastly different scales of measurement—one scale is a day, the other seventy years. Neither time-sense is destroyed; they exist together; we are aware both of our seventy years and of the daffodils' day; but we *feel* that we and they live and die together. And finally this unifying feeling is strong enough to include still another time-sense, the hour of summer's rain and morning's dew. In fact our feeling had already accepted the statement that we grow and die as quickly

As you, or anything.

In effect, our feeling has destroyed all our sense of relativity, by which we are aware of time and on which is based our feeling of the sadness of quick death. There remains only the feeling of the sweet-sadness of all quick deaths, a feeling undisturbed by the differences between a day, seventy years, and an hour.

Many of the statements in this poem, if taken logically or literally, are nonsense. Good poems are often full of such nonsense.

After this heavy-handed explanation, the reader may be more than ever aware of the difference between description and poetic evocation. He will want to turn to the poem, to the delicacy and lightness of its rhythms, to the simplicity and clarity of its diction, to the subtle and graceful movement of its feeling.

44, W. C. Bryant, *The Yellow Violet*, 1821. Consider this comment: 'The poet says that, because he dislikes the newly-rich who forget their friends of poorer days, he will notice the yellow violet in May as well as in April. The statement of the poet is nonsense.' It is no more nonsense than statements in *To Daffodils*. Why is this not a good poem?

45, William Blake, '*Ah, Sunflower, weary of time*,' 1794. Consider the images in this and the two following poems. The rhythm of this poem is a skillful balance of pattern and variations. One variation in particular is repeated often enough to become a kind of pattern-variation. Can you hear it? In l. 1, what is the double meaning of *time*? Compare the central experience with that of poem No. 32, *To Night*.

46, P. B. Shelley, *To a Skylark*, 1820. Consider the separate effectiveness of each of the many images. Can you use them to create a coherent experience? What is contributed by the rhythmic pattern of the stanza?

47, Thomas Hardy, *The Darkling Thrush*, 1902. This was written in December 1900, at the end of the century. Has the poet's feeling (ll. 1–16) changed at the end of the poem? Consider in l. 29 *trembled through*.

GROUP FIVE

48–90. This is a group of love poems, nearly all arranged in chronological order. In most of them the sound of the words is important in creating the reader's experience. Read each poem aloud until you catch the underlying pattern of rhythm. Notice how the actual sounds are counterpointed against this pattern. Sometimes the pattern-rhythm is vigorous enough to force itself on the sound of your voice, in spite of the opposing tendency to vary the stresses to conform to ordinary pronunciation or to the sense meaning of the phrases. Can you, in reading aloud, allow both of these tendencies to operate? This problem is discussed in the essay in Part X.

As an example of the problem, listen to the sound of poem No. 52. The pattern-rhythm in every line is four iambic feet, the rhythm which is actually heard in ll. 6–7:

> *Thĕre chérrĭes grów whĭch nóne măy búy*
> *Tĭll 'chérrў rípe' thĕmsélvĕs dŏ crý.*

Repeat these lines aloud until the rhythm becomes a kind of meaningless chant, and then chant ll. 1–2. You will stress them like this:

> There is a garden in her face
> Where roses and white lilies grow.

This is not the right reading of these lines. It puts the sound-stress on two words whose meaning is not important and which would not be stressed in our ordinary speech rhythm—namely, *in* and *and*. And it puts no sound-stress on *white*, which both meaning and speech-habits would normally require us to stress. Your voice cannot meet the requirements of meaning and speech-habits without destroying, momentarily, the pattern-rhythm of the lines. But the pattern-rhythm has not entirely disappeared: it still is 'running through your head.' You are aware of it, just as in dancing when the sound of the music ceases for a few moments you are aware of the rhythm, and continue to move to the rhythm. This double-awareness is the skill you need most in reading poems aloud.

48, Anonymous, '*Western wind, when will thou blow*.' Written about 1500.

49, John Lyly, '*Cupid and my Campaspe played*,' 1632. A song from *Alexander and Campaspe*. Poems Nos. 49–53 are Elizabethan lyrics. The feeling is light and graceful, sometimes intricate and witty, often extravagant. Images and rhythms are of like quality.

50, Thomas Campion, '*Rose-cheeked Laura*,' 1602. *Concent*, l. 6, means playing or singing together in harmony. Campion, a superb writer of rhymed lyrics and songs, wrote this poem to show that rhyme was unnecessary in lyric poems. He described the measure of the stanza as follows: l. 1, two feet, the first either a spondee or trochee; ll. 2, 3, four feet, the first either a spondee or trochee, the other three trochees; l. 4, two feet, both trochees. Campion does not mention the second foot of l. 1. Probably he intended it to be heard as a dactyl, or possibly with an unstressed syllable between two stressed. Try reading the poem aloud as Campion directed. What does Campion do with the quality of sound?

51, Thomas Campion, '*Follow your saint*,' 1601.

52, Thomas Campion, '*There is a garden in her face*,' about 1617. *Cherry-ripe* was the cry of street venders in London.

53, George Peele, '*Fair and fair and twice so fair*,' 1584. A song from *Arraignment of Paris*. Paris, a shepherd, son of King Priam of Troy, was married to

Œnone, a nymph. Later he deserted her for Helen of Troy. This poem has a very strongly marked and regular rhythm. What is the effect?

54, Edmund Spenser, *Prothalamion*, 1596. The title means 'a song sung before a wedding.' This was written to celebrate the double wedding of the two daughters of the Earl of Worcester. To sing the praises of the two ladies, Spenser tells of their journey up the Thames on a ceremonial visit, not long before the wedding, to Essex House, where their future husbands greeted them. The ladies are two white swans. Spenser liked intricate stanzas, which gave him room to create elaborate effects of rhyme, of sustained and various verbal music, and of descriptive details. He also liked the effect of antiquated words and spelling, which is here preserved. The refrain ending each stanza catches his joy in the beauty of the river.

l. 12. *rutty*. Rooty.

l. 67. *Somers-heat*. Somerset, a county.

l. 137. *a stately place*. Essex House, formerly the residence of Spenser's patron, the Earl of Leicester.

l. 145. *a noble peer*. The Earl of Essex, who had just returned from Cadiz upon which he had led a brilliant attack.

l. 173. *twins of Jove*. Castor and Pollux, who became the constellation Gemini.

55, Ben Jonson, '*Drink to me only with thine eyes*,' 1616. Jonson entitled this poem *Song, to Celia*. Here the first line is used as a title, to avoid confusion with poem No. 59, which Jonson also called *Song, to Celia*. The feeling and statements in this poem are extravagant; the handling of image and sound is marked by order, care, restraint, and balance. What is the total experience?

56, Ben Jonson, '*Still to be neat, still to be dressed*,' 1616. A song from *Epicœne, or the Silent Woman*. This and the two following poems are on the same theme.

57, Robert Herrick, *Delight and Disorder*, 1648.

58, Robert Herrick, *Upon Julia's Clothes*, 1648.

59, Ben Jonson, '*Come, my Celia, let us prove*,' 1607. For the title, see poem No. 55, notes above. This and poem No. 60 have the same theme. Are there differences of feeling and attitude?

60, Robert Herrick, *To the virgins, to make much of time*, 1648. How is the humorous tone achieved?

61, Robert Herrick, *Cherry-ripe*, 1648.

62–67. These poems are based on the view that love and ladies are not all they are usually supposed to be. How does the feeling about this situation differ in the several poems?

62, John Donne, '*Go and catch a falling star*,' 1633. Donne entitled this poem simply *Song*. Legend said the mandrake was half-human in form and nature. Is the poet's feeling bitter or amused?

63, Sir John Suckling, '*Why so pale and wan, fond lover?*,' 1646. The original title is simply *Song*. Do the rhythm and rhyme support the tone of feeling?

64, Sir John Suckling, '*Out upon it! I have loved*,' 1659.

65, Anonymous, *Song, By a Person of Quality*, 1733. Variously attributed to Alexander Pope and Jonathan Swift.

66, Thomas Moore, '*The time I've lost in wooing*,' 1808. Compare this with poem No. 64.

67, A. E. Housman, '*Is my team plowing*,' 1896.

68, Robert Herrick, *To Perilla*, 1648. This and the next three poems are to be taken as by lovers grown old. See also poems Nos. 34 and 35.

69, W. B. Yeats, *When You Are Old*, 1893. The speaker will be dead when the woman is old.

70, Ella Wheeler Wilcox, *Friendship after Love*, 1883.

71, Robert Burns, *John Anderson, My Jo*, 1790. The Scotch words mean: *jo*, sweetheart; *brent*, smooth; *beld*, bald; *pow*, head; *cantie*, happy. Many of Burns's lyrics were written for old melodies. The five love poems here are full of his gift of song in line and stanza, and his genius in finding images to express exquisite and tender feeling.

72, Robert Burns, '*O, wert thou in the cauld blast*,' 1800. The Scotch words mean: *airt*, direction, quarter; *bield*, shelter.

73, Robert Burns, *Ae Fond Kiss*, 1792. The Scotch words mean: *ae*, one; *wage*, pledge; *ilka*, every.

74, Robert Burns, *Ye Flowery Banks*, 1808. The Scotch words mean: *fause*, false; *wist na*, knew not; *aft*, often; *staw*, stole.

75, Robert Burns, '*O, my luv is like a red, red rose*,' 1796.

76, Lord Byron, '*There be none of Beauty's daughters*,' 1816. Byron gave this the title *Stanzas for Music*.

77, Lord Byron, '*She walks in beauty*,' 1815.

78, Lord Byron, '*So, we'll go no more a-roving*,' 1830.

79, P. B. Shelley, '*When the lamp is shattered*,' 1824.

80, P. B. Shelley, '*Music, when soft voices die*,' 1824.

81, Alfred Tennyson, '*Now sleeps the crimson petal*,' 1847. Danaë was a Greek princess whose father imprisoned her in a bronze tower so that suitors might not come near her; but Zeus, who loved her, came down to her in the form of a shower of gold; their son was Perseus.

The experience of this poem is a very delicately balanced and sustained association between images and feeling. This quality of delicate balance of feeling and image is supported by formal balance, in grammar, rhythm, alliteration, vowel tone, and the grouping of lines. The repeated order of image and feeling is a kind of echo-structure, or like the full sound of a gong (the sensory image) followed by the reverberations of the tones (the feeling). There is complete and simple reliance on 'objective correlatives'; every quality of the feeling is given solely by the image. The poem is worth close study of its imagery and sound. A fine sense of form controls the details and the whole poem.

82, E. A. Poe, *To Helen*, 1831.
l. 2. *Nicèan barks*. What Poe meant to refer to is not clear. Probably he had in mind the magic ships of the Phæacians, which carried Ulysses, at the end of his perilous wanderings, back to his home in Ithaca.
l. 7. *hyacinth hair*. The epithet used by Homer to describe luxuriant curling tresses.
l. 8. *Naiad*. Graceful water nymphs of Greek legend.
l. 14. *Psyche*. Greek princess whom Cupid loved, coming to her at night so that she could not see him; at length one night she held a lamp over him asleep and saw his beauty. Psyche was a personification of the Soul.

83, E. A. Poe, *The Sleeper*, 1831.

84 a–e. James Joyce, from *Chamber Music*, 1918. *Chamber Music* is a series of thirty-six lyrics. Behind them is a shadowy story of love that began with the freshness of spring, that reached its full joy even though it alienated the man's friend, and that at the fall of the year died in the woman. The feeling is communicated in delicate rhythms and simple words, and in brief images full of

overtones of meaning. In the first of these five poems the person in bright cap and streamers suggests a combination of two traditional figures: Pan, the Greek god of woods and fields who loved the music and dance of spring festivals; the medieval troubadour singing his love songs, villanelles, and roundelays.

85, A. E. Housman, '*White in the moon the long road lies,*' 1896. Compare the rhythms of ll. 5–6 and ll. 7–8.

86, Ezra Pound, *Na Audiart*, 1909.
    l. 24. i.e. in illumined manuscript (author's note).
    l. 35. Reincarnate (author's note).

Group Six

87–96. These are songs from Shakespeare's plays. Their rhythms and refrains are full of the joy of singing. They give an extraordinary sense of lively pleasure in things, from the homely details of *Winter* to the delicate fairy world of '*Where the bee sucks.*' In the last three the world of man is observed more seriously, but song is always present. Two other songs by Shakespeare are poems Nos. 5 and 7.

87, William Shakespeare, *Spring*, 1598. From *Love's Labour's Lost*, written about 1590. This and the following poem are set in contrast. *Cuckoo* is a word of fear because a man whose wife is unfaithful is called a 'cuckold,' derived from the French name for the bird.

88, William Shakespeare, *Winter*, 1598. From *Love's Labour's Lost*, written about 1590. Greasy Joan cools the pot by skimming or stirring; roasted crabapples hiss in the ale.

89, William Shakespeare, '*Hark, hark! the lark,*' 1623. From *Cymbeline*, written about 1610. *Those springs* of l. 3 are the dew.

90, William Shakespeare, '*Where the bee sucks,*' 1623. From *The Tempest*, written about 1611. This is sung by Ariel, an airy spirit.

91, William Shakespeare, '*Tell me where is fancy bred,*' 1600. From *The Merchant of Venice*, written about 1596. *Fancy* means love.

92, William Shakespeare, '*It was a lover and his lass,*' 1623. From *As You Like It*, written about 1599.

93, William Shakespeare, '*Who is Silvia?,*' 1623. From *The Two Gentlemen of Verona*, written about 1591.

94, William Shakespeare, '*Take, O take those lips away,*' 1623. From *Measure for Measure*, written about 1603. *Forsworn* means either 'renounced' or 'false to an oath.' Which meaning fits the context here? What is the meaning of *seals*?

95, William Shakespeare, '*When that I was and a little tiny boy,*' 1623. From *Twelfth-Night*, written about 1601. In l. 1 *and* is without meaning, an expletive. *Toss-pots* are drunkards.

96, William Shakespeare, '*Blow, blow, thou winter wind,*' 1623. From *As You Like It*, written about 1599.

GROUP SEVEN

97, Matthew Arnold, *Philomela*, 1853. Poems Nos. 97, 98, and 99 have a common 'subject,' the Nightingale.

The story of the Nightingale was told by Ovid. Philomela and Procne were sisters, princesses in Athens. When Procne married Tereus, king of Thrace, Philomela went with her to that wild country, whose capital was Daulis, near the river Cephissus. Later Tereus fell violently in love with Philomela, violated her, and cut out her tongue to prevent her betraying him. But she wove the story into a piece of tapestry; in revenge Procne killed her little son Itys (Itylus) and served the cooked flesh to his father. The two women fled; as Tereus pursued them, they prayed for aid and were turned into birds, Philomela into a nightingale, Procne into a swallow. (In Greek versions of the story, Philomela became a swallow, Procne a nightingale.) The legend is one of the most terrible stories of violent, barbaric passion. The song of the nightingale, usually heard at night when all is still, seems to many listeners to be full of tragic beauty. Arnold has reversed the roles of the sisters, making Philomela the wife of Tereus.

98, A. C. Swinburne, *Itylus*, 1866. Both this poem and the one above try to communicate to us the experience of the nightingale. What are the differences in the experiences and in the means used to communicate them?

99, Robert Bridges, *Nightingales*, 1893. How is the intention here different from those of the two poems above? What is the metrical pattern of this poem?

GROUP EIGHT

100–105. These six poems were written between 1802 and 1819 by four poets who are usually put in the same classification, Romantic Poets. In each poem a feeling of sadness or dejection is an important element in the experience. Notice carefully the differences in the causes and qualities of the sadness or dejection. Does the term 'Romantic' have any meaning when used to describe all these poems?

100, John Keats, *Ode on Melancholy*, 1820. Poems Nos. 100, 101, 102 were all written in May 1819. They arose out of a persistent kind of experience which dominated Keats's feelings, attitudes, and thoughts during that time. Each of them is a unique experience, but each of them is also, as it were, a facet of a larger experience. This larger experience is an intense awareness of both the joy and pain, the happiness and the sorrow, of human life as the poet sees them in others and feels them in himself. This awareness is not only feeling; it becomes also thought, a kind of brooding contemplation of the lot of human beings, who must satisfy their desire for happiness in a world where joy and pain are inevitably and inextricably tied together. This union of joy and pain is the fundamental fact of human experience that Keats has observed and accepted as true. The 'plain sense' of the *Ode on Melancholy* is a statement of that observed and accepted fact. What is the feeling or attitude toward that fact? Is the feeling of this poem an instance of the fact itself? Is Keats's 'acceptance' of the fact a *complete* experience—intellectual, sensuous, emotional?

l. 1. *go not*. That is, if you want to experience the most profound melancholy, *the wakeful anguish of the soul*, do not try to find it in Lethe, etc.

l. 7. *Psyche*. Psyche, the Soul, who appeared often as a beautiful butterfly, was the wife of Cupid.

l. 8. *mysteries*. Rites of religious worship.

ll. 27–8. This is a very important statement. Do you understand it clearly?

101, John Keats, *Ode to a Nightingale*, 1820. The *Ode to Melancholy*, we have said, has for its 'plain sense' (the skeleton of its structure) the statement that joy and melancholy are tied together in human experience. This is a statement of relationship, an abstract idea. And in the last stanza Keats is thinking and feeling primarily about abstractions—Melancholy, Beauty, Joy, Pleasure, Delight. In the *Ode to a Nightingale* the experience is not on the level of abstractions, but on the level of immediate, 'concrete' sensations and feelings. In short, here is a complete experience about which we can *later* think and from which we can *later* deduce or abstract a conclusion or idea, the idea of the *Ode to Melancholy*.

The key to understanding the *Ode to a Nightingale* is seeing that the experience is not static, that it moves and changes. The outline of the movement is simple. In the first stanza the experience is the immediate sensations and feelings of joy-pain arising from hearing the song of an actual nightingale (*aching pleasure nigh, turning to poison . . . burst Joy's grape . . . taste the sadness of her might . . . her cloudy trophies*). Then, from l. 11 to l. 50 Keats deliberately tries to break this union of joy-pain, tries to live not as a human being but as a nightingale. He is driven to attempt this by the pain of the joy-pain experience; he *rebels* against the fundamental fact of human experience which he had *accepted* in the *Ode on Melancholy*; he wishes to 'escape' from the actual world, to experience only the pure joy of the nightingale-world. He can do this by using his power of day-dreaming and thus moving into the world of fantasy. In ll. 11–20 he wishes to do this by *day-dreaming about* wine (he does *not* want to get drunk)—wine which tradition has associated with pure joy. But for the moment he cannot enter the world of fantasy without being aware of the actual world from which he wishes to escape. On the threshold of fantasy he pauses to look back, to feel the pure pain (without joy) of contemplating the lot of all men, where time means only painful change and death,

> *Where but to think is to be full of sorrow*
> *And leaden-eyed despairs.*

Under the compulsion of this enormously increased realization of pain, he turns a second time to escape into fantasy; he day-dreams a world of pure joy (ll. 31–50), realized through pure sensation alone. But in this fantasy-world he hears a fantasy-nightingale; and his day-dreaming, picking up from the actual world a remembrance of another means of release from pain, moves out of sensory experience into death, where for him time ceases to exist. But Time *itself* continues, actual and audible as the song of the nightingale. Here is the crux of the experience of the poem (ll. 61–70). The nightingale changes once again, no longer the fantasy-nightingale, and becomes time-as-sound, becomes therefore immortal, a voice sounding through all time. And now the experience is that of realizing the lot of all men in this voice-as-time: time, which was once (ll. 21–30) painful change and death, is now a beautiful voice sounding forever over the passing generations below, over the joy and suffering of men, over the pain of Ruth—and over the pain of Keats. This is the final experience, a realization of the union of joy and pain, an *emotional acceptance* of this union as true and beautiful. The poem has moved from a realization of this union as an immediate and momentary experience (ll. 1–10), through an emotional rebellion against pain and an escape into fantasy-joy (ll. 11–50), to a new realization (ll. 51–70) of this union and to a complete acceptance of the human lot as true and beautiful. The nightingale, or rather, the song of the nightingale is the central 'objective correlative' which Keats used to obtain this experience and which he used to communicate this experience.

And when the nightingale ceases to sing and flies away (ll. 71–80), the experience is over. What follows is not a part of the coherent experience we have traced. It is an aftermath of that experience. Now he only *remembers* the experience of ll. 51–70 and he doubts its validity. Was this full realization and acceptance of joy-pain as true and beautiful—was this a *vision*, a genuine insight into the meaning of human life? Or was it only a *waking dream*, a daydream, a fantasy? Am I *now* awake to the true meaning of human life? Or was I awake to it in ll. 51–70? And am I *now* asleep to it? Keats, in his ordinary self, might well have doubted the validity of his vision. Fully to accept the unity of pain and joy as true and beautiful, to *experience* this unity, is a rare and great achievement. To communicate it fully is to create a great poem. To read the poem fully is to create a great experience.

102, John Keats, *Ode on a Grecian Urn*, 1820. As in the preceding poem, the central experience of this poem is completed in the next to last stanza. The experience itself begins with the same desire to create a world of pure joy; the world of fantasy here is the life of the people on the urn. Keats sees them as being, at once and the same time, both marble figures and people alive in ancient Greece. For them time is suspended; they cannot move or change physically; but their inner life of desire and feeling remains, although it too cannot change, since time is suspended. As in the *Ode to a Nightingale*, the world of painful actuality is set in sharp contrast to the fantasy world of joy. There is no union of joy and pain—until ll. 31–40. And here the experience undergoes a change very much like that in the previous poem in ll. 61–70. His imagination creates a scene that is not depicted on the urn, the little town emptied of its folk. And this town, silent and desolate, becomes an image whose meaning is both beauty and pain. The suspension of time, which earlier had created pure joy, now suddenly creates pain forevermore. And Keats accepts the complete experience and knows and feels it is true and beautiful.

The last stanza is the aftermath, the remembering of the vision. The marble urn is now merely marble, a *silent form, Cold Pastoral*. But Keats remembers that his imagination did use the urn to create an experience which, like the thought of eternity, is *out of thought*, out of the reach of the *dull brain* which *perplexes and retards*—an experience which befriends us when we must accept our woes in time by showing us the beauty of woe when time is suspended. The Truth which was declared by the *Ode on Melancholy*, that the human lot is joy and pain together, is experienced as Beauty in the *Nightingale* and the *Grecian Urn. Beauty is truth, truth beauty.* If we know that, we have accepted and understood what we most need to accept and understand.

The meaning of the statement *Beauty is truth, truth beauty* has been hotly debated *as if Keats had written it as an isolated remark.* Its meaning can be understood only *in the poem.* One other common comment on the *Ode on a Grecian Urn* should be noticed, that Keats here asserts that Art is superior to Nature. Keats is not thinking or feeling or talking about the urn as a work of art. As a remark on this poem, the comment is irrelevant; in any context, it is probably without meaning.

103, William Wordsworth, *Ode: Intimations of Immortality*, 1807. When first published in 1807 this poem was entitled simply *Ode*; in 1815 the subtitle was added. It has caused frequent misunderstanding of the poem. Here the word *Immortality* does not mean life after death or life before birth; Wordsworth intended it to mean that human consciousness, the power of our mind and imagination, is infinite and can create experiences that are beyond things existing in time and space. The poem concerns what Coleridge called our 'modes of inmost being.'

Today we should say that the poem deals with the psychology of childhood experience. The chief characteristic of such experience in Wordsworth's own life was, as he wrote, the 'dream-like vividness and splendor which invest objects of sight.' The child does not see things as they are seen by mature people. The child's mind *creates* a 'dream-like vividness and splendor.' The mental *power* to create (Wordsworth believed) is what makes us human. Even when this power creates falsely, as in childhood, it is of first importance, because the power cannot develop unless it is exercised. And so the child's creative power is the beginning, the source, of mature power. The child loves the dream-like things of his world, and his power to feel affection and 'primal sympathy' grows into our mature power to love the world about us. *The Child is father of the Man.* The man does not falsify the world; he sees it truly and he understands it by the power of his mind and imagination to *create*, that is, to perceive (as we say) the relation of thing to thing and the relation of things to us. This mature power can create experience that starts from but is not limited by things, so that

> *To me the meanest flower that blows can give*
> *Thoughts that do often lie too deep for tears.*

The main structure of the poem is simple. In ll. 1–57 the poet remembers his dream-like experience as a child and regrets its loss. Then in ll. 129–203 he states his evaluation of that early experience and tells how the remembrance of it, and the powers which then began to operate, now enable him to find permanent and mature understanding and happiness.

We omitted ll. 58–128 from the outline of the structure because they are one vast 'image' through which the poet tries to communicate the experiences of the child. The 'image' is an ancient idea, that each soul lived in Heaven before it came to live at 'birth' in an earthly body. The poet, in effect, says: the ecstatic experiences of a child are so un-earthly that it is *as if* he had come from a heavenly life and *as if* he still felt the heavenly emotions even when he is looking with his physical eyes at things on earth. Wordsworth did not 'believe' in the idea of the pre-natal existence of the soul in Heaven, any more than he 'believed' Greek myths which he used in poems. The idea was sufficiently well known, he wrote, to allow him 'to make for my purpose the best use of it I could as a poet." *As a poet*, he used it as an 'image.' He develops it in great detail. He expected this long passage would enable the reader to comprehend more fully the child's experience and the poet's sense of its importance.

104, S. T. Coleridge, *Dejection: An Ode*, 1802. The lady who is addressed is Wordsworth's sister, Dorothy, a very dear friend of Coleridge.

105, P. B. Shelley, *Ode to the West Wind*, 1820. Shelley's personal life had been full of painful experiences; but more important to him, his poems, through which he hoped to inspire people to desire a more humane life, had been almost ignored. This poem, although full of surging emotion, has a beautiful architectural structure. Study the relations of the details to the whole experience.

GROUP NINE

106–14. The poems in this group have common elements, both in the experience and in the imagery, so that comparative study will give the reader a better comprehension of the full meaning of each and of the means of communicating it. Most of them have as part of the experience an awareness of modern life, of the feeling of confusion it creates in sensitive and thoughtful people, and of the need for finding some stable values in a shifting and changing world. The desire for love and comradeship between individuals is particularly strong.

The sea is often used here as an 'objective correlative.' Notice just how it functions in each poem. In particular notice whether the sea is used as an image to express the experience or whether the sea is used to prove the validity of the experience. In argument a recognized method of proving a point is analogy; the proof is effective when the similarity between the two objects can be made to seem complete; the proof can be smashed by showing a lack of similarity in important respects. Inexperienced readers of poems often assume that an image is used as an analogy. For instance, this comment was made on poem No. 106, *Dover Beach*: 'Arnold says the modern world has lost Faith, that the Sea of Faith, which was once at full tide, is now at low tide. Arnold feels very discouraged, which is strange. He ought to remember that the sea always comes back at high tide.' Another reader understood the poem to say just that: 'Although there is confusion now because the sea of faith is at low tide, Arnold says that, if they will just be true to one another through these dark days, the sea of faith will return at the full tide.'

The method of imagery in good poems is not the method of analogy. Imagery is not used to prove anything. An image does not correspond, point by point, to the object. Indeed a poem controls our response to the image in such a way that other possible responses to other 'points' of the image do not occur to us. A reader who expects an image to be an analogy cannot respond to the image properly, and often he is led woefully astray. Analogy is common in poor poems, particularly in didactic poems which urge us to think and feel as we *ought* to, or which *prove* that platitudes are true.

Consider the use of the sea in poems Nos. 106, 107, and 109.

106, Matthew Arnold, *Dover Beach*, 1867.

107, Archibald MacLeish, '*Dover Beach*'—*A Note to that Poem*, 1936.

108, A. E. Housman, *Hell Gate*, 1922. The *conductor* is Satan; the gate is guarded, as in Milton's *Paradise Lost*, by Sin, once a beautiful woman but now hideous, and Death, her son.

109, A. H. Clough, '*Say not the struggle naught availeth*,' 1849.

110, Matthew Arnold, '*Yes! in the sea of life enisled*,' 1852.

111, A. E. Housman, *The Land of Biscay*, 1936.

112, Louis MacNeice, *Leaving Barra*, 1935. Barra is an island in the Hebrides.

113, Archibald MacLeish, *Speech to Those who Say Comrade*, 1936.

114, Stephen Spender, '*oh young men oh young comrades*,' 1933.

Group Ten

115, W. H. Auden, '*Hearing of harvests rotting*,' 1938. This poem and the next are written in the verse form known as the 'sestina,' which was invented in France in the thirteenth century. What are the requirements of the form?

116, Ezra Pound, *Sestina: Altaforte*, 1909.

Group Eleven

117, John Milton, *L'Allegro*, 1645. This poem and No. 118, *Il Penseroso*, are companion poems. Notice that they are closely parallel in the plan of development, in the measure, and (in spite of the opposing pleasures) in the general tone of feeling.

l. 2. *Cereberus*. Monstrous dog guarding Hades, the *Stygian* or hateful region.

l. 10. *Cimmerian*. Land of darkness, beyond the Ocean Stream.

l. 29. *Hebe*. Goddess of Youth, cupbearer to the gods.

ll. 83–8. The four names are conventional names in pastoral poems.

l. 132. *Sock*. Low-heeled shoe, symbol of comedy.

l. 136. *Lydian*. Sweet, tender music.

l. 145. *Orpheus*. Orpheus' music persuaded Pluto to release Orpheus' wife, Eurydice, from Hades; but he disobeyed instructions, looked back to see if she followed, and she had to remain.

118, John Milton, *Il Penseroso*, 1645.

   l. 10. *Morpheus*. God of dreams.

   l. 18. *Memnon*. Handsome Ethiopian king in Trojan war.

   l. 19. *Queen*. Cassiopeia, who became a constellation.

   l. 23. *Vesta*. Goddess of the hearth.

   l. 24. *Saturn*. Father of Jove, who overthrew him.

   l. 59. *Cynthia*. The moon.

   l. 87. The constellation Bear never sets.

   l. 88. *Hermes*. Mythical Egyptian philosopher.

   l. 102. *Buskind*. Buskin, high-heeled shoe, symbol of tragedy.

   ll. 104–15. Milton wishes that he might read Musaeus' lost verses and that Chaucer might finish his Squire's Tale.

   l. 124. *Boy*. Cephalus, loved by Aurora, the Dawn.

   l. 154. *Genius*. Guardian spirit.

119, Thomas Gray, *Elegy Written in a Country Churchyard*, 1751.

120 a–p, Alfred Tennyson, from *In Memoriam*, 1850. *In Memoriam* is a collection of 133 poems, arranged to tell the story of a man's grief at the death of his dearest friend, of his religious doubts, and of his recovery of faith. *In Memoriam* is not actual autobiography, although it is based on Tennyson's experiences after the death in Vienna in 1833 of his very close friend, Arthur Henry Hallam. His body was brought from Italy by sea to England, where it was buried at Clevedon on the Severn River.

The poems were written over a period of seventeen years. The sixteen poems given here were not selected to be representative of the whole story told in *In Memoriam*. Each was chosen for its own excellence as a poem. Nos. 120h, i, and j show the influence upon Tennyson of the new discoveries and theories of geology and biology, especially the evidence of the struggle for survival between individuals and of the disappearance of many species (*types* is his word) in past geologic ages. Tennyson is a master-craftsman in his images, rhythm, sound, and organization. Special study of poem No. 120e will reveal his skill.

121, Edward Fitzgerald, *The Rubáiyát of Omar Khayyám*, 1859–79. *Rubáiyát* means 'Quatrains.' Omar Khayyám (Omar the tent maker) was a Persian poet and astronomer of the eleventh century. The English poem is a very free translation from the Persian. The organization of the poem is a rapidly shifting series of meditations. Each stanza is independent, with its own comment fully stated, usually in its own set of images. The prevailing attitude of Omar is a kind of fatalism, skeptical of all efforts to know, and sympathetic toward all efforts to enjoy. While he scoffs gently at any explanation of life as spiritual, he often regards the sensuous as having an almost mystical significance.

GROUP TWELVE

122, Anonymous, '*Sumer is icumen in*,' written about 1275. This is among the earliest English lyrics known, a song in the musical form known as a *Rota* or *Rondel*. The words are a greeting to the spring, full of pure joy and fun.

l. 3. *med*. Meadow.

l. 8. *verteth*. Harbors in the green.

l. 12. *swik*. Cease.

123, Ezra Pound, *Ancient Music*, 1916. Some six centuries later Mr. Pound also has fun.

II

SONNETS

The organization of an experience to give it form is the most funda-mental aim of a poet. The most important kind of form, of course, is in the relation of the various elements of the experience to each other and to the whole experience. But the experience can exist for the reader only through language, and the poet must therefore extend his concern with form to include language. The inner form of the poem cannot be separated from its language-form.

A study of poems using the same language-form will reveal this unity of inner and outer form. The sonnet is especially useful for this purpose. Most of our best poets, from the sixteenth century to the present, have used it.

The sonnet form was borrowed from Italy by Elizabethan poets. It came to mean a poem of fourteen five-stress iambic lines, arranged according to either of two definite rhyme schemes or their modifica-tions. There are thus two kinds of sonnets, called the Italian and the English. The Italian sonnet has two divisions, the first eight lines, called the octave, and the last six, called the sestet: abba abba, cde cde. The arrangement of rhymes in the sestet is not fixed, but varies a great deal; there are nearly always three rhyme-sounds. The English sonnet organizes its rhymes into three quatrains and a couplet: abab, cdcd, efef, gg.

In the Italian type, the whole sonnet should contain, without ir-relevant detail, a single thought or feeling. The subject matter is (the-oretically) organized according to a pattern: the first quatrain introduces the subject; the second develops the subject further; then a pause or turn, and the sestet develops the thought or feeling in a new direction or considers the subject from another point of view. No English poets follow this scheme strictly and most of them vary it considerably. Poems Nos. 147–148g follow the theoretical plan rather closely.

note

The English sonnet does not have, even theoretically, the severe organization of the Italian. The subject matter is frequently presented according to the rhyme scheme of three quatrains and a couplet. But the practice of poets varies a great deal. Some English sonnets use the 'turn' at the end of the second quatrain. Shakespeare had a fairly definite way of organizing the material, especially in the couplet. For a discussion of a typical Shakespeare sonnet, see the essay in Part X.

124a–d, Sir Philip Sidney, from *Astrophel and Stella*, 1591. This sequence of 108 sonnets was inspired by Sidney's love for Penelope Devereux. '*Loving in truth*' is in lines of twelve syllables, instead of the usual ten. In '*Come sleep! O sleep*,' l. 5, *prease* means 'press, crowd.'

124d, Sir Philip Sidney, '*Leave me, O love*,' 1598.

125, Samuel Daniel, '*Care-charmer sleep*,' 1623. Compare this with poem No. 124c.

126a–e, Edmund Spenser, from *Amoretti*, 1595. Spenser left a record of the courtship of his wife, Elizabeth Boyle, in this sequence of 88 sonnets. Spenser's own spelling is retained here. Notice that the poet, using the Shakespearean type of sonnet, links successive quatrains together with a common rhyme-sound. In '*Lyke as a ship*,' l. 10, Helice is the constellation Great Bear.

127a–p, William Shakespeare, from *Shakespeare's Sonnets*, 1609. Most of these 154 poems are addressed to a man, the others to a woman. We cannot know certainly who they were; nor does the story of possible events behind the poems concern us here. These sixteen sonnets are independent of whatever actual occasion may have inspired them. They are Shakespeare's contemplation of universal and recurrent events—the destructive power of time, the decay of beauty, absence, old age, death, the power of love to lift us above time, the degradation of spirit by overbearing physical passion.

These are some of the 'themes' of the poems; only in a very loose way are they connected with the two persons, usually in the concluding couplet. The important poetic experience is usually in the first twelve lines, the three quatrains. (See the discussion of poem No. 127i in Part X, *On Reading Poems.*)

The reader should compare sonnets which have the same 'subject,' to discover the particular quality of each experience. He should come to sense the development of thought, feeling, and image within the rigid form, the quatrain: in no other sonnets are the substance and form so fused together. Shakespeare was extraordinarily sensitive to the weight and color of words, to the variety of tone and overtone in their meanings. He enjoys playing with words, seriously and lovingly. Shakespeare's language should be studied closely; only then do these poems yield their full enjoyment.

127c, '*When to the sessions of sweet silent thought.*'
    l. 6. *dateless*. Endless.
    l. 10. *tell*. Count.
Words here are made to do very complex service. Compare the effect with the effect of the more simple use of words in poem No. 127b.

127d, '*Full many a glorious morning have I seen.*'
    l. 6. *rack*. Cloud-fragments.
    l. 12. *region*. The upper air.
    l. 14. *stain*. Be darkened.
Compare the steady development and application of the image here with the circling of the three images in No. 127i.

127e, '*Like as the waves make toward the pebbled shore.*'
    l. 5. *Nativity*. Birth. The image is of the sun crawling up the sky and then setting.
    l. 7. *Crooked*. Evil.
    l. 8. *confound*. Destroy.
    l. 9. *flourish*. Outer adornment.
    l. 11. *nature's truth*. Natural excellence.

127f, '*When I have seen by Time's fell hand defaced.*'
    l. 8. The shore increases its abundance by the loss sustained by the ocean, and *vice versa.*
    l. 9. Here *state* means condition; in l. 10, greatness.

127l, '*Not mine own fears, nor the prophetic soul.*'
    ll. 5–8. Perhaps an allusion to the prophecy of the death of Queen Elizabeth, which proved false.
    l. 10. *subscribes*. Submits.
    l. 11. *insults*. Exults over other dead.

127n, '*Let me not to the marriage of true minds.*' This is Shakespeare's most impressive poem on the enduring quality of love. The vehemence of the feeling breaks the usual organization of sentences into quatrains.

l. 5. *mark*. Landmark to guide ships.

l. 8. The star's altitude can be calculated, but its riches are unknowable.

127o, '*Th' expense of spirit in a waste of shame*.' The passionate anger and revulsion forces the language into abrupt and condensed statement.

l. 1. *expense*. Expenditure, waste. The line has many overtones of meaning arising from a number of suggested images.

l. 11. *in proof*. In expectation.

127p, '*Poor soul, the center of my sinful earth*.'

l. 2. *rebel powers*. Earthly, physical desires.

l. 8. *charge*. Body on which you have spent much.

l. 11. *terms*. Periods of time.

128, Wright Thomas, '*When shrill winds shriek*.' Written 1933.

129, John Donne, '*Death, be not proud*,' 1633. Compare this with poem No. 127p.

130, John Milton, '*How soon hath Time the suttle theef of youth*,' 1645. Milton later gave this the title *On His Being Arrived to His Twenty-third Year*. Notice the 'turn' of the thought at l. 9.

131, John Milton, *On His Deceased Wife*, 1673. Milton's wife died in childbirth. Alcestis gave her life for her husband, but Hercules snatched her from Death's grasp and restored her, veiled, to her husband.

132, John Milton, '*When I consider how my light is spent*,' 1673. Milton became totally blind when he was forty-four years of age; this was written three years later.

l. 3. *talent*. See the parable of the talents, Matthew xxv, 14–30.

l. 8. *fondly*. Impulsively, foolishly.

l. 13. *post*. Travel rapidly.

l. 14. Would the meaning of the line change if *stand* were changed to 'sit'?

133, John Milton, *On the late Massacre in Piedmont*, 1673. Milton hated the high authorities of the Catholic Church (and of the Church of England) as tyrants. In 1655 the Duke of Savoy persecuted the Protestants living in Piedmont, who were supposed to have kept the primitive Christianity of the Apostles.

l. 4. When England was a Catholic country.

l. 12. *triple Tyrant*. The Pope, wearing his triple crowns.

l. 14. *Babylonian wo*. The woe pronounced in Revelations against Babylon, whose modern counterpart, Milton thought, was the Church of Rome.

[Poems 134–141]

134, William Wordsworth, *London, 1802*, 1807. Is there coherence in the images of ll. 1–8? of ll. 9–14?

135, William Wordsworth, '*O friend! I know not which way I must look*,' 1807. Wordsworth gave this the title *Written in London, September, 1802*. The friend is Coleridge. Where does the 'turn' of the thought come? Does the poem lose in effectiveness by abandoning the balance of octave against sestet?

136, William Wordsworth, '*The world is too much with us*,' 1807. This sonnet observes the pattern of organizing the experience into two well defined quatrains and a sestet. What quality does this contribute to the whole? Proteus was a sea-god, herdsman of sea monsters, and Triton a merman in Greek legend. Why does Wordsworth wish to see and hear them?

This and the two sonnets above are on the same theme. Which is the most effective poem? Contrast the ways in which images are used.

137, William Wordsworth, '*It is a beauteous evening*,' 1807. The child is Wordsworth's daughter. *In Abraham's bosom* means 'in the presence of God.' Is the central experience of this poem Wordsworth's feeling for the scene or his idea about the child's spiritual nature? Do the feeling and the idea fuse into a unified experience? Compare the child here with the child in poem No. 103.

138, William Wordsworth, *Composed upon Westminster Bridge*, 1807. Consider the relative power of evoking emotion of ll. 4–5 and ll. 6–9. Part of the effectiveness of ll. 12–14 is in the implied contrast. What is the contrast?

139, William Wordsworth, *On the Extinction of the Venetian Republic*, 1807. Venice had existed as an independent republic from the ninth century until conquered by Napoleon in 1797. Annually from 1177, the Doge of Venice threw a ring into the sea, symbol of her control over the sea. By 1797 Venice had been declining from its glory for several centuries.

140, William Wordsworth, *Thought of a Briton on the Subjugation of Switzerland*, 1807. Napoleon had conquered Switzerland in 1798 and in 1807 was master of Europe, except Britain. Considering only your experience in reading this poem and the preceding poem, do you feel more moved by the fall of Venice or of Switzerland? Why?

141, John Keats, *On First Looking into Chapman's Homer*, 1817. Keats could not read Greek; but he had read translations of Homer before he discovered Chapman's. Apollo was, among other things, god of poetry. Is there any relation between the imagery of ll. 1–8 and ll. 11–14? What is the effect of the image of ll. 9–10 coming between the two passages? Balboa, not Cortez, discovered the Pacific. Does Keats's error reduce the effectiveness of the image? Consider the rhythm of l. 14.

142, John Keats, *To Sleep*, 1848. Written 1819. Compare poems Nos. 124c, 125, and 142 for their images and sound.

143, John Keats, '*When I have fears that I may cease to be*,' 1848. Written in 1818. What is Keats's experience recorded in ll. 12–14? Do these lines recreate the experience? Is it the same kind of experience that Keats had in each of the quatrains?

144, John Keats, '*Bright star*,' 1848. Written in 1819. In ll. 2–8 Keats creates in magnificent images the loneliness which he does not wish to have. Does this tend to destroy the unity of the whole poem? Does your practice in reading sonnets help you to feel the unity of the poem?

145, Elizabeth B. Browning, '*When our two souls stand up*,' 1850. Why is silence dear?

146, Elizabeth B. Browning, '*How do I love thee?*,' 1850. Is any one of these *ways* (l. 1) like the way of love in the preceding poem?

147, Christina Rossetti, *Remember*, 1862. Does the sonnet form make the communication of this experience more effective? Compare this poem with No. 127h.

148a–g, D. G. Rossetti, from *The House of Life*, 1869–81. This is a sequence of 101 sonnets expressing Rossetti's love for his wife and his grief after her early death. Rossetti liked to repeat images which held a particular meaning for him. For instance, the reflection of his wife's eyes in water (*Lovesight*, l. 9) came to symbolize her living presence. After her death the image (*Willowwood*) adds ironic poignancy to his grief. Notice also the image of whirling wind. Rossetti's use at times of sustained rhythms, alliteration, and vowel music is notable.

149, George Meredith, *Lucifer in Starlight*, 1883. Why is a realization of Lucifer's hugeness necessary for the full response to this poem?

150, Henry W. Longfellow, *Dante*, 1845. Compare Longfellow's conception of Dante's character with Wordsworth's tribute to Milton, poem No. 134.

151a–f, Henry W. Longfellow, *Divina Commedia*, 1865–7. Longfellow wrote these six sonnets to accompany his translation of Dante's *Divine Com-*

edy. In his great poem Dante leaves the world of the living and is led through Hell, Purgatory, and Paradise; in each place he hears from the souls the stories of their lives on earth. In Paradise he is met by Beatrice, whom he had loved since her death with an intense spiritual worship that illuminated his whole life and work. In these sonnets Longfellow sees Dante's poem as a great cathedral which he daily enters and in which he comes to know the events and people of the poem.

152, George Santayana, '*As in the Midst of Battle*,' 1894. In this and the next poem Santayana, a philosopher, shows how a good craftsman can use the sonnet conventions to make serious thought clear and impressive.

153, George Santayana, *The Rustic at the Play*, 1894.

154, Elinor Wylie, '*I hereby swear that to uphold your house*,' 1929. Does the extended and detailed image communicate the feeling with sufficient flexibility and freshness to the end?

155, Edna St. Vincent Millay, '*What lips my lips have kissed*,' 1920. For comment on this poem, see introductory Notes to Part VI, *Serious Wit and Symbolism*.

156, Louis MacNeice, '*You who will soon be unrecapturable*,' 1935.

III

NARRATIVE AND DRAMATIC POEMS

A pure narrative is a series of statements which informs us that certain events occurred in sequence. A detailed military report of the actions of a regiment during a battle is a pure narrative. We learn the military reasons for the actions of the men, but we do not learn who they are, what they thought and felt, what they wanted to do, etc. The report does not interest us unless we are interested in military affairs.

There are no pure narratives in literature. No one would find them interesting enough to write or to read. But narrative poems have been told and written in all ages, from the most primitive times to the present. Probably the most permanently interesting thing in the world is people in action. When few people could write or read, narrative poems were made up, and sung or said, and remembered for generations, almost word for word. These are called folk ballads. There are nine of them here. They were made up in England and Scotland about the fifteenth century, although they were not written down until many generations later. Their spelling and dialect words show their folk origin. (One old ballad, poem No. 158, is given in modern spelling.) Many of these stories are found in the ballads of various countries of Europe. In them we see the customs and superstitions, the ways of acting and feeling, of medieval people. But the human experiences of these poems are permanently interesting.

When the people that we come to know in poems have definite individuality, the poem has dramatic as well as narrative interest. The hero of a ballad is usually typical rather than individual, but his story has some dramatic quality. The hero of *Andrea del Sarto* is a unique person, and the dramatic element of the poem is our center of interest. The two elements, in varying proportions, are in all these poems. Together they make a poem of a person in action.

It might be well to remember Mr. Eliot's remark that emotion is evoked by 'objective correlatives,' which may be 'a set of objects, a situation, a chain of events.' In most of these poems, the emotions of the poet (or the speaker, if the poem is in the first person) are a part of the experience that the reader should re-create.

157, Anonymous, *Sir Patrick Spens*.
  l. 8. *braid*. Long.
  l. 31. *owre*. Ere.

158, Anonymous, *Lord Randall*.

159, Anonymous, *Mary Hamilton*.
  l. 7. *laigh*. Low.
  l. 16. *greet*. Grieve.

160, Anonymous, *The Wife of Usher's Well*.
  l. 7. *carline*. Old woman.
  l. 20. *birk*. Birch.
  l. 21. *syke*. Ditch.
  l. 22. *sheugh*. Ditch.
  l. 42. *channerin*. Fretting.
  l. 46. *byre*. Cow-barn.

161, Anonymous, *The Bailiff's Daughter of Islington.*
l. 22. *puggish.* Ragged.

162, Anonymous, *Young Waters.*
l. 2. *round tables.* A game.
l. 13. *Gowden-graithd.* Golden harnessed.
l. 21. *laird.* Landholder.
l. 32. *maun.* Must.
l. 49. *heiding-hill.* Beheading mound.

163, Anonymous, *Bonny Barbara Allan.*
l. 3. *hooly.* Slowly.

164, Anonymous, *Johnie Armstrong.*
l. 1. *Westmerland*, Westmorland, an English county.
l. 10. *sicke a won.* Such a one.

165, Anonymous, *A Lyke-Wake Dirge.* A dirge sung at the watch over a corpse.
l. 3. *fleet.* Floor? flute? sleet?
l. 7. *Whinny-muir.* The moor of prickly shrubs.
l. 19. *Brig.* Bridge.

166, Michael Drayton, *Ballad of Agincourt*, 1619. A strongly marked measure carries this along. What is it?

167, Ezra Pound, *Ballad of the Goodly Fere*, 1909. *Fere* means mate, companion. Simon Zelotes, one of the twelve apostles, usually called the Canaanite; Zelotes also means a zealot. Pound's conception of Christ and the meaning of his acts finds expression in narrative and dramatic form. How are these two fused together? What do the last two lines do in the poem? Compare this poem with poems Nos. 286–90.

168, John Keats, *La Belle Dame Sans Merci*, 1820. The title means 'The Beautiful Lady without Pity.' What is the effect of the short fourth line? What are the details that set the tone?

169, D. G. Rossetti, *The Blessed Damozel*, 1850. Notice the images which create the scene. How do the words in parentheses contribute to the narrative? What happens at the end?

170, William Morris, *The Haystack in the Floods*, 1858. How is the feeling of pity for Jehane aroused? How is it controlled? On what charge will Jehane be tried in Paris?

171, William Morris, *The Gillyflower of Gold*, 1858. The refrain is 'the beautiful yellow gillyflower.' What meaning does it gather as the poem moves along? *Honneur aux fils des preux* is the cry raised for the victor, 'honor to the sons of valiant knights.'

172, S. T. Coleridge, *The Rime of the Ancient Mariner*, 1798. In the *Biographia Literaria* Coleridge said that his aim was to write a poem in which 'the incidents and agents were to be, in part at least, supernatural; and the excellence aimed at was to consist in the interesting of the [reader's] affections by the dramatic truth of such emotions, as would naturally accompany such situations, supposing them real.' He wished to create 'persons and characters supernatural, or at least romantic; and yet so to transfer from our inward nature a human interest and a semblance of truth sufficient to procure for these shadows of imagination that willing suspension of disbelief for the moment, which constitutes poetic faith.' Coleridge answered a criticism that the poem did not have a moral: 'in my judgment the poem had too much; and that the only, or chief fault, if I might say so, was the intrusion of the moral sentiment so openly on the reader as a principle or cause of action in a work of pure imagination. It ought to have had no more moral than the *Arabian Nights'* tale of the merchant sitting down to eat dates by the side of a well and throwing the shells aside; and lo! a genie starts up and says he *must* kill the aforesaid merchant *because* one of the date shells had, it seems, put out the eye of the genie's son.'

173, Samuel Daniel, *Ulysses and the Siren*, 1605. This and the following poem are based on incidents and characters in Homer's *Odyssey*, the story of Ulysses' (Odysseus') wanderings on his return from the Siege of Troy. The two poems deal with certain ideas about admirable human attitudes and actions. *Ulysses and the Siren* is direct argument. The sirens were beautiful female creatures who sang to lure sailors onto a rocky coast; in Homer Ulysses enjoyed their singing but escaped by stuffing his men's ears so that they sailed past safely. In this poem Ulysses wins by persuasive speech.

174, Alfred Tennyson, *Ulysses*, 1842. In Homer's story Ulysses' life has been full of great achievements that should have satisfied any man's desire for action, and Ulysses returns home to his faithful wife, Penelope, content to live at rest. But Tennyson, following Dante's invention, creates a different Ulysses. This one has ideas and attitudes much like those of the argument in *Ulysses and the Siren*. What has Tennyson done in order to create a dramatic, rather than an argumentative, poem?

Tennyson said that this poem, written in the midst of his grief at Hallam's death, expressed his feeling of the need for 'going forward and braving the struggle of life.' Tennyson found an 'objective correlative' for his feeling in the aged Ulysses in a specific situation, speaking to his men, remembering the actions of the past and foreseeing the actions of the future. That is, *Ulysses* is a dramatic poem.

175, Alfred Tennyson, *The Lotos-Eaters*, 1842. The fruit of the lotus tree produced intense lassitude, in Homer's story, when Ulysses and his men ate of it. In this poem Tennyson writes a kind of counterpoint to *Ulysses*. Study the contrast in dominant feeling, in diction, sentence structure, rhythm, use of imagery, and word music. The Choric Song is built on alternating feelings: pleasure in living here and the pain of further travel. At the end the desire for pleasure finds its justification in a vision of the gods and of all men.

176, Alfred Tennyson, *Tithonus*, 1860. Tithonus, a prince of Troy, married the goddess of the dawn, Aurora, who asked the gods to give him immortality but forgot to ask eternal youth for him. Tennyson imagined what Tithonus must feel, withered to a shadow, still in love with the beauty of the dawn, to whom he speaks. Notice how color becomes an image of his feeling. The poem shows Tennyson's craftsmanship in creating exquisite overtones of meaning by the sounds of words.

177, Robert Browning, *My Last Duchess*, 1842. Browning's interest in human personality found ample material in the people of the Italian Renaissance. They speak in this and the two following poems. Here Browning has combined the dramatic and narrative elements to create, in brief space, a clearly realized person. To whom is the Duke speaking?

178, Robert Browning, *Andrea del Sarto*, 1855. Andrea del Sarto was a great painter in Florence in the sixteenth century. His work is excellent, except that often the eyes of his people are blurred, rarely showing anything of their inner personalities. He is speaking to his young wife.

l. 105. *The Urbinate*. Raphael.

l. 130. *Agnolo*. Michelangelo.

l. 149. *Francis*. Francis I, King of France, for whom Andrea worked a year; later Andrea bought a house for Lucrezia with money Francis had entrusted to him for buying pictures.

l. 220. *Cousin*. Polite word for lover.

179, Robert Browning, *Fra Lippo Lippi*, 1855. Fra Lippo (1406–69), a monk, was a great painter of Florence whose pictures clearly show his interest in mundane things. He painted a great deal for his own monastery, for ecclesiastical officials, and for churches. Compare his opinion of the spiritual with Andrea's. Notice also the differences in the language of the two men.

l. 17. *Cosimo*. Cosimo de Medici (1389–1464), the leading citizen of Florence.

l. 189. *Giotto*. An early painter who did not try to represent the physical exactly.

l. 347. Fra Lippo describes one of his great pictures, *The Coronation of the Virgin.*

180, Ezra Pound, *Cino*, 1909. Compare the method of narrative of this with that of the three preceding poems. Notice that, though he is much influenced by Browning, Pound has condensed and intensified his 'story' to a far greater degree. The 'archaic' English is not really archaic at all but an attempt to augment the medieval quality of the poem.

181, Amy Lowell, *Patterns*, 1916.

182, E. A. Robinson, *Richard Cory*, 1897.

183, E. A. Robinson, *Miniver Cheevy*, 1910.

184, E. A. Robinson, *Mr. Flood's Party*, 1921.

185, Robert Frost, *The Tuft of Flowers*, 1913.

186, Robert Frost, *Mending Wall*, 1914.

187, Robert Frost, *West-Running Brook*, 1928.

188, Archibald MacLeish, *Frescoes for Mr. Rockefeller's City . . .*, 1933. This poem owes its title to a heated public controversy. Diego Rivera, the great Mexican painter, had been commissioned to paint murals on American life for Rockefeller City; the owners refused to allow the murals to remain, claiming that they were Marxist propaganda glorifying the worker and satirizing the wealthy. This poem offers itself to Mr. Rockefeller's City to replace Rivera's frescoes. It is MacLeish's version of what America is and who built America.

189, Christopher Marlowe, *Hero and Leander*, 1598. Marlowe left this poem unfinished, as printed here, at his death in 1793. It was completed by George Chapman.
First Sestiad
l. 56. *Colchis.* Country of the Golden Fleece.
ll. 73–75. Narcissus.
l. 107. *star.* The moon, Diana.
l. 114. *shaggy-footed race.* Centaurs.
l. 158. *turtles' blood.* Turtle-doves, sacred to Venus.
Second Sestiad
l. 123. *in a diameter.* With direct rays.
l. 155. *god.* Neptune.

l. 179. *Helle.* Fleeing from her stepmother, she was drowned in the waters later named for her, Hellespont.

l. 292. *which made.* Ancient notions held that strife or war made all things.

l. 305. *Erycine.* Venus.

190, John Keats, *The Eve of St. Agnes*, 1820. A transcript of seven stanzas of the manuscript of this poem is given in Part VIII.

St. Agnes was a Roman virgin, a martyr; St. Agnes Day is January 21. Keats based his poem on the superstition that a girl could foresee her future husband if she performed certain rites on the eve of St. Agnes; if she went to bed without looking behind her and lay on her back with her hands under her head, he would appear in her dream, kiss her, and feast with her.

191, John Keats, *Hyperion*, 1820. If *Hyperion* had been finished it would have been an epic narrative of a change of dynasties in the Greek gods. The Greeks believed that the world began as Chaos, from which emerged Uranus (the Sky, male) and Gæa (Earth, female). Their children were the Titans (Earth-born); the leader among them, Saturn (or Cronus), overthrew his parents and ruled as King (with Rhea as Queen) of the new dynasty, whose lower gods were his brother and sister Titans. Then the children of Saturn, led by Zeus (Jove), rebelled and overthrew the Titan dynasty. This War of the Titans, lasting ten years, and the change to the new dynasty make the subject of Keats's poem.

An epic poem is a story of great events and heroic characters. The action usually moves slowly. The manner of writing is dignified. The story carries important meanings. Milton's *Paradise Lost* was written 'to justify the ways of God to man.' Keats sees in his story a central idea about the nature of the world: that it steadily progresses from the less beautiful to the more beautiful. This interpretation of the change in dynasties is spoken by Oceanus, Book II, ll. 167–243. Following the epic tradition, Keats begins the poem in the middle of the action: the War is almost finished, Saturn has been defeated with all the lesser gods except Hyperion, who still rules the Sun. The poem opens with Saturn sitting alone, dazed and still; he is summoned by Thea, wife of Hyperion, to a council of the defeated gods underground, where they have been imprisoned by Zeus.

Book I

l. 146. *Olympus.* Home of the new gods.

l. 164. The scene shifts to Hyperion's palace of the Sun, at sunset. Hyperion rides on a winged ball of fire. The description of the palace suggests a magnificent sunset.

l. 304. *Cœlus.* Another name for Uranus, the Sky, Hyperion's father.

Book II

l. 4. *Cybele.* Another name for Rhea (also Ops), wife of Saturn. Many of the Titans are described in the following lines.

[Poem 191]

l. 166. The council begins, each speaker presenting a philosophy. Oceanus is wise; Clymene is sensitive to beauty but cannot think clearly; Enceladus knows only brute force.

Book III

l. 13. *the Father of all verse.* Apollo, new god of the sun, wisdom, poetry, song, and other civilized arts. He is still a youth, capable of beautiful song, but not yet possessed of knowledge. When he suddenly acquires knowledge from Mnemosyne (Memory, a goddess of the old dynasty, the link between the old and the new) Apollo achieves godhood. Keats also meant that when a young poet accepts knowledge, a painful process, he becomes a mature poet. See Notes to poems Nos. 100–102.

Keats probably intended to continue the story by telling of the final counterattack of the old gods and the permanent establishment of the new gods in power.

IV

SATIRIC POEMS

Perhaps the most important thing to remember in reading satiric poems is that the poet is not trying to give an objective, balanced, and just estimate of a person or of a set of events. He is trying to make us *feel* as *he* does toward the person or events. For this purpose he focuses our attention only on those facts which will evoke these feelings and attitudes, or he may invent imaginary facts. If he appears to be giving a balanced and just estimate, that is just a weapon used to make us more willing to yield to his feeling. To 'damn with faint praise' is an effective way to damn. The phrase occurs in Pope's *Epistle to Dr. Arbuthnot*, in his portrait of Addison, one of our most brilliant examples of how a satirist can use apparent objectivity as a deadly weapon. The intention of the poet should be clearly seen and constantly kept in mind. Often he may not wish us to dislike a person, but merely to be amused at him. Pope's attitude toward Belinda in *The Rape of the Lock* is good-natured amusement.

Some kind of laughter is frequently the response the reader should have. Serious satire aims to make the person seem ridiculous. A frequent device is the incongruity between the supposed worth of the person and the situation which the poet invents for him. Incongruous images are often used.

In elaborate satiric poetry, such as *The Rape of the Lock*, the reader is expected to be aware of several meanings at once. When Belinda

[Poem 192]

faces herself at the dressing table, we understand that she is literally making up her face; the poet also makes it clear that this is a religious ceremony, worship at the altar; his language reminds us that he is telling a heroic story of great significance, and that she is getting ready for battle. In Byron's *Vision of Judgment* the events have meanings arising out of their similarity to or contrast with events in Southey's poem, in *Paradise Lost*, and in the Bible. Reading satiric poetry exercises our wits.

A satiric poem is frequently occasional, that is, it arises out of a specific occasion and refers to details of that occasion and of the contemporary life of which it is a part. Readers several generations later do not understand these references unless they happen to be well acquainted with the earlier period. In general, however, readers today can enjoy satiric poems of the past much more fully than might be supposed. Many of the references in part explain their own meaning. A few notes will frequently do much to enable the reader to understand the meaning of the reference. A satiric poet usually delivers so many thrusts at his subject that we can fail to see some and yet enjoy the art of an expert swordsman.

192, John Dryden, *Mac Flecknoe*, 1682. The sub-title is *A Satire on the True Blue Protestant Poet*, *T. S.*, i.e. Thomas Shadwell. Just before writing this poem Dryden had issued two vigorous political satires, part of the warfare between the Whig and Tory parties. One of the answers was by Thomas Shadwell, a former friend and a well-known dramatist, in a poem which was a violent and scurrilous personal attack on Dryden. The counterattack was *Mac Flecknoe*. In the poem, Mac Flecknoe, a very dull writer of plays who had died recently, is seeking a successor to his throne of dullness—and Shadwell is his choice. Many of Shadwell's plays are referred to: *Epsom Wells*, *Psyche*, *The Miser*, *The Humorists*, *Love's Kingdom*, *The Virtuoso*.

l. 29. *Heywood and Shirley*. Dramatist of the previous generation.

l. 43. *Arion*. Famous Greek musician; thrown in the sea, he enchanted the Dolphins, who carried him to land on their backs.

l. 64. *Augusta*. London.

l. 74. *Nursery*. A theatrical training school for boys and girls.

l. 151. *George*. Sir George Etheridge, a fine dramatist, who created the characters mentioned next.

l. 163. *Sedley*. Sir Charles Sedley, who had written a Prologue for *Epsom Wells*.

l. 168. *Sir Formal*. Sir Formal Trifle, florid orator in *The Virtuoso*,

l. 179. *Prince Nicander*. A character in *Psyche*.

l. 212. *Bruce and Longville*. Characters in *The Virtuoso* who dropped the orating Sir Formal through a trap-door.

193, Allen Tate, *Mr. Pope*, 1928. This poem, of course, is not a satire, but an appreciation of Pope's genius.

194, Alexander Pope, *Epistle to Dr. Arbuthnot*, 1735. In his *Advertisement* Pope describes this poem as 'a sort of bill of complaint, begun many years since, and drawn up by snatches, as the several occasions offered' and now completed and published because 'some Persons of Rank and Fortune' had recently attacked not only his poems but his '*Person, Morals*, and *Family*.' This is his answer to these attacks in particular, and his defense of his aims and position as a man of letters.

Pope was a master craftsman of verse form. His couplets, however, are not easy to read properly. A full discussion of the way to read them will be found in the note to poem No. 201.

The poem is in the form of a dialogue between Pope and his intimate friend Dr. Arbuthnot.

l. 1. Pope tells his servant to keep out would-be poets who plague him. They are the objects of his satire until l. 122.

l. 2. *Bedlam*. Insane asylum in London.

l. 48. *Prologue*. A Prologue by Pope would greatly help a play by an unknown writer.

l. 79. *Dunciad*. Pope's poem satirizing petty writers.

l. 97. *Bavius*. Stock name for a bad poet.

l. 99. *Sappho*. The name of the Greek poetess. Pope means Lady Mary Wortley Montague, once his close friend but now his bitter enemy, who was one of the 'Persons of Rank' that had slandered him.

l. 115. *Ammon's great son*. Alexander the Great.

l. 120. *Maro*. Vergil.

l. 123. Here Pope begins his account of his life as a poet.

ll. 133–9. These names are of writers famous when Pope was young.

l. 147. *Fanny*. Lord Hervey, whom Pope flays in ll. 303–31.

ll. 191–212. *Atticus* is Joseph Addison, perhaps the most influential literary man of his day. He had befriended Pope, but later (Pope believed) had tried to injure his literary reputation. The portrait of Atticus may not be fair to Addison, but it is the most brilliant satirical characterization in English poetry.

l. 228. *Bufo*. Portrait of a vain but parsimonious patron of letters, probably the Earl of Halifax.

l. 254. *Gay*. A poet. Pope wrote the epitaph for his tomb.

ll. 297–8. A fictional passage in one of Pope's poems had been falsely interpreted by gossip to refer to the Duke of Chandos.

ll. 302–31. *Sporus* is Lord Hervey, who had joined Lady Mary in defaming Pope's character and family. He was the perfect fop, effeminate to the point of painting his face. He drank ass's milk to improve his health.

    l. 332. Pope resumes the account of his literary career.

    195, Alexander Pope, *The Rape of the Lock*, 1714. Pope wrote this poem, at the request of his friend Caryl, to turn light ridicule on an incident that had caused a feud between two families: a young man had snipped a love-lock from the head of a young lady, Arabella Fermor. Pope related the incident in a mock-heroic or mock-epic poem. With it he printed a letter to the young lady.

MADAM,
    It will be in vain to deny that I have some regard for this piece, since I dedicate it to You. Yet you may bear me witness, it was intended only to divert a few young Ladies, who have good sense and good humour enough to laugh not only at their sex's little unguarded follies, but at their own. But as it was communicated with the air of a Secret, it soon found its way into the world. An imperfect copy having been offer'd to a Bookseller, you had the good-nature for my sake to consent to the publication of one more correct: This I was forc'd to, before I had executed half my design, for the Machinery was entirely wanting to compleat it.
    The Machinery, Madam, is a term invented by the Critics, to signify that part which the Deities, Angels, or Dæmons are made to act in a Poem: For the ancient Poets are in one respect like many modern Ladies: let an action be never so trivial in itself, they always make it appear of the utmost importance. These Machines I determined to raise on a very new and odd foundation, the Rosicrucian doctrine of Spirits.
    I know how disagreeable it is to make use of hard words before a Lady; but 'tis so much the concern of a Poet to have his works understood, and particularly by your Sex, that you must give me leave to explain two or three difficult terms.
    The Rosicrucians are a people I must bring you acquainted with. The best account I know of them is in a French book call'd *Le Comte de Gabalis*, which both in its title and size is so like a Novel, that many of the Fair Sex have read it for one by mistake. According to these Gentlemen, the four Elements are inhabited by Spirits, which they call Sylphs, Gnomes, Nymphs, and Salamanders. The Gnomes or Dæmons of Earth delight in mischief; but the Sylphs, whose habitation is in the Air, are the best-condition'd creatures imaginable. For they say, any mortals may enjoy the most intimate familiarities with these gentle Spirits, upon a condition very easy to all true Adepts, an inviolate preservation of Chastity.
    As to the following Canto's, all the passages of them are as fabulous, as the Vision at the beginning, or the Transformation at the end; (except the loss of your Hair, which I always mention with reverence). The Human persons are as fictitious as the airy ones; and the character of Belinda, as it is now manag'd, resembles you in nothing but in Beauty.
    If this Poem had as many Graces as there are in your Person, or in your Mind, yet I could never hope it should pass thro' the world half so Uncensur'd as You have done. But let its fortune be what it will, mine is happy enough, to have given me this occasion of assuring you that I am, with the truest esteem, MADAM,
        Your most obedient, Humble Servant,
                        A. POPE.

The descriptions of the life of the polite society of the time are clear enough not to need explanation. The parody of the incidents and art of the heroic poem is notable in many passages. Supernatural agents protect the heroine, who worships her own image at the dressing table. The card game is a battle. Umbriel goes to the underworld, the Cave of Spleen, for magic help. Belinda's friend, Thalestris, appeals to the heroic Sir Plume for aid. The climax comes in a great battle, fought with smiles, frowns, and snuff; Belinda draws her weapon, a bodkin, whose history is told at length. And Belinda's name is made immortal.

196, Lord Byron, *The Vision of Judgment*, 1822. When George III, who began his reign in 1760, died in 1820, Robert Southey the Poet Laureate wrote a poem, *A Vision of Judgment*, describing the arrival of the King's soul in heaven, its triumph over old enemies brought from Hell to accuse it, and its entrance into eternal life. The poem, untrue to history in its fulsome praise of the King, is dull with platitudinous sanctity. It enraged Byron, who despised both the King and Southey. The two poets had for years quarreled in print; lately Southey had attacked Byron as the leader of the 'Satanic School' of poets. With glee Byron seized the opportunity to write a parody of Southey's poem. He has several aims: to give a true estimate of George's reign, to destroy Southey with ridicule, to have good-natured fun with the popular notion of heavenly affairs derived from Milton's *Paradise Lost*. Above all, Byron wanted to enjoy himself.

l. 63. In his old age George was blind and, at times, insane.

l. 92. George II concealed and ignored his father's will.

l. 156. *parvenu*. Upstart. St. Paul was not one of the Apostles.

l. 224. Johanna Southcote announced that she was with child by immaculate conception; she had the dropsy.

l. 377. George opposed Catholic Emancipation, the right to hold political office.

l. 393. *Cerberus*. The dog that guarded Hell.

l. 520. *Wilkes*. John Wilkes, a popular political leader, who violently criticized George, was imprisoned, and later was elected Lord Mayor of London. Southey had described Wilkes, and other opponents of George, as speechless with shame before the King's soul.

l. 585. *Junius*. The writer of *The Letters of Junius*, which effectively attacked George, has never been identified.

l. 769. Southey held radical political views but later turned very conservative.

V

PASTORAL POEMS

i

Pastoral is perhaps the most artificial and conventional of the forms of poetry. Yet, like most conventional arts, it was intended at one time to be realistic and natural. Just as the highly stylized conventions of classic tragedy grew out of the religious rituals of ancient Greece, so the typical aspects of pastoral poetry had their origin in the real life of shepherds.

Pastoral poetry has its beginnings in the songs of real shepherds in the island of Sicily many centuries before Christ. The sunny climate, the hillsides covered with soft grasses, the frequent springs and natural caverns by the shores of the sea somehow combined with the relatively leisurely life of the young men and women who tended sheep and goats to inspire simple songs of love and joy, or occasionally of grief for a dead shepherd. The songs these shepherds sang were never written down and we have lost both the tunes and the words. We can reconstruct them only from scattered remarks in the histories of a later Greek time, and from the literary poems of Theocritus. It is to Theocritus, who lived in the third century B.C., that the pastoral tradition owes its origin.

Theocritus was born in Sicily, but lived the greater part of his life in cities, especially Alexandria which was a great intellectual capital in the time of the Ptolemies. His songs, called *idylls* (a Greek word meaning *little pictures*), were written of the life which he had known as a boy and to which he looked back with the typical longing of a country boy forced to live in a bustling city. He made these idylls mainly for his own pleasure, and he tried to put into them faithful images of real pastoral life. They were deservedly popular, and like most arts which are both original and popular they were soon widely imitated. The most important of the imitators were Bion and Moschus, both of whom were nearly contemporary with Theocritus. (Moschus's *Lament for Bion* will be found below in the note on *Pastoral Elegy*. These poets were of the city, and their pastorals had little of the freshness and naturalness of their master; but they set conventional patterns and adapted the pastoral to new uses which have never been lost to the tradition. They, in turn, were imitated by the Roman poet Virgil, who, in his *Eclogues*, raised pastoral to a plane of high poetry.

After Virgil the poets of pastoral are legion. With the beginning of the Christian era, the poets naturally combined their songs of the shepherd's life with the new symbolism of the shepherd which the New Testament offered; and in the period between the fall of Rome and the beginnings of the Italian Renascence literally hundreds of poems were written which work a Christian meaning into the older pagan materials of pastoral. But during this long period nearly all of the lyrical quality of the pagan poetry was lost, as pastoral became more and more purely didactic.

Together with most of the forms of classical Greek poetry pastoral was revived during the Renascence, first by the Italians, to whom Boccaccio had given the lead even earlier, and then by the French and English. It comes into English during the sixteenth century, toward the end of which Edmund Spenser and Sir Philip Sidney (the latter in his prose romance *Arcadia*), like Virgil in the earlier time, raised it again to very high levels of importance. For nearly a century pastoral was one of the most popular forms of poetry and most of the poets tried their hand at it. It was revived briefly at the beginning of the eighteenth century by John Gay and Alexander Pope and then almost entirely died out of English poetry. Louis MacNeice's *Eclogue by a Five-Barred Gate* is a remarkable poem in our time if only because it is so isolated.

ii

The Conventions of Pastoral: There are three chief kinds of pastoral: the lyric, the dramatic, and the elegiac. In the following paragraphs the typical materials of the first two kinds are discussed; the elegiac is treated in detail in the notes to *Lycidas*, poem No. 205.

Pastoral lyrics are for the most part love poems. They deal with simple situations and uncomplicated passions and draw many of their comparisons from nature. Typical themes are the stirring of new life in the spring, the need to make love before age removes the desire, coy flirtation, the dejection of the rejected suitor, and rivalry for a pretty shepherdess. Conventional images draw parallels between spring and youth and between autumn and age, liken feminine beauty to the beauties of nature, especially flowers, and picture the shepherd as a minstrel playing upon his oaten pipe. The setting is a kind of wonderful land of greenness, sunshine, and mild weather, which bears little resemblance to any real place. The names of the shepherds and shepherdesses are drawn from the early Greek poems: Corin, Thyrsis, Philemon, Corinna, Phyllis, etc. The measure of the verse is usually simple and musical, nearly always rhyming, and many pastorals have in fact been set to music.

These are the qualities which all pastoral lyrics have in common, and the excellence of a pastoral lyric will generally depend upon the original twists which a poet may give to the old materials or the fresh beauty with which he may shape them. There are no finer examples in English than the poems of Marlowe and Ralegh (*The Passionate Shepherd* and *The Nymph's Reply*, Nos. 197 and 198). But during the Renascence the poets began to use the symbols and conventions of pastoral as a disguise for other matters. They began, that is to say, to write of real people and real situations, using the pastoral names and places instead of the real ones. The disguise was thin but safe, and soon even sharp satire was clothed in the old conventions. Examples of this use of pastoral are discussed in the notes to *Lycidas* and *Adonais*, poems Nos. 205 and 206. The most important poem of this kind in English is Spenser's *The Faerie Queene*, in which the tales of chivalry are supplemented by a great deal of pastoral which contains allegory of the court life and politics of Queen Elizabeth's time.

Dramatic pastoral is cast in the form of monologue, dialogue, or sometimes of three-way and even four-way conversation. The speeches are generally interspersed with short lyrics or songs to accompany a dance. The settings and names are the same as those of the lyric pastoral; but the themes are usually philosophical. Typical subjects for discussion are the meaning of death, the fleeting quality of time, the advantages of various rural occupations as compared with the life of a shepherd, and the meaning of happiness. The weather is often represented as in keeping with the subject of the discussion. If the shepherds are to talk of joy or love or happiness they will meet on a wonderful morning in May. If they are to meditate upon human misery or debate the meaning of death they will meet in the cold of winter or during wind and storm. Here again, the poets of the Renascence saw the possibilities of pastoral convention as a convenient disguise for real problems and real people, and again Spenser's *The Faerie Queene* is the most important example. But these conventions are seldom better used than in MacNeice's *Eclogue by a Five-Barred Gate* where the two shepherds meet with Death himself. The time is spring, but that is fitting because Death is seducing them with illusions of new life.

iii

The reading of pastoral requires, more than most poetry, an acceptance of convention. Unless we can forget for the moment the careful description of external nature which marks the poetry of Wordsworth and other Romantics, or the attempt to imitate the talk of real people which is found in much modern poetry, to mention only two examples, we shall not get very far with pastoral. We must not expect to find the rather complicated emotions and psychological situations of much Romantic and modern poetry and all real life; nor must we look for too much depth of feeling. Rather, pastoral should be read in something of the spirit in which we listen to the formal music of Bach, Haydn, or Mozart, paying heed to the skill with which the conventions are handled and taking pleasure in the recognition of enduring symbols. Indeed, anyone who has learned to take pleasure in Beethoven's *Pastoral Symphony* (Symphony No. 6 in F Major) will find a similar pleasure in pastoral poetry. The poet has deliberately accepted limits within which he will work, and we should not expect him to exceed them. We should judge him rather by the skill and the beauty with which he fills them. The central experience of a pastoral poem is generally a simple and unified thing; but no kind of poetry better illustrates the essential difference between the language of poetry and the language of prose. The experience and the beauty are dependent upon the conventions, and the exercise of prose paraphrase will quickly show that the two are inseparable.

197, Christopher Marlowe, *The Passionate Shepherd to His Love*, 1600. This should be read together with the next poem. Ralegh supplies the other side of Marlowe's picture. In this poem the conventional pastoral pleasures of young love in a life of leisure are celebrated, as the shepherd woos his sweetheart. Ralegh, on the other hand, makes an equally delightful lyric out of equally conventional references to the passage of time and the folly and fickleness of mankind. Compare the central idea in the two poems and notice how each depends upon conventional images such as those discussed in the introductory paragraphs above.

198, Sir Walter Ralegh, *The Nymph's Reply to the Shepherd*, 1600.

199, Robert Herrick, *Corinna's Going A-Maying*, 1648. (Probably written many years earlier.)

200, Robert Herrick, *To Phyllis, To Love and Live with Him*, 1648. (Probably written many years earlier.)

201, Alexander Pope, *Summer: The Second Pastoral, or Alexis*, 1709. Pope's four pastorals, one for each of the seasons, were said by him to have been written when he was only sixteen. Though this may well be an exaggeration, they were certainly written at a very early age. The chief problem in reading this poem, as well as nearly all of Pope's work, is the understanding of the so-called *heroic couplet*, the measure in which the poem is written. Since the time of Wordsworth there has been a tendency to judge the heroic couplet as a monotonous measure scarcely more musical than prose. Some critics have even denied that it is poetry at all. Whatever it may have been in lesser hands, the couplet of Pope needs only a careful ear to prove the mistake which such critics make. It is not an easy measure to read, but the beauty of such a poem as this well repays the effort to learn. The chief difficulty is, of course, the rhyme scheme. Read with emphasis upon each rhyme word, the couplet will no doubt have a soporific effect which eventually becomes quite unpleasant. But read with a natural emphasis on the major words of the line, regardless of their position, the rhymes will fall into harmonies which are often exquisite and subtle. The *punctuation* in Pope's couplets must be strictly observed. He never uses a comma when he means a semi-colon, or a colon when he means a period; that is to say, each mark of punctuation carries with it clear instructions for the pause in reading as exactly as the notes in a musical score are definite guides to the musician. The comma indicates the shortest pause, the semi-colon a slightly longer, the colon still a longer, and the period a full stop. The paragraph indentations are guides to a shift in subject matter, and naturally call for an even longer pause. The punctuation at the end of the line must be observed with special care, according to this scheme, and the whole effect is spoiled if a line which has no concluding punctuation is read as though it had. This poem, which is filled with the conventional materials of pastoral, becomes even more artificial for being poured into the couplet mold. But like the strict forms of Mozart, in the hands of Pope the artifice serves only to enhance the freshness of the music.

l. 9. *O Garth.* Dr. Garth, physician, poet, and friend of Pope, to whom the poem is dedicated.

ll. 73–6. These lines, set to Handel's music, make one of the high points in English song.

202, William Collins, *Ode to Evening*, 1746. This poem is especially remarkable for its unique measure. The diction is conventional, and the strain of melancholy (an eighteenth-century specialty) is not uncommon in pastoral at any time; but the whole effect depends mainly upon the slow and deliberate quality of the unrhymed iambic lines: five beats in the first two, and three in the last two of each stanza.

l. 2. *chaste Eve*. The subject, which is repeated several times, finds its main verb in *teach*, l. 15.

203, Matthew Arnold, *The Scholar-Gypsy*, 1853. This poem is a good illustration of the use of pastoral convention as a light cloak for narrative or philosophical meditation, in this case both.

l. 31. *Glanvil's book*. Arnold's explanatory note quotes the following passage from Joseph Glanvil's *The Vanity of Dogmatizing*, 1661:

There was very lately a lad in the University of Oxford, who was by his poverty forced to leave his studies there; and at last to join himself to a company of vagabond gypsies. Among these extravagant people, by the insinuating subtility of his carriage, he quickly got so much of their love and esteem as that they discovered to him their mystery. After he had been a pretty while exercised in the trade, there chanced to ride by a couple of scholars, who had formerly been of his acquaintance. They quickly spied out their old friend among the gypsies; and he gave them an account of the necessity which drove him to that kind of life, and told them that the people he went with were not such imposters as they were taken for, but that they had a traditional kind of learning among them, and could do wonders by the power of imagination, their fancy binding that of others: that himself had learned much of their art, and when he had compassed the whole secret, he intended, he said, to leave their company, and give the world an account of what he had learned.

204, Louis MacNeice, *Eclogue by a Five-Barred Gate*, 1935. The term *eclogue* is derived from a Greek word meaning *to select*. It is generally used to describe a pastoral poem which picks out or selects a conversation among two or more shepherds. The central experience of this poem is vastly more complicated than is usually the case in the dramatic pastoral. It is a modern feeling about death and should strike a responsive chord in most readers. Compare the poem with No. 115, '*Hearing of harvests rotting in the valleys*,' by MacNeice's friend W. H. Auden. Notice that much of the familiar convention of pastoral is here, but directly ridiculed. Notice, too, that the setting is the English countryside in which there are such present-day symbols as 'telephone wires,' a far cry from the Arcadias of the older pastoral.

The three poems which are grouped at the conclusion of this section fall into a special category of pastoral, the *elegy*. The term is borrowed from a Greek word meaning a *song of mourning* and goes back, as a literary form, at least to the time of Bion and Moschus who were mentioned in the introductory notes. The structure of the pastoral elegy is based upon a primitive ritual of burial which, in turn, is probably a vestige of even earlier vegetation rites. The elements of the typical structure are best studied in one of the classical models used by Milton, Shelley, and Arnold in the three poems presented here. Here is the *Lament for Bion* with which Moschus mourned the passing of his fellow poet. (The text is taken from the translation of Andrew Lang in his *Theocritus, Bion, and Moschus.*)

Wail, let me hear you wail, ye woodland glades, and thou Dorian water; and weep ye rivers, for Bion, the well beloved! Now all ye green things, mourn, and now ye groves lament him, ye flowers now in sad clusters breathe yourselves away. Now redden ye roses in your sorrow, and now wax red ye windflowers, now thou hyacinth, whisper the letters on thee graven, and add a deeper *ai ai* to thy petals; he is dead, the beautiful singer.
Begin, ye Sicilian Muses, begin the dirge.

Ye nightingales that lament among the thick leaves of the trees, tell ye to the Sicilian waters of Arethusa the tidings that Bion the herdsman is dead, and that with Bion song too has died, and perished hath the Dorian minstrelsy.
Begin, ye Sicilian Muses, begin the dirge.

Ye Strymonian swans, sadly wail ye by the waters, and chant with melancholy notes the dolorous song, even such a song as in his time with voice like yours he was wont to sing. And tell again to the Œagrian maidens, tell to all the Nymphs Bistonian, how that he hath perished, the Dorian Orpheus.
Begin, ye Sicilian Muses, begin the dirge.

No more to his herds he sings, that beloved herdsman, no more 'neath the lonely oaks he sits and sings, nay, but by Pluteus's side he chants a refrain of oblivion. The mountains too are voiceless: and the heifers that wander by the bulls lament and refuse their pasture.
Begin, ye Sicilian Muses, begin the dirge.

Thy sudden doom, O Bion, Apollo himself lamented, and the Satyrs mourned thee, and the Priapi in sable raiment, and the Panes sorrow for thy song, and the fountain fairies in the wood made moan, and their tears turned to rivers of waters. And Echo in the rocks laments that thou art silent, and no more she mimics thy voice. And in sorrow for thy fall the trees cast down

[689]

their fruit, and all the flowers have faded. From the ewes hath flowed no fair milk, nor honey from the hives, nay, it hath perished for mere sorrow in the wax, for now hath thy honey perished, and no more it behooves men to gather the honey of the bees.

Begin, ye Sicilian Muses, begin the dirge.

Not so much did the dolphin mourn beside the sea-banks, nor ever sang so sweet the nightingale on the cliffs, nor so much lamented the swallow on the long ranges of the hills, nor shrilled so loud the halcyon o'er his sorrows;

Begin, ye Sicilian Muses, begin the dirge.

Nor so much, by the grey sea-waves, did ever the sea-bird sing, nor so much in the dells of dawn did the bird of Memnon bewail the son of Morning, fluttering around his tomb, as they lamented for Bion dead.

Nightingales, and all the swallows that once he was wont to delight, that he would teach to speak, they sat over against each other on the boughs and kept moaning, and the birds sang in answer, 'Wail, ye wretched ones, even ye!'

Begin, ye Sicilian Muses, begin the dirge.

Who, ah who will ever make music on thy pipe, O thrice desired Bion, and who will put his mouth to the reeds of thine instrument? who is so bold?

For still thy lips and still thy breath survive, and Echo, among the reeds, doth still feed upon thy songs. To Pan shall I bear the pipe? Nay, perchance even he would fear to set his mouth to it, lest, after thee, he should win but the second prize.

Begin, ye Sicilian Muses, begin the dirge.

Yea, and Galatea laments thy song, she whom once thou wouldst delight, as with thee she sat by the sea-banks. For not like the Cyclops didst thou sing —him fair Galatea ever fled, but on thee she still looked more kindly than on the salt water. And now hath she forgotten the wave, and sits on the lonely sands, but still she keeps thy kine.

Begin, ye Sicilian Muses, begin the dirge.

All the gifts of the Muses, herdsman, have died with thee, the delightful kisses of maidens, the lips of boys; and woful round thy tomb the loves are weeping. But Cypris loves thee far more than the kiss wherewith she kissed the dying Adonis.

Begin, ye Sicilian Muses, begin the dirge.

This, O most musical of rivers, is thy second sorrow, this, Meles, thy new woe. Of old didst thou lose Homer, that sweet mouth of Calliope, and men say thou didst bewail thy goodly son with streams of many tears, and didst fill all the salt sea with the voice of thy lamentation—now again another son thou weepest, and in a new sorrow art thou wasting away.

Begin, ye Sicilian Muses, begin the dirge.

Both were beloved of the fountains, and one ever drank of the Pegasean fount, but the other would drain a draught of Arethusa. And the one sang

the fair daughter of Tyndarus, and the mighty son of Thetis, and Menelaus Atreus's son, but that other,—not of wars, not of tears, but of Pan, would he sing, and of herdsmen would he chant, and so singing, he tended the herds. And pipes he would fashion, and would milk the sweet heifer, and taught lads how to kiss, and Love he cherished in his bosom and woke the passion of Aphrodite.

Begin, ye Sicilian Muses, begin the dirge.

Every famous city laments thee, Bion, and all the towns. Ascra laments thee far more than her Hesiod, and Pindar is less regretted by the forests of Bœotia. Nor so much did pleasant Lesbos mourn for Alcaeus, nor did the Teian town so greatly bewail her poet, while for thee more than for Archilochus doth Paros yearn, and not for Sappho, but still for thee doth Mytilene wail her musical lament;

[Here seven verses are lost.]

And in Syracuse Theocritus; but I sing thee the dirge of an Ausonian sorrow, I that am no stranger to the pastoral song, but heir of the Doric Muse which thou didst teach thy pupils. This was thy gift to me; to others didst thou leave thy wealth, to me thy minstrelsy.

Begin, ye Sicilian Muses, begin the dirge.

Ah me, when the mallows wither in the garden, and the green parsley, and the curled tendrils of the anise, on a later day they live again, and spring in another year; but we men, we the great and mighty, or wise, when once we have died, in hollow earth we sleep, gone down into silence; a right long, and endless, and unawakening sleep. And thou too, in the earth wilt be lapped in silence, but the nymphs have thought good that the frog should eternally sing. Nay, him I would not envy, for 'tis no sweet song he singeth.

Begin, ye Sicilian Muses, begin the dirge.

Poison came, Bion, to thy mouth, thou didst know poison. To such lips as thine did it come, and was not sweetened? What mortal was so cruel that could mix poison for thee, or who could give thee the venom that heard thy voice? surely he had no music in his soul.

Begin, ye Sicilian Muses, begin the dirge.

But justice hath overtaken them all. Still for this sorrow I weep, and bewail thy ruin. But ah, if I might have gone down like Orpheus to Tartarus, or as once Odysseus, or Alcides of yore, I too would speedily have come to the house of Pluteus, that thee perchance I might behold, and if thou singest to Pluteus, that I might hear what is thy song. Nay, sing to the Maiden some strain of Sicily, sing some sweet pastoral lay.

And she too is Sicilian, and on the shores by Aetna she was wont to play, and she knew the Dorian strain. Not unrewarded will the singing be; and as once to Orpheus's sweet minstrelsy she gave Eurydice to return with him, even so will she send thee too, Bion, to the hills. But if I, even I, and my piping had aught availed, before Pluteus I too would have sung.

In this, as in most of the elegies, the lamentation is presented through the song of a single shepherd, the dear friend of the dead shepherd. But his song is in several parts, all closely related. (1) The poet calls upon the Muses to lift their voices in a funeral dirge, for the scene is the burial of the dead shepherd. (2) The poet exhorts the trees, flowers, and creatures of the scene to join in the lament. (3) The poet himself makes the chief 'speech,' in which he celebrates the virtues of the dead shepherd and reviews his life in general terms. (4) The poet explains the manner of the shepherd's death. (5) The poet assures us that the spirit of the shepherd is not dead, but is, rather, elevated to a higher life. (In many elegies, for example *Lycidas*, the mourners are represented as decking the casket with flowers just before the poet sings of the elevation of the soul of the dead shepherd.) Within the various sections of the elegy the poet explains his personal relation to the dead shepherd and calls attention to the living people who, though not present at the burial service, are also lamenting the loss of the beloved shepherd. In most cases, as in this, all of Nature as well as the gods are exhorted to join in the lamentation.

205, John Milton, *Lycidas*, 1637. This was one of several poems contributed to a memorial volume published by friends of Edward King, whom Milton had known as a student at the University of Cambridge and who was drowned in the Irish Sea. Perhaps no single poem in English has been so lavishly praised; but it offers a number of difficulties for the modern reader. The following brief commentary is intended as a guide for reading the poem intelligently, not as a full analysis.

(1) *Structure.* The poem, like the *Lament for Bion*, is built upon the pastoral funeral service, and falls into several divisions which correspond to the steps in the ritual. ll. 1–14 contain the statement of the subject, the fact that Lycidas is dead and that Milton feels that he must make an expression of his grief. ll. 15–49: The poet calls upon the Muses to commence the dirge, and explains his relation to the dead shepherd. ll. 50–84: The poet, who is the chief mourner, now makes his own address, complaining that the nymphs of the countryside in which Lycidas had kept his sheep failed to protect him from the sea. He goes on to sing of the fleeting quality of earthly fame, but takes heart that true fame is heavenly and cannot die. ll. 85–102: Triton (the 'Herald of the Sea') reports that Neptune, god of the sea, is not to be blamed for the death; and Hippotades, son of Aeolus, god of the wind, likewise exonerates the winds. The blame is cast upon the ship itself, which must have been built during an inauspicious time. ll. 103–31: The procession of mourn-

ers continues with the speeches of Camus (god of the river Cam and of Cambridge where Lycidas and his elegist had been students together) and St. Peter. ll. 132–64: The speeches over, the mourners deck the bier with flowers. There can be no burial of course, since there is no corpse. ll. 165–85: Now comes the elevation, the poet singing of the real triumph of the soul of the dead shepherd which is now in heaven; and the service is over. ll. 186–93: The poem concludes with the idea of the continuity of life, in spite of the particular death. This is the formal, conventional structure of the poem and it is on this level that the reader should first grasp it.

(2) *Themes*. Into the form, as outlined, Milton works several themes, of which two are of major importance: *death by water*, and the *life of single purpose*. Death by water, of course, runs through the whole poem. Edward King was drowned in the Irish Sea and Milton himself was about to go to Italy by water, so that he is especially impressed by the fact of drowning. He recalls the story of Orpheus in one of the finest images of the poem, ll. 58–63. Orpheus, the first Greek lyric poet, according to the old myth, aroused the anger of the Thracian women when he refused to pay attention to them after the death of his wife Eurydice. They hurled rocks and trees at him, but the beauty of his song caused them to remain suspended in mid-air. But the women set up a hideous roar which drowned his song and brought about his death. They then dismembered his body and threw it into the river Hebrus. The head of Orpheus, however, floated down the river to the island of Lesbos where Sappho was to write the next great lyric poetry. This evidently signifies the continuity of the tradition; and Milton uses it for that purpose in *Lycidas*. The images in the elevation passage (ll. 165–85) give water a different meaning. For just as the sun seems to sink into the sea at night and to rise again from it in the morning, so Lycidas, though drowned, is raised to heaven, where the streams are filled with Nectar; and his 'genius' has returned to guard the place where he had lived upon earth and to protect 'all that wander in that perilous flood.' His body has been washed pure under the sea and water is no longer dreadful to him (ll. 154–8). The second theme, the life of single or dedicated purpose, also unites Milton with King. For just as King was preparing to be a clergyman (mourned for this reason by St. Peter), so Milton is preparing for the life of a great poet, a life in which he must 'strictly meditate the thankles Muse' and, again like King, place his hope of lasting fame in heaven rather than the world. This circumstance permits Milton to berate the corrupt clergy, through the mouth of St. Peter, as well as to make a kind of statement of faith as he sings of Lycidas raised to heaven.

(3) *Measure*. The poem is written in iambic measure, but varies the ordinary five stress line with lines of three stresses. The rhyming is 'free,' that is to say, it follows no strict pattern and allows the poet to build his harmonies without restriction. In reading *Lycidas* the paragraphing should be carefully observed, for the indentations mark changes in subject in much the same way that the various parts of a sonata mark changes of theme.

[Poem 206]

ll. 1–2. *Laurels. Myrtles. Ivy.* Traditional symbols of the poet.

l. 15. *Sisters of the sacred well.* The Muses.

l. 29. *Batt'ning.* Fattening.

l. 34. *Satyrs. Fauns.* Animals of Greek myth used here to symbolize King's fellow students at Cambridge. *Damoetas* (l. 36) probably refers to a well-loved teacher at Cambridge.

ll. 37–8. *now thou art gon.* Notice the trick of repetition by which Milton gets some of his most musical effects. Cf. *Muse her self* (ll. 58–9), and *That sing, and singing* (l. 180).

l. 77. *Phoebus.* The god of the sun is also the god of poetry.

l. 85. *Arethuse.* A spring in the island of Sicily, often referred to by Theocritus and other early pastoral poets.

l. 86. *Mincius.* A river in Italy on which Virgil had lived.

l. 99. *Panope.* A sea nymph.

l. 109. *The Pilot of the Galilean lake.* St. Peter, keeper of the gates of heaven.

ll. 113–30. The pastoral imagery here refers directly to Christ and the Church who are often represented as a shepherd and his flock. *The grim Woolf* may stand for the Roman Catholic Church, which Milton hated. The most satisfactory explanation for the *two-handed engine* is that of E. M. W. Tillyard who thinks it signifies the rod of Christ (*Milton*, 1930, 387). St. Peter mourns the passing of Lycidas because King was a promising young clergyman of a kind that Milton thought might save the Church from corruption.

l. 132. *Alpheus.* The chief river of Peloponnesus. According to the Greek myth the spirit of this river was masculine and in love with the feminine spirit of Arethusa(e).

ll. 151–3. Milton imagines that Lycidas is returned for burial, as the mourners deck the empty bier with flowers.

l. 160. *Bellerus.* Land's End in Cornwall, a craggy place which looks straight south to Spain (Namancos and Bayona).

l. 163. *Look homeward Angel now.* The poet urges the angel of the 'guarded Mount' to look nearer England and care for the drowned shepherd.

l. 164. *Dolphins.* Milton is suggesting the story of Arion who was cast into the sea but brought to shore by dolphins whom he had charmed with his song. See poem No. 299, note.

ll. 172–81. Milton deliberately mixes his reference to Christ and the saints with images which belong to the pagan home of the gods, Olympus.

206, Percy Bysshe Shelley, *Adonais*, 1821. Keats died of tuberculosis in Rome during his twenty-sixth year, 1821. Shelley, it was proved long ago, was mistaken in thinking that harsh reviews of his poems, particularly *Endymion*, had killed Keats. After a study of the conventions of pastoral and, especially, a detailed analysis of *Lycidas*, *Adonais* should offer little reading difficulty. It follows the elegiac form quite closely, and a comparison with

Moschus's *Lament for Bion* will show that Shelley sometimes borrows directly from his models. A comparison of *Adonais* and *Lycidas* is a valuable study in the experience of poetry. Notice that though both Shelley and Milton refer to themselves almost as much as they do to the dead shepherds they are lamenting, there is a personal quality in *Adonais*, not always pleasing, which is totally lacking in Milton's poem. Can this be accounted for in terms of the methods used? Or does it depend upon theme?

207, Matthew Arnold, *Thyrsis*, 1866. This is the third of the great English elegies. Notice that the chief difference in method is that Arnold refers to the actual places, rivers, etc. which he associates with Clough; while Milton and Shelley disguise them in conventional pastoral names. Is Arnold's poem somewhat lacking in the smooth, singing quality which marks *Lycidas* and *Adonais*? Can this, if it is true, be explained in terms of the imagery or the measure?

VI

POEMS OF SERIOUS WIT AND SYMBOLISM

i

In most of the poems of this Part and of the following Part there is a sharp difference of kind from much of the verse we have been studying. Let us take an illustration, one in which the contrast is between poems of more or less equal interest and complexity of experience. Here are two poems which have as their general subject the perception of the passage of time. The first is by Robert Herrick:

> *Fair daffodils, we weep to see*
> *You haste away so soon;*
> *As yet the early rising sun*
> *Has not attained his noon.*
> *Stay, stay*
> *Until the hasting day*
> *Has run*
> *But to the even-song;*
> *And, having prayed together, we*
> *Will go with you along.*

We have short time to stay, as you;
We have as short a spring,
As quick a growth to meet decay,
As you, or anything.
We die
As your hours do, and dry
Away
Like to the summer's rain,
Or as the pearls of morning's dew,
Ne'er to be found again.

And this is a stanza from a poem of Louis MacNeice:

The sunlight on the garden
Hardens and grows cold,
We cannot cage the minute
Within its nets of gold;
When all is told
We cannot beg for pardon.

Herrick's poem is justly famous and enduring. A universal experience of the growth and decay of man is communicated to us by means of an extended comparison with an object of common observation, namely, the daffodil. But notice that it is precisely the *extension* of the comparison which makes the poem. We are given the experience in full detail. The problem of reading the poem is the problem of perceiving with our mind's eye the changes in the life of the daffodil, and then making a comparison by recollecting the corresponding changes in the life of man. The additional point, of the *brevity* of man's life, is brought home to us by our perception of the obviously brief life of the flower. We need, that is to say, an active *visual* imagination and a normally intelligent understanding of the temporal condition of human life in order to realize the full experience of the poem. But what of the lines of MacNeice? When we bring these same tools to bear upon them we find that we make little headway. We can *see* sunlight on a garden well enough; but we cannot *see* it *hardening*. We can see nets of gold; but we cannot see a minute or imagine it being caged. In short we cannot actually make the comparisons at all. But some-

[696]

how the poet has communicated with us directly; he has brought to sharp focus in our consciousness an experience about the terrible speed of time. And when we ask ourselves how he has done it we are forced to the conclusion that in spite of what we have just said, we *have* somehow made the comparisons and imagined the experiences. We do in fact know what he means by the sunlight hardening and by caging a minute within golden nets. But we have not understood him by means of impossible sensory reactions; we have got beyond or beside or perhaps through sensory experience into intellectual experience. We have understood what we could not imagine. And that is precisely the point. Whereas in the Herrick poem we responded to the experience communicated by following the comparison through with our visual imagination, in the lines of MacNeice we have responded to the experience by understanding a comparison which we could not follow through at all. It is the impossibility of the thing which makes the poem, paradoxical as that may be. The problem of reading the lines is sharply different from reading Herrick's; it is the problem of grasping intellectually the impossibility of a sensory experience. The meaning of the lines is thus not the comparison but *the implication of the impossibility of the comparison.* It is the impossibility, that is to say, which gives to the poem its feverish urgency and makes us almost feel time as an immediate and tangible thing. The trick by which this is managed is called *wit*: the pointing out of the implications of trying to compare things which cannot be compared in the imagination. We may sum up the matter by saying that *the poet in using wit is forcing upon us an intellectual experience by showing us the limitations of sensory experience.* He calls to our attention a similarity, which only the mind can grasp, between apparently dissimilar things.

✓ Wit is one of the most important devices of poetry, and an ability to read it is essential to the enjoyment and comprehension of much of the best poetry in English. In this Part the first large group of poems is taken from the seventeenth century, a time when wit flourished as at no other time in the history of English literature; while the second large group is taken from the work of our own contemporaries, who for various reasons have thought it desirable, in order to reinvigorate the tradition, to revive the old device once more. But it should be understood that a certain amount of wit is to be found in almost any period of literary history.

[697]

Even a cursory reading of any of the poems in this Part of Donne, or Eliot, or Auden, for example, will show that they are sharply different from the narrative or pastoral or most of the lyrical poems of the earlier Parts in still another way. Let us follow out the implications of a simple comparison. Here is a passage from a sonnet of Edna St. Vincent Millay:

> *And in my heart there stirs a quiet pain*
> *For unremembered lads that not again*
> *Will turn to me at midnight with a cry.*

And this is taken from T. S. Eliot's *The Love Song of J. Alfred Prufrock*:

> *No! I am not Prince Hamlet, nor was meant to be;*
> *Am an attendant lord, one that will do*
> *To swell a progress, start a scene or two,*
> *Advise the prince; no doubt, an easy tool,*
> *Deferential, glad to be of use,*
> *Politic, cautious, and meticulous;*
> *Full of high sentence, but a bit obtuse;*
> *At times, indeed, almost ridiculous—*
> *Almost, at times, the Fool.*

Millay's lines are a relatively simple statement of a simple experience. The diction is clear and the measure is smooth and harmonious; and a feeling of nostalgia, of romantic sadness, is immediately stirred in the reader. Whether we take it seriously or regard the feeling as mere sentimentality will depend largely upon our previous experience and our general attitudes. In any case the problem of reading the lines is scarcely more than the recognition of an ordinary feeling about love and the hearing of the harmony and rhythm of the measure. Even though we may never have seen these lines before, they will seem somehow familiar.

But when we turn to the lines from Eliot it is clear at once that language is being put to a new use. The lines are striking whether, at first, we like them or not. One thing we grasp upon the first reading: these lines are about somebody *in particular*, not anybody in general; somebody with a distinct inferiority complex is describing himself. Now if we are accustomed by long habit to reading poems which require no more attention than the lines of Millay it is probable that we shall let it go at that: this is a passage in which a man explains that he feels inferior. But we ought not to be satisfied with that response. We ought, rather, to be disturbed by a number of questions: why is Prince Hamlet mentioned? what does 'start a scene or two' mean? why is 'Fool' capitalized? (Notice that no such disturbing questions are raised by Millay's lines.) The first thing that will occur to us is that *all the questions suggest the theater and Shakespeare*; for scenes belong in plays, and Hamlet and Fools are characters in the plays of Shakespeare. If we have not read Shakespeare, of course, we shall not be able to progress beyond our first reading; but among persons of ordinary culture some knowledge of Shakespeare's plays is hardly too much for the poet to expect. Once we have begun to think of Shakespeare our minds will begin to construct trains of association about Hamlet, the theater, and Shakespeare's fools. And this is precisely the poet's purpose in bringing these names and phrases into his poem; in fact he relies for his chief effect upon the associations which we will be stimulated to make. We recall the character and situation of Hamlet, and we recollect the contrast between that unhappy prince and the minor lords of the Danish court who do in fact 'swell a progress, start a scene or two,' only to give way upon the entrance of the tragic hero. It is this contrast between the hero and his satellites which lies at the center of the whole passage, contrast plus the tenuous suggestion that there is something about the speaker which is not wholly unlike Hamlet himself. And then there is the Fool. We remember, now, that the Fool, in *King Lear* for example, is a very considerable character. It is the peculiar situation of the Fool that simply because convention held him 'out of his head' he could say things which had in them more method than madness, could make sweeping criticisms of the great lords and even of the King himself, without fear that he would be held responsible for his words. He provides a brilliant choral commentary, sharply satirical in the main, upon the whole action. And there is something of the Fool in the speaker of Eliot's poem. We know now a great deal about that speaker; he has become a sharply defined character; not simply a man with an inferiority complex, but a man with a very particular kind of inferiority and a very particular kind of wisdom. He is now a really interesting person. We are a long way from the simple but vague sort of emotion of the Millay poem; yet we are nearer, perhaps, to meaningful experience. But this is not the whole of the Eliot passage. If we are steeped in English literature we may have read the letters of Laurence Sterne, the eighteenth-century author of *Tristram Shandy*. And we shall be delighted to discover that the reference of the passage is not simply to Shakespeare, but also to a letter of Sterne. In fact we shall see that the first two lines are actually a quotation from Sterne in a letter about himself. Our perception of Eliot's Mr. Prufrock will now be enormously heightened by the recollection of the character and opinions of Laurence Sterne and the realization that Prufrock is in certain ways like Sterne.

It is hardly necessary to carry the analysis farther. The very great difference between the two kinds of verse is abundantly clear. In the one case the process of reading is elementary and requires no more than superficial attention; while in the other we must use our store of culture, our eyes, and our minds all with the closest attention. For we have presented not one level of experience only, but at least three. Nor must we allow ourselves to think of the Eliot poem as an exercise in literary detection. The full experience, and therefore pleasure, of the poem comes at the point when we have learned how to read well enough *to respond to all three levels of the poem simultaneously.*

It will have been observed that the first big step that we took in reading the Prufrock passage beyond the superficial level was the recognition of the connection between Hamlet and Prufrock, involving as it did the reconstruction of the Hamlet situation and character in our imagination. Hamlet served us as *symbol* for a whole segment of our previous experience which the poet wished us to bring to bear upon the poem in order that we might perceive the character of Prufrock. By means of this symbol our imagination was stimulated to do the poet's work for him, or, better, to do the work which the poet had himself done in his imagination. This response made it possible for the poet to tell us a great deal in a very few words and to tell it with a great deal more accuracy than he could have done in a long explanatory passage. In addition we had the distinct pleasure of re-creating in our own minds the scenes and recollecting the ideas which the poet wished us to associate with Prufrock. The poetical technique which Eliot has used here is known as *symbolism*. The definition of symbol-

[700]

ism has long been the cause of critical warfare; but our analysis offers us a simple definition which is certainly sufficient for ordinary purposes: *symbolism is the reliance upon symbols rather than explanatory statement or expanded comparison for the communication of experience in a poem.* Many of the poems in this section and the following section of religious poems are primarily symbolist poems. Symbolism is not at all a new technique (it was used abundantly in classical Greek poetry); but in comparatively recent times it has been revived, and many of the best poems of our own time rely heavily upon it. This is especially true of Eliot and W. B. Yeats.

It is the belief of such distinguished contemporary poets as W. H. Auden, Louis MacNeice, and T. S. Eliot that there are certain vitally important experiences which can be communicated only by means of wit or symbols or, often, both. Such experiences are often ambiguous and sometimes obscure; but it is the great virtue of the method of serious wit and symbolism that they can be communicated directly and immediately through a poem when it would be impossible to explain them at all in prose or in ordinary expository or didactic poetry. It is perhaps significant, we may add, that wit and symbolism have tended to distinguish poetry written during periods like our own which are shot through with violent contrasts, severe tensions, and difficult ambiguities of experience; whereas during periods in which there is a general acceptance of religious and intellectual attitudes there is likely to be relatively little wit. In studying the poems in this and the following Part the student will do well to compare them constantly with the simpler and more expanded kinds of poems found in other Parts.

208, John Donne, *The Flea*, 1633. In this and the following nine poems of Donne notice how concrete images are used to communicate experiences which are primarily intellectual or moral rationalizations of passion. The method, however, is rarely the simple simile. The most common device is wit; when a witty metaphor is explored and analyzed in its full implications, the poetry is called *metaphysical* by analogy with the intellectual speculations of philosophy (e.g. ll. 16–18).

209, John Donne, *The Bait*, 1633. Compare this poem with Nos. 197 and 198. Donne's wit has seized upon the simple and beautiful love song of Marlowe and given it a wholly new twist, remarkably different from Ralegh's parodic *Reply*. A valuable exercise is to write out an analysis of the difference in the quality of the experience among the three poems.

210, John Donne, *The Ecstasy*, 1633. Notice that the passion of this poem and the 'metaphysical' speculation are inseparably bound up together. An interesting experiment is to observe how completely the poem is lost, and the experience with it, when a prose translation is attempted.

211, John Donne, *The Good-morrow*, 1633.

212, John Donne, *The Anniversary*, 1633.

213, John Donne, *Song: Sweetest love, I do not go*, 1633. Compare this poem with Nos. 50 and 51 of Thomas Campion.

214, John Donne, *A Valediction Forbidding Mourning*, 1633. In this, as in *The Ecstasy*, notice how passionately Donne insists that there is something ideal or spiritual in his love, over and above physical passion, yet how strong at the same time the physical passion really is.

215, John Donne, *The Funeral*, 1633.

216, John Donne, *A Nocturnal upon St. Lucy's Day*, 1633.
    l. 21. *limbecke*. An alembic, an apparatus for distillation.
    l. 39. *the Goat*. Capricorn, the tenth sign of the Zodiac into which the sun enters at the winter solstice. In medieval allegory a goat is the sign of lust, and Capricorn is represented on ancient monuments by the figure of a goat.

217, John Donne, *On His Mistress*, 1633.

218, John Cleveland, *Mark Antony*, 1677. Notice how this poem depends for its effect upon the repeated reference in the refrain to Mark Antony, symbol of intense and passionate loving.
    ll. 34–44. Compare this stanza with the method of Donne in the preceding poems.
    l. 40. *ingeny*. Ingenuity.

219, Andrew Marvell, *To His Coy Mistress*, 1681. The chief thing to read in this poem is the complexity of the central experience. It begins as a conventional love poem in which the lover tries to persuade his mistress to give in to his entreaties. But with the introduction of the image of the chariot in l. 21, the poet becomes obsessed by the terrible onrush of time, and the love theme becomes scarcely more than an illustration of the effect which time has upon human life. Love is not forgotten for a moment, yet it is so carefully and intensely blended with the theme of the passage and destruction of time that the quality with which the poem began is wholly transformed. A more or less light love poem has become a poem of terrible seriousness. Notice that the entire structure of the poem depends upon wit.

220, Archibald MacLeish, *You, Andrew Marvell*, 1929. In this remarkable contemporary poem, MacLeish has taken his inspiration from the experience of the onrush of time which he received while reading Marvell's poem and built it into his own, quite different, poem. In *To His Coy Mistress* time was expressed through auditory and visual images primarily; here the poet uses a single image, or situation, which arouses a *feeling* of time, almost as though it were something which the poet feels moving over him. The sequence of visual images is secondary, yet it contributes to this effect.

221, Andrew Marvell, *The Mower to the Glow-worms*, 1681.

222, Walter Savage Landor, *Past Ruin'd Ilion Helen Lives*, 1831. This and the following poem are noteworthy because so much meaning is distilled from so few words.

223, Walter Savage Landor, *On Seeing a Hair of Lucretia Borgia*, 1837. Lucretia Borgia (1480–1519) was Duchess of Ferrara and notorious for her use of poison to murder her enemies.

224, Ralph Waldo Emerson, *Days*, 1857.

225, Stephen Spender, *The Express*, 1933. This and the following poem have similar subjects. Study the very different qualities of experience. Transcriptions of the MS of this poem are given in Part IX. VIII

226, Emily Dickinson, *I Like to See it Lap the Miles*, 1890.

227, Emily Dickinson, *There's a Certain Slant of Light*, 1890. In this and the two following poems notice the similarity in method with the poems of Donne. Miss Dickinson is the more remarkable for having written her poems at a time when nearly all poetry was in the more expanded and explanatory style which we have studied in earlier parts of this book.

228, Emily Dickinson, *I Died for Beauty*, 1890.

229, Emily Dickinson, *I Heard a Fly Buzz When I Died*, 1890.

230, Gerard Manley Hopkins, *The Leaden Echo and the Golden Echo*, 1918. (Though his poems were not published until 1918, Hopkins wrote during the seventies and eighties of the previous century.) This and the following eight poems should be studied together. They form a group of very different kinds of poems all dealing in one way or another with the problem of beauty. (See also poem No. 127 g.) The style of Hopkins, which is here at its most typical, has been of great influence upon contemporary poets, especially W. H. Auden and C. Day Lewis. Its chief characteristics are its rhythm and its originality of diction. Hopkins called his measure 'Sprung Rhythm,' by which he meant that he was not holding his verse within the bounds of traditional syllabic units (Iambic, Trochaic, Dactylic, etc.) but permitting the syllables to be sprung loose. He allowed anywhere from one to four syllables to the foot, and sometimes more, but stressed the first syllable. He often marks the stress so that his intention will not be missed. The stress is often unnatural but never uninteresting. He writes of his verse lining in Sprung Rhythm that 'if the first [line] has one or more syllables at its end the other must have so many the less at its beginning; and in fact the scanning runs on without break from the beginning, say, of a stanza to the end, and all the stanza is one long strain, though written in lines asunder.' (*Author's Preface* to the collected poems.)

231, T. Sturge Moore, *The Leaden Echo and the Golden Echo*, 1930. Study this poem carefully and compare it with the Hopkins original. The important questions are these: what differences do you *hear* in the two poems? and what difference, if any, does what you *hear* make to what you *understand*? Which poem seems to communicate the richer experience? Here is what Mr. Moore writes about his poem: 'Though, as you may decide, his [Hopkins's] lavish outlay in words attained more music, my spare rescension has retained most of his felicities, discarded his most ludicrous redundances, and achieved an inherent music which reads itself without the aid of marks and so asks far less indulgence: yet 547 words have become 204.' ('Style or Beauty in Literature,' *The Criterion*, IX, July 1930.)

232, Conrad Aiken, '*All lovely things will have an ending*,' 1916.

233, A. E. Housman, '*With Rue My Heart is Laden*,' 1896. For an analysis of this poem see Part X, *On Reading Poems*.

234, Edna St. Vincent Millay, '*Euclid alone has looked on Beauty bare*,' 1920. Euclid is, of course, the great geometer of the fifth century B.C. Miss Millay is referring to his perception of the abstract beauty of pure line or symmetry.

235, Christopher Marlowe, '*What is beauty*,' from *Tamburlaine*, c.1587.

236, John Masefield, *On Growing Old*, 1913. Compare the expansion of emotion in this poem with the compression of emotion in the poem of Housman. Which do you prefer? Why?

237, Wallace Stevens, *Peter Quince at the Clavier*, 1923.

238, Robert Browning, *A Toccata of Galuppi's*, 1855.

239, Gerard Manley Hopkins, *Spring and Fall*, 1918. What is the significance of the title? Compare the poem with this passage from the sermons of John Donne:

No man is an Iland, intire of it selfe; every man is a peece of the Continent, a part of the maine; if a Clod bee washed away by the Sea, Europe is the lesse, as well as if a Promontorie were, as well as if a Mannor of thy friends or thine owne were; any mans death diminishes me, because I am involved in Mankinde; And therefore never send to know for whom the bell tolls; It tolls for thee.

240, Gerard Manley Hopkins, *The Windhover*, 1918. Why is the subtitle of this poem *To Christ our Lord*?
    l. 4. *wimpling*. Rippling.
    l. 12. *sillion*. An archaic word which sometimes means *ridge* and sometimes *furrow*. Here the image would seem to require *furrow*.

241, James Joyce, *Ecce Puer*, 1936. The apparent simplicity of this poem is very misleading. Does the central experience in fact come through even upon a thorough reading? If so, how would you define it?

242, Elinor Wylie, *O Virtuous Light*, 1929.

243, Thomas Hardy, *Dead 'Wessex,' the Dog, to the Household*,

244, John Crowe Ransom, *Janet Waking*,

245, John Crowe Ransom, *Here Lies a Lady*,

246, Archibald MacLeish, *The Too-Late Born*, 1926.

247, C. Day Lewis, *Moving In*, 1935. Many of the poems of Lewis have as their theme some aspect or experience of the so-called 'class-struggle.' Lewis is himself prominently identified with the left-Socialist side in politics and economics. Notice however that this poem is not at all rhetorical propaganda.
    l. 1. Observe Lewis's debt to Gerard Manley Hopkins in such a line as this.

248, C. Day Lewis, *'Rest from loving,'* 1931.

249, Stephen Spender, *'I hear the cries of evening,'* 1934. Spender, like Lewis, often uses left-wing attitudes and experiences for the mood or substance of his poems. Yet, as in this poem, there is very often a kind of pure lyrical statement which has led some critics to liken him to Shelley.

250, Stephen Spender, '*Not palaces, an era's crown*,' 1934.

251, Stephen Spender, '*He will watch the hawk*,' 1934.

252, W. H. Auden, '*Sir, no man's enemy*,' 1934. In this and the following group of poems by Auden study especially the syntax. Sometimes an apparent obscurity is owing merely to the omission of a connecting word; but more often there is a deliberate ambiguity which has seemed to many good judges of poetry a true reflection of the ambiguities of our time. Study also the influences of T. S. Eliot and Hopkins as they are to be found in these poems. This poem is a sonnet in form. How does it differ from such sonnets as those studied in Part II? What is the effect of the 'off-rhymes'?

l. 8. What is the image in this line?

l. 14. What is the purpose of 'New styles of architecture' in the context of the whole poem?

253, W. H. Auden, '*Doom is dark and deeper*,' 1934.

254, W. H. Auden, '*Between attention*,' 1934.

255, W. H. Auden, '*Control of the passes*,' 1934.

256, W. H. Auden, '*Consider this and in our time*,' 1934.

l. 52. Notice how the poem seems to reach a climax at this line; yet *that day* is never defined. Is the poem therefore obscure?

257, W. H. Auden, '*Where do They come from?*,' 1940. See Part VIII for a transcription of the manuscript of this poem.

258, Louis MacNeice, *The Hebrides*, 1937. MacNeice is generally identified with Lewis, Spender, and Auden, who are his friends; but his style differs greatly from theirs. Perhaps the most remarkable thing about this poem is its quiet dignity. How is it achieved? Notice that in this and the two following poems the central images are those of time. How do they differ from the images of time in Marvell's *To His Coy Mistress* or MacLeish's *You, Andrew Marvell*? Compare them with Auden's '*Consider this and in our time*.'

259, Louis MacNeice, *Song: 'The sunlight on the garden*,' 1937. Study the structure of this poem carefully, especially the rhyme scheme. Is the remarkable unity of the poem artificial, or does it hold a unified experience? For discussion of the imagery, see the Introduction to this Part. Compare this poem, with reference to wit, with poem No. 156.

260, Louis MacNeice, *Bagpipe Music*, 1937. Notice the juxtaposition of frivolous with serious images. Is the effect of the poem mixed or unified? How much depends upon the concluding image of the barometer?

261, Ezra Pound, *Portrait d'une Femme*, 1912. This poem should be read together with the next. In what ways are the poems similar? In what different?
l. 1. The Sargasso Sea is remarkable because the floating sea-weed gives it the appearance of land.

262, T. S. Eliot, *Portrait of a Lady*, 1917.

263, T. S. Eliot, *The Love Song of J. Alfred Prufrock*, 1917. This is one of the most important and influential of modern poems. Though its subject is no more than a character sketch its overtones raise it to the level of serious poetry, and its technique of blending wit with symbolism set a model for a whole generation of English and American poets. The epigraph is from Dante:

> *If I thought my answer were to one who ever*
> *could return to the world, this flame should*
> *shake no more;*
> *But since none ever did return alive from this*
> *depth, if what I hear be true, without fear of*
> *infamy I answer thee.*
> (*Inferno*, XXVII, 61–6)

l. 29. *works and days*. This is the title of the great poem of Hesiod, written in the eighth century B.C.
ll. 73–4. What is the function of this image in the context of the whole poem?
l. 82. John the Baptist. See Matthew xiv, 8.
ll. 111–19. See the Introduction to this Part.

264, T. S. Eliot, *Sweeney Among the Nightingales*, 1920. The motto is from the *Agamemnon* of Aeschylus; it is the cry of Agamemnon when his wife, Clytemnestra, kills him: 'Ah me! I have been smitten deep with a mortal blow.' Notice that the terrible contrast of the last stanza in this poem is doubly effective because the theme is not broken off but continued.
l. 7. *Raven*. Bird of death in the old myths.
l. 9. *Orion and the Dog*. Constellations.
l. 35. *nightingales*. Symbol of purity and beauty, suggesting the legend of Philomela. See poems Nos. 97, 98, 99 and notes.

l. 38. *Agamemnon*. Greek tyrant and leader of the attack upon Troy in Greek myth. He was murdered by his wife Clytemnestra and her lover Aegisthus.

265, T. S. Eliot, *Marina*, 1930. Marina is the name of the daughter of Pericles, Prince of Tyre, in Shakespeare's *Pericles*. She was born at sea and separated by shipwreck from her father, who sought her many years by land and water until he found her, a young woman, beautiful, kind and loving; their reunion is full of exquisite tenderness of feeling. Eliot conceived the speaker in this poem to be an old man like Pericles, dazed with a joy long desired and now almost incredible, a daze in which his recollections of the places and peoples of his wandering years mingle with the present half-realization of this daughter he made. The Latin heading may be translated, 'What is this place, this region, this expanse of the world?'

VII

POEMS OF RELIGIOUS EXPERIENCE

A glance at the table of contents for this Part will show that the word *religious* is here given very great latitude. Some of the poems deal with essentially Christian experience or attitudes; some are pagan; and some communicate some sort of denial of any supernatural order whatever. But all the poems have this in common: they try to communicate some feeling, attitude, or experience involving the great problems of religion, God, other-worldliness, the immortality of the soul, and supernatural standards of conduct, whether the experience in any particular poem is positive or negative. Experience of this kind has been one of the chief subjects of poetry from the very earliest times; and English poetry is especially rich in it. In the seventeenth century, for example, much of the most significant English poetry was primarily religious, as the poems of Donne, Vaughan, Herbert, and Crashaw abundantly illustrate, while the great work of Milton rests largely upon the Christian myth itself. Again, in the nineteenth century most of the major poets were concerned with the relation between religion and social conduct, or the implications of science with reference to religion. In our own time such poets as T. S. Eliot and William Butler Yeats have felt that their poetry, written in an age of intellectual anarchy, needed the support of religious myth. Eliot has found his way back to Christianity, while Yeats has constructed his own elaborate myth.

The reading of religious poetry requires precisely the same skills that we need to read any other kind of poetry: attention, the awakening of the imagination to receive images of sight, sound, taste, touch, and smell; hearing the harmonies of words, and the skill of perceiving the relation of the part to the whole structure. But there is one pitfall in reading religious poetry which is not often found in other kinds: religious poems often deal with matters of belief and controversy about which we may feel strongly. The danger is that we may let what we think is a disagreement with the poet interfere with our enjoyment of his poem. This not only deprives us of the pleasure of some of the world's best literature, but is, in addition, a serious failure of intelligence. The stuff of religious poetry, as in any other poetry, is human experience; and it is just as stupid for us to object to a particular belief which may be found in a poem as it would be to object to Greek temples because they were not dedicated to Jehovah, or to object to a Raphael madonna because one happens not to believe in the Virgin Birth. The error which lies at the bottom of such judgments of poetry is taking the poem as theology or as metaphysics; whereas in fact a poem is not theology or metaphysics but a poem. And as a poem it must be judged by its own standards, just as we judge a painting in terms of line and color. We are not required to *like* religious poems, of course; but we cannot decide that question until we have learned to *read* them.

266, Thomas Nashe, '*Adieu, farewell earth's bliss,*' 1600.
   l. 19. *Helen.* Greek princess, wife of Menelaus, who was abducted by Paris and for whose release the Trojan War was fought in Greek mythology.
   l. 23. *Hector.* Trojan hero and son of King Priam.

267, Alfred, Lord Tennyson, *Crossing the Bar*, 1889.
   l. 15. Is the figure of the *pilot* appropriate for Christ in this context?

268, John Donne, *Good Friday, 1613. Riding Westward*, 1633. Notice in this and the following poem how the 'metaphysical' style of the love poems of Donne in Part VI is here put to quite different but equally effective use.

269, John Donne, '*At the round earth's imagined corners,*' 1633.

270, Henry Vaughan, *The Night*, 1655. Compare this with poem No. 17 and note.

l. 5. See John iii, 1, 2.

l. 50. How does the whole structure of the poem build toward this image?

271, Henry Vaughan, *The Waterfall*, 1655.

272, Henry Vaughan, *Mount of Olives*, 1655.

273, Henry Vaughan, *The World*, 1655. What qualities do all four of these poems of Vaughan have in common? How does his experience differ from Donne's in the poems above?

274, George Herbert, *The Pulley*, 1633. What is the significance of the title?

275, Thomas Traherne, *Eden*, 1910. (Traherne's poems were discovered in manuscript in 1910. He lived from 1636 to 1674.)

276, Thomas Traherne, *Wonder*, 1910. Compare Traherne's experience of nature with that of Wordsworth as we have it in the next poem.

277, William Wordsworth, *Tintern Abbey*, 1798. (The full title is *Lines Composed a Few Miles above Tintern Abbey, on Revisiting the Banks of the Wye during a Tour. July 13, 1798.*)

l. 116. *dear Friend*. Wordsworth's sister Dorothy.

278, John Milton, *On the Morning of Christs Nativity*, 1645, written 1629. Study the measure and imagery of this poem especially. Is it more impressive for its technical excellence or for deeply felt experience?

l. 89. *Pan*. In Greek mythology the patron god of shepherds, hunters, and fishermen.

l. 102. *Cynthia*. Artemis, goddess of the moon.

ll. 176–8. The oracle of Apollo at Delphi was a sacred place in Greek mythology.

l. 191. *Lars*. Lares. The Roman gods of particular localities. *Lemures*. In Roman mythology malevolent spirits or ghosts.

l. 194. *Flamins*. Flamens were priests in Roman religion.

l. 197. *Peor, and Baalim*. Local gods of the ancient Semitic peoples.

l. 200. *Ashtaroth*. Astarte, Phoenician goddess of fertility and sexual love.

l. 203. *Hammon*. Ammon, a name given to the Greek god Zeus as worshipped in Egypt and Libya.

l. 204. *Thamuz*. Babylonian god of fertility and vegetation.

l. 205. *Moloch*. A Semitic god whose worship involved human sacrifice.

l. 212. *Isis*. Egyptian goddess of fertility. *Orus*. Horus, son of Isis. *Anubis*. Son of Isis, represented as a dog or jackal.

l. 213. *Osiris*. Husband of Isis and chief god of the Egyptian hierarchy.

l. 226. *Typhon*. A monster of Greek mythology who was supposed to have been the father of such other monsters as the Chimera and the Sphinx.

279, William Blake, *The Divine Image*, 1789.

280, William Blake, '*And did those feet in ancient time*' (from *Milton*), 1808.

281, William Blake, *Holy Thursday*, 1794.

282, William Blake, *The Tiger*, 1794. This and the following two poems should be read together. What quality of experience is common to all three? Compare the images of animals in this poem and *The Waste Places*.

283, Edwin Arlington Robinson, *The Sheaves*, 1916. Study the central experience of this poem carefully. Does the concluding image seem appropriate to it?

284, James Stephens, *The Waste Places*, 1915.

285, Alexander Pope, *Eloïsa to Abelard*, 1717. Pope prefaced this poem with the following Argument:

Abelard and Eloïsa flourished in the twelfth Century; they were two of the most distinguished Persons of their age in learning and beauty, but for nothing more famous than for their unfortunate passion. After a long course of calamities, they retired each to a several Convent, and consecrated the remainder of their days to religion. It was many years after this separation, that a letter of Abelard's to a Friend, which contained the history of his misfortune, fell into the hands of Eloïsa. This awakening all her Tenderness, occasioned those celebrated letters (out of which the following is partly extracted) which gives so lively a picture of the struggles of grace and nature, virtue and passion.

Does the passionate tension between Eloïsa's love of God and her love of Abelard seem deeply felt or merely sentimental? How much of the quality of the experience depends upon the original materials, and how much upon Pope's handling of them?

286, A. E. Housman, *Easter Hymn*, 1936. This and the five poems following form a group of short lyrics which have as their subject some kind of ironic or angry experience of religion, especially of the meaning of Christ. Are any of them blasphemous? any sentimental? How does the quality of imagery in the poem by Emily Dickinson differ from all the others? See poem No. 17, *For My Funeral*.

287, T. S. Eliot, *Journey of the Magi*. The opening lines are quoted from a sermon of Bishop Lancelot Andrewes (1555–1626), one of the translators of the *Authorized Version* of the Bible.

288, Edna St. Vincent Millay, *To Jesus on His Birthday*, 1928.

289, A. E. Housman, *The Carpenter's Son*, 1896.

290, A. E. Housman, '*The chestnut casts his flambeaux*,' 1922.

291, Robinson Jeffers, *Shine, Perishing Republic*, 1924.

292, Emily Dickinson, '*Of course I prayed*,' 1924.

293, Elinor Wylie, *Hymn to Earth*, 1929.

294, Francis Thompson, *The Kingdom of God*, 1913. This poem, by one of the few great Roman Catholic poets of England, was written about 1895.

295, Coventry Patmore, *The Toys*, 1877. Notice that the *subject* of this poem is one which makes it difficult for the poet not to fall into sentimentality; yet the *experience* is deep and genuine. How is the effect managed?

296, Gerard Manley Hopkins, '*I wake and feel the fell of dark, not day*,' 1919. What are the meanings of 'dark' and 'light' in the context of the whole poem? Notice that the images which follow, though almost violently unlike the contrast between dark and light, nevertheless fill out and complete the expression of the experience of the poem.

297, Gerard Manley Hopkins, *Pied Beauty*, 1919. 'Pied' means having two or more colors in blotches. The poem is constructed by listing a number of things which are pied. Notice, however, that the experience is communicated and *explained* by these things; it is not *of* them.

l. 3. *stipple*. A method of painting or drawing by which shades of light and dark are suggested by dots or splotches.

298, William Butler Yeats, *Sailing to Byzantium*, 1928. This should be read together with the following poem. The imagery of both poems is almost entirely symbolist; and the central symbol is, of course, Byzantium. Byzantium (Constantinople) was the capital of the eastern Roman Empire and its great period of art and architecture was during the fifth and sixth centuries. But the poet by no means intends to have us contrast the present time with ancient Byzantium; nor does he mean that he prefers the latter. Byzantium is used, on several levels, as a symbol for things of the mind and spirit as opposed to ordinary sensuous experience. These qualities Yeats associates primarily with the arts of Byzantium, ll. 26–9. The forms which 'Grecian gold-smiths make' are to be contrasted with the images of sensuous and sensual ex-perience (including fertility) in the first stanza, because they are timeless, fixed, and permanent in their shape and significance. They were created by artists who copied forms from their own imaginations rather than from ex-ternal nature. Byzantine art was thus abstract, and, according to Yeats, per-manent because it was of the spirit and not the flesh; while the images of the first stanza belong to 'Whatever is begotten, born, and dies.' The poem as-sumes a soul independent of the body which is subject to a series of births, deaths, and rebirths in different shapes and forms. Although ll. 21–4 may in-deed refer to the poet's own feeling of age and lack of animal vitality, the ex-perience of the poem is much more general in its implications than that. The 'dying animal,' that is to say, means any organic life, as opposed to 'monu-ments of unaging intellect.' The poet has felt that the whole world is in a state of decay, and, as *The Second Coming* (poem No. 300) shows, is moving toward some kind of rebirth. In order not to be caught in the whirling chaos of this present world's end it is better to set one's mind toward things which are permanent and at the same time beautiful, to be valued even though in their time of creation they served only to 'keep a drowsy Emperor awake.'

The chief reason that Yeats used the symbolism of Byzantium, ancient art, mosaic, fire, etc. is that he wished to avoid any suggestion to the reader's mind of the descriptions of the world which modern physics gives us. Yeats had no belief in science, and when it tried to explain 'the first and last things' of life, he hated it. He relied upon his own somewhat mystical 'vision,' forti-fied by his reading of the great books of the past. This and the following two poems were set by Yeats in the context of his own elaborate myth, which he described in a prose book called *A Vision* (1925); and there the curious reader may find special meanings which he attached to fire, blood, the moon, and other symbols. But the poems, when read with real attention, communicate directly and are extraordinarily impressive to an alert and sympathetic mind.

l. 1. *That.* The poet uses the demonstrative because he represents him-self as having arrived at 'Byzantium.' The reference, of course, is to the here and now of our world.

l. 8. i.e. works of art which, like those of Byzantium, are not dependent upon the world of sense.

l. 19. *perne in a gyre.* Yeats imagined that the whole world, at the present time, was whirling at great velocity in the manner of a gyre, i.e. like a tor-nado, spirally about its axis. By *perne* Yeats probably means to move in the manner of a hawk, i.e. circling and then swooping. The image thus conveys the idea of moving in such a manner as to pierce through the gyre in order to reach the poet who is caught in it by the accident of having been born into the present-day world. See *The Second Coming*, l. 1.

l. 24. *artifice of eternity.* From Yeats's point of view eternity would be abstract and artificial, that is, of the mind or spirit rather than of anything attached to sensory experience. Compare l. 8.

l. 30. *golden bough.* Though there is probably no specific reference here to the golden bough which Aeneas, by command of the Cumaean Sybil, plucked before he entered the underworld in Greek myth, Yeats certainly wishes the reader to recall that the *golden bough* is associated with primitive religion and myth. (See Sir James George Frazer, *The Golden Bough*, 1890.)

299, William Butler Yeats, *Byzantium*, 1930. Although this poem depends more directly upon *A Vision* and is certainly more difficult than *Sailing to Byzantium*, it is equally true that the central experience in its full impact comes through with careful reading to a reader of reasonable intelligence, even though he may have no previous knowledge of Yeats. The chief task is to grasp the structure of the poem, for once this is achieved the details fall readily into place. The poet represents himself, now, as having arrived in Byzantium, i.e. having, for the moment, got loose from the 'dying animal' of his body and reached the 'artifice of eternity.' The experience of the poem is thus a blending together of his observation of the stream of sensuous life from which he is now detached, of the actual feeling of severance from the sensuous world in which others are struggling for freedom, and his observation or perception of the images which belong in eternity. In other words, the poem is an attempt to say what it is like to be in Yeats's symbolic Byzantium. The first stanza is a statement of the contrast between the violent and meaningless complexity of experience in the world of sense and the permanent perfection of the 'monuments of unaging intellect,' such as a 'moonlit dome.' The images of day ('unpurged' because he has not permanently got rid of them'), that is ordinary experience, recede as does the sound of a gong rung from a great cathedral; and the poet now, in the second stanza, sees an image which belongs not to time but to eternity. (The word *image* is used deliberately and ambivalently. In l. 1 it indicates that the experiences of this world are illusions and unreal, while in l. 9 it suggests that the poet does not really *see* this spirit from the other-world, but *imagines* that he does.) He calls it 'death-in-life' because it has no sensuous life but belongs to the higher, abstract life; he calls it 'life-in-death' because he sees it only for a moment, remembering that he still belongs in the world of here and now. The third stanza describes the image in terms of the 'forms' which 'Grecian goldsmiths make,' recalling that those forms depend upon the intellect and not upon natural objects. In stanza four the quality of the abstract and perfect 'life' of Yeats's Byzantium is contrasted with the life of the historical Byzantium of Roman imperial history. 'Midnight' is the time imagined for the appearance of Yeats's images because the city of living beings would be still; and the meaning is that the people of historical Byzantium had no more appreciation of the otherworld which their artists were making than do we of this time who are no better than tattered coats upon sticks. In the final stanza the poet is speaking of the plight of those spirits which are trying, with a desperate but futile intensity, to escape from the 'mire' of ordinary life by means which are themselves sensuous. But only 'The smithies of the Emperor' can break the flood, the smithies in which the 'forms' of the 'Grecian goldsmiths' are forged.

ll. 1–4. The poet is in Byzantium in two senses: (1) the historical Byzantium of the Emperor filled with the 'unpurged images of day,' and (2) the symbolic Byzantium of the intellect into which in ll. 5–8 he moves as the images recede. The experience is like the dying away of the sound of a great gong.

l. 11. *Hades' bobbin.* Hades is taken here in its ancient sense of the afterworld where spirits exist as 'shades,' not at all in the more common sense of Hell. (See note to poem No. 3.) The spirit, which is likened to a 'bobbin bound in mummy cloth,' is placed in Hades simply to show that it has passed beyond the world of sense.

ll. 17–19. Compare with ll. 25–30 of *Sailing to Byzantium.*

l. 20. *cocks of Hades.* Just as the crowing of a rooster, according to the old myths, would drive away ghosts, so the crowing of the cocks in Hades would drive away the figures of the physical world.

l. 33. The reference here is to the myth of Arion who was forced by robbers to leap into the sea but was rescued by a dolphin. However, from Yeats's point of view, the dolphin belongs to the world of sense and escape from that world is therefore impossible by its agency. The experience here is of the futility of trying to escape by any means other than the pure intellect symbolized by the 'smithies of the Emperor.'

l. 40. *dolphin-torn.* The sea of life, the world about us, is torn by our mistaken belief that we can escape from it by any sensory experience. *gong-tormented.* The sound of the gong, which receded in stanza I and thus allowed the poet to enter the Byzantium of the imagination, is ever present in the world of sense.

300, William Butler Yeats, *The Second Coming*, 1921. Although this poem has a good deal of the same mythological basis as *Sailing to Byzantium* and *Byzantium*, it is a much more direct poetic statement. The structure of the poem is strictly logical, even though the experience is prophetic. The first stanza describes the poet's impression of the present, and the second explains the terrible inference which his vision has forced him to make. There is a terrible irony in the manner with which the poet treats the Christian myth and faith, irony amounting to denial of that myth and faith. For *spiritus mundi*, by which Yeats understood a great racial memory into which the human mind could pierce at moments of mystical intuition, is a thoroughly pagan conception.

Compare this poem with Millay's *To Jesus on His Birthday* and Housman's *Easter Hymn.* Yeats's poem seems to cut more deeply and to have a more terrifying effect because he is imagining a world and a history in which Christianity is only one of many phases or cycles, where two thousand years can be described as 'stony sleep,' while Millay and Housman tend to equate the Christian era with significant human history and then to object, rather petulantly, that Christianity has not been better than it has been.

ll. 1–2. The image here is primarily that of a trained falcon in characteristic flight (see note to l. 19 of *Sailing to Byzantium*) which is unable to hear the commands of its master on the ground; but secondarily, and more significantly, the image is of the motion of the whole world of living beings. The poet's vision has told him that the gyre of the present cannot continue much longer; its center will not hold and it will fly in all directions. It follows, from Yeats's point of view, that some tremendous event, such as a second coming, must be near at hand.

l. 6. *ceremony of innocence.* What is the image here, and how does it function in the context of the stanza?

l. 12. *Spiritus mundi.* Literally *spirit of the world.* See introductory paragraph above. Yeats believed that all experience and history, past, present, future, were preserved in a great racial spirit or memory which exists everywhere but is not subject to sensory perception. However an intuitive perception was possible, and at moments of mystical experience, such as this, the future might be revealed.

301, T. S. Eliot, *The Waste Land*, 1922. In many ways this is the pivotal poem of the twentieth century. It is at once the most discussed, the most criticized and the most admired poem of our times; but in spite of the endless controversy which surrounds it, there is no doubt that the ability to read it marks full maturity in the art of reading poems. And it is equally true that the full experience of the poem is abundantly worth the effort it requires. But the difficulties of the poem have been, on the whole, very greatly exaggerated. A reader with an awakened imagination and a sensitive ear will find that the central themes and experience come through even on a first reading, especially if the poem is heard read aloud by someone who knows it well. It remains to master the details by study and gradually learn to place them in their proper structural function.

Much of the imagery is drawn from a book called *From Ritual to Romance* by Jessie L. Weston (1920), which is a study of the anthropological sources of the legend of the Holy Grail. According to that legend a man called the Fisher King ruled over the Waste Land (whence Eliot gets his title). The land was barren and dry and was to remain so until a knight of purity should arrive to heal the Fisher King, who is wounded in the genital organs. This story goes back to very primitive times, but persisted through to the Christian era, and in the Middle Ages was worked into the cycle of stories about King Arthur and his Knights of the Round Table. Here it was connected with another story, of the Holy Grail (the chalice supposed to have been used at the Last Supper), the Grail becoming the means of healing the Fisher

King. Several of the knights of Arthur's court, according to various versions of the legend, are supposed to have accomplished the adventure; but in the best versions it is Sir Perceval who is the hero. (Cf. Wagner's opera *Parsifal*.) Eliot's references are usually to stories and tales and poems of which Perceval is the hero. The hero, in any case, sets forth for the Waste Land, encountering on the way many adventures which involve conflicts with evil knights and temptations of the flesh, hunger and lust. In the heart of the Waste Land the knight comes upon the Chapel Perilous where he meets the most difficult of his various trials, and, if successful, arrives next day at the Grail Castle where he heals and releases the Fisher King. This results in the return of fertility to the land. Miss Weston showed that the origin of this myth was to be found in primitive rites of fertility and vegetation, especially in the near East and along the Nile river. That is to say, the story of the Holy Grail has come down with many changes from the ritual performed by primitive men in the hope of bringing rain and sun, of bringing spring after winter, life after apparent death. And it is the sexual symbolism of the legend which Eliot has seized upon for the heart of his poem.

In Eliot's conception the world of our time is a waste land, barren and dry of the water of life; it needs a Grail Knight to deliver it from spiritual death. But the knight can go only so far as the Chapel Perilous (ll. 385–8), for the poet does not see any real hope of revival, and at the conclusion of the poem the Fisher King is still 'Fishing, with the arid plain behind me.' This is the central symbolism of the poem, and all the rest of the details are either related to it or suggested by it in one way or another. But the poem is not constructed as a modern version of the Grail story; and this is the chief difficulty which the innocent reader meets. If he expects a logically developed narrative in which an old story is used as a kind of allegory for the modern situation, he will be quite frustrated in his attempts to read the poem intelligently. The method, on the contrary, is that of freely associated ideas and images, having the center from which they radiate in the symbol of the Waste Land. Let us make an analysis of an important passage in order to discover how this is managed.

The first section of Part II, 'A Game of Chess' (ll. 77–138) presents a scene of modern luxury, a woman of wealth and position in her boudoir waiting for her lover. The lover arrives and a desultory conversation ensues. The theme of the lines is a theme of futility, aimlessness, purposelessness, and sterility.

> 'What shall I do now? What shall I do?'
> 'I shall rush out as I am, and walk the street
> 'With my hair down, so. What shall we do tomorrow?
> 'What shall we ever do?'

The woman apparently has no appreciation of the great beauty of her surroundings. She does not look forward to her lover's arrival with any genuine emotion; and when he does come she can think of nothing to say. He, for his part, is represented simply as thinking, either aloud or to himself, and taking no pleasure in being with her. They have nothing to do and the best suggestions offered are 'hot water at ten,' 'a closed car at four,' and 'a game of chess.' These things are apparent to any intelligent reader; on this level the experience is clear. This is simply one of the illustrations which Eliot has used to characterize the modern waste land.

But the great richness of the whole passage depends upon the imaginative associations which the poet has made and indicated to his reader. Let us examine it in detail. The description of the room (ll. 77–108) is made from quotations, allusions, and suggestions from no less than four of the great books of the world: Shakespeare's *Antony and Cleopatra*, the *Aeneid*, *Paradise Lost*, and Ovid's *Metamorphoses*. The first line alludes by direct quotation to the description which Enobarbus gives of the manner in which Cleopatra first went to meet Mark Antony (see note to l. 77 below). The reader recalls the tremendous love story of these two people who risked whole empires (and lost them) to realize their love. In a moment (l. 92) the word 'laquearia' suggests the description Virgil gives in Book I of the *Aeneid* of the feast with which Dido, Queen of Carthage, greeted Aeneas (see note to this line, below). Six lines later the phrase 'sylvan scene' recalls Milton's description of Eden in Book IV of *Paradise Lost*; and the picture itself is a representation of the myth of Philomela, heroine of the terrible tale which Ovid recounts in his *Metamorphoses* (see note to l. 99, below). The song of the nightingale comes back into the poem at l. 204.

In this setting, which is made to suggest the richness and meaningfulness of the great love stories of the past, the woman talks with her lover (ll. 111–14). She tells him to think; and he does,

> *I think we are in rats' alley*
> *Where the dead men lost their bones.*

The passage carries us forward to ll. 187–95 where rats and bones emerge into major importance as central symbols of the waste land. As the empty colloquy proceeds, she asks him to remember, and he remembers 'Those are pearls that were his eyes.' This carries us back to the fortune-telling of Mme Sosostris in Part I, and beyond that to the song of Ariel in Shakespeare's *Tempest* from which the line is taken (see note to l. 48, below). This great scene from *The Tempest* is in the poet's mind all the time, and we meet it again in ll. 191–2 and 257. But in the waste land even Shakespeare no longer has meaning; there is only that 'Shakespeherian rag,' 'so elegant, so intelligent.' There is nothing of value, not even anything desired, in the midst of all this splendor; nothing to do but play a game of chess and wait 'for a knock upon the door.' But in the English theater of Shakespeare's time there was a very important game of chess; and it is this of which the poet is now thinking.

[Poem 301]

In Thomas Middleton's *Women Beware Women* a game of chess was used to distract attention while a girl was violated (see note to l. 138, below).

It will be noticed that the associations which the poet wishes us to make take us, in each case, to something of sexual significance; and this is the purpose of the passage. It is also the theme which holds the passage in the context of the Grail myth. For the land, in that myth, was waste because of sterility; and so also is our present-day land waste because of sterility, spiritual sterility. For primitive peoples sexual symbolism stood for life itself, because they depended entirely upon the seasons and good weather for the crops which they all cultivated. For them the winter meant death, the spring life; the winter was a waste land, but the spring brought rebirth. Their myth expressed their deepest concerns. For us it is not a question of food, but of faith. We have no faith, and it follows that our appetites will not be satisfied by food or sexual indulgence. As the passage we have been studying shows, we have no more zest for life. The passage suggests further that a part at least of our difficulty lies in our having allowed the great tradition of our culture (indicated by the references to Shakespeare, Milton, Virgil, and Ovid) to die away. It is the *unawareness* of the woman which is so terrible; and the poet wishes us to grasp this fact by the contrast of the woman and her setting with the great scenes of the past suggested by the allusions.

The method of allusion in this passage is typical of the whole poem; and the notes which follow are intended to supply what is needed in order to make the required associations. The theme of sexual sterility and meaninglessness occurs often, but it is not the only theme. For example, 'death by water' can be traced through the poem in much the same manner, as can the idea of the swift rush of time, or the inconsequential quality of modern business activity, or the unreality of a modern city when compared with the spiritual wisdom of the ages. An interesting and illuminating study is the comparison of this poem with *Lycidas*. It will be noticed that Milton relies very heavily upon allusion to classic literature just as Eliot does; and it may be further observed that both poems have 'death by water' as a central theme, deliberately playing upon the physical (H_2O) and symbolic ('water of life') meanings of the word water.

Eliot has observed that the remarkable thing about poetry is that it can communicate *before* it is understood; and no poem better illustrates the truth of this statement than does *The Waste Land*. The mastery of the reading of *The Waste Land* means moving from an initial experience of the terrifying futility of modern living to ever richer perception and experience as the many levels of meaning are comprehended. It may be that in the end the reader will be dissatisfied with the poem. He may feel that it is unnecessarily complicated, too much a *tour de force*; or he may feel (with Eliot) that the life it describes is unendurable without some sort of faith, faith perhaps in the social and personal ethos of democracy, like that of Archibald MacLeish, or faith in the Christian myth, to which Eliot has himself returned. But however that may be, it is certain that a sensitive person cannot fully read *The Waste Land* without feeling that his experience of both art and life has been vastly enriched.

NOTES

Many of these notes are by Eliot; most have been expanded and a considerable number added, in parentheses.

The motto (Petronius, *Satyricon*, chap. 48) is part of a scoffing account of the wonders of an earlier heroic age. The Sibyl of Cumae had once uttered divine wisdom; now she is withered, hung in a cage, full of despair, and derided by boys. 'Yes, and I myself with my own eyes saw the Sibyl of Cumae hanging in a cage; and when the boys cried at her: "Sibyl, what do you want?", she used to reply, "I want to die." '

l. 12. ('I am no Russian, I come from Litau, true German.')

l. 20. Cf. Ezekiel II, 1. ('And He said unto me, Son of Man, stand upon thy feet, and I will speak unto thee.' God always calls Ezekiel 'Son of Man.')

l. 23. Cf. Ecclesiastes XII, 5. (The coming of death: 'Also when they shall be afraid of that which is high, and fears shall be in the way, and the almond tree shall flourish, and the grasshopper shall be a burden, and desire shall fail: because man goeth to his long home, and the mourners go about the streets: Or ever the silver cord be loosed, or the golden bowl be broken, or the pitcher be broken at the fountain, or the wheel broken at the cistern. Then shall the dust return to the earth as it was: and the spirit shall return unto God who gave it. Vanity of vanities, saith the preacher; all is vanity.')

ll. 31–4. Wagner's *Tristan and Isolde*, I, verses 5–8. ('Fresh blows the wind to the homeland; my Irish child, where do you tarry?' Sailor's song.)

l. 42. *Ibid.* III, verse 24. ('Sea, desolate and empty.')

ll. 46–55. I am not familiar [Eliot says] with the exact constitution of the Tarot pack of cards, from which I have obviously departed to suit my own convenience. [The Tarot pack of cards, used by fortune-tellers, is of very primitive and very obscure origins. It was, however, certainly a part of ancient vegetation rituals; and its suits, Cup, Lance, Sword, and Dish, are symbols which are found in the Grail legend itself.] The Hanged Man, a member of the traditional pack, fits my purpose in two ways: because he is associated in my mind with the Hanged God of Frazer [*The Golden Bough*, a study of primitive religions], and because I associate him with the hooded figure in the passage of the disciples to Emmaus in Part V. The Phoenician Sailor and the Merchant appear later; also the 'crowds of people,' and Death by Water is executed in Part IV. The man with Three Staves (an authentic member of the Tarot pack) I associate, quite arbitrarily, with the Fisher King himself.

l. 48. (Shakespeare's *Tempest*, I, 2, 387–404. Prospero has sent Ariel, an airy spirit, to bring Ferdinand, Prince of Naples, who has been shipwrecked, his father apparently drowned; Prospero intends Ferdinand to fall in love with his daughter, Miranda; Ariel, invisible, guides Ferdinand by singing:

FERDINAND:
Where should this music be? i' the air or the earth?
It sounds no more: and, sure, it waits upon
Some god o' the island. Sitting on a bank,
Weeping again the king my father's wreck,
This music crept by me upon the waters,
Allaying both their fury and my passion
With its sweet air: thence I have follow'd it,
Or it hath drawn me rather. But 'tis gone.
No, it begins again.
        Ariel sings:
        Full fathom five thy father lies;
        Of his bones are coral made;
        Those are pearls that were his eyes:
        Nothing of him that doth fade
        But doth suffer a sea-change
        Into something rich and strange.
        Sea-nymphs hourly ring his knell:
        Burthen: *Ding-dong.*
        Hark! Now I hear them,—ding-dong, bell.)

l. 55. (*The Hanged Man*. In most of the primitive religions there was a hanged or maimed god. Cf. Christianity. See ll. 322–30, where the disciples on the journey to Emmaus *do not see* Christ.)

ll. 60–62. Cf. Baudelaire: 'Fourmillante cité,' etc.

('*Swarming city, city full of dreams,*
Where the spectre in full day walks with the passer-by.'

Fleurs du Mal, poem 93: '*The Seven Old Men.*' Baudelaire tells of going out in a foul, yellow fog into the slums, meeting an old man, evil-eyed, bent, 'hostile to life'; then six others exactly like him pass in the fog; Baudelaire hurried home shuddering, locked himself in, half-mad: 'these seven hideous monsters had the look of eternal beings.')

l. 63. Cf. Dante's *Inferno*, III, 55–7. (Just inside the Gate of Hell, Dante sees a crowd of people, wailing; they had 'lived without blame, and without praise, they had never lived; from cowardice they made the great refusal; hateful to God and to His enemies'; Hell will not receive them, they wail because they 'have no hope of death, and their blind life is so mean that they are envious of every other lot,

        . . . *so long a train*
        of people that I should never have believed
        that death had undone so many.')

[Poem 301]

l. 64. Cf. *Inferno*, IV, 25–7. (In the first circle of Hell, Dante sees the heathen, not in pain, but 'neither sad nor joyful'; 'without hope we live in desire';

> *No plaint could be heard, except of sighs,*
> *which caused the eternal air to tremble.*)

ll. 68–9. A phenomenon which I have often noticed [Eliot writes].

ll. 74–5. (Cf. poem No. 8. This song is sung by the mad Cornelia to her son Flamineo; she is preparing for burial the corpse of another son, Marcello, who has been murdered by Flamineo.)

l. 76. See Baudelaire, Preface to *Fleurs du Mal*. ('Hypocrite reader!—my double,—my brother!' The Preface is addressed 'To the Reader.' After describing the foul souls in 'us,' he says one uglier monster waits:

> *Boredom—his eye full of involuntary tears,*
> *He dreams of gallows, smoking his pipe.*
> *You know him, reader, this dainty monster,*
> *—Hypocrite reader,—my double,—my brother!*)

l. 77. Cf. Shakespeare's *Antony and Cleopatra*, II, 2, 190. (Enobarbus tells how Cleopatra first came to meet Mark Antony, to overwhelm him with sensuous appeal; the two are famous for their passionate and romantic love:

> *The barge she sat in, like a burnished throne,*
> *Burn'd on the water; the poop was beaten gold;*
> *Purple the sails, and so perfumed that*
> *The winds were love-sick with them; the oars were silver,*
> *Which to the tune of flutes kept stroke, and made*
> *The water which they beat to follow faster,*
> *As amorous of their strokes. For her own person,*
> *It beggar'd all description: she did lie*
> *In her pavilion—cloth-of-gold of tissue—*
> *O'er-picturing that Venus where we see*
> *The fancy outwork nature: on each side her*
> *Stood pretty dimpled boys, like smiling Cupids,*
> *With divers-colour'd fans, whose wind did seem*
> *To glow the delicate cheeks which they did cool,*
> *And what they undid did.*
>   (*O, rare for Antony!*)
> *Her gentlewomen, like the Nereides,*
> *So many mermaids, tended her i' the eyes,*
> *And made their bends adornings: at the helm*
> *A seeming mermaid steers: the silken tackle*
> *Swell with the touches of those flower-soft hands,*
> *That rarely frame the office. From the barge*

A strange invisible perfume hits the sense
Of the adjacent wharfs. The city cast
Her people out upon her; and Antony
Enthron'd i' the market-place, did sit alone,
Whistling to the air; which, but for vacancy,
Had gone to gaze on Cleopatra too
And made a gap in nature . . .

Age cannot wither her, nor custom stale
Her infinite variety: other women cloy
The appetites they feed: but she makes hungry
Where most she satisfies:)

l. 92. *laquearia*. See *Aeneid*, I, 726. ('lighted lamps hang from the fretted ceiling [laquearia] of gold, and flaming torches drive out the night.' This is the gorgeous feast given by Dido, Queen of Carthage, to Aeneas when he arrives; Venus has sent Cupid to smite Dido with love for Aeneas at this welcoming feast. Later when he left Carthage, Dido in grief killed herself—one of the great tragic lovers of legend.)

l. 98. *sylvan scene*. See Milton, *Paradise Lost*, IV, 140. ('sylvan scene' begins the description of the Garden of Eden, in which are Adam and Eve,

> *. . . the loveliest pair*
> *That ever since in love's embraces met,*
> *Adam the goodliest of men since born*
> *His sons, the fairest of her daughters Eve.*

They tell of their simple and joyous life, and of their happy love, recalling their first meeting; Milton then writes a famous passage in praise of wedded love, ending

> *Here Love his golden shaft employs, here lights*
> *His Constant Lamp, and waves his purple wings,*
> *Reigns here and revels . . .*
> *These lulled by Nightingales embracing slept*
> *And on their naked limbs the flowery roof*
> *Shower'd roses, which the morn repaired.*

Eliot's style in lines 95–102 reminds one strongly of Milton's.)

ll. 99–103. See Ovid, *Metamorphoses*, VI, Philomela. (See poems Nos. 97, 98, 99, and notes. In poetry the nightingale's song is represented by 'jug jug' and 'Tereu.')

l. 100. (Cf. ll. 203–6.)

ll. 108–10. (Compare Shelley's

> *Like the bright hair uplifted from the head*
> *Of some fierce Maenad . . . [Ode to the West Wind]*

The Maenades were, with satyrs and others, semi-human followers of Dionysus [Bacchus], who was primarily a god of fertility; the Maenades, with wild
hair streaming, danced themselves into a frenzy in the wild and savage orgies
of Dionysus.)

l. 115. Cf. l. 195.

l. 126. Cf. ll. 37, 48.

l. 138. Cf. the game of chess in Middleton's *Women beware Women*. (Act
II, Sc. ii, where Livia and Bianca's mother play chess, distracting the
mother's attention while Bianca is being seduced.)

l. 172. (*Hamlet*, V, v, 71. Ophelia, insane, wanders in before the King and
Queen, singing old ballads of the burial of loved ones and of the betrayal of
trusting maids; as she leaves, she says, 'And so I thank you for your good
counsel. Come, my coach! Good night, ladies; good night, sweet ladies; good
night, good night.')

l. 175. ('The nymphs are departed.' Pastoral love poetry is full of scenes
such as this from Milton's *Comus*:

> *The sounds, and seas with all their finny drove*
> *Now to the moon in wavering morrice move,*
> *And on the tawny sands and shelves,*
> *Trip the pert fairies and the dapper elves;*
> *By dimpled brook, and fountain brim,*
> *The wood-nymphs deckt with daisies trim,*
> *Their merry wakes and pastimes keep:*
> *What hath night to do with sleep?*
> *Night hath better sweets to prove,*
> *Venus now wakes, and wak'ns love.*)

ll. 175–6. See Spenser, *Prothalamion*. (See poem No. 54. The title means
'A Marriage Song.' Notice especially the river-nymphs, the river itself, and
the refrain line.)

l. 182. (Psalm 137. 'By the rivers of Babylon, there we sat down, yea, we
wept, when we remembered Zion. We hanged our harps upon the willows in
the midst thereof. For they that carried us away captive required of us a song;
and they that wasted us required of us mirth, saying, Sing us one of the songs
of Zion. How shall we sing the Lord's song in a strange land? If I forget thee,
O Jerusalem, let my right hand forget her cunning.')

l. 185. (Cf. poem No. 219, ll. 21–4.)

ll. 191–2. (See *Tempest*, speech of Ferdinand, note to line 48, above.)

ll. 197–9. Cf. Day, *Parliament of Bees*:

> *When of the sudden, listening, you shall hear,*
> *A noise of horns and hunting, which shall bring*
> *Actaeon to Diana in the spring,*
> *Where all shall see her naked skin . . .*

[Poem 301]

(A 'vain-glorious reveller' is describing his future magnificent house; on the ceiling would be a forest, upsidedown, in which the Actaeon-Diana story would be enacted. Actaeon while hunting came upon Diana, goddess of chastity, bathing naked; for this sacrilege, he was turned into a stag and killed by his own dogs.)

ll. 199–201. I do not know the origin of the ballad from which these lines are taken; it was reported to me from Sydney, Australia [writes Eliot]. (It sounds as if it were sung to the tune of a popular American song, 'Pretty Red Wing,' which opens, 'Oh the moon shone bright on pretty Red Wing.')

l. 202. See Verlaine, *Parsifal*. (Parsifal attains his quest, finds the Holy Grail, and in a robe of gold worships the glorious symbol, the pure vessel where shines the true blood, and in the chapel of the Holy Grail he hears—

'And—O, the voices of children singing in the choir-loft.')

l. 207. (Cf. l. 60, note, above.)

l. 209. (Cf. l. 52.)

l. 210. The currants were quoted at a price 'carriage and insurance free to London'; and the Bill of Lading etc. were to be handed to the buyer upon payment of the sight draft. (Eliot, who once worked in a London bank, knows the liturgy of commerce.)

l. 218. *Tiresias*. Tiresias, although a mere spectator and not indeed a 'character,' is yet the most important personage in the poem, uniting all the rest. Just as the one-eyed merchant, seller of currants, melts into the Phoenician Sailor, and the latter is not wholly distinct from Ferdinand Prince of Naples, so all the women are one woman, and the two sexes meet in Tiresias. What Tiresias *sees*, in fact, is the substance of the poem. The whole passage from Ovid is of great anthropological interest:

(It chanced that Jove, while warmed with wine, put care aside and bandied good-humored jests with Juno in an idle hour. 'I maintain,' he said, 'that your pleasure in love is greater than we [male gods] enjoy.' She held the opposite view. And so they decided to ask the judgment of wise Tiresias. He knew both sides of love. For once, with a blow of his staff he had outraged two huge serpents mating in the green forest; and, wonderful to relate, from man he was changed into a woman, and in that form spent seven years. In the eighth year he saw the same serpents again and said, 'Since in striking you there is such magic power as to change the nature of the giver of the blow, now will I strike you once more.' So saying, he struck the serpents and his former state was restored and he became as he had been born. He therefore, being asked to arbitrate the playful dispute of the gods, took sides with Jove. Saturnia [Juno], they say, grieved more deeply than she should and than the issue warranted, and condemned the arbitrator to perpetual blindness. But the Almighty Father [for no god may undo what another god has done] in return for his loss of sight gave Tiresias the power to know the future, lightening the penalty by the honor.

Tiresias became a very famous seer in the city of Thebes, and lived for seven generations; when Thebes was destroyed in war, he was killed; his shade went to Hades, where he retained his prophetic power, being visited by Ulysses for advice.)

l. 221. This may not appear as exact as Sappho's lines, but I had in mind the 'long-shore' or 'dory' fisherman, who returns at nightfall.

(Eliot wishes to recall a famous poem of Sappho, the Greek poetess, to the evening star:

> *Hesperus, you bring home all things that the shining*
> *morning scattered; you bring the sheep, you bring the*
> *goat, you bring the child to the mother.*

Among other poets, Byron paraphrased the poem [*Don Juan*, III, st. 107]:

> *Oh, Hesperus! thou bringest all good things—*
> *Home to the weary, to the hungry cheer,*
> *To the young bird the parent's brooding wings,*
> *The welcome stall to the o'erlabor'd steer;*
> *Whate'er of peace about our hearthstone clings,*
> *Whate'er our household gods protect of dear,*
> *Are gather'd round us by thy look of rest;*
> *Thou bring'st the child, too, to the mother's breast.*)

See also poem No. 19.

l. 224. (Keats in the *Ode to a Nightingale* imagined the bird's song to be

> *The same that oft-times hath*
> *Charmed magic casements, opening on the foam*
> *Of perilous seas, in faery lands forlorn.*)

l. 234. (Bradford. A manufacturing city which produced many 'newly rich' men, assertive, but uncertain of their manners.)

ll. 253–6. See Goldsmith, the song in *The Vicar of Wakefield*.

> (*When lovely woman stoops to folly*
> *And finds too late that men betray,*
> *What charm can soothe her melancholy,*
> *What art can wash her guilt away?*
>
> *The only art her guilt to cover,*
> *To hide her shame from every eye,*
> *To give repentance to her lover*
> *And wring his bosom—is to die.*)

l. 257. See *The Tempest*. (Note to line 48, above.)

l. 264. The interior of St. Magnus Martyr is to my mind one of the finest among Wren's interiors. See *The Proposed Demolition of Nineteen City Churches*.

ll. 266–306. The song of the (three) Thames-daughters begins here.

From ·line 292 to 306 inclusive they speak in turn. See *Götterdämmerung*, III, i: the Rhine-daughters. (At the opening of Wagner's *Das Rheingold* the three Rhine-daughters sing joyously of the gold which they guard, using the refrain 'Weialala' etc. of lines 277, 290. In his *Götterdämmerung*, III, i, they lament the loss of the Rhinegold and their former joy.)

l. 279. See Froude, *Elizabeth*, Vol. I, ch. 4, letter of De Quadra to Philip of Spain: 'In the afternoon we were in a barge, watching the games on the river. [The Queen] was alone with Lord Robert and myself on the poop, when they began to talk nonsense, and went so far that Lord Robert [Leicester] at last said, as I was on the spot there was no reason why they should not be married if the queen pleased.'

ll. 293–4. Cf. Dante's *Purgatorio*, V, 133. (As Dante begins the ascent to the Mount of Purgatory, he meets the souls of the violently slain who repented and made their peace with God at the last moment; Dante promises to bear news of these souls to their friends on earth and implore their prayers. Among them is 'La Pia'; legend says she was born in Siena and became the wife of a nobleman who, wishing to marry another woman, placed her in a house in the malarial marshes of Maremma until she died of the fever; to Dante she says only a few words, long memorable for their simple poignancy:

> *Pray, when thou shalt return to the world,*
> *And art rested from thy long journey,*
>
> *Remember me, who am La Pia;*
> *Siena made me, Maremma unmade me:*
> *'Tis known to him who, first plighting troth,*
> *Had wedded me with his gem.*)

ll. 294–300. (Richmond and Kew are popular places for holiday-making on the river above London. Moorgate is a slum area of London. Margate is a popular sea-side resort near London.)

l. 307. See St. Augustine's *Confessions*: 'to Carthage then I came, where a cauldron of unholy loves sang all about mine ears.'

l. 308. (Eliot notes that these words are taken from Buddha's *Fire Sermon*, which corresponds in importance to the *Sermon on the Mount*. See Henry Clarke Warren, *Buddhism in Translation*.)

l. 312. From St. Augustine's *Confessions* again. The collocation of these two representatives of eastern and western asceticism, as the culmination of this part of the poem, is not an accident. (Eliot says, remember, that Mr. Eugenides, l. 207, melts into Phlebas, and Phlebas into Ferdinand Prince of Naples. Compare ll. 312–21 with Ariel's song, note to line 48.)

ll. 322–76. In the first part of Part V three themes are employed: the journey to Emmaus, the approach to the Chapel Perilous (see Miss Weston's book), and the present [1922] decay of eastern Europe.

ll. 322–65. (This journey through the waste land begins with the recollection of the events leading to the crucifixion of Christ, the disillusionment and despair of the disciples; after Mary had reported the Resurrection, which the disciples think an idle tale not to be believed, two of them started on a journey to Emmaus; Jesus appeared but they did not know him, until he told them, at evening, when he broke bread with them, blessed it, and vanished. See Luke, 22–24.)

ll. 357–8. (Eliot notes that the song of the Hermit-thrush, unequaled in 'purity and sweetness of tone and exquisite modulation,' has been called a 'water-dripping song.')

ll. 359–65. The following lines were stimulated by the account of one of the Antarctic expeditions (I forget which, but I think one of Shackleton's): it was related that the party of explorers, at the extremity of their strength, had the constant delusion that there was *one more member* than could actually be counted.

ll. 368–76. Cf. Hermann Hesse, *Blick ins Chaos*: (*A Look at Chaos*: Already half of Europe, already at least half of Eastern Europe, is on the way to Chaos, traveling drunken in an illusion of holy ecstasy along the edge of the abyss, and celebrates this by singing, singing drunken hymns, as Dmitri Karamasoff [cf. Dostoevsky, *The Brothers Karamazov*] sang. Over these songs the insulted burgher laughs, the saint and the seer hear them with tears.')

ll. 378–379. (Cf. ll. 108–10, and note above; also l. 255.)

ll. 382–4. (Cf. bells of ll. 67, 286–7; the upsidedown scene of Diana-Actaeon, l. 197, note; the voices chanting of l. 202 and note.)

ll. 385–95. (The approach to the Chapel Perilous. In the legends of the Holy Grail, the Grail Knight endures a night of terror at the Chapel Perilous: a cemetery full of ghosts, a dead body in the Chapel, a black hand that kills all who come—supernatural and evil power aroused. This is a test of the Knight's fitness to achieve his Quest of the Holy Grail, which he does on the following day. During the night a thunder-storm rages. The crowing of the cock was popularly supposed to have power to force evil spirits to depart. See *Hamlet*, I, ii, 158:

> *Some say that ever 'gainst that season comes*
> *Wherein our Saviour's birth is celebrated,*
> *The bird of dawning singeth all night long;*
> *And then, they say, no spirit dare stir abroad;*
> *The nights are wholesome; then no planets strike,*
> *No fairy takes, nor witch hath power to charm,*
> *So hallow'd and so gracious is the time.*)

l. 401. 'Datta, dayadhvam, damyata' (Give, sympathize, control.) The fable of the meaning of the Thunder is found in the *Brihadaranyaka-Upanishad*, v, 1. A translation is found in Deussen's *Sechzig Upanishads des Veda*, p. 489. (The Vedic Books are the sacred books of wisdom of the Hindus, written in Sanskrit about 1000 B.C., the earliest literature in the Indo-European [Aryan] languages.)

    ll. 402–4. (Cf. poem No. 263.)

    l. 407. Cf. Webster, *The White Devil*, v, 6:

> *. . . they'll remarry*
> *Ere the worm pierce your winding-sheet, ere the spider*
> *Make a thin curtain for your epitaphs.*

    l. 411. Cf. *Inferno*, XXXIII, 46: ('And below I heard the outlet of the horrible tower locked up.' In the lowest circle of Hell, Dante finds the traitors. The story of Ugolino of Pisa is perhaps the most horrible ever told. Dante finds him gnawing the head of Ruggieri. In life Ugolino had betrayed his own grandson in a conspiracy with Ruggieri, who later betrayed Ugolino, putting him in prison with four sons and grandsons. One night, after a prophetic dream, Ugolino tells Dante, he

'awoke before the dawn, I heard my sons, who were with me, weeping in their sleep and asking for bread. Thou art right cruel, if thou dost not grieve already at the thought of what my heart foreboded; and if thou weepest not, at what art thou used to weep? They were awake now, and the hour approaching at which our food used to be brought us, and each was anxious from his dream,

and below I heard the outlet of the horrible tower locked up;

whereat I looked into the faces of my sons, without uttering a word. I did not weep: so stony I grew within; they wept; and my little Anselm said: "Thou lookest so, father, what ails thee?" But I shed no tear, nor answered all that day, nor the next night, till another sun came forth upon the world. When a small ray was sent into the doleful prison, and I discerned in their four faces the aspect of my own, I bit on both my hands for grief. And they thinking that I did it from desire of eating, of a sudden rose up, and said: "Father, it will give us much less pain, if thou wilt eat of us: thou didst put upon us this miserable flesh, and do thou strip it off." Then I calmed myself, in order not to make them more unhappy; that day and the next we were all mute. Ah, hard earth! why didst thou not open? When we had come to the fourth day, Gaddo threw himself out at my feet, saying: "My father! why don't you help me?" There he died; and even as thou seest me, saw I the three fall one by one, between the fifth and the sixth: whence I betook me, already blind, to groping over each, and for three days called them, after they were dead; then fasting had more power than grief. When he had spoken this, with eyes distorted he seized the miserable skull again with his teeth, which as a dog's were strong upon the bone.')

    l. 411. Cf. also F. H. Bradley, *Appearance and Reality*, p. 346: 'My external sensations are no less private to myself than are my thoughts or my feelings. In either case my experience falls within my own circle, a circle closed on the outside; and, with all its elements alike, every sphere is opaque to the others which surround it . . . In brief, regarded as an existence which appears in a soul, the whole world for each is peculiar and private to that soul.'

l. 415. *Coriolanus.* (Coriolanus, a great Roman general and hero of Shakespeare's play, through his pride and the citizens' ingratitude, was exiled from Rome; enraged, he joined the enemy, the Volscians, and attacked Rome; his Roman mother and wife and son finally persuaded him to spare Rome; he went back to the Volscians, a stranger, a traitor both to them and to Rome; they killed him.)

l. 424. See Weston: *From Ritual to Romance*; chapter on the Fisher King. (In the Grail legends, the illness of the Fisher King caused his land to be waste and parched by drought. Cf. ll. 187–90.)

l. 427. See Dante's *Purgatorio*, xxvi, 148. ('Then he dived back into that fire which refines them.' In Purgatory, Dante comes to those who indulged their carnal appetites, among them the Provencal poet, Arnaut Daniel, who willingly suffers torment so that he may enter Heaven;

> *'I am Arnaut that weep and go a-singing; in thought*
> *I see my past madness, and I see with joy the day which*
> *I await before me. Now I pray you, by that Goodness*
> *which guideth you to the summit of the stairway, be*
> *mindful in due time of my pain.' Then he dived back*
> *into that fire which refines them.*

Cf. the fire of lust of l. 308.)

l. 428. See *Pervigilium Veneris*, 90. Cf. Philomela in Parts II and III. (*When shall I be like the swallow*. This poem tells how, on this 'Night of Venus,' all nature rejoices; even the Nightingale sings as if she had no terrible memories—all rejoice but the poet:

> *She is singing: I am silent. When will spring awake in me?*
> *When shall I be like the swallow and from dumb distress be free?*
> *I have lost the Muse by silence: me Apollo heedeth not.*

The refrain in the poem, a chant by happy creatures, is:

> *Are ye loveless or love-lorn? Yours be love to-morrow morn!*)

l. 429. See Gerard de Nerval, Sonnet *El Desdichado*. (Gerard, who lived much in a world of illusions, expressing a moment of wearied grief, wrote:

> *I am the gloomy one,—the widower,—the unconsoled,*
> *The Prince of Aquitaine at the ruined tower.*)

l. 431. See Kyd's *Spanish Tragedy*, iv, i, 67. (Hieronymo is driven into periods of insanity by grief for his murdered son; he writes a play to give himself, as an actor, a chance to kill the murderers; just then the King sends the murderers to request him to present an entertainment at court; Hieronymo agrees to fill the need, 'Why then I'll fit you.' His scheme succeeds, he bites off his own tongue to avoid confessing, and then kills himself in a violent scene in which the dead outnumber the living.)

l. 433. Shantih. Repeated as here, a formal ending to an Upanishad (a part of the sacred Vedic Books). 'The Peace which passeth understanding' is our equivalent to this word.

VIII

THE CREATION OF POEMS

The material in this Part shows four poets at work, one revising a published poem, and three creating poems as they write. The latter poems are given in transcriptions of the original manuscripts. To assist the reader in following the transcription, a number has been placed opposite the first word of each line that the poet started to write; the interlinear corrections are printed above or below the original line in approximately the same position they occupy in the manuscript. Each illegible word is indicated by a question mark in a blank space. Words or letters within parentheses were, in the manuscript, written over the word or letters preceding the parenthesis (except in Spender's *The Express*, in which the poet himself uses the parenthesis). Brackets indicate material added by the editors (except in *The Express*, in which they indicate words or letters written over the preceding letters). The six successive drafts of Spender's *The Express* are called A, B, C, etc.; letters are also used in stanzas 24 and 26 of Keats's *The Eve of St. Agnes*, in which Keats starts several separate drafts of each stanza. All of the evidence that a manuscript reveals concerning the deletions and revisions cannot be shown in print. In the notes to each poem, some of this evidence is described.

Revisions and early drafts of poems, showing poets at work, can be very helpful to readers. Even a rapid glance at this material will be useful in correcting some general notions about poets and poems that often prevent effective reading. One source of such notions is the belief that the words of the poem are given to the poet by an inspiration and are therefore to be understood by a similar gift to the reader, who communes with the poet. The words of a poem are the means of communing, not the means of communication. Careful study of a poem is 'tearing it to pieces.' This attitude frequently causes the communist reader to use the poem as a springboard into a poem of his own. It also causes the reader who doesn't like poetry to regard a poem as a remote and unapproachable secret, whose revelation, if it come not at first glance, will come not at all; his highest praise for a poem is that it is easy to understand.

The study of manuscripts will also help to correct a more sophisticated error: that a poet creates a poem somewhere in his consciousness and then finds words to express it. The main object in reading is to get past the words and discover what the poet really meant. The words are just one way of expressing the poem; possibly other words, which the reader is sometimes willing to supply, could express the poem better. Many readers suffering from this error have an incurable itch to rewrite the poem so that the experience will be more adequately expressed. What they are really doing, of course, is assuming that the poem exists apart from the words, that they can understand it in spite of the ineffective words. 'This is a good poem but it is poorly expressed.' Such a statement means 'This poem suggests to me another poem, similar but better.' The other poem is not infrequently worse.

No one who studies these revisions and early drafts will deny that a poet has special gifts that often amount to genius, and that his creative power is fundamentally a mysterious power. This is true even if the genius does not operate until the fourth revision; the only fact of importance is that it does operate. But the poem which this power creates is not mysterious. It is a communication of experience that is communicable. All that we readers have are the poet's words—and they are enough, if we will use them. We cannot properly use them if we take them vaguely or at a glance. We must use them, as far as we can, as the poet used them. They are our only means of access to the poet's experience; for us, he thought and felt only in words. Whatever of wordless thought and feeling existed in the poet has been changed, developed, and shaped by the words he used. No doubt some part of his original thought or feeling escaped verbalization— but with this part we have no concern. Actually both the poet and the reader are concerned only with the experience which these words mean. If the poet is concerned with any other experience, he must write another poem, using other words.

We have said that, in the creation of a poem, the words do not simply *express* an already fixed experience. The words themselves change and shape the experience. To take a simple example, in the last line of stanza 30 of *The Eve of St. Agnes*, Keats is describing the place from which the *spiced daintes* come: he writes *wealthy Samarchand*, which is, presumably, his first feeling about the place. After he has finished the line, he goes back and deletes *wealthy*. Why? Is he merely revising his language? No, he is revising his notion of Samarchand—it is now *glutted*. Now, it might well be that in reality, but the word rather takes the delectable edge off the *spiced daintes* of the midnight feast. Keats deletes the word and revises his notion of Samarchand *in this poem*—and now it is *silken*. His feeling about Samarchand in this poem, obviously, is not fixed until he calls it *silken*. And thereafter, to Keats the meaning of Samarchand in this line is not *wealthy* or *glutted*, but *silken*. What he may have felt about Samarchand on other occasions is irrelevant. Now, the reader of the published poem has only *silken*. And whatever he may think about Samarchand on other occasions, here it can mean to him only *silken*. He must let this partic- ular word stimulate and control his experience here. And so it is with every word in a poem. The reader must use that word and no other. For him, as for the poet, the words of a poem, if properly used, com- municate the experience. Close study of a poem, fixing the attention on every word, cannot tear a good poem to pieces. On the contrary, if the reader has sufficient skill in using words, it is the only way in which he can create the full experience in his consciousness.

One further general observation about these revisions and drafts may be briefly made. They show the poet as a craftsman, an artist. He uses the instrument that other people have largely created, lan- guage. He works within the conditions he chooses to accept—within the metrical pattern of line, the rhyme scheme of stanza, the length of stanza, etc. He tries, in less fixed ways, to shape his original im- pulse into a form in which details unite to make a coherent whole, whose total meaning is self-sustained and complete. Whatever the value of his experience, he is an expert craftsman. And since he is working with material which all people have (human experience) and since his tool is the greatest of human tools (language) we can watch him with genuine interest—and discover knowledge from every movement of his thought and feeling and language.

And finally we may realize that, when so much effort and skill goes into the creation of a poem, we cannot hope to read it without being willing ourselves to contribute effort and skill. We can learn from these revisions and drafts a great deal about the kind of effort and skill we need to have as readers. As we watch Tennyson or Keats or Spender or Auden at the work of creating a poem, we should try to 'follow' him by always asking, What is he doing? And why?

302, Alfred Tennyson, *The Lady of Shalott* (1833 Version), 1833. Tennyson's *Poems*, which included this poem, was dated 1833. It was issued, however, in December 1832, and is sometimes referred to as of that year. The volume was severely criticized by the reviewers. Tennyson revised *The Lady of Shalott* and printed the revised version in his *Poems* of 1842.

303, Alfred Tennyson, *The Lady of Shalott* (1842 version), 1842.

304, John Keats, *From the Manuscript of* THE EVE OF ST. AGNES. This manuscript, now in the Widener Library at Harvard University, contains the whole poem; the first seven stanzas are not in Keats's hand. The rest of the manuscript is almost certainly the first draft of the poem, written in January–April 1819. In the seven stanzas here transcribed we can see Keats creating the poem as he writes. The final draft of each stanza is almost identical with the text as printed in 1820, which is included in this book as poem No. 190.

Professor M. R. Ridley, in his *Keats' Craftsmanship*, has discussed the creation of these stanzas in great detail. His conjectures concerning the poet's reasons for making the many revisions are acute and illuminating.

STANZA 24: Several heavy diagonal lines are used to delete the whole of Draft A and the whole of Draft B. In Draft A, l. 4., after Keats had written *upon*, he deleted it and inserted the colon after *gules*.

STANZA 26: Several heavy diagonal lines are used to delete the whole of Draft A and the whole of Draft B. Before starting the third draft of the stanza, Keats postponed for a moment a difficult job by counting the stanzas he had completed; for the first time he placed a number at the head of a stanza.

STANZA 27.

l. 1. The words *forth she slips* are vigorously deleted by diagonal lines, as if Keats suddenly realized their comic implications.

l. 2. In the final version, Keats indicated that the words *She lay* are to be shifted to the end of the line.

STANZA 29. In ll. 9–10 the verbs were first written in the past tense, and then changed to the present.

STANZA 30.

l. 6. Keats intended the last word to be 'cinnamon'; as often in this manuscript, his haste confused his fingers.

l. 7. The revisions here are crowded together and almost obliterated by deletion marks. Previous editors have not ventured to print some of the most obscured words. We can trace with some assurance the order of the revisions up to a certain point, when Keats abandoned the line without writing out the final version, although the line was probably clear in his head. He first wrote, with only the deletion of *from*, the line

And sugar'd dates that o'er Euphrates fard

Then he dropped down the normal space and began what was intended as l. 8

And Manna wild and

Here he stopped and apparently decided to put both dates and manna in one line. He deleted the original l. 7, deleted by two diagonal marks the first *And*, and started to change *wild* to *and*; but instead he deleted *Manna wild and*, and immediately above these words began the line anew

Manna and daites in Bragine wild transferrd

This is an iambic pentameter line, with the proper rhyme at the end. But no *Bragine* ever sailed the seas, and Keats seems to have discovered his error at once. (Professor Ridley hesitantly read *Peaches* where we read *Bragine*.) He deleted *wild transferrd*, and wrote *transferred* so close above the phrase that the whole is a tangled mess of letters. Then he deleted this *transferred*, and, shifting higher, wrote *in Brigantine transferred*, which gave him a proper line. But he was not satisfied with plain manna and dates; he deleted *in Brigantine transferred* and then, underneath his *Bragine*, wrote *and Manna*. Then he deleted by four diagonal lines all of the words of the last half of the line. The revisions do not clearly reveal what happened after this. Keats wrote once more the name of his ship, *Bragantine*, only to delete it at once. Then came *sugar'd dates transferrd*, which probably indicates that Keats had postponed the troublesome ship and now intended the line to be

And Manna wild and sugar'd dates transferrd

He then went on to begin l. 8

In Brigantine from Fez

At this point he seems to have decided to put the ship back into l. 7 and to change it to *argosy*. Since there was literally no room in the line for *argosy*, he wrote it in the left margin. Then he deleted *sugar'd*—and there his pen stopped. It is clear, however, that the words had reached the form of the printed text

Manna and dates in argosy transferr'd

Such are the workings of what is sometimes called poetic inspiration.

305, Stephen Spender, *The Manuscript of* THE EXPRESS. These six drafts of the poem are in a work-book of the poet now in the Lockwood Memorial Library of the University of Buffalo. While the first part of the poem may have been worked out in previous drafts, it seems obvious that these six drafts show the entire composition of at least the last half of the poem. The final draft is almost identical with the text printed in Spender's *Poems* (New York, 1934), which is given here as poem No. 225.

No editorial matter has been inserted in the transcription of the lines. The parenthesis which first appears in Draft B, l. 18, is the poet's. Letters or words in brackets are written in the manuscript over the preceding letters or words.

DRAFT B.

l. 18. The words *Her passengers* are written in the left margin before *Travellers go.*

DRAFT C.

l. 6. The word *And* is written in the margin before *The.*

ll. 17-26. The passage is deleted by a large X.

ll. 27-9. The passage is deleted by diagonal lines.

ll. 30-33. An arrow in the left margin points to this passage.

DRAFT D.

l. 22. The word *oh* is written in the margin before *They.*

l. 31. The words *They watch* are written in the margin before *The images.*

ll. 28-9. This passage was the first to suffer deletion, by a waving horizontal line.

ll. 17-34. This passage is deleted by a large X and a long curving vertical line.

DRAFT E.

l. 20. The first revision makes this line read

And parallels like white bursts from guns

The whole of Draft E is deleted by a curving vertical line.

DRAFT F. This draft, as corrected, differs from the printed text only slightly; four commas are changed, and one word altered in ll. 13 and 19.

306, W. H. Auden, *The Manuscript of* WHERE DO THEY COME FROM? The manuscript is in the Lockwood Memorial Library of the University of Buffalo. It is probably the first draft of the poem. It should be compared with the final text printed in *Another Time* (1940), which is given here as poem No. 257. In the transcription each stanza is numbered to correspond with the same stanza in the printed text; notice that stanzas 5 and 6 are reversed in position.

[Poem 306]

The poem was first printed in *The Atlantic Monthly*, September 1939. There it has the title *Crisis*, and is headed by a quotation from Dante:

> *Of my sowing such straw I reap. O human folk,*
> *why set the heart there where exclusion of*
> *partnership is necessary?*
> —*Purgatorio*, XIV, *85–7*

PART X

ON READING POEMS

X

ON READING POEMS

I

In certain ways the art of reading poetry is like the art of listening to music: a trained listener, for example, listens to a Mozart Concerto or a Brahms Symphony with very great pleasure; but if we should ask him whether he likes 'music' he would reply that he likes Mozart or Brahms, not simply 'music.' There is, for him, no such thing as music; there are only musical compositions of which he likes many and dislikes others, even though he may have mastered the art of listening to most of them. And it is so with reading poetry. Before we set out to read a poem we ought to realize that there is really no such thing as 'poetry'; there are only poems, of which we shall like many and dislike others. 'Poetry' is a word which stands for our generalized idea of *all* poems, for our abstract notion, for our summary of all the poems we know anything about and those we do not know about. As such it is a useful word, but it is *only a word*. And it is not a word which stands for any *thing* that we can point to and say 'There it is.' We may say that *Hamlet*, *Paradise Lost*, the *Iliad* of Homer, and Sandburg's *Fog* are poetry, and this is often a useful convenience; but the poems are obviously so very different that we are not helped in reading them by knowing that they are 'poetry.' 'Poetry,' this is to say, stands for something in the subjective world, the world of our minds; it is an idea in our minds. If we start to read a *particular poem* as 'poetry' we shall expect *this* poem to be whatever our notion of poetry happens to be. When we say 'I don't like poetry,' we are describing the general effect of displeasure left in our recollection by reading poems. And if we 'do not like poetry' we shall not like *this* poem. Our position is hopeless; we shall never learn to like poems and one of the highest pleasures of the human mind will be permanently cut off from us. On the other hand, we shall get into the same sort of difficulty if we are satisfied to say that we 'like poetry'; for in that case we shall in all probability read the particular poem with our minds only partly awake, assuming that we like it because we like 'poetry.' We may never actually come to a full comprehension of the poem at all, and hence never fully enjoy it.

If our notion of poetry is clear and strong, it will try to force the particular poem we are reading to conform to it. For example, 'poetry is all emotion'; therefore this poem will be all emotion. Or, 'poetry is smooth in sound'; therefore this poem should be smooth in sound. 'Poetry is all right for women but not for men.' 'Poetry is written by long-haired dreamers.' 'Poetry is good because it is cultural.' 'Poetry is ruined by careful study.' These notions, and dozens of others, are created by our actual reading of poems, or by what we read about poetry, or by the notions about poetry that we hear from our friends or teachers, etc. Our notion may be pleasant or distasteful, adequate or narrow, justified or unjustified, but whatever it is it sets up expectations that are not useful to us in reading a particular poem—but, in fact, quite the opposite. Even when we expect to enjoy the poem in *certain ways* our reading of the poem will be distorted. For if it cannot be forced to fit these ways, we may even say 'This isn't poetry.'

The danger of bringing abstract notions to the reading of a poem is never greater than when it is a question of notions about a particular author. For example, 'Tennyson was a Victorian sentimentalist'; therefore this poem will be sentimental. Or, 'Shakespeare was a great genius'; therefore this poem is perfect, wonderful, and probably beyond my powers of comprehension. Or again, 'modern poetry is always very difficult and obscure'; therefore I shall not be able to understand this poem of W. H. Auden. The truth of the matter is that the only really useful expectation that a reader can bring to a poem is that it will be in certain ways unique, a thing in itself, and will provide him with a new experience. We might even make a parody of Gertrude Stein, 'a poem is a poem is a poem is a poem.'

Reading a poem is an activity, not a passive reception. The reader must create; he must, in fact, *create a poem* where none existed before—that is, in his own consciousness. No one can do this for him. That this is true is clear if we ask the question: where is a poem? Is it in the mind of the poet? It *was*, but whether it is now or not is of no concern to us—the poet may well be dead. Is the poem in the ink marks on a page of this book? Obviously not. Is it in the sound waves made by someone speaking? No—these are just a succession of condensed and rarified states of air. The fact is that a poem is not in existence at all until we create it in our consciousness; and this is the true meaning of 'reading' a poem. In this essay (and throughout the book), *when we speak of a 'poem' we mean the experience which the reader creates in his mind by using the words of the poet, and by 'reading' we mean the process by which he creates the poem.*

II

It is obvious that the reader of a poem needs certain skills which are used in the creation of a poem. These skills are the special talents of the poet, but they are also possessed, in lesser degree, by everybody else. And, fortunately, they can be increased, like other skills, by training and exercise, and by understanding something of their nature and of the activities in which they are used. The most important of these activities is in *using language.* The reader, as well as the poet, must have skill in using the medium of communication between them. The poet is conscious of an experience; to him, from the point at which he starts to write, the poem is not the original experience but the experience which *these words* 'mean' to him. The reader must use these words, in reverse order so to speak, to create in himself an experience. The first aim of the good reader, it follows, is to use the words of the poet to create in himself an experience which resembles as nearly as possible the experience which the words 'meant' to the poet, to *re-create* the experience of the poet. This resemblance, of course, can never be complete; that fact must be accepted. But we ought not therefore to conclude that the reader should rest content with creating an experience vaguely like that of the poet. Nor does it follow that a number of readers cannot reach a reasonably close agreement on what the poem 'means.' We *should* conclude, on the other hand, that our comprehension of the poem is tentative, that we can come to a closer comprehension if we can know what it 'means' to others, and that careful study of a poem will not tear it to pieces but will, rather, enable us to create an experience more nearly like that of the poet and hence to enjoy it more fully (or to dislike it for honest reasons). Above all, we should conclude that skill in the use of language is of first importance to the reader as well as to the poet.

Most of us assume that we have a good deal of this skill in language, at least as readers. But the truth is not so flattering. Nearly everyone needs to use language much more effectively if he wishes to become a good reader. We can increase our efficiency by observing what happens when we read a poem, that is, when we create an experience by using the words of a poet. Here are words for us to use in creating a poetic experience:

1. *That time of year thou mayst in me behold*
2. *When yellow leaves, or none, or few, do hang*
3. *Upon those boughs which shake against the cold,*
4. *Bare ruin'd choirs, where late the sweet birds sang.*
5. *In me thou see'st the twilight of such day*
6. *As after sunset fadeth in the west,*
7. *Which by and by black night doth take away,*
8. *Death's second self, that seals up all in rest.*
9. *In me thou see'st the glowing of such fire,*
10. *That on the ashes of his youth doth lie,*
11. *As the death-bed whereon it must expire,*
12. *Consum'd with that which it was nourish'd by.*
13. *This thou perceiv'st, which makes thy love more strong,*
14. *To love that well which thou must leave ere long.*

An element of the experience of this poem is what we may call its *plain sense*, that part of its total meaning which can be summarized in prose: 'You know that I am growing old; therefore you love me more, since you must soon leave me.' We can call this plain sense the skeleton of the experience. The skeleton has an important function in any structure: it holds the other parts together. And it is by understanding the skeleton that we understand the general shape of the structure. In most poems (not in all) this plain sense meaning is of considerable importance; but it is never more than the skeleton of the experience. A person, as we see him, is not that particular person because of his bone-frame; his individuality, to us, is his whole appearance. So the plain sense of this poem might be the skeleton of a hundred poems, each different. The poem is itself unique, because of the flesh and blood (so to speak) on its skeleton—that is, the meaning of all the words working together as a whole. In our discussion of this experience, however, we can for convenience notice separately other elements of the whole.

The plain sense of the first twelve lines is 'You know that I am growing old.' It is said three different times, ll. 1–4, 5–8, and 9–12. But the whole meaning of ll. 1–4 is not the same as that of the other lines. What are the elements of the whole meaning of ll. 1–4? One is the sight of trees in early winter shaken by cold winds. This is the sight of the year growing old, as I am growing old. You remember that in the summer sweet birds sang in these branches, now bare, ruined—like the ruins of a cathedral, the broken arches of its choir, under which sweet voices once sang. This remembering and these sights of the dying year may make you feel as you feel when you know that I am growing old. I do not say what you feel: I say I am that time of year—those yellow leaves, or none, or few—hanging leaves—boughs shaking in the cold wind, bare, ruined—bare, ruined choirs—once the leaves of summer, sweet songs in trees and choir. The meaning of ll. 1–4 is the whole experience—plain sense, the sights, the sounds, the feelings. All these are present simultaneously in our consciousness as a unified experience; and our responses to them are continuously interacting—the aging man, the leaves, the boughs, the wind, the cold, the ruined choirs, and the remembrance of summer, birds, singing voices. This interaction is especially effective when the desolation of the cathedral is added, together with the contrasting joyousness of song both of the birds in summer and of the cathedral singers. This is brought about rapidly (in one line) so that the compression and condensation of a new sight (ruined choir) of desolation suddenly set against an earlier happiness, and the mental task of understanding 'sweet birds' as both birds and choir-singers, force into intense activity our creative ability, our power to fuse all these elements together into a unified experience of plain sense, sights, sounds, and feeling. Of these elements the first three, while they are important and necessary, are functioning here chiefly for the sake of the *feeling*. The feeling is not stated, named, or described. The reader must *create* it through his response to the plain sense, sights, and sounds. This is a typical occurrence in a poem.

It is so typical and important that it deserves special consideration for a moment. We all know, in our everyday lives, how difficult it is to tell someone just what emotion or feeling we had at a certain moment yesterday. We can describe it directly only in very crude terms, by stating or naming it—'I was happy, joyous, cheerful, ecstatic, merry, etc.' Dozens of such words fail to express the emotion; the person to whom we are talking hardly understands at all, and certainly does not himself feel the emotion. To put the matter in the terms of this essay, he could not use our words to create in himself a similar experience. And this is what a poet wishes his words to be used for; he wishes his words to *communicate* his experience to the reader. Now, in everyday life, if we really wish our hearer to share our emotion, we quite naturally (with no thought of being a poet) do one of two things, or both. We may say 'I felt like a million dollars—I had that wonderful feeling you get when the pain of a terrible headache suddenly leaves—I felt like writing a poem.' Or we may set about describing all the circumstances of yesterday's moment—the things about us, the events, what she looked like, what she said, what we said. Or we may use both methods. What we are forced to do to communicate our feeling is what the poet is forced to do. In this poem the feeling of growing old is not stated or described; to communicate the feeling to us the poet describes *things* that arouse in us this feeling—leaves, branches; and then, to reinforce our feeling about these things, he shows us other *things*—choirs, birds. The feeling about the aging man is communicated through wintry branches which are communicated (in part) by choirs and birds. Here is the answer to a question often asked in all good faith by inexperienced readers, 'Why doesn't the poet just say that his friend should feel sad because the poet is growing old, instead of beating about the bush and puzzling me with talk about branches, choirs, and birds?' *Neither we nor the poet can communicate feeling directly.* Mr. T. S. Eliot has said this excellently, and given us a useful term for the *things* in a poem.

The only way of expressing emotion in the form of art [for example the art of poetry] is by finding an 'objective correlative'; in other words, a set of objects, a situation, a chain of events which shall be the formula of that *particular* emotion; such that when the external facts, which must terminate in sensory experience, are given, the emotion is immediately evoked.[1]

In ll. 1–4 of this poem the branches, choirs, and birds are the objective correlatives of the emotion.

We have said that in these lines the plain sense, sights, and sounds are functioning chiefly for the sake of the feeling. Earlier we said that the skeleton of the whole poem was the plain sense and that the sense of ll. 1–4 was 'You know I am growing old.' We can now see that this

1. T. S. Eliot, *Selected Essays*, Harcourt Brace and Co., 1932, 124.

plain sense is not the skeleton of the whole poem, or the most important part, or even the most important part of ll. 1–4. Notice the plain sense of the whole poem: 'You know that I am growing old; therefore you love me more, since you must soon leave me.' The word 'therefore' means that greater love (in the person addressed by the poet) is aroused by his knowing that the poet is growing old; but this result is not likely unless the 'knowing' first arouses *feelings* in him—the feelings that are in ll. 1–4. These feelings are therefore an even more important part of the experience in ll. 1–4 than is the plain sense. And this, too, is typical of a great many poems: although the plain sense meaning is important, it often functions chiefly for the sake of the feeling that accompanies it. A poet may even make statements whose plain sense is nonsense to many readers (or to all): if the reader understands that the statement is not made for its own sake (that is, to assert its truth) but for the sake of expressing feeling, the poet may succeed excellently in his purpose, which is to communicate an experience. Hyperbole is an example of this. Robert Burns, trying to communicate to his sweetheart his feeling of love, wrote:

> *And I will luve thee still, my dear,*
> *Till a' the seas gang dry.*

No one doubts that his sweetheart understood the meaning of that nonsense.

The function of ll. 5–8 is to sharpen and focus still more immediately the experience which the reader has already had from ll. 1–4. The plain sense is 'You see that I am approaching death,' but this is very far from the whole meaning of the lines. Upon this skeleton the poet builds two comparisons, one immediate and the other implied. He is not only like the dying year, as he has already said, but like the 'twilight' of day, that ambiguous period just before the blackness of night hides the day forever. But the blackness of night suggests that other blackness which engulfs everyone in the end, death itself. The reader is now forced to intensify his imaginative activity of recreation by moving rapidly from the larger conception of the year to the narrower image of day, while, in addition, he must recollect that night is like death because it swallows up light (which is like life) in blackness.

The plain sense of ll. 9–12 is simply a more emphatic statement of the plain sense of the previous four lines. But here the plain sense is of almost no importance at all. The purport of the lines is to bring the whole experience into final and complete focus upon an image of fire: for a fire is 'Consumed with that which it was nourished by.' A dying fire lies upon the ashes of its youth, yet it still glows, preserving light and life; and so too the poet still retains within himself the spent energies of his youth, yet retains light and life. But the inevitability of a fire's dying out brings almost unendurably to the reader the experience of the inevitability of the life of a man dying out of his body.

The experience is now complete and it remains only to draw the conclusion, to interpret its meaning. And the concluding couplet performs just that function: it makes a direct statement which does not need to be translated into prose. But after reading the poem with this thoroughness we do not make the mistake of supposing that it performs any *other function*. The couplet is not a statement of the 'meaning' of the whole poem; it is a statement of the 'meaning' of the *experience* of the poem. It has no meaning at all until the experience of ll. 1–12 has been fully re-created in the consciousness of the reader.

III

We may summarize what we have said so far by recalling our central statement about poems: *a poem is not 'poetry' but a particular experience communicated through words, and it is only a poem when someone is reading it.* Reading, we have said, means the re-creation in the consciousness of the reader of the experience which the poet has tried to communicate to him by means of language. And we have studied a poem in detail to discover how we need to be able to *use language* in order to read a poem. This, as we have said, is one of the skills necessary to the art of reading poems. But there are a number of other skills of almost equal importance.

These are mainly the skills of the imagination. From the point of view of the psychologist the problem of the imagination is an exceedingly difficult one; but our purpose requires only a very simple definition. *By imagination we mean the power of forming mental images which correspond to the experiences of the senses.* That is to say, the power of seeing pictures, hearing sounds, touching things, smelling smells, and tasting things in our minds. In reading poems we need all five of these skills; and they must be highly developed. For without them we shall not be able to re-create the experience of a poem at all; we shall read only on a *verbal* level. We shall be able to comprehend only the idea, that part of a poem which can be translated into prose; and, as we have seen, that part is often of only very minor importance. Many people do not exercise their imagination at all, and many do not use it beyond the formation of visual images. But the richness of a poem often requires the ability to imagine several sensations at once. The poet relies on our having this ability.

Let us examine a passage from a poem which will illustrate the enormous importance of these skills. Here is a descriptive passage from Mr. T. S. Eliot's *The Waste Land* which has a major function in the poem:

1. *The Chair she sat in, like a burnished throne,*
2. *Glowed on the marble, where the glass*
3. *Held up by standards wrought with fruited vines*
4. *From which a golden Cupidon peeped out*
5. *(Another hid his eyes behind his wing)*
6. *Doubled the flames of sevenbranched candelabra*
7. *Reflecting light upon the table as*
8. *The glitter of her jewels rose to meet it,*
9. *From satin cases poured in rich profusion;*
10. *In vials of ivory and colored glass*
11. *Unstoppered, lurked her strange synthetic perfumes,*
12. *Unguent, powdered, or liquid—troubled, confused*
13. *And drowned the sense in odors; stirred by the air*
14. *That freshened from the window, these ascended*
15. *In fattening the prolonged candle-flames,*
16. *Flung their smoke into the laquearia,*
17. *Stirring the pattern on the coffered ceiling.*
18. *Huge sea-wood fed with copper*
19. *Burned green and orange, framed by the colored stone,*
20. *In which sad light a carvèd dolphin swam.*
21. *Above the antique mantel was displayed*
22. *As though a window gave upon the sylvan scene*
23. *The change of Philomel, by the barbarous king*
24. *So rudely forced; yet there the nightingale*
25. *Filled all the desert with inviolable voice*
26. *And still she cried, and still the world pursues,*
27. *'Jug Jug' to dirty ears.*

The primary impression of this scene is, naturally enough, *visual*.[1]
But we are not asked to imagine the whole room, its general shape
and furnishings. We are expected, rather, to imagine certain specific
qualities of the whole picture. In ll. 1–9 the center of the experience is
a complex image of light—'burnished,' 'glowed,' 'flames,' 'light,'
'glitter.' Incidentally we should 'see' the chair and the looking glass
with the figuring on the standards which support it. The glass itself
is central to the whole effect because it reflects the light from the candles, doubles it, and causes the glitter of the jewels. In ll. 10–12 the
image is primarily one of *smell*; but this time the image is not specific.
It is an experience which troubles, confuses, and drowns the sense in
odors. An indirect image of touch is now introduced by the fresh air
from the open window, which forces the odors upward at the same
time that it stirs the smoke from the candle flames and alters the pattern on the ceiling. The sensitive reader will *feel* the air as he *watches*
what it does, and will observe the additional details of the room
which are now offered, the laquearia (sunken panels) of the coffered
(deeply paneled) ceiling (ll. 13–17). ll. 18–27 introduce more light,
this time from the fire which is burning in the beautiful colors of drift-
wood blaze, and ask us to look at a picture within the larger picture
which is the whole passage. For above the mantel there is a picture
which depicts the story of Philomela, the heroine of Greek myth who
was changed into a nightingale. And now (ll. 24–27) we must *hear* the
song of the bird in order to complete our experience of the room.

It will be noticed that the re-creation of this scene, as we allowed
the poet's words to stimulate our imagination, required us to form
images of all our senses except taste (and it would be a simple matter
to show how an image of taste can be used in a poem). The process
by which we make the re-creation is not unlike the process by which
we remember places where we have been. If our memory of a place
is clear, we will probably have stored up images not only of how it
looked, but of how it *smelt*, of what sounds we *heard* there, and what
things we may have *felt* there; whereas if the recollection is not so
clear, it is probable that we will have only a visual image, or an auditory image, etc. which, however sharp it may be in itself, does not

1. For a detailed discussion of the method of composition of this passage and explanation of certain of the puzzling references in it see the Notes to *The Waste
Land*, poem No. 301.

provide us with a full re-creation of the place as we originally experienced it. Much of the effect of the scene we have been examining is an effect of light and is re-created by our *visual* imagination; and it is by means of the visual imagination that we bring the objects into the picture and place them in relation to the light. It is probable that a great many readers will re-create the scene to this extent. But a much smaller number would go beyond this point, to the point of smelling the perfumes and powders (all that is needed here is some recollection of the confused odor of many cosmetics together); and only a few will hear the song of the nightingale. Yet the scene is simply not re-created without *all* these acts of the imagination. And the poet absolutely requires us to realize the scene fully because he intends, by the sound of the nightingale, for example, to communicate to us much more than a scene. The function, in fact, of the whole passage is to make a vital contrast between the opulence of her surroundings and the heróic love which they suggest and the woman who is seated before the glass (who is not described at all). In short, if we do not fully re-create the passage as an experience in our own consciousness, we shall pretty completely miss the experience of the whole section of the poem and hence of the whole poem.

IV

In addition to the skills in the use of language and the imagination, the reader of poems needs one further skill, that of the *ear*. Nearly all poems are written in what is called *measure*; that is, the words are arranged according to the quality or quantity of their accents. And the reader must *hear* the beats and follow the rhythm in much the same manner that a listener to musical compositions is always conscious of the *time* of the music. It is probable that the poems of primitive men were organized in measure in order to make them memorable; and, though measure has long been used for many more subtle reasons, that is still an important reason for its use. Although we now read poems *to ourselves* out of books, it is still true that the full effect of a good poem can only be realized by *hearing* it read aloud. We might almost say that a poem is not a poem until someone is reading it, not only in the sense we used earlier, but in the sense of actually reading it aloud. At the very least the reader must imagine that he hears the poem; and it is here that he will be most helped by measure.

We may take a line or two from the passage we have been studying in the previous section of this essay. The first line,

> *The Chair she sat in, like a burnished throne*

could have been written,

> *The Chair in which she was sitting was like a*
> *burnished throne*

but a large part of its effectiveness would have been lost. It would simply not have been memorable as it is in measure, and it would not have pleased the ear. We may mark the accents in the line,

> *The Chair she sat in, like a bur nished throne,*

Notice that they fall regularly on every second syllable. Now observe the accenting of the second line,

> *Glowed on the mar ble where the glass*

and of the third,

> *Held up by stan dards wrought with frui ted vines*

If we divide each line into parts (feet) of two syllables each it is clear that the second line differs from the other two in two respects: it begins with an accented syllable, and it contains only four accents. The rest of the line, however, is similar to the others. And all three are so much alike that we are led to expect that line four will follow the same pattern. We are not to be disappointed. Our ear has caught a definite rhythmic pattern and it has become impressed upon our consciousness. Our pleasure is twofold: (1) the *recognition* by the ear of the pattern (which is often pleasurable in itself) as a recurrent element of the poem is accentuated by the variations of beat which the poet introduces; we discover that he is *counterpointing* the irregular line against the pattern of the regular line which he has set up in our consciousness; and (2) the rather slow and dignified pace of the lines is harmonious with the stately luxury of the experience of the room itself. In general it may be said, in connection with the second point, that the poet tries to build his poem in a measure which is suitable to the experience he is trying to communicate; but it is dangerous to speculate much further on the relation between sound and sense.

The chief function of measure, or rhythm, is to set up a pattern which the reader will recognize as it recurs and to counterpoint it in such manner that an effect is achieved not unlike the counterpointing of melody in music. What is required of the reader is that he recognize by ear the pattern of regularity and retain it in his consciousness all through the reading of the poem while, at the same time, he hears distinctly the actual accents in the line, whether they are regular or not. There are, of course, a great many measures and combinations of measures in verse; but, whether the measure of a particular poem is the very common measure which Eliot uses in the passage we have examined or something quite different, the principle is the same.

Another skill which the ear is called upon to exercise is the recognition of the *quality* of the sounds of words. The simplest qualitative appeal which the poet makes is *rhyme*. Rhyme belongs to poetry from the very earliest time because it helps greatly in fitting words to music; but it is often used for its own sake in poems which are not intended to be sung. *Rhyme is the repetition according to pattern of harmonious vowel and consonantal sounds.* In general rhyme offers the reader little difficulty of recognition; but there are many poems in which it is easy to miss subtleties of rhyming effect. This is especially true of the so-called 'heroic couplet' used by such poets as Dryden and Pope.[1] In reading Pope, for example, the 'monotony' which so many readers confess to feeling is not the fault of Pope but of the reader. When the punctuation marks are carefully observed and the beat is placed upon the proper words in the line, the end rhymes will be found to fall into graceful and delicate harmonies which are so far from monotony that one forgets that he is reading couplets at all.

Rhyme is capable of almost endless variation; and it is interesting to observe that contemporary poets are still experimenting with it, sometimes with extraordinarily good results. Here is a stanza from a poem of Louis MacNeice in which the rhymes are especially effective:

> *Our freedom as free* lances
> Advances *towards its* end;
> *The earth compels,* upon it
> Sonnets *and birds* descend;
> *And soon, my* friend
> *We shall have no time for* dances.[2]

1. See Note to Pope's *Summer*, poem No. 201, for a discussion of the problems of reading the heroic couplet.
2. See poem No. 259 and Introduction to Part VI.

In this poem notice that the sound 'free' is repeated in the first line. It is not a rhyme because the harmony of the words is broken by the ending 'dom'; yet the quality of the sounds catches the ear and adds to the pleasant effect of the line. The poet has at his command a large number of such devices, and the accomplished reader will, in the long run and with continued practice, come to recognize and take pleasure in most of them. But it is an error of the first magnitude to study poems in terms of the special devices of the poet's craft. For one thing, there is the obvious danger of failing to re-create the experience of the poem at all because of too much attention to methods by which effects are obtained. And, perhaps more important, it is safe to say that from the poet's point of view (and hence rightly also from the reader's) the devices bear an organic relation to the experience of the poem, are functional to it. The poet begins, as we have said, with an experience which he wishes to communicate, not with a bag of tricks. And the reader must read the poem in 'the same spirit in which the author writ.' [1]

It will be useful at this point to sum up our discussion by performing a simple but interesting experiment. Let us read a poem carefully and then see what happens when we try to translate it into prose. Here is a famous poem by A. E. Housman:

> *With rue my heart is laden*
> *For golden friends I had,*
> *For many a rose-lipt maiden*
> *And many a lightfoot lad.*
>
> *By brooks too broad for leaping*
> *The lightfoot boys are laid;*
> *The rose-lipt girls are sleeping*
> *In fields where roses fade.*

The experience of this poem is a simple one; yet it is one of the deepest of the human heart. And the simplicity of its structure is deceiving; for when we read it with the fullness required in order to recreate the experience, a great many things happen in our consciousness. The complicated process begins immediately. The plain sense of the first line is 'I feel sad,' but the effect of the line is much more than this. Rue is a bitter herb used in medicinal preparations and

1. A convenient list of the common terms of versification, with brief definitions, will be found in Appendix I.

would therefore, taken by itself, provide us with an image of *taste*. But it is likened to a burden which is laid upon something else, the heart. And a burden provides us with an image of *touch* or weight. The juxtaposition is logically impossible. But that is exactly the point: the feeling of grief is 'unbearable.' The whole statement of the cause of this grief is contained in the single word 'had' in the next line, and this is amplified by the word 'golden' which characterizes what the poet 'had.' The plain sense is that the poet's friends are dead; but this plain sense does not communicate the feeling at all; that feeling is re-created in our minds by the relation between the words 'golden friends' and 'had,' and, in turn, depends upon our having experienced the grief of the first line. The third line amplifies the second, and so does the fourth; but *nothing* is actually added to the plain sense. The experience, however, is greatly enriched by the two lines, for we create in our minds generalized images of fresh and blooming girls and vital young men. Our experience of 'golden' is amplified; and now the experience of all three lines is enormously enriched again, when they are taken together, if we recollect the famous song of Shakespeare of which Housman is thinking:

> *Golden lads and girls all must,*
> *As chimney-sweepers, come to dust.*

He is not imitating Shakespeare here. It is simply that his experience has called to his mind a similar experience of another poet which he (Housman) has re-created in his mind no doubt many times; and we, for our part, recognize that there is a quality of universality about the experience which brings Housman and Shakespeare close together. Yet the two poems are quite different when taken as *specific* experiences. Shakespeare's image of the sooty chimney-sweeper has nothing in common with the images Housman uses. It is only the *generalized* experience of grief at the loss of friends which brings the two poems into close relation. The effect is largely to call to our minds a feeling of the continuity of human experience in terms of human loss and grief.

The plain sense of ll. 5–6 is that the boys are dead and will never return; and ll. 7–8 suggest that the same is true of the girls. But the tension which the image of 'brooks too broad for leaping' evokes produces a feeling of utter hopelessness which is not in the plain sense at all. And the image of 'fields where roses fade' so sharpens the feeling of death to the blooming girls that even 'sleeping' seems a vicious understatement of what has actually happened to them. The whole poem now re-created as a single experience, and rendered memorable by the simple three-beat rhythm and the simple but appropriate rhyme scheme, evokes in our consciousness a feeling of the finality of death and the grief of the living so inextricably intertwined and so poignant that no reader can remain unmoved. And the poem has inevitably achieved a place among the great lyric poems of our language.

And now here is a statement of the plain sense, a prose translation:

> *I am greatly saddened because my friends, fresh and*
> *vital girls and boys, are gone.*

> *The boys are dead and will not return; the girls too*
> *are forever dead.*

The experience, it hardly needs to be said, is simply not there. What remains is no more than a banal statement of a fact which everyone knows. We should not therefore conclude that poetry is superior to prose, or that some things are poetical and others prosaic. What we should grasp is the fundamental distinction between the language of poetry and the language of prose, the difference between receiving information through the medium of language and re-creating an experience which is communicated by means of language.

v

But mastery of these skills of language, imagination, and ear is not all that is needed in the art of reading poems. We ought also to be able to distinguish more or less readily among good poems and poor poems. We ought, that is to say, to have some standards for judgment and evaluation, to take our pleasure from poems with discrimination. And it must be admitted immediately that there is no problem in literature which is at once so difficult of solution and so often attempted. At least since the time of Aristotle critics have tried to set up standards of evaluation, and almost invariably they have landed themselves in the quicksand of metaphysical speculation.

But it may be observed that some, at least, of the difficulties will be eliminated with the genuine *reading* of poems in the sense with which we have dealt in this essay, and with the recognition that *poetry* is an abstraction, not a thing. This is to say that the common procedure of critics, the setting up of definitions of 'poetry' and the judgment of specific poems with reference to the definition, is a procedure which puts the cart before the horse. The error involved is the assumption that poetry is what we think it ought to be, which leads us to ignore what a specific poem really is. Thus we may decide that poetry should represent man as a creature exercising free choice among difficult possibilities of action; it follows that poems in which man seems to be conditioned by things beyond his control are inferior poems. Or we may decide that poetry ought to teach us moral lessons; it follows that poems which do not teach us moral lessons are inferior poems. And we could pile up examples of the application of such preconceptions. But in any case we are forced, through this error, to reject as inferior very many poems which, by some other standards, are possibly very fine poems. We shall also, as we have shown earlier in this essay, be placing barriers between ourselves and the poem which make it impossible for us to re-create the experience, impossible to *read* the poem at all. No one, it seems evident, would maintain that we should judge a poem without having read it.

The secret of wise discrimination among poems is to be found in the nature of an actual poem. As we have shown in the preceding pages, a poem is an attempt to communicate an experience or group of experiences through the medium of language so that the reader may re-create the experience for himself, or at least create a new experience in his consciousness which is more or less like that of the poet. It follows, then, that the real measure of the value of a poem must be twofold: (1) the clarity of the actual communication, and (2) the value of the experience communicated. Thus we may safely reject as inferior a poem which offers us insufficient materials for the re-creation of its experience, a poem in which the images are unclear or confused, or in which the parts are so unrelated as not to form a whole. And such poems we should, obviously, reject, whether they contain an 'idea' with which we agree or not. For to judge such a poem by an 'idea' which it seems to state is to judge it as though it were prose. On the other hand, if, with a thorough reading, we are able to re-create the experience with clarity we must consider the poem as having achieved the first of the two values, and we must proceed to judge it in the light of the second. We must ask the question now, what is the value of the experience which the poem has communicated to us?

The only limit to the subject matter of poems is the limit of human experience itself. And we ought, therefore, to be very careful not to assume that the experience of a poem is valid because we like it or invalid because we do not like it, any more than we would assume that an experience of life is valid because we like it or invalid because we do not like it. The test of an experience of life is its truth (psychological, emotional, intellectual, physical), and truth should likewise be the test of the experience of a poem. It follows that there will be many 'good' poems (i.e. *true* poems) which we do not like, just as there are pictures which are true but which do not please us, and there are many true experiences of life which we cannot like. There is, this is to say, no *special* problem involved in the evaluation of the experience of a poem. The problem is moral and social, and a man will judge the experience of a poem, as he judges the experience of life, in terms of his general moral and social attitudes. But only a very narrow and uncultured reader will permit his moral or social judgment of the experience of a poem to interfere with his enjoyment of it as a true and interesting and perhaps beautiful experience. He will many times disagree with the moral or social judgment of the poet, but he will not reject the poem any more than he would reject the enjoyment of a beautiful Roman Catholic cathedral simply because, as a Baptist, he disagrees with the religion for which the cathedral is used. Concomitantly it might be said that, as a Baptist might well derive the fullest satisfaction from a very beautiful Baptist church, a reader will find his greatest enjoyment from the poem which provides him with an experience which fits into his moral and social scale of values. But even here it is essential to remember that the poem is not good because it finds a place in his scale of values but because it is a true poem.

The test of a good poem (not a poem we 'like'), then, is that it shall communicate a true and interesting experience in a manner which is pleasurable to the ear and to the imagination. The language of such a poem will necessarily be appropriate to the experience, because it will be functional to the experience. A dull, ordinary, or simply uninter-

[758]

esting experience will not make a good poem by the use of out-of-the-ordinary or striking words. A good poem is so absolutely a *whole* thing that no separation can be made between the experience and the language which communicates it, the one is a direct function of the other. Conversely, a true experience may be reduced to the level of inferior poetry if the poet is careless in his use of language or permits the special qualities of his experience to be lost in inadequate or banal or trite images. It follows that the initial experience, the perception and sensitivity of the poet, is the *sine qua non* of a good poem; and it may be said in a general way that an experience clearly defined and sensitively realized in the imagination of a man who is skilled in the uses of language will produce a good poem, will permit the reader to acquire for himself an enjoyable and valuable experience. The art of *making* poems is only completed by the parallel art of *reading* poems.

VI

It may be well to conclude with a word or two of caution. We have been speaking throughout this essay of 'experience,' and it may be that some readers will tend to identify experience solely with the activities, perceptions, feelings of individual, personal life. In this case what we have said would seem to argue that poetry is a purely personal or subjective art. This is very far from our intention. In one sense, to be sure, all experience is personal, since it is what happens to persons. But in another sense, as soon as experience is recognized by others as true it ceases to be personal, becomes impersonal. There are, it is true, a small number of poems, sometimes much admired by certain critics, which are so exclusively personal that they do not communicate anything to an ordinary intelligent reader. But, on any realistic view, these are certainly bad poems. Poems may be relatively more subjective than objective, that is, more specific than general, or they may be very general, so general as to seem not to communicate the experience of an individual person at all; but in any case, if they are good poems, they will be impersonal. However original a good poem may be, it will bear some direct relation to the whole continuity and tradition of the experience of the race. It will be unique, yet at the same time a part of a larger whole. It will suggest the infinite variety and flux of human experience at the same time that it assures us once more of the recurring patterns of that experience. And, though Plato ruled poetry out of his ideal commonwealth, it may not be too much to say that a good poem is one of the best keys we have to that paradox of human life which so fascinated him: permanence in the midst of change, the One in the Many.

APPENDIX I

TERMS OF VERSIFICATION

syllables. The phonetic units of words. a·bout, tel·e·phone. The syllable always contains a vowel sound, but not always consonants.

stress. Emphasis upon a certain syllable. ă·bóut, tél·ĕ·phŏne, néed·less·lў.

foot. The phonetic unit of a line of verse, consisting of two or more syllables.

'To máke | ă mán | tŏ méet | thĕ mór | tăl néed.'
The common kinds of feet are:

iambic. Two syllables, the stress falling on the second.

'To máke | ă mán | tŏ méet | thĕ mór | tăl néed.'

anapestic. Three syllables, the stress falling on the third.

'Ĭn thĕ mórn | ĭng ŏf lífe.'

Iambic and anapestic feet are said to be *rising* because the reader moves *toward* the stress.

trochaic. Two syllables, the stress falling on the first.

'Thén lĕt | wíng ĕd | fán cў | wán dĕr.'

dactylic. Three syllables, the stress falling on the first.

'Thís ĭs thĕ | fór ĕst prím | ĕ văl, thĕ | múr mŭr ĭng | pínes ănd the | hém lŏcks.'

Trochaic and dactylic feet are said to be *falling* because the reader moves *away* from the stress.

spondaic. Two syllables, both stressed. This is sometimes called *level stress.*

'Mán, bírd, | beást, físh, | flésh, fówl.'

pyrrhic. Two syllables, both unstressed.

'Nót sŏ | mŭch lífe | ăs ŏn | ă súm | mĕr's dáy.'

Spondaic and pyrrhic feet seldom occur except as variations on the iambic or trochaic foot.

measure (meter). The pattern by which feet (of whatever kind) are arranged to form a line of verse. The common measures in English poems are:

dimeter. Two feet to the line.

   'Ŏf thĕ | dárk pást
   Ă chíld | ĭs bórn.'

trimeter. Three feet to the line.

   'Thĕ Ráin | bŏw cómes | ănd góes,
   Ănd lóve | lў ĭs | thĕ Róse,'

tetrameter. Four feet to the line.

   'Háp pŭ | fíeld ŏr | móss ў | cáv ĕrn
   Chóic ĕr | thăn thĕ | Mér măid | táv ĕrn?'

pentameter. Five feet to the line.

   'Thĕ mínd | ĭs ĭts | ówn pláce, | ănd ín | ĭt sélf
   Căn máke | ă Heáv'n | ŏf Héll, | ă Héll | ŏf Heáv'n.'

hexameter. Six feet to the line.

   'Fóol săid | mў múse | tŏ mé, | lŏok ĭn | thў heárt | ănd wríte.'

caesura. An internal pause, sometimes slight, which interrupts the regular flow of a line, not necessarily indicated by punctuation.

   'Nŏt már | blĕ, ‖ nŏr | thĕ gíld | ĕd món | ŭ ménts
   Ŏf prín | cĕs, ‖ shăll | oŭt líve | thĭs pówer | fŭl ríme;
   Bŭt yóu | shăll shíne | mŏre bríght ‖ ĭn thése | cŏn ténts
   Thăn ún | swĕpt stóne, ‖ bĕ smeár'd | wĭth slút | tĭsh tíme.'

feminine ending. A line of iambic or anapestic feet with an extra un-stressed syllable at the end is said to have a *feminine ending*.

   'Ănd só | făre wéll | tŏ thĕ lít | tlĕ góod | yŏu beár mĕ,'

end-stopped line. A line with a complete or nearly complete syntactical pause at the end.

   'Nów ĭs | thĕ wín | tĕr ŏf | oŭr dís | cŏn tént
   Máde glór | ĭous súm | mĕr bў | thĭs sún | ŏf Yórk;'

run-on line. A line of which the syntax 'runs on' without pause to the following line.

   'Gíve mĕ | mў róbe, | pút ón | mў crówn; | Ĭ háve

Ĭm mŏr | tăl lŏng | ĭngs ĭn | mĕ. Nŏw | nŏ mŏre
The juĭce | ŏf Ĕg | ypt's grăpe | shăll mŏist | thĭs lĭp.'

rhyme. Repetition of the same sound or sounds. When the repetition occurs at the conclusion of two or more lines it is called *end-rhyme*; when the repetition occurs within the lines it is called *internal rhyme*. The repetition of the same sound or sounds in the first syllables of words is known as *alliteration*. The repetition of the same vowel sounds with different consonants is called *assonance*. *Consonance* is the repetition of consonantal sounds when the vowel sounds differ. The repetition of both vowel and consonant sounds is called *rhyme proper*.

end-rhyme:
"'Tis hard to say, if greater want of *skill*
Appear in writing or in judging *ill*;'

internal rhyme:
'The sunlight on the *garden*
Hardens and grows cold,'

alliteration:
'*L*ooking and *l*oving our behaviors pass
The *st*ones, the *st*eels and the polished glass;'

assonance:
'And all the summer through the *water saunter*.'

consonance:
'Send to us power and light, a sovereign *touch*
Curing the intolerable neural *itch*,'

rhyme proper:
(See *end-rhyme* above.)

masculine rhyme. Rhyme-proper when single, stressed syllables are used. *stark, mark.*

feminine rhyme. Rhyme-proper when the rhyme falls upon a stressed syllable followed by one or more unstressed syllables. *singing, bringing.*

onomatopoeia. When the sound of a word is supposed to echo or suggest the meaning.
'The moan of doves in immemorial elms,'

blank verse. Unrhymed iambic pentameter.

alexandrine. Iambic hexameter with caesura after second, third, or fourth stress.

[763]

free verse. Irregular rhythms following no fixed metrical pattern.

stanza. The arrangement of lines according to a fixed pattern, usually marked by end-rhyme. (But see poem No. 202, *Ode to Evening*, and note.) The common stanza forms are:

couplet. Stanza of two lines with end-rhyme.

octosyllabic couplet. Couplet of iambic tetrameter.

heroic couplet. Couplet of iambic pentameter. Often (as in Pope) heroic couplets are 'closed,' that is, the couplet contains a complete thought. A *triplet* is a variation in a poem of heroic couplets in which three rhyming lines are used.

terza rima. Three line stanzas rhyming *a b a*, in which the *b* rhyme becomes the *a* rhyme of the following stanza. *a b a , b c b, c d c.*

quatrain. Four line stanza.

ballad stanza. Quatrain of alternating four and three stress lines, rhyming *a b c b* (sometimes *a b a b*).

rhyme royal. Seven line stanza of iambic pentameter, rhyming *a b a b b c c.*

ottava rima. Eight line stanza of iambic pentameter, rhyming *a b a b a b c c.*

Spenserian stanza. Nine line iambic stanza of which the first eight are pentameter and the last is alexandrine, rhyming *a b a b b c b-c c.*

sonnet. See introduction to Part II. 665

APPENDIX II

NOTES ON VERSIFICATION[1]

Gerard Manley Hopkins

Common English rhythm, called Running Rhythm [here] . . . , is measured by feet of either two or three syllables and (putting aside the imperfect feet at the beginning and end of lines and also some unusual measures, in which feet seem to be paired together and double or composite feet to arise) never more or less.

Every foot has one principal stress or accent, and this or the syllable it falls on may be called the Stress of the foot and the other part, the one or two unaccented syllables, the Slack. Feet (and the rhythms made out of them) in which the stress comes first are called Falling Feet and Falling Rhythms, feet and rhythm in which the slack comes first are called Rising Feet and Rhythms, and if the stress is between two slacks there will be Rocking Feet and Rhythms. These distinctions are real and true to nature; but for the purposes of scanning it is a great convenience to follow the example of music and take the stress always first, as the accent or the chief accent always comes first in a musical bar. If this is done there will be in common English verse only two possible feet—the so-called accentual Trochee and Dactyl, and correspondingly only two possible uniform rhythms, the so-called Trochaic and Dactylic. But they may be mixed and then what the Greeks called a Logaoedic Rhythm arises. These are the facts and according to these the scanning of ordinary regularly-written English verse is very simple indeed and to bring in other principles is here unnecessary.

But because verse written strictly in these feet and by these principles will become same and tame the poets have brought in licences and departures from rule to give variety, and especially when the natural rhythm is rising, as in the common ten-syllable or five-foot verse, rhymed or blank. These irregularities are chiefly Reversed

1 Selected from 'Author's Preface.' Gerard Manley Hopkins, *Poems*, ed. Robert Bridges, 2nd ed., Oxford University Press, London, 1930. Reprinted by permission of the Oxford University Press.

[765]

Feet and Reversed or Counterpoint Rhythm, which two things are two steps or degrees of licence in the same kind. By a reversed foot I mean the putting the stress where, to judge by the rest of the measure, the slack should be and the slack where the stress, and this is done freely at the beginning of a line and, in the course of a line, after a pause; only scarcely ever in the second foot or place and never in the last, unless when the poet designs some extraordinary effect; for these places are characteristic and sensitive and cannot well be touched. But the reversal of the first foot and of some middle foot after a strong pause is a thing so natural that our poets have generally done it, from Chaucer down, without remark and it commonly passes unnoticed and cannot be said to amount to a formal change of rhythm, but rather is that irregularity which all natural growth and motion shows. If however the reversal is repeated in two feet running, especially so as to include the sensitive second foot, it must be due either to great want of ear or else is a calculated effect, the super-inducing or *mounting* of a new rhythm upon the old; and since the new or mounted rhythm is actually heard and at the same time the mind naturally supplies the natural or standard foregoing rhythm, for we do not forget what the rhythm is that by rights we should be hearing, two rhythms are in some manner running at once and we have something answerable to counterpoint in music, which is two or more strains of tune going on together, and this is Counterpoint Rhythm. Of this kind of verse Milton is the great master and the choruses of *Samson Agonistes* are written throughout in it—but with the disadvantage that he does not let the reader clearly know what the ground-rhythm is meant to be and so they have struck most readers as merely irregular. And in fact if you counterpoint throughout, since one only of the counter rhythms is actually heard, the other is really destroyed or cannot come to exist, and what is written is one rhythm only and probably Sprung Rhythm, of which I now speak.

Sprung Rhythm, as used in this book, is measured by feet of from one to four syllables, regularly, and for particular effects any number of weak or slack syllables may be used. It has one stress, which falls on the only syllable, if there is only one, or, if there are more, then scanning as above, on the first, and so gives rise to four sorts of feet, a monosyllable and the so-called accentual Trochee, Dactyl, and the First Paeon. And there will be four corresponding natural rhythms;

but nominally the feet are mixed and any one may follow any other. And hence Sprung Rhythm differs from Running Rhythm in having or being only one nominal rhythm, a mixed or 'logaoedic' one, instead of three, but on the other hand in having twice the flexibility of foot, so that any two stresses may either follow one another running or be divided by one, two, or three slack syllables. But strict Sprung Rhythm cannot be counterpointed. In Sprung Rhythm, as in logaoedic rhythm generally, the feet are assumed to be equally long or strong and their seeming inequality is made up by pause or stressing.

Remark also that it is natural in Sprung Rhythm for the lines to be *rove over*, that is for the scanning of each line immediately to take up that of the one before, so that if the first has one or more syllables at its end the other must have so many the less at its beginning; and in fact the scanning runs on without break from the beginning, say, of a stanza to the end and all the stanza is one long strain, though written in lines asunder.

Two licences are natural to Sprung Rhythm. The one is rests, as in music; [see poem No.230, l.2.] . . . The other is *hangers* or *outrides*, that is one, two, or three slack syllables added to a foot and not counting in the nominal scanning. They are so called because they seem to hang below the line or ride forward or backward from it in another dimension than the line itself, according to a principle needless to explain here. . . .

Note on the nature and history of Sprung Rhythm—Sprung Rhythm is the most natural of things. For (1) it is the rhythm of common speech and of written prose, when rhythm is perceived in them. (2) It is the rhythm of all but the most monotonously regular music, so that in the words of choruses and refrains and in songs written closely to music it arises. (3) It is found in nursery rhymes, weather saws, and so on; because, however these may have been once made in running rhythm, the terminations having dropped off by the change of language, the stresses come together and so the rhythm is sprung. (4) It arises in common verse when reversed or counterpointed, for the same reason. . . .

INDEX OF AUTHORS

The references are to the numbers of the poems.

INDEX TO TITLES AND FIRST LINES

References immediately following the entries are to page numbers, those in the outer column are to the notes.

[771]

[772]

[773]

[780]